HARDPRESS.NET
HOME OF HARD-TO-FIND BOOKS

The Debates in the Several State Conventions on the Adoption of the Federal Constitution
by Jonathan Elliot

Address:
HardPress
8345 NW 66TH ST #2561
MIAMI FL 33166-2626
USA
Email: info@hardpress.net

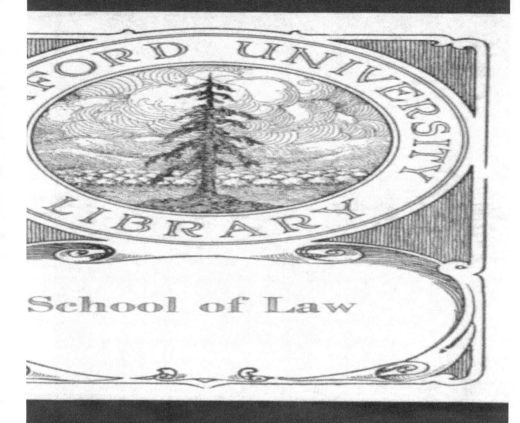

THE

DEBATES

IN THE SEVERAL

STATE CONVENTIONS

ON THE ADOPTION OF THE

FEDERAL CONSTITUTION,

AS RECOMMENDED BY THE

GENERAL CONVENTION AT PHILADELPHIA,

IN

1787.

TOGETHER WITH THE

JOURNAL OF THE FEDERAL CONVENTION,

LUTHER MARTIN'S LETTER.

YATES'S MINUTES,

CONGRESSIONAL OPINIONS,

VIRGINIA AND KENTUCKY RESOLUTIONS OF '98 - '9.

AND

OTHER ILLUSTRATIONS OF THE CONSTITUTION

IN FIVE VOLUMES.

VOL. IV.

SECOND EDITION, WITH CONSIDERABLE ADDITIONS.

COLLECTED AND REVISED FROM CONTEMPORARY PUBLICATIONS,

By JONATHAN ELLIOT.

PUBLISHED UNDER THE SANCTION OF CONGRESS.

PHILADELPHIA:

J. B. LIPPINCOTT & CO.

1876.

Entered according to Act of Congress, in the year one thousand eight hundred
and thirty-six,
By JONATHAN ELLIOT,
in the Clerk's Office of the District Court of the District of Columbia.

CONTENTS.

INDEX.

BY SPEAKERS' NAMES.

NORTH CAROLINA.

SOUTH CAROLINA.

DEBATES

IN

THE CONVENTION

OF THE

STATE OF NORTH CAROLINA,

ON THE

ADOPTION OF THE FEDERAL CONSTITUTION.

At a Convention, begun and held at Hillsborough, the 21st day of July, in the year of our Lord one thousand seven hundred and eighty-eight, and of the Independence of America the 13th, in pursuance of a resolution of the last General Assembly, for the purpose of deliberating and determining on the proposed Plan of Federal Government, —

A MAJORITY of those who were duly elected as members of this Convention being met at the church, they proceeded to the election of a president, when his excellency, Samuel Johnston, Esq., was unanimously chosen, and conducted to the chair accordingly.

The house then elected Mr. John Hunt and Mr. James Taylor clerks to the Convention, and also appointed door-keepers, &c.

The house then appointed a select committee to prepare and propose certain *rules* and *regulations* for the government of the Convention in the discussion of the Constitution.

The committee consisted of Messrs. Davie, Person, Iredell, I. M'Donald, Battle, Spaight, and the Hon. Samuel Spencer, Esq.

The Convention then appointed a committee of three members from each district, as a committee of privileges and elections, consisting of Messrs. Spencer, Irwin, Caldwell, Person, A. Mebane, Joseph Taylor, M'Dowell, J. Brown, J. Johnston, Davie, Peebles, E. Gray, Gregory, Iredell, Cabarrus, I. G. Blount, Keais, B. Williams, T. Brown, Maclaine, Foster, Clinton, J. Willis, Grove, J. Stewart, Martin, and Tipton

The Convention then adjourned till to-morrow morning.

TUESDAY, *July* 22, 1788.

The Convention met according to adjournment.

The committee appointed for that purpose reported certain rules and regulations for the government of the Convention, which were twice read, and, with the exception of one article, were agreed to, and are as fol-lows, viz: —

"1. When the president assumes the chair, the members shall take their seats.

"2. At the opening of the Convention, each day, the minutes of the preceding day shall be read, and be in the power of the Convention to be corrected, after which any business addressed to the chair may be proceeded upon.

"3. No member shall be allowed to speak but in his place, and, after rising and addressing himself to the president, shall not proceed until permitted by the president.

"4. No member speaking shall be interrupted but by a call to order by the president, or by a member through the president.

"5. No person shall pass between the president and the person speaking.

"6. No person shall be called upon for any words of heat, but on the day on which they were spoken.

"7. No member to be referred to in debate by name.

"8. The president shall be heard without interruption, and when he rises, the member up shall sit down.

"9. The president himself, or by request, may call to order any member who shall transgress the rules; if a second time, the president may refer to him by name; the Convention may then examine and censure the member's conduct, he being allowed to extenuate or justify.

"10. When two or more members are up together, the president shall determine who rose first.

"11. A motion made and seconded shall be repeated by the president. A motion shall be reduced to writing if the president requires it. A motion may be withdrawn by the member making it, before any decision is had upon it.

"12. The name of him who makes, and the name of him who seconds, the motion, shall be entered upon the minutes.

"13. No member shall depart the service of the house without leave.

"14. Whenever the house shall be divided upon any question, two or more tellers shall be appointed by the president, to number the members on each side.

"15. No member shall come into the house, or remove from one place to another, with his hat on, except those of the Quaker profession.

"16. Every member of a committee shall attend at the call of his chairman.

"17. The yeas and nays may be called and entered on the minutes, when any two members require it.

"18. Every member actually attending the Convention shall be in his place at the time to which the Convention stands adjourned, or within half an hour thereof."

Mr Lenoir moved, and was seconded by Mr. Person, that the return for Dobbs county should be read, which was accordingly read; whereupon Mr. Lenoir presented the petition of sundry of the inhabitants of Dobbs county, complaining of an illegal election in the said county, and praying relief; which being also read, on motion of Mr. Lenoir, seconded by Mr. Davie, *Resolved*, That the said petition be referred to the committee of elections.

Mr. Spaight presented the deposition of Benjamin Caswell, sheriff of Dobbs county, and a copy of the poll of an election held in the said county, for members to this Convention, and the depositions of William

Croom, Neil Hopkins, Robert White, John Hartsfield, Job Smith, and Frederick Baker, which, being severally read, were referred to the committee of elections.

Mr. Cabarrus presented the depositions of Charles Markland, Jun., and Luther Spalding, relative to the election of Dobbs county; which, being read, were referred to the committee of elections.

The Convention then adjourned to 10 o'clock to-morrow morning.

WEDNESDAY, *July* 23, 1788.

The house met according to adjournment.

Mr. Gregory, from the committee of elections, to whom were referred the returns from Dobbs county, and sundry other papers, and the petition of sundry of the inhabitants of Dobbs county relative to the election of the said county, delivered in a report; which, being read, was agreed to in the following words, viz: —

" *Resolved*, That it is the opinion of this committee, that the sitting members returned from the county of Dobbs vacate their seats, as it does not appear that a majority of the county approved of a new election under the recommendation of his excellency, the governor; but the contrary is more probable.

" That it appears to this committee, that there was a disturbance and riot at the first election, (which was held on the days appointed by the resolve of the General Assembly,) before all the tickets could be taken out of the box, and the box was then taken away by violence; at which time it appears there were a sufficient number of tickets remaining in the box to have given a majority of the whole poll to five others of the candidates, besides those who had a majority of the votes at the time when the disturbance and riot happened. It is, therefore, the opinion of this committee, that the sheriff could have made no return of any five members elected; nor was there any evidence before the committee by which they could determine, with certainty, which candidates had a majority of votes of the other electors.

" The committee are therefore of opinion that the first election is void, as well as the latter."

On a motion made by Mr. Galloway, seconded by Mr. Macon, —

" *Resolved*, That the Bill of Rights and Constitution of this state, the Articles of Confederation, the resolve of Congress of the 21st of February, 1787, recommending a Convention of Delegates to meet at Philadelphia the second Monday in May, 1787, for the purpose of revising the said Articles of Confederation, together with the act of Assembly of this state, passed at Fayetteville, the 6th day of January, 1787, entitled 'An act for appointing deputies from this state to a Convention proposed to be held in the city of Philadelphia in May next, for the purpose of revising the Federal Constitution;' as also the resolve of Congress of the 28th September last, accompanying the report of the Federal Convention, together with the said report, and the resolution of the last General Assembly, be now read."

The Bill of Rights and Constitution of this state, the Articles of Confederation, the act of Assembly of this state above referred to, and the resolution of Congress of the 28th September last, were accordingly read.

The honorable the president then laid before the Convention official accounts of the ratification of the proposed Federal Constitution by the states of Massachusetts and South Carolina; which were ordered to be filed with the secretary, subject to the perusal of the members

Mr. JAMES GALLOWAY moved that the Constitution should be discussed clause by clause.

Mr. WILLIE JONES moved that the question upon the Constitution should be immediately put. He said that the Constitution had so long been the subject of the deliberation of every man in this country, and that the members of the Convention had had such ample opportunity to consider it, that he believed every one of them was prepared to give his vote then upon the question; that the situation of the public funds would not admit of lavishing the public money, but required the utmost economy and frugality; that, as there was a large representation from this state, an immediate decision would save the country a considerable sum of money. He thought it, therefore, prudent to put the question immediately.

He was seconded by Mr. PERSON, who added to the reasoning of Mr. Jones, that he should be sorry if any man had come hither without having determined in his mind a question which must have been so long the object of his consideration.

Mr. IREDELL then arose, and addressed the president thus: —

Mr. President, I am very much surprised at the motion which has been made by the gentleman from Halifax. I am greatly astonished at a proposal to decide immediately, without the least deliberation, a question which is perhaps the greatest that ever was submitted to any body of men. There is no instance of any convention upon the continent, in which the subject has not been fully debated, except in those states which adopted the Constitution unanimously. If it be thought proper to debate at large an act of Assembly, trivial in its nature, and the operation of which may continue but a few months, are we to decide on this great and important question without a moment's consideration? Are we to give a dead vote upon it? If so, I would wish to know why we are met together. If it is to be resolved now by dead votes, it would have been better that every elector, instead of voting for persons to come here, should, in their respective counties, have voted or balloted for or against the Constitution. A decision by that mode would have been as rational and just as by this, and would have been better on economical principles, as it would have saved the public the expense of our meeting here.

This is a subject of great consideration. It is a Constitution which has been formed after much deliberation. It has had the sanction of men of the first characters for their probity and understanding. It has also had the solemn ratification of ten states in the Union. A Constitution like this, sir, ought not to be adopted or rejected in a moment. If, in consequence of either, we should involve our country in misery and distress, what excuse could we make for our conduct? Is it reconcilable with our duty to our constituents? Would it be a conscientious discharge of that trust which they have so implicitly reposed in us? Shall it be said, sir, of the representatives of North Carolina, that near three hundred of them assembled for the express purpose of deliberating upon the most important question that ever came before a people, refused to discuss it, and discarded all reasoning as useless? It is undoubtedly to be lamented that any addition should be made to the public expense, especially at this period, when the public funds are so low; but if it be ever necessary on any occasion, it is necessary on this, when the question perhaps involves the safety or ruin of our country. For my own part, I should not choose to determine on any question without mature reflection; and on this occasion, my repugnance to a hasty decision is equal to the magnitude of the subject. A gentleman has said, he should be sorry if any member had come here without having determined in his mind on a subject he had so long considered. I should be sorry, sir, that I could be capable of coming to this house predetermined for or against the Constitution. I readily confess my present opinion is strongly in its favor. I have listened to every objection, that I had an opportunity of hearing, with attention, but have not yet heard any that I thought would justify its rejection, even if it had not been adopted by so many states. But notwithstanding this favorable opinion I entertain of it, I have not come here resolved, at all events, to vote for its adoption. I have come here for information, and to judge, after all that can be said upon it, whether it really merits my attachment or not. My constituents did me the honor to elect me unanimously, without the least solicitation on my part. They probably chose me because my sentiments were the same with their own. But highly as I value this honor, and much as I confess my ambition prompted me to aspire to it, had I been told that I should not be elected unless I promised to obey their directions, I should have disdained to serve on such dishonorable terms. Sir, I shall vote perfectly independent, and shall certainly avow a change of my present opinion, if I can be convinced it is a wrong one. I shall not, in such a case, be restrained by the universal opinion of the part of the country from which I came. I shall not be afraid to go back, and tell my constituents, "Gentlemen, I have been convinced I was in an error. I found, on consideration, that the opinion which I had taken up was ill founded, and have voted according to my sincere sentiments at the time, though contrary to your wishes." I know that the honor and integrity of my constituents are such, that they would approve of my acting on such principles, rather than any other. They are the principles, however, I think it my duty to act upon, and shall govern my conduct.

This Constitution ought to be discussed in such a manner that every possible light may be thrown upon it. If those gentlemen who are so sanguine in their opinion that it is a bad government will freely unfold to us the reasons on which their opinion is founded, perhaps we may all concur in it. I flatter myself that this Convention will imitate the conduct of the conventions of other states, in taking the best possible method of considering its merits, by debating it article by article. Can it be supposed that any gentlemen here are so obstinate and tenacious of their opinion, that they will not recede from it when they hear strong reasons offered? Has not every gentleman here, almost, received useful knowledge from a communication with others? Have not many of the members of this house, when members of Assembly, frequently changed their opinions on subjects of legislation? If so, surely a subject of so complicated a nature, and which involves such serious consequences, as this, requires the most ample discussion, that we may derive every information that can enable us to form a proper judgment. I hope, therefore, that we shall imitate the laudable example of the other states, and go into a committee of the whole house, that the Constitution may be discussed clause by clause.

I trust we shall not go home and tell our constituents that we met at Hillsborough, were afraid to enter into a discussion of the subject, but precipitated a decision without a moment's consideration.

Mr. WILLIE JONES. Mr. President, my reasons for proposing an immediate decision were, that I was prepared to give my vote, and believed that others were equally prepared as myself. If gentlemen differ from me in the propriety of this motion, I will submit. I agree with the gentleman that economical considerations are not of equal importance with the magnitude of the subject. He said that it would have been better, at once, for the electors to vote in their respective counties than to decide it here without discussion. Does he forget that the act of Assembly points out another mode?

Mr. IREDELL replied, that what he meant was, that the Assembly might as well have required that the electors should vote or ballot for or against the Constitution in their respective counties, as for the Convention to decide it in this precipitate manner.

Mr. JAMES GALLOWAY. Mr. President, I had no supposition that the gentleman on my right (Mr. Jones) was afraid of a discussion. It is not so with me, nor do I believe that it is so with any gentleman here. I do not like such reflections, and am surprised that gentlemen should make them.

Mr. IREDELL declared that he meant not to reflect on any gentleman; but, for his part, he would by no means choose to go home and tell his constituents that he had voted without any previous consideration.

After some desultory conversation, the Convention adjourned till to-morrow, 10 o'clock.

THURSDAY, *July* 24, 1788.

The Convention met according to adjournment.

Rev. Mr. CALDWELL. Mr. President, the subject before us is of a complicated nature. In order to obviate the difficulty attending its discussion, I conceive that it will be necessary to lay down such rules or maxims as ought to be the fundamental principles of every free government: and after laying down such rules, to compare the Constitution with them, and see whether it has attended to them; for if it be not founded on such principles, it cannot be proper for our adoption. [Here he read those rules which he said appeared to him most proper.]

Mr. JAMES GALLOWAY. Mr. President, I had the

honor yesterday of proposing the mode which I thought most eligible for our proceeding. I wish the subject to be fairly, coolly, and candidly discussed, that we may not go away without knowing why we came hither. My intention is, that we should enter into a committee of the whole house, where we shall be at liberty to discuss it. Though I do not object to the proposition of the honorable member, as the groundwork of our proceeding, I hope he will withdraw his motion, and I shall second him in the committee.

Mr. CALDWELL had no objection to that proposition.

Mr. PERSON opposed the motion of entering into a committee. He conceived it would be a useless waste of time, as they would be obliged to reconsider the whole Constitution in Convention again.

Mr. DAVIE largely expatiated on the necessity of entering into a committee. He said, that the legislature, in voting so large a representation, did not mean that they should go away without investigating the subject, but that their collective information should be more competent to a just decision; that the best means was, to deliberate and confer together like plain, honest men. He did not know how the ardor of opposition might operate upon *some* gentlemen, yet he trusted that others had temper and moderation. He hoped that the motion of the member from Rockingham would be agreed to, and that the Constitution would be discussed clause by clause. He then observed, that, if they laid down a number of original principles, they must go through a double investigation; that it would be necessary to establish these original principles, and compare them with the Constitution; that it was highly improbable that they should agree on those principles; that he had a respect for the understanding of the honorable member, and trusted he would reflect, that difference in opinion arose from the nature of things; and that a great deal of time might be taken up to no purpose, if they should neither agree on those principles nor their application. He said, he hoped they would not treat this important business like a military enterprise, but proceed upon it like a deliberative body, and that the debates would be conducted with decency and moderation.

The Convention then resolved itself into a committee of the whole house, Mr. Elisha Battle in the chair.

Mr. CALDWELL. Mr. Chairman, those *maxims* which I conceive to be the fundamental principles of every safe and free government, are — 1st. A government is a compact between the rulers and the people. 2d. Such a compact ought to be lawful in itself. 3d. It ought to be lawfully executed. 4th. Unalienable rights ought not to be given up, if not necessary. 5th. The compact ought to be mutual. And, 6th. It ought to be plain, obvious, and easily understood. Now, sir, if these principles be just, by comparing the Constitution with them, we shall be able to judge whether it is fit for our adoption.

Mr. IREDELL. Mr. Chairman, I concur entirely in the sentiments lately urged by the gentleman from Halifax, and am convinced we shall be involved in very great difficulties if we adopt the principles offered by the gentleman from Guilford. To show the danger and impolicy of this proceeding, I think I can convince the committee in a moment, that his very first principle is erroneous. In other countries, where the origin of government is obscure, and its formation different from ours, government may be deemed a contract between the rulers and the people. What is the consequence? A compact cannot be annulled but by the consent of both parties; therefore, unless the rulers are guilty of oppression, the people, on the principle of a compact, have no right to new-model their government. This is held to be the principle of some monarchical governments in Europe. Our government is founded on much nobler principles. The people are known with certainty to have originated it themselves. Those in power are their servants and agents; and the people, without their consent, may new-model their government whenever they think proper, not merely because it is oppressively exercised, but because they think another form will be more conducive to their welfare. It is upon the footing of this very principle that we are now met to consider of the Constitution before us. If we attempt to lay down any rules here, it will take us as much time to establish their validity as to consider the system itself.

Mr. CALDWELL observed, that, though this government did not resemble the European governments, it still partook of the nature of a compact; that he conceived those principles which he proposed to be just, but was willing that any others, which should be thought better, should be substituted in their place.

Mr. MACLAINE. Mr. Chairman, the gentleman has taken his principles from sources which cannot hold here. In England, the government is a compact between the king and the people. I hope it is not so here. We shall have no officers in the situation of a king. The people here are the origin of all power. Our governors are elected temporarily. We can remove them occasionally, and put others in their stead. We do not bind ourselves. We are to consider whether this system will promote our happiness.

Mr. GOUDY. Mr. Chairman, I wonder that these gentlemen, learned in the law, should quibble upon words. I care not whether it be called a *compact, agreement, covenant, bargain,* or what. Its intent is a concession of power, on the part of the people, to their rulers. We know that private interest governs mankind generally. Power belongs originally to the people; but if rulers be not well guarded, that power may be usurped from them. People ought to be cautious in giving away power. These gentlemen say there is no occasion for general rules: every one has one for himself. Every one has an unalienable right of thinking for himself. There can be no inconvenience from laying down general rules. If we give away more power than we ought, we put ourselves in the situation of a man who puts on an iron glove, which he can never take off till he breaks his arm. Let us beware of the iron glove of tyranny. Power is generally taken from the people by imposing on their understanding, or by fetters. Let us lay down certain rules to govern our proceedings. It will be highly proper, in my opinion, and I very much wonder that gentlemen should object to it.

Mr. IREDELL. Mr. Chairman, the gentleman who spoke last mistook what the gentleman from Wilmington and myself have said. In my opinion, there ought to be a line drawn, as accurately as possible, between the power which is given and that which is retained. In this system, the line is most accurately drawn by the positive grant of the powers of the general government. But a compact between the rulers and the ruled, which gentlemen compare this government with, is certainly not the principle of our government. Will any man say that, if there be a compact, it can be altered without the consent of both parties ?   Those who govern, unless they grossly abuse their trust, (which is held an implied violation of the compact, and therefore a dissolution of it,) have a right to say they do not choose the government should be changed.   But have any of the officers of our government a right to say so if the people choose to change it ?   Surely they have not.   Therefore, as a general principle, it can never apply to a government where the people are avowedly the fountain of all power.   I have no manner of objection to the most explicit declaration that all power depends upon the people ; because, though it will not strengthen their rights, it may be the means of fixing them on a plainer foundation.   One gentleman has said that we were quibbling upon words.   If I know my own heart, I am incapable of quibbling on words.   I act on as independent principles as any gentleman upon the floor.   If I make use of quibbles, there are gentlemen here who can correct me.

If my premises are wrong, let them be attacked.   If my conclusions be wrong, let me be put right.   I am sorry that, in debating on so important a subject, it could be thought that we were disputing about words.   I am willing to apply as much time as is necessary for our deliberations.   I have no objection to any regular way of discussing the subject ; but this way of proceeding will waste time, and not answer any purpose.   Will it not be in the power of any gentleman, in the course of the debates, to say that this plan militates against those principles which the reverend gentleman recommends?   Will it not be more proper to urge its incompatibility with those principles during that discussion, than to attempt to establish their exclusive validity previous to our entering upon the new plan of government ?   By the former mode, those rules and the Constitution may be considered together.   By the latter, much time may be wasted to no purpose.   I trust, therefore, that the reverend gentleman will withdraw his motion.

Mr. RUTHERFORD.   Mr. Chairman, I conceive those maxims will be of utility.   I wish, as much as any one, to have a full and free discussion of the subject.   To facilitate this desirable end, it seems highly expedient that some groundwork should be laid, some line drawn, to guide our proceedings.   I trust, then, that the reverend gentleman's proposal will be agreed to.

Mr. SPENCER. I conceive that it will retard the business to accede to the proposal of the learned gentleman. The observation which has been made in its behalf does not apply to the present circumstances. When there is a king or other governor, there is a compact between him and the people. It is then a covenant. But in this case, in regard to the government which it is proposed we should adopt, there are no governors or rulers, we being the people who possess all power. It strikes me that, when a society of free people agree on a plan of government, there are no governors in existence; but those who administer the government are their servants. Although several of those principles are proper, I hope they will not be part of one discussion, but that every gentleman will consider and discuss the subject with all the candor, moderation, and deliberation, which the magnitude and importance of the subject require.

Mr. CALDWELL observed, that he would agree that any other word should be substituted to the word *compact*; but, after all that had been said, the Constitution appeared to him to be of the nature of a compact. It could not be fully so called till adopted and put in execution; when so put in execution, there were actual governors in existence.

Mr. DAVIE. Mr. President, what we have already said may convince the reverend gentleman what a long time it will take us to discuss the subject in the mode which he has proposed: those few solitary propositions which he has put on paper, will make but a small part of the principles of this Constitution. I wish the gentleman to reflect how dangerous it is to confine us to any particular rules. This system is most extensive in its nature, involving not only the principles of governments in general, but the complicated principles of federal governments. We should not, perhaps, in a week lay down all the principles essential to such a Constitution. Any gentleman may, in the course of the investigation, mention any maxims he thinks proper, and compare them with the Constitution. It would take us more time to establish these principles, than to consider the Constitution itself. It will be wrong to tie any man's hands. I hope the question will be put.

Mr. PERSON insisted on the propriety of the principles, and that they ought to be laid on the table with the Declaration of Rights, Constitution of the state, and the Confederation.

Mr LENOIR approved of the principles, but disapproved of being bound by any rules.

Mr. MACLAINE was of the same opinion as to the impropriety of being bound.

Mr. JAMES GALLOWAY wished to leave the hands of the members free, but he thought these principles were unexceptionable. He saw no inconvenience in adopting them, and wished they would be agreed to.

Mr. LENOIR answered, that the matter had been largely debated. He said, that he thought the previous question ought to be put, whether they should lay down certain principles to be governed by, or leave every man to judge as his own breast suggested.

After some little altercation, the previous question was put — for the principles, 90 ; against them, 163 ; majority against them, 73.

His excellency, Gov. JOHNSTON, then moved to discuss it by sections. This was opposed, because it would take up too much time.

After some altercation about the mode of considering the Constitution, Mr. IREDELL arose, and spoke as follows : —

Mr. President, whatever delay may attend it, a discussion is indispensable. We have been sent hither, by the people, to consider and decide this important business for them. This is a sacred trust, the honor and importance of which, I hope, are deeply impressed on every member here. We ought to discuss this Constitution thoroughly in all its parts. It was useless to come hither, and dishonorable, unless we discharge that trust faithfully. God forbid that any one of us should be determined one way or the other. I presume that every man thinks it his duty to hold his mind open to conviction ; that whatever he may have heard, whether against or for the Constitution, he will recede from his present opinion, if reasons of sufficient validity are offered. The gentleman from Granville has told us, that we had since March to consider it, and that he hoped every member was ready to give his vote upon it. 'Tis true, we have had since that time to consider it, and I hope every member has taken pains to inform himself. I trust they have conscientiously considered it ; that they have read on both sides of the question, and are resolved to vote according to the dictates of their consciences. I can truly say, that I believe there are few members in this house who have taken more pains to con-

2

sider it than myself. But I am still by no means confident that I am right. I have scarcely ever conversed on the subject with any man of understanding, who has not thrown some new light upon the subject which escaped me before. Those gentlemen who are so self-sufficient that they believe that they are never in the wrong, may arrogate infallibility to themselves, and conclude deliberation to be useless. For my part, I have often known myself to be in the wrong, and have ever wished to be corrected. There is nothing dishonorable in changing an opinion. Nothing is more fallible than human judgment. No gentleman will say that his is not fallible. Mine, I am sure, has often proved so. The serious importance of the subject merits the utmost attention; an erroneous decision may involve truly awful and calamitous consequences. It is incumbent on us, therefore, to decide it with the greatest deliberation. The Constitution is at least entitled to a regular discussion. It has had the sanction of many of the best and greatest men upon the continent — of those very men to whom, perhaps, we owe the privilege of debating now. It has also been adopted by ten states since. Is it probable that we are less fallible than they are? Do we suppose our knowledge and wisdom to be superior to their aggregate wisdom and information? I agree that this question ought to be determined on the footing of reason, and not on that of authority; and if it be found defective and unwise, I shall be for rejecting it; but it is neither decent nor right to refuse it a fair trial. A system supported by such characters merits at least a serious consideration. I hope, therefore, that the Constitution will be taken up paragraph by paragraph. It will then be in the power of any gentlemen to offer his opinion on every part, and by comparing it with other opinions, he may obtain useful information. If the Constitution be so defective as it is represented, then the inquiry will terminate in favor of those who oppose it. But if, as I believe and hope, it be discovered to be so formed as to be likely to promote the happiness of our country, then I hope the decision will be, accordingly, in its favor. Is there any gentleman so indifferent to a union with our sister states, as to hazard disunion rashly, without considering the consequences? Had my opinion been different from what it is, I am sure I should have hesitated and reflected a long time before I had offered it against such respectable authorities. I am sorry for the expense which may be incurred, when the community is so distressed ; but this is a trivial consideration compared to the consequences of a rash proceeding upon this important question.   Were any member to determine against it without proper consideration, and afterwards, upon his return home, on an impartial consideration, to be convinced it was a good system, his reflections on the temerity and precipitation of his conduct might destroy his peace of mind forever.   I doubt not the members in general who condemn it, do so from a sincere belief that the system is a bad one ; but at the same time, I believe there are many who are ready to relinquish that opinion, if they can be convinced it is erroneous, and that they sincerely wish for a fair and full discussion of the subject.   For these reasons I am of opinion that the motion made by the honorable member is proper to be adopted.

Mr. RUTHERFORD was surprised at the arguments used by gentlemen, and wished to know how they should vote, whether on the paragraphs, and how the report should be made when the committee rose.

His excellency, Gov. JOHNSTON.   If we reject any one part, we reject the whole.   We are not to form a constitution, but to say whether we shall adopt a Constitution to which ten states have already acceded.   If we think it a bad government, it is not binding to us ; we can reject it. If it be proper for our adoption, we may adopt it.   But a rejection of a single article will amount to a rejection of the whole.

Mr. RUTHERFORD.   The honorable gentleman has mistaken me.   Sorry I am that it is so late taken up by North Carolina, if we are to be influenced and persuaded in this manner.   I am unhappy to hear gentlemen of learning and integrity preach up the doctrine of adoption by ten states. Sir, it is my opinion that we ought to decide it as if no state had adopted it.   Are we to be thus intimidated into a measure of which we may disapprove ?

The question was then put, and carried by a great majority, to discuss the Constitution clause by clause.

The preamble of the Constitution was then read.

Mr. CALDWELL.   Mr. Chairman, if they mean, *We, the people*, — the people at large, — I conceive the expression is improper.   Were not they who framed this Constitution the representatives of the legislatures of the different states?. In my opinion, they had no power, from the people at large, to use their name, or to act for them. They were not delegated for that purpose.

Mr. MACLAINE. The reverend gentleman has told us, that the expression, *We, the people*, is wrong, because the gentlemen who framed it were not the representatives of the people. I readily grant that they were delegated by states. But they did not think that they were the people, but intended it for the people, at a future day. The sanction of the state legislatures was in some degree necessary. It was to be submitted by the legislatures to the people; so that, when it is adopted, it is the act of the people. When it is the act of the people, their name is certainly proper. This is very obvious and plain to any capacity.

Mr. DAVIE. Mr. Chairman, the observation of the reverend gentleman is grounded, I suppose, on a supposition that the Federal Convention exceeded their powers. This objection has been industriously circulated; but I believe, on a candid examination, the prejudice on which this error is founded will be done away. As I had the honor, sir, to be a member of the Convention, it may be expected I would answer an objection personal in its nature, and which contains rather a reflection on our conduct, than an objection to the merits of the Constitution. After repeated and decisive proofs of the total inefficiency of our general government, the states deputed the members of the Convention to revise and strengthen it. And permit me to call to your consideration that, whatever form of confederate government they might devise, or whatever powers they might propose to give this new government, no part of it was binding until the whole Constitution had received the solemn assent of the people. What was the object of our mission? "To decide upon the most effectual means of removing the defects of our federal union." This is a general, discretional authority to propose any alteration they thought proper or necessary. Were not the state legislatures afterwards to review our proceedings? Is it not immediately through their recommendation that the plan of the Convention is submitted to the people? And this plan must still remain a dead letter, or receive its operation from the fiat of this Convention. Although the Federal Convention might recommend the concession of the most extensive powers, yet they could not put one of them into execution. What have the Convention done that can merit this species of censure? They have only recommended a plan of government containing some additional powers to those enjoyed under the present feeble system; amendments not only necessary, but which were the express object of the deputation. When we investigate this system candidly and accurately, and compare all its parts with one another, we shall find it absolutely necessary to confirm these powers, in order to secure the tranquillity of the states and the liberty of the people. Perhaps it would be necessary, to form a true judgment of this important question, to state some events, and develop some of those defects, which gave birth to the late Convention, and which have produced this revolution in our federal government. With the indulgence of the committee, I will attempt this detail with as much precision as I am capable of. The general objects of the union are, 1st, to protect us against foreign invasion; 2d, to defend us against internal commotions and insurrections; 3d, to promote the commerce, agriculture, and manufactures, of America. These objects are requisite to make us a safe and happy people, and they cannot be attained without a firm and efficient system of union.

As to the first, we cannot obtain any effectual protection from the present Confederation. It is indeed universally acknowledged, that its inadequacy in this case is one of its greatest defects. Examine its ability to repel invasion. In the late glorious war, its weakness was unequivocally experienced. It is well known that Congress had a *discretionary right* to raise men and money; but they had no power to do either. In order to preclude the necessity of examining the whole progress of its imbecility, permit me to call to your recollection one single instance. When the last great stroke was made which humbled the pride of Britain, and put us in possession of peace and independence, so low were the finances and credit of the United States, that our army could not move from Philadelphia, until the minister of his most Christian majesty was prevailed upon to draw bills to defray the expense of the expedition. These were not obtained on the credit or interest of Congress, but by the personal influence of the commander-in-chief.

Had this great project miscarried, what fatal events might

have ensued! It is a very moderate presumption, that what has once happened may happen again. The next important consideration, which is involved in the external powers of the Union, are *treaties*. Without a power in the federal government to compel the performance of our engagements with foreign nations, we shall be perpetually involved in destructive wars. The Confederation is extremely defective in this point also. I shall only mention the British treaty as a satisfactory proof of this melancholy fact. It is well known that, although this treaty was ratified in 1784, it required the sanction of a law of North Carolina in 1787; and that our enemies, presuming on the weakness of our federal government, have refused to deliver up several important posts within the territories of the United States, and still hold them, to our shame and disgrace. It is unnecessary to reason on facts, the perilous consequences of which must in a moment strike every mind capable of reflection.

The next head under which the general government may be considered, is the regulation of commerce. The United States should be empowered to compel foreign nations into commercial regulations that were either founded on the principles of justice or reciprocal advantages. Has the present Confederation effected any of these things? Is not our commerce equally unprotected abroad by arms and negotiation? Nations have refused to enter into treaties with us. What was the language of the British court on a proposition of this kind? Such as would insult the pride of any man of feeling and independence. — "You can make engagements, but you cannot compel your citizens to comply with them. We derive greater profits from the present situation of your commerce than we could expect under a treaty; and you have no kind of power that can compel us to surrender any advantage to you." This was the language of our enemies; and while our government remains as feeble as it has been, no nation will form any connection with us that will involve the relinquishment of the least advantage. What has been the consequence? A general decay of trade, the rise of imported merchandise, the fall of produce, and an uncommon decrease of the value of lands. Foreigners have been reaping the benefits and emoluments which our citizens ought to enjoy An unjustifiable perversion of justice has pervaded almost all the states, and every thing presented to

our view a spectacle of public poverty and private wretch-
edness!

While this is a true representation of our situation, can our
general government recur to the ordinary expedient of *loans?*
During the late war, large sums were advanced to us by
foreign states and individuals. Congress have not been
enabled to pay even the interest of these debts, with honor
and punctuality. The requisitions made on the states have
been every where unproductive, and some of them have not
paid a stiver. These debts are a part of the price of our
liberty and independence — debts which ought to be regarded with gratitude and discharged with honor. Yet
many of the individuals who lent us money in the hour
of our distress, are now reduced to indigence in consequence of our delinquency. So low and hopeless are the
finances of the United States, that, the year before last,
Congress were obliged to borrow money even to pay the
interest of the principal which we had borrowed before.
This wretched resource of turning interest into principal, is
the most humiliating and disgraceful measure that a nation
could take, and approximates with rapidity to absolute ruin.
Yet it is the inevitable and certain consequence of such a
system as the existing Confederation.

There are several other instances of imbecility in that
system. It cannot secure to us the enjoyment of our own
territories, or even the navigation of our own rivers. The
want of power to establish a uniform rule for naturalization
through the United States is also no small defect, as it must
unavoidably be productive of disagreeable controversies with
foreign nations. The general government ought in this, as
in every other instance, to possess the means of preserving
the peace and tranquillity of the Union. A striking proof
of the necessity of this power recently happened in Rhode
Island: A man who had run off with a vessel and cargo, the
property of some merchants in Holland, took sanctuary in
that place: application was made for him as a citizen of the
United Netherlands by the minister, but, as he had taken the
oath of allegiance, the state refused to deliver him up, and
protected him in his villany. Had it not been for the peculiar situation of the states at that time, fatal consequences
might have resulted from such a conduct, and the contemptible state of Rhode Island might have involved the whole
Union in a war.

The encroachments of some states on the rights of others, and of all on those of the Confederacy, are incontestable proofs of the weakness and imperfection of that system. Maryland lately passed a law granting exclusive privileges to her own vessels, contrary to the Articles of the Confederation. Congress had neither power nor influence to alter it; all they could do was to send a contrary recommendation. It is provided, by the 6th Article of the Confederation, that no compact shall be made between two or more states without the consent of Congress; yet this has been recently violated by Virginia and Maryland, and also by Pennsylvania and New Jersey. North Carolina and Massachusetts have had a considerable body of forces on foot, and those in this state raised for two years, notwithstanding the express provision in the Confederation that no force should be kept up by any state in time of peace.

As to internal tranquillity, — without dwelling on the unhappy commotions in our own back counties, — I will only add that, if the rebellion in Massachusetts had been planned and executed with any kind of ability, that state must have been ruined; for Congress were not in a situation to render them any assistance.

Another object of the federal union is, to promote the agriculture and manufactures of the states — objects in which we are so nearly concerned. Commerce, sir, is the nurse of both. The merchant furnishes the planter with such articles as he cannot manufacture himself, and finds him a market for his produce. Agriculture cannot flourish if commerce languishes; they are mutually dependent on each other. Our commerce, as I have before observed, is unprotected abroad, and without regulation at home, and in this and many of the states ruined by partial and iniquitous laws — laws which, instead of having a tendency to protect property and encourage industry, led to the depreciation of the one, and destroyed every incitement to the other — laws which basely warranted and legalized the payment of just debts by *paper*, which represents nothing, or property of very trivial value.

These are some of the leading causes which brought forward this new Constitution. It was evidently necessary to infuse a greater portion of strength into the national government. But Congress were but a single body, with whom it was dangerous to lodge additional powers. Hence arose the necessity of a different organization. In order to form some balance, the departments of goverument were separated, and as a necessary check, the legislative body was composed of *two branches.* Steadiness and wisdom are better insured when there is a second branch, to balance and check the first. The stability of the laws will be greater when the popular branch, which might be influenced by local views, or the violence of party, is checked by another, whose longer continuance in office will render them more experienced, more temperate, and more competent to decide rightly.

The Confederation derived its sole support from the state legislatures. This rendered it weak and ineffectual. It was therefore necessary that the foundations of this government should be laid on the broad basis of the people. Yet the state governments are the pillars upon which this government is extended over such an immense territory, and are essential to its existence. The House of Representatives are immediately elected by the people. The senators represent the sovereignty of the states; they are directly chosen by the state legislatures, and no legislative act can be done without their concurrence. The election of the executive is in some measure under the control of the legislatures of the states, the electors being appointed under their direction.

The difference, in point of magnitude and importance, in the members of the confederacy, was an additional reason for the division of the legislature into two branches, and for establishing an equality of suffrage in the Senate. The protection of the small states against the ambition and influence of the larger members, could only be effected by arming them with an equal power in one branch of the legislature. On a contemplation of this matter, we shall find that the jealousies of the states could not be reconciled any other way. The lesser states would never have concurred unless this check had been given them, as a security for their political existence, against the power and encroachments of the great states. It may be also proper to observe, that the executive is separated in its functions from the legislature, as well as the nature of the case would admit, and the judiciary from both.

Another radical vice in the old system, which was necessary to be corrected, and which will be understood without a long deduction of reasoning, was, that it legislated on states, instead of individuals; and that its powers could not be executed but by fire or by the sword — by military force, and not by the intervention of the civil magistrate. Every one who is acquainted with the relative situation of the states, and the genius of our citizens, must acknowledge that, if the government was to be carried into effect by military force, the most dreadful consequences would ensue. It would render the citizens of America the most implacable enemies to one another. If it could be carried into effect against the small states, yet it could not be put in force against the larger and more powerful states. It was therefore absolutely necessary that the influence of the magistrate should be introduced, and that the laws should be carried home to individuals themselves.

In the formation of this system, many difficulties presented themselves to the Convention.

Every member saw that the existing system would ever be ineffectual, unless its laws operated on individuals, as military coercion was neither eligible nor practicable. Their own experience was fortified by their knowledge of the inherent weakness of all confederate governments. They knew that all governments merely federal had been short-lived, or had existed from principles extraneous from their constitutions, or from external causes which had no dependence on the nature of their governments. These considerations determined the Convention to depart from that solecism in politics — the principle of legislation for states in their political capacities.

The great extent of country appeared to some a formidable difficulty; but a confederate government appears, at least in theory, capable of embracing the various interests of the most extensive territory. Founded on the state governments solely, as I have said before, it would be tottering and inefficient. It became, therefore, necessary to bottom it on the people themselves, by giving them an immediate interest and agency in the government. There was, however, some real difficulty in conciliating a number of jarring interests, arising from the incidental but unalterable difference in the states in point of territory, situation, climate, and rivalship in commerce. Some of the states are very extensive, others very limited : some are manufacturing states, others merely agricultural : some of these are exporting states, while the carrying and navigation business are in the possession of others. It was not easy to reconcile such a multiplicity of

discordant and clashing interests.   Mutual concessions w're
necessary to come to any concurrence.   A plan that would
promote the exclusive interests of a few states would be injurious to others.   Had each state obstinately insisted on
the security of its particular local advantages, we should
never have come to a conclusion.   Each, therefore, amicably
and wisely relinquished its particular views.   The Federal
Convention have told you, that the Constitution which they
formed " was the result of a spirit of amity, and of that
mutual deference and concession which the peculiarity of
their political situation rendered indispensable."   I hope the
same laudable spirit will govern this Convention in their
decision on this important question.

    The business of the Convention was to amend the Con-
federation by giving it additional powers.   The present form
of Congress being a single body, it was thought unsafe to
augment its powers, without altering its organization.   The
act of the Convention is but a mere proposal, similar to the
production of a private pen.   I think it a government which,
if adopted, will cherish and protect the happiness and liberty
of America ; but I hold my mind open to conviction.   I
am ready to recede from my opinion if it be proved to be
ill-founded.   I trust that every man here is equally ready to
change an opinion he may have improperly formed.   The
weakness and inefficiency of the old Confederation produced
the necessity of calling the Federal Convention.   Their plan
is now before you ; and I hope, on a deliberate consideration,
every man will see the necessity of such a system.   It has
been the subject of much jealousy and censure out of doors.
I hope gentlemen will now come forward with their objections, and that they will be thrown out and answered with
candor and moderation.

    Mr. CALDWELL wished to know why the gentlemen
who were delegated by the states, styled themselves *We,
the people.*   He said that he only wished for information.

    Mr. IREDELL answered, that it would be easy to satisfy
the gentleman ; that the style, *We, the people*, was not to
be applied to the members themselves, but was to be the
style of the Constitution, when it should be ratified in their
respective states.

    Mr. JOSEPH TAYLOR.   Mr. Chairman, the very
wording of this Constitution seems to carry with it an

assumed power. *We, the people*, is surely an assumed power. Have they said, We, the delegates of the people? It seems to me that, when they met in Convention, they assumed more power than was given them. Did the people give them the power of using their name? This power was in the people. They did not give it up to the members of the Convention. If, therefore, they had not this power, they assumed it. It is the interest of every man, who is a friend to liberty, to oppose the assumption of power as soon as possible. I see no reason why they assumed this power. Matters may be carried still farther. This is a consolidation of all the states. Had it said, *We, the states*, there would have been a federal intention in it. But, sir, it is clear that a consolidation is intended. Will any gentleman say that a consolidated government will answer this country? It is too large. The man who has a large estate cannot manage it with convenience. I conceive that, in the present case, a consolidated government can by no means suit the genius of the people. The gentleman from Halifax (Mr. Davie) mentioned reasons for such a government. They have their weight, no doubt; but at a more convenient time we can show their futility. We see plainly that men who come from New England are different from us. They are ignorant of our situation; they do not know the state of our country. They cannot with safety legislate for us. I am astonished that the servants of the legislature of North Carolina should go to Philadelphia, and, instead of speaking of the *state* of North Carolina, should speak of the *people*. I wish to stop power as soon as possible; for they may carry their assumption of power to a more dangerous length. I wish to know where they found the power of saying *We, the people*, and of consolidating the states.

Mr. MACLAINE. Mr. Chairman, I confess myself astonished to hear objections to the preamble. They say that the delegates to the Federal Convention assumed powers which were not granted them; that they ought not to have used the words *We, the people*. That they were not the delegates of the people, is universally acknowledged. The Constitution is only a mere proposal. Had it been binding on us, there might be a reason for objecting. After they had finished the plan, they proposed that it should be recommended to the people by the several state legislatures

If the people approve of it, it becomes their act. Is not this merely a dispute about words, without any meaning whatever? Suppose any gentleman of this Convention had drawn up this government, and we thought it a good one; we might respect his intelligence and integrity, but it would not be binding upon us. We might adopt it if we thought it a proper system, and then it would be our act. Suppose it had been made by our enemies, or had dropped from the clouds; we might adopt it if we found it proper for our adoption. By whatever means we found it, it would be our act as soon as we adopted it. It is no more than a blank till it be adopted by the people. When that is done here, is it not the people of the state of North Carolina that do it, joined with the people of the other states who have adopted it? The expression is, then, right. But the gentleman has gone farther, and says that the people of New England are different from us. This goes against the Union altogether. They are not to legislate for us; we are to be represented as well as they. Such a futile objection strikes at all union. We know that without union we should not have been debating now. I hope to hear no more objections of this trifling nature, but that we shall enter into the spirit of the subject at once.

Mr. CALDWELL observed, that he only wished to know why they had assumed the name of the people.

Mr. JAMES GALLOWAY. Mr. Chairman, I trust we shall not take up more time on this point. I shall just make a few remarks on what has been said by the gentleman from Halifax. He has gone through our distresses, and those of the other states. As to the weakness of the Confederation, we all know it. A sense of this induced the different states to send delegates to Philadelphia. They had given them certain powers; we have seen them, they are now upon the table. The result of their deliberations is now upon the table also. As they have gone out of the line which the states pointed out to them, we, the people, are to take it up and consider it. The gentlemen who framed it have exceeded their powers, and very far. They will be able, perhaps, to give reasons for so doing. If they can show us any reasons, we will, no doubt, take notice of them. But, on the other hand, if our civil and religious liberties are not secured, and proper checks provided, we have the power in our own hands to do with it as we think proper. I hope gentlemen will permit us to proceed.

The clerk then read the 1st section of the 1st article.

Mr. CALDWELL. Mr. Chairman, I am sorry to be objecting, but I apprehend that all the legislative powers granted by this Constitution are not vested in a Congress consisting of the Senate and the House of Representatives, because the Vice-President has a right to put a check on it. This is known to every gentleman in the Convention. How can all the legislative powers granted in that Constitution be vested in the Congress, if the Vice-President is to have a vote in case the Senate is equally divided? I ask for information, how it came to be expressed in this manner, when this power is given to the Vice-President.

Mr. MACLAINE declared, that he did not know what the gentleman meant.

Mr. CALDWELL said, that the Vice-President is made a part of the legislative body, although there was an express declaration, that all the legislative powers were vested in the Senate and House of Representatives, and that he would be glad to know how these things consisted together.

Mr. MACLAINE expressed great astonishment at the gentleman's criticism. He observed, that the Vice-President had only a casting vote in case of an equal division in the Senate — that a provision of this kind was to be found in all deliberative bodies — that it was highly useful and expedient — that it was by no means of the nature of a check which impedes or arrests, but calculated to prevent the operation of the government from being impeded — that, if the gentleman could show any legislative power to be given to any but the two houses of Congress, his objection would be worthy of notice.

Some other gentlemen said, they were dissatisfied with Mr. Maclaine's explanation — that the Vice-President was not a member of the Senate, but an officer of the United States, and yet had a legislative power, and that it appeared to them inconsistent — that it would have been more proper to have given the casting vote to the President.

His excellency, Gov. JOHNSTON, added to Mr. Maclaine's reasoning, that it appeared to him a very good and proper regulation — that, if one of the Senate was to be appointed Vice-President, the state which he represented would either lose a vote if he was not permitted to vote on every occasion, or if he was, he might, in some instances, have two votes — that the President was already possessed of the power of preventing the passage of a law by a bare majority ; yet laws were said not to be made by the President, but by the two houses of Congress exclusively.

Mr. LENOIR. Mr. Chairman, I have a greater objection on this ground than that which has just been mentioned. I mean, sir, the legislative power given to the President himself. It may be admired by some, but not by me. He, sir, with the Senate, is to make treaties, which are to be the supreme law of the land. This is a legislative power given to the President, and implies a contradiction to that part which says that all legislative power is vested in the two houses.

Mr. SPAIGHT answered, that it was thought better to put that power into the hands of the senators as representatives of the states — that thereby the interest of every state was equally attended to in the formation of treaties — but that it was not considered as a legislative act at all.

Mr. IREDELL. Mr. Chairman, this is an objection against the inaccuracy of the sentence. I humbly conceive it will appear accurate on a due attention. After a bill is passed by both houses, it is to be shown to the President. Within a certain time, he is to return it. If he disapproves of it, he is to state his objections in writing ; and it depends on Congress afterwards to say whether it shall be a law or not. Now, sir, I humbly apprehend that, whether a law passes by a bare majority, or by two thirds, (which are required to concur after he shall have stated objections,) what gives active operation to it is, the will of the senators and representatives. The President has no power of legislation. If he does not object, the law passes by a bare majority; and if he objects, it passes by two thirds. His power extends only to cause it to be reconsidered, which secures a greater probability of its being good. As to his power with respect to treaties, I shall offer my sentiments on it when we come properly to it.

Mr. MACLAINE intimated, that if any gentleman was out of order,* it was the gentleman from Wilkes (Mr. Le-

---

- * Something had been said about order, which was not distinctly heard

noir) — that treaties were the supreme law of the land in all countries, for the most obvious reasons — that laws, or legislative acts, operated upon individuals, but that treaties acted upon states — that, unless they were the supreme law of the land, they could have no validity at all — that the President did not act in this case as a legislator, but rather in his executive capacity.

Mr. LENOIR replied that he wished to be conformable to the rules of the house ; but he still thought the President was possessed of legislative powers, while he could make treaties, joined with the Senate.

Mr. IREDELL. Mr. Chairman, I think the gentleman is in order. When treaties are made, they become as valid as legislative acts. I apprehend that every act of the government, legislative, executive, or judicial, if in pursuance of a constitutional power, is the law of the land. These different acts become the acts of the state by the instrumentality of its officers. When, for instance, the governor of this state grants a pardon, it becomes the law of the land, and is valid. Every thing is the law of the land, let it come from what power it will, provided it be consistent with the Constitution.

Mr. LENOIR answered, that that comparison did not hold.

Mr. IREDELL continued. If the governor grants a pardon, it becomes a law of the land. Why? Because he has power to grant pardons by the Constitution. Suppose this Constitution is adopted, and a treaty made ; that treaty is the law of the land. Why? Because the Constitution grants the power of making treaties.

Several members expressed dissatisfaction at the inconsistency (as they conceived it) of the expressions, when —

Mr. JAMES GALLOWAY observed, that their observations would be made more properly when they come to that clause which gave the casting vote to the Vice-President, and the qualified negative to the President.

The first three clauses of the 2d section read.

Mr. MACLAINE. Mr. Chairman, as many objections have been made to biennial elections, it will be necessary to obviate them. I beg leave to state their superiority to annual elections. Our elections have been annual for some years. People are apt to be attached to old customs. An nual elections may be proper in our state governments, but not in the general government. The seat of government is at a considerable distance; and in case of a disputed election it would be so long before it could be settled, that the state would be totally without representation. There is another reason, still more cogent, to induce us to prefer biennial to annual elections. The objects of state legislation are narrow and confined, and a short time will render a man sufficiently acquainted with them ; but those of the general government are infinitely more extensive, and require a much longer time to comprehend them. The representatives to the general government must be acquainted not only with the internal situation and circumstances of the United States, but also with the state of our commerce with foreign nations, and our relative situation to those nations. They must know the relative situation of those nations to one another, and be able to judge with which of them, and in what manner, our commerce should be regulated. These are good reasons to extend the time of elections to two years. I believe you remember, — and perhaps every member here remembers, — that this country was very happy under biennial elections. In North Carolina, the representatives were formerly chosen by ballot biennially. It was changed under the royal government, and the mode pointed out by the king. Notwithstanding the contest for annual elections, perhaps biennial elections would still be better for this country. Our laws would certainly be less fluctuating.

Mr. SHEPPERD observed, that he could see no propriety in the friends of the new system making objections, when none were urged by its opposers ; that it was very uncommon for a man to make objections and answer them himself ; and that it would take an immense time to mention every objection which had been mentioned in the country.

Mr. MACLAINE. It is determined already by the Convention to debate the Constitution section by section. Are we then to read it only ? Suppose the whole of it is to be passed over without saying any thing ; will not that amount to a dead vote ? Sir, I am a member of this Convention ; and if objections are made here, I will answer them to the best of my ability. If I see gentlemen pass by in silence such parts as they vehemently decry out of doors, or such parts as have been loudly complained of in the country, I shall answer them also.

After some desultory conversation, Mr. WILLIE JONES observed, that he would easily put the friends of the Constitution in a way of discussing it. Let one of them, said he, make objections and another answer them.

Mr. DAVIE. Mr. Chairman, I hope that reflections of a personal nature will be avoided as much as possible. What is there in this business should make us jealous of each other? We are all come hither to serve one common cause of one country. Let us go about it openly and amicably. There is no necessity for the employment of underhanded means. Let every objection be made. Let us examine the plan of government submitted to us thoroughly. Let us deal with each other with candor. I am sorry to see so much impatience so early in the business.

Mr. SHEPPERD answered, that he spoke only because he was averse to unnecessary delays, and that he had no finesse or design at all.

Mr. RUTHERFORD wished the system to be thoroughly discussed. He hoped that he should be excused in making a few observations, in the Convention, after the committee rose, and that he trusted gentlemen would make no reflections.

Mr. BLOODWORTH declared, that every gentleman had a right to make objections in both cases, and that he was sorry to hear reflections made.

Mr. GOUDY. Mr. Chairman, this clause of taxation will give an advantage to some states over the others. It will be oppressive to the Southern States. Taxes are equal to our representation. To augment our taxes, and increase our burdens, our negroes are to be represented. If a state has fifty thousand *negroes*, she is to send one representative for them. I wish not to be represented with negroes, especially if it increases my burdens.

Mr. DAVIE. Mr. Chairman, I will endeavor to obviate what the gentleman last up said. I wonder to see gentlemen so precipitate and hasty on a subject of such awful importance. It ought to be considered, that some of us are slow of apprehension, or not having those quick conceptions, and luminous understandings, of which other gentlemen may be possessed. The gentleman "does not wish to be repre sented with negroes." This, sir, is an unhappy species of population; but we cannot at present alter their situation. The Eastern States had great jealousies on this subject. They insisted that their cows and horses were equally entitled to representation; that the one was property as well as the other. It became our duty, on the other hand, to acquire as much weight as possible in the legislation of the Union; and, as the Northern States were more populous in whites, this only could be done by insisting that a certain proportion of our slaves should make a part of the computed population. It was attempted to form a rule of representation from a compound ratio of wealth and population; but, on consideration, it was found impracticable to determine the comparative value of lands, and other property, in so extensive a territory, with any degree of accuracy; and population alone was adopted as the only practicable rule or criterion of representation. It was urged by the deputies of the Eastern States, that a representation of two fifths would be of little utility, and that their entire representation would be unequal and burdensome — that, in a time of war, slaves rendered a country more vulnerable, while its defence devolved upon its free inhabitants. On the other hand, we insisted that, in time of peace, they contributed, by their labor, to the general wealth, as well as other members of the community — that, as rational beings, they had a right of representation, and, in some instances, might be highly useful in war. On these principles the Eastern States gave the matter up, and consented to the regulation as it has been read. I hope these reasons will appear satisfactory. It is the same rule or principle which was proposed some years ago by Congress, and assented to by twelve of the states. It may wound the delicacy of the gentleman from Guilford, (Mr. Goudy,) but I hope he will endeavor to accommodate his feelings to the interest and circumstances of his country.

Mr. JAMES GALLOWAY said, that he did not object to the representation of negroes, so much as he did to the fewness of the number of representatives. He was surprised how we came to have but five, including those intended to represent negroes. That, in his humble opinion, North Carolina was entitled to that number independent of the negroes.

Mr. SPAIGHT endeavored to satisfy him, that the Con-

vention had no rule to go by in this case — that they could
not proceed upon the ratio mentioned in the Constitution
till the enumeration of the people was made — that some
states had made a return to Congress of their numbers, and
others had not — that it was mentioned that we had had
time, but made no return — that the present number was
only temporary — that in three years the actual census would
be taken, and our number of representatives regulated accordingly.

His excellency, Gov. JOHNSTON, was perfectly satisfied with the temporary number.   He said that it could
not militate against the people of North Carolina, because
they paid in proportion; that no great inconvenience could
happen, in three years, from their paying less than their full
proportion; that they were not very flush of money, and that
he hoped for better times in the course of three years.

The rest of the 2d section read.

Mr. JOSEPH TAYLOR objected to the provision made
for impeaching.   He urged that there could be no security
from it, as the persons accused were triable by the Senate,
who were a part of the legislature themselves; that, while
men were fallible, the senators were liable to errors, especially
in a case where they were concerned themselves.

Mr. IREDELL.   Mr. Chairman, I was going to observe
that this clause, vesting the power of impeachment in the
House of Representatives, is one of the greatest securities
for a due execution of all public offices.   Every government
requires it.   Every man ought to be amenable for his conduct, and there are no persons so proper to complain of the
public officers as the representatives of the people at large.
The representatives of the people know the feelings of the
people at large, and will be ready enough to make complaints.   If this power were not provided, the consequences
might be fatal.   It will be not only the means of punishing
misconduct, but it will prevent misconduct.   A man in public office who knows that there is no tribunal to punish him,
may be ready to deviate from his duty; but if he knows
there is a tribunal for that purpose, although he may be a
man of no principle, the very terror of punishment will perhaps deter him.   I beg leave to mention that every man has
a right to express his opinion, and point out any part of the
Constitution which he either thinks defective, or has heard

represented to be so.   What will be the consequence if they
who have objections do not think proper to communicate
them, and they are not to be mentioned by others?   Many
gentlemen have read many objections, which perhaps have
made impressions on their minds, though they are not communicated to us.   I therefore apprehend that the member
was perfectly regular in mentioning the objections made out
of doors.   Such objections may operate upon the minds of
gentlemen, who, not being used to convey their ideas in
public, conceal them out of diffidence.

Mr. BLOODWORTH wished to be informed, whether
this sole power of impeachment, given to the House of Representatives, deprived the state of the power of impeaching
any of its members.

Mr. SPAIGHT answered, that this impeachment extended only to the officers of the United States — that it
would be improper if the same body that impeached had
the power of trying — that, therefore, the Constitution had
wisely given the power of impeachment to the House of
Representatives, and that of trying impeachments to the
Senate.

Mr. JOSEPH TAYLOR.   Mr. Chairman, the objection
is very strong.   If there be but one body to try, where are
we?   If any tyranny or oppression should arise, how are
those who perpetrated such oppression to be tried and punished?   By a tribunal consisting of the very men who assist
in such tyranny.   Can any tribunal be found, in any community, who will give judgment against their own actions?
Is it the nature of man to decide against himself?   I am
obliged to the worthy member from New Hanover for assist-
ing me with objections.   None can impeach but the representatives; and the impeachments are to be determined by
the senators, who are one of the branches of power which
we dread under this Constitution.

His excellency, Gov. JOHNSTON.   Mr. Chairman, the
worthy member from Granville surprises me by his objection.
It has been explained by another member, that only officers
of the United States were impeachable.   I never knew any
instance of a man being impeached for a legislative act; nay,
I never heard it suggested before.   No member of the House
of Commons, in England, has ever been impeached before
the Lords, nor any lord, for a legislative misdemeanor.   A

representative is answerable to no power but his constituents. He is accountable to no being under heaven but the people who appointed him.

Mr. TAYLOR replied, that it now appeared to him in a still worse light than before.

Mr. BLOODWORTH observed, that as this was a Constitution for the United States, he should not have made the observation he did, had the subject not been particularly mentioned — that the words " sole power of impeachment " were so general, and might admit of such a latitude of construction, as to extend to every legislative member upon the continent, so as to preclude the representatives of the different states from impeaching.

Mr. MACLAINE. Mr. Chairman, if I understand the gentleman rightly, he means that Congress may impeach all the people or officers of the United States. If the gentleman will attend, he will see that this is a government for confederated states ; that, consequently, it can never intermeddle where no power is given. I confess I can see no more reason to fear in this case than from our own General Assembly. A power is given to our own state Senate to try impeachments. Is it not necessary to point out some tribunal to try great offences ? Should there not be some mode of punishment for the offences of the officers of the general government ? Is it not necessary that such officers should be kept within proper bounds ? The officers of the United States are excluded from offices of honor, trust, or profit, under the United States, on impeachment for, and conviction of, high crimes and misdemeanors. This is certainly necessary. This exclusion from offices is harmless in comparison with the regulation made, in similar cases, in our own government. Here it is expressly provided how far the punishment shall extend, and that it shall extend no farther. On the contrary, the limits are not marked in our own Constitution, and the punishment may be extended too far. I believe it is a certain and known fact, that members of the legislative body are never, as such, liable to impeachment, but are punishable by law for crimes and misdemeanors in their personal capacity. For instance ; the members of Assembly are not liable to impeachment, but, like other people, are amenable to the law for crimes and misdemeanors committed as individuals. But in Congress, a member of either house can be no officer.

Gov. JOHNSTON. Mr. Chairman, I find that making objections is useful. I never thought of the objection made by the member from New Hanover. I never thought that impeachments extended to any but officers of the United States. When you look at the judgment to be given on impeachments, you will see that the punishment goes no farther than to remove and disqualify civil officers of the United States, who shall, on impeachment, be convicted of high misdemeanors. Removal from office is the punishment — to which is added future disqualification. How could a man be removed from office who had no office ? An officer of this state is not liable to the United States. Congress could not disqualify an officer of this state. No body can disqualify, but that body which creates. We have nothing to apprehend from that article. We are perfectly secure as to this point. I should laugh at any judgment they should give against any officer of our own.

Mr. BLOODWORTH. From the complexion of the paragraph it appeared to me to be applicable only to officers of the United States ; but the gentleman's own reasoning convinces me that he is wrong. He says he would laugh at them. Will the gentleman laugh when the extension of their powers takes place ? It is only by our adoption they can have any power.

Mr. IREDELL. Mr. Chairman, the argument of the gentleman last up is founded upon misapprehension. Every article refers to its particular object. We must judge of expressions from the subject matter concerning which they are used. The sole power of impeachment extends only to objects of the Constitution. The Senate shall only try impeachments arising under the Constitution. In order to confirm and illustrate that position, the gentleman who spoke before explained it in a manner perfectly satisfactory to my apprehension — " under this Constitution." What is the meaning of these words ? They signify those arising under the government of the United States. When this government is adopted, there will be two governments to which we shall owe obedience. To the government of the Union, in certain defined cases — to our own state government in every other case. If the general government were to disqualify me from any office which I held in North Carolina under its laws, I would refer to the Constitution, and say that they violated it, as it only extended to officers of the United States.

Mr. BLOODWORTH. The penalty is only removal from office. It does not mention from what office. I do not see any thing in the expression that convinces me that I was mistaken. I still consider it in the same light.

Mr. PORTER wished to be informed, if every officer, who was a creature of that Constitution, was to be tried by the Senate — whether such officers, and those who had complaints against them, were to go from the extreme parts of the continent to the seat of government, to adjust disputes.

Mr. DAVIE answered, that impeachments were confined to cases under the Constitution, but did not descend to petty offices ; that if the gentleman meant that it would be troublesome and inconvenient to recur to the federal courts in case of oppressions by officers, and to carry witnesses such great distances, he would satisfy the gentleman, that Congress would remove such inconveniences, as they had the power of appointing inferior tribunals, where such disputes would be tried.

Mr. J. TAYLOR. Mr. Chairman, I conceive that, if this Constitution be adopted, we shall have a large number of officers in North Carolina under the appointment of Congress. We shall undoubtedly, for instance, have a great number of tax-gatherers. If any of these officers shall do wrong, when we come to fundamental principles, we find that we have no way to punish them but by going to Congress, at an immense distance, whither we must carry our witnesses. Every gentleman must see, in these cases, that oppressions will arise. I conceive that they cannot be tried elsewhere. I consider that the Constitution will be explained by the word "sole." If they did not mean to retain a general power of impeaching, there was no occasion for saying the "sole power." I consider therefore that oppressions will arise. If I am oppressed, I must go to the House of Representatives to complain. I consider that, when mankind are about to part with rights, they ought only to part with those rights which they can with convenience relinquish, and not such as must involve them in distresses.

In answer to Mr. Taylor, Mr. SPAIGHT observed that, though the power of impeachment was given, yet it did not say that there was no other manner of giving redress — that it was very certain and clear that, if any man was injured by an officer of the United States, he could get redress by a suit at law.

Mr. MACLAINE. Mr. Chairman, I confess I never heard before that a tax-gatherer was worthy of impeachment. It is one of the meanest and least offices. Impeachments are only for high crimes and misdemeanors. If any one is injured in his person or property, he can get redress by a suit at law. Why does the gentleman talk in this manner? It shows what wretched shifts gentlemen are driven to. I never heard, in my life, of such a silly objection. A poor, insignificant, petty officer amenable to impeachment!

Mr. IREDELL. Mr. Chairman, the objection would be right if there was no other mode of punishing. But it is evident that an officer may be tried by a court of common law. He may be tried in such a court for common-law offences, whether impeached or not. As it is to be presumed that inferior tribunals will be constituted, there will be no occasion for going always to the Supreme Court, even in cases where the federal courts have exclusive jurisdiction. Where this exclusive cognizance is not given them, redress may be had in the common-law courts in the state; and I have no doubt such regulations will be made as will put it out of the power of officers to distress the people with impunity.

Gov. JOHNSTON observed, that men who were in very high offices could not be come at by the ordinary course of justice; but when called before this high tribunal and convicted, they would be stripped of their dignity, and reduced to the rank of their fellow-citizens, and then the courts of common law might proceed against them.

FRIDAY, *July* 25, 1788.

The Convention met according to adjournment.

Mr. BATTLE in the chair. 1st article of the 3d section read.

Mr. CABARRUS wished to be informed of the reason why the *senators* were to be elected for so long a time.

Mr. IREDELL. Mr. Chairman, I have waited for some time in hopes that a gentleman better qualified than myself

4

would explain this part. Every objection to every part of this Constitution ought to be answered as fully as possible.

I believe, sir, it was the general sense of all America, with the exception only of one state, in forming their own state constitutions, that the legislative body should be divided into two branches, in order that the people might have a double security. It will often happen that, in a single body, a bare majority will carry exceptionable and pernicious measures. The violent faction of a party may often form such a majority in a single body, and by that means the particular views or interests of a part of the community may be consulted, and those of the rest neglected or injured. Is there a single gentleman in this Convention, who has been a member of the legislature, who has not found the minority in the most important questions to be often right? Is there a man here, who has been in either house, who has not at some times found the most solid advantages from the coöperation or opposition of the other? If a measure be right, which has been approved of by one branch, the other will probably confirm it; if it be wrong, it is fortunate that there is another branch to oppose or amend it. These principles probably formed one reason for the institution of a Senate, in the form of government before us. Another arose from the peculiar nature of that government, as connected with the government of the particular states.

The general government will have the protection and management of the general interests of the United States. The local and particular interests of the different states are left to their respective legislatures. All affairs which concern this state only are to be determined by our representatives coming from all parts of the state; all affairs which concern the Union at large are to be determined by representatives coming from all parts of the Union. Thus, then, the general government is to be taken care of, and the state governments to be preserved. The former is done by a numerous representation of the people of each state, in proportion to its importance. The latter is effected by giving each state an equal representation in the Senate. The people will be represented in one house, the state legislatures in the other.

Many are of the opinion that the power of the Senate is

too great ; but I cannot think so, considering the great weight which the House of Representatives will have. Several reasons may be assigned for this. The House of Representatives will be more numerous than the Senate. They will represent the immediate interests of the people. They will originate all money bills, which is one of the greatest securities in any republican government. The respectability of their constituents, who are the free citizens of America, will add great weight to the representatives ; for a power derived from the people is the source of all real honor, and a demonstration of confidence which a man of any feeling would be more ambitious to possess, than any other honor or any emolument whatever. There is, therefore, always a danger of such a house becoming too powerful, and it is necessary to counteract its influence by giving great weight and authority to the other. I am warranted by well-known facts in my opinion that the representatives of the people at large will have more weight than we should be induced to believe from a slight consideration.

The British government furnishes a very remarkable instance to my present purpose. In that country, sir, is a king, who is hereditary — a man, who is not chosen for his abilities, but who, though he may be without principles or abilities, is by birth their sovereign, and may impart the vices of his character to the government. His influence and power are so great, that the people would bear a great deal before they would attempt to resist his authority. He is one complete branch of the legislature — may make as many peers as he pleases, who are immediately members of another branch ; he has the disposal of almost all offices in the kingdom, commands the army and navy, is head of the church, and has the means of corrupting a large proportion of the representatives of the people, who form the third branch of the legislature. The House of Peers, which forms the second branch, is composed of members who are hereditary, and, except as to money bills, (which they are not allowed either to originate or alter,) hath equal authority with the other house. The members of the House of Commons, who are considered to represent the people, are elected for seven years, and they are chosen by a small proportion of the people, and, I believe I may say, a large majority of them by actual corruption. Under these circumstances, one would suppose their influence, compared to that of the king and the lords, was very inconsiderable. But the fact is, that they have, by degrees, increased their power to an astonishing degree, and, when they think proper to exert it, can command almost any thing they please. This great power they enjoy, by having the name of representatives of the people, and the exclusive right of originating money bills. What authority, then, will our representatives not possess, who will really represent the people, and equally have the right of originating money bills?

The manner in which our Senate is to be chosen gives us an additional security. Our senators will not be chosen by a king, nor tainted by his influence. They are to be chosen by different legislatures in the Union. Each is to choose two. It is to be supposed that, in the exercise of this power, the utmost prudence and circumspection will be observed. We may presume that they will select two of the most respectable men in the state, two men who had given the strongest proofs of attachment to the interests of their country. The senators are not to hold estates for life in the legislature, nor to transmit them to their children. Their families, friends, and estates, will be pledges for their fidelity to their country. Holding no office under the United States, they will be under no temptation of that kind to forget the interest of their constituents. There is every probability that men elected in this manner will, in general, do their duty faithfully. It may be expected, therefore, that they will coöperate in every laudable act, but strenuously resist those of a contrary nature. To do this to effect, their station must have some permanency annexed to it.

As the representatives of the people may probably be more popular, and it may be sometimes necessary for the Senate to prevent factious measures taking place, which may be highly injurious to the real interests of the public, the Senate should not be at the mercy of every popular clamor. Men engaged in arduous affairs are often obliged to do things which may, for the present, be disapproved of, for want of full information of the case, which it is not in every man's power immediately to obtain. In the mean time, every one is eager to judge, and many to condemn; and thus many an action is for a time unpopular, the true policy and justice of which afterwards very plainly appear. These observations apply even to acts of legislation concerning domestic policy : they apply much more forcibly to the case of foreign negotiations, which will form one part of the business of the Senate. I hope we shall not be involved in the labyrinths of foreign politics. But it is necessary for us to watch the conduct of European powers, that we may be on our defence and ready in case of an attack. All these things will require a continued attention ; and, in order to know whether they were transacted rightly or not, it must take up a considerable time.

A certain permanency in office is, in my opinion, useful for another reason. Nothing is more unfortunate for a nation than to have its affairs conducted in an irregular manner. Consistency and stability are necessary to render the laws of any society convenient for the people. If they were to be entirely conducted by men liable to be called away soon, we might be deprived, in a great measure, of their utility ; their measures might be abandoned before they were fully executed, and others, of a less beneficial tendency, substituted in their stead. The public also would be deprived of that experience which adds so much weight to the greatest abilities.

The business of a senator will require a great deal of knowledge, and more extensive information than can be acquired in a short time. This can be made evident by facts well known. I doubt not the gentlemen of this house, who have been members of Congress, will acknowledge that they have known several instances of men who were members of Congress, and were there many months before they knew how to act, for want of information of the real state of the Union. The acquisition of full information of this kind must employ a great deal of time ; since a general knowledge of the affairs of all the states, and of the relative situation of foreign nations, would be indispensable. Responsibility, also, would be lessened by a short duration ; for many useful measures require a good deal of time, and continued operations, and no man should be answerable for the ill success of a scheme which was taken out of his hands by others.

For these reasons, I hope it will appear that six years are not too long a duration for the Senate. I hope, also, it will be thought that, so far from being injurious to the liberties and interest of the public, it will form an additional security to both, especially when the next clause is taken up, by which we shall see that one third of the Senate is to go out every second year, and two thirds must concur in the most important cases; so that, if there be only one honest man among the two thirds that remain, added to the one third which has recently come in, this will be sufficient to prevent the rights of the people being sacrificed to any unjust ambition of that body.

I was in hopes some other gentleman would have explained this paragraph, because it introduces an entire change in our system; and every change ought to be founded on good reasons, and those reasons made plain to the people. Had my abilities been greater, I should have answered the objection better. I have, however, done it in the best manner in my power, and I hope the reasons I have assigned will be satisfactory to the committee.

Mr. MACLAINE. Mr. Chairman, a gentleman yesterday made some objections to the power of the Vice-President, and insisted that he was possessed of legislative powers; that, in case of equality of voice in the Senate, he had the deciding vote, and that of course he, and not the Senate legislated. I confess I was struck with astonishment at such an objection, especially as it came from a gentleman of character. As far as my understanding goes, the Vice-President is to have no acting part in the Senate, but a mere casting vote. In every other instance, he is merely to preside in the Senate in order to regulate their deliberations. I think there is no danger to be apprehended from him in particular, as he is to be chosen in the same manner with the President, and therefore may be presumed to possess a great share of the confidence of all the states. He has been called a useless officer. I think him very useful, and I think the objection very trifling. It shows the uniform opposition gentlemen are determined to make. It is very easy to cavil at the finest government that ever existed.

Mr. DAVIE. Mr. Chairman, I will state to the committee the reasons upon which this officer was introduced. I had the honor to observe to the committee, before, the causes of the particular formation of the Senate — that it was owing, with other reasons, to the *jealousy* of the states, and, particularly, to the extreme jealousy of the lesser states of the power and influence of the larger members of the confederacy. It was in the Senate that the several political interests of the states were to be preserved, and where all their powers were to be perfectly balanced. The commercial jealousy between the Eastern and Southern States had a principal share in this business. It might happen, in important cases, that the voices would be equally divided Indecision might be dangerous and inconvenient to the public. It would then be necessary to have some person who should determine the question as impartially as possible. Had the Vice-President been taken from the representation of any of the states, the vote of that state would have been under local influence in the second. It is true he must be chosen from some state; but, from the nature of his election and office, he represents no one state in particular, but all the states. It is impossible that any officer could be chosen more impartially. He is, in consequence of his election, the creature of no particular district or state, but the officer and representative of the Union. He must possess the confidence of the states in a very great degree, and consequently be the most proper person to decide in cases of this kind. These, I believe, are the principles upon which the Convention formed this officer.

6th clause of the 3d section read.

Mr. JAMES GALLOWAY wished gentlemen to offer their objections. That they must have made objections to it, and that they ought to mention them here.

Mr. JOHN BLOUNT said, that the sole power of impeachment had been objected to yesterday, and that it was urged, officers were to be carried from the farthest parts of the states to the seat of government. He wished to know if gentlemen were satisfied.

Mr. MACLAINE. Mr. Chairman, I have no inclination to get up a second time, but some gentlemen think this subject ought to be taken notice of. I recollect it was mentioned by one gentleman, that petty officers might be impeached. It appears to me, sir, to be the most horrid ignorance to suppose that every officer, however trifling his office, is to be impeached for every petty offence; and that every man, who should be injured by such petty officers, could get no redress but by this mode of impeachment, at the seat of government, at the distance of several hundred miles, whither he would be obliged to summon a great number of witnesses. I hope every gentleman in this committee must see plainly that impeachments cannot extend to inferior officers of the United States. Such a construction cannot be supported without a departure from the usual and well-known practice both in England and America. But this clause empowers the House of Representatives, which is the grand inquest of the Union at large, to bring great offenders to justice. It will be a kind of state trial for high crimes and misdemeanors. I remember it was objected yesterday, that the House of Representatives had the sole power of impeachment. The word "sole" was supposed to be so extensive as to include impeachable offences against particular states. Now, for my part, I can see no impropriety in the expression. The word relates to the general objects of the Union. It can only refer to offences against the United States; nor can it be tortured so as to have any other meaning, without a perversion of the usual meaning of language. The House of Representatives is to have the sole power of impeachment, and the Senate the sole power of trying. And here is a valuable provision, not to be found in other governments.

In England, the Lords, who try impeachments, declare solemnly, upon honor, whether the persons impeached be guilty or not. But here the senators are on oath. This is a very happy security. It is further provided, that, when the President is tried, (for he is also liable to be impeached,) the chief justice shall preside in the Senate; because it might be supposed that the Vice-President might be connected, together with the President, in the same crime, and would therefore be an improper person to judge him. It would be improper for another reason. On the removal of the President from office, it devolves on the Vice-President. This being the case, if the Vice-President should be judge, might he not look at the office of President, and endeavor to influence the Senate against him? This is a most excellent caution. It has been objected by some, that the President is in no danger from a trial by the Senate, because he does nothing without its concurrence. It is true, he is expressly restricted not to make treaties without the concurrence of two thirds of the senators present, nor appoint officers without the concurrence of the Senate, (not requiring two thirds.)

The concurrence of all the senators, however, is not required in either of those cases. They may be all present when he is impeached, and other senators in the mean time introduced The chief justice, we ought to presume, would not countenance a collusion. One dissenting person might divulge their misbehavior. Besides, he is impeachable for his own misdemeanors, and as to their concurrence with him, it might be effected by misrepresentations of his own, in which case they would be innocent, though he be guilty. I think, therefore, the Senate a very proper body to try him. Notwithstanding the mode pointed out for impeaching and trying, there is not a single officer but may be tried and indicted at common law; for it is provided, that a judgment, in cases of impeachment, shall not extend farther than to removal from office, and disqualification to hold and enjoy any office of honor, trust, or profit, under the United States; but the party convicted shall, nevertheless, be liable and subject to indictment, trial, judgment, and punishment, according to law. Thus you find that no offender can escape the danger of punishment. Officers, however, cannot be oppressed by an unjust decision of a bare majority; for it further provides, that no person shall be convicted without the concurrence of two thirds of the members present; so that those gentlemen who formed this government have been particularly careful to distribute every part of it as equally as possible. As the government is solely instituted for the United States, so the power of impeachment only extends to officers of the United States. The gentleman who is so much afraid of impeachment by the federal legislature, is totally mistaken in his principles.

Mr. J. TAYLOR. Mr. Chairman, my apprehension is, that this clause is connected with the other, which gives the sole power of impeachment, and is very dangerous. When I was offering an objection to this part, I observed that it was supposed by some, that no impeachments could be preferred but by the House of Representatives. I concluded that perhaps the collectors of the United States, or gatherers of taxes, might impose on individuals in this country, and that these individuals might think it too great a distance to go to the seat of federal government to get redress, and would therefore be injured with impunity. I observed that there were some gentlemen, whose abilities are great, who con-

strue it in a different manner. They ought to be kind
enough to carry their construction not to the mere letter, but
to the meaning. I observe that, when these great men are
met in Congress, in consequence of this power, they will
have the power of appointing all the officers of the United
States. My experience in life shows me that the friends of
the members of the legislature will get the offices. These
senators and members of the House of Representatives will
appoint their friends to all offices. These officers will be
great men, and they will have numerous deputies under
them. The receiver-general of the taxes of North Carolina
must be one of the greatest men in the country. Will he
come to me for his taxes? No. He will send his deputy,
who will have special instructions to oppress me. How am
I to be redressed? I shall be told that I must go to Congress, to get him impeached. This being the case, whom
am I to impeach? A friend of the representatives of North
Carolina. For, unhappily for us, these men will have too
much weight for us; they will have friends in the government who will be inclined against us, and thus we may be
oppressed with impunity.

I was sorry yesterday to hear personal observations drop
from a gentleman in this house. If we are not of equal
ability with the gentleman, he ought to possess charity towards us, and not lavish such severe reflections upon us in
such a declamatory manner.

These are considerations I offer to the house. These oppressions may be committed by these officers. I can see no
mode of redress. If there be any, let it be pointed out.
As to personal aspersions, with respect to me, I despise them.
Let him convince me by reasoning, but not fall on detraction
or declamation.

Mr. MACLAINE. Mr. Chairman, if I made use of any
asperity to that gentleman yesterday, I confess I am sorry for
it. It was because such an observation came from a gentleman of his profession. Had it come from any other gentleman in this Convention, who is not of his profession, I
should not be surprised. But I was surprised that it should
come from a gentleman of the law, who must know the contrary perfectly well. If his memory had failed him, he might
have known by consulting his library. His books would
have told him that no petty officer was ever impeachable

When such trivial, ill-founded objections were advanced, by persons who ought to know better, was it not sufficient to irritate those who were determined to decide the question by a regular and candid discussion ?

Whether or not there will be a receiver-general in North Carolina, if we adopt the Constitution, I cannot take upon myself to say. I cannot say how Congress will collect their money. It will depend upon laws hereafter to be made. These laws will extend to other states as well as to us. Should there be a receiver-general in North·Carolina, he certainly will not be authorized to oppress the people. His deputies can have no power that he could not have himself. As all collectors and other officers will be bound to act according to law, and will, in all probability, be obliged to give security for their conduct, we may expect they will not dare to oppress. The gentleman has thought proper to lay it down as a principle, that these receivers-general will give special orders to their deputies to oppress the people. The President is the superior officer, who is to see the laws put in execution. He is amenable for any maladministration in his office. Were it possible to suppose that the President should give wrong instructions to his deputies, whereby the citizens would be distressed, they would have redress in the ordinary courts of common law. But, says he, parties injured must go to the seat of government of the United States, and get redress there. I do not think it will be necessary to go to the seat of the general government for that purpose. No persons will be obliged to attend there, but on extraordinary occasions; for Congress will form regulations so as to render it unnecessary for the inhabitants to go thither, but on such occasions.

My reasons for this conclusion are these : I look upon it as the interest of all the people of America, except those in the vicinity of the seat of government, to make laws as easy as possible for the people, with respect to local attendance. They will not agree to drag their citizens unnecessarily six or seven hundred miles from their homes. This would be equally inconvenient to all except those in the vicinity of the seat of government, and therefore will be prevented But, says the gentleman from Granville, what redress have we when we go to that place ? These great officers will be the friends of the representatives of North Carolina. It is possible they may, or they may not. They have the power to appoint officers for each state from what place they please. It is probable they will appoint them out of the state in which they are to act. I will, however, admit, for the sake of argument, that those federal officers who will be guilty of misdemeanors in this state will be near relations of the representatives and senators of North Carolina. What then ? Are they to be tried by them only ? Will they be the near friends of the senators and representatives of the other states ? If not, his objection goes for nothing. I do not understand what he says about detraction and declamation. My character is well known. I am no declaimer ; but when I see a gentleman, ever so respectable, betraying his trust to the public, I will publish it loudly ; and I say this is not detraction or declamation.

Gov. JOHNSTON. Mr. Chairman, impeachment is very different in its nature from what the learned gentleman from Granville supposes it to be. If an officer commits an offence against an individual, he is amenable to the courts of law. If he commits crimes against the state, he may be indicted and punished. Impeachment only extends to high crimes and misdemeanors in a *public office*. It is a mode of trial pointed out for great misdemeanors against the public. But I think neither that gentleman nor any other person need be afraid that officers who commit oppressions will pass with impunity. It is not to be apprehended that such officers will be tried by their cousins and friends. Such cannot be on the jury at the trial of the cause ; it being a principle of law that no person interested in a cause, or who is a relation of the party, can be a juror in it. This is the light in which it strikes me. Therefore the objection of the gentleman from Granville must necessarily fall to the ground on that principle.

Mr. MACLAINE. Mr. Chairman, I must obviate some objections which have been made. It was said, by way of argument, that they could impeach and remove any officer, whether of the United States or any particular state. This was suggested by the gentleman from New Hanover. Nothing appears to me more unnatural than such a construction. The Constitution says, in one place, that the House of Representatives shall have the sole power of impeachment. In the clauses under debate, it provides that the Senate shall have the sole power to try all impeachments, and then subjoins, that judgment, in cases of impeachment, shall not extend further than to removal from office, and disqualification to hold and enjoy any office of honor, trust, or profit, under the United States.   And in the 4th section of the 2d article, it says that the President, Vice-President, and all civil officers of the United States, shall be removed from office on impeachment for, and conviction of, treason, bribery, or other high crimes and misdemeanors.

Now, sir, what can be more clear and obvious than this? The several clauses relate to the same subject, and ought to be considered together.   If considered separately and unconnectedly, the meaning is still clear.   They relate to the government of the Union altogether.   Judgment on impeachment only extends to removal from office, and future disqualification to hold offices *under the United States.*   Can those be removed from offices, and disqualified to hold offices under the United States, who actually held no office under the United States?   The 4th section of the 2d article provides expressly for the removal of the President, Vice-President, and all civil officers of the United States, on impeachment and conviction.   Does not this clearly prove that none but officers of the United States are impeachable?   Had any other been impeachable, why was not provision made for the case of their conviction?   Why not point out the punishment in one case as well as in others?   I beg leave to observe, that this is a Constitution which is not made with any reference to the government of any particular state, or to officers of particular states, but to the government of the United States at large.

We must suppose that every officer here spoken of must be an officer of the United States.   The words discover the meaning as plainly as possible.   The sentence which provides that "judgment, in cases of impeachment, shall not extend further than to removal from office," is joined by a conjunction copulative to the other sentence, — "and disqualification to hold and enjoy any office of honor, trust, or profit, under the United States," — which incontrovertibly proves that officers of the United States only are referred to. No other grammatical construction can be put upon it. But there is no necessity to refer to grammatical constructions, since the whole plainly refers to the government of

the United States at large. The general government cannot intermeddle with the internal affairs of the state governments. They are in no danger from it. It has been urged
that it has a tendency to a consolidation. On the contrary, it
appears that the state legislatures must exist in full force,
otherwise the general government cannot exist itself. A
consolidated government would never secure the happiness
of the people of this country. It would be the interest of
the people of the United States to keep the general and individual governments as separate and distinct as possible.

Mr. BLOODWORTH. Mr. Chairman, I confess I am
obliged to the honorable gentleman for his construction.
Were he to go to Congress, he might put that construction
on the Constitution. But no one can say what construction
Congress will put upon it. I do not distrust him, but I
distrust them. I wish to leave no dangerous latitude of
construction.

The 1st clause of the 4th section read.

Mr. SPENCER. Mr. Chairman, it appears to me that
this clause, giving this control over the time, place, and
manner, of holding elections, to Congress, does away the
right of the people to choose the representatives every second year, and impairs the right of the state legislatures to
choose the senators. I wish this matter to be explained.

Gov. JOHNSTON. Mr. Chairman, I confess that I am
a very great admirer of the new Constitution, but I cannot
comprehend the reason of this part. The reason urged is,
that every government ought to have the power of continuing itself, and that, if the general government had not this
power, the state legislatures might neglect to regulate elections, whereby the government might be discontinued. As
long as the state legislatures have it in their power not to
choose the senators, this power in Congress appears to me
altogether useless, because they can put an end to the general government by refusing to choose senators. But I do
not consider this such a blemish in the Constitution as that
it ought, for that reason, to be rejected. I observe that every state which has adopted the Constitution, and recommended amendments, has given directions to remove this
objection; and I hope, if this state adopts it, she will do
the same.

Mr. SPENCER. Mr. Chairman, it is with great reluctance that 1 rise upon this important occasion.   I have considered with some attention the subject before us.   I have paid attention to the Constitution itself, and to the writings on both sides.   I considered it on one side as well as on the other, in order to know whether it would be best to adop. it or not.   I would not wish to insinuate any reflections on those gentlemen who formed it.   I look upon it as a great performance.   It has a great deal of merit in it, and it is, perhaps, as much as any set of men could have done.   Even if it be true, what gentlemen have observed, that the gentlemen who were delegates to the Federal Convention were not instructed to form a new constitution, but to amend the Confederation, this will be immaterial, if it be proper to be adopted.   It will be of equal benefit to us, if proper to be adopted in the whole, or in such parts as will be necessary, whether they were expressly delegated for that purpose or not.   This appears to me to be a reprehensible clause ; because it seems to strike at the state legislatures, and seems to take away that power of elecitons which reason dictates they ought to have among themselves.   It apparently looks forward to a consolidation of the government of the United States, when the state legislatures may entirely decay away.

   This is one of the grounds which have induced me to make objections to the new form of government.   It appears to me that the state governments are not sufficiently secured; and that they may be swallowed up by the great mass of powers given to Congress.   If that be the case, such power should not be given ; for, from all the notions which we have concerning our happiness and well-being, the state governments are the basis of our happiness, security, and prosperity.   A large extent of country ought to be divided into such a number of states as that the people may conveniently carry on their own government.   This will render the government perfectly agreeable to the genius and wishes of the people.   If the United States were to consist of ten times as many states, they might all have a degree of harmony.   Nothing would be wanting but some cement for their connection.   On the contrary, if all the United States were to be swallowed up by the great mass of powers given to Congress, the parts that are more distant in this great empire would be governed with less and less energy. It would not suit the genius of the people to assist in the government. Nothing would support government, in such a case as that, but military coercion. Armies would be necessary in different parts of the United States. The expense which they would cost, and the burdens which they would render necessary to be laid upon the people, would be ruinous. I know of no way that is likely to produce the happiness of the people, but to preserve, as far as possible, the existence of the several states, so that they shall not be swallowed up.

It has been said that the existence of the state governments is essential to that of the general government, because they choose the senators. By this clause, it is evident that it is in the power of Congress to make any alterations, except as to the place of choosing senators. They may alter the time from six to twenty years, or to any time ; for they have an unlimited control over the time of elections. They have also an absolute control over the election of the representatives. It deprives the people of the very mode of choosing them. It seems nearly to throw the whole power of election into the hands of Congress. It strikes at the mode, time, and place, of choosing representatives. It puts all but the place of electing senators into the hands of Congress. This supersedes the necessity of continuing the state legislatures. This is such an article as I can give no sanction to, because it strikes at the foundation of the governments on which depends the happiness of the states and the general government. It is with reluctance I make the objection. I have the highest veneration for the characters of the framers of this Constitution. I mean to make objections only which are necessary to be made. I would not take up time unnecessarily. As to this matter, it strikes at the foundation of every thing. I may say more when we come to that part which points out the mode of doing without the agency of the state legislatures.

Mr. IREDELL. Mr. Chairman, I am glad to see so much candor and moderation. The liberal sentiments expressed by the honorable gentleman who spoke last command my respect. No time can be better employed than in endeavoring to remove, by fair and just reasoning, every objection which can be made to this Constitution. I apprehend that the honorable gentleman is mistaken as to the extent of the operation of this clause.   He supposes that the control of the general government over elections looks forward to a consolidation of the states, and that the general word *time* may extend to twenty, or any number of years. In my humble opinion, this clause does by no means warrant such a construction.   We ought to compare other parts with it.   Does not the Constitution say that representatives shall be chosen every second year ?   The right of choosing them, therefore, reverts to the people every second year.   No instrument of writing ought to be construed absurdly, when a rational construction can be put upon it.   If Congress can prolong the election to any time they please, why is it said that representatives shall be chosen every second year? *They must be chosen every second year*; but whether in the month of March, or January, or any other month, may be ascertained, at a future time, by regulations of Congress. The word *time* refers only to the particular month and day within the two years.   I heartily agree with the gentleman, that, if any thing in this Constitution tended to the annihilation of the state government, instead of exciting the admiration of any man, it ought to excite the resentment and execration.   No such wicked intention ought to be suffered. But the gentlemen who formed the Constitution had no such object ; nor do I think there is the least ground for that jealousy.   The very existence of the general government depends on that of the state governments.   The state legislatures are to choose the senators.   Without a Senate there can be no Congress.   The state legislatures are also to direct the manner of choosing the President.   Unless, therefore, there are state legislatures to direct that manner, no President can be chosen.   The same observation may be made as to the House of Representatives, since, as they are to be chosen by the electors of the most numerous branch of each state legislature, if there are no state legislatures, there are no persons to choose the House of Representatives.   Thus it is evident that the very existence of the general government depends on that of the state legislatures, and of course, that their continuance cannot be endangered by it.

An occasion may arise when the exercise of this ultimate power in Congress may be necessary ; as, for instance, if a state should be involved in war, and its legislature could not assemble, (as was the case of South Carolina, and occasion ally of some other states, during the late war ;) it might also be useful for this reason — lest a few powerful states should combine, and make regulations concerning elections which might deprive many of the electors of a fair exercise of their rights, and thus injure the community, and occasion great dissatisfaction.   And it seems natural and proper that every government should have in itself the means of its own preservation.   A few of the great states might combine to prevent any election of representatives at all, and thus a majority might be wanting to do business ; but it would not be so easy to destroy the government by the non-election of senators, because one third only are to go out at a time, and all the states will be equally represented in the Senate.   It is not probable this power would be abused ; for, if it should be, the state legislatures would immediately resent it, and their authority over the people will always be extremely great.   These reasons induce me to think that the power is both necessary and useful.   But I am sensible great jealousy has been entertained concerning it ; and as perhaps the danger of a combination, in the manner I have mentioned, to destroy or distress the general government, is not very probable, it may be better to incur the risk, than occasion any discontent by suffering the clause to continue as it now stands.   I should, therefore, not object to the recommendation of an amendment similar to that of other states — that this power in Congress should only be exercised when a state legislature neglected or was disabled from making the regulations required.

Mr. SPENCER.   Mr. Chairman, I did not mean to insinuate that designs were made, by the honorable gentlemen who composed the Federal Constitution, against our liberties.   I only meant to say that the words in this place were exceeding vague.   It may admit of the gentleman's construction ; but it may admit of a contrary construction. In a matter of so great moment, words ought not to be so vague and indeterminate.   I have said that the states are the basis on which the government of the United States ought to rest, and which must render us secure.   No man wishes more for a federal government than I do.   I think it necessary for our happiness ; but at the same time, when we form a government which must entail happiness or misery on posterity, nothing is of more consequence than settling it so as to exclude animosity and a contest between the general and individual governments. With respect to the mode here mentioned, they are words of very great extent. This clause provides that a Congress may at any time alter such regulations, except as to the places of choosing senators. These words are so vague and uncertain, that it must ultimately destroy the whole liberty of the United States. It strikes at the very existence of the states, and supersedes the necessity of having them at all. I would therefore wish to have it amended in such a manner as that the Congress should not interfere but when the states refused or neglected to regulate elections.

Mr. BLOODWORTH. Mr. Chairman, I trust that such learned arguments as are offered to reconcile our minds to such dangerous powers will not have the intended weight. The House of Representatives is the only democratical branch. This clause may destroy representation entirely. What does it say? " The times, places, and manner, of holding elections for senators and representatives, shall be prescribed in each state by the legislature thereof; but the Congress may at any time, by law, make or alter such regulations, except as to the places of choosing senators." Now, sir, does not this clause give an unlimited and unbounded power to Congress over the times, places, and manner, of choosing representatives? They may make the time of election so long, the place so inconvenient, and the manner so oppressive, that it will entirely destroy representation. I hope gentlemen will exercise their own understanding on this occasion, and not let their judgment be led away by these shining characters, for whom, however, I have the highest respect. This Constitution, if adopted in its present mode, must end in the subversion of our liberties. Suppose it takes place in North Carolina; can farmers elect them? No, sir. The elections may be in such a manner that men may be appointed who are not representatives of the people. This may exist, and it ought to be guarded against. As to the place, suppose Congress should order the elections to be held in the most inconvenient place in the most inconvenient district; could every person entitled to vote attend at such a place? Suppose they should order it to be laid off into so many districts, and order the election to be held within each district, yet may not their power over the manner of election enable them to exclude from voting every description of men they please? The democratic branch is so much endangered, that no arguments can be made use of to satisfy my mind to it. The honorable gentleman has amused us with learned discussions, and told us he will condescend to propose amendments. I hope the representatives of North Carolina will never swallow the Constitution till it is amended.

Mr. GOUDY. Mr. Chairman, the invasion of these states is urged as a reason for this clause. But why did they not mention that it should be only in cases of invasion? But that was not the reason, in my humble opinion. I fear it was a combination against our liberties. I ask, when we give them the purse in one hand, and the sword in another, what power have we left? It will lead to an aristocratical government, and establish tyranny over us. We are freemen, and we ought to have the privileges of such.

Gov. JOHNSTON. Mr. Chairman, I do not impute any impure intentions to the gentlemen who formed this Constitution. I think it unwarrantable in any one to do it. I believe that were there twenty conventions appointed, and as many constitutions formed, we never could get men more able and disinterested than those who formed this; nor a constitution less exceptionable than that which is now before you. I am not apprehensive that this article will be attended with all the fatal consequences which the gentleman conceives. I conceive that Congress can have no other power than the states had. The states, with regard to elections, must be governed by the articles of the Constitution; so must Congress. But I believe the power, as it now stands, is unnecessary. I should be perfectly satisfied with it in the mode recommended by the worthy member on my right hand. Although I should be extremely cautious to adopt any constitution that would endanger the rights and privileges of the people, I have no fear in adopting this Constitution, and then proposing amendments. I feel as much attachment to the rights and privileges of my country as any man in it; and if I thought any thing in this Constitution tended to abridge these rights, I would not agree to it. I cannot conceive that this is the case. I have not the least doubt but it will be adopted by a very great

majority of the states.   For states who have been as jealous
of their liberties as any in the world have adopted it, and
they are some of the most powerful states.   We shall have
the assent of all the states in getting amendments.   Some
gentlemen have apprehensions that Congress will immediately conspire to destroy the liberties of their country.   The
men of whom Congress will consist are to be chosen from
among ourselves.   They will be in the same situation with
us.   They are to be bone of our bone and flesh of our flesh.
They cannot injure us without injuring themselves.   I have
no doubt but we shall choose the best men in the community.   Should different men be appointed, they are
sufficiently responsible.   I therefore think that no danger is
to be apprehended.

Mr. M'DOWALL.   Mr. Chairman, I have the highest
esteem for the gentleman who spoke last.   He has amused
us with the fine characters of those who formed that government.   Some were good, but some were very imperious,
aristocratical, despotic, and monarchical.   If parts of it are
extremely good, other parts are very bad.

The freedom of election is one of the greatest securities
we have for our liberty and privileges.   It was supposed by
the member from Edenton, that the control over elections
was only given to Congress to be used in case of invasion.
I differ from him.   That could not have been their intention,
otherwise they could have expressed it.   But, sir, it points
forward to the time when there will be no state legislatures
— to the consolidation of all the states.   The states will be
kept up as boards of elections.   I think the same men could
make a better constitution ; for good government is not the
work of a short time.   They only had their own wisdom.
Were they to go now, they would have the wisdom of the
United States.   Every gentleman who must reflect on this
must see it.   The adoption of several other states is urged.
I hope every gentleman stands for himself, will act according to his own judgment, and will pay no respect to the
adoption by the other states.   It may embarrass us in some
political difficulties, but let us attend to the interest of our
constituents.

Mr. IREDELL answered, that he stated the case of
invasion as only one reason out of many for giving the ultimate control over elections to Congress.

Mr. DAVIE. Mr. Chairman, a consolidation of the states is said by some gentlemen to have been intended. They insinuate that this was the cause of their giving this power of elections. If there were any seeds in this Constitution which might, one day, produce a consolidation, it would, sir, with me, be an insuperable objection, I am so perfectly convinced that so extensive a country as this can never be managed by one consolidated government. The Federal Convention were as well convinced as the members of this house, that the state governments were absolutely necessary to the existence of the federal government. They considered them as the great massy pillars on which this political fabric was to be extended and supported; and were fully persuaded that, when they were removed, or should moulder down by time, the general government must tumble into ruin. A very little reflection will show that no department of it can exist without the state governments.

Let us begin with the House of Representatives. Who are to vote for the federal representatives? Those who vote for the state representatives. If the state government vanishes, the general government must vanish also. This is the foundation on which this government was raised, and without which it cannot possibly exist.

The next department is the Senate. How is it formed? By the states themselves. Do they not choose them? Are they not created by them? And will they not have the interest of the states particularly at heart? The states, sir, can put a final period to the government, as was observed by a gentleman who thought this power over elections unnecessary. If the state legislatures think proper, they may refuse to choose senators, and the government must be destroyed.

Is not this government a nerveless mass, a dead carcase, without the executive power? Let your representatives be the most vicious demons that ever existed; let them plot against the liberties of America; let them conspire against its happiness, — all their machinations will not avail if not put in execution. By whom are their laws and projects to be executed? By the President. How is he created? By electors appointed by the people under the direction of the legislatures — by a union of the interest of the people and the state governments. The state governments can put a *veto*, at any time, on the general government, by ceasing to continue the executive power. Admitting the representatives or senators could make corrupt laws, they can neither execute them themselves, nor appoint the executive. Now, sir, I think it must be clear to every candid mind, that no part of this government can be continued after the state governments lose their existence, or even their present forms. It may also be easily proved that all federal governments possess an inherent weakness, which continually tends to their destruction. It is to be lamented that all governments of a federal nature have been short-lived.

Such was the fate of the Achæan league, the Amphictyonic council, and other ancient confederacies ; and this opinion is confirmed by the uniform testimony of all history. There are instances in Europe of confederacies subsisting a considerable time ; but their duration must be attributed to circumstances exterior to their government. The Germanic confederacy would not exist a moment, were it not for fear of the surrounding powers, and the interest of the emperor. The history of this confederacy is but a series of factions, dissensions, bloodshed, and civil war. The confederacies of the Swiss, and United Netherlands, would long ago have been destroyed, from their imbecility, had it not been for the fear, and even the policy, of the bordering nations. It is impossible to construct such a government in such a manner as to give it any probable longevity. But, sir, there is an excellent principle in this proposed plan of federal government, which none of these confederacies had, and to the want of which, in a great measure, their imperfections may be justly attributed — I mean the principle of representation. I hope that, by the agency of this principle, if it be not immortal, it will at least be long-lived. I thought it necessary to say this much to detect the futility of that unwarrantable suggestion, that we are to be swallowed up by a great consolidated government. Every part of this federal government is dependent on the constitution of the state legislatures for its existence. The whole, sir, can never swallow up its parts. The gentleman from Edenton (Mr. Iredell) has pointed out the reasons of giving this control over elections to Congress, the principal of which was, to prevent a dissolution of the government by designing states. If all the states were equally possessed of absolute power over their elections, without any control of Congress, danger might be justly apprehended where one state possesses as much terri-

tory as four or five others; and some of them, being thinly
peopled now, will daily become more numerous and formidable.   Without this control in Congress, those large states
might successfully combine to destroy the general government.   It was therefore necessary to control any combination of this kind.

Another principal reason was, that it would operate, in
favor of the people, against the ambitious designs of the federal Senate.   I will illustrate this by matter of fact.   The
history of the little state of Rhode Island is well known.   An
abandoned faction have seized on the reins of government,
and frequently refused to have any representation in Congress.   If Congress had the power of making the law of
elections operate throughout the United States, no state
could withdraw itself from the national councils, without the
consent of a majority of the members of Congress.   Had this
been the case, that trifling state would not have withheld its
representation.   What once happened may happen again;
and it was necessary to give Congress this power, to keep the
government in full operation.   This being a federal government, and involving the interests of several states, and some
acts requiring the assent of more than a majority, they ought
to be able to keep their representation full.   It would have
been a solecism, to have a government without *any means* of
self-preservation.   The Confederation is the only instance
of a government without such means, and is a nerveless system, as inadequate to every purpose of government as it is to
the security of the liberties of the people of America.   When
the councils of America have this power over elections, they
can, in spite of any faction in any particular state, give the
people a representation.   Uniformity in matters of election
is also of the greatest consequence.   They ought all to be
judged by the same law and the same principles, and not to
be different in one state from what they are in another.   At
present, the manner of electing is different in different states.
Some elect by ballot, and others *viva voce*.   It will be more
convenient to have the manner uniform in all the states.   I
shall now answer some observations made by the gentleman
from Mecklenburg.   He has stated that this power over
elections gave to Congress power to lengthen the time for
which they were elected.   Let us read this clause coolly,
all prejudice aside, and determine whether this construction

be warrantable. The clause runs thus: " The times, places, and manner, of holding elections for senators and representatives, shall be prescribed in each state by the legislature thereof; but the Congress may at any time, by law, make or alter such regulations, except as to the place of choosing senators." I take it as a fundamental principle, which is beyond the reach of the general or individual governments to alter, that the representatives shall be chosen every second year, and that the tenure of their office shall be for two years ; that senators be chosen every sixth year, and that the tenure of their office be for six years. I take it also as a principle, that the electors of the most numerous branch of the state legislatures are to elect the federal representatives. Congress has ultimately no power over elections, but what is primarily given to the state legislatures. If Congress had the power of prolonging the time, &c., as gentlemen observe, the same powers must be completely vested in the state legislatures. I call upon every gentleman candidly to declare, whether the state legislatures have the power of altering the time of elections for representatives from two to four years, or senators from six to twelve ; and whether they have the power to require any other qualifications than those of the most numerous branch of the state legislatures ; and also whether they have any other power over the manner of elections, any more than the mere mode of the act of choosing ; or whether they shall be held by sheriffs, as contradistinguished from any other officer ; or whether they shall be by votes, as contradistinguished from ballots, or any other way. If gentlemen will pay attention, they will find that, in the latter part of this clause, Congress has no power but what was given to the states in the first part of the same clause. They may alter the manner of holding the election, but cannot alter the tenure of their office. They cannot alter the nature of the elections ; for it is established, as fundamental principles, that the electors of the most numerous branch of the state legislature shall elect the federal representatives, and that the tenure of their office shall be for two years ; and likewise, that the senators shall be elected by the legislatures, and that the tenure of their office shall be for six years. When gentlemen view the clause accurately, and see that Congress have only the same power which was in the state legislature, they will not be alarmed. The

6

learned doctor on my right (Mr. Spencer) has also said that
Congress might lengthen the time of elections.   I am willing to appeal to grammatical construction and punctuation.
Let me read this, as it stands on paper.   [Here he read the
clause different ways, expressing the same sense.]   Here,
in the first part of the clause, this power over elections is
given to the states, and in the latter part the same power is
given to Congress, and extending only to the time of *holding*, the place of *holding*, and the manner of *holding*, the
elections.   Is this not the plain, literal, and grammatical
construction of the clause?   Is it possible to put any other
construction on it, without departing from the natural order,
and without deviating from the general meaning of the words,
and every rule of grammatical construction?   Twist it, torture it, as you may, sir, it is impossible to fix a different sense
upon it.   The worthy gentleman from New Hanover, (whose
ardor for the liberty of his country I wish never to be damped,)
has insinuated that high characters might influence the members on this occasion.   I declare, for my own part, I wish
every man to be guided by his own conscience and understanding, and by nothing else.   Every man has not been
bred a politician, nor studied the science of government;
yet, when a subject is explained, if the mind is unwarped by
prejudice, and not in the leading-strings of other people,
gentlemen will do what is right.   Were this the case, I
would risk my salvation on a right decision.

Mr. CALDWELL.   Mr. Chairman, those things which
can be may be.   We know that, in the British government,
the members of Parliament were eligible only for three
years.   They determined they might be chosen for seven
years.   If Congress can alter the time, manner, and place,
I think it will enable them to do what the British Parliament once did.   They have declared that the elections
of senators are for six years, and of representatives for two
years.   But they have said there was an exception to this
general declaration, viz., that Congress can alter them.   If
the Convention only meant that they should alter them in
such a manner as to prevent a discontinuation of the government, why have they not said so?   It must appear to
every gentleman in this Convention, that they can alter
the elections to what time they please.   And if the British
Parliament did once give themselves the power of sitting
four years longer than they had a right to do, Congress,

having a standing army, and the command of the militia, may, with the same propriety, make an act to continue the members for twenty years, or even for their natural lives. This construction appears perfectly rational to me. I shall therefore think that this Convention will never swallow such a government, without securing us against danger.

Mr. MACLAINE. Mr. Chairman, the reverend gentleman from Guilford has made an objection which astonishes me more than any thing I have heard. He seems to be acquainted with the history of England, but he ought to consider whether his historical references apply to this country. He tells us of triennial elections being changed to septennial elections. This is an historical fact we well know, and the occasion on which it happened is equally well known. They talk as loudly of constitutional rights and privileges in England as we do here, but they have no written constitution. They have a common law,— which has been altered from year to year, for a very long period, — Magna Charta, and bill of rights. These they look upon as their constitution. Yet this is such a constitution as it is universally considered Parliament can change. Blackstone, in his admirable Commentaries, tells us that the power of the Parliament is transcendent and absolute, and can do and undo every thing that is not naturally impossible. The act, therefore, to which the reverend gentleman alludes, was not unconstitutional. Has any man said that the legislature can deviate from this Constitution? The legislature is to be guided by the Constitution. They cannot travel beyond its bounds. The reverend gentleman says, that, though the representatives are to be elected for two years, they may pass an act prolonging their appointment for twenty years, or for natural life, without any violation of the Constitution. Is it possible for any common understanding or sense to put this construction upon it? Such an act, sir, would be a palpable violation of the Constitution: were they to attempt it, sir, the country would rise against them. After such an unwarrantable suggestion as this, any objection may be made to this Constitution. It is necessary to give power to the government. I would ask that gentleman who is so much afraid it will destroy our liberties, why he is not as much afraid of our state legislature; for they have much more power than we are now proposing to give this general government. They have an unlimited control over the purse and sword ; yet no complaints are made. Why is he not as much afraid that our legislature will call out the militia to destroy our liberties? Will the militia be called out by the general government to enslave the people — to enslave their friends, their families, themselves? The idea of the militia being made use of, as an instrument to destroy our liberties, is almost too absurd to merit a refutation. It cannot be supposed that the representatives of our general government will be worse men than the members of our state government. Will we be such fools as to send our greatest rascals to the general government? We must be both fools as well as villains to do so.

Gov. JOHNSTON. Mr. Chairman, I shall offer some observations on what the gentleman said. A parallel has been drawn between the British Parliament and Congress. The powers of Congress are all circumscribed, defined, and clearly laid down. So far they may go, but no farther. But, sir, what are the powers of the British Parliament? They have no written constitution in Britain. They have certain fundamental principles and legislative acts, securing the liberty of the people ; but these may be altered by their representatives, without violating their constitution, in such manner as they may think proper. Their legislature existed long before the science of government was well understood. From very early periods, you find their Parliament in full force. What is their Magna Charta? It is only an act of Parliament. Their Parliament can, at any time, alter the whole or any part of it. In short, it is no more binding on the people than any other act which has passed. The power of the Parliament is, therefore, unbounded. But, sir, can Congress alter the Constitution? They have no such power. They are bound to act by the Constitution. They dare not recede from it. At the moment that the time for which they are elected expires, they may be removed. If they make bad laws, they will be removed ; for they will be no longer worthy of confidence. The British Parliament can do every thing they please. Their bill of rights is only an act of Parliament, which may be, at any time, altered or modified, without a violation of the constitution. The people of Great Britain have no constitution to control their legislature. The king, lords, and commons, can do what they please.

Mr. CALDWELL observed, that whatever nominal powers the British Parliament might possess, yet they had infringed the liberty of the people in the most flagrant manner, by giving themselves power to continue four years in Parliament longer than they had been elected for — that though they were only chosen for three years by their constituents, yet they passed an act that representatives should, for the future, be chosen for seven years — that this Constitution would have a dangerous tendency — that this clause would enable them to prolong their continuance in office as long as they pleased — and that, if a constitution was not agreeable to the people, its operation could not be happy.

Gov. JOHNSTON replied, that the act to which allusion was made by the gentleman was not unconstitutional ; but that, if Congress were to pass an act prolonging the terms of elections of senators or representatives, it would be clearly unconstitutional.

Mr. MACLAINE observed, that the act of Parliament referred to was passed on urgent necessity, when George I. ascended the throne, to prevent the Papists from getting into Parliament ; for parties ran so high at that time, that Papists enough might have got in to destroy the act of settlement which excluded the Roman Catholics from the succession to the throne.

Mr. SPENCER. The gentleman from Halifax said, that the reason of this clause was, that some states might be refractory. I profess that, in my opinion, the circumstances of Rhode Island do not appear to apply. I cannot conceive the particular cause why Rhode Island should not send representatives to Congress. If they were united in one government, is it presumed that they would waive the right of representation ? I have not the least reason to doubt they would make use of the privilege. With respect to the construction that the worthy member put upon the clause, were that construction established, I would be satisfied ; but it is susceptible of a different explanation. They may alter the mode of election so as to deprive the people of the right of choosing. I wish to have it expressed in a more explicit manner.

Mr. DAVIE. Mr. Chairman, the gentleman has certainly misconceived the matter, when he says " that the circumstances of Rhode Island do not apply." It is a fact well known of which, perhaps, he may not be possessed, that the state of Rhode Island has not been regularly represented for several years, owing to the character and particular views of the prevailing party. By the influence of this faction, who are in possession of the state government, the people have been frequently deprived of the benefit of a representation in the Union, and Congress often embarrassed by their absence. The same evil may again result from the same cause ; and Congress ought, therefore, to possess constitutional power to give the people an opportunity of electing representatives, if the states neglect or refuse to do it. The gentleman from Anson has said, " that this clause is susceptible of an explanation different from the construction I put upon it." I have a high respect for his opinion, but that alone, on this important occasion, is not satisfactory : we must have some *reasons* from him to support and sanction this opinion. He is a professional man, and has held an office many years, the nature and duties of which would enable him to put a different construction on this clause, if it is capable of it.

This clause, sir, has been the occasion of much groundless alarm, and has been the favorite theme of declamation out of doors. I now call upon the gentlemen of the opposition to show that it contains the mischiefs with which they have alarmed and agitated the public mind, and I defy them to support the construction they have put upon it by one single plausible reason. The gentleman from New Hanover has said, in objection to this clause, " that Congress may appoint the most inconvenient place in the most inconvenient district, and make the manner of election so oppressive as entirely to destroy representation." If this is considered as possible, he should also reflect that the state legislatures may do the same thing. But this can never happen, sir, until the whole mass of the people become corrupt, when all parchment securities will be of little service. Does that gentleman, or any other gentleman who has the smallest acquaintance with human nature or the spirit of America, suppose that the people will passively relinquish privileges, or suffer the usurpation of powers unwarranted by the Constitution ? Does not the right of electing representatives revert to the people every second year ? There is nothing in this clause that can impede or destroy this reversion ; and although the particular time of year, the particular place in a county or a district, or the particular mode in which elections are to be held, as whether by vote or ballot, be left to Congress to direct, yet this can never deprive the people of the *right* or *privilege* of election.   He has also added, " that the democratical branch was in danger from this clause ; " and, with some other gentlemen, took it for granted that an aristocracy must arise out of the general government.   This, I take it, from the very nature of the thing, can never happen. Aristocracies grow out of the combination of a few powerful families, where the country or people upon which they are to operate are immediately under their influence ; whereas the interest and influence of this government are too weak, and too much diffused, ever to bring about such an event. The confidence of the people, acquired by a wise and virtuous conduct, is the only influence the members of the federal government can ever have.   When aristocracies are formed, they will arise within the individual states.   It is therefore absolutely necessary that Congress should have a constitutional power to give the people at large a representation in the government, in order to break and control such dangerous combinations.   Let gentlemen show when and how this aristocracy they talk of is to arise out of this Constitution.   Are the first members to perpetuate themselves ? Is the Constitution to be attacked by such absurd assertions as these, and charged with defects with which it has no possible connection ?

Mr. BLOODWORTH.   Mr. Chairman, the gentleman has mistaken me.   When we examine the gentleman's arguments, they have no weight.   He tells us that it is not probable " that an aristocracy can arise."   I did not say that it would.   Various arguments are brought forward in support of this article.   They are vague and trifling.   There is nothing that can be offered to my mind which will reconcile me to it while this evil exists — while Congress have this control over elections.   It was easy for them to mention that this control should only be exerted when the state would neglect, or refuse, or be unable in case of invasion, to regulate elections.   If so, why did they not mention it expressly ?

It appears to me that some of their general observations imply a contradiction.   Do they not tell us that there is no ounger of a consolidation ? that Congress can exist no longer than the states — the massy pillars on which it is said to be raised ? Do they not also tell us that the state governments are to secure us against Congress ? At another time, they tell us that it was unnecessary to secure our liberty by giving them power to prevent the state governments from oppressing us. We know that there is a corruption in human nature. Without circumspection and carefulness, we shall throw away our liberties. Why is this general expression used on this great occasion ? Why not use expressions that were clear and unequivocal ? If I trust my property with a man and take security, shall I then barter away my rights ?

Mr. SPENCER. Mr. Chairman, this clause may operate in such a manner as will abridge the liberty of the people. It is well known that men in power are apt to abuse it, and extend it if possible. From the ambiguity of this expression, they may put such construction upon it as may suit them. I would not have it in such a manner as to endanger the rights of the people. But it has been said that this power is necessary to preserve their existence. There is not the least doubt but the people will keep them from losing their existence, if they shall behave themselves in such a manner as will merit it.

Mr. MACLAINE. Mr. Chairman, I thought it very extraordinary that the gentleman who was last on the floor should say that Congress could do what they please with respect to elections, and be warranted by this clause. The gentleman from Halifax (Mr. Davie) has put that construction upon it which reason and common sense will put upon it. Lawyers will often differ on a point of law, but people will seldom differ about so very plain a thing as this. The clause enables Congress to alter such regulations as the states shall have made with respect to elections. What would he infer from this ? What is it to alter ? It is to alter the time, place, and manner, established by the legislatures, if they do not answer the purpose. Congress ought to have power to perpetuate the government, and not the states, who might be otherwise inclined. I will ask the gentleman — and I wish he may give me a satisfactory answer — if the whole is not in the power of the people, as well when the elections are regulated by Congress, as when by the states. Are not both the agents of the people, ame-

nable to them ? Is there any thing in this Constitution which
gives them the power to perpetuate the sitting members ?
Is there any such strange absurdity ?   If the legislature of
this state has the power to fix the time, place, and manner,
of holding elections, why not place the same confidence in
the general government ?   The members of the general government, and those of the state legislature, are both chosen
by the people.   They are both from among the people, and are
in the same situation.   Those who served in the state legislature are eligible, and may be sent to Congress.   If the elections be regulated in the best manner in the state government,
can it be supposed that the same man will lose all his virtue,
his character and principles, when he goes into the general
government, in order to deprive us of our liberty ?

The gentleman from New Hanover seems to think it
possible Congress will so far forget themselves as to point
out such improper seasons of the year, and such inconvenient
places for elections, as to defeat the privilege of the democratic branch altogether.   He speaks of inconsistency in the
arguments of the gentlemen.   I wish he would be consistent
himself.   If I do not mistake the politics of that gentleman,
it is his opinion that Congress had sufficient power under
the Confederation.   He has said, without contradiction, that
we should be better without the Union than with it ; that it
would be better for us to be by ourselves than in the Union.
His antipathy to a general government, and to the Union, is
evidently inconsistent with his predilection for a federal
democratic branch.   We should have no democratic part of
the government at all, under such a government as he would
recommend.   There is no such part in the old Confederation.   The body of the people had no agency in that system.
The members of the present general government are selected
by the state legislatures, and have the power of the purse,
and other powers, and are not amenable to the people at large.
Although the gentleman may deny my assertions, yet this
argument of his is inconsistent with his other assertions and
doctrines.   It is impossible for any man in his senses to
think that we can exist by ourselves, separated from our
sister states.   Whatever gentlemen may pretend to say on
this point, it must be a matter of serious alarm to every
reflecting mind, to be disunited from the other states.

Mr. BLOODWORTH begged leave to wipe off the assertion of the gentleman; that he could not account for any expression which he might drop among a laughing, jocose people, but that it was well known he was for giving power to Congress to regulate the trade of the United States; that he had said that Congress had exercised power not given them by the Confederation, and that he was accurate in the assertion; that he was a freeman, and was under the control of no man.

Mr. MACLAINE replied, that he meant no aspersions; that he only meant to point out a fact; that he had committed mistakes himself in argument, and that he supposed the gentleman not more infallible than other people.

Mr. J. TAYLOR wished to know why the states had control over the place of electing senators, but not over that of choosing the representatives.

Mr. SPAIGHT answered, that the reason of that reservation was to prevent Congress from altering the places for holding the legislative assemblies in the different states.

Mr. JAMES GALLOWAY. Mr. Chairman, in the beginning I found great candor in the advocates of this government, but it is not so towards the last. I hope the gentleman from Halifax will not take it amiss, if I mention how he brought the motion forward. They began with dangers. As to Rhode Island being governed by a faction, what has that to do with the question before us? I ask, What have the state governments left for them, if the general government is to be possessed of such extensive powers, without control or limitation, without any responsibility to the states? He asks, How is it possible for the members to perpetuate themselves? I think I can show how they can do it. For instance, were they to take the government as it now stands organized. We send five members to the House of Representatives in the general government. They will go, no doubt, from or near the seaports. In other states, also, those near the sea will have more interest, and will go forward to Congress; and they can, without violating the Constitution, make a law continuing themselves, as they have control over the place, time, and manner, of elections. This may happen; and where the great principles of liberty are endangered, no general, indeterminate, vague expression ought to be suffered. Shall we pass over this article as it is now? They will be able to perpetuate themselves as well as if it had expressly said so.

Mr. STEELE. Mr. Chairman, the gentleman has said
that the five representatives which this state shall be entitled
to send to the general government, will go from the sea-
shore. What reason has he to say they will go from the
sea-shore? The time, place, and manner, of holding elections are to be prescribed by the legislatures. Our legislature is to regulate the first election, at any event. They
will regulate it as they think proper. They may, and most
probably will, lay the state off into districts. Who are to
vote for them? Every man who has a right to vote for a
representative to our legislature will ever have a right to
vote for a representative to the general government. Does
it not expressly provide that the electors in each state shall
have the qualifications requisite for the most numerous branch
of the state legislature? Can they, without a most manifest
violation of the Constitution, alter the qualifications of the
electors? The power over the manner of elections does not
include that of saying who shall vote : — the Constitution expressly says that the qualifications which entitle a man to
vote for a state representative. It is, then, clearly and indubitably fixed and determined *who* shall be the electors;
and the power over the manner only enables them to determine *how* these electors shall elect — whether by ballot, or
by vote, or by any other way. Is it not a maxim of universal jurisprudence, of reason and common sense, that an
instrument or deed of writing shall be so construed as to give
validity to all parts of it, if it can be done without involving
any absurdity? By construing it in the plain, obvious way
I have mentioned, all parts will be valid. By the way, gentlemen suggest the most palpable contradiction, and absurdity will follow. To say that they shall go from the sea-
shore, and be able to perpetuate themselves, is a most
extravagant idea. Will the members of Congress deviate
from their duty without any prospect of advantage to themselves? What interest can they have to make the place of
elections inconvenient? The judicial power of that government is so well constructed as to be a check. There was
no check in the old Confederation. Their power was, in
principle and theory, transcendent. If the Congress make
laws inconsistent with the Constitution, independent judges
will not uphold them, nor will the people obey them. A
universal resistance will ensue. In some countries, the

arbitrary disposition of rulers may enable them to overturn
the liberties of the people ; but in a country like this, where
every man is his own master, and where almost every man
is a freeholder, and has the right of election, the violations
of a constitution will not be passively permitted.   Can it be
supposed that in such a country the rights of suffrage will be
tamely surrendered ?   Is it to be supposed that 30,000 free
persons will send the most abandoned wretch in the district
to legislate for them in the general legislature ?   I should
rather think they would choose men of the most respectable
characters.

                                   SATURDAY, *July* 26, 1788.

    Mr. KENNION in the chair.   The 5th section of the 1st
article read.
    Mr. STEELE observed, that he had heard objections to
the 3d clause of this section, with respect to the periodical
publication of the Journals, the entering the yeas and nays
on them, and the suppression of such parts as required
secrecy — that he had no objection himself, for that he
thought the necessity of publishing their transactions was an
excellent check, and that every principle of prudence and
good policy pointed out the necessity of not publishing such
transactions as related to military arrangements and war —
that this provision was exactly similar to that which was in
the old Confederation.
    Mr. GRAHAM wished to hear an explanation of the
words " from time to time," whether it was a short or a long
time, or how often they should be obliged to publish their
proceedings.
    Mr. DAVIE answered, that they would be probably pub-
lished after the rising of Congress, every year — that if they
sat two or three times, or oftener, in the year, they might be
published every time they rose — that there could be no
doubt of their publishing them as often as it would be convenient and proper, and that they would conceal nothing but
what it would be unsafe to publish.   He further observed, that
some states had proposed an amendment, that they should
be published annually ;   but he thought it very safe and
proper as it stood — that it was the sense of the Convention
that they should be published at the end of every session.
The gentleman from Salisbury had said, that in this particu-

lar it resembled the old Confederation.   Other gentlemen have said there is no similarity at all.   He therefore wished the difference to be stated.

Mr. IREDELL remarked, that the provision in the clause under consideration was similar in meaning and substance to that in the Confederation — that in time of war it was absolutely necessary to conceal the operations of government; otherwise no attack on an enemy could be premeditated with success, for the enemy could discover our plans soon enough to defeat them — that it was no less imprudent to divulge our negotiations with foreign powers, and the most salutary schemes might be prevented by imprudently promulgating all the transactions of the government indiscriminately.

Mr. J. GALLOWAY wished to obviate what gentlemen had said with regard to the similarity of the old Confederation to the new system, with respect to the publication of their proceedings.   He remarked, that, at the desire of one member from any state, the yeas and nays were to be put on the Journals, and published by the Confederation; whereas, by this system, the concurrence of one fifth was necessary.

To this it was answered, that the alteration was made because experience had showed, when any two members could require the yeas and nays, they were taken on many trifling occasions; and there was no doubt one fifth would require them on every occasion of importance.

The 6th section read without any observations.

1st clause of the 7th section likewise read without any observations.

2d clause read.

Mr. IREDELL.   Mr. Chairman, this is a novelty in the Constitution, and is a regulation of considerable importance.   Permit me to state the reasons for which I imagine this regulation was made.   They are such as, in my opinion, fully justify it.

One great alteration proposed by the Constitution — and which is a capital improvement on the Articles of Confederation — is, that the executive, legislative, and judicial powers should be separate and distinct.   The best writers, and all the most enlightened part of mankind, agree that it is essential to the preservation of liberty, that such distinction and separation of powers should be made. But this distinction would have very little efficacy if each power had no means to defend itself against the encroachment of the others.

The British constitution, the theory of which is much admired, but which, however, is in fact liable to many objections, has divided the government into three branches. The king, who is hereditary, forms one branch, the Lords and Commons the two others; and no bill passes into a law without the king's consent. This is a great constitutional support of his authority. By the proposed Constitution, the President is of a very different nature from a monarch. He is to be chosen by electors appointed by the people; to be taken from among the people; to hold his office only for the short period of four years; and to be personally responsible for any abuse of the great trust reposed in him.

In a republican government, it would be extremely dangerous to place it in the power of one man to put an absolute negative on a bill proposed by two houses, one of which represented the people, and the other the states of America. It therefore became an object of consideration, how the executive could defend itself without being a competent part of the legislature. This difficulty was happily remedied by the clause now under our consideration. The executive is not entirely at the mercy of the legislature; nor is it put in the power of the executive entirely to defeat the acts of those two important branches. As it is provided in this clause, if a bare majority of both houses should pass a bill which the President thought injurious to his country, it is in his power — to do what? Not to say, in an arbitrary, haughty manner, that he does not approve of it — but, if he thinks it a bad bill, respectfully to offer his reasons to both houses; by whom, in that case, it is to be reconsidered, and not to become a law unless two thirds of both houses shall concur; which they still may, notwithstanding the President's objection. It cannot be presumed that he would venture to oppose a bill, under such circumstances, without very strong reasons. Unless he was sure of a powerful support in the legislature, his opposition would be of no effect; and as his reasons are to be put on record, his fame is committed both to the present times and to posterity.

The exercise of this power, in a time of violent factions,

might be possibly hazardous to himself; but he can have no
ill motive to exert himself in the face of a violent opposition.
Regard to his duty alone could induce him to oppose, when
it was probable two thirds would at all events overrule him.
This power may be usefully exercised, even when no ill
intention prevails in the legislature.   It might frequently
happen that, where a bare majority had carried a pernicious
bill, if there was an authority to suspend it, upon a cool
statement of reasons, many of that majority, on a reconsideration, might be convinced, and vote differently.   I
therefore think the method proposed is a happy medium between the possession of an absolute negative, and the executive having no control whatever on acts of legislation;
and at the same time that it serves to protect the executive
from ill designs in the legislature, it may also answer the
purposes of preventing many laws passing which would be
immediately injurious to the people at large.   It is a strong
guard against abuses in all, that the President's reasons are
to be entered at large on the Journals, and, if the bill
passes notwithstanding, that the yeas and nays are also
to be entered.   The public, therefore, can judge fairly between them.

The 1st clause of the 8th section read.

Mr. SPENCER.   Mr. Chairman, I conceive this power
to be too extensive, as it embraces all possible powers of
taxation, and gives up to Congress every possible article of
taxation that can ever happen.   By means of this, there will
be no way for the states of receiving or collecting taxes at
all, but what may interfere with the collections of Congress.
Every power is given over our money to those over whom
we have no immediate control.   I would give them powers
to support the government, but would not agree to annihilate
the state governments in an article which is most essential
to their existence.   I would give them power of laying imposts; and I would give them power to lay and collect excises.   I confess that this is a kind of tax so odious to a free
people, that I should with great reluctance agree to its
exercise; but it is obvious that, unless such excises were
admitted, the public burden will be all borne by those parts
of the community who do not manufacture for themselves.
So manifest an inequality would justify a recurrence to this
species of taxes.

How are direct taxes to be laid? By a poll tax, assessments on land or other property? Inconvenience and oppression will arise from any of them. I would not be understood that I would not wish to have an efficient government for the United States. I am sensible that laws operating on individuals cannot be carried on against states; because, if they do not comply with the general laws of the Union, there is no way to compel a compliance but force. There must be an army to compel them. Some states may have some excuse for non-compliance. Others will feign excuses. Several states may perhaps be in the same predicament. If force be used to compel them, they will probably call for foreign aid; and the very means of defence will operate to the dissolution of the system, and to the destruction of the states. I would not, therefore, deny that Congress ought to have the power of taking out of the pockets of the individuals at large, if the states fail to pay those taxes in a convenient time. If requisitions were to be made on the several states, proportionate to their abilities, the several state legislatures, knowing the circumstances of their constituents, and that they would ultimately be compelled to pay, would lay the tax in a convenient manner, and would be able to pay their quotas at the end of the year. They are better acquainted with the mode in which taxes can be raised, than the general government can possibly be.

It may happen, for instance, that if ready money cannot be immediately received from the pockets of individuals for their taxes, their estates, consisting of lands, negroes, stock, and furniture, must be set up and sold at vendue. We can easily see, from the great scarcity of money at this day, that great distresses must happen. There is no hard money in the country. It must come from other parts of the world. Such property would sell for one tenth part of its value. Such a mode as this would, in a few years, deprive the people of their estates. But, on the contrary, if articles proper for exportation were either specifically taken for their taxes immediately by the state legislature, or if the collection should be deferred till they had disposed of such articles, no oppression or inconvenience would happen. There is no person so poor but who can raise something to dispose of For a great part of the United States, those articles which are proper for exportation would answer the purpose. I would have a tax laid on estates where such articles could not be had, and such a tax to be by instalments for two or more years.

I would admit, if the quotas were not punctually paid at the end of the time, that Congress might collect taxes, because this power is absolutely necessary for the support of the general government.   But I would not give it in the first instance ; for nothing would be more oppressive, as in a short time people would be compelled to part with their property.   In the other case, they would part with none but in such a manner as to encourage their industry.   On the other hand, if requisitions, in cases of emergency, were proposed to the state assemblies, it would be a measure of convenience to the people, and would be a means of keeping up the importance of the state legislatures, and would conciliate their affections ; and their knowledge of the ultimate right of Congress to collect taxes would stimulate their exertions to raise money.   But if the power of taxation be given in the first instance to Congress, the state legislatures will be liable to be counteracted by the general government in all their operations.   These are my reasons for objecting to this article.

Gov. JOHNSTON.   Mr. Chairman, this clause is objected to ; and it is proposed to alter it in such a manner, that the general government shall not have power to lay taxes in the first instance, but shall apply to the states, and, in case of refusal, that direct taxation shall take place ; that is to say, that the general government should pass an act to levy money on the United States, and if the states did not, within a limited time, pay their respective proportions, the officers of the United States should proceed to levy money on the inhabitants of the different states.   The question has been agitated by the conventions in different states, and some very respectable states have proposed that there should be an amendment, in the manner which the worthy member last up has proposed.   But, sir, although I pay very great respect to the opinions and decisions of the gentlemen who composed those conventions, and although they were wise in many instances, I cannot concur with them in this particular.   It appears to me that it will be attended with many inconveniences.   It seems to me probable that the money arising from duties and excises will be, in general, sufficient to answer all the ordinary purposes of government; but in cases of emergency, it will be necessary to lay direct taxes. In cases of emergency, it will be necessary that these taxes should be a responsible and established fund to support the credit of the United States; for it cannot be supposed that, from the ordinary sources of revenue, money can be brought into our treasury in such a manner as to answer pressing dangers; nor can it be supposed that our credit will enable us to procure any loans, if our government is limited in the means of procuring money. But, if the government have it in their power to lay those taxes, it will give them credit to borrow money on that security, and for that reason it will not be necessary to lay so heavy a tax; for, if the tax is sufficiently productive to pay the interest, money may always be had in consequence of that security. If the state legislatures must be applied to, they must lay a tax for the full sum wanting. This will be much more oppressive than a tax laid by Congress; for I presume that no state legislature will have as much credit individually as the United States conjointly; therefore, viewing it in this light, a tax laid by Congress will be much easier than a tax laid by the states. Another inconvenience which will attend this proposed amendment is, that these emergencies may happen a considerable time before the meeting of some state legislatures, and previous to their meeting, the schemes of the government may be defeated by this delay. A considerable time will elapse before the state can lay the tax, and a considerable time before it be collected; and perhaps it cannot be collected at all. One reason which the worthy member has offered in favor of the amendment was, that the general legislature cannot lay a tax without interfering with the taxation of the state legislature. It may happen that the taxes of both may be laid on the same article; but I hope and believe that the taxes to be laid on by the general legislature will be so very light that it will be no inconvenience to the people to pay them; and if you attend to the probable amount of the impost, you must conclude that the small addition to the taxes will not make them so high as they are at this time. Another reason offered by the worthy member in support of the amendment is, that the state legislature may direct taxes to be paid in specific articles. We had full experience of this in the late war

I call on the house to say, whether it was not the most oppressive and least productive tax ever known in the state. Many articles were lost, and many could not be disposed of so as to be of any service to the people. Most articles are perishable, and therefore cannot answer. Others are difficult to transport, expensive to keep, and very difficult to dispose of. A tax payable in tobacco would answer very well in some parts of the country, and perhaps would be more productive than any other ; yet we feel that great losses have been sustained by the public on this article. A tax payable in any kind of grain would answer very little purpose, grain being perishable. A tax payable in pitch and tar would not answer. A mode of this kind would not be at all eligible in this state : the great loss on the specific articles, and inconvenience in disposing of them, would render them productive of very little.

He says that this would be a means of keeping up the importance of the state legislatures. I am afraid it would have a different effect. If requisitions should not be complied with at the time fixed, the officers of Congress would then immediately proceed to make their collections. We know that several causes would inevitably produce a failure. The states would not, or could not, comply. In that case, the state legislature would be disgraced. After having done every thing for the support of their credit and importance without success, would they not be degraded in the eyes of the United States? Would it not cause heart-burnings between particular states and the United States? The inhabitants would oppose the tax-gatherers. They would say, "We are taxed by our own state legislature for the proportionate quota of our state ; we will not pay you also." This would produce insurrections and confusion in the country. These are the reasons which induce me to support this clause. It is perhaps particularly favorable to this state. We are not an importing country: very little is here raised by imposts. Other states, who have adopted the Constitution, import for us. Massachusetts, South Carolina, Maryland, and Virginia, are great importing states. From them we procure foreign goods, and by that means they are generally benefited ; for it is agreed upon by all writers that the consumer pays the impost.

Do we not, then, pay a tax in support of their revenue in

proportion to our consumption of foreign articles? Do we not know that this, in our present situation, is without any benefit to us? Do we not pay a second duty when these goods are imported into this state? We now pay double duties. It is not to be supposed that the merchant will pay the duty without wishing to get interest and profit on the money he lays out. It is not to be presumed that he will not add to the price a sum sufficient to indemnify himself for the inconvenience of parting with the money he pays as a duty. We therefore now pay a much higher price for European manufactures than the people do in the great importing states. Is it not laying heavy burdens on the people of this country, not only to compel them to pay duties for the support of the importing states, but to pay a second duty on the importation into this state by our own merchants? By adoption, we shall participate in the amount of the imposts. Upon the whole, I hope this article will meet with the approbation of this committee, when they consider the necessity of supporting the general government, and the many inconveniences, and probable if not certain inefficacy, of requisitions.

Mr. SPENCER. Mr. Chairman, I cannot, notwithstanding what the gentleman has advanced, agree to this clause unconditionally. The most certain criterion of happiness that any people can have, is to be taxed by their own immediate representatives, — by those representatives who intermix with them, and know their circumstances, — not by those who cannot know their situation. Our federal representatives cannot sufficiently know our situation and circumstances. The worthy gentleman said that it would be necessary for the general government to have the power of laying taxes, in order to have credit to borrow money. But I cannot think, however plausible it may appear, that his argument is conclusive. If such emergency happens as will render it necessary for them to borrow money, it will be necessary for them to borrow before they proceed to lay the tax. I conceive the government will have credit sufficient to borrow money in the one case as well as the other. If requisitions be punctually complied with, no doubt they can borrow; and if not punctually complied with, Congress can ultimately lay the tax.

I wish to have the most easy way for the people to pay

their taxes. The state legislature will know every method and expedient by which the people can pay, and they will recur to the most convenient. This will be agreeable to the people, and will not create insurrections and dissensions in the country. The taxes might be laid on the most productive articles: I wish not, for my part, to lay them on perishable articles. There are a number of other articles besides those which the worthy gentleman enumerated. There are, besides tobacco, hemp, indigo, and cotton. In the Northern States, where they have manufactures, a contrary system from ours would be necessary. There the principal attention is paid to the giving their children trades. They have few articles for exportation. By raising the tax in this manner, it will introduce such a spirit of industry as cannot fail of producing happy consequences to posterity. He objected to the mode of paying taxes in specific articles. May it not be supposed that we shall gain something by experience, and avoid those schemes and methods which shall be found inconvenient and disadvantageous? If expenses should be incurred in keeping and disposing of such articles, could not those expenses be reimbursed by a judicious sale? Cannot the legislature be circumspect as to the choice and qualities of the objects to be selected for raising the taxes due to the Continental treasury? The worthy gentleman has mentioned that, if the people should not comply to raise the taxes in this way, then, if they were subject to the law of Congress, it would throw them into confusion. I would ask every one here, if there be not more reason to induce us to believe that they would be thrown into confusion, in case the power of Congress was exercised by Congress in the first instance, than in the other case. After having so long a time to raise the taxes, it appears to me there could be no kind of doubt of a punctual compliance. The right of Congress to lay taxes ultimately, in case of non-compliance with requisitions, would operate as a penalty, and would stimulate the states to discharge their quotas faithfully. Between these two modes there is an immense difference. The one will produce the happiness, ease, and prosperity of the people; the other will destroy them, and produce insurrections.

Mr. SPAIGHT. Mr. Chairman, it was thought absolutely necessary for the support of the general government to give it power to raise taxes. Government cannot exist without certain and adequate funds. Requisitions cannot be depended upon. For my part, I think it indifferent whether I pay the tax to the officers of the continent or to those of the state. I would prefer paying to the Continental officers, because it will be less expensive.

The gentleman last up has objected to the propriety of the tax being laid by Congress, because they could not know the circumstances of the people. The state legislature will have no source or opportunity of information which the members of the general government may not have. They can avail themselves of the experience of the state legislature. The gentleman acknowledges the inefficacy of requisitions, and yet recommends them. He has allowed that laws cannot operate upon political bodies without the agency of force. His expedient of applying to the states in the first instance will be productive of delay, and will certainly terminate in a disappointment to Congress. But the gentleman has said that we had no hard money, and that the taxes might be paid in specific articles. It is well known that if taxes are not raised in medium, the state loses by it. If the government wishes to raise one thousand pounds, they must calculate on a disappointment by specific articles, and will therefore impose taxes more in proportion to the expected disappointment. An individual can sell his commodities much better than the public at large. A tax payable in any produce would be less productive, and more oppressive to the people, as it would enhance the public burdens by its inefficiency. As to abuses by the Continental officers, I apprehend the state officers will more probably commit abuses than they. Their conduct will be more narrowly watched, and misconduct more severely punished. They will be therefore more cautious.

Mr. SPENCER, in answer to Mr. Spaight, observed, that, in case of war, he was not opposed to this article, because, if the states refused to comply with requisitions, there was no way to compel them but military coercion, which would induce refractory states to call for foreign aid, which might terminate in the dismemberment of the empire. But he said that he would not give the power of direct taxation to Congress in the first instance, as he thought the states would lay the taxes in a less oppressive manner.

Mr. WHITMILL HILL. Mr. Chairman, the subject now before us is of the highest importance. The object of all government is the protection, security, and happiness of the people. To produce this end, government must be possessed of the necessary means.

Every government must be empowered to raise a sufficient revenue ; but I believe it will be allowed, on all hands, that Congress has been hitherto altogether destitute of that power so essential to every government. I believe, also, that it is generally wished that Congress should be possessed of power to raise such sums as are requisite for the support of the Union, though gentlemen may differ with regard to the mode of raising them.

Our past experience shows us that it is in vain to expect any possible efficacy from requisitions. Gentlemen recommend these, as if their inutility had not been experienced. But do we not all know what effects they have produced? Is it not to them that we must impute the loss of our credit and respectability? It is necessary, therefore, that government have recourse to some other mode of raising a revenue. Had, indeed, every state complied with requisitions, the old Confederation would not have been complained of; but as the several states have already discovered such repugnancy to comply with federal engagements, it must appear absolutely necessary to free the general government from such a state of dependence.

The debility of the old system, and the necessity of substituting another in its room, are the causes of calling this Convention.

I conceive, sir, that the power given by that clause is absolutely necessary to the existence of the government. Gentlemen say that we are in such a situation that we cannot pay taxes. This, sir, is not a fair representation, in my opinion. The honest people of this country acknowledge themselves sufficiently able and willing to pay them. Were it a private contract, they would find means to pay them. The honest part of the community complain of the acts of the legislature. They complain that the legislature makes laws, not to suit their constituents, but themselves. The legislature, sir, never means to pay a just debt, as their constituents wish to do. Witness the laws made in this country. I will, however, be bold enough to say, that it is the wish of the honest people to pay those taxes which are necessary for the support of the government. We have for a long time waited, in hope that our legislature would point out the manner of supporting the general government, and relieving us from our present ineligible situation. Every body was convinced of the necessity of this; but how is it to be done? The legislature have pointed out a mode — their old, favorite mode — they have made paper money; purchased tobacco at an extravagant price, and sold it at a considerable loss; they have received about a dollar in the pound. Have we any ground to hope that we shall be in a better situation?

Shall we be bettered by the alternative proposed by gentlemen — by levying taxes in specific articles? How will you dispose of them? Where is the merchant to buy them? Your business will be put into the hands of a commissioner, who, having no business of his own, will grasp at it eagerly; and *he*, no doubt, will *manage* it. But if the payment of the tax be left to the people, — if individuals are told that they must pay such a certain proportion of their income to support the general government, — then each will consider it as a debt; he will exert his ingenuity and industry to raise it; he will use no agent, but depend on himself. By these means the money will certainly be collected. I will pledge myself for its certainty. As the legislature has never heretofore called upon the people, let the general government apply to individuals : it cannot *depend* upon states. If the people have articles, they can receive money for them. Money is said to be scarce; but, sir, it is the want of industry which is the source of our indigence and difficulties. If people would be but active, and exert every power, they might certainly pay, and be in easy circumstances; and the people are disposed to do so; — I mean the good part of the community, which, I trust, is the greater part of it.

Were the money to be paid into our treasury first, instead of recommitting it to the Continental treasury, we should apply it to discharge our own pressing demands; by which means, a very small proportion of it would be paid to Congress. And if the tax were to be laid and collected by the several states, what would be the consequence? Congress must depend upon twelve funds for its support. The general government must depend on the contingency of succeeding in twelve different applications to twelve different bodies. What a slender and precarious dependence would this be ! The states, when called upon to pay these demands of Congress, would fail; they would pay every other demand before those of Congress. They have hitherto done it. Is not this a true statement of facts ? How is it with the Continental treasury? The true answer to this question must hurt every friend to his country.

I came in late ; but I believe that a gentleman (Governor Johnston) said, that if the states should refuse to pay requisitions, and the Continental officers were sent to collect, the states would be degraded, and the people discontented. I believe this would be the case. The states, by acting dishonestly, would appear in the most odious light ; and the people would be irritated at such an application, after a rejection by their own legislature. But if the taxes were to be raised of individuals, I believe they could, without any difficulty, be paid in due time.

But, sir, the United States wish to be established and known among other nations. This will be a matter of great utility to them. We might then form advantageous connections. When it is once known among foreign nations that our general government and our finances are upon a respectable footing, should emergencies happen, we can borrow money of them without any disadvantage. The lender would be sure of being reimbursed in time. This matter is of the highest consequence to the United States. Loans must be recurred to sometimes. In case of war they would be necessary. All nations borrow money on pressing occasions.

The gentleman who was last up mentioned many specific articles which could be paid by the people in discharge of their taxes. He has, I think, been fully answered. He must see the futility of such a mode. When our wants would be greatest, these articles would be least productive ; I mean in time of war. But we still have means ; such means as honest and assiduous men will find. He says that Congress cannot lay the tax to suit us. He has forgotten that Congress are acquainted with us — go from us — are situated like ourselves. I will be bold to say, it will be most their own interest to behave with propriety and moderation. Their own interest will prompt them to lay

8

taxes moderately; and nothing but the last necessity will urge them to recur to that expedient.

This is a most essential clause. Without money, government will answer no purpose. Gentlemen compare this to a foreign tax. It is by no means the case. It is laid by ourselves. Our own representatives lay it, and will, no doubt, use the most easy means of raising it, possible. Why not trust our own representatives? We might, no doubt, have confidence in them on this occasion, as well as every other. If the Continental treasury is to depend on the states, as usual, it will be always poor. But gentlemen are jealous, and unwilling to trust government, though they are their own representatives. Their maxim is, Trust them with no power. This holds against all government. Anarchy will ensue if government be not trusted. I think that I know the sentiments of the honest, industrious part of the community, as well as any gentleman in this house. They wish to discharge these debts, and are able. If they can raise the interest of the public debt, it is sufficient. They will not be called upon for more than the interest, till such time as the country be rich and populous. The principal can then be paid with great facility.

We can borrow money with ease, and on advantageous terms, when it shall be known that Congress will have that power which all governments ought to have. Congress will not pay their debts in paper money. I am willing to trust this article to Congress, because I have no reason to think that our government will be better than it has been. Perhaps I have spoken too liberally of the legislature before: but I do not expect that they will ever, without a radical change of men and measures, wish to put the general government on a better footing. It is not the poor man who opposes the payment of those just debts to which we owe our independence and political existence, but the rich miser. Not the poor, but the rich, shudder at the idea of taxes. I have no dread that Congress will distress us; nor have I any fear that the tax will be embezzled by officers. Industry and economy will be promoted, and money will be easier got than ever it has been yet. The taxes will be paid by the people when called upon. I trust that all honest, industrious people will think, with me, that Congress ought to be possessed of the power of applying immediately to the people for its support, without the interposition of the state legislatures. I have no confidence in the legislature: the people do not suppose them to be honest men.

Mr. STEELE was decidedly in favor of the clause. A government without revenue he compared to a poor, forlorn, dependent individual, and said that the one would be as helpless and contemptible as the other. He wished the government of the Union to be on a respectable footing. Congress, he said, showed no disposition to tax us — that it was well known that a poll tax of eighteen pence per poll, and six pence per hundred acres of land, was appropriated and offered by the legislature to Congress — that Congress was solicited to send the officers to collect those taxes, but they refused — that if this power was not given to Congress, the people must be oppressed, especially in time of war — that, during the last war, provisions, horses, &c., had been taken from the people by force, to supply the wants of government — that a respectable government would not be under the necessity of recurring to such unwarrantable means — that such a method was unequal and oppressive to the last degree. The citizens, whose property was pressed from them, paid all the taxes; the rest escaped. The press-masters went often to the poorest, and not to the richest citizens, and took their horses, &c. This disabled them from making a crop the next year. It would be better, he said, to lay the public burdens equally upon the people. Without this power, the other powers of Congress would be nugatory. He added, that it would, in his opinion, give strength and respectability to the United States in time of war, would promote industry and frugality, and would enable the government to protect and extend commerce, and consequently increase the riches and population of the country.

Mr. JOSEPH M'DOWALL. Mr. Chairman, this is a power that I will never agree to give up from the hands of the people of this country. We know that the amount of the imposts will be trifling, and that the expenses of this government will be very great; consequently the taxes will be very high. The tax-gatherers will be sent, and our property will be wrested out of our hands. The Senate is most dangerously constructed. Our only security is the House of Representatives. They may be continued at Congress

eight or ten years.   At such a distance from their homes,
and for so long a time, they will have no feeling for, nor
any knowledge of, the situation of the people.   If elected
from the seaports, they will not know the western part of
the country, and *vice versa*.   Two coöperative powers cannot exist together.   One must submit.   The inferior must
give up to the superior.   While I am up, I will say something to what has been said by the gentleman to ridicule the
General Assembly.   He represents the legislature in a very
opprobrious light.   It is very astonishing that the people
should choose men of such characters to represent them.   If
the people be virtuous, why should they put confidence in
men of a contrary disposition?   As to paper money, it was
the result of necessity.   We were involved in a great war.
What money had been in the country was sent to other
parts of the world.   What would have been the consequence
if paper money had not been made?   We must have been
undone.   Our political existence must have been destroyed.
The extreme scarcity of specie, with other good causes,
particularly the solicitation of the officers to receive it at its
nominal value, for their pay, produced subsequent emissions.
He tells us that all the people wish this power to be given
— that the mode of payment need only be pointed out, and
that they will willingly pay.   How are they to raise the
money?   Have they it in their chests?   Suppose, for instance, there be a tax of two shillings per hundred laid on
land ; where is the money to pay it?   We have it not.   I
am acquainted with the people.   I know their situation.
They have no money.   Requisitions may yet be complied
with.   Industry and frugality may enable the people to pay
moderate taxes, if laid by those who have a knowledge of
their situation, and a feeling for them.   If the tax-gatherers
come upon us, they will, like the locusts of old, destroy us.
They will have pretty high salaries, and exert themselves to
oppress us.   When we consider these things, we should be
cautious.   They will be weighed, I trust, by the House.
Nothing said by the gentlemen on the other side has obviated my objections.

    Gov. JOHNSTON.   Mr. Chairman, the gentleman who
was last up, still insists on the great utility which would re
sult from that mode which has hitherto been found ineffect
ual.   It is amazing that past experience will not instruct
him.   When a merchant follows a similar mode, — when he

purchases dear and sells cheap, — he is called a swindler and must soon become a bankrupt. This state deserves that most disgraceful epithet. We are swindlers; we gave three pounds per hundred weight for tobacco, and sold it three dollars per hundred weight, after having paid very considerable expenses for transporting and keeping it. The United States are bankrupts. They are considered such in every part of the world. They borrow money, and promise to pay : they have it not in their power, and they are obliged to ask of the people, whom they owe, to lend them money to pay the very interest. This is disgraceful and humiliating. By these means we are paying compound interest. No private fortune, however great, — no estate, however affluent, — can stand this most destructive mode. This has proceeded from the inefficacy of requisitions. Shall we continue the same practice? Shall we not rather struggle to get over our misfortunes? I hope we shall.

Another member, on the same side, says that it is improper to take the power of taxation out of the hands of the people. I deny that it is taken out of their hands by this system. Their immediate representatives lay these taxes. Taxes are necessary for every government. Can there be any danger when these taxes are laid by the representatives of the people? If there be, where can political safety be found? But it is said that we have a small proportion of that representation. Our proportion is equal to the proportion of money we shall have to pay. It is therefore a full proportion ; and unless we suppose that all the members of Congress shall combine to ruin their constituents, we have no reason to fear. It is said (I know not from what principle) that our representatives will be taken from the seacoast, and will not know in what manner to lay the tax to suit the citizens of the western part of the country. I know not whence that idea arose. The gentlemen from the westward are not precluded from voting for representatives. They have it, therefore, in their power to send them from the westward, or the middle part of the state. They are more numerous, and can send them, or the greater part of them. I do not doubt but they will send the most proper, and men in whom they can put confidence, and will give them, from time to time, instructions to enlighten their minds.

Something has been said with regard to their paper money. I think very little can be done in favor of it; much may be said, very justly, in favor of it.

Every man of property — every man of considerable transactions, whether a merchant, planter, mechanic, or of any other condition — must have felt the baneful influence of that currency. It gave us relief for a moment. It assisted us in the prosecution of a bloody war. It is destructive, however, in general, in the end. It was struck, in the last instance, for the purpose of paying the officers and soldiers. The motive was laudable.

I then thought, and still do, that those gentlemen might have had more advantage by not receiving that kind of payment. It would have been better for them, and for the country, had it not been emitted. We have involved ourselves in a debt of £200,000. We have not, with this sum, honestly and fairly paid £50,000. Was this right? But, say they, there was no circulating medium. This want was necessary to be supplied. It is a doubt with me whether the circulating medium be increased by an emission of paper currency. Before the emission of the paper money, there was a great deal of hard money among us. For thirty years past, I had not known so much specie in circulation as we had at the emission of paper money, in 1783. That medium was increasing daily. People from abroad bring specie; for, thank God, our country produces articles which are every where in demand. There is more specie in the country than is generally imagined; but the proprietors keep it locked up. No man will part with his specie. It lies in his chest. It is asked, Why not lend it out? The answer is obvious — that, should he once let it get out of his power, he never can recover the whole of it. If he bring suit, he will obtain a verdict for one half of it. This is the reason of our poverty. The scarcity of money must be, in some degree, owing to this; and the specie which is now in this country might as well be in any other part of the world. If our trade was once on a respectable footing, we should find means of paying that enormous debt.

Another observation was made, which has not yet been answered, viz., that the demands of the United States will be smaller than those of the states, for this reason — the United States will only make a demand of the interest of the public debts: the states must demand both principal and interest:

for I presume no state can, on an emergency, produce, without the aid of individuals, a sum sufficient for that purpose; but the United States can borrow, on the credit of the funds arising from their power of laying taxes, such sums as will be equal to the emergency.

There will be always credit given, where there is good security. No man, who is not a miser, will hesitate to trust where there is a respectable security; but credulity itself would not trust where there was no kind of security, but an absolute certainty of losing. Mankind wish to make their money productive; they will therefore lend it where there is a security and certainty of recovering it, and no longer keep it hoarded in strong boxes.

This power is essential to the very existence of the government. Requisitions are fruitless and idle. Every expedient proposed as an alternative, or to qualify this power, is replete with inconvenience. It appears to me, therefore, upon the whole, that this article stands much better, as it is, than in any other manner.

Mr. IREDELL. Mr Chairman, I do not presume to rise to discuss this clause, after the very able, and, in my opinion, unanswerable arguments which have been urged in favor of it; but merely to correct an error which fell from a respectable member (Mr. M'Dowall) on the other side.

It was, that Congress, by interfering with the mode of elections, might continue themselves in office. I thought that this was sufficiently explained yesterday. There is nothing in the Constitution to empower Congress to continue themselves longer than the time specified. It says, expressly, that the House of Representatives shall consist of members chosen for two years, and that the Senate shall be composed of senators chosen for six years. At the expiration of these terms, the right of election reverts to the people and the states; nor is there any thing in the Constitution to warrant a contrary supposition. The clause alluded to has no reference to the duration of members in Congress, but merely as to the time and manner of their election.

Now that I am up, I beg leave to take notice of a suggestion, that Congress could as easily borrow money when they had the ultimate power of laying taxes, as if they possessed it in the first instance. I entirely differ from that

opinion.   Had Congress the immediate power, tnere would
be no doubt the money would be raised.   In the other mode,
doubts might be entertained concerning it.   For can any man
suppose that if, for any reasons, the state legislatures did
not think proper to pay their quotas, and Congress should be
compelled to lay taxes, it would not raise alarms in the
state ?   Is it not reasonable the people would be more apt
to side with their state legislature, who indulged them, than
with Congress, who imposed taxes upon them ?   They would
say, " Had we been able to pay, our state legislature would
have raised the money.   They know and feel for our distresses ; but Congress have no regard for our situation, and
have imposed taxes on us we are unable to bear."   This is,
sir, what would probably happen.   Language like this would
be the high road to popularity.   In all countries, particularly
in free ones, there are many ready to catch at such opportunities of making themselves of consequence with the people.
General discontent would probably ensue, and a serious
quarrel take place between the general and the state governments.   Foreigners, who would view our situation narrowly
before they lent their money, would certainly be less willing
to risk it on such contingencies as these, than if they knew
there was a direct fund for their payment, from which no ill
consequences could be apprehended.   The difference between those who are able to borrow, and those who are not,
is extremely great.   Upon a critical emergency, it may be
impossible to raise the full sum wanted immediately upon
the people.   In this case, if the public credit is good, they
may borrow a certain sum, and raise for the present only
enough to pay the interest, deferring the payment of the
principal till the public is more able to bear it.   In the other
case, where no money can be borrowed, there is no resource,
if the whole sum cannot be raised immediately.   The difference, perhaps, may be stated as twenty to one.   A hundred thousand pounds, therefore, may be wanted in the one
case ; five thousand pounds may be sufficient, for the present,
in the other.   Sure this is a difference of the utmost moment.
I should not have risen at all, were it not for the strong impression which might have been made by the error committed by the worthy gentleman on the other side.   I hope
I shall be excused for the time I have taken up with the additional matter, though it was only stating what had been
urged with great propriety before.

Mr. GOUDY. Mr. Chairman, this is a dispute whether Congress shall have great, enormous powers. I am not able to follow these learned gentlemen through all the labyrinths of their oratory. Some represent us as rich, and not honest; and others again represent us as honest, and not rich. We have no gold or silver, no substantial money, to pay taxes with. This clause, with the clause of elections, will totally destroy our liberties. The subject of our consideration therefore is, whether it be proper to give any man, or set of men, an unlimited power over our purse, without any kind of control. The purse-strings are given up by this clause. The sword is also given up by this system. Is there no danger in giving up both? There is no danger, we are told. It may be so; but I am jealous and suspicious of the liberties of mankind. And if it be a character which no man wishes but myself, I am willing to take it. Suspicions, in small communities, are a pest to mankind; but in a matter of this magnitude, which concerns the interest of millions yet unborn, suspicion is a very noble virtue. Let us see, therefore, how far we give power; for when it is once given, we cannot take it away. It is said that those who formed this Constitution were great and good men. We do not dispute it. We also admit that great and learned people have adopted it. But I have a judgment of my own; and, though not so well informed always as others, yet I will exert it when manifest danger presents itself. When the power of the purse and the sword is given up, we dare not think for ourselves. In case of war, the last man and the last penny would be extorted from us. That the Constitution has a tendency to destroy the state governments, must be clear to every man of common understanding. Gentlemen, by their learned arguments, endeavor to conceal the danger from us. I have no notion of this method of evading arguments, and of clouding them over with rhetoric, and, I must say, sophistry too. But I hope no man will be led astray with them.

Gov. JOHNSTON observed, that if any sophistical arguments had been made use of, they ought to be pointed out; and nobody could doubt that it was in the power of a learned divine (alluding to Mr. Caldwell) to show their sophistry.

Gov. Johnston, being informed of his mistake in taking Mr. Goudy for Mr. Caldwell, apologized for it.

Mr PORTER. Mr Chairman, I must say that I think the gentleman last up was wrong; for the other gentleman was, in my opinion, right. This is a money clause. I would fain know whence this power originates. I have heard it said that the legislature were villains, and that this power was to be exercised by the representatives of the people. When a building is raised, it should be on solid ground. Every gentleman must agree that we should not build a superstructure on a foundation of villains. Gentlemen say that the mass of the people are honest. I hope gentlemen will consider that we should build the structure on the people, and not on the representatives of the people. Agreeably to the gentleman's argument, (Mr Hill,) our representatives will be mere villains. I expect that very learned arguments, and powerful oratory, will be displayed on this occasion. I expect that the great cannon from Halifax (meaning Mr Davie) will discharge fire-balls among us; but large batteries are often taken by small arms.

Mr. BLOODWORTH wished that gentlemen would desist from making personal reflections. He was of opinion that it was wrong to do so, and incompatible with their duty to their constituents; that every man had a right to display his abilities, and he hoped they would no longer reflect upon one another.

From the 2d to the 8th clause read without any observation.

9th clause read

Several members wished to hear an explanation of this clause. Mr. MACLAINE looked upon this as a very valuable part of the Constitution, because it consulted the ease and convenience of the people at large; for that, if the Supreme Court were at one fixed place, and no other tribunals established, nothing could possibly be more injurious; that it was therefore necessary that Congress should have power to constitute tribunals in different states, for the trial of common causes, and to have appeals to the Supreme Court in matters of more magnitude — that that was his idea, but, if not satisfactory, he trusted other gentlemen would explain it — that it would be more explained when they came to the judiciary.

The 10th and 11th clauses read without any observation.

12th clause read

Mr. IREDELL. Mr. Chairman, this clause is of so much importance, that we ought to consider it with the most serious attention. It is a power vested in Congress, which, in my opinion, is absolutely indispensable; yet there have been, perhaps, more objections made to it than any other power vested in Congress. For my part, I will observe generally that, so far from being displeased with that jealousy and extreme caution with which gentlemen consider every power proposed to be given to this government, they give me the utmost satisfaction.

I believe the passion for liberty is stronger in America than in any other country in the world. Here every man is strongly impressed with its importance, and every breast glows for the preservation of it. Every jealousy, not incompatible with the indispensable principles of government, is to be commended; but these principles must at all events be observed. The powers of government ought to be competent to the public safety. This, indeed, is the primary object of all governments. It is the duty of gentlemen who form a constitution to take care that no power should be wanting which the safety of the community requires. The exigencies of the country must be provided for, not only in respect to common and usual cases, but for occasions which do not frequently occur. If such a provision is not made, critical occasions may arise, when there must be either a usurpation of power, or the public safety eminently endangered; for, besides the evils attending a frequent change of a constitution, the case may not admit of so slow a remedy. In considering the powers that ought to be vested in any government, possible abuses ought not to be pointed out, without at the same time considering their use. No power, of any kind or degree, can be given but what may be abused; we have, therefore, only to consider whether any particular power is absolutely necessary. If it be, the power must be given, and we must run the risk of the abuse, considering our risk of this evil as one of the conditions of the imperfect state of human nature, where there is no good without the mixture of some evil. At the same time, it is undoubtedly our duty to guard against abuses as much as possible. In America, we enjoy peculiar blessings; the people are distinguished by the possession of freedom in a very high degree, unmixed with those oppressions the freest countries in Europe suffer. But we ought to consider that in this country, as well as in others, it is equally necessary to restrain and suppress internal commotions, and to guard against foreign hostility. There is, I believe, no government in the world without a power to raise armies. In some countries in Europe, a great force is necessary to be kept up, to guard against those numerous armies maintained by many sovereigns there, where an army belonging to one government alone sometimes amounts to two hundred thousand or four hundred thousand men. Happily, we are situated at a great distance from them, and the inconsiderable power to the north of us is not likely soon to be very formidable. But though our situation places us at a remote danger, it cannot be pretended we are in no danger at all. I believe there is no man who has written on this subject, but has admitted that this power of raising armies is necessary in time of war; but they do not choose to admit of it in a time of peace. It is to be hoped that, in time of peace, there will not be occasion, at any time, but for a very small number of forces; possibly, a few garrisons may be necessary to guard the frontiers, and an insurrection like that lately in Massachusetts might require some troops. But a time of war is the time when the power would probably be exerted to any extent. Let us, however, consider the consequences of a limitation of this power to a time of war only. One moment's consideration will show the impolicy of it in the most glaring manner. We certainly ought to guard against the machinations of other countries. We know not what designs may be entertained against us; but surely, when known, we ought to endeavor to counteract their effects. Such designs may be entertained in a time of profound peace, as well as after a declaration of war. Now suppose, for instance, our government had received certain intelligence that the British government had formed a scheme to attack New York, next April, with ten thousand men; would it not be proper immediately to prepare against it?——and by so doing the scheme might be defeated. But if Congress had no such power, because it was a time of peace, the place must fall the instant it was attacked; and it might take years to recover what might at first have been seasonably defended. This restriction, therefore, cannot take place with safety to the community, and the power must of course be left to the direction of the general government. I hope there will be little necessity for the exercise of this power; and I trust that the universal resentment and resistance of the people will meet every attempt to abuse this or any other power. That high spirit for which they are distinguished, I hope, will ever exist; and it probably will as long as we have a republican form of government. Every man feels a consciousness of a personal equality and independence. Let him look at any part of the continent, — he can see no superiors. This personal independence is the surest safeguard of the public freedom. But is it probable that our own representatives, chosen for a limited time, can be capable of destroying themselves, their families and fortunes, even if they have no regard to their public duty? When such considerations are involved, surely it is very unlikely that they will attempt to raise an army against the liberties of their country. Were we to establish an hereditary nobility, or a set of men who were to have exclusive privileges, then, indeed, our jealousy might be well grounded. But, fortunately, we have no such. The restriction contended for, of no standing army in time of peace, forms a part of our own state Constitution. What has been the consequence? In December, 1786, the Assembly flagrantly violated it, by raising two hundred and one men, for two years, for the defence of Davidson county. I do not deny that the intention might have been good, and that the Assembly really thought the situation of that part of the country required such a defence. But this makes the argument still stronger against the impolicy of such a restriction, since our own experience points out the danger resulting from it; for I take it for granted, that we could not at that time be said to be in a state of war. Dreadful might the condition of this country be without this power. We must trust our friends or trust our enemies. There is one restriction on this power, which I believe is the only one that ought to be put upon it.

Though Congress are to have the power of raising and supporting armies, yet they cannot appropriate money for that purpose for a longer time than two years. Now, we will suppose that the majority of the two houses should be capable of making a bad use of this power, and should appropriate more money to raise an army than is necessary

The appropriation, we have seen, cannot be constitutional for
more than two years.   Within that time it might command
obedience.   But at the end of the second year from the first
choice, the whole House of Representatives must be re-
chosen, and also one third of the Senate.   The people,
being inflamed with the abuse of power of the old members,
would turn them out with indignation.   Upon their return
home, they would meet the universal execrations of their
fellow-citizens.   Instead of the grateful plaudits of their
country, so dear to every feeling mind, they would be treated
with the utmost resentment and contempt;   their names
would be held in everlasting infamy;   and their measures
would be instantly reprobated and changed by the new
members.   In two years, a system of tyranny certainly could
not succeed in the face of the whole people;   and the appropriation could not be with any safety for less than that
period.   If it depended on an annual vote, the consequence
might be, that, at a critical period, when military operations
were necessary, the troops would not know whether they
were entitled to pay or not, and could not safely act till
they knew that the annual vote had passed.   To refuse this
power to the government, would be to invite insults and
attacks from other nations.   Let us not, for God's sake, be
guilty of such indiscretion as to trust our enemies' mercy,
but give, as is our duty, a sufficient power to government to
protect their country, — guarding, at the same time, against
abuses as well as we can.   We well know what this country
suffered by the ravages of the British army during the war.
How could we have been saved but by an army?   Without
that resource we should soon have felt the miserable consequences;   and this day, instead of having the honor — the
greatest any people ever enjoyed — to choose a government
which our reason recommends, we should have been groaning under the most intolerable tyranny that was ever felt.
We ought not to think these dangers are entirely over.   The
British government is not friendly to us.   They dread the
rising glory of America.   They tremble for the West Indies,
and their colonies to the north of us.   They have counteracted us on every occasion since the peace.   Instead of a
liberal and reciprocal commerce, they have attempted to
confine us to a most narrow and ignominious one.   Their
pride is still irritated with the disappointment of their en-

deavors to enslave us. They know that, on the record of history, their conduct towards us must appear in the most disgraceful light. Let it also appear, on the record of history, that America was equally wise and fortunate in peace as well as in war. Let it be said that, with a temper and unanimity unexampled, they corrected the vices of an imperfect government, and framed a new one on the basis of justice and liberty; that, though all did not concur in approving the particular structure of this government, yet that the minority peaceably and respectfully submitted to the decision of the greater number. This is a spectacle so great, that, if it should succeed, this must be considered the greatest country under heaven; for there is no instance of any such deliberate change of government in any other nation that ever existed. But how would it gratify the pride of our enemy to say, "We could not conquer you, but you have ruined yourselves. You have foolishly quarrelled about trifles. You are unfit for any government whatever. You have separated from us, when you were unable to govern yourselves, and you now deservedly feel all the horrors of anarchy." I beg pardon for saying so much. I did not intend it when I began. But the consideration of one of the most important parts of the plan excited all my feelings on the subject. I speak without any affectation in expressing my apprehension of foreign dangers: the belief of them is strongly impressed on my mind. I hope, therefore, the gentlemen of the committee will excuse the warmth with which I have spoken. I shall now take leave of the subject. I flatter myself that gentlemen will see that this power is absolutely necessary, and must be vested somewhere; that it can be vested nowhere so well as in the general government; and that it is guarded by the only restriction which the nature of the thing will admit of.

Mr. HARDIMAN desired to know, if the people were attacked or harassed in any part of the state, — if on the frontiers, for instance, — whether they must not apply to the state legislature for assistance.

Mr. IREDELL replied, that he admitted that application might be immediately made to the state legislature, and that, by the plan under consideration, the strength of the Union was to be exerted to repel invasions of foreign enemies and suppress domestic insurrections; and that the possibility of an instantaneous and unexpected attack, in time of profound peace, illustrated the danger of restricting the power of raising and supporting armies.

The rest of the 8th section read without any observation.

1st clause of the 9th section read.

Mr. J. M'DOWALL wished to hear the reasons of this restriction.

Mr. SPAIGHT answered, that there was a contest between the Northern and Southern States; that the Southern States, whose principal support depended on the labor of slaves, would not consent to the desire of the Northern States to exclude the importation of slaves absolutely; that South Carolina and Georgia insisted on this clause, as they were now in want of hands to cultivate their lands; that in the course of twenty years they would be fully supplied; that the trade would be abolished then, and that, in the mean time, some tax or duty might be laid on.

Mr. M'DOWALL replied, that the explanation was just such as he expected, and by no means satisfactory to him, and that he looked upon it as a very objectionable part of the system.

Mr. IREDELL. Mr. Chairman, I rise to express sentiments similar to those of the gentleman from Craven. For my part, were it practicable to put an end to the importation of slaves immediately, it would give me the greatest pleasure; for it certainly is a trade utterly inconsistent with the rights of humanity, and under which great cruelties have been exercised. When the entire abolition of slavery takes place, it will be an event which must be pleasing to every generous mind, and every friend of human nature; but we often wish for things which are not attainable. It was the wish of a great majority of the Convention to put an end to the trade immediately; but the states of South Carolina and Georgia would not agree to it. Consider, then, what would be the difference between our present situation in this respect, if we do not agree to the Constitution, and what it will be if we do agree to it. If we do not agree to it, do we remedy the evil? No, sir, we do not. For if the Constitution be not adopted, it will be in the power of every state to continue it forever. They may or may not abolish it, at their discretion. But if we adopt the Constitution, the trade must cease after twenty years, if Con-

gress declare so, whether particular states please so or not ;
surely, then, we can gain by it.   This was the utmost that
could be obtained.   I heartily wish more could have been
done.   But as it is, this government is nobly distinguished
above others by that very provision.   Where is there another
country in which such a restriction prevails ?   We, therefore, sir, set an example of humanity, by providing for the
abolition of this inhuman traffic, though at a distant period.
I hope, therefore, that this part of the Constitution will not
be condemned because it has not stipulated for what was
impracticable to obtain.

Mr. SPAIGHT further explained the clause.   That the
limitation of this trade to the term of twenty years was a
compromise between the Eastern States and the Southern
States.   South Carolina and Georgia wished to extend the
term.   The Eastern States insisted on the entire abolition
of the trade.   That the state of North Carolina had not
thought proper to pass any law prohibiting the importation
of slaves, and therefore its delegation in the Convention did
not think themselves authorized to contend for an immediate
prohibition of it.

Mr. IREDELL added to what he had said before, that
the states of Georgia and South Carolina had lost a great
many slaves during the war, and that they wished to supply
the loss.

Mr. GALLOWAY.   Mr. Chairman, the explanation giv-
en to this clause does not satisfy my mind.   I wish to see
this abominable trade put an end to.   But in case it be
thought proper to continue this abominable traffic for twenty
years, yet I do not wish to see the tax on the importation
extended to all persons whatsoever.   Our situation is different from the people to the north.   We want citizens ;
they do not.   Instead of laying a tax, we ought to give a
bounty to encourage foreigners to come among us.   With
respect to the abolition of slavery, it requires the utmost
consideration.   The property of the Southern States consists
principally of slaves.   If they mean to do away slavery altogether, this property will be destroyed.   I apprehend it
means to bring forward manumission.   If we must manu-
mit our slaves, what country shall we send them to ?   It is
impossible for us to be happy, if, after manumission, they
are to stay among us.

Mr. IREDFLL. Mr. Chairman, the worthy gentleman, I believe, has misunderstood this clause, which runs in the following words: "The migration or importation of such persons as any of the states now existing shall think proper to admit, shall not be prohibited by the Congress prior to the year 1808; but a tax or duty may be imposed on such importation, not exceeding ten dollars for each person." Now, sir, observe that the Eastern States, who long ago have abolished slaves, did not approve of the expression *slaves*; they therefore used another, that answered the same purpose. The committee will observe the distinction between the two words *migration* and *importation*. The first part of the clause will extend to persons who come into this country as free people, or are brought as slaves. But the last part extends to slaves only. The word *migration* refers to free persons; but the word *importation* refers to slaves, because free people cannot be said to be imported. The tax, therefore, is only to be laid on slaves who are imported, and not on free persons who migrate. I further beg leave to say that the gentleman is mistaken in another thing. He seems to say that this extends to the abolition of slavery. Is there any thing in this Constitution which says that Congress shall have it in their power to abolish the slavery of those slaves who are now in the country? Is it not the plain meaning of it, that after twenty years they may prevent the future importation of slaves? It does not extend to those now in the country. There is another circumstance to be observed. There is no authority vested in Congress to restrain the states, in the interval of twenty years, from doing what they please. If they wish to prohibit such importation, they may do so. Our next Assembly may put an entire end to the importation of slaves.

The rest of the 9th section read without any observation. Article 2d, section 1st.

Mr. DAVIE. Mr. Chairman, I must express my astonishment at the precipitancy with which we go through this business. Is it not highly improper to pass over in silence any part of this Constitution which has been loudly objected to? We go into a committee to have a freer discussion. I am sorry to see gentlemen hurrying us through, and suppressing their objections, in order to bring them forward at an unseasonable hour. We are assembled here to deliberate for our own common welfare, and to decide upon a question of infinite importance to our country. What is the cause of this silence and gloomy jealousy in gentlemen of the opposition? This department has been universally objected to by them. The most virulent invectives, the most opprobrious epithets, and the most indecent scurrility, have been used and applied against this part of the Constitution. It has been represented as incompatible with any degree of freedom. Why, therefore, do not gentlemen offer their objections now, that we may examine their force, if they have any? The clause meets my entire approbation. I only rise to show the principle on which it was formed. The principle is, the separation of the executive from the legislative — a principle which pervades all free governments. A dispute arose in the Convention concerning the reëligibility of the President. It was the opinion of the deputation from this state, that he should be elected for five or seven years, and be afterwards ineligible. It was urged, in support of this opinion, that the return of public officers into the common mass of the people, where they would feel the tone they had given to the administration of the laws, was the best security the public had for their good behavior; that it would operate as a limitation to his ambition, at the same time that it rendered him more independent; that when once in possession of that office, he would move heaven and earth to secure his reëlection, and perhaps become the cringing dependant of influential men; that our opinion was supported by some experience of the effects of this principle in several of the states. A large and very respectable majority were of the contrary opinion. It was said that such an exclusion would be improper for many reasons; that if an enlightened, upright man had discharged the duties of the office ably and faithfully, it would be depriving the people of the benefit of his ability and experience, though they highly approved of him; that it would render the President less ardent in his endeavors to acquire the esteem and approbation of his country, if he knew that he would be absolutely excluded after a given period; and that it would be depriving a man of singular merit even of the rights of citizenship. It was also said, that the day might come, when the confidence of America would be put in one man, and that it might be dangerous to exclude such a man from the service of his country. It was urged, likewise, that no undue influence could take place in his election; that, as he was to be elected on the same day throughout the United States, no man could say to himself, *I am to be the man.* Under these considerations, a large, respectable majority voted for it as it now stands. With respect to the unity of the executive, the superior energy and secrecy wherewith one person can act, was one of the principles on which the Convention went. But a more predominant principle was, the more obvious responsibility of one person. It was observed that, if there were a plurality of persons, and a crime should be committed, when their conduct came to be examined, it would be impossible to fix the fact on any one of them, but that the public were never at a loss when there was but one man. For these reasons, a great majority concurred in the unity, and reëligibility also, of the executive. I thought proper to show the spirit of the deputation from this state. However, I heartily concur in it as it now stands, and the mode of his election precludes every possibility of corruption or improper influence of any kind.

Mr. JOSEPH TAYLOR thought it improper to object on every trivial case; that this clause had been argued on in some degree before, and that it would be a useless waste of time to dwell any longer upon it; that if they had the power of amending the Constitution, every part need not be discussed, as some were not objectionable; and that, for his own part, he would object when any essential defect came before the house.

2d, 3d, and 4th clauses read.

Mr. J. TAYLOR objected to the power of Congress to determine the time of choosing the electors, and to determine the time of electing the President, and urged that it was improper to have the election on the same day throughout the United States; that Congress, not satisfied with their power over the time, place, and manner of elections of representatives, and over the time and manner of elections of senators, and their power of raising an army, wished likewise to control the election of the electors of the President; that by their army, and the election being on the same day in all the states, they might compel the electors to vote as they please.

Mr. SPAIGHT answered, that the time of choosing the

electors was to be determined by Congress, for the sake of regularity and uniformity; that, if the states were to determine it, one might appoint it at one day, and another at another, &c.; and that the election being on the same day in all the states, would prevent a combination between the electors.

Mr. IREDELL. Mr. Chairman, it gives me great astonishment to hear this objection, because I thought this to be a most excellent clause. Nothing is more necessary than to prevent every danger of influence. Had the time of election been different in different states, the electors chosen in one state might have gone from state to state, and conferred with the other electors, and the election might have been thus carried on under undue influence. But by this provision, the electors must meet in the different states on the same day, and cannot confer together. They may not even know who are the electors in the other states. There can be, therefore, no kind of combination. It is probable that the man who is the object of the choice of thirteen different states, the electors in each voting unconnectedly with the rest, must be a person who possesses, in a high degree, the confidence and respect of his country.

Gov. JOHNSTON expressed doubts with respect to the persons by whom the electors were to be appointed. Some, he said, were of opinion that the people at large were to choose them, and others thought the state legislatures were to appoint them.

Mr. IREDELL was of opinion that it could not be done with propriety by the state legislatures, because, as they were to direct the manner of appointing, a law would look very awkward, which should say, "They gave the power of such appointments to themselves."

Mr. MACLAINE thought the state legislatures might direct the electors to be chosen in what manner they thought proper, and they might direct it to be done by the people at large.

Mr. DAVIE was of opinion, that it was left to the wisdom of the legislatures to direct their election in whatever manner they thought proper.

Mr. TAYLOR still thought the power improper with respect to the time of choosing the electors. This power appeared to him to belong properly to the state legislatures, nor could he see any purpose it could answer but that of an augmentation of the congressional powers, which, he said, were too great already; that by this power they might prolong the elections to seven years, and that, though this would be in direct opposition to another part of the Constitution, sophistry would enable them to reconcile them.

Mr. SPAIGHT replied, that he was surprised that the gentleman objected to the power of Congress to determine the time of choosing the electors, and not to that of fixing the day of the election of the President; that the power in the one case could not possibly answer the purpose of uniformity without having it in the other; that the power, in both cases, could be exercised properly only by one general superintending power; that, if Congress had not this power, there would be no uniformity at all, and that a great deal of time would be taken up in order to agree upon the time.

MONDAY, *July* 28, 1788.

The 2d section of the 2d article read.

Mr. IREDELL. Mr. Chairman, this part of the Constitution has been much objected to. The office of superintending the execution of the laws of the Union is an office of the utmost importance. It is of the greatest consequence to the happiness of the people of America, that the person to whom this great trust is delegated should be worthy of it. It would require a man of abilities and experience; it would also require a man who possessed, in a high degree, the confidence of his country. This being the case, it would be a great defect, in forming a constitution for the United States, if it was so constructed that, by any accident, an improper person could have a chance to obtain that office. The committee will recollect that the President is to be elected by electors appointed by each state, according to the number of senators and representatives to which the state may be entitled in the Congress; that they are to meet on the same day throughout the states, and vote by ballot for two persons, one of whom shall not be an inhabitant of the same state with themselves. These votes are afterwards to be transmitted, under seal, to the seat of the general government. The person who has the greatest number of votes, if it be a majority of the whole, will be the President. If more than one have a majority, and equal votes, the House of Representatives

are to choose one of them.   If none have a majority of votes,
then the House of Representatives are to choose which of the
persons they think proper, out of the five highest on the list.
The person having the next greatest number of votes is to
be the Vice-President, unless two or more should have equal
votes, in which case the Senate is to choose one of them for
Vice-President.   If I recollect right, these are the principal
characteristics.   Thus, sir, two men will be in office at the
same time ; the President, who possesses, in the highest degree, the confidence of his country, and the Vice-President,
who is thought to be the next person in the Union most fit
to perform this trust.   Here, sir, every contingency is provided for.   No faction or combination can bring about the
election.   It is probable that the choice will always fall upon
a man of experienced abilities and fidelity.   In all human
probability, no better mode of election could have been
devised.

The rest of the 1st section read without any observations.
2d section read.

Mr. IREDELL.   Mr. Chairman, I was in hopes that
some other gentleman would have spoken to this clause.
It conveys very important powers, and ought not to be
passed by.   I beg leave, in as few words as possible, to speak
my sentiments upon it.   I believe most of the governors of
the different states have powers similar to those of the President.   In almost every country, the executive has the command of the military forces.   From the nature of the thing, the
command of armies ought to be delegated to one person only.
The secrecy, despatch, and decision, which are necessary in
military operations, can only be expected from one person.
The President, therefore, is to command the military forces
of the United States, and this power I think a proper one ;
at the same time it will be found to be sufficiently guarded.
A very material difference may be observed between this
power, and the authority of the king of Great Britain under
similar circumstances.   The king of Great Britain is not
only the commander-in-chief of the land and naval forces,
but has power, in time of war, to raise fleets and armies.
He has also authority to declare war.   The President has
not the power of declaring war by his own authority, nor
that of raising fleets and armies.   These powers are vested
in other hands.   The power of declaring war is expressly

given to Congress, that is, to the two branches of the legislature — the Senate, composed of representatives of the state legislatures, the House of Representatives, deputed by the people at large. They have also expressly delegated to them the powers of raising and supporting armies, and of providing and maintaining a navy.

With regard to the militia, it must be observed, that though he has the command of them when called into the actual service of the United States, yet he has not the power of calling them out. The power of calling them out is vested in Congress, for the purpose of executing the laws of the Union. When the militia are called out for any purpose, some person must command them ; and who so proper as that person who has the best evidence of his possessing the general confidence of the people? I trust, therefore, that the power of commanding the militia, when called forth into the actual service of the United States, will not be objected to.

The next part, which says " that he may require the opinion in writing of the principal officers," is, in some degree, substituted for a council. He is only to consult them if he thinks proper. Their opinion is to be given him in writing. By this means he will be aided by their intelligence ; and the necessity of their opinions being in writing, will render them more cautious in giving them, and make them responsible should they give advice manifestly improper. This does not diminish the responsibility of the President himself.

They might otherwise have colluded, and opinions have been given too much under his influence.

It has been the opinion of many gentlemen, that the President should have a council. This opinion, probably, has been derived from the example in England. It would be very proper for every gentleman to consider attentively whether that example ought to be imitated by us. Although it be a respectable example, yet, in my opinion, very satisfactory reasons can be assigned for a departure from it in this Constitution.

It was very difficult, immediately on our separation from Great Britain, to disengage ourselves entirely from ideas of government we had been used to. We had been accustomed to a council under the old government, and took it for granted we ought to have one under the new. But examples ought not to be implicitly followed ; and the reasons which prevail in Great Britain for a council do not apply equally to us.   In that country, the executive authority is vested in a magistrate who holds it by birthright.   He has great powers and prerogatives, and it is a constitutional maxim, *that he can do no wrong.*   We have experienced that he can do wrong, yet no man can say so in his own country.   There are no courts to try him for any high crimes ; nor is there any constitutional method of depriving him of his throne.   If he loses it, it must be by a general resistance of his people, contrary to *forms* of law, as at the revolution which took place about a hundred years ago.   It is, therefore, of the utmost moment in that country, that whoever is the instrument of any act of government should be personally responsible for it, since the king is not ; and, for the same reason, that no act of government should be exercised but by the instrumentality of some person who can be accountable for it.   Every thing, therefore, that the king does, must be by some *advice*, and the adviser of course answerable.   Under our Constitution we are much happier.

No man has an authority to injure another with impunity. No man is better than his fellow-citizens, nor can pretend to any superiority over the meanest man in the country.   If the President does a single act by which the people are prejudiced, he is punishable himself, and no other man merely to screen him.   If he commits any misdemeanor in office, he is impeachable, removable from office, and incapacitated to hold any office of honor, trust, or profit.   If he commits any crime, he is punishable by the laws of his country, and in capital cases may be deprived of his life.   This being the case, there is not the same reason here for having a council which exists in England.   It is, however, much to be desired, that a man who has such extensive and important business to perform should have the means of some assistance to enable him to discharge his arduous employment.   The advice of the principal executive officers, which he can at all times command, will, in my opinion, answer this valuable purpose.   He can at no time want advice, if he desires it, as the principal officers will always be on the spot.   Those officers, from their abilities and experience, will probably be able to give as good, if not better, advice than any coun-sellors would do ; and the solemnity of the advice in writing,

10

which must be preserved, would be a great check upon them.

Besides these considerations, it was difficult for the Convention to prepare a council that would be unexceptionable. That jealousy which naturally exists between the different states enhanced this difficulty. If a few counsellors were to be chosen from the Northern, Southern, or Middle States, or from a few states only, undue preference might be given to those particular states from which they should come. If, to avoid this difficulty, one counsellor should be sent from each state, this would require great expense, which is a consideration, at this time, of much moment, especially as it is probable that, by the method proposed, the President may be equally well advised without any expense at all.

We ought also to consider that, had he a council by whose advice he was bound to act, his responsibility, in all such cases, must be destroyed. You surely would not oblige him to follow their advice, and punish him for obeying it. If called upon on any occasion of dislike, it would be natural for him to say, " You know my council are men of integrity and ability : I could not act against their opinions, though I confess my own was contrary to theirs." This, sir, would be pernicious. In such a situation, he might easily combine with his council, and it might be impossible to fix a fact upon him. It would be difficult often to know whether the President or counsellors were most to blame. A thousand plausible excuses might be made, which would escape detection. But the method proposed in the Constitution creates no such embarrassment. It is plain and open. And the President will personally have the credit of good, or the censure of bad measures ; since, though he may ask advice, he is to use his own judgment in following or rejecting it. For all these reasons, I am clearly of opinion that the clause is better as it stands than if the President were to have a council. I think every good that can be derived from the institution of a council may be expected from the advice of these officers, without its being liable to the disadvantages to which, it appears to me, the institution of a council would be.

Another power that he has is to grant pardons, except in cases of impeachment. I believe it is the sense of a great part of America, that this power should be exercised by their

governors. It is in several states on the same footing
that it is here. It is the genius of a republican government
that the laws should be rigidly executed, without the influence of favor or ill-will — that, when a man commits a
crime, however powerful he or his friends may be, yet he
should be punished for it ; and, on the other hand, though
he should be universally hated by his country, his real guilt
alone, as to the particular charge, is to operate against him.
This strict and scrupulous observance of justice is proper in
all governments ; but it is particularly indispensable in a
republican one, because, in such a government, the law is
superior to every man, and no man is superior to another.
But, though this general principle be unquestionable, surely
there is no gentleman in the committee who is not aware
that there ought to be exceptions to it ; because there may
be many instances where, though a man offends against the
letter of the law, yet peculiar circumstances in his case may
entitle him to mercy. It is impossible for any general law
to foresee and provide for all possible cases that may arise ;
and therefore an inflexible adherence to it, in every instance,
might frequently be the cause of very great injustice. For
this reason, such a power ought to exist somewhere ; and
where could it be more properly vested, than in a man who
had received such strong proofs of his possessing the highest
confidence of the people ? This power, however, only refers
to offences against the United States, and not against
particular states. Another reason for the President possessing this authority, is this : it is often necessary to convict
a man by means of his accomplices. We have sufficient
experience of that in this country. A criminal would often
go unpunished, were not this method to be pursued against
him. In my opinion, till an accomplice's own danger is
removed, his evidence ought to be regarded with great
diffidence. If, in civil causes of property, a witness must
be entirely disinterested, how much more proper is it he
should be so in cases of life and death ! This power is
naturally vested in the President, because it is his duty to
watch over the public safety ; and as that may frequently
require the evidence of accomplices to bring great offenders
to justice, he ought to be intrusted with the most effectual
means of procuring it.

I beg leave further to observe, that, for another reason, I

think there is a propriety in leaving this power to the general discretion of the executive magistrate, rather than to fetter it in any manner which has been proposed. It may happen that many men, upon plausible pretences, may be seduced into very dangerous measures against their country. They may aim, by an insurrection, to redress imaginary grievances, at the same time believing, upon false suggestions, that their exertions are necessary to save their country from destruction. Upon cool reflection, however, they possibly are convinced of their error, and clearly see through the treachery and villany of their leaders. In this situation, if the President possessed the power of pardoning, they probably would throw themselves on the equity of the government, and the whole body be peaceably broken up. Thus, at a critical moment, the President might, perhaps, prevent a civil war. But if there was no authority to pardon, in that delicate exigency, what would be the consequence? The principle of self-preservation would prevent their parting. Would it not be natural for them to say, " We shall be punished if we disband. Were we sure of mercy, we would peaceably part. But we know not that there is any chance of this. We may as well meet one kind of death as another. We may as well die in the field as at the gallows." I therefore submit to the committee if this power be not highly necessary for such a purpose.

We have seen a happy instance of the good effect of such an exercise of mercy in the state of Massachusetts, where, very lately, there was so formidable an insurrection. I believe a great majority of the insurgents were drawn into it by false artifices. They at length saw their error, and were willing to disband. Government, by a wise exercise of lenity, after having shown its power, generally granted a pardon ; and the whole party were dispersed. There is now as much peace in that country as in any state in the Union.

A particular instance which occurs to me shows the utility of this power very strongly. Suppose we were involved in war. It would be then necessary to know the designs of the enemy. This kind of knowledge cannot always be procured but by means of spies — a set of wretches whom all nations despise, but whom all employ ; and, as they would assuredly be used against us, a principle of self-defence would urge and justify the use of them on our part. Suppose, therefore, the President could prevail upon a man of some importance to go over to the enemy, in order to give him secret information of his measures. He goes off privately to the enemy. He feigns resentment against his country for some ill usage, either real or pretended, and is received, possibly, into favor and confidence. The people would not know the purpose for which he was employed. In the mean time, he secretly informs the President of the enemy's designs, and by this means, perhaps, those designs are counteracted, and the country saved from destruction. After his business is executed, he returns into his own country, where the people, not knowing he had rendered them any service, are naturally exasperated against him for his supposed treason. I would ask any gentleman whether the President ought not to have the power of pardoning this man. Suppose the concurrence of the Senate, or any other body, was necessary; would this obnoxious person be properly safe? We know in every country there is a strong prejudice against the executive authority. If a prejudice of this kind, on such an occasion, prevailed against the President, the President might be suspected of being influenced by corrupt motives, and the application in favor of this man be rejected. Such a thing might very possibly happen when the prejudices of party were strong; and therefore no man, so clearly entitled as in the case I have supposed, ought to have his life exposed to so hazardous a contingency.

The power of impeachment is given by this Constitution, to bring great offenders to punishment. It is calculated to bring them to punishment for crime which it is not easy to describe, but which every one must be convinced is a high crime and misdemeanor against the government. This power is lodged in those who represent the great body of the people, because the occasion for its exercise will arise from acts of great injury to the community, and the objects of it may be such as cannot be easily reached by an ordinary tribunal. The trial belongs to the Senate, lest an inferior tribunal should be too much awed by so powerful an accuser. After trial thus solemnly conducted, it is not probable that it would happen once in a thousand times, that a man actually convicted would be entitled to mercy; and if the President had the power of pardoning in such a case, this great check upon high officers of state would lose much of its influence. It seems, therefore, proper that the general power of pardoning should be abridged in this particular instance. The punishment annexed to this conviction on impeachment can only be removal from office, and disqualification to hold any place of honor, trust, or profit. But the person convicted is further liable to a trial at common law, and may receive such common-law punishment as belongs to a description of such offences, if it be punishable by that law. I hope, for the reasons I have stated, that the whole of this clause will be approved by the committee. The regulations altogether, in my opinion, are as wisely contrived as they could be. It is impossible for imperfect beings to form a perfect system. If the present one may be productive of possible inconveniences, we are not to reject it for that reason, but inquire whether any other system could be devised which would be attended with fewer inconveniences, in proportion to the advantages resulting. But we ought to be exceedingly attentive in examining, and still more cautious in deciding, lest we should condemn what may be worthy of applause, or approve of what may be exceptionable. I hope that, in the explanation of this clause, I have not improperly taken up the time of the committee.

Mr. MILLER acknowledged that the explanation of this clause by the member from Edenton had obviated some objections which he had to it; but still he could not entirely approve of it. He could not see the necessity of vesting this power in the President. He thought that his influence would be too great in the country, and particularly over the military, by being the commander-in-chief of the army, navy, and militia. He thought he could too easily abuse such extensive powers, and was of opinion that Congress ought to have power to direct the motions of the army. He considered it as a defect in the Constitution, that it was not expressly provided that Congress should have the direction of the motions of the army.

Mr. SPAIGHT answered, that it was true that the command of the army and navy was given to the President; but that Congress, who had the power of raising armies, could certainly prevent any abuse of that authority in the President — that they alone had the means of supporting armies, and that the President was impeachable if he in any manner abused his trust. He was surprised that any objection should be made to giving the command of the army to one man ; that it was well known that the direction of an army could not be properly exercised by a numerous body of men ; that Congress had, in the last war, given the exclusive command of the army to the commander-in-chief, and that if they had not done so, perhaps the independence of America would not have been established.

Mr. PORTER. Mr. Chairman, there is a power vested in the Senate and President to make treaties, which shall be the supreme law of the land. Which among us can call them to account? I always thought that there could be no proper exercise of power without the suffrage of the people ; yet the House of Representatives has no power to intermeddle with treaties. The President and seven senators, as nearly as I can remember, can make a treaty which will be of great advantage to the Northern States, and equal injury to the Southern States. They might give up the rivers and territory of the Southern States. Yet, in the preamble of the Constitution, they say *all the people* have done it. I should be glad to know what power there is of calling the President and Senate to account.

Mr. SPAIGHT answered that, under the Confederation, two thirds of the states might make treaties ; that, if the senators from all the states attended when a treaty was about to be made, two thirds of the states would have a voice in its formation. He added, that he would be glad to ask the gentleman what mode there was of calling the present Congress to account.

Mr. PORTER repeated his objection. He hoped that gentlemen would not impose on the house ; that the President could make treaties with two thirds of the senate ; that the President, in that case, voted rather in a legislative than in an executive capacity, which he thought impolitic.

Gov. JOHNSTON. Mr. Chairman, in my opinion, if there be any difference between this Constitution and the Confederation, with respect to treaties, the Constitution is more safe than the Confederation. We know that two members from each state have a right, by the Confederation, to give the vote of that state, and two thirds of the states have a right also to make treaties. By this Constitution, two thirds of the senators cannot make treaties without the concurrence of the President. Here is, then, an additional guard. The calculation that seven or eight senators, with the President, can make treaties, is totally erroneous. Fourteen is a quorum; two thirds of which are ten. It is upon the improbable supposition that they will not attend, that the objection is founded that ten men, with the President, can make treaties. Can it be reasonably supposed that they will not attend when the most important business is agitated — when the interests of their respective states are most immediately affected?

Mr. MACLAINE observed, that the gentleman was out of order with his objection — that they had not yet come to the clause which enables the Senate and President to make treaties.

The 2d clause of the 2d section read.

Mr. SPENCER. Mr. Chairman, I rise to declare my disapprobation of this, likewise. It is an essential article in our Constitution, that the legislative, the executive, and the supreme judicial powers, of government, ought to be forever separate and distinct from each other. The Senate, in the proposed government of the United States, are possessed of the legislative authority in conjunction with the House of Representatives. They are likewise possessed of the sole power of trying all impeachments, which, not being restrained to the officers of the United States, may be intended to include all the officers of the several states in the Union. And by this clause they possess the chief of the executive power; they are, in effect, to form treaties, which are to be the law of the land; and they have obviously, in effect, the appointment of all the officers of the United States. The President may nominate, but they have a negative upon his nomination, till he has exhausted the number of those he wishes to be appointed. He will be obliged, finally, to acquiesce in the appointment of those whom the Senate shall nominate, or else no appointment will take place. Hence it is easy to perceive that the President, in order to do any business, or to answer any purpose in this department of his office, and to keep himself out of perpetual hot water, will be under a necessity to form a connection with that powerful body, and be contented to put himself at the head of the leading members who compose it. I do not expect, at this day, that the outline and organization of this proposed government will be materially

altered.   But I cannot but be of opinion that the government would have been infinitely better and more secure, if
the President had been provided with a standing council,
composed of one member from each of the states, the duration of whose office might have been the same as that of
the President's office, or for any other period that might
have been thought more proper ; for it can hardly be supposed, if two senators can be sent from each state, who are
fit to give counsel to the President, that one such cannot
be found in each state qualified for that purpose.   Upon this
plan, one half the expense of the Senate, as a standing
council to the President in the recess of Congress, would
evidently be saved ; each state would have equal weight in
this council, as it has now in the Senate.   And what renders this plan the more eligible is, that two very important consequences would result from it, which cannot result from the
present plan.   The first is, that the whole executive department, being separate and distinct from that of the legislative and judicial, would be amenable to the justice of the
land : the President and his council, or either or any of
them, might be impeached, tried, and condemned, for any
misdemeanor in office.   Whereas, on the present plan proposed, the Senate, who are to advise the President, and
who, in effect, are possessed of the chief executive powers,
let their conduct be what it will, are not amenable to the
public justice of their country : if they may be impeached,
there is no tribunal invested with jurisdiction to try them.
It is true that the proposed Constitution provides that, when
the President is tried, the chief justice shall preside.   But
I take this to be very little more than a farce.   What can
the Senate try him for ?   For doing that which they have
advised him to do, and which, without their advice, he would
not have done.   Except what he may do in a military capacity — when, I presume, he will be entitled to be tried by
a court martial of general officers — he can do nothing in the
executive department without the advice of the Senate, unless it be to grant pardons, and adjourn the two Houses of
Congress to some day to which they cannot agree to adjourn
themselves — probably to some term that may be convenient to the leading members of the Senate.

I cannot conceive, therefore, that the President can ever
be tried by the Senate with any effect, or to any purpose

for any misdemeanor in his office, unless it should extend to high treason, or unless they should wish to fix the odium of any measure on him, in order to exculpate themselves; the latter of which I cannot suppose will ever happen.

Another important consequence of the plan I wish had taken place is that, the office of the President being thereby unconnected with that of the legislative, as well as the judicial, he would have that independence which is necessary to form the intended check upon the acts passed by the legislature before they obtain the sanction of laws. But, on the present plan, from the necessary connection of the President's office with that of the Senate, I have little ground to hope that his firmness will long prevail against the overbearing power and influence of the Senate, so far as to answer the purpose of any considerable check upon the acts they may think proper to pass in conjunction with the House of Representatives; for he will soon find that, unless he inclines to compound with them, they can easily hinder and control him in the principal articles of his office. But, if nothing else could be said in favor of the plan of a standing council to the President, independent of the Senate, the dividing the power of the latter would be sufficient to recommend it; it being of the utmost importance towards the security of the government, and the liberties of the citizens under it. For I think it must be obvious to every unprejudiced mind, that the combining in the Senate the power of legislation, with a controlling share in the appointment of all the officers of the United States, (except those chosen by the people,) and the power of trying all impeachments that may be found against such officers, invests the Senate at once with such an enormity of power, and with such an overbearing and uncontrollable influence, as is incompatible with every idea of safety to the liberties of a free country, and is calculated to swallow up all other powers, and to render that body a despotic aristocracy.

Mr. PORTER recommended the most serious consideration when they were about to give away power; that they were not only about to give away power to legislate or make laws of a supreme nature, and to make treaties, which might sacrifice the most valuable interests of the community, but to give a power to the general government to drag the inhabitants to any part of the world as long as they pleased;

that they ought not to put it in the power of any man, or any set of men, to do so; and that the representation was defective, being not a substantial, immediate representation. He observed that, as treaties were the supreme law of the land, the House of Representatives ought to have a vote in making them, as well as in passing them.

Mr. J. M'DOWALL. Mr. Chairman : permit me, sir, to make a few observations, to show how improper it is to place so much power in so few men, without any responsibility whatever. Let us consider what number of them is necessary to transact the most important business. Two thirds of the members present, with the President, can make a treaty. Fourteen of them are a quorum, two thirds of which are ten. These ten may make treaties and alliances. They may involve us in any difficulties, and dispose of us in any manner, they please. Nay, eight is a majority of a quorum, and can do every thing but make treaties. How unsafe are we, when we have no power of bringing those to an account! It is absurd to try them before their own body. Our lives and property are in the hands of eight or nine men. Will these gentlemen intrust their rights in this manner?

Mr. DAVIE. Mr. Chairman, although treaties are mere conventional acts between the contracting parties, yet, by the law of nations, they are the supreme law of the land to their respective citizens or subjects. All civilized nations have concurred in considering them as paramount to an ordinary act of legislation. This concurrence is founded on the reciprocal convenience and solid advantages arising from it. A due observance of treaties makes nations more friendly to each other, and is the only means of rendering less frequent those mutual hostilities which tend to depopulate and ruin contending nations. It extends and facilitates that commercial intercourse, which, founded on the universal protection of private property, has, in a measure, made the world one nation.

The power of making treaties has, in all countries and governments, been placed in the executive departments. This has not only been grounded on the necessity and reason arising from that degree of secrecy, design, and despatch, which is always necessary in negotiations between nations, but to prevent their being impeded, or carried into effect, by the violence, animosity, and heat of parties, which too

often infect numerous bodies. Both of these reasons preponderated in the foundation of this part of the system. It
is true, sir, that the late treaty between the United States
and Great Britain has not, in some of the states, been held
as the supreme law of the land. Even in this state, an act
of Assembly passed to declare its validity. But no doubt
that treaty was the supreme law of the land without the
sanction of the Assembly; because, by the Confederation,
Congress had power to make treaties. It was one of those
original rights of sovereignty which were vested in them;
and it was not the deficiency of constitutional authority in
Congress to make treaties that produced the necessity of a
law to declare their validity; but it was owing to the entire
imbecility of the Confederation.

On the principle of the propriety of vesting this power in
the executive department, it would seem that the whole
power of making treaties ought to be left to the President,
who, being elected by the people of the United States at
large, will have their general interest at heart. But that
jealousy of executive power which has shown itself so
strongly in all the American governments, would not admit
this improvement. Interest, sir, has a most powerful influence over the human mind, and is the basis on which all the
transactions of mankind are built. It was mentioned before
that the extreme jealousy of the little states, and between
the commercial states and the non-importing states, produced the necessity of giving an equality of suffrage to the
Senate. The same causes made it indispensable to give to
the senators, as representatives of states, the power of
making, or rather ratifying, treaties. Although it militates
against every idea of just proportion that the little state of
Rhode Island should have the same suffrage with Virginia,
or the great commonwealth of Massachusetts, yet the small
states would not consent to confederate without an equal
voice in the formation of treaties. Without the equality,
they apprehended that their interest would be neglected or
sacrificed in negotiations. This difficulty could not be got
over. It arose from the unalterable nature of things. Every
man was convinced of the inflexibility of the little states in
this point. It therefore became necessary to give them an
absolute equality in making treaties.

The learned gentleman on my right, (Mr. Spencer,) after

saying that this was an enormous power, and that blending the different branches of government was dangerous, said, that such accumulated powers were inadmissible, and contrary to all the maxims of writers. It is true, the great Montesquieu, and several other writers, have laid it down as a maxim not to be departed from, that the legislative, executive, and judicial powers should be separate and distinct. But the idea that these gentlemen had in view has been misconceived or misrepresented. An absolute and complete separation is not meant by them. It is impossible to form a government upon these principles. Those states who had made an absolute separation of these three powers their leading principle, have been obliged to depart from it. It is a principle, in fact, which is not to be found in any of the state governments. In the government of New York, the executive and judiciary have a negative similar to that of the President of the United States. This is a junction of all the three powers, and has been attended with the most happy effects. In this state, and most of the others, the executive and judicial powers are dependent on the legislature. Has not the legislature of this state the power of appointing the judges? Is it not in their power also to fix their compensation? What independence can there be in persons who are obliged to be obsequious and cringing for their office and salary? Are not our judges dependent on the legislature for every morsel they eat? It is not difficult to discern what effect this may have on human nature. The meaning of this maxim I take to be this — that the whole legislative, executive, and judicial powers should not be exclusively blended in any one particular instance. The Senate try impeachments. This is their only judicial cognizance. As to the ordinary objects of a judiciary — such as the decision of controversies, the trial of criminals, &c. — the judiciary is perfectly separate and distinct from the legislative and executive branches. The House of Lords, in England, have great judicial powers; yet this is not considered as a blemish in their constitution. Why? Because they have not the whole legislative power. Montesquieu, at the same time that he laid down this maxim, was writing in praise of the British government. At the very time he recommended this distinction of powers, he passed the highest eulogium on a constitution wherein they were all partially blended. So

that the meaning of the maxim, as laid down by him and
other writers, must be, that these three branches must
not be entirely blended in one body. And this system
before you comes up to the maxim more completely than
the favorite government of Montesquieu. The gentleman
from Anson has said that the Senate destroys the independence of the President, because they must confirm the
nomination of officers. The necessity of their interfering in
the appointment of officers resulted from the same reason
which produced the equality of suffrage. In other countries,
the executive or chief magistrate, alone, nominates and
appoints officers. The small states would not agree that
the House of Representatives should have a voice in the
appointment to offices; and the extreme jealousy of all the
states would not give it to the President alone. In my
opinion, it is more proper as it is than it would be in either
of those cases. The interest of each state will be equally
attended to in appointments, and the choice will be more
judicious by the junction of the Senate to the President.
Except in the appointments of officers, and making of treaties, he is not joined with them in any instance. He is perfectly independent of them in his election. It is impossible
for human ingenuity to devise any mode of election better
calculated to exclude undue influence. He is chosen by the
electors appointed by the people. He is elected on the
same day in every state, so that there can be no possible combination between the electors. The affections of the people can be the only influence to procure his election. If he
makes a judicious nomination, is it to be presumed that the
Senate will not concur in it? Is it to be supposed the legislatures will choose the most depraved men in the states to
represent them in Congress? Should he nominate unworthy
characters, can it be reasonably concluded that they will
confirm it? He then says that the senators will have influence to get themselves reëlected; nay, that they will be
perpetually elected.

I have very little apprehension on this ground. I take it
for granted that the man who is once a senator will very
probably be out for the next six years. Legislative influence changes. Other persons rise, who have particular connections to advance them to office. If the senators stay six
years out of the state governments, their influence will be

greatly diminished. It will be impossible for the most influential character to get himself reëlected after being out of the country so long. There will be an entire change in six years. Such futile objections, I fear, proceed from an aver sion to any general system. The same learned gentleman says that it would be better, were a council, consisting of one from every state, substituted to the Senate. Another gentleman has objected to the smallness of this number. This shows the impossibility of satisfying all men's minds. I beg this committee to place these two objections together, and see their glaring inconsistency. If there were thirteen counsellors, in the manner he proposes, it would destroy the responsibility of the President. He must have acted also with a majority of them. A majority of them is seven, which would be a quorum. A majority of these would be four, and every act to which the concurrence of the Senate and the President is necessary could be decided by these four. Nay, less than a majority — even one — would suffice to enable them to do the most important acts. This, sir, would be the effect of this council. The dearest interests of the community would be trusted to two men. Had this been the case, the loudest clamors would have been raised, with justice, against the Constitution, and these gentlemen would have loaded their own proposition with the most virulent abuse.

On a due consideration of this clause, it appears that this power could not have been lodged as safely any where else as where it is. The honorable gentleman (Mr. M'Dowall) has spoken of a consolidation in this government. That is a very strange inconsistency, when he points out, at the same time, the necessity of lodging the power of making treaties with the representatives, where the idea of a consolidation can alone exist; and when he objects to placing it in the Senate, where the federal principle is completely preserved. As the Senate represents the sovereignty of the states, whatever might affect the states in their political capacity ought to be left to them. This is the certain means of preventing a consolidation. How extremely absurd is it to call that disposition of power a consolidation of the states, which must to all eternity prevent it! I have only to add the principle upon which the General Convention went — that the power of making treaties could nowhere be so safely

lodged as in the President and Senate; and the extreme
jealousy subsisting between some of the states would not
admit of it elsewhere.   If any man will examine the operation of that jealousy, in his own breast, as a citizen of North
Carolina, he will soon feel the inflexibility that results from
it, and perhaps be induced to acknowledge the propriety
of this arrangement.

Mr. M'DOWALL declared, that he was of the same opinion as before, and that he believed the observations which
the gentleman had made, on the apparent inconsistency of
his remarks, would have very little weight with the committee; that giving such extensive powers to so few men in
the Senate was extremely dangerous; and that he was not
the more reconciled to it from its being brought about by
the inflexibility of the small, pitiful states to the north.   He
supposed that eight members in the Senate from those states,
with the President, might do the most important acts.

Mr. SPAIGHT.   Mr. Chairman, the gentleman objects
to the smallness of the number, and to their want of responsibility.   He argues as if the senators were never to attend, and as if the northern senators were to attend more
regularly than those from the south.   Nothing can be more
unreasonable than to suppose that they will be absent on
the most important occasions.   What responsibility is there
in the present Congress that is not in the Senate?   What
responsibility is there in our state legislature?   The senators
are as responsible as the members of our legislature.   It is
to be observed. that though the senators are not impeachable,
yet the President is.   He may be impeached and punished
for giving his consent to a treaty, whereby the interest of
the community is manifestly sacrificed.

Mr. SPENCER.   Mr. Chairman, the worthy gentleman
from Halifax has endeavored to obviate my objections against
the want of responsibility in the President and senators,
and against the extent of their power.   He has not removed
my objections.   It is totally out of their power to show any degree of responsibility.   The executive is tried by his advisers.
The reasons I urged are so cogent and strong with me, that
I cannot approve of this clause.   I can see nothing of any
weight against them.   [Here Mr. Spencer spoke so low that
he could not distinctly be heard.]   I would not give the
President and senators power to make treaties, because it

destroys their responsibility. If a bad treaty be made, and he impeached for it, the Senate will not pronounce sentence against him, because they advised him to make it. If they had legislative power only, it would be unexceptionable; but when they have the appointment of officers, and such extensive executive powers, it gives them such weight as is inadmissible. Notwithstanding what gentlemen have said in defence of the clause, the influence of the Senate still remains equally formidable to me. The President can do nothing unless they concur with him. In order to obtain their concurrence, he will compromise with them. Had there been such a council as I mentioned, to advise him, the Senate would not have had such dangerous influence, and the responsibility of the President would have been secured. This seems obviously clear to be the case.

Mr. PORTER. Mr. Chairman, I only rise to make one observation on what the gentleman has said. He told us, that if the Senate were not amenable, the President was. I beg leave to ask the gentleman if it be not inconsistent that they should punish the President, whom they advised themselves to do what he is impeached for. My objection still remains. I cannot find it in the least obviated.

Mr. BLOODWORTH desired to be informed whether treaties were not to be submitted to the Parliament in Great Britain before they were valid.

Mr. IREDELL. Mr. Chairman, the objections to this clause deserve great consideration. I believe it will be easy to obviate the objections against it, and that it will be found to have been necessary, for the reasons stated by the gentleman from Halifax, to vest this power in some body composed of representatives of states, where their voices should be equal; for in this case the sovereignty of the states is particularly concerned, and the great caution of giving the states an equality of suffrage in making treaties, was for the express purpose of taking care of that sovereignty, and attending to their interests, as political bodies, in foreign negotiations. It is objected to as improper, because, if the President or Senate should abuse their trust, there is not sufficient responsibility, since he can only be tried by the Senate, by whose advice he acted; and the Senate cannot be tried at all. I beg leave to observe that, when any man is impeached, it must be for an error of the heart, and not of the head.   God forbid that a man, in any country in the world, should be liable to be punished for want of judgment. This is not the case here.   As to errors of the heart, there is sufficient responsibility.   Should these be committed, there is a ready way to bring him to punishment.   This is a responsibility which answers every purpose that could be desired by a people jealous of their liberty.   I presume that, if the President, with the advice of the Senate, should make a treaty with a foreign power, and that treaty should be deemed unwise, or against the interest of the country, yet if nothing could be objected against it but the difference of opinion between them and their constituents, they could not justly be obnoxious to punishment.   If they were punishable for exercising their own judgment, and not that of their constituents, no man who regarded his reputation would accept the office either of a senator or President.   Whatever mistake a man may make, he ought not to be punished for it, nor his posterity rendered infamous.   But if a man be a villain, and wilfully abuse his trust, he is to be held up as a public offender, and ignominiously punished.   A public officer ought not to act from a principle of fear.   Were he punishable for want of judgment, he would be continually in dread; but when he knows that nothing but real guilt can disgrace him, he may do his duty firmly, if he be an honest man; and if he be not, a just fear of disgrace may, perhaps, as to the public, have nearly the effect of an intrinsic principle of virtue.   According to these principles, I suppose the only instances, in which the President would be liable to impeachment, would be where he had received a bribe, or had acted from some corrupt motive or other.   If the President had received a bribe, without the privity or knowledge of the Senate, from a foreign power, and, under the influence of that bribe, had address enough with the Senate, by artifices and misrepresentations, to seduce their consent to a pernicious treaty, — if it appeared afterwards that this was the case, would not that Senate be as competent to try him as any other persons whatsoever?   Would they not exclaim against his villany?   Would they not feel a particular resentment against him, for being made the instrument of his treacherous purposes?   In this situation, if any objection could be made against the Senate as a proper tribunal, it might more properly be made by the President himself, lest their resentment should operate too strongly, rather than by the public, on the ground of a supposed partiality. The President must certainly be punishable for giving false information to the Senate. He is to regulate all intercourse with foreign powers, and it is his duty to impart to the Senate every material intelligence he receives. If it should appear that he has not given them full information, but has concealed important intelligence which he ought to have communicated, and by that means induced them to enter into measures injurious to their country, and which they would not have consented to had the true state of things been disclosed to them, — in this case, I ask whether, upon an impeachment for a misdemeanor upon such an account, the Senate would probably favor him. With respect to the impeachability of the Senate, that is a matter of doubt. There have been no instances of impeachment for legislative misdemeanors; and we shall find, upon examination, that the inconveniences resulting from such impeachments would more than preponderate the advantages. There is no greater honor in the world than being the representative of a free people. There is no trust on which the happiness of the people has a greater dependence. Yet who ever heard of impeaching a member of the legislature for any legislative misconduct? It would be a great check on the public business, if a member of the Assembly was liable to punishment for his conduct as such. Unfortunately, it is the case, not only in other countries, but even in this, that division and differences in opinion will continually arise. On many questions there will be two or more parties. These often judge with little charity of each other, and attribute every opposition to their own system to an ill motive. We know this very well from experience; but, in my opinion, this constant suspicion is frequently unjust. I believe, in general, both parties really think themselves right, and that the majority of each commonly act with equal innocence of intention. But, with the usual want of charity in these cases, how dangerous would it be to make a member of the legislature liable to impeachment! A mere difference of opinion might be interpreted, by the malignity of party, into a deliberate, wicked action.

It therefore appears to me at least very doubtful whether it would be proper to render the Senate impeachable at all · especially as, in the branches of executive government, where their concurrence is required, the President is the primary agent, and plainly responsible, and they, in fact, are but a council to validate proper, or restrain improper, conduct in him ; but if a senator is impeachable, it could only be for corruption, or some other wicked motive, in which case, surely those senators who had acted from upright motives would be competent to try him.   Suppose there had been such a council as was proposed, consisting of thirteen, one from each state, to assist the President in making treaties, &c. ; more general alarm would have been excited, and stronger opposition made to this Constitution, than even at present.   The power of the President would have appeared more formidable, and the states would have lost one half of their security ; since, instead of two representatives, which each has now for those purposes, they would have had but one.   A gentleman from New Hanover has asked whether it is not the practice, in Great Britain, to submit treaties to Parliament, before they are esteemed as valid.   The king has the sole authority, by the laws of that country, to make treaties.   After treaties are made, they are frequently discussed in the two houses, where, of late years, the most important measures of government have been narrowly examined.   It is usual to move for an address of approbation ; and such has been the complaisance of Parliament for a long time, that this seldom hath been withheld.   Sometimes they pass an act in conformity to the treaty made ; but this, I believe, is not for the mere purpose of confirmation, but to make alterations in a particular system, which the change of circumstances requires.   The constitutional power of making treaties is vested in the crown ; and the power with whom a treaty is made considers it as binding, without any act of Parliament, unless an alteration by such is provided for in the treaty itself, which I believe is sometimes the case.   When the treaty of peace was made in 1763, it contained stipulations for the surrender of some islands to the French.   The islands were given up, I believe, without any act of Parliament.   The power of making treaties is very important, and must be vested somewhere, in order to counteract the dangerous designs of other countries, and to be able to terminate a war when it is begun.   Were it known that our government was weak, two or more European powers might combine against us.   Would it not be politic to have some power in this country, to obviate this danger by a treaty? If this power was injudiciously limited, the nations where the power was possessed without restriction would have greatly the advantage of us in negotiation; and every one must know, according to modern policy, of what moment an advantage in negotiation is. The honorable member from Anson said that the accumulation of all the different branches of power in the Senate would be dangerous. The experience of other countries shows that this fear is without foundation. What is the Senate of Great Britain opposed to the House of Commons, although it be composed of an hereditary nobility, of vast fortunes, and entirely independent of the people? Their weight is far inferior to that of the Commons. Here is a strong instance of the accumulation of powers of the different branches of government without producing any inconvenience. That Senate, sir, is a separate branch of the legislature, is the great constitutional council of the crown, and decides on lives and fortunes in impeachments, besides being the ultimate tribunal for trying controversies respecting private rights. Would it not appear that all these things should render them more formidable than the other house? Yet the Commons have generally been able to carry every thing before them. The circumstance of their representing the great body of the people, alone gives them great weight. This weight has great authority added to it, by their possessing the right (a right given to the people's representatives in Congress) of exclusively originating money bills. The authority over money will do every thing. A government cannot be supported without money. Our representatives may at any time compel the Senate to agree to a reasonable measure, by withholding supplies till the measure is consented to. There was a great debate, in the Convention, whether the Senate should have an equal power of originating money bills. It was strongly insisted, by some, that they should; but at length a majority thought it unadvisable, and the clause was passed as it now stands. I have reason to believe that our representatives had a great share in establishing this excellent regulation, and in my opinion they deserve the public thanks for it. It has been objected that this power must necessarily injure the people, inasmuch as a bare majority of the Senate might alone be assembled, and eight would be sufficient for a decision. This is on a suppositior

that many of the senators would neglect attending. It is to
be hoped that the gentlemen who will be honored with seats
in Congress will faithfully execute their trust, as well in attending as in every other part of their duty. An objection
of this sort will go against all government whatever. Possible abuse, and neglect of attendance, are objections which
may be urged against any government which the wisdom of
man is able to construct. When it is known of how much
importance attendance is, no senator would dare to incur the
universal resentment of his fellow-citizens by grossly absent-
ing himself from his duty. Do gentlemen mean that it ought
to have been provided, by the Constitution, that the whole
body should attend before particular business was done?
Then it would be in the power of a few men, by neglecting
to attend, to obstruct the public business, and possibly bring
on the destruction of their country. If this power be improperly vested, it is incumbent on gentlemen to tell us in
what body it could be more safely and properly lodged.

· I believe, on a serious consideration, it will be found that
it was necessary, for the reasons mentioned by the gentleman from Halifax, to vest the power in the Senate, or in
some other body representing equally the sovereignty of the
states, and that the power, as given in the Constitution, is
not likely to be attended with the evils which some gentlemen apprehend. The only real security of liberty, in any
country, is the jealousy and circumspection of the people
themselves. Let them be watchful over their rulers. Should
they find a combination against their liberties, and all other
methods appear insufficient to preserve them, they have,
thank God, an ultimate remedy. That power which created the government can destroy it. Should the government,
on trial, be found to want amendments, those amendments
can be made in a regular method, in a mode prescribed by
the Constitution itself. Massachusetts, South Carolina, New
Hampshire, and Virginia, have all proposed amendments;
but they all concurred in the necessity of an immediate
adoption. A constitutional mode of altering the Constitution itself is, perhaps, what has never been known among
mankind before. We have this security, in addition to the
natural watchfulness of the people, which I hope will never
be found wanting The objections I have answered deserved all possible attention; and for my part, I shall always

respect that jealousy which arises from the love of public liberty.

Mr. SPENCER. Mr. Chairman, I think that no argument can be used to show that this power is proper. If the whole legislative body — if the House of Representatives do not interfere in making treaties, I think they ought at least to have the sanction of the whole Senate. The worthy gentleman last up has mentioned two cases wherein he supposes that impeachments will be fairly tried by the senators. He supposes a case where the President had been guilty of corruption, and by that means had brought over and got the sanction of two thirds of the senators; and that, if it should be afterwards found that he brought them over by artifices, they would be a proper body to try him. As they will be ready to throw the odium off their own shoulders on him, they may pronounce sentence against him. He mentions another case, where, if a majority was obtained by bribing some of the senators, those who were innocent might try those who were guilty. I think that these cases will happen but rarely in comparison to other cases, where the senators may advise the President to deviate from his duty, and where a majority of them may be guilty. And should they be tried by their own body when thus guilty, does not every body see the impropriety of it? It is universally disgraceful, odious, and contemptible, to have a trial where the judges are accessory to the misdemeanor of the accused. Whether the accusation against him be true or not, if afraid for themselves, they will endeavor to throw the odium upon him. There is an extreme difference between the case of trying this officer and that of trying their own members. They are so different, that I consider they will always acquit their own members; and if they condemn the President, it will be to exonerate themselves. It appears to me that the powers are too extensive, and not sufficiently guarded. I do not wish that an aristocracy should be instituted. An aristocracy may arise out of this government, though the members be not hereditary. I would therefore wish that every guard should be placed, in order to prevent it. I wish gentlemen would reflect that the powers of the Senate are so great in their legislative and judicial capacities, that, when added to their executive powers, particularly their interference in the appointment of all officers in the continent, they will render their power so enormous as to enable them to destroy our rights and privileges. This, sir, ought to be strictly guarded against.

Mr. IREDELL. Mr. Chairman, the honorable gentleman must be mistaken. He suggests that an aristocracy will arise out of this government. Is there any thing like an aristocracy in this government? This insinuation is uncandidly calculated to alarm and catch prejudices. In this government there is not the least symptom of an aristocracy, which is, where the government is in a select body of men entirely independent of the people; as, for instance, an hereditary nobility, or a senate for life, filling up vacancies by their own authority. Will any member of this government hold his station by any such tenure? Will not all authority flow, in every instance, directly or indirectly from the people? It is contended, by that gentleman, that the addition of the power of making treaties to their other powers, will make the Senate dangerous; that they would be even dangerous to the representatives of the people. The gentleman has not proved this in theory. Whence will he adduce an example to prove it? What passes in England directly disproves his assertion. In that country, the representatives of the people are chosen under undue influence; frequently by direct bribery and corruption. They are elected for seven years, and many of the members hold offices under the crown — some during pleasure, others for life. They are also not a genuine representation of the people, but, from a change of circumstances, a mere shadow of it. Yet, under these disadvantages, they having the sole power of originating money bills, it has been found that the power of the king and lords is much less considerable than theirs. The high prerogatives of the king, and the great power and wealth of the lords, have been more than once mentioned in the course of the debates. If, under such circumstances, such representatives, — mere shadows of representatives, — by having the power of the purse, and the sacred name of the people, to rely upon, are an overmatch for the king and lords, who have such great hereditary qualifications, we may safely conclude that our own representatives, who will be a genuine representation of the people, and having equally the right of originating money bills, will, at least, be a match for the Senate, possessing qualifications so inferior to those of the House of Lords in England.

It seems to be forgotten that the Senate is placed there for a very valuable purpose — as a guard against any attempt of consolidation. The members of the Convention were as much averse to consolidation as any gentleman on this floor; but without this institution, (I mean the Senate, where the suffrages of the states are equal,) the danger would be greater. There ought to be some power given to the Senate to counteract the influence of the people by their biennial representation in the other house, in order to preserve completely the sovereignty of the states. If the people, through the medium of their representatives, possessed a share in making treaties and appointing officers, would there not be a greater balance of power in the House of Representatives than such a government ought to possess? It is true that it would be very improper if the Senate had authority to prevent the House of Representatives from protecting the people. It would be equally so if the House of Representatives were able to prevent the Senate from protecting the sovereignty of the states. It is probable that either house would have sufficient authority to prevent much mischief. As to the suggestion of a tendency to aristocracy, it is totally groundless. I disdain every principle of aristocracy. There is not a shadow of an aristocratical principle in this government. The President is only chosen for four years — liable to be impeached — and dependent on the people at large for his reëlection. Can this mode of appointment be said to have an aristocratical principle in it? The Senate is chosen by the legislatures. Let us consider the example of other states, with respect to the construction of their Senate. In this point, most of them differ; though they almost all concur in this, that the term of election for senators is longer than that for representatives. The reason of this is, to introduce stability into the laws, and to prevent that mutability which would result from annual elections of both branches. In New York, they are chosen for three years; in Virginia, they are chosen for four years; and in Maryland, they are chosen for five years. In this Constitution, although they are chosen for six years, one third go out every second year, (a method pursued in some of the state constitutions,) which at the same time secures stability to the laws, and a due dependence on the state legislatures. Will any man say that there are any aristocratical principles in a body who

12

have no power independent of the people, and whereof one third of the members are chosen, every second year, by a wise and select body of electors? I hope, therefore, that it will not be considered that there are any aristocratical principles in this government, and that it will be given up as a point not to be contended for. The gentleman contends that a council ought to be instituted in this case. One objection ought to be compared with another. It has been objected against the Constitution that it will be productive of great expense. Had there been a council, it would have been objected that it was calculated for creating new offices, and increasing the means of undue influence. Though he approves of a council, others would not. As to offices, the Senate has no other influence but a restraint on improper appointments. The President proposes such a man for such an office. The Senate has to consider upon it. If they think him improper, the President must nominate another, whose appointment ultimately again depends upon the Senate. Suppose a man nominated by the President; with what face would any senator object to him without a good reason? There must be some decorum in every public body. He would not say, "I do not choose this man, because a friend of mine wants the office." Were he to object to the nomination of the President, without assigning any reason, his conduct would be reprobated, and still might not answer his purpose. Were an office to be vacant, for which a hundred men on the continent were equally well qualified, there would be a hundred chances to one whether his friend would be nominated to it. This, in effect, is but a restriction on the President. The power of the Senate would be more likely to be abused were it vested in a council of thirteen, of which there would be one from each state. One man could be more easily influenced than two. We have therefore a double security. I am firmly of opinion that, if you take all the powers of the President and Senate together, the vast influence of the representatives of the people will preponderate against them in every case where the public good is really concerned.

Mr. BLOODWORTH. Mr. Chairman, I confess I am sorry to take up any time. I beg leave to make a few observations; for it would be an Herculean task, and disagreeable to this committee, to mention every thing. It has indeed been objected, and urged, that the responsibility of the Senate was not sufficient to secure the states. When we consider the length of the term for which they are elected, and the extent of their powers, we must be persuaded that there is no real security. A gentleman has said that the Assembly of North Carolina are rogues. It is, then, probable that they may be corrupted. In this case, we have not a sufficient check on those gentlemen who are gone six years. A parallel is drawn between them and the members of our Assembly ; but if you reflect a moment, you will find that the comparison is not good. There is a responsibility in the members of the Assembly: at the end of a year they are liable to be turned out. This is not the case with the senators. I beg gentlemen to consider the extreme difference between the two cases. Much is said about treaties. I do not dread this so much as what will arise from the jarring interests of the Eastern, Southern, and the Middle States. They are different in soil, climate, customs, produce, and every thing. Regulations will be made evidently to the disadvantage of some part of the community, and most probably to ours. I will not take up more of the time of the committee.

3d clause of the 2d section of the 2d article read.

Mr. MACLAINE. It has been objected to this part, that the power of appointing officers was something like a monarchical power. Congress are not to be sitting at all times ; they will only sit from time to time, as the public business may render it necessary. Therefore the executive ought to make temporary appointments, as well as receive ambassadors and other public ministers. This power can be vested nowhere but in the executive, because he is perpetually acting for the public ; for, though the Senate is to advise him in the appointment of officers, &c., yet, during the recess, the President must do this business, or else it will be neglected ; and such neglect may occasion public inconveniences. But there is an objection made to another part, that has not yet been read. His power of adjourning both houses, when they disagree, has been by some people construed to extend to any length of time. If gentlemen look at another part of the Constitution, they will find that there is a positive injunction, that the Congress must meet at *least once* in every year ; so that he cannot, were he so inclined, prevent their meeting within a year. One of the best provisions contained in it is, that he shall commission all officers of the United States, and shall take care that the laws be faithfully executed. If he takes care to see the laws faithfully executed, it will be more than is done in any government on the continent ; for I will venture to say that our government, and those of the other states, are, with respect to the execution of the laws, in many respects mere ciphers.

Rest of the article read without any observations.

Article 3d, 1st and 2d sections, read.

Mr. SPENCER. Mr. Chairman, I have objections to this article. I object to the exclusive jurisdiction of the federal court in all cases of law and equity arising under the Constitution and the laws of the United States, and to the appellate jurisdiction of controversies between the citizens of different states, and a few other instances. To these I object, because I believe they will be oppressive in their operation. I would wish that the federal court should not interfere, or have any thing to do with controversies to the decision of which the state judiciaries might be fully competent, nor with such controversies as must carry the people a great way from home. With respect to the jurisdiction of cases arising under the Constitution, when we reflect on the very extensive objects of the plan of government, the manner in which they may arise, and the multiplicity of laws that may be made with respect to them, the objection against it will appear to be well founded. If we consider nothing but the articles of taxation, duties, and excises, and the laws that might be made with respect to these, the cases will be almost infinite. If we consider that it is in contemplation that a stamp duty shall take place throughout the continent ; that all contracts shall be on stamp paper ; that no contracts shall be of validity but what would be thus stamped, — these cases will be so many that the consequences would be dreadful. It would be necessary to appoint judges to the federal Supreme Court, and other inferior departments, and such a number of inferior courts in every district and county, with a correspondent number of officers, that it would cost an immense expense without any apparent necessity, which must operate to the distress of the inhabitants. There will be, without any manner of doubt, clashings and animosities between the jurisdiction of the federal courts and of the state courts, so that they will keep the country in hot water. It has been said that the impropriety of this was mentioned by some in the Convention. I cannot see the reasons of giving the federal courts jurisdiction in these cases; but I am sure it will occasion great expense unnecessarily. The state judiciaries will have very little to do. It will be almost useless to keep them up. As all officers are to take an oath to support the general government, it will carry every thing before it. This will produce that consolidation through the United States which is apprehended. I am sure that I do not see that it is possible to avoid it. I can see no power that can keep up the little remains of the power of the states. Our rights are not guarded. There is no declaration of rights, to secure to every member of the society those unalienable rights which ought not to be given up to any government. Such a bill of rights would be a check upon men in power. Instead of such a bill of rights, this Constitution has a clause which may warrant encroachments on the power of the respective state legislatures. I know it is said that what is not given up to the United States will be retained by the individual states. I know it ought to be so, and should be so understood; but, sir, it is not *declared* to be so. In the Confederation it is expressly declared that all rights and powers, of any kind whatever, of the several states, which are not given up to the United States, are expressly and absolutely retained, to be enjoyed by the states. There ought to be a bill of rights, in order that those in power may not step over the boundary between the powers of government and the rights of the people, which they may do when there is nothing to prevent them. They may do so without a bill of rights; notice will not be readily taken of the encroachments of rulers, and they may go a great length before the people are alarmed. Oppression may therefore take place by degrees; but if there were express terms and bounds laid down, when these were passed by, the people would take notice of them, and oppressions would not be carried on to such a length. I look upon it, therefore, that there ought to be something to confine the power of this government within its proper boundaries. I know that several writers have said that a bill of rights is not necessary in this country; that some states had them

not, and that others had.   To these I answer, that those
states that have them not as bills of rights, strictly so called,
have them in the frame of their constitution, which is nearly
the same.

There has been a comparison made of our situation with
Great Britain.   We have no crown, or prerogative of a king,
like the British constitution.   I take it, that the subject has
been misunderstood.   In Great Britain, when the king attempts to usurp the rights of the people, the declaration and
bill of rights are a guard against him.   A bill of rights
would be necessary here to guard against our rulers.   I wish
to have a bill of rights, to secure those unalienable rights,
which are called by some respectable writers the *residuum*
of human rights, which are never to be given up.   At the
same time that it would give security to individuals, it would
add to the general strength.   It might not be so necessary
to have a bill of rights in the government of the United
States, if such means had not been made use of as endanger a consolidation of all the states ; but at any event, it
would be proper to have one, because, though it might not
be of any other service, it would at least satisfy the minds
of the people.   It would keep the states from being swallowed up by a consolidated government.   For the reasons I
before gave, I think that the jurisdiction of the federal court,
with respect to all cases in law and equity, and the laws of
Congress, and the appeals in all cases between citizens
of different states, &c., is inadmissible.   I do not see the
necessity that it should be vested with the cognizance of all
these matters.   I am desirous, and have no objection to
their having one Supreme Federal Court for general matters ;
but if the federal courts have cognizance of those subjects
which I mentioned, very great oppressions may arise.   Nothing can be more oppressive than the cognizance with respect
to controversies between citizens of different states.   In all
cases of appeal, those persons who are able to pay had better pay down in the first instance, though it be unjust, than
be at such a dreadful expense by going such a distance to
the Supreme Federal Court.   Some of the most respectable
states have proposed, by way of amendments, to strike out
a great part of these two clauses.   If they be admitted as
they are, it will render the country entirely unhappy.   On
the contrary, I see no inconvenience from reducing the

power as has been proposed. I am of opinion that it is inconsistent with the happiness of the people to admit these two clauses. The state courts are sufficient to decide the common controversies of the people, without distressing them by carrying them to such far-distant tribunals. If I did not consider these two clauses to be dangerous, I should not object to them. I mean not to object to any thing that is not absolutely necessary. I wish to be candid, and not be prejudiced or warped.

Mr. SPAIGHT. Mr. Chairman, the gentleman insinuates that differences existed in the Federal Convention respecting the clauses which he objects to. Whoever told him so was wrong; for I declare that, in that Convention, the unanimous desire of all was to keep separate and distinct the objects of the jurisdiction of the federal from that of the state judiciary. They wished to separate them as judiciously as possible, and to consult the ease and convenience of the people. The gentleman objects to the cognizance of all cases in law and equity arising under the Constitution and the laws of the United States. This objection is very astonishing. When any government is established, it ought to have power to enforce its laws, or else it might as well have no power. What but that is the use of a judiciary? The gentleman, from his profession, must know that no government can exist without a judiciary to enforce its laws, by distinguishing the disobedient from the rest of the people, and imposing sanctions for securing the execution of the laws. As to the inconvenience of distant attendance, Congress has power of establishing inferior tribunals in each state, so as to accommodate every citizen. As Congress have it in their power, will they not do it? Are we to elect men who will wantonly and unnecessarily betray us?

Mr. MACLAINE. Mr. Chairman, I hoped that some gentleman more capable than myself would have obviated the objections to this part. The objections offered by the gentleman appear to me totally without foundation. He told us that these clauses tended to a consolidation of the states. I cannot see how the states are to be consolidated by establishing these two clauses. He enumerated a number of cases which would be involved within the cognizance of the federal courts; customs, excises, duties, stamp duties — a stamp on every article, on every contract — in order to bring all persons into the federal court; and said that there would be necessarily courts in every district and county, which would be attended with enormous and needless expense, for that the state courts could do every thing. He went on further, and said that there would be a necessity of having sheriffs and other officers in these inferior departments. A wonderful picture indeed, drawn up in a wonderful manner! I will venture to say that the gentleman's suggestions are not warranted by any reasonable construction of the Constitution. The laws can, in general, be executed by the officers of the states. State courts and state officers will, for the most part, probably answer the purpose of Congress as well as any other. But the gentleman says that the state courts will be swallowed up by the federal courts. This is only a general assertion, unsupported by any probable reasons or arguments. The objects of each are separate and distinct. I suppose that whatever courts there may be, they will be established according to the convenience of the people. This we must suppose from the mode of electing and appointing the members of the government. State officers will as much as possible be employed, for one very considerable reason — I mean, to lessen the expense. But he imagines that the oath to be taken by officers will tend to the subversion of our state governments and of our liberty. Can any government exist without fidelity in its officers? Ought not the officers of every government to give some security for the faithful discharge of their trust? The officers are only to be sworn to support the Constitution, and therefore will only be bound by their oath so far as it shall be strictly pursued. No officer will be bound by his oath to support any act that would violate the principles of the Constitution.

The gentleman has wandered out of his way to tell us — what has so often been said out of doors — that there is no declaration of rights; that consequently all our rights are taken away. It would be very extraordinary to have a bill of rights, because the powers of Congress are expressly defined; and the very definition of them is as valid and efficacious a check as a bill of rights could be, without the dangerous implication of a bill of rights. The powers of Congress are limited and enumerated. We say we have given them those powers, but we do not say we have given them more

We retain all those rights which we have not given away to the general government. The gentleman is a professional man. If a gentleman had made his last will and testament, and devised or bequeathed to a particular person the sixth part of his property, or any particular specific legacy, could it be said that that person should have the whole estate? If they can assume powers not enumerated, there was no occasion for enumerating any powers. The gentleman is learned. Without recurring to his learning, he may only appeal to his common sense; it will inform him that, if we had all power before, and give away but a part, we still retain the rest. It is as plain a thing as possibly can be, that Congress can have no power but what we expressly give them. There is an express clause which, however disingenuously it has been perverted from its true meaning, clearly demonstrates that they are confined to those powers which are given them. This clause enables them to " make all laws which shall be necessary and proper for carrying into execution the foregoing powers, and all other powers vested by this Constitution in the government of the United States, or any department or officers thereof." This clause specifies that they shall make laws to carry into execution *all the powers vested* by this Constitution; consequently, they can make no laws to execute any other power. This clause gives no new power, but declares that those already given are to be executed by proper laws. I hope this will satisfy gentlemen.

Gov. JOHNSTON. Mr. Chairman, the learned member from Anson says that the federal courts have exclusive jurisdiction of all cases in law and equity arising under the Constitution and laws of the United States. The opinion which I have always entertained is, that they will, in these cases, as well as in several others, have concurrent jurisdiction with the state courts, and not exclusive jurisdiction. I see nothing in this Constitution which hinders a man from bringing suit wherever he thinks he can have justice done him. The jurisdiction of these courts is established for some purposes with which the state courts have nothing to do, and the Constitution takes no power from the state courts which they now have. They will have the same business which they have now, and if so, they will have enough to employ their time. We know that the gentlemen who preside in our superior courts have more business than they can determine. Their complicated jurisdiction, and the great extent of country, occasions them a vast deal of business. The addition of the business of the United States would be no manner of advantage to them. It is obvious to every one that there ought to be one Supreme Court for national purposes. But the gentleman says that a bill of rights was necessary. It appears to me, sir, that it would have been the highest absurdity to undertake to define what rights the people of the United States were entitled to; for that would be as much as to say they were entitled to nothing else. A bill of rights may be necessary in a monarchical government, whose powers are undefined. Were we in the situation of a monarchical country? No, sir. Every right could not be enumerated, and the omitted rights would be sacrificed, if security arose from an enumeration. The Congress cannot assume any other powers than those expressly given them, without a palpable violation of the Constitution. Such objections as this, I hope, will have no effect on the minds of any members in this house. When gentlemen object, generally, that it tends to consolidate the states and destroy their state judiciaries, they ought to be explicit, and explain their meaning. They make use of contradictory arguments. The Senate represents the states, and can alone prevent this dreaded consolidation; yet the powers of the Senate are objected to. The rights of the people, in my opinion, cannot be affected by the federal courts. I do not know how inferior courts will be regulated. Some suppose the state courts will have this business. Others have imagined that the continent would be divided into a number of districts, where courts would be held so as to suit the convenience of the people. Whether this or some other mode will be appointed by Congress, I know not; but this I am sure of, that the state judiciaries are not divested of their present judicial cognizance, and that we have every security that our ease and convenience will be consulted. Unless Congress had this power, their laws could not be carried into execution.

Mr. BLOODWORTH. Mr. Chairman, the worthy gentleman up last has given me information on the subject which I had never heard before. Hearing so many opinions, I did not know which was right. The honorable gentleman has said that the state courts and the courts of the United States would have concurrent jurisdiction. I beg the committee to reflect what would be the consequence of such measures. It has ever been considered that the trial by jury was one of the greatest rights of the people. I ask whether, if such causes go into the federal court, the trial by jury is not cut off, and whether there is any security that we shall have justice done us. I ask if there be any security that we shall have juries in civil causes. In criminal cases there are to be juries, but there is no provision made for having civil causes tried by jury. This concurrent jurisdiction is inconsistent with the security of that great right. If it be not, I would wish to hear how it is secured. I have listened with attention to what the learned gentlemen have said, and have endeavored to see whether their arguments had any weight; but I found none in them. Many words have been spoken, and long time taken up; but with me they have gone in at one ear, and out at the other. It would give me much pleasure to hear that the trial by jury was secured.

Mr. J. M'DOWALL. Mr. Chairman, the objections to this part of the Constitution have not been answered to my satisfaction yet. We know that the trial by a jury of the vicinage is one of the greatest securities for property. If causes are to be decided at such a great distance, the poor will be oppressed; in land affairs, particularly, the wealthy suitor will prevail. A poor man, who has a just claim on a piece of land, has not substance to stand it. Can it be supposed that any man, of common circumstances, can stand the expense and trouble of going from Georgia to Philadelphia, there to have a suit tried? And can it be justly determined without the benefit of a trial by jury? These are things which have justly alarmed the people. What made the people revolt from Great Britain? The trial by jury, that great safeguard of liberty, was taken away, and a stamp duty was laid upon them. This alarmed them, and led them to fear that greater oppressions would take place. We then resisted. It involved us in a war, and caused us to relinquish a government which made us happy in every thing else. The war was very bloody, but we got our independence. We are now giving away our dear-bought rights. We ought to consider what we are about to do before we determine.

Mr. SPAIGHT. Mr. Chairman, the trial by jury was not forgotten in the Convention ; the subject took up a considerable time to investigate it. It was impossible to make any one uniform regulation for all the states, or that would include all cases where it would be necessary. It was impossible, by one expression, to embrace the whole. There are a number of equity and maritime cases, in some of the states, in which jury trials are not used. Had the Convention said that all causes should be tried by a jury, equity and maritime cases would have been included. It was therefore left to the legislature to say in what cases it should be used ; and as the trial by jury is in full force in the state courts, we have the fullest security.

Mr. IREDELL. Mr. Chairman, I have waited a considerable time, in hopes that some other gentleman would fully discuss this point. I conceive it to be my duty to speak on every subject whereon I think I can throw any light ; and it appears to me that some things ought to be said which no gentleman has yet mentioned. The gentleman from New Hanover said that our arguments went in at one ear, and out at the other. This sort of language, on so solemn and important an occasion, gives me pain. [Mr. Bloodworth here declared that he did not mean to convey any disrespectful idea by such an expression ; that he did not mean an absolute neglect of their arguments, but that they were not sufficient to convince him ; that he should be sorry to give pain to any gentleman ; that he had listened, and still would listen, with attention, to what would be said. Mr. Iredell then continued.] I am by no means surprised at the anxiety which is expressed by gentlemen on this subject. Of all the trials that ever were instituted in the world, this, in my opinion, is the best, and that which I hope will continue the longest. If the gentlemen who composed the Convention had designedly omitted it, no man would be more ready to condemn their conduct than myself. But I have been told that the omission of it arose from the difficulty of establishing one uniform, unexceptionable mode ; this mode of trial being different, in many particulars, in the several states. Gentlemen will be pleased to consider that there is a material difference between an article fixed in the Constitution, and a regulation by law. An article in the Constitution, however inconvenient it may prove by experience, can only be altered by altering the Constitution itself, which manifestly is a thing that ought not to be done often. When regulated by law, it can easily be occasionally altered so as best to suit the conveniences of the people. Had there been an article in the Constitution taking away that trial, it would justly have excited the public indignation. It is not taken away by the Constitution. Though that does not provide expressly for a trial by jury in civil cases, it does not say that there shall not be such a trial. The reasons of the omission have been mentioned by a member of the late General Convention, (Mr. Spaight.) There are different practices in regard to this trial in different states. In some cases, they have no juries in admiralty and equity cases; in others, they have juries in these cases, as well as in suits at common law. I beg leave to say that, if any gentleman of ability and knowledge of the subject will only endeavor to fix upon any one rule that would be pleasing to all the states under the impression of their present different habits, he will be convinced that it is impracticable. If the practice of any particular state had been adopted, others, probably, whose practice had been different, would have been discontented. This is a consequence that naturally would have ensued, had the provision been made in the Constitution itself. But when the regulation is to be by law, — as that law, when found injudicious, can be easily repealed, a majority may be expected to agree upon some method, since some method or other must be first tried, and there is a greater chance of the favorite method of one state being in time preferred. It is not to be presumed that the Congress would dare to deprive the people of this valuable privilege. Their own interest will operate as an additional guard, as none of them could tell how soon they might have occasion for such a trial themselves. The greatest danger from ambition is in criminal cases. But here they have no option. The trial must be by jury, in the state wherein the offence is committed; and the writ of *habeas corpus* will in the mean time secure the citizen against arbitrary imprisonment, which has been the principal source of tyranny in all ages.

As to the clause respecting cases arising under the Constitution and the laws of the Union, which the honorable member objected to, it must be observed, that laws are useless unless they are executed. At present, Congress have powers which they cannot execute. After making laws which affect the dearest interest of the people, in the constitutional mode, they have no way of enforcing them. The situation of those gentlemen who have lately served in Congress must have been very disagreeable. Congress have power to enter into negotiations with foreign nations, but cannot compel the observance of treaties that they make. They have been much distressed by their inability to pay the pressing demands of the public creditors. They have been reduced so low as to borrow principal to pay interest. Such are the unfortunate consequences of this unhappy situation! These are the effects of the pernicious mode of requisitions! Has any state fully paid its quota? I believe not, sir. Yet I am far from thinking that this has been owing altogether to an unwillingness to pay the debts. It may have been in some instances the case, but I believe not in all. Our state legislature has no way of raising any considerable sums but by laying direct taxes. Other states have imports of consequence. These may afford them a considerable relief; but our state, perhaps, could not have raised its full quota by direct taxes, without imposing burdens too heavy for the people to bear. Suppose, in this situation, Congress had proceeded to enforce their requisitions, by sending an army to collect them; what would have been the consequence? *Civil war*, in which the innocent must have suffered with the guilty. Those who were willing to pay would have been equally distressed with those who were unwilling. Requisitions thus having failed of their purpose, it is proposed, by this Constitution, that, instead of collecting taxes by the sword, application shall be made by the government to the individual citizens. If any individual disobeys, the courts of justice can give immediate relief. This is the only natural and effectual method of enforcing laws. As to the danger of concurrent jurisdictions, has any inconvenience resulted from the concurrent jurisdictions, in sundry cases, of the superior and county courts of this state? The inconvenience of attending at a great distance, which has been so much objected to, is one which would be so general, that there is no doubt but that a majority would always feel themselves and their constituents personally interested in preventing it. I have no doubt, therefore, that proper care will be taken to lessen this evil as much as possible; and, in particular, that an appeal to the Supreme Court will not be allowed but in cases of great importance, where the object may be adequate to the expense. The Supreme Court may possibly be directed to sit alternately in different parts of the Union.

The propriety of having a Supreme Court in every government must be obvious to every man of reflection. There can be no other way of securing the administration of justice uniformly in the several states. There might be, otherwise, as many different adjudications on the same subject as there are states. It is to be hoped that, if this government be established, connections still more intimate than the present will subsist between the different states. The same measure of justice, therefore, as to the objects of their common concern, ought to prevail in all. A man in North Carolina, for instance, if he owed £100 here, and was compellable to pay it in good money, ought to have the means of recovering the same sum, if due to him in Rhode Island, and not merely the nominal sum, at about an eighth or tenth part of its intrinsic value. To obviate such a grievance as this, the Constitution has provided a tribunal to administer equal justice to all.

A gentleman has said that the stamp act, and the taking away of the trial by jury, were the principal causes of resistance to Great Britain, and seemed to infer that opposition would therefore be justified on this part of the system. The stamp act was much earlier than the immediate cause of our independence. But what was the great ground of opposition to the stamp act? Surely it was because the act was not passed by our own representatives, but by those of Great Britain. Under this Constitution, taxes are to be imposed by our own representatives in the General Congress. The fewness of their numbers will be compensated by the weight and importance of their characters. Our representatives will be in proportion to those of the other states. This case is certainly not like that of taxation by a foreign legislature. In respect to the trial by jury, its being taken away, in certain cases, was, to be sure, one of the causes assigned in the Declaration of Independence. But that was done by a foreign legislature, which might continue it so forever; and therefore jealousy was justly excited. But this Constitution has not taken it away, and it is left to the discretion of our own legislature to act, in this respect, as their wisdom shall direct. In Great Britain, the people speak of the trial by jury with admiration. No monarch, or minister, however arbitrary in his principles, would dare to attack that noble palladium of liberty. The enthusiasm of the people in its favor would, in such a case, produce general resistance. That trial remains unimpaired there, although they have a considerable standing army, and their Parliament has authority to abolish it, if they please. But wo to those who should attempt it! If it be secure in that country, under these circumstances, can we believe that Congress either would or could take it away in this? Were they to attempt it, their authority would be instantly resisted. They would draw down on themselves the resentment and detestation of the people. They and their families, so long as any remained in being, would be held in eternal infamy, and the attempt prove as unsuccessful as it was wicked.

With regard to a bill of rights, this is a notion originating in England, where no written constitution is to be found, and the authority of their government is derived from the most remote antiquity. Magna Charta itself is no constitution, but a solemn instrument ascertaining certain rights of individuals, by the legislature for the time being; and every article of which the legislature may at any time alter. This, and a bill of rights also, the invention of later times, were occasioned by great usurpations of the crown, contrary, as was conceived, to the principles of their government, about which there was a variety of opinions. But neither that instrument, nor any other instrument, ever attempted to abridge the authority of Parliament, which is supposed to be without any limitation whatever. Had their constitution been fixed and certain, a bill of rights would have been useless, for the constitution would have shown plainly the extent of that authority which they were disputing about. Of what use, therefore, can a bill of rights be in this Constitution, where the people expressly declare how much power they do give, and consequently retain all they do not? It is a declaration of particular powers by the people to their representatives, for particular purposes. It may be considered as a great power of attorney, under which no power can be exercised but what is expressly given. Did any man ever hear, before, that at the end of a power of attorney it was said that the attorney should not exercise more power than was the.e given him?   Suppose, for instance, a man had lands in the counties of Anson and Caswell, and he should give another a power of attorney to sell his lands in Anson, would the other have any authority to sell the lands in Caswell?—or could he, without absurdity, say, "'Tis true you have not expressly authorized me to sell the lands in Caswell; but as you had lands there, and did not say I should not, I thought I might as well sell those lands as the other."   A bill of rights, as I conceive, would not only be incongruous, but dangerous. No man, let his ingenuity be what it will, could enumerate all the individual rights not relinquished by this Constitution. Suppose, therefore, an enumeration of a great many, but an omission of some, and that, long after all traces of our present disputes were at an end, any of the omitted rights should be invaded, and the invasion be complained of; what would be the plausible answer of the government to such a complaint?   Would they not naturally say, "We live at a great distance from the time when this Constitution was established.   We can judge of it much better by the ideas of it entertained at the time, than by any ideas of our own.   The bill of rights, passed at that time, showed that the people did not think every power retained which was not given, else this bill of rights was not only useless, but absurd.   But we are not at liberty to charge an absurdity upon our ancestors, who have given such strong proofs of their good sense, as well as their attachment to liberty.   So long as the rights enumerated in the bill of rights remain unviolated, you have no reason to complain.   This is not one of them."   Thus a bill of rights might operate as a snare rather than a protection.   If we had formed a general legislature, with undefined powers, a bill of rights would not only have been proper, but necessary; and it would have then operated as an exception to the legislative authority in such particulars. It has this effect in respect to some of the American constitutions, where the powers of legislation are general.   But where they are powers of a particular nature, and expressly defined, as in the case of the Constitution before us, I think, for the reasons I have given, a bill of rights is not only unnecessary, but would be absurd and dangerous.

Mr. J. M'DOWALL.   Mr. Chairman, the learned gentleman made use of several arguments to induce us to believe that the trial by jury, in civil cases, was not in danger, and observed that, in criminal cases, it is provided that the trial is to be in the state where the crime was committed. Suppose a crime is committed at the Mississippi; the man may be tried at Edenton. They ought to be tried by the people of the vicinage; for when the trial is at such an immense distance, the principal privilege attending the trial by jury is taken away; therefore the trial ought to be limited to a district or certain part of the state. It has been said, by the gentleman from Edenton, that our representatives will have virtue and wisdom to regulate all these things. But it would give me much satisfaction, in a matter of this importance, to see it absolutely secured. The depravity of mankind militates against such a degree of confidence. I wish to see every thing fixed.

Gov. JOHNSTON. Mr. Chairman, the observations of the gentleman last up confirm what the other gentleman said. I mean that, as there are dissimilar modes with respect to the trial by jury in different states, there could be no general rule fixed to accommodate all. He says that this clause is defective, because the trial is not to be by a jury of the vicinage. Let us look at the state of Virginia, where, as long as I have known it, the laws have been executed so as to satisfy the inhabitants, and, I believe, as well as in any part of the Union. In that country, juries are summoned every day from the by-standers. We may expect less partiality when the trial is by strangers; and were I to be tried for my property or life, I would rather be tried by disinterested men, who were not biased, than by men who were perhaps intimate friends of my opponent. Our mode is different from theirs; but whether theirs be better than ours or not, is not the question. It would be improper for our delegates to impose our mode upon them, or for theirs to impose their mode upon us. The trial will probably be, in each state, as it has been hitherto used in such state, or otherwise regulated as conveniently as possible for the people. The delegates who are to meet in Congress will, I hope, be men of virtue and wisdom. If not, it will be our own fault. They will have it in their power to make necessary regulations to accommodate the inhabitants of each state. In the Constitution, the general principles only are laid down. It will be the object of the future legislation to Congress to

make such laws as will be most convenient for the people.
With regard to a bill of rights, so much spoken of, what the
gentleman from Edenton has said, I hope, will obviate the
objections against the want of it.   In a monarchy, all power
may be supposed to be vested in the monarch, except what
may be reserved by a bill of rights.   In England, in every
instance where the rights of the people are not declared,
the prerogative of the king is supposed to extend.   But in
this country, we say that what rights we do not give away
remain with us.

Mr. BLOODWORTH.   Mr. Chairman, the footing on
which the trial by jury is, in the Constitution, does not satisfy me.   Perhaps I am mistaken ; but if I understand the
thing right, the trial by jury is taken away.   If the Supreme
Federal Court has jurisdiction both as to law and fact, it appears to me to be taken away.   The honorable gentleman
who was in the Convention told us that the clause, as it now
stands, resulted from the difficulty of fixing the mode of trial.
I think it was easy to have put it on a secure footing.   But,
if the genius of the people of the United States is so dissimilar that our liberties cannot be secured, we can never
hang long together.   Interest is the band of social union ;
and when this is taken away, the Union itself must dissolve.

Mr. MACLAINE.   Mr. Chairman, I do not take the interest of the states to be so dissimilar ; I take them to be
all nearly alike, and inseparably connected.   It is impossible
to lay down any constitutional rule for the government of all
the different states in each particular.   But it will be easy
for the legislature to make laws to accommodate the people
in every part of the Union, as circumstances may arise.
Jury trial is not taken away in such cases where it may be
found necessary.   Although the Supreme Court has cognizance of the appeal, it does not follow but that the trial by
jury may be had in the court below, and the testimony transmitted to the Supreme Court, who will then finally determine,
on a review of all the circumstances.   This is well known
to be the practice in some of the states.   In our own state,
indeed, when a cause is instituted in the county court, and
afterwards there is an appeal upon it, a new trial is had in
the superior court, as if no trial had been had before.   In
other countries, however, when a trial is had in an inferior
court, and an appeal is taken, no testimony can be given in

the court above, but the court determines upon the circumstances appearing upon the record. If I am right, the plain inference is, that there may be a trial in the inferior courts, and that the record, including the testimony, may be sent to the Supreme Court. But if there is a necessity for a jury in the Supreme Court, it will be a very easy matter to empanel a jury at the bar of the Supreme Court, which may save great expense, and be very convenient to the people. It is impossible to make every regulation at once. Congress, who are our own representatives, will undoubtedly make such regulations as will suit the convenience and secure the liberty of the people.

Mr. IREDELL declared it as his opinion that there might be juries in the Superior Court as well as in the inferior courts, and that it was in the power of Congress to regulate it so.

TUESDAY, *July* 29, 1788.

Mr. KENNION in the chair.

Mr. SPENCER. Mr. Chairman, I hope to be excused for making some observations on what was said yesterday, by gentlemen, in favor of these two clauses. The motion which was made that the committee should rise, precluded me from speaking then. The gentlemen have showed much moderation and candor in conducting this business; but I still think that my observations are well founded, and that some amendments are necessary. The gentleman said, all matters not given up by this form of government were retained by the respective states. I know that it ought to be so; it is the general doctrine, but it is necessary that it should be expressly declared in the Constitution, and not left to mere construction and opinion. I am authorized to say it was heretofore thought necessary. The Confederation says, expressly, that all that was not given up by the United States was retained by the respective states. If such a clause had been inserted in this Constitution, it would have superseded the necessity of a bill of rights. But that not being the case, it was necessary that a bill of rights, or something of that kind, should be a part of the Constitution. It was observed that, as the Constitution is to be a delegation of power from the several states to the United States, a bill of rights was unnecessary. But it will be noticed that this is a different case.

The states do not act in their political capacities, but the government is proposed for individuals. The very caption of the Constitution shows that this is the case. The expression, " We, the people of the United States," shows that this government is intended for individuals ; there ought, therefore, to be a bill of rights. I am ready to acknowledge that the Congress ought to have the power of executing its laws. Heretofore, because all the laws of the Confederation were binding on the states in their political capacities, courts had nothing to do with them ; but now the thing is entirely different. The laws of Congress will be binding on individuals, and those things which concern individuals will be brought properly before the courts. In the next place, all the officers are to take an oath to carry into execution this general government, and are bound to support every act of the government, of whatever nature it may be. This is a fourth reason for securing the rights of individuals. It was also observed that the federal judiciary and the courts of the states, under the federal authority, would have concurrent jurisdiction with respect to any subject that might arise under the Constitution. I am ready to say that I most heartily wish that, whenever this government takes place, the two jurisdictions and the two governments — that is, the general and the several state governments — may go hand in hand, and that there may be no interference, but that every thing may be rightly conducted. But I will never concede that it is proper to divide the business between the two different courts. I have no doubt that there is wisdom enough in this state to decide the business, without the necessity of federal assistance to do our business. The worthy gentleman from Edenton dwelt a considerable time on the observations on a bill of rights, contending that they were proper only in monarchies, which were founded on different principles from those of our government ; and, therefore, though they might be necessary for others, yet they were not necessary for us. I still think that a bill of rights is necessary. This necessity arises from the nature of human societies. When individuals enter into society, they give up some rights to secure the rest. There are certain human rights that ought not to be given up, and which ought in some manner to be secured. With respect to these great essential rights, no latitude ought to be left. They are the most inestimable gifts of the great Creator, and therefore ought not to be destroyed, but ought to be secured. They ought to be secured to individuals in consideration of the other rights which they give up to support society.

The trial by jury has been also spoken of. Every person who is acquainted with the nature of liberty need not be informed of the importance of this trial. Juries are called the bulwarks of our rights and liberty; and no country can ever be enslaved as long as those cases which affect their lives and property are to be decided, in a great measure, by the consent of twelve honest, disinterested men, taken from the respectable body of yeomanry. It is highly improper that any clause which regards the security of the trial by jury should be any way doubtful. In the clause that has been read, it is ascertained that criminal cases are to be tried by jury in the states where they are committed. It has been objected to that clause, that it is not sufficiently explicit. I think that it is not. It was observed that one may be taken to a great distance. One reason of the resistance to the British government was, because they required that we should be carried to the country of Great Britain, to be tried by juries of that country. But we insisted on being tried by juries of the vicinage, in our own country. I think it therefore proper that something explicit should be said with respect to the vicinage.

With regard to that part, that the Supreme Court shall have appellate jurisdiction both as to law and fact, it has been observed that, though the federal court might decide without a jury, yet the court below, which tried it, might have a jury. I ask the gentleman what benefit would be received in the suit by having a jury trial in the court below, when the verdict is set aside in the Supreme Court. It was intended by this clause that the trial by jury should be suppressed in the superior and inferior courts. It has been said, in defence of the omission concerning the trial by jury in civil cases, that one general regulation could not be made; that in several cases the constitution of several states did not require a trial by jury, — for instance, in cases of equity and admiralty, — whereas in others it did, and that, therefore, it was proper to leave this subject at large. I am sure that, for the security of liberty, they ought to have been at the pains of drawing some line. I think that the respectable

body who formed the Constitution should have gone so far
as to put matters on such a footing as that there should be
no danger.   They might have provided that all those cases
which are now triable by a jury should be tried in each state
by a jury, according to the mode usually practised in such
state.   This would have been easily done, if they had been
at the trouble of writing five or six lines.   Had it been done,
we should have been entitled to say that our rights and liberties were not endangered.   If we adopt this clause as it is, I
think, notwithstanding what gentlemen have said, that there
will be danger.   There ought to be some amendments to it,
to put this matter on a sure footing.   There does not appear
to me to be any kind of necessity that the federal court
should have jurisdiction in the body of the country.   I am
ready to give up that, in the cases expressly enumerated, an
appellate jurisdiction (except in one or two instances) might
be given.   I wish them also to have jurisdiction in maritime
affairs, and to try offences committed on the high seas.   But
in the body of a state, the jurisdiction of the courts in that
state might extend to carrying into execution the laws of
Congress.   It must be unnecessary for the federal courts to
do it, and would create trouble and expense which might be
avoided.   In all cases where appeals are proper, I will agree
that it is necessary there should be one Supreme Court.
Were those things properly regulated, so that the Supreme
Court might not be oppressive, I should have no objection
to it.

Mr. DAVIE.   Mr. Chairman, yesterday and to-day I
have given particular attention to the observations of the gentleman last up.   I believe, however, that, before we take
into consideration these important clauses, it will be necessary to consider in what manner laws can be executed.   For
my own part, I know but two ways in which the laws can
be executed by any government.   If there be any other, it
is unknown to me.   The first mode is coercion by military
force, and the second is coercion through the judiciary.
With respect to coercion by force, I shall suppose that it is
so extremely repugnant to the principles of justice and the
feelings of a free people, that no man will support it.   It
must, in the end, terminate in the destruction of the liberty
of the people.   I take it, therefore, that there is no rational
way of enforcing the laws but by the instrumentality of the

judiciary.   From these premises we are left only to consider how far the jurisdiction of the judiciary ought to extend.   It appears to me that the judiciary ought to be competent to the decision of any question arising out of the Constitution itself.   On a review of the principles of all free governments, it seems to me also necessary that the judicial power should be coëxtensive with the legislative.

It is necessary in all governments, but particularly in a federal government, that its judiciary should be competent to the decision of all questions arising out of the constitution.   If I understand the gentleman right, his objection was not to the defined jurisdiction, but to the general jurisdiction, which is expressed thus : " The judicial power shall extend to all cases in law and equity arising under this Constitution, the laws of the United States, and treaties made, or which shall be made, under their authority ; " and also the appellate jurisdiction in some instances.   Every member who has read the Constitution with attention must observe that there are certain fundamental principles in it, both of a positive and negative nature, which, being intended for the general advantage of the community, ought not to be violated by any future legislation of the particular states.   Every member will agree that the positive regulations ought to be carried into execution, and that the negative restrictions ought not to disregarded or violated.   Without a judiciary, the injunctions of the Constitution may be disobeyed, and the positive regulations neglected or contravened.   There are certain prohibitory provisions in this Constitution, the wisdom and propriety of which must strike every reflecting mind, and certainly meet with the warmest approbation of every citizen of this state.   It provides, " that no state shall, without the consent of Congress, lay any imposts or duties on imports or exports, except what may be absolutely necessary for executing its inspection laws ; that no preference shall be given, by any regulation of commerce or revenue, to the ports of one state over those of another ; and that no state shall emit bills of credit, make any thing but gold and silver coin a tender in payment of debts, pass any bill of attainder, *ex post facto* law, or law impairing the obligation of contracts."   These restrictions ought to supersede the laws of particular states.   With respect to the prohibitory provision — that no duty or impost shall be laid by any particular state—which is so highly in favor of us and the other non-importing states, the importing states might make laws laying duties notwithstanding, and the Constitution might be violated with impunity, if there were no power in the general government to correct and counteract such laws. This great object can only be safely and completely obtained by the instrumentality of the federal judiciary. Would not Virginia, who has raised many thousand pounds out of our citizens by her imposts, still avail herself of the same advantage if there were no constitutional power to counteract her regulations? If cases arising under the Constitution were left to her own courts, might she not still continue the same practices? But we are now to look for justice to the controlling power of the judiciary of the United States. If the Virginians were to continue to oppress us by laying duties, we can be relieved by a recurrence to the general judiciary. This restriction in the Constitution is a fundamental principle, which is not to be violated, but which would have been a dead letter, were there no judiciary constituted to enforce obedience to it. Paper money and private contracts were in the same condition. Without a general controlling judiciary, laws might be made in particular states to enable its citizens to defraud the citizens of other states. Is it probable, if a citizen of South Carolina owed a sum of money to a citizen of this state, that the latter would be certain of recovering the full value in their courts? That state might in future, as they have already done, make pine-barren acts to discharge their debts. They might say that our citizens should be paid in sterile, inarable lands, at an extravagant price. They might pass the most iniquitous instalment laws, procrastinating the payment of debts due from their citizens, for years—nay, for ages. Is it probable that we should get justice from their own judiciary, who might consider themselves obliged to obey the laws of their own state? Where, then, are we to look for justice? To the judiciary of the United States. Gentlemen must have observed the contracted and narrow-minded regulations of the individual states, and their predominant disposition to advance the interests of their own citizens to the prejudice of others. Will not these evils be continued if there be no restraint? The people of the United States have one common interest; they are all members of the same community, and ought to have justice administered to them equally in every part of the continent, in the same manner, with the same despatch, and on the same principles. It is therefore absolutely necessary that the judiciary of the Union should have jurisdiction in all cases arising in law and equity under the Constitution. Surely there should be somewhere a constitutional authority for carrying into execution constitutional provisions; otherwise, as I have already said, they would be a dead letter.

With respect to their having jurisdiction of all cases arising under the laws of the United States, although I have a very high respect for the gentleman, I heard his objection to it with surprise. I thought, if there were any political axiom under the sun, it must be, that the judicial power ought to be coëxtensive with the legislative. The federal government ought to possess the means of carrying the laws into execution. This position will not be disputed. A government would be a *felo de se* to put the execution of its laws under the control of any other body. If laws are not to be carried into execution by the interposition of the judiciary, how is it to be done?

I have already observed that the mind of every honest man, who has any feeling for the happiness of his country, must have the highest repugnance to the idea of military coercion. The only means, then, of enforcing obedience to the legislative authority must be through the medium of the officers of peace. Did the gentleman carry his objection to the extension of the judicial power to treaties? It is another principle, which I imagine will not be controverted, that the general judiciary ought to be competent to the decision of all questions which involve the general welfare or peace of the Union. It was necessary that treaties should operate as laws upon individuals. They ought to be binding upon us the moment they are made. They involve in their nature not only our own rights, but those of foreigners. If the rights of foreigners were left to be decided ultimately by thirteen distinct judiciaries, there would necessarily be unjust and contradictory decisions. If our courts of justice did not decide in favor of foreign citizens and subjects when they ought, it might involve the whole Union in a war: there ought, therefore, to be a paramount tribunal, which should have ample power to carry them into effect. To the decision of all causes which might involve the peace of the Union may be referred, also, that of controversies between the citizens or subjects of foreign states and the citizens of the United States. It has been laid down by all writers that the denial of justice is one of the just causes of war. If these controversies were left to the decision of particular states, it would be in their power, at any time, to involve the continent in a war, usually the greatest of all national calamities. It is certainly clear that where the peace of the Union is affected, the general judiciary ought to decide. It has generally been given up, that all cases of admiralty and maritime jurisdiction should also be determined by them. It has been equally ceded, by the strongest opposers to this government, that the federal courts should have cognizance of controversies between two or more states, between a state and the citizens of another state, and between the citizens of the same state claiming lands under the grant of different states. Its jurisdiction in these cases is necessary to secure impartiality in decisions, and preserve tranquillity among the states. It is impossible that there should be impartiality when a party affected is to be judge.

The security of impartiality is the principal reason for giving up the ultimate decision of controversies between citizens of different states. It is essential to the interest of agriculture and commerce that the hands of the states should be bound from making paper money, instalment laws, or *pine-barren acts*. By such iniquitous laws the merchant or farmer may be defrauded of a considerable part of his just claims. But in the federal court, real money will be recovered with that speed which is necessary to accommodate the circumstances of individuals. The tedious delays of judicial proceedings, at present, in some states, are ruinous to creditors. In Virginia, many suits are twenty or thirty years spun out by legal ingenuity, and the defective construction of their judiciary. A citizen of Massachusetts or this country might be ruined before he could recover a debt in that state. It is necessary, therefore, in order to obtain justice, that we recur to the judiciary of the United States, where justice must be equally administered, and where a debt may be recovered from the citizen of one state as soon as from the citizen of another.

As to a bill of rights, which has been brought forward in

a manner I cannot account for, it is unnecessary to say any thing. The learned gentleman has said that, by a concurrent jurisdiction, the laws of the United States must necessarily clash with the laws of the individual states, in consequence of which the laws of the states will be obstructed, and the state governments absorbed. This cannot be the case. There is not one instance of a power given to the United States, whereby the internal policy or administration of the states is affected. There is no instance that can be pointed out wherein the internal policy of the state can be affected by the judiciary of the United States. He mentioned impost laws. It has been given up, on all hands, that, if there was a necessity of a federal court, it was on this account. Money is difficult to be got into the treasury. The power of the judiciary to enforce the federal laws is necessary to facilitate the collection of the public revenues. It is well known, in this state, with what reluctance and backwardness collectors pay up the public moneys. We have been making laws after laws to remedy this evil, and still find them ineffectual. Is it not, therefore, necessary to enable the general government to compel the delinquent receivers to be punctual? The honorable gentleman admits that the general government ought to legislate upon individuals, instead of states.

Its laws will otherwise be ineffectual, but particularly with respect to treaties. We have seen with what little ceremony the states violated the peace with Great Britain. Congress had no power to enforce its observance. The same cause will produce the same effect. We need not flatter ourselves that similar violations will always meet with equal impunity. I think he must be of opinion, upon reflection, that the jurisdiction of the federal judiciary could not have been constructed otherwise with safety or propriety. It is necessary that the Constitution should be carried into effect, that the laws should be executed, justice equally done to all the community, and treaties observed. These ends can only be accomplished by a general, paramount judiciary. These are my sentiments, and if the honorable gentleman will prove them erroneous, I shall readily adopt his opinions.

Mr. MACLAINE. Mr. Chairman, I beg leave to make a few observations. One of the gentleman's objections to the Constitution now under consideration is, that it is not the act of the states, but of the people ; but that it ought to be the act of the states ; and he instances the delegation of power by the states to the Confederation, at the commencement of the war, as a proof of this position. I hope, sir, that all power is in the people, and not in the state governments. If he will not deny the authority of the people to delegate power to agents, and to devise such a government as a majority of them thinks will promote their happiness, he will withdraw his objection. The people, sir, are the only proper authority to form a government. They, sir, have formed their state governments, and can alter them at pleasure. Their transcendent power is competent to form this or any other government which they think promotive of their happiness. But the gentleman contends that there ought to be a bill of rights, or something of that kind — something declaring expressly, that all power not expressly given to the Constitution ought to be retained by the states ; and he produces the Confederation as an authority for its necessity. When the Confederation was made, we were by no means so well acquainted with the principles of government as we are now. We were then jealous of the power of our rulers, and had an idea of the British government when we entertained that jealousy. There is no people on earth so well acquainted with the nature of government as the people of America generally are. We know now that it is agreed upon by most writers, and men of judgment and reflection, that all power is in the people, and immediately derived from them. The gentleman surely must know that, if there be certain rights which never can, nor ought to, be given up, these rights cannot be said to be given away, merely because we have omitted to say that we have not given them up. Can any security arise from declaring that we have a right to what belongs to us ? Where is the necessity of such a declaration ? If we have this inherent, this unalienable, this indefeasible title to those rights, if they are not given up, are they not retained ? If Congress should make a law beyond the powers and the spirit of the Constitution, should we not say to Congress, "You have no authority to make this law. There are limits beyond which you cannot go. You cannot exceed the power prescribed by the Constitution. You are amenable to us for your conduct. This act is unconstitutional. We will disregard it, and punish you for the attempt."

But the gentleman seems to be most tenacious of the judicial power of the states. The honorable gentleman must know, that the doctrine of reservation of power not relinquished, clearly demonstrates that the judicial power of the states is not impaired. He asks, with respect to the trial by jury, "When the cause has gone up to the superior court, and the verdict is set aside, what benefit arises from having had a jury trial in the inferior court?" I would ask the gentleman, "What is the reason, that, on a special verdict or case agreed, the decision is left to the court?" There are a number of cases where juries cannot decide. When a jury finds the fact specially, or when it is agreed upon by the parties, the decision is referred to the court. If the law be against the party, the court decides against him; if the law be for him, the court judges accordingly. He, as well as every gentleman here, must know that, under the Confederation, Congress set aside juries. There was an appeal given to Congress : did Congress determine by a jury? Every party carried his testimony in writing to the judges of appeal, and Congress determined upon it.

The distinction between matters of law and of fact has not been sufficiently understood, or has been intentionally misrepresented. On a demurrer in law, in which the facts are agreed upon by the parties, the law arising thereupon is referred to the court. An inferior court may give an erroneous judgment; an appeal may be had from this court to the Supreme Federal Court, and a right decision had. This is an instance wherein it can have cognizance of matter of law solely. In cases where the existence of facts has been first disputed by one of the parties, and afterwards established as in a special verdict, the consideration of these facts, blended with the law, is left to the court. In such cases, inferior courts may decide contrary to justice and law, and appeals may be had to the Supreme Court. This is an instance wherein it may be said they have jurisdiction both as to law and fact. But where facts only are disputed, and where they are once established by a verdict, the opinion of the judges of the Supreme Court cannot, I conceive, set aside these facts ; for I do not think they have the power so to do by this Constitution.

The federal court has jurisdiction only in some instances. There are many instances in which no court but the state courts can have any jurisdiction whatsoever, except where parties claim land under the grant of different states, or the subject of dispute arises under the Constitution itself. The state courts have exclusive jurisdiction over every other possible controversy that can arise between the inhabitants of their own states ; nor can the federal courts intermeddle with such disputes, either originally or by appeal. There is a number of other instances, where, though jurisdiction is given to the federal court, it is not taken away from the state courts. If a man in South Carolina owes me money, I can bring suit in the courts of that state, as well as in any inferior federal court. I think gentlemen cannot but see the propriety of leaving to the general government the regulation of the inferior federal tribunals. This is a power which our own state legislature has. We may trust Congress as well as them.

Mr. SPENCER answered, that the gentleman last up had misunderstood him. He did not object to the caption of the Constitution, but he instanced it to show that the United States were not, merely as states, the objects of the Constitution ; but that the laws of Congress were to operate upon individuals, and not upon states. He then continued : I do not mean to contend that the laws of the general government should not operate upon individuals. I before observed that this was necessary, as laws could not be put in execution against states without the agency of the sword, which, instead of answering the ends of government, would destroy it. I endeavored to show that, as the government was not to operate against states, but against individuals, the rights of individuals ought to be properly secured. In order to constitute this security, it appears to me there ought to be such a clause in the Constitution as there was in the Confederation, expressly declaring, that every power, jurisdiction, and right, which are not given up by it, remain in the states. Such a clause would render a bill of rights unnecessary. But as there is no such clause, I contend that there should be a bill of rights, ascertaining and securing the great rights of the states and people. Besides my objection to the revision of facts by the federal court, and the insecurity of jury trial, I consider the concurrent jurisdiction of those courts with the state courts as extremely dangerous. It must be obvious to every one that, if they have such a concurrent jurisdiction, they must in time take away the business from the state courts entirely. I do not deny the propriety of having federal courts ; but they should be confined to federal business, and ought not to interfere in those cases where the state courts are fully competent to decide. The state courts can do their business without federal assistance. I do not know how far any gentleman may suppose that I may, from my office, be biased in favor of the state jurisdiction. I am no more interested than any other individual. I do not think it will affect the respectable office which I hold. Those courts will not take place immediately, and even when they do, it will be a long time before their concurrent jurisdiction will materially affect the state judiciaries. I therefore consider myself as disinterested. I only wish to have the government so constructed as to promote the happiness, harmony, and liberty, of every individual at home, and render us respectable as a nation abroad. I wish the question to be decided coolly and calmly — with moderation, candor, and deliberation.

Mr. MACLAINE replied, that the gentleman's objections to the want of a bill of rights had been sufficiently answered; that the federal jurisdiction was well guarded, and that the federal courts had not, in his opinion, cognizance, in any one case, where it could be alone vested in the state judiciaries with propriety or safety. The gentleman, he said, had acknowledged that the laws of the Union could not be executed under the existing government ; and yet he objected to the federal judiciary's having cognizance of such laws, though it was the only probable means whereby they could be enforced. The treaty of peace with Great Britain was the supreme law of the land ; yet it was disregarded, for want of a federal judiciary. The state judiciaries did not enforce an observance of it. The state courts were highly improper to be intrusted with the execution of the federal laws, as they were bound to judge according to the state laws, which might be repugnant to those of the Union.

Mr. IREDELL. Mr. Chairman, I beg leave to make a few observations on some remarks that have been made on this part of the Constitution. The honorable gentleman said that it was very extraordinary that the Convention should not have taken the trouble to make an addition of five or six lines, to secure the trial by jury in civil cases.   Sir, if by the addition, not only of five or six lines, but of five or six hundred lines, this invaluable object could have been secured, I should have thought the Convention criminal in omitting it; and instead of meriting the thanks of their country, as I think they do now, they might justly have met with its resentment and indignation.   I am persuaded the omission arose from the real difficulty of the case.   The gentleman says that a mode might have been provided, whereby the trial by jury might have been secured satis-factorily to all the states.   I call on him to show that mode. I know of none; nor do I think it possible for any man to devise one to which some states would not have objected.   It is said, indeed, that it might have been provided that it should be as it had been heretofore.   Had this been the case, surely it would have been highly incongruous.

The trial by jury is different in different states.   It is reg-ulated in one way in the state of North Carolina, and in another way in the state of Virginia.   It is established in a different way from either in several other states.   Had it, then, been inserted in the Constitution, that the trial by jury should be as it had been heretofore, there would have been an example, for the first time in the world, of a judiciary belonging to the same government being different in differ-ent parts of the same country.   What would you think of an act of Assembly which should require the trial by jury to be had in one mode in the county of Orange, and in another mode in Granville, and in a manner different from both in Chatham?   Such an act of Assembly, so manifestly inju-dicious, impolitic, and unjust, would be repealed next year.

But what would you say of our Constitution, if it au-thorized such an absurdity?   The mischief, then, could not be removed without altering the Constitution itself.   It must be evident, therefore, that the addition contended for would not have answered the purpose.   If the method of any particular state had been established, it would have been objected to by others, because, whatever inconveniences it might have been attended with, nothing but a change in the Constitution itself could have removed them; whereas, as it is now, if any mode established by Congress is found in-convenient, it can easily be altered by a single act of legis-

lation   Let any gentleman consider the difficulties in which
the Convention was placed.   A union was absolutely necessary.   Every thing could be agreed upon except the regulation of the trial by jury in civil cases.   They were all
anxious to establish it on the best footing, but found they
could fix upon no permanent rule that was not liable to great
objections and difficulties.   If they could not agree among
themselves, they had still less reason to believe that all the
states would have unanimously agreed to any one plan that
could be proposed.   They, therefore, thought it better to
leave all such regulations to the legislature itself, conceiving
there could be no real danger, in this case, from a body composed of our own representatives, who could have no temptation to undermine this excellent mode of trial in civil cases,
and who would have, indeed, a personal interest, in common
with others, in making the administration of justice between
man and man secure and easy.

In criminal cases, however, no latitude ought to be allowed.   In these the greatest danger from any government
subsists, and accordingly it is provided that there shall be
a trial by jury, in all such cases, in the state wherein the
offence is committed.   I thought the objection against the
want of a bill of rights had been obviated unanswerably.
It appears to me most extraordinary.   Shall we give up any
thing but what is positively granted by that instrument?
It would be the greatest absurdity for any man to pretend
that, when a legislature is formed for a particular purpose, it
can have any authority but what is so expressly given to it,
any more than a man acting under a power of attorney could
depart from the authority it conveyed to him, according to
an instance which I stated when speaking on the subject
before.   As for example : — if I had three tracts of land, one
in Orange, another in Caswell, and another in Chatham,
and I gave a power of attorney to a man to sell the two
tracts in Orange and Caswell, and he should attempt to sell
my land in Chatham, would any man of common sense suppose he had authority to do so?   In like manner, I say, the
future Congress can have no right to exercise any power
but what is contained in that paper.   Negative words, in
my opinion, could make the matter no plainer than it was
before.   The gentleman says that unalienable rights ought
not to be given up.   Those rights which are unalienable

are not alienated. They still remain with the great body
of the people. If any right be given up that ought not to
be, let it be shown. Say it is a thing which affects your
country, and that it ought not to be surrendered : this
would be reasonable. But when it is evident that the exercise of any power not given up would be a usurpation, it
would be not only useless, but dangerous, to enumerate a
number of rights which are not intended to be given up ;
because it would be implying, in the strongest manner, that
every right not included in the exception might be impaired
by the government without usurpation ; and it would be
impossible to enumerate every one. Let any one make
what collection or enumeration of rights he pleases, I will
immediately mention twenty or thirty more rights not contained in it.

　　Mr. BLOODWORTH. Mr. Chairman, I have listened
with attention to the gentleman's arguments ; but whether
it be for want of sufficient attention, or from the grossness
of my ideas, I cannot be satisfied with his defence of the
omission, with respect to the trial by jury. He says that
it would be impossible to fall on any satisfactory mode of
regulating the trial by jury, because there are various customs relative to it in the different states. Is this a satisfactory cause for the omission ? Why did it not provide that
the trial by jury should be preserved in civil cases ? It has
said that the trial should be by jury in criminal cases ; and
yet this trial is different in its manner in criminal cases in
the different states. If it has been possible to secure it in
criminal cases, notwithstanding the diversity concerning it,
why has it not been possible to secure it in civil cases ?
I wish this to be cleared up. By its not being provided for,
it is expressly provided against. I still see the necessity of
a bill of rights. Gentlemen use contradictory arguments on
this subject, if I recollect right. Without the most express
restrictions, Congress may trample on your rights. Every
possible precaution should be taken when we grant powers.
Rulers are always disposed to abuse them. I beg leave to
call gentlemen's recollection to what happened under our
Confederation. By it, nine states are required to make a
treaty ; yet seven states said that they could, with propriety,
repeal part of the instructions given our secretary for foreign
affairs, which prohibited him from making a treaty to give

up the Mississippi to Spain, by which repeal the rest of his instructions enabled him to make such treaty. Seven states actually did repeal the prohibitory part of these instructions, and they insisted it was legal and proper. This was in fact a violation of the Confederation. If gentlemen thus put what construction they please upon words, how shall we be redressed, if Congress shall say that all that is not expressed is given up, and they assume a power which is expressly inconsistent with the rights of mankind? Where is the power to pretend to deny its legality? This has occurred to me, and I wish it to be explained.

Mr. SPENCER. Mr. Chairman, the gentleman expresses admiration as to what we object with respect to a bill of rights, and insists that what is not given up in the Constitution is retained. He must recollect I said, yesterday, that we could not guard with too much care those essential rights and liberties which ought never to be given up. There is no express negative — no fence against their being trampled upon. They might exceed the proper boundary without being taken notice of. When there is no rule but a vague doctrine, they might make great strides, and get possession of so much power that a general insurrection of the people would be necessary to bring an alteration about. But if a boundary were set up, when the boundary is passed, the people would take notice of it immediately. These are the observations which I made; and I have no doubt that, when he reflects, he will acknowledge the necessity of it. I acknowledge, however, that the doctrine is right; but if that Constitution is not satisfactory to the people, I would have a bill of rights, or something of that kind, to satisfy them.

Mr. LOCKE. Mr. Chairman, I wish to throw some particular light upon the subject, according to my conceptions. I think the Constitution neither safe nor beneficial, as it grants powers unbounded with restrictions. One gentleman has said that it was necessary to give cognizance of causes to the federal court, because there was partiality in the judges of the states; that the state judges could not be depended upon in causes arising under the Constitution and laws of the Union. I agree that impartiality in judges is indispensable; but I think this alteration will not produce more impartiality than there is now in our courts, whatever evils it may bring forth. Must there not be judges in the federal

courts, and those judges taken from some of the states?
The same partiality, therefore, may be in them. For my
part, I think it derogatory to the honor of this state to give
this jurisdiction to the federal courts. It must be supposed
that the same passions, dispositions, and failings of humanity
which attend the state judges, will be equally the lot of the
federal judges. To justify giving this cognizance to those
courts, it must be supposed that all justice and equity are
given up at once in the states. Such reasoning is very
strange to me. I fear greatly for this state, and for other
states. I find there has a considerable stress been laid upon
the injustice of laws made heretofore. Great reflections are
thrown on South Carolina for passing *pine-barren* and *instalment* laws, and on this state for making paper money. I
wish those gentlemen who made those observations would
consider the necessity which compelled us in a great measure
to make such money. I never thought the law which authorized it a good law. If the evil could have been avoided,
it would have been a very bad law; but necessity, sir, justified it in some degree. I believe I have gained as little by
it as any in this house. If we are to judge of the future by
what we have seen, we shall find as much or more injustice
in Congress than in our legislature. Necessity compelled
them to pass the law, in order to save vast numbers of people from ruin. I hope to be excused in observing that it
would have been hard for our late Continental army to lay
down their arms, with which they had valiantly and successfully fought for their country, without receiving or being
promised and assured of some compensation for their past
services. What a situation would this country have been in,
if they had had the power over the *purse* and *sword!* If
they had the powers given up by this Constitution, what a
wretched situation would this country have been in! Congress was unable to pay them, but passed many resolutions
and laws in their favor, particularly one that each state should
make up the depreciation of the pay of the Continental line,
who were distressed for the want of an adequate compensation for their services. This state could not pay her proportion in specie. To have laid a tax for that purpose would
have been oppressive. What was to be done? The only
expedient was to pass a law to make paper money, and make
it a tender. The Continental line was satisfied, and ap-

proved of the measure, it being done at their instance in some degree. Notwithstanding it was supposed to be highly beneficial to the state, it is found to be injurious to it. Saving expense is a very great object, but this incurred much expense. This subject has for many years embroiled the state; but the situation of the country, and the distress of the people are so great, that the public measures must be accommodated to their circumstances with peculiar delicacy and caution, or another insurrection may be the consequence. As to what the gentleman said of the trial by jury, it surprises me much to hear gentlemen of such great abilities speak such language. It is clearly insecure, nor can ingenuity and subtle arguments prove the contrary. I trust this country is too sensible of the value of liberty, and her citizens have bought it too dearly, to give it up hastily.

Mr. IREDELL. Mr. Chairman, I hope some other gentleman will answer what has been said by the gentlemen who have spoken last. I only rise to answer the question of the member from New Hanover — which was, if there was such a difficulty, in establishing the trial by jury in civil cases, that the Convention could not concur in any mode, why the difficulty did not extend to criminal cases? I beg leave to say, that the difficulty, in this case, does not depend so much on the mode of proceeding, as on the difference of the subjects of controversy, and the laws relative to them. In some states, there are no juries in admiralty and equity cases. In other states, there are juries in such cases. In some states, there are no distinct courts of equity, though in most states there are. I believe that, if a uniform rule had been fixed by the Constitution, it would have displeased some states so far that they would have rejected the Constitution altogether. Had it been declared generally, as the gentleman mentioned, it would have included equity and maritime cases, and created a necessity of deciding them in a manner different from that in which they have been decided heretofore in many of the states; which would very probably have met with the disapprobation of those states.

We have been told, and I believe this was the real reason, why they could not concur in any general rule. I have great respect for the characters of those gentlemen who formed the Convention, and I believe they were not capable of overlooking the importance of the trial by jury, much less of designedly plotting against it. But I fully believe that the real difficulty of the thing was the cause of the omission. I trust sufficient reasons have been offered, to show that it is in no danger. As to criminal cases, I must observe that the great instrument of arbitrary power is criminal prosecutions. By the privileges of the *habeas corpus*, no man can be confined without inquiry; and if it should appear that he has been committed contrary to law, he must be discharged. That diversity which is to be found in civil controversies, does not exist in criminal cases. That diversity which contributes to the security of property in civil cases, would have pernicious effects in criminal ones. There is no other safe mode to try these but by a jury. If any man had the means of trying another his own way, or were it left to the control of arbitrary judges, no man would have that security for life and liberty which every freeman ought to have. I presume that in no state on the continent is a man tried on a criminal accusation but by a jury. It was necessary, therefore, that it should be fixed, in the Constitution, that the trial should be by jury in criminal cases; and such difficulties did not occur in this as in the other case. The worthy gentleman says, that by not being provided for in civil cases, it is expressly provided against, and that what is not expressed is given up. Were it so, no man would be more against this Constitution than myself. I should detest and oppose it as much as any man. But, sir, this cannot be the case. I beg leave to say that that construction appears to me absurd and unnatural. As it could not be fixed either on the principles of uniformity or diversity, it must be left to Congress to modify it. If they establish it in any manner by law, and find it inconvenient, they can alter it. But I am convinced that a majority of the representatives of the people will never attempt to establish a mode oppressive to their constituents, as it will be their own interest to take care of this right. But it is observed that there ought to be a fence provided against future encroachments of power. If there be not such a fence, it is a cause of objection. I readily agree that there ought to be such a *fence*. The instrument ought to contain such a definition of authority as would leave no doubt; and if there be any ambiguity, it ought not to be admitted. He says this construction is not agreeable to the people, though he acknowledges it is a right one.

In my opinion, there is no man, of any reason at all, but must be satisfied with so clear and plain a definition. If the Congress should claim any power not given them, it would be as bare a usurpation as making a king in America. If this Constitution be adopted, it must be presumed the instrument will be in the hands of every man in America, to see whether authority be usurped; and any person by inspecting it may see if the power claimed be enumerated. If it be not, he will know it to be a usurpation.

Mr. MACLAINE. Mr. Chairman, a gentleman lately up (Mr. Locke) has informed us of his doubts and fears respecting the federal courts. He is afraid for this state and other states. He supposes that the idea of cognizance of the laws of the Union to federal courts, must have arisen from suspicions of partiality and want of common integrity in our state judges. The worthy gentleman is mistaken in his construction of what I said. I did not personally reflect on the members of our state judiciary; nor did I impute the impropriety of vesting the state judiciaries with exclusive jurisdiction over the laws of the Union, and cases arising under the Constitution, to any want of probity in the judges. But if they be the judges of the local or state laws, and receive emoluments for acting in that capacity, they will be improper persons to judge of the laws of the Union. A federal judge ought to be solely governed by the laws of the United States, and receive his salary from the treasury of the United States. It is impossible for any judges, receiving pay from a single state, to be impartial in cases where the local laws or interests of that state clash with the laws of the Union, or the general interests of America. We have instances here which prove this partiality in such cases. It is also so in other states. The gentleman has thrown out something very uncommon. He likens the power given by this Constitution to giving the late army the purse and the sword. I am much astonished that such an idea should be thrown out by that gentleman, because his respectability is well known. If he considers for a moment, he must see that his observation is bad, and that the comparison is extremely absurd and improper. The purse and the sword must be given to every government. The sword is given to the executive magistrate; but the purse remains, by this Constitution, in the representatives of the people. We know very well that they cannot raise one shilling but by the consent of the representatives of the people. Money bills do not even originate in the Senate; they originate solely in the other house. Every appropriation must be by law. We know, therefore, that no executive magistrate or officer can appropriate a shilling, but as he is authorized by law. With respect to paper money, the gentleman has acted and spoken with great candor. He was against paper money from the first emission. There was no other way to satisfy the late army but by paper money, there being not a shilling of specie in the state. There were other modes adopted by other states, which did not produce such inconveniences. There was, however, a considerable majority of that assembly who adopted the idea, that not one shilling more paper money should be made, because of the evil consequences that must necessarily follow. The experience of this country, for many years, has proved that such emissions involve us in debts and distresses, destroy our credit, and produce no good consequences; and yet, contrary to all good policy, the evil was repeated.

With respect to our public security and paper money, the apprehensions of gentlemen are groundless. I believe this Constitution cannot affect them at all. In the 10th section of the 1st article, it is provided, among other restrictions, "that no state shall emit bills of credit, make any thing but gold and silver coin a tender in payment of debts, or pass any law impairing the obligation of contracts." Now, sir, this has no retrospective view. It looks to futurity. It is conceived by many people, that the moment this new Constitution is adopted, our present paper money will sink to nothing. For my part, I believe that, instead of sinking, it will appreciate. If we adopt, it will rise in value, so that twenty shillings of it will be equal to two Spanish milled dollars and a half. Paper money is as good as gold and silver where there are proper funds to redeem it, and no danger of its being increased. Before the late war, our paper money fluctuated in value. Thirty-six years ago, when I came into this country, our paper money was at seven shillings to the dollar. A few years before the late war, the merchants of Great Britain remonstrated to the ministry of that country, that they lost much of their debts by paper money losing its value. This

caused an order to be made through all the states not to
pass any money bills whatever.   The effect of this was, that
our paper money appreciated.   At the commencement of
the war, our paper money in circulation was equal to gold
or silver.   But it is said that, on adoption, all debts contracted heretofore must then be paid in gold or silver coin.
I believe that, if any gentleman will attend to the clause
above recited, he will find that it has no retrospective, but
a prospective view.   It does not look back, but forward.   It
does not destroy the paper money which is now actually
made, but prevents us from making any more.   This is
much in our favor, because we may pay in the money we
contracted for, (or such as is equal in value to it ;) and the
very restriction against an increase of it will add to its
value.   It is in the power of the legislature to establish a
scale of depreciation, to fix the value of it.   There is nothing
against this in the Constitution.   On the contrary, it favors
it.   I should be much injured if it was really to be the case
that the paper money should sink.   After the Constitution
was adopted, I should think myself, as a holder of our paper
money, possessed of Continental security.   I am convinced
our money will be good money ; and if I was to speculate
in any thing, I would in paper money, though I never did
speculate.   I should be satisfied that I should make a profit.
Why say that the state security will be paid in gold and
silver after all these things are considered ?   Every real,
actual debt of the state ought to be discharged in real, and
not nominal value, at any rate.

Mr. BASS took a general view of the original and appellate jurisdiction of the federal court.   He considered the
Constitution neither necessary nor proper.   He declared
that the last part of the 1st paragraph of the 2d section
appeared to him totally inexplicable.   He feared that dreadful oppression would be committed by carrying people too
great a distance to decide trivial causes.   He observed that
gentlemen of the law and men of learning did not concur in
the explanation or meaning of this Constitution.   For his
part, he said, he could not understand it. although he took
great pains to find out its meaning, and although he flattered
himself with the possession of common sense and reason
He always thought that there ought to be a compact be
tween the governors and governed.   Some called this a

compact ; others said it was not.   From the contrariety of
opinions, he thought the thing was either uncommonly difficult, or absolutely unintelligible.   He wished to reflect on
no gentleman, and apologized for his ignorance, by observing that he never went to school, and had been born
blind ; but he wished for information, and supposed that
every gentleman would consider his desire as laudable.

Mr. MACLAINE first, and then Mr. IREDELL, endeavored to satisfy the gentleman, by a particular explanation
of the whole paragraph.   It was observed that, if there
should be a controversy between this state and the king of
France or Spain, it must be decided in the federal court.
Or if there should arise a controversy between the French
king, or any other foreign power, or one of their subjects or
citizens, and one of our citizens, it must be decided there
also.   The distinction between the words *citizen* and *subject*
was explained — that the former related to individuals of
popular governments, the latter to those of monarchies ; as,
for instance, a dispute between this state, or a citizen of it,
and a person in Holland.   The words *foreign citizen* would
properly refer to such persons.   If the dispute was between
this state and a person in France or Spain, the words *foreign
subject* would apply to this ; and all such controversies might
be decided in the federal court — that the words *citizens or
subjects*, in that part of the clause, could only apply to
foreign citizens or foreign subjects; and another part of the
constitution made this plain, by confining disputes, in general, between citizens of the same state, to the single case
of their claiming lands under grants of different states.

The last clause of the 2d section under consideration.

Mr. MACLAINE.   Mr. Chairman, an objection was
made yesterday by a gentleman against this clause, because
it confined the trial to the state ; and he observed that a
person on the Mississippi might be tried in Edenton.

Gentlemen ought to consider that it was impossible for
the Convention, when devising a general rule for all the
states, to descend to particular districts.   The trial by jury
is secured generally, by providing that the trial shall be in
the state where the crime was committed.   It is left to
Congress to make such regulations, by law, as will suit the
circumstances of each state.   It would have been impolitic
to fix the mode of proceeding, because it would alter the

present mode of proceeding, in such cases, in this state, or in several others; for there is such a dissimilarity in the proceedings of different states, that it would be impossible to make a general law which would be satisfactory to the whole. But as the trial is to be in the state, there is no doubt but it will be the usual and common mode practised in the state.

3d section read without any observation.

Article 4th. The 1st section, and two first clauses of the 2d section, read without observation.

The last clause read.

Mr. IREDELL begged leave to explain the reason of this clause. In some of the Northern States they have emancipated all their *slaves*. If any of our slaves, said he, go there, and remain there a certain time, they would, by the present laws, be entitled to their freedom, so that their masters could not get them again. This would be extremely prejudicial to the inhabitants of the Southern States; and to prevent it, this clause is inserted in the Constitution. Though the word *slave* is not mentioned, this is the meaning of it. The northern delegates, owing to their particular scruples on the subject of slavery, did not choose the word *slave* to be mentioned.

The rest of the 4th article read without any observation.

Article 5th.

Mr. IREDELL. Mr. Chairman, this is a very important clause. In every other constitution of government that I have ever heard or read of, no provision is made for necessary amendments. The misfortune attending most constitutions which have been deliberately formed, has been, that those who formed them thought their wisdom equal to all possible contingencies, and that there could be no error in what they did. The gentlemen who framed this Constitution thought with much more diffidence of their capacities; and, undoubtedly, without a provision for amendment it would have been more justly liable to objection, and the characters of its framers would have appeared much less meritorious. This, indeed, is one of the greatest beauties of the system, and should strongly recommend it to every candid mind. The Constitution of any government which cannot be regularly amended when its defects are experienced, reduces the people to this dilemma — they must either submit to its oppressions, or bring about amendments, more or less, by a civil war. Happy this, the country we live in! The Constitution before us, if it be adopted, can be altered with as much regularity, and as little confusion, as any act of Assembly; not, indeed, quite so easily, which would be extremely impolitic; but it is a most happy circumstance, that there is a remedy in the system itself for its own fallibility, so that alterations can without difficulty be made, agreeable to the general sense of the people. Let us attend to the manner in which amendments may be made. The proposition for amendments may arise from Congress itself, when two thirds of both houses shall deem it necessary. If they should not, and yet amendments be generally wished for by the people, two thirds of the legislatures of the different states may require a general convention for the purpose, in which case Congress are under the necessity of convening one. Any amendments which either Congress shall propose, or which shall be proposed by such general convention, are afterwards to be submitted to the legislatures of the different states, or conventions called for that purpose, as Congress shall think proper, and, upon the ratification of three fourths of the states, will become a part of the Constitution. By referring this business to the legislatures, expense would be saved; and in general, it may be presumed, they would speak the genuine sense of the people. It may, however, on some occasions, be better to consult an immediate delegation for that special purpose. This is therefore left discretionary. It is highly probable that amendments agreed to in either of these methods would be conducive to the public welfare, when so large a majority of the states consented to them. And in one of these modes, amendments that are now wished for may, in a short time, be made to this Constitution by the states adopting it.

It is, however, to be observed, that the 1st and 4th clauses in the 9th section of the 1st article are protected from any alteration till the year 1808; and in order that no consolidation should take place, it is provided that no state shall, by any amendment or alteration, be ever deprived of an equal suffrage in the Senate without its own consent. The first two prohibitions are with respect to the census, (according to which direct taxes are imposed,) and with respect to the importation of slaves. As to the first, it must be observed, that there is a material difference between the Northern and Southern States. The Northern States have been much longer settled, and are much fuller of people, than the Southern, but have not land in equal proportion, nor scarcely any slaves. The subject of this article was regulated with great difficulty, and by a spirit of concession which it would not be prudent to disturb for a good many years. In twenty years, there will probably be a great alteration, and then the subject may be reconsidered with less difficulty and greater coolness. In the mean time, the compromise was upon the best footing that could be obtained. A compromise likewise took place in regard to the importation of slaves. It is probable that all the members reprobated this inhuman traffic; but those of South Carolina and Georgia would not consent to an immediate prohibition of it — one reason of which was, that, during the last war, they lost a vast number of negroes, which loss they wish to supply. In the mean time, it is left to the states to admit or prohibit the importation, and Congress may impose a limited duty upon it.

Mr. BASS observed, that it was plain that the introduction of amendments depended altogether on Congress.

Mr. IREDELL replied, that it was very evident that it did not depend on the will of Congress; for that the legislatures of two thirds of the states were authorized to make application for calling a convention to propose amendments, and, on such application, it is provided that Congress *shall* call such convention, so that they will have no option.

Article 6th. 1st clause read without any observation.

2d clause read.

Mr. IREDELL. This clause is supposed to give too much power, when, in fact, it only provides for the execution of those powers which are already given in the foregoing articles. What does it say? That " this Constitution, and the laws of the United States which shall be made in pursuance thereof, and all treaties made, or which shall be made, under the authority of the United States, shall be the supreme law of the land; and the judges in every state shall be bound thereby, any thing in the constitution or laws of any state to the contrary notwithstanding." What is the meaning of this, but that, as we have given power, we will support the execution of it? We should act like children, to give power and deny the legality of executing it. It is saying no more than that, when we adopt the government, we will maintain and obey it ; in the same manner as if the Constitution of this state had said that, when a law is passed in conformity to it, we must obey that law. Would this be objected to ? Then, when the Congress passes a law consistent with the Constitution, it is to be binding on the people. If Congress, under pretence of executing one power, should, in fact, usurp another, they will violate the Constitution. I presume, therefore, that this explanation, which appears to me the plainest in the world, will be entirely satisfactory to the committee.

Mr. BLOODWORTH. Mr. Chairman, I confess his explanation is not satisfactory to me. I wish the gentleman had gone farther. I readily agree that it is giving them no more power than to execute their laws. But how far does this go ? It appears to me to sweep off all the constitutions of the states. It is a total repeal of every act and constitution of the states. The judges are sworn to uphold it. It will produce an abolition of the state governments. Its sovereignty absolutely annihilates them.

Mr. IREDELL. Mr. Chairman, every power delegated to Congress is to be executed by laws made for that purpose. It is necessary to particularize the powers intended to be given, in the Constitution, as having no existence before ; but, after having enumerated what we give up, it follows, of course, that whatever is done, by virtue of that authority, is legal without any new authority or power. The question, then, under this clause, will always be, whether Congress has exceeded its authority. If it has not exceeded it, we must obey, otherwise not. This Constitution, when adopted, will become a part of our state Constitution ; and the latter must yield to the former only in those cases where power is given by it. It is not to yield to it in any other case whatever. For instance, there is nothing in the Constitution of this state establishing the authority of a federal court. Yet the federal court, when established, will be as constitutional as the superior court is now under our Constitution. It appears to me merely a general clause, the amount of which is that, when they pass an act, if it be in the execution of a power given by the Constitution, it shall be binding on the people, otherwise not. As to the sufficiency or extent of the power, that is another consideration, and has been discussed before.

Mr. BLOODWORTH. This clause will be the destruction of every law which will come in competition with the laws of the United States. Those laws and regulations which have been, or shall be, made in this state, must be destroyed by it, if they come in competition with the powers of Congress. Is it not necessary to define the extent of its operation? Is not the force of our tender-laws destroyed by it? The worthy gentleman from Wilmington has endeavored to obviate the objection as to the Constitution's destroying the credit of our paper money, and paying debts in coin, but unsatisfactorily to me. A man assigns, by legal action, a bond to a man in another state; could that bond be paid by money? I know it is very easy to be wrong. I am conscious of being frequently so. I endeavor to be open to conviction. This clause seems to me too general, and I think its extent ought to be limited and defined. I should suppose every reasonable man would think some amendments to it were necessary.

Mr. MACLAINE. Mr. Chairman, that it will destroy the state sovereignty is a very popular argument. I beg leave to have the attention of the committee. Government is formed for the happiness and prosperity of the people at large. The powers given it are for their own good. We have found, by several years' experience, that government, taken by itself nominally, without adequate power, is not sufficient to promote their prosperity. Sufficient powers must be given to it. The powers to be given the general government are proposed to be withdrawn from the authority of the state governments, in order to protect and secure the Union at large. This proposal is made to the people. No man will deny their authority to delegate powers and recall them, in all free countries. But, says the gentleman last up, the construction of the Constitution is in the power of Congress, and it will destroy the sovereignty of the state governments. It may be justly said that it diminishes the power of the state legislatures, and the diminution is necessary to the safety and prosperity of the people; but it may be fairly said that the members of the general government,—the President, senators, and representatives,—whom we send thither, by our free suffrages, to consult our common interest, will not wish to destroy the state governments, because the existence of the general government will depend on that of the state governments.

But what is the sovereignty, and who is Congress? One branch, the people at large ; and the other branch, the states by their representatives. Do people fear the delegation of power to themselves — to their own representatives? But he objects that the laws of the Union are to be the supreme laws of the land. Is it not proper that their laws should be the laws of the land, and paramount to those of any particular state ?— or is it proper that the laws of any particular state should control the laws of the United States? Shall a part control the whole? To permit the local laws of any state to control the laws of the Union, would be to give the general government no powers at all. If the judges are not to be bound by it, the powers of Congress will be nugatory. This is self-evident and plain. Bring it home to every understanding ; it is so clear it will force itself upon it. The worthy gentleman says, in contradiction to what I have observed, that the clause which restrains the states from emitting paper money, &c., will operate upon the present circulating paper money, and that gold and silver must pay paper contracts. The clause cannot possibly have a retrospective view. It cannot affect the existing currency in any manner, except to enhance its value by the prohibition of future emissions. It is contrary to the universal principles of jurisprudence, that a law or constitution should have a retrospective operation, unless it be expressly provided that it shall. Does he deny the power of the legislature to fix a scale of depreciation as a criterion to regulate contracts made for depreciated money? As to the question he has put, of an assigned bond, I answer that it can be paid with paper money. For this reason, the assignee can be in no better situation than the assignor. If it be regularly transferred, it will appear what person had the bond originally, and the present possessor can recover nothing but what the original holder of it could. Another reason which may be urged is, that the federal courts could have no cognizance of such a suit. Those courts have no jurisdiction in cases of debt between the citizens of the same state. The assignor being a citizen of the same state with the debtor, and assigning it to a citizen of another state, to avoid the intent of the Constitu-

16

tion, the assignee can derive no advantage from the assignment, except what the assignor had a right to; and consequently the gentleman's objection falls to the ground.

Every gentleman must see the necessity for the laws of the Union to be paramount to those of the separate states, and that the powers given by this Constitution must be executed. What, shall we ratify a government and then say it shall not operate? This would be the same as not to ratify. As to the amendments, the best characters in the country, and those whom I most highly esteem, wish for amendments. Some parts of it are not organized to my wish. But I apprehend no danger from the structure of the government. One gentleman (Mr. Bass) said he thought it neither necessary nor proper. For my part, I think it essential to our very existence as a nation, and our happiness and prosperity as a free people. The men who composed it were men of great abilities and various minds. They carried their knowledge with them. It is the result, not only of great wisdom and mutual reflection, but of "mutual deference and concession." It has trifling faults, but they are not dangerous. Yet at the same time I declare that, if gentlemen propose amendments, if they be not such as would destroy the government entirely, there is not a single member here more willing to agree to them than myself.

Mr. DAVIE. Mr. Chairman: permit me, sir, to make a few observations on the operation of the clause so often mentioned. This Constitution, as to the powers therein granted, is constantly to be the supreme law of the land. Every power ceded by it must be executed, without being counteracted by the laws or constitutions of the individual states. Gentlemen should distinguish that it is not the supreme law in the exercise of a power not granted. It can be supreme only in cases consistent with the powers specially granted, and not in usurpations. If you grant any power to the federal government, the laws made in pursuance of that power must be supreme, and uncontrolled in their operation. This consequence is involved in the very nature and necessity of the thing. The only rational inquiry is, whether those powers are necessary, and whether they are properly granted. To say that you have vested the federal government with power to legislate for the Union, and then deny the supremacy of the laws, is a solecism in terms. With respect to its operation on our own paper money, I believe that a little consideration will satisfy every man that it cannot have the effect asserted by the gentleman from New Hanover. The Federal Convention knew that several states had large sums of paper money in circulation, and that it was an interesting property, and they were sensible that those states would never consent to its immediate destruction, or ratify any system that would have that operation. The mischief already done could not be repaired : all that could be done was, to form some limitation to this great political evil. As the paper money had become private property, and the object of numberless contracts, it could not be destroyed or intermeddled with in that situation, although its baneful tendency was obvious and undeniable. It was, however, effecting an important object to put bounds to this growing mischief. If the states had been compelled to sink the paper money instantly, the remedy might be worse than the disease. As we could not put an immediate end to it, we were content with prohibiting its future increase, looking forward to its entire extinguishment when the states that had an emission circulating should be able to call it in by a gradual redemption.

In Pennsylvania, their paper money was not a tender in discharge of private contracts. In South Carolina, their bills became eventually a tender ; and in Rhode Island, New York, New Jersey, and North Carolina, the paper money was made a legal tender in all cases whatsoever. The other states were sensible that the destruction of the circulating paper would be a violation of the rights of private property, and that such a measure would render the accession of those states to the system absolutely impracticable. The injustice and pernicious tendency of this disgraceful policy were viewed with great indignation by the states which adhered to the principles of justice. In Rhode Island, the paper money had depreciated to eight for one, and a hundred per cent. with us. The people of Massachusetts and Connecticut had been great sufferers by the dishonesty of Rhode Island, and similar complaints existed against this state. This clause became in some measure a preliminary with the gentlemen who represented the other states. " You have," said they, " by your iniquitous laws and paper emissions shamefully defrauded our citizens. The Confederation pre-

vented our compelling you to do them justice; but before
we confederate with you again, you must not only agree to
be honest, but put it out of your power to be otherwise."
Sir, a member from Rhode Island itself could not have set
his face against such language. The clause was, I believe,
unanimously assented to: it has only a future aspect, and
can by no means have a retrospective operation; and I
trust the principles upon which the Convention proceeded
will meet the approbation of every honest man.

Mr. CABARRUS. Mr. Chairman, I contend that the
clause which prohibits the states from emitting bills of credit
will not affect our present paper money. The clause has no
retrospective view. This Constitution declares, in the most
positive terms, that no *ex post facto* law shall be passed by
the general government. Were this clause to operate retrospectively, it would clearly be *ex post facto*, and repugnant
to the express provision of the Constitution. How, then,
in the name of God, can the Constitution take our paper
money away? If we have contracted for a sum of money,
we ought to pay according to the nature of our contract.
Every honest man will pay in specie who engaged to pay it.
But if we have contracted for a sum of paper money,
it must be clear to every man in this committee, that we
shall pay in paper money. This is a Constitution for the
future government of the United States. It does not look
back. Every gentleman must be satisfied, on the least
reflection, that our paper money will not be destroyed. To
say that it will be destroyed, is a popular argument, but not
founded in fact, in my opinion. I had my doubts, but on
consideration, I am satisfied.

Mr. BLOODWORTH. Mr. Chairman, I beg leave to
ask if the payment of sums now due be *ex post facto*. Will
it be an *ex post facto* law to compel the payment of money
now due in silver coin? If suit be brought in the federal
court against one of our citizens, for a sum of money, will
paper money be received to satisfy the judgment? I inquire
for information; my mind is not yet satisfied. It has been
said that we are to send our own gentlemen to represent us,
and that there is not the least doubt they will put that construction on it which will be most agreeable to the people
they represent. But it behoves us to consider whether they
can do so if they would, when they mix with the body of

Congress.   The Northern States are much more populous than the Southern ones.   To the north of the Susquehannah there are thirty-six representatives, and to the south of it only twenty-nine.   They will always outvote us.   Sir, we ought to be particular in adopting a Constitution which may destroy our currency, when it is to be the supreme law of the land, and prohibits the emission of paper money.   I am not, for my own part, for giving an indefinite power.   Gentlemen of the best abilities differ in the construction of the Constitution.   The members of Congress will differ too.   Human nature is fallible.   I am not for throwing ourselves out of the Union ; but we ought to be cautious by proposing amendments.   The majority in several great adopting states was very trifling.   Several of them have proposed amendments, but not in the mode most satisfactory to my mind. I hope this Convention never will adopt it till the amendments are actually obtained.

Mr. IREDELL.   Mr. Chairman, with respect to this clause, it cannot have the operation contended for.   There is nothing in the Constitution which affects our present paper money.   It prohibits, for the future, the emitting of any, but it does not interfere with the paper money now actually in circulation in several states.   There is an express clause which protects it.   It provides that there shall be no *ex post facto* law.   This would be *ex post facto*, if the construction contended for were right, as has been observed by another gentleman.   If a suit were brought against a man in the federal court, and execution should go against his property, I apprehend he would, under this Constitution, have a right to pay our paper money, there being nothing in the Constitution taking away the validity of it.   Every individual in the United States will keep his eye watchfully over those who administer the general government, and no usurpation of power will be acquiesced in.   The possibility of usurping powers ought not to be objected against it.   Abuse may happen in any government.   The only resource against usurpation is the inherent right of the people to prevent its exercise.   This is the case in all free governments in the world.   The people will resist if the government usurp powers not delegated to it.   We must run the risk of abuse. We must take care to give no more power than is necessary·

but, having given that, we must submit to the possible dangers arising from it.

With respect to the great weight of the Northern States, it will not, on a candid examination, appear so great as the gentleman supposes. At present, the regulation of our representation is merely temporary. Whether greater or less, it will hereafter depend on actual population. The extent of this state is very great, almost equal to that of any state in the Union; and our population will probably be in proportion. To the north of Pennsylvania, there are twenty-seven votes. To the south of Pennsylvania, there are thirty votes, leaving Pennsylvania out. Pennsylvania has eight votes. In the division of what is called the northern and southern interests, Pennsylvania does not appear to be decidedly in either scale. Though there may be a combination of the Northern States, it is not certain that the interests of Pennsylvania will coincide with theirs. If, at any time, she join us, we shall have thirty-eight against twenty-seven. Should she be against us, they will have only thirty-five to thirty. There are two states to the northward, who have, in some respect, a similarity of interests with ourselves. What is the situation of New Jersey? It is, in one respect, similar to ours. Most of the goods they use come through New York, and they pay for the benefit of New York, as we pay for that of Virginia. It is so with Connecticut; so that, in every question between importing and non-importing states, we may expect that two of the Northern States would probably join with North Carolina. It is impossible to destroy altogether this idea of separate interests. But the difference between the states does not appear to me so great as the gentleman imagines; and I beg leave to say, that, in proportion to the increase of population, the Southern States will have greater weight than the Northern, as they have such large quantities of land still uncultivated, which is not so much the case to the north. If we should suffer a small temporary inconvenience, we shall be compensated for it by having the weight of population in our favor in future.

Mr. BLOODWORTH. Mr. Chairman, when I was in Congress, the southern and northern interests divided at Susquehannah. I believe it is so now. The advantage to be gained by future population is no argument at all. Do we gain any thing when the other states have an equality of members in the Senate, notwithstanding the increase of members in the House of Representatives? This is no consequence at all. I am sorry to mention it, but I can produce an instance which will prove the facility of misconstruction. [Here Mr. Bloodworth cited an instance which took place in Congress with respect to the Indian trade, which, not having been distinctly heard, is omitted.]

They may trample on the rights of the people of North Carolina if there be not sufficient guards and checks. I only mentioned this to show that there may be misconstructions, and that, in so important a case as a constitution, every thing ought to be clear and intelligible, and no ground left for disputes.

Mr. CALDWELL. Mr. Chairman, it is very evident that there is a great necessity for perspicuity. In the sweeping clause, there are words which are not plain and evident. It says that " this Constitution, and the laws of the United States which shall be made in pursuance thereof, &c., shall be the supreme law of the land." The word *pursuance* is equivocal and ambiguous ; a plainer word would be better. They may pursue bad as well as good measures, and therefore the word is improper ; it authorizes bad measures. Another thing is remarkable, — that gentlemen, as an answer to every improper part of it, tell us that every thing is to be done by our own representatives, who are to be good men. There is no security that they will be so, or continue to be so. Should they be virtuous when elected, the laws of Congress will be unalterable. These laws must be annihilated by the same body which made them. It appears to me that the laws which they make cannot be altered without calling a convention. [Mr. Caldwell added some reasons for this opinion, but spoke too low to be heard.]

Gov. JOHNSTON. Mr. Chairman, I knew that many gentlemen in this Convention were not perfectly satisfied with every article of this Constitution ; but I did not expect that so many would object to this clause. The Constitution must be the supreme law of the land; otherwise, it would be in the power of any one state to counteract the other states, and withdraw itself from the Union. The laws made in pursuance thereof by Congress ought to be the supreme law of the land ; otherwise, any one state might repeal the laws

of the Union at large.   Without this clause, the whole Constitution would be a piece of blank paper.   Every treaty
should be the supreme law of the land ; without this, any
one state might involve the whole Union in war.   The
worthy member who was last up has started an objection
which I cannot answer.   I do not know a word in the English language so good as the word *pursuance*, to express the
idea meant and intended by the Constitution.   Can any one
understand the sentence any other way than this ?   When
Congress makes a law in virtue of their constitutional
authority, it will be an actual law.   I do not know a more
expressive or a better way of representing the idea by words.
Every law consistent with the Constitution will have been
made in pursuance of the powers granted by it.   Every
usurpation or law repugnant to it cannot have been made in
pursuance of its powers.   The latter will be nugatory and
void.   I am at a loss to know what he means by saying the
laws of the Union will be unalterable.   Are laws as immutable as constitutions ?   Can any thing be more absurd than
assimilating the one to the other ?   The idea is not war
ranted by the Constitution, nor consistent with reason.

Mr. J. M'DOWALL wished to know how the taxes are
to be paid which Congress were to lay in this state.   He
asked if paper money would discharge them.   He calculated
that the taxes would be higher, and did not know how they
could be discharged ; for, says he, every man is to pay so
much more, and the poor man has not the money locked up
in his chest.   He was of opinion that our laws could be repealed entirely by those of Congress.

Mr. MACLAINE.   Mr. Chairman, taxes must be paid in
gold or silver coin, and not in imaginary money.   As to the
subject of taxation, it has been the opinion of many intelligent men that there will be no taxes laid immediately, or, if
any, that they will be very inconsiderable.   There will be no
occasion for it, as proper regulations will raise very large
sums of money.   We know that Congress will have sufficient
power to make such regulations.   The moment that the
Constitution is established, Congress will have credit with
foreign nations.   Our situation being known, they can borrow any sum.   It will be better for them to raise any money
they want at present by borrowing than by taxation.   It is
well known that in this country gold and silver vanish when

paper money is made. When we adopt, if ever, gold and silver will again appear in circulation. People will not let their hard money go, because they know that paper money cannot repay it. After the war, we had more money in gold and silver, in circulation, than we have nominal money now. Suppose Congress wished to raise a million of money more than the imposts. Suppose they borrow it. They can easily borrow it in Europe at four per cent. The interest of that sum will be but £40,000. So that the people, instead of having the whole £1,000,000 to pay, will have but £40,000 to pay, which will hardly be felt. The proportion of £40,000 for this state would be a trifle. In seven years' time, the people would be able, by only being obliged to pay the interest annually, to save money, and pay the whole principal, perhaps, afterwards, without much difficulty. Congress will not lay a single tax when it is not to the advantage of the people at large. The western lands will also be a considerable fund. The sale of them will aid the revenue greatly, and we have reason to believe the impost will be productive.

Mr. J. M'DOWALL. Mr. Chairman, instead of reasons and authorities to convince me, assertions are made. Many respectable gentlemen are satisfied that the taxes will be higher. By what authority does the gentleman say that the impost will be productive, when our trade is come to nothing? Sir, borrowing money is detrimental and ruinous to nations. The interest is lost money. We have been obliged to borrow money to pay interest! We have no way of paying additional and extraordinary sums. The people cannot stand them. I should be extremely sorry to live under a government which the people could not understand, and which it would require the greatest abilities to understand. It ought to be plain and easy to the meanest capacity. What would be the consequence of ambiguity? It may raise animosity and revolutions, and involve us in bloodshed. It becomes us to be extremely cautious.

Mr. MACLAINE. Mr. Chairman, I would ask the gentleman what is the state of our trade. I do not pretend to a very great knowledge in trade, but I know something of it. If our trade be in a low situation, it must be the effect of our present weak government. I really believe that Congress will be able to raise almost what sums they please by

the impost.   I know it will, though the gentleman may call
it assertion.   I am not unacquainted with the territory or
resources of this country.   The resources, under proper regulations, are very great.   In the course of a few years, we
can raise money without borrowing a single shilling.   It is
not disgraceful to borrow money.   The richest nations have
recurred to loans on some emergencies.   I believe, as much
as I do in my existence, that Congress will have it in their
power to borrow money if our government be such as people
can depend upon.   They have been able to borrow now
under the present feeble system.   If so, can there be any
doubt of their being able to do it under a respectable government?

Mr. M'DOWALL replied, that our trade was on a contemptible footing; that it was come almost to nothing, and
lower in North Carolina than any where; that therefore little could be expected from the impost.

Mr. J. GALLOWAY.   Mr. Chairman, I should make no
objection to this clause were the powers granted by the Constitution sufficiently defined; for I am clearly of opinion that
it is absolutely necessary for every government, and especially for a general government, that its laws should be the
supreme law of the land.   But I hope the gentlemen of the
committee will advert to the 10th section of the 1st article.
This is a negative which the Constitution of our own state
does not impose upon us.   I wish the committee to attend
to that part of it which provides that no state shall pass
any law which will impair the obligation of contracts.   Our
public securities are at a low ebb, and have been so for many
years.   We well know that this country has taken those securities as specie.   This hangs over our heads as a contract.   There is a million and a half in circulation at least.
That clause of the Constitution may compel us to make
good the nominal value of these securities.   I trust this
country never will leave it to the hands of the general government to redeem the securities which they have already
given.   Should this be the case, the consequence will be,
that they will be purchased by speculators, when the citizens
will part with them, perhaps for a very trifling consideration.
Those speculators will look at the Constitution, and see that
they will be paid in gold and silver.   They will buy them
at a half-crown in the pound, and get the full nominal value

for them in gold and silver.   I therefore wish the committee to consider whether North Carolina can redeem those securities in the manner most agreeable to her citizens, and justifiable to the world, if this Constitution be adopted.

Mr. DAVIE. Mr. Chairman, I believe neither the 10th section, cited by the gentleman, nor any other part of the Constitution, has vested the general government with power to interfere with the public securities of any state. I will venture to say that the last thing which the general government will attempt to do will be this. They have nothing to do with it. The clause refers merely to contracts between individuals. That section is the best in the Constitution. It is founded on the strongest principles of justice. It is a section, in short, which I thought would have endeared the Constitution to this country. When the worthy gentleman comes to consider, he will find that the general government cannot possibly interfere with such securities. How can it? It has no negative clause to that effect. Where is there a negative clause, operating negatively on the states themselves? It cannot operate retrospectively, for this would be repugnant to its own express provisions. It will be left to ourselves to redeem them as we please. We wished we could put it on the shoulders of Congress, but could not. Securities may be higher, but never less. I conceive, sir, that this is a very plain case, and that it must appear perfectly clear to the committee that the gentleman's alarms are groundless.

WEDNESDAY, *July* 30, 1788.

The last clause of the 6th article read.

Mr. HENRY ABBOT, after a short exordium, which was not distinctly heard, proceeded thus: Some are afraid, Mr. Chairman, that, should the Constitution be received, they would be deprived of the privilege of worshipping God according to their consciences, which would be taking from them a benefit they enjoy under the present constitution. They wish to know if their religious and civil liberties be secured under this system, or whether the general government may not make laws infringing their religious liberties. The worthy member from Edenton mentioned sundry political reasons why treaties should be the supreme law of the land. It is feared, by some people, that, by the power of making treaties, they might make a treaty engaging with foreign powers to adopt the Roman Catholic religion in the United States, which would prevent the people from worshipping God according to their own consciences. The worthy member from Halifax has in some measure satisfied my mind on this subject. But others may be dissatisfied. Many wish to know what *religion* shall be established. I believe a majority of the community are Presbyterians. I am, for my part, against any exclusive establishment; but if there were any, I would prefer the Episcopal. The exclusion of religious tests is by many thought dangerous and impolitic. They suppose that if there be no religious test required, pagans, deists, and Mahometans might obtain offices among us, and that the senators and representatives might all be pagans. Every person employed by the general and state governments is to take an oath to support the former. Some are desirous to know how and by whom they are to swear, since no religious tests are required — whether they are to swear by Jupiter, Juno, Minerva, Proserpine, or Pluto. We ought to be suspicious of our liberties. We have felt the effects of oppressive measures, and know the happy consequences of being jealous of our rights. I would be glad some gentleman would endeavor to obviate these objections, in order to satisfy the religious part of the society. Could I be convinced that the objections were well founded, I would then declare my opinion against the Constitution. [Mr. Abbot added several other observations, but spoke too low to be heard.]

Mr. IREDELL. Mr. Chairman, nothing is more desirable than to remove the scruples of any gentleman on this interesting subject. Those concerning religion are entitled to particular respect. I did not expect any objection to this particular regulation, which, in my opinion, is calculated to prevent evils of the most pernicious consequences to society. Every person in the least conversant in the history of mankind, knows what dreadful mischiefs have been committed by religious persecutions. Under the color of religious tests, the utmost cruelties have been exercised. Those in power have generally considered all wisdom centred in themselves; that they alone had a right to dictate to the rest of mankind; and that all opposition to their tenets was profane and impious. The consequence of this intolerant spirit had been, that each church has in turn set itself up against every other ; and persecutions and wars of the most implacable and bloody nature have taken place in every part of the world. America has set an example to mankind to think more modestly and reasonably — that a man may be of different religious sentiments from our own, without being a bad member of society. The principles of toleration, to the honor of this age, are doing away those errors and prejudices which have so long prevailed, even in the most intolerant countries. In the Roman Catholic countries, principles of moderation are adopted which would have been spurned at a century or two ago. I should be sorry to find, when examples of toleration are set even by arbitrary governments, that this country, so impressed with the highest sense of liberty, should adopt principles on this subject that were narrow and illiberal.

I consider the clause under consideration as one of the strongest proofs that could be adduced, that it was the intention of those who formed this system to establish a general religious liberty in America. Were we to judge from the examples of religious tests in other countries, we should be persuaded that they do not answer the purpose for which they are intended. What is the consequence of such in England ? In that country no man can be a member in the House of Commons, or hold any office under the crown, without taking the sacrament according to the rites of the Church. This, in the first instance, must degrade and profane a rite which never ought to be taken but from a sincere principle of devotion. To a man of base principles, it is made a mere instrument of civil policy. The intention was, to exclude all persons from offices but the members of the Church of England. Yet it is notorious that dissenters qualify themselves for offices in this manner, though they never conform to the Church on any other occasion ; and men of no religion at all have no scruple to make use of this qualification. It never was known that a man who had no principles of religion hesitated to perform any rite when it was convenient for his private interest. No test can bind such a one. I am therefore clearly of opinion that such a discrimination would neither be effectual for its own purposes, nor, if it could, ought it by any means to be made. Upon the principles I have stated, I confess the restriction on the power of Congress, in this particular, has my hearty approbation. They certainly have no authority to interfere in the establishment of any religion whatsoever; and I am astonished that any gentleman should conceive they have. Is there any power given to Congress in matters of religion? Can they pass a single act to impair our religious liberties? If they could, it would be a just cause of alarm. If they could, sir, no man would have more horror against it than myself. Happily, no sect here is superior to another. As long as this is the case, we shall be free from those persecutions and distractions with which other countries have been torn. If any future Congress should pass an act concerning the religion of the country, it would be an act which they are not authorized to pass, by the Constitution, and which the people would not obey. Every one would ask, "Who authorized the government to pass such an act? It is not warranted by the Constitution, and is barefaced usurpation." The power to make treaties can never be supposed to include a right to establish a foreign religion among ourselves, though it might authorize a toleration of others.

But it is objected that the people of America may, perhaps, choose representatives who have no religion at all, and that pagans and Mahometans may be admitted into offices. But how is it possible to exclude any set of men, without taking away that principle of religious freedom which we ourselves so warmly contend for? This is the foundation on which persecution has been raised in every part of the world. The people in power were always right, and every body else wrong. If you admit the least difference, the door to persecution is opened. Nor would it answer the purpose, for the worst part of the excluded sects would comply with the test, and the best men only be kept out of our counsels. But it is never to be supposed that the people of America will trust their dearest rights to persons who have no religion at all, or a religion materially different from their own. It would be happy for mankind if religion was permitted to take its own course, and maintain itself by the excellence of its own doctrines. The divine Author of our religion never wished for its support by worldly authority. Has he not said that the gates of hell shall not prevail against it? It made much greater progress for itself, than when supported by the greatest authority upon earth.

It has been asked by that respectable gentleman (Mr

Abbot) what is the meaning of that part, where it is said that the United States shall *guaranty* to every state in the Union a republican form of government, and why a *guaranty* of religious freedom was not included. The meaning of the guaranty provided was this : There being thirteen governments confederated upon a republican principle, it was essential to the existence and harmony of the confederacy that each should be a republican government, and that no state should have a right to establish an aristocracy or monarchy. That clause was therefore inserted to prevent any state from establishing any government but a republican one. Every one must be convinced of the mischief that would ensue, if any state had a right to change its government to a monarchy. If a monarchy was established in any one state, it would endeavor to subvert the freedom of the others, and would, probably, by degrees succeed in it. This must strike the mind of every person here, who recollects the history of Greece, when she had confederated governments. The king of Macedon, by his arts and intrigues, got himself admitted a member of the Amphictyonic council, which was the superintending government of the Grecian republics ; and in a short time he became master of them all. It is, then, necessary that the members of a confederacy should have similar governments. But consistently with this restriction, the states may make what change in their own governments they think proper. Had Congress undertaken to guaranty religious freedom, or any particular species of it, they would then have had a pretence to interfere in a subject they have nothing to do with. Each state, so far as the clause in question does not interfere, must be left to the operation of its own principles.

There is a degree of jealousy which it is impossible to satisfy. Jealousy in a free government ought to be respected ; but it may be carried to too great an extent. It is impracticable to guard against all possible danger of people's choosing their officers indiscreetly. If they have a right to choose, they may make a bad choice.

I met, by accident, with a pamphlet, this morning, in which the author states, as a very serious danger, that the pope of Rome might be elected President. I confess this never struck me before ; and if the author had read all the qualifications of a President, perhaps his fears might have

been quieted.   No man but a native, or who has resided fourteen years in America, can be chosen President.   I know
not all the qualifications for pope, but I believe he must be
taken from the college of cardinals ; and probably there are
many previous steps necessary before he arrives at this dignity.   A native of America must have very singular good
fortune, who, after residing fourteen years in his own country,
should go to Europe, enter into Romish orders, obtain the
promotion of cardinal, afterwards that of pope, and at length
be so much in the confidence of his own country as to be
elected President.   It would be still more extraordinary if
he should give up his popedom for our presidency.   Sir, it is
impossible to treat such idle fears with any degree of gravity.
Why is it not objected, that there is no provision in the Constitution against electing one of the kings of Europe President ?   It would be a clause equally rational and judicious.

I hope that I have in some degree satisfied the doubts of
the gentleman.   This article is calculated to secure universal religious liberty, by putting all sects on a level — the only
way to prevent persecution.   I thought nobody would have
objected to this clause, which deserves, in my opinion, the
highest approbation.   This country has already had the
honor of setting an example of civil freedom, and I trust it
will likewise have the honor of teaching the rest of the world
the way to religious freedom also.   God grant both may be
perpetuated to the end of time !

Mr. ABBOT, after expressing his obligations for the explanation which had been given, observed that no answer
had been given to the question he put concerning the form
of an *oath*.

Mr. IREDELL.   Mr. Chairman, I beg pardon for having
omitted to take notice of that part which the worthy gentleman has mentioned.   It was by no means from design, but
from its having escaped my memory, as I have not the conveniency of taking notes.   I shall now satisfy him in that
particular in the best manner in my power.

According to the modern definition of an oath, it is considered a "solemn appeal to the Supreme Being, for the truth
of what is said, by a person who believes in the existence of
a Supreme Being and in a future state of rewards and punishments, according to that form which will bind his conscience most."   It was long held that no oath could be

administered but upon the New Testament, except to a Jew, who was allowed to swear upon the Old. According to this notion, none but Jews and Christians could take an oath; and heathens were altogether excluded. At length, by the operation of principles of toleration, these narrow notions were done away. Men at length considered that there were many virtuous men in the world who had not had an opportunity of being instructed either in the Old or New Testament, who yet very sincerely believed in a Supreme Being, and in a future state of rewards and punishments. It is well known that many nations entertain this belief who do not believe either in the Jewish or Christian religion. Indeed, there are few people so grossly ignorant or barbarous as to have no religion at all. And if none but Christians or Jews could be examined upon oath, many innocent persons might suffer for want of the testimony of others. In regard to the form of an oath, that ought to be governed by the religion of the person taking it. I remember to have read an instance which happened in England, I believe in the time of Charles II. A man who was a material witness in a cause, refused to swear upon the book, and was admitted to swear with his uplifted hand. The jury had a difficulty in crediting him; but the chief justice told them, he had, in his opinion, taken as strong an oath as any of the other witnesses, though, had he been to swear himself, he should have kissed the book. A very remarkable instance also happened in England, about forty years ago, of a person who was admitted to take an oath according to the rites of his own country, though he was a heathen. He was an East Indian, who had a great suit in chancery, and his answer upon oath to a bill filed against him was absolutely necessary. Not believing either in the Old or New Testament, he could not be sworn in the accustomed manner, but was sworn according to the form of the Gentoo religion, which he professed, by touching the foot of a priest. It appeared that, according to the tenets of this religion, its members believed in a Supreme Being, and in a future state of rewards and punishments. It was accordingly held by the judges, upon great consideration, that the oath ought to be received; they considering that it was probable those of that religion were equally bound in conscience by an oath according to their form of swearing, as they themselves were by one of theirs; and that it would be a reproach to the justice of the country, if a man, merely because he was of a different religion from their own, should be denied redress of an injury he had sustained. Ever since this great case, it has been universally considered that, in administering an oath, it is only necessary to inquire if the person who is to take it, believes in a Supreme Being, and in a future state of rewards and punishments. If he does, the oath is to be administered according to that form which it is supposed will bind his conscience most. It is, however, necessary that such a belief should be entertained, because otherwise there would be nothing to bind his conscience that could be relied on; since there are many cases where the terror of punishment in this world for perjury could not be dreaded. I have endeavored to satisfy the committee. We may, I think, very safely leave religion to itself; and as to the form of the oath, I think this may well be trusted to the general government, to be applied on the principles I have mentioned.

Gov. JOHNSTON expressed great astonishment that the people were alarmed on the subject of religion. This, he said, must have arisen from the great pains which had been taken to prejudice men's minds against the Constitution. He begged leave to add the following few observations to what had been so ably said by the gentleman last up.

I read the Constitution over and over, but could not see one cause of apprehension or jealousy on this subject. When I heard there were apprehensions that the pope of Rome could be the President of the United States, I was greatly astonished. It might as well be said that the king of England or France, or the Grand Turk, could be chosen to that office. It would have been as good an argument. It appears to me that it would have been dangerous, if Congress could intermeddle with the subject of religion. True religion is derived from a much higher source than human laws. When any attempt is made, by any government, to restrain men's consciences, no good consequence can possibly follow. It is apprehended that Jews, Mahometans, pagans, &c., may be elected to high offices under the government of the United States. Those who are Mahometans, or any others who are not professors of the Christian religion, can never be elected to the office of President, or other high office, but in one of two cases. First, if the people of America lay aside the Christian religion altogether, it may happen.   Should this unfortunately take place, the people will choose such men as think as they do themselves. Another case is, if any persons of such descriptions should, notwithstanding their religion, acquire the confidence and esteem of the people of America by their good conduct and practice of virtue, they may be chosen.   I leave it to gentlemen's candor to judge what probability there is of the people's choosing men of different sentiments from themselves.

But great apprehensions have been raised as to the influence of the Eastern States.   When you attend to circumstances, this will have no weight.   I know but two or three states where there is the least chance of establishing any particular religion.   The people of Massachusetts and Connecticut are mostly Presbyterians.   In every other state, the people are divided into a great number of sects.   In Rhode Island, the tenets of the Baptists, I believe, prevail.   In New York, they are divided very much : the most numerous are the Episcopalians and the Baptists.   In New Jersey, they are as much divided as we are.   In Pennsylvania, if any sect prevails more than others, it is that of the Quakers. In Maryland, the Episcopalians are most numerous, though there are other sects.   In Virginia, there are many sects ; you all know what their religious sentiments are.   So in all the Southern States they differ ; as also in New Hampshire. I hope, therefore, that gentlemen will see there is no cause of fear that any one religion shall be exclusively established.

Mr. CALDWELL thought that some danger might arise. He imagined it might be objected to in a political as well as in a religious view.   In the first place, he said, there was an invitation for Jews and pagans of every kind to come among us.   At some future period, said he, this might endanger the character of the United States.   Moreover, even those who do not regard religion, acknowledge that the Christian religion is best calculated, of all religions, to make good members of society, on account of its morality.   I think, then, added he, that, in a political view, those gentlemen who formed this Constitution should not have given this invitation to Jews and heathens.   All those who have any religion are against the emigration of those people from the eastern hemisphere.

Mr SPENCER was an advocate for securing every unalienable right, and that of worshipping God according to the dictates of conscience in particular. He therefore thought that no one particular religion should be established. Religious tests, said he, have been the foundation of persecutions in all countries. Persons who are conscientious will not take the oath required by religious tests, and will therefore be excluded from offices, though equally capable of discharging them as any member of the society. It is feared, continued he, that persons of bad principles, deists, atheists, &c., may come into this country; and there is nothing to restrain them from being eligible to offices. He asked if it was reasonable to suppose that the people would choose men without regarding their characters. Mr. Spencer then continued thus: Gentlemen urge that the want of a test admits the most vicious characters to offices. I desire to know what test could bind them. If they were of such principles, it would not keep them from enjoying those offices. On the other hand, it would exclude from offices conscientious and truly religious people, though equally capable as others. Conscientious persons would not take such an oath, and would be therefore excluded. This would be a great cause of objection to a religious test. But in this case, as there is not a religious test required, it leaves religion on the solid foundation of its own inherent validity, without any connection with temporal authority; and no kind of oppression can take place. I confess it strikes me so. I am sorry to differ from the worthy gentleman. I cannot object to this part of the Constitution. I wish every other part was as good and proper.

Gov. JOHNSTON approved of the worthy member's candor. He admitted a possibility of Jews, pagans, &c., emigrating to the United States; yet, he said, they could not be in proportion to the emigration of Christians who should come from other countries; that, in all probability, the children even of such people would be Christians; and that this, with the rapid population of the United States, their zeal for religion, and love of liberty, would, he trusted, add to the progress of the Christian religion among us.

The 7th article read without any objection against it.

Gov. JOHNSTON, after a short speech, which was not distinctly heard, made a motion to the following effect —

That this committee, having fully deliberated on the Constitution proposed for the future government of the United States of America, by the Federal Convention lately held at Philadelphia, on the 17th day of September last, and having taken into their serious consideration the present critical situation of America, which induces them to be of opinion, that though certain amendments to the said Constitution may be wished for, yet that those amendments should be proposed subsequent to the ratification on the part of this state, and not previous to it, — they therefore recommend that the Convention do ratify the Constitution, and at the same time propose amendments, to take place in one of the modes prescribed by the Constitution.

Mr. LENOIR. Mr. Chairman, I conceive that I shall not be out of order to make some observations on this last part of the system, and take some retrospective view of some other parts of it. I think it not proper for our adoption, as I consider that it endangers our liberties. When we consider this system collectively, we must be surprised to think that any set of men, who were delegated to amend the Confederation, should propose to annihilate it; for that and this system are utterly different, and cannot exist together. It has been said that the fullest confidence should be put in those characters who formed this Constitution. We will admit them, in private and public transactions, to be good characters. But, sir, it appears to me, and every other member of this committee, that they exceeded their powers. Those gentlemen had no sort of power to form a new constitution altogether; neither had the citizens of this country such an idea in their view. I cannot undertake to say what principles actuated them. I must conceive they were mistaken in their politics, and that this system does not secure the unalienable rights of freemen. It has some aristocratical and some monarchical features, and perhaps some of them intended the establishment of one of these governments. Whatever might be their intent, according to my views, it will lead to the most dangerous aristocracy that ever was thought of — an aristocracy established on a constitutional bottom! I conceive (and I believe most of this committee will likewise) that this is so dangerous, that I should like as well to have no constitution at all. Their powers are almost unlimited.

A constitution ought to be understood by every one. The most humble and trifling characters in the country have a right to know what foundation they stand upon. I confess I do not see the end of the powers here proposed, nor

VOL. IV.   26

the reasons for granting them. The principal end of a constitution is to set forth what must be given up for the community at large, and to secure those rights which ought never to be infringed. The proposed plan secures no right ; or, if it does, it is in so vague and undeterminate a manner, that we do not understand it. My constituents instructed me to oppose the adoption of this Constitution. The principal reasons are as follow : The right of representation is not fairly and explicitly preserved to the people, it being easy to evade that privilege as provided in this system, and the terms of election being too long. If our General Assembly be corrupt, at the end of the year we can make new men of them by sending others in their stead. It is not so here. If there be any reason to think that human nature is corrupt, and that there is a disposition in men to aspire to power, they may embrace an opportunity, during their long continuance in office, by means of their powers, to take away the rights of the people. The senators are chosen for six years, and two thirds of them, with the President, have most extensive powers. They may enter into a dangerous combination. And they may be continually reëlected. The President may be as good a man as any in existence, but he is but a man. He may be corrupt. He has an opportunity of forming plans dangerous to the community at large. I shall not enter into the *minutiæ* of this system, but I conceive, whatever may have been the intention of its framers, that it leads to a most dangerous aristocracy. It appears to me that, instead of securing the sovereignty of the states, it is calculated to melt them down into one solid empire. If the citizens of this state like a consolidated government, I hope they will have virtue enough to secure their rights. I am sorry to make use of the expression, but it appears to me to be a scheme to reduce this government to an aristocracy. It guaranties a republican form of government to the states ; when all these powers are in Congress, it will only be a form. It will be past recovery, when Congress has the power of the purse and the sword. The power of the sword is in explicit terms given to it. The power of direct taxation gives the purse. They may prohibit the trial by jury, which is a most sacred and valuable right. There is nothing contained in this Constitution to bar them from it. The federal courts have also appellate cognizance of law and fact ; the sole cause of which is to deprive the people of that trial, which it is optional in them to grant or not. We find no provision against infringement on the rights of conscience. Ecclesiastical courts may be established, which will be destructive to our citizens. They may make any establishment they think proper. They have also an exclusive legislation in their ten miles square, to which may be added their power over the militia, who may be carried thither and kept there for life. Should any one grumble at their acts, he would be deemed a traitor, and perhaps taken up and carried to the exclusive legislation, and there tried without a jury. We are told there is no cause to fear. When we consider the great powers of Congress, there is great cause of alarm. They can disarm the militia. If they were armed, they would be a resource against great oppressions. The laws of a great empire are difficult to be executed. If the laws of the Union were oppressive, they could not carry them into effect, if the people were possessed of proper means of defence.

It was cried out that we were in a most desperate situation, and that Congress could not discharge any of their most sacred contracts. I believe it to be the case. But why give more power than is necessary? The men who went to the Federal Convention went for the express purpose of amending the government, by giving it such additional powers as were necessary. If we should accede to this system, it may be thought proper, by a few designing persons, to destroy it, in a future age, in the same manner that the old system is laid aside. The Confederation was binding on all the states. It could not be destroyed but with the consent of all the states. There was an express article to that purpose. The men who were deputed to the Convention, instead of amending the old, as they were solely empowered and directed to do, proposed a new system. If the best characters departed so far from their authority, what may not be apprehended from others, who may be agents in the new government?

It is natural for men to aspire to power — it is the nature of mankind to be tyrannical; therefore it is necessary for us to secure our rights and liberties as far as we can. But it is asked why we should suspect men who are to be chosen by ourselves, while it is their interest to act justly, and while

men have self-interest at heart.   I think the reasons which
I have given are sufficient to answer that question.   We
ought to consider the depravity of human nature, the predominant thirst of power which is in the breast of every
one, the temptations our rulers may have, and the unlimited
confidence placed in them by this system.   These are the
foundation of my fears.   They would be so long in the general government that they would forget the grievances of
the people of the states.

But it is said we shall be ruined if separated from the
other states, which will be the case if we do not adopt.   If
so, I would put less confidence in those states.   The states
are all bound together by the Confederation, and the rest
cannot break from us without violating the most solemn
compact.   If they break that, they will this.

But it is urged that we ought to adopt, because so many
other states have.   In those states which have patronized
and ratified it, many great men have opposed it.   The motives of those states I know not.   It is the goodness of the
Constitution we are to examine.   We are to exercise our
own judgments, and act independently.   And as I conceive
we are not out of the Union, I hope this Constitution will
not be adopted till amendments are made.   Amendments
are wished for by the other states.   It was urged here that the
President should have power to grant reprieves and pardons.
This power is necessary with proper restrictions.   But the
President may be at the head of a combination against the
rights of the people, and may reprieve or pardon the whole.
It is answered to this, that he cannot pardon in cases of
impeachment.   What is the punishment in such cases?
Only removal from office and future disqualification.   It
does not touch life or property.   He has power to do away
punishment in every other case.   It is too unlimited, in my
opinion.   It may be exercised to the public good, but may
also be perverted to a different purpose.   Should we get
those who will attend to our interest, we should be safe
under any Constitution, or without any.   If we send men
of a different disposition, we shall be in danger.   Let us
give them only such powers as are necessary for the good of
the community.

The President has other great powers.   He has the nomination of all officers, and a qualified negative on the laws

He may delay the wheels of government. He may drive the Senate to concur with his proposal. He has other extensive powers. There is no assurance of the liberty of the press. They may make it treason to write against the most arbitrary proceedings. They have power to control our elections as much as they please. It may be very oppressive on this state, and all the Southern States.

Much has been said of taxation, and the inequality of it on the states. But nothing has been said of the mode of furnishing men. In what proportion are the states to furnish men? Is it in proportion to the whites and blacks? I presume it is. This state has one hundred thousand blacks. By this Constitution, fifty negroes are equal to thirty whites. This state, therefore, besides the proportion she must raise for her white people, must furnish an additional number for her blacks, in proportion as thirty is to fifty. Suppose there be a state to the northward that has sixty thousand persons; this state must furnish as many men for the blacks as that whole state, exclusive of those she must furnish for her whites. Slaves, instead of strengthening, weaken the state; the regulation, therefore, will greatly injure it, and the other Southern States. There is another clause which I do not, perhaps, understand. The power of taxation seems to me not to extend to the lands of the people of the United States; for the rule of taxation is the number of the whites and three fifths of the blacks. Should it be the case that they have no power of taxing this object, must not direct taxation be hard upon the greater part of this state? I am not confident that it is so, but it appears to me that they cannot lay taxes on this object. This will oppress the poor people who have large families of whites, and no slaves to assist them in cultivating the soil, although the taxes are to be laid in proportion to three fifths of the negroes, and all the whites. Another disadvantage to this state will arise from it. This state has made a contract with its citizens. The public securities and certificates I allude to. These may be negotiated to men who live in other states. Should that be the case, these gentlemen will have demands against this state on that account. The Constitution points out the mode of recovery; it must be in the federal court only, because controversies between a state and the citizens of another state are cognizable only in the federal courts.

18

They cannot be paid but in gold and silver. Actual specie will be recovered in that court. This would be an intolerable grievance without remedy.

I wish not to be so understood as to be so averse to this system, as that I should object to all parts of it, or attempt to reflect on the reputation of those gentlemen who formed it; though it appears to me that I would not have agreed to any proposal but the amendment of the Confederation. If there were any security for the liberty of the people, I would, for my own part, agree to it. But in this case, as millions yet unborn are concerned, and deeply interested in our decision, I would have the most positive and pointed security. I shall therefore hope that, before this house will proceed to adopt this Constitution, they will propose such amendments to it as will make it complete; and when amendments are adopted, perhaps I will be as ready to accede to it as any man. One thing will make it aristocratical. Its powers are very indefinite. There was a very necessary clause in the Confederation, which is omitted in this system. That was a clause declaring that every power, &c., not given to Congress, was reserved to the states. The omission of this clause makes the power so much greater. Men will naturally put the fullest construction on the power given them. Therefore lay all restraint on them, and form a plan to be understood by every gentleman of this committee, and every individual of the community.

Mr. SPAIGHT. Mr. Chairman, I am one of those who formed this Constitution. The gentleman says, we exceeded our powers. I deny the charge. We were sent with a full power to amend the existing system. This involved every power to make every alteration necessary to meliorate and render it perfect. It cannot be said that we arrogated powers altogether inconsistent with the object of our delegation. There is a clause which expressly provides for future amendments, and it is still in your power. What the Convention has done is a mere proposal. It was found impossible to improve the old system without changing its very form; for by that system the three great branches of government are blended together. All will agree that the concession of a power to a government so constructed is dangerous. The proposing a new system, to be established by the assent and ratification of nine states, arose from the necessity of the case. It was thought extremely hard that one state, or even three or four states, should be able to prevent necessary alterations. The very refractory conduct of Rhode Island, in uniformly opposing every wise and judicious measure, taught us how impolitic it would be to put the general welfare in the power of a few members of the Union. It was, therefore, thought by the Convention, that, if so great a majority as nine states should adopt it, it would be right to establish it. It was recommended by Congress to the state legislatures to refer it to the people of their different states. Our Assembly has confirmed what they have done, by proposing it to the consideration of the people. It was there, and not here, that the objection should have been made. This Convention is therefore to consider the Constitution, and whether it be proper for the government of the people of America; and had it been proposed by any one individual, under these circumstances, it would be right to consider whether it be good or bad. The gentleman has insinuated that this Constitution, instead of securing our liberties, is a scheme to enslave us. He has produced no proof, but rests it on his bare assertion — an assertion which I am astonished to hear, after the ability with which every objection has been fully and clearly refuted in the course of our debates. I am, for my part, conscious of having had nothing in view but the liberty and happiness of my country; and I believe every member of that Convention was actuated by motives equally sincere and patriotic.

He says that it will tend to aristocracy. Where is the aristocratical part of it? It is ideal. I always thought that an aristocracy was that government where the few governed the many, or where the rulers were hereditary. This is a very different government from that. I never read of such an aristocracy. The first branch are representatives chosen freely by the people at large. This must be allowed upon all hands to be democratical. The next is the Senate, chosen by the people, in a secondary manner, through the medium of their delegates in the legislature. This cannot be aristocratical. They are chosen for six years, but one third of them go out every second year, and are responsible to the state legislatures. The President is elected for four years. By whom? By those who are elected in such manner as the state legislatures think proper. I hope the gentleman will not pretend to call this an aristocratical feature. The privilege of representation is secured in the most positive and unequivocal terms, and cannot be evaded. The gentleman has again brought on the trial by jury. The Federal Convention, sir, had no wish to destroy the trial by jury. It was three or four days before them. There were a variety of objections to any one mode. It was thought impossible to fall upon any one mode but/what would produce some inconveniences. I cannot now recollect all the reasons given. Most of them have been amply detailed by other gentlemen here. I should suppose that, if the representatives of twelve states, with many able lawyers among them, could not form any unexceptionable mode, this Convention could hardly be able to do it. As to the subject of religion, I thought what had been said would fully satisfy that gentleman and every other. No power is given to the general government to interfere with it at all. Any act of Congress on this subject would be a usurpation.

No sect is preferred to another. Every man has a right to worship the Supreme Being in the manner he thinks proper. No test is required. All men of equal capacity and integrity, are equally eligible to offices. Temporal violence might make mankind wicked, but never religious. A test would enable the prevailing sect to persecute the rest. I do not suppose an infidel, or any such person, will ever be chosen to any office, unless the people themselves be of the same opinion. He says that Congress may establish ecclesiastical courts. I do not know what part of the Constitution warrants that assertion. It is impossible. No such power is given them. The gentleman advises such amendments as would satisfy him, and proposes a mode of amending before ratifying. If we do not adopt first, we are no more a part of the Union than any foreign power. It will be also throwing away the influence of our state to propose amendments as the condition of our ratification. If we adopt first, our representatives will have a proportionable weight in bringing about amendments, which will not be the case if we do not adopt. It is adopted by ten states already. The question, then, is, not whether the Constitution be good, but whether we will or will not confederate with the other states. The gentleman supposes that the liberty of the press is not secured. The Constitution does not take it away.

It says nothing of it, and can do nothing to injure it. But it is secured by the constitution of every state in the Union in the most ample manner.

He objects to giving the government exclusive legislation in a district not exceeding ten miles square, although the previous consent and cession of the state within which it may be, is required. Is it to be supposed that the representatives of the people will make regulations therein dangerous to liberty? Is there the least color or pretext for saying that the militia will be carried and kept there for life? Where is there any power to do this? The power of calling forth the militia is given for the common defence; and can we suppose that our own representatives, chosen for so short a period, will dare to pervert a power, given for the general protection, to an absolute oppression? But the gentleman has gone farther, and says, that any man who will complain of their oppressions, or write against their usurpation, may be deemed a traitor, and tried as such in the ten miles square, without a jury. What an astonishing misrepresentation! Why did not the gentleman look at the Constitution, and see their powers? Treason is there defined. It says, expressly, that treason against the United States shall consist only in levying war against them, or in adhering to their enemies, giving them aid and comfort. Complaining, therefore, or writing, cannot be treason. [Here Mr. Lenoir rose, and said he meant misprision of treason.] The same reasons hold against that too. The liberty of the press being secured, creates an additional security. Persons accused cannot be tried without a jury; for the same article provides that "the trial of all crimes shall be by jury." They cannot be carried to the ten miles square; for the same clause adds, "and such trial shall be held in the state where the said crimes shall have been committed." He has made another objection, that land might not be taxed, and the other taxes might fall heavily on the poor people. Congress has a power to lay taxes, and no article is exempted or excluded. The proportion of each state may be raised in the most convenient manner. The census or enumeration provided is meant for the salvation and benefit of the Southern States. It was mentioned that land ought to be the only object of taxation. As an acre of land in the Northern States is worth many acres in the Southern States, this would have greatly

oppressed the latter.   It was then judged that the number
of people, as therein provided, was the best criterion for fixing the proportion of each state, and that proportion in each
state to be raised in the most easy manner for the people.
But he has started another objection, which I never heard
before — that Congress may call for men in proportion to the
number of negroes.   The article with respect to requisitions
of men is entirely done away.   Men are to be raised by
bounty.   Suppose it had not been done away.   The Eastern
States could not impose on us a man for every black.   It
was not the case during the war, nor ever could be.   But the
quotas of men are entirely done away.

Another objection which he makes is, that the federal
courts will have cognizance of contracts between this state
and citizens of another state; and that public securities,
negotiated by our citizens to those of other states, will be
recoverable in specie in those courts against this state.
They cannot be negotiated.   What do these certificates say?
Merely that the person therein named shall, for a particular
service, receive so much money.   They are not negotiable.
The money must be demanded for them in the name of those
therein mentioned.   No other person has a right.   There
can be no danger. therefore, in this respect.   The gentleman has made several other objections; but they have been
so fully answered and clearly refuted by several gentlemen in
the course of the debates, that I shall pass them by unnoticed.
I cannot, however, conclude without observing that I am
amazed he should call the powers of the general government
indefinite.   It is the first time I heard the objection.   I will
venture to say they are better defined than the powers of
any government he ever heard of.

Mr. J. M'DOWALL.   Mr. Chairman, I was in hopes
that amendments would have been brought forward to the
Constitution before the idea of adopting it had been thought
of or proposed.   From the best information, there is a great
proportion of the people in the adopting states averse to it as
it stands.   I collect my information from respectable authority.   I know the necessity of a federal government.   I therefore wish this was one in which our liberties and privileges
were secured; for I consider the Union as the rock of our
political salvation.   I am for the strongest federal government.   A bill of rights ought to have been inserted, to ascertain our most valuable and unalienable rights.

The 1st clause of the 4th section gives the Congress an unlimited power over elections. This matter was not cleared up to my satisfaction. They have full power to alter it from one time of the year to another, so as that it shall be impossible for the people to attend. They may fix the time in winter, and the place at Edenton, when the weather will be so bad that the people cannot attend. The state governments will be mere boards of election. The clause of elections gives the Congress power over the time and manner of choosing the Senate. I wish to know why reservation was made of the place of choosing senators, and not also of electing representatives. It points to the time when the states shall be all consolidated into one empire. Trial by jury is not secured. The objections against this want of security have not been cleared up in a satisfactory manner. It is neither secured in civil nor criminal cases. The federal appellate cognizance of law and fact puts it in the power of the wealthy to recover unjustly of the poor man, who is not able to attend at such extreme distance, and bear such enormous expense as it must produce. It ought to be limited so as to prevent such oppressions.

I say the trial by jury is not sufficiently secured in criminal cases. The very intention of the trial by jury is, that the accused may be tried by persons who come from the vicinage or neighborhood, who may be acquainted with his character. The substance, therefore, of this privilege is taken away.

By the power of taxation, every article capable of being taxed may be so heavily taxed that the people cannot bear the taxes necessary to be raised for the support of their state governments. Whatever law we may make, may be repealed by their laws. All these things, with others, tend to make us one general empire. Such a government cannot be well regulated. When we are connected with the Northern States, who have a majority in their favor, laws may be made which will answer their convenience, but will be oppressive to the last degree upon the Southern States. They differ in climate, soil, customs, manners, &c. A large majority of the people of this country are against this Constitution, because they think it replete with dangerous defects. They ought to be satisfied with it before it is adopted; otherwise it cannot operate happily. Without the affections of the people, it will not have sufficient energy. To enforce its execution, recourse must be had to arms and bloodshed. How much better would it be if the people were satisfied with it! From all these considerations, I now rise to oppose its adoption; for I never will agree to a government that tends to the destruction of the liberty of the people.

Mr. WILSON wished that the Constitution had excluded Popish priests from offices. As there was no test required, and nothing to govern them but honor, he said that when their interest clashed with their honor, the latter would fly before the former.

Mr. LANCASTER. Mr. Chairman, it is of the utmost importance to decide this great question with candor and deliberation. Every part of this Constitution has been elucidated. It hath been asserted, by several worthy gentlemen, that it is the most excellent Constitution that ever was formed. I could wish to be of that opinion if it were so. The powers vested therein were very extensive. I am apprehensive that the power of taxation is unlimited. It expressly says that Congress shall have the power to lay taxes, &c. It is obvious to me that the power is unbounded, and I am apprehensive that they may lay taxes too heavily on our lands, in order to render them more productive. The amount of the taxes may be more than our lands will sell for. It is obvious that the lands in the Northern States, which gentlemen suppose to be more populous than this country, are more valuable and better cultivated than ours; yet their lands will be taxed no higher than our lands. A rich man there, from report, does not possess so large a body of land as a poor man to the southward. If so, a common poor man here will have much more to pay for poor land, than the rich man there for land of the best quality. This power, being necessarily unequal and oppressive, ought not to be given up. I shall endeavor to be as concise as possible. We find that the ratification of nine states shall be sufficient for its establishment between the states so ratifying the same. This, as has been already taken notice of, is a violation of the Confederation. We find that, by that system, no alteration was to take place, except it was ratified by every state in the Union. Now, by comparing this last article of the Constitution to that part of the Confederation, we find a most flagrant violation. The Articles of Confederation were sent out with all solemnity on so solemn an occasion, and were to be always binding on the states; but, to our astonishment, we see that nine states may do away the force of the whole. I think, without exaggeration, that it will be looked upon, by foreign nations, as a serious and alarming change.

How do we know that, if we propose amendments, they shall be obtained after actual ratification? May not these amendments be proposed with equal propriety, and more safety, as the condition of our adoption? If they violate the 13th article of the Confederation in this manner, may they not, with equal propriety, refuse to adopt amendments, although agreed to and wished for by two thirds of the states? This violation of the old system is a precedent for such proceedings as these. That would be a violation destructive to our felicity. We are now determining a question deeply affecting the happiness of millions yet unborn. It is the policy of freemen to guard their privileges. Let us, then, as far as we can, exclude the possibility of tyranny. The President is chosen for four years; the senators for six years. Where is our remedy for the most flagrant abuses? It is thought that North Carolina is to have an opportunity of choosing one third of their senatorial members, and all their representatives, once in two years. This would be the case as to senators, if they should be of the first class; but, at any rate, it is to be after six years. But if they deviate from their duty, they cannot be excluded and changed the first year, as the members of Congress can now by the Confederation. How can it be said to be safe to trust so much power in the hands of such men, who are not responsible or amenable for misconduct?

As it has been the policy of every state in the Union to guard elections, we ought to be more punctual in this case. The members of Congress now may be recalled. But in this Constitution they cannot be recalled. The continuance of the President and Senate is too long. It will be objected, by some gentlemen, that, if they are good, why not continue them? But I would ask, How are we to find out whether they be good or bad? The individuals who assented to any bad law are not easily discriminated from others. They will, if individually inquired of, deny that they gave it their approbation; and it is in their power to conceal their transactions as long as they please.

There is also the President's conditional negative on the laws. After a bill is presented to him, and he disapproves of it, it is to be sent back to that house where it originated, for their consideration. Let us consider the effects of this for a few moments. Suppose it originates in the Senate, and passes there by a large majority; suppose it passes in the House of Representatives unanimously; it must be transmitted to the President. If he objects, it is sent back to the Senate; if two thirds do not agree to it in the Senate, what is the consequence? Does the House of Representatives ever hear of it afterwards? No, it drops, because it must be passed by two thirds of both houses; and as only a majority of the Senate agreed to it, it cannot become a law. This is giving a power to the President to over-rule fifteen members of the Senate and every member of the House of Representatives. These are my objections. I look upon it to be unsafe to drag each other from the most remote parts in the state to the Supreme Federal Court, which has appellate jurisdiction of causes arising under the Constitution, and of controversies between citizens of different states. I grant, if it be a contract between a citizen of Virginia and a citizen of North Carolina, the suit must be brought here; but may they not appeal to the Supreme Court, which has cognizance of law and fact? They may be carried to Philadelphia. They ought to have limited the sum on which appeals should lie. They may appeal on a suit for only ten pounds. Such a trifling sum as this would be paid by a man who thought he did not owe it, rather than go such a distance. It would be prudence in him so to do. This would be very oppressive.

I doubt my own judgment; experience has taught me to be diffident; but I hope to be excused and put right if I be mistaken.

The power of raising armies is also very exceptionable. I am not well acquainted with the government of other countries, but a man of any information knows that the king of Great Britain cannot raise and support armies. He may call for and raise men, but he has no money to support them. But Congress is to have power to raise and support armies. Forty thousand men from North Carolina could not be refused without violating the Constitution. I wish amendments to these parts. I agree it is not our business to inquire whether the continent be invaded or not. The general legislature ought to superintend the care of this Treaties are to be the supreme law of the land. This has been sufficiently discussed : it must be amended some way or other. If the Constitution be adopted, it ought to be the supreme law of the land, and a perpetual rule for the governors and governed. But if treaties are to be the supreme law of the land, it may repeal the laws of different states, and render nugatory our bill of rights.

As to a religious test, had the article which excludes it provided none but what had been in the states heretofore, I would not have objected to it. It would secure religion. Religious liberty ought to be provided for. I acquiesce with the gentleman, who spoke, on this point, my sentiments better than I could have done myself. For my part, in reviewing the qualifications necessary for a President, I did not suppose that the pope could occupy the President's chair. But let us remember that we form a government for millions not yet in existence. I have not the art of divination. In the course of four or five hundred years, I do not know how it will work. This is most certain, that Papists may occupy that chair, and Mahometans may take it. I see nothing against it. There is a disqualification, I believe, in every state in the Union — it ought to be so in this system. It is said that all power not given is retained. I find they thought proper to insert negative clauses in the Constitution, restraining the general government from the exercise of certain powers. These were unnecessary if the doctrine be true, that every thing not given is retained. From the insertion of these we may conclude the doctrine to be fallacious. Mr. Lancaster then observed, that he would disapprove of the Constitution as it then stood. His own feelings, and his duty to his constituents, induced him to do so. Some people, he said, thought a delegate might act independently of the people. He thought otherwise, and that every delegate was bound by their instructions, and if he did any thing repugnant to their wishes, he betrayed his trust. He thought himself bound by the voice of the people, whatever other gentlemen might think. He would cheerfully agree to adopt, if he thought it would be of general utility ; but as he thought it would have a contrary effect, and as he believed a great majority of the people were against it, he would oppose its adoption.

Mr. WILLIE JONES was against ratifying in the man ner proposed. He had attended, he said, with patience to the debates of the speakers on both sides of the question. One party said the Constitution was all perfection. The other party said it wanted a great deal of perfection. For his part, he thought so. He treated the dangers which were held forth in case of non-adoption, as merely ideal and fanciful. After adding other remarks, he moved that the previous question might be put, with an intention, as he said, if that was carried, to introduce a resolution which he had in his hand, and which he was then willing to read if gentlemen thought proper, stipulating for certain amendments to be made previous to the adoption by this state.

Gov. JOHNSTON begged gentlemen to recollect that the proposed amendments could not be laid before the other states unless we adopted and became part of the Union.

Mr. TAYLOR wished that the previous question might be put, as it would save much time. He feared the motion first made was a manœuvre or contrivance to impose a constitution on the people which a majority disapproved of.

Mr. IREDELL wished the previous should be withdrawn, and that they might debate the first question. The great importance of the subject, and the respectability of the gentleman who made the motion, claimed more deference and attention than to decide it in the very moment it was introduced, by getting rid of it by the previous question. A decision was now presented in a new form by a gentleman of great influence in the house, and gentlemen ought to have time to consider before they voted precipitately upon it

A desultory conversation now arose. Mr. J. GALLO-WAY wished the question to be postponed till to-morrow morning.

Mr. J. M'DOWALL was for immediately putting the question. Several gentlemen expatiated on the evident necessity of amendments.

Gov. JOHNSTON declared that he disdained all manœuvres and contrivance ; that an intention of imposing an improper system on the people, contrary to their wishes, was unworthy of any man. He wished the motion to be fairly and fully argued and investigated. He observed that the very motion before them proposed amendments to be made : that they were proposed as they had been in other states

He wished, therefore, that the motion for the previous question should be withdrawn.

Mr. WILLIE JONES could not withdraw his motion. Gentlemen's arguments, he said, had been listened to attentively, but he believed no person had changed his opinion. It was unnecessary, then, to argue it again. His motion was not conclusive. He only wished to know what ground they stood on — whether they should ratify it unconditionally or not.

Mr. SPENCER wished to hear the arguments and reasons for and against the motion. Although he was convinced the house wanted amendments, and that all had nearly determined the question in their own minds, he was for hearing the question argued, and had no objection to the postponement of it till to-morrow.

Mr. IREDELL urged the great importance of consideration ; that the consequence of the previous question, if carried, would be an exclusion of this state out of the Union. He contended that the house had no right to make a conditional ratification ; and, if excluded from the Union, they could not be assured of an easy admission at a future day, though the impossibility of existing out of the Union must be obvious to every thinking man. The gentleman from Halifax had said that his motion would not be conclusive. For his part, he was certain it would be tantamount to immediate decision. He trusted gentlemen would consider the propriety of debating the first motion at large.

Mr. PERSON observed, that the previous question would produce no inconvenience. The other party, he said, had all the debating to themselves, and would probably have it again, if they insisted on further argument. He saw no propriety in putting it off till to-morrow, as it was not customary for a committee to adjourn with two questions before them.

Mr. SHEPHERD declared that, though he had made up his mind, and believed other gentlemen had done so, yet he had no objection to giving gentlemen an opportunity of displaying their abilities, and convincing the rest of their error if they could. He was for putting it off till to-morrow.

Mr. DAVIE took notice that the gentleman from Granville had frequently used ungenerous insinuations, and had taken much pains out of doors to irritate the minds of his countrymen against the Constitution. He called upon gentlemen to act openly and aboveboard, adding that a contrary conduct, on this occasion, was extremely despicable.   He came thither, he said, for the common cause of his country, and he knew no party, but wished the business to be conducted with candor and moderation.   The previous question he thought irregular, and that it ought not to be put till the other question was called for ; that it was evidently intended to preclude all further debate, and to precipitate the committee upon the resolution which it had been suggested was immediately to follow, which they were not then ready to enter upon ; that he had not fully considered the consequences of a conditional ratification, but at present they appeared to him alarmingly dangerous, and perhaps equal to those of an absolute rejection.

Mr. WILLIE JONES observed, that he had not intended to take the house by surprise ; that, though he had his motion ready, and had heard of the motion which was intended for ratification, he waited till that motion should be made, and had afterwards waited for some time, in expectation that the gentleman from Halifax, and the gentleman from Edenton, would both speak to it.   He had no objection to adjourning, but his motion would be still before the house.

Here there was a great cry for the question.

Mr. IREDELL.   [The cry for the question still continuing.]   Mr. Chairman, I desire to be heard, notwithstanding the cry of " The question! the question !"   Gentlemen have no right to prevent any member from speaking to it, if he thinks fit.   [The house subsided into order.]   Unimportant as I may be myself, my constituents are as respectable as those of any member in the house.   It has, indeed, sir, been my misfortune to be under the necessity of troubling the house much oftener than I wished, owing to a circumstance which I have greatly regretted — that so few gentlemen take a share in our debates, though many are capable of doing so with propriety.   I should have spoken to the question at large before, if I had not fully depended on some other gentleman doing it ; and therefore I did not prepare myself by taking notes of what was said.   However, I beg leave now to make a few observations.   I think this Constitution safe.   I have not heard a single objection which, in my opinion, showed that it was dangerous.   Some particular parts have been objected to, and amendments pointed out.

Though I think it perfectly safe, yet, with respect to any amendments which do not destroy the substance of the Constitution, but will tend to give greater satisfaction, I should approve of them, because I should prefer that system which would most tend to conciliate all parties. On these principles, I am of opinion that some amendments should be proposed.

The general ground of the objections seems to be, that the power proposed to the general government may be abused. If we give no power but such as may not be abused, we shall give none; for all delegated powers may be abused. There are two extremes equally dangerous to liberty. These are *tyranny* and *anarchy*. The medium between these two is the true government to protect the people. In my opinion, this Constitution is well calculated to guard against both these extremes. The possibility of general abuses ought not to be urged, but particular ones pointed out. A gentleman who spoke some time ago (Mr. Lenoir) observed, that the government might make it treason to write against the most arbitrary proceedings. He corrected himself afterwards, by saying he meant *misprision of treason*. But in the correction he committed as great a mistake as he did at first. Where is the power given to them to do this? They have power to define and punish piracies and felonies committed on the high seas, and offences against the law of nations. They have no power to define any other crime whatever. This will show how apt gentlemen are to commit mistakes. I am convinced, on the part of the worthy member, it was not designed, but arose merely from inattention.

Mr. LENOIR arose, and declared, that he meant that those punishments might be inflicted by them within the ten miles square, where they would have exclusive powers of legislation.

Mr. IREDELL continued: They are to have exclusive power of legislation, — but how? Wherever they may have this district, they must possess it from the authority of the state within which it lies; and that state may stipulate the conditions of the cession. Will not such state take care of the liberties of its own people? What would be the consequence if the seat of the government of the United States, with all the archives of America, was in the power of any one particular state? Would not this be most unsafe and humiliating? Do we not all remember that, in the year 1783, a band of soldiers went and insulted Congress? The sovereignty of the United States was treated with indignity. They applied for protection to the state they resided in, but could obtain none. It is to be hoped such a disgraceful scene will never happen again; but that, for the future, the national government will be able to protect itself. The powers of the government are particularly enumerated and defined: they can claim no others but such as are so enumerated. In my opinion, they are excluded as much from the exercise of any other authority as they could be by the strongest negative clause that could be framed. A gentleman has asked, What would be the consequence if they had the power of the purse and sword? I ask, In what government under heaven are these not given up to some authority or other? There is a necessity of giving both the purse and the sword to every government, or else it cannot protect the people.

But have we not sufficient security that those powers shall not be abused? The immediate power of the purse is in the immediate representatives of the people, chosen every two years, who can lay no tax on their constituents but what they are subject to at the same time themselves. The power of taxation must be vested somewhere. Do the committee wish it to be as it has been? Then they must suffer the evils which they have done. Requisitions will be of no avail. No money will be collected but by means of military force. Under the new government, taxes will probably be much lighter than they can be under our present one. The impost will afford vast advantages, and greatly relieve the people from direct taxation. In time of peace, it is supposed by many, the imposts may be alone sufficient; but in the time of war, it cannot be expected they will. Our expenses would be much greater, and our ports might be blocked up by the enemy's fleet. Think, then, of the advantage of a national government possessed of energy and credit. Could government borrow money to any advantage without the power of taxation? If they could secure funds, and wanted immediately, for instance, £100,000, they might borrow this sum, and immediately raise only money to pay the interest of it. If they could not, the £100,000 must be instantly raised, however distressing to the people,

or our country perhaps overrun by the enemy. Do not gen
tlemen see an immense difference between the two cases?
It is said that there ought to be jealousy in mankind. I
admit it as far as is consistent with prudence; but unlimited
jealousy is very pernicious.

We must be contented if powers be as well guarded as
the nature of them will permit. In regard to amending
before or after the adoption, the difference is very great. I
beg leave to state my idea of that difference. I mentioned,
one day before, the adoption by ten states. When I did so,
it was not to influence any person with respect to the merits
of the Constitution, but as a reason for coolness and deliberation. In my opinion, when so great a majority of the
American people have adopted it, it is a strong evidence in
its favor; for it is not probable that ten states would have
agreed to a bad constitution. If we do not adopt, we are
no longer in the Union with the other states. We ought to
consider seriously before we determine our connection with
them. The safety and happiness of this state depend upon
it. Without that union, what would have been our condition
now? A striking instance will point out this very clearly.
At the beginning of the late war with Great Britain, the Parliament thought proper to stop all commercial intercourse
with the American provinces. They passed a general prohibitory act, from which New York and North Carolina were at
first excepted. Why were they excepted? They had been
as active in opposition as the other states; but this was an
expedient to divide the Northern from the Middle States, and
to break the heart of the Southern. Had New York and
North Carolina been weak enough to fall into this snare, we
probably should not now have been an independent people.
[Mr. Person called to order, and intimated that the gentleman meant to reflect on the opposers of the Constitution,
as if they were friendly to the British interest. Mr. Iredell warmly resented the interruption, declaring he was
perfectly in order, that it was disorderly to interrupt him;
and, in respect to Mr. Person's insinuation as to his intention, he declared, in the most solemn manner, he had
no such, being well assured the opposers of the Constitution
were equally friendly to the independence of America as its
supporters. He then proceeded:]

I say, they endeavored to divide us. North Carolina and

New York had too much sense to be taken in by their artifices.   Union enabled us then to defeat their endeavors:
union will enable us to defeat all the machinations of our
enemies hereafter.   The friends of their country must lament
our present unhappy divisions.   Most free countries have lost
their liberties by means of dissensions among themselves.
They united in war and danger.   When peace and apparent
security came, they split into factions and parties, and thereby
became a prey to foreign invaders.   This shows the necessity of union.   In urging the danger of disunion so strongly,
I beg leave again to say, that I mean not to reflect on any
gentleman whatsoever, as if his wishes were directed to so
wicked a purpose.   I am sure such an insinuation as the gentleman from Granville supposed I intended, would be unjust,
as I know some of the warmest opposers of Great Britain
are now among the warmest opponents of the proposed Constitution.   Such a suggestion never entered my head ; and I
can say with truth that, warmly as I am attached to this
Constitution, and though I am convinced that the salvation
of our country depends upon the adoption of it, I would not
procure its success by one unworthy action or one ungenerous word.   A gentleman has said that we ought to deter
mine in the same manner as if no state had adopted the
Constitution.   The general principle is right ; but we ought
to consider our peculiar situation.   We cannot exist by ourselves.   If we imitate the examples of some respectable
states that have proposed amendments subsequent to their
ratification, we shall add our weight to have these amendments carried, as our representatives will be in Congress · to
enforce them.   Gentlemen entertain a jealousy of the Eastern States.   To withdraw ourselves from the Southern
States will be increasing the northern influence.   The loss
of one state may be attended with particular prejudice.   It
will be a good while before amendments of any kind can
take place; and in the mean time, if we do not adopt, we
shall have no share or agency in their transactions, though
we may be ultimately bound by them.   The first session of
Congress will probably be the most important of any for
many years.   A general code of laws will then be established in execution of every power contained in the Constitution.   If we ratify, and propose amendments, our representatives will be there to act in this important business.   If

we do not, our interest may suffer; nor will the system be afterwards altered merely to accommodate our wishes. Besides that, one house may prevent a measure from taking place, but both must concur in repealing it. I therefore think an adoption proposing subsequent amendments far safer and more desirable than the other mode; nor do I doubt that every amendment, not of a local nature, nor injuring essentially the material power of the Constitution, but principally calculated to guard against misconstruction the real liberties of the people, will be readily obtained.

The previous question, after some desultory conversation, was now put: for it, 183; against it, 84; majority in favor of the motion, 99.

Thursday, *July* 31, 1788.

Gov. JOHNSTON. Mr. Chairman, it appears to me that, if the motion made yesterday, by the gentleman from Halifax, be adopted, it will not answer the intention of the people. It determines nothing with respect to the Constitution. We were sent here to determine upon it. [Here his excellency read the resolution of the Assembly under which the Convention met.] If we do not decide upon the Constitution, we shall have nothing to report to Congress. We shall be entirely out of the Union, and stand by ourselves. I wish gentlemen would pause a moment before they decide so awful a question. To whom are we to refer these amendments which are to be proposed as the condition of our adoption? The present Congress have nothing to do with them. Their authority extends only to introduce the new government, not to receive any proposition of amendments. Shall we present them to the new Congress? In what manner can that be done? We shall have no representatives to introduce them. We may indeed appoint ambassadors to the United States of America, to represent what scruples North Carolina has in regard to their Constitution. I know no other way. A number of states have proposed amendments to the Constitution, and ratified in the mean time. These will have great weight and influence in Congress, and may prevail in getting material amendments proposed. We shall have no share in voting upon any of these amendments; for, in my humble opinion, we shall be entirely out of the Union, and can be considered only as a foreign power. It is true, the United States may admit us hereafter. But they may admit us on terms unequal and disadvantageous to us. In the mean time, many of their laws, by which we shall be hereafter bound, may be particularly injurious to the interests of this state, as we shall have no share in their formation. Gentlemen say they will not be influenced by what others have done. I must confess that the example of great and good men, and wise states, has great weight with me.

It is said there is a probability New York will not adopt this Constitution. Perhaps she may not. But it is generally supposed that the principal reason of her opposing it arises from a selfish motive. She has it now in her power to tax indirectly two contiguous states. Connecticut and New Jersey contribute to pay a great part of the taxes of that state, by consuming large quantities of goods, the duties of which are now levied for the benefit of New York only. A similar policy may induce the United States to lay restrictions on us, if we are out of the Union. These considerations ought to have great weight with us. We can derive very little assistance from any thing New York will do on our behalf. Her views are diametrically opposite to ours. That state wants all her imposts for her own exclusive support. It is our interest that all imposts should go into the general treasury. Should Congress receive our commissioners, it will be a considerable time before this business will be decided on. It will be some time after Congress meets before a convention is appointed, and some time will elapse before the convention meets. What they will do, will be transmitted to each of the states, and then a convention, or the legislature, in each state, will have to ratify it ultimately. This will probably take up eighteen months or two years. In the mean time, the national government is going on. Congress will appoint all the great officers, and will proceed to make laws and form regulations for the future government of the United States. This state, during that time, will have no share in their proceedings, or any negative on any business before them. Another inconvenience which will arise is this: we shall be deprived of the benefit of the impost, which, under the new government, is an additional fund; all the states having a common right to it. By being in the Union we should have a right to our proportionate share of all the duties and imposts collected in all the states. But by adopting this resolution, we shall lose the benefit of this, which is an object worthy of attention. Upon the whole, I can see no possible good that will result to this state from following the resolution before us. I have not the vanity to think that any reasons I offer will have any weight. But I came from a respectable county to give my reasons for or against the Constitution. They expect them from me, and to suppress them would be a violation of my duty.

Mr. WILLIE JONES. Mr. Chairman, the gentleman last up has mentioned the resolution of Congress now lying before us, and the act of Assembly under which we met here, which says that we should deliberate and determine on the Constitution. What is to be inferred from that? Are we to ratify it at all events? Have we not an equal right to reject? We do not determine by neither rejecting nor adopting. It is objected we shall be out of the Union. So I wish to be. We are left at liberty to come in at any time. It is said we shall suffer a great loss for want of a share of the impost. I have no doubt we shall have it when we come in, as much as if we adopted now. I have a resolution in my pocket, which I intend to introduce if this resolution is carried, recommending it to the legislature to lay an impost, for the use of Congress, on goods imported into this state, similar to that which may be laid by Congress on goods imported into the adopting states. This shows the committee what is my intention, and on what footing we are to be. This being the case, I will forfeit my life that we shall come in for a share. It is said that all the offices of Congress will be filled, and we shall have no share in appointing the officers. This is an objection of very little importance. Gentlemen need not be in such haste. If left eighteen months or two years without offices, it is no great cause of alarm. The gentleman further said that we could send no representatives, but must send ambassadors to Congress, as a foreign power. I assert the contrary; and that, whenever a convention of the states is called, North Carolina will be called upon like the rest. I do not know what these gentlemen would desire.

I am very sensible that there is a great majority against the Constitution. If we take the question as they propose they know it would be rejected, and bring on us all the dreadful consequences which they feelingly foretell, but which can never in the least alarm me. I have endeavored to fall in with their opinions, but could not. We have a right, in plain terms, to refuse it if we think proper. I have, in my proposition, adopted, word for word, the Virginia amendments, with one or two additional ones. We run no risk of being excluded from the Union when we think proper to come in. Virginia, our next neighbor, will not oppose our admission. We have a common cause with her. She wishes the same alterations. We are of the greatest importance to her. She will have great weight in Congress; and there is no doubt but she will do every thing she can to bring us into the Union. South Carolina and Georgia are deeply interested in our being admitted. The Creek nation would overturn these two states without our aid. They cannot exist without North Carolina. There is no doubt we shall obtain our amendments, and come into the Union when we please. Massachusetts, New Hampshire, and other states, have proposed amendments. New York will do also, if she ratifies. There will be a majority of the states, and the most respectable, important, and extensive states also, desirous of amendments, and favorable to our admission.

As great names have been mentioned, I beg leave to mention the authority of Mr. Jefferson, whose great abilities and respectability are well known. When the Convention sat in Richmond, in Virginia, Mr. Madison received a letter from him. In that letter he said he wished nine states would adopt it, not because it deserved ratification, but to preserve the Union. But he wished that the other four states would reject it, that there might be a certainty of obtaining amendments. Congress may go on, and take no notice of our amendments; but I am confident they will do nothing of importance till a convention be called. If I recollect rightly, amendments may be ratified either by conventions or the legislatures of the states. In either case, it may take up about eighteen months. For my part, I would rather be eighteen years out of the Union than adopt it in its present defective form.

Gov. JOHNSTON. Mr. Chairman, I wish to clear myself from the imputation of the gentleman last up. If any part of my conduct warrants his aspersion, — if ever I hunted after offices, or sought public favors to promote private inter-est, — let the instances be pointed out.   If I know myself I never did.   It is easy for any man to throw out illibera and ungenerous insinuations.   I have no view to offices under this Constitution.   My views are much humbler.   When I spoke of Congress establishing offices, I meant great offices, the establishment of which might affect the interests of the states ; and I added that they would proceed to make laws, deeply affecting us, without any influence of our own.   As to the appointment of the officers, it is of no importance to me who is an officer, if he be a good man.

Mr. JONES replied, that in every publication one might see ill motives assigned to the opposers of the Constitution. One reason assigned for their opposition was, that they feared the loss of their influence, and diminution of their importance. He said, that it was fair its opposers should be permitted to retort, and assign a reason equally selfish for the conduct of its friends.   Expectation to offices might influence them, as well as the loss of office and influence might bias the others. He intended no allusion to that gentleman, for whom he de-clared he had the highest respect.

Mr. SPENCER rose in support of the motion of the gen-tleman from Halifax.   He premised, that he wished no res-olution to be carried without the utmost deliberation and candor.   He thought the proposition was couched in such modest terms as could not possibly give offence to the other states ; that the amendments it proposed were to be laid be-fore Congress, and would probably be admitted, as they were similar to those which were wished for and proposed by several of the adopting states.   He always thought it more proper, and agreeable to prudence, to propose amend-ments previous, rather than subsequent, to ratification.   He said that, if two or more persons entered into a copartnership, and employed a scrivener to draw up the articles of copart-nership in a particular form, and, on reading them, they found them to be erroneous, — it would be thought very strange if any of them should say, " Sign it first, and we shall have it altered hereafter."   If it should be signed before altera-tion, it would be considered as an act of indiscretion.   As, therefore, it was a principle of prudence, in matters of pri-vate property, not to assent to any obligation till its errors were removed, he thought the principle infinitely more neces-

sary to be attended to in a matter which concerned such a
number of people, and so many millions yet unborn.   Gentlemen said they should be out of the Union.   He observed,
that they were before confederated with the other states by
a solemn compact, which was not to be dissolved without
the consent of every state in the Union.   North Carolina
had not assented to its dissolution.   If it was dissolved, it
was not their fault, but that of the adopting states.   It was
a maxim of law that the same solemnities were necessary to destroy, which were necessary to create, a deed
or contract.   He was of opinion that, if they should
be out of the Union by proposing previous amendments,
they were as much so now.   If the adoption by nine
states enabled them to exclude the other four states, he
thought North Carolina might then be considered as excluded.
But he did not think that doctrine well founded.   On the
contrary, he thought each state might come into the Union
when she thought proper.   He confessed it gave him some
concern, but he looked on the short exclusion of eighteen
months — if it might be called exclusion — as infinitely less
dangerous than an unconditional adoption.   He expected
the amendments would be adopted, and when they were,
this state was ready to embrace it.   No great inconvenience
could result from this.   [Mr. Spencer made some other remarks, but spoke too low to be heard.]

. Mr. IREDELL.   Mr. Chairman, in my opinion, this is a
very awful moment.   On a right decision of this question
may possibly depend the peace and happiness of our country
for ages.   Whatever be the decision of the house on this subject, it ought to be well weighed before it is given.   We
ought to view our situation in all its consequences, and determine with the utmost caution and deliberation.   It has been
suggested, not only out of doors, but during the course of the
debates, that, if we are out of the Union, it will be the fault
of other states, and not ours.   It is true that, by the Articles
of Confederation, the consent of each state was necessary
for any alteration.   It is also true that the consent of nine
states renders the Constitution binding on them.   The unhappy consequences of that unfortunate article in this Confederation produced the necessity of this article in the Constitution.   Every body knows that, through the peculiar
obstinacy of Rhode Island, many great advantages were lost.

Notwithstanding her weakness, she uniformly opposed every regulation for the benefit and honor of the Union at large. The other states were driven to the necessity of providing for their own security and welfare, without waiting for the consent of that little state. The deputies from twelve states unanimously concurred in opinion that the happiness of all America ought not to be sacrificed to the caprice and obstinacy of so inconsiderable a part.

It will often happen, in the course of human affairs, that the policy which is proper on common occasions fails, and that laws which do very well in the regular administration of a government cannot stand when every thing is going into confusion. In such a case, the safety of the community must supersede every other consideration, and every subsisting regulation which interferes with that must be departed from, rather than that the people should be ruined. The Convention, therefore, with a degree of manliness which I admire, dispensed with a unanimous consent for the present change, and at the same time provided a permanent remedy for this evil, not barely by dispensing with the consent of one member in future alterations, but by making the consent of nine sufficient for the whole, if the rest did not agree, considering that the consent of so large a number ought in reason to govern the whole; and the proportion was taken from the old Confederation, which in the most important cases required the consent of nine, and in every thing, except the alteration of the Constitution, made that number sufficient. It has been objected, that the adoption of this government would be improper, because it would interfere with the oath of allegiance to the state. No oath of allegiance requires us to sacrifice the safety of our country. When the British government attempted to establish a tyranny in America, the people did not think their oath of allegiance bound them to submit to it. I had taken that oath several times myself, but had no scruple to oppose their tyrannical measures. The great principle is, The safety of the people is the supreme law. Government was originally instituted for their welfare, and whatever may be its form, this ought to be its object. This is the fundamental principle on which our government is founded. In other countries, they suppose the existence of original compact, and infer that, if the sovereign violates his part of it, the

20*

people have a right to resist. If he does not, the government must remain unchanged, unless the sovereign consents to an alteration. In America, our governments have been clearly created by the people themselves. The same authority that created can destroy; and the people may undoubtedly change the government, not because it is ill exercised, but because they conceive another form will be more conducive to their welfare. I have stated the reasons for departing from the rigid article in the Confederation requiring a unanimous consent. We were compelled to do this, or see our country ruined. In the manner of the dispensation, the Convention, however, appear to have acted with great prudence, in copying the example of the Confederation in all other particulars of the greatest moment, by authorizing nine states to bind the whole. It is suggested, indeed, that, though ten states have adopted this new Constitution, yet, as they had no right to dissolve the old Articles of Confederation, these still subsist, and the old Union remains, of which we are a part. The truth of that suggestion may well be doubted, on this ground: when the principles of a constitution are violated, the constitution itself is dissolved, or may be dissolved at the pleasure of the parties to it. Now, according to the Articles of Confederation, Congress had authority to demand money, in a certain proportion, from the respective states, to answer the exigencies of the Union. Whatever requisitions they made for that purpose were constitutionally binding on the states. The states had no discretion except as to the mode of raising the money. Perhaps every state has committed repeated violations of the demands of Congress. I do not believe it was from any dishonorable intention in many of the states; but whatever was the cause, the fact is, such violations were committed. The consequence is that, upon the principle I have mentioned, (and in which I believe all writers agree,) the Articles of Confederation are no longer binding. It is alleged that, by making the consent of nine sufficient to form a government for themselves, the first nine may exclude the other four. This is a very extraordinary allegation. When the new Constitution was proposed, it was proposed to the thirteen states in the Union. It was desired that all should agree, if possible; but if that could not be obtained, they took care that nine states might at least save themselves from destruction.   Each, undoubtedly, had a right on the first proposition, because it was proposed to them all.   The only doubt can be, whether they had a right afterwards.   In my opinion, when any state has once rejected the Constitution, it cannot claim to come in afterwards as a matter of right.

If it does not, in plain terms, reject, but refuses to accede for the present, I think the other states may regard this as an absolute rejection, and refuse to admit us afterwards but at their pleasure, and on what terms they please.   Gentlemen wish for amendments.   On this subject, though we may differ as to the necessity of amendments, I believe none will deny the propriety of proposing some, if only for the purpose of giving more general satisfaction.   The question, then, is, whether it is most prudent for us to come into the Union immediately, and propose amendments, (as has been done in the other states,) or to propose amendments, and be out of the Union till all these be agreed to by the other states.   The consequences of either resolution I beg leave to state.   By adopting, we shall be in the Union with our sister states, which is the only foundation of our prosperity and safety.   We shall avoid the danger of a separation, a danger of which the latent effects are unknown.   So far am I convinced of the necessity of the Union, that I would give up many things against my own opinion to obtain it. If we sacrificed it by a rejection of the Constitution, or a refusal to adopt, (which amounts, I think, nearly to the same thing,) the very circumstance of disunion may occasion animosity between us and the inhabitants of the other states, which may be the means of severing us forever.

We shall lose the benefit which must accrue to the other states from the new government.   Their trade will flourish; goods will sell cheap; their commodities will rise in value; and their distresses, occasioned by the war, will gradually be removed.   Ours, for want of these advantages, will continue. Another very material consequence will result from it : we shall lose our share of the imposts in all the states, which, under this Constitution, is to go into the federal treasury. It is the particular local interest of this state to adopt, on this account, more, perhaps, than that of any other member of the Union.   At present, all these imposts go into the respective treasury of each state, and we well know our own are of little conseq ience, compared to those of the other states in general. The gentleman from Halifax (Mr. Jones) has offered an expedient to prevent the loss of our share of the impost. In my opinion, that expedient will not answer the purpose. The amount of duties on goods imported into this state is very little ; and if these resolutions are agreed to, it will be less. I ask any gentleman whether the United States would receive, from the duties of this state, so much as would be our proportion, under the Constitution, of the duties on goods imported in all the states. Our duties would be no manner of compensation for such proportion. What would be the language of Congress on our holding forth such an offer ? "If you are willing to enjoy the benefits of the Union, you must be subject to all the laws of it. We will make no partial agreement with you." This would probably be their language. I have no doubt all America would wish North Carolina to be a member of the Union. It is of importance to them. But we ought to consider whether ten states can do longer without one, or one without ten. On a competition, which will give way ? The adopting states will say, " Other states had objections as well as you ; but rather than separate, they agreed to come into the Union, trusting to the justice of the other states for the adoption of proper amendments afterwards. One most respectable state, Virginia, has pursued this measure, though apparently averse to the system as it now stands. But you have laid down the condition on which alone you will come into the Union. We must accede to your particular propositions, or be disunited from you altogether. Is it fit that North Carolina shall dictate to the whole Union ? We may be convinced by your reason, but our conduct will certainly not be altered by your resistance."

I beg leave to say, if Virginia thought it right to adopt and propose amendments, under the circumstances of the Constitution at that time, surely it is much more so for us in our present situation. That state, as was justly observed, is a most powerful and respectable one. Had she held out, it would have been a subject of most serious alarm. But she thought the risk of losing the union altogether too dangerous to be incurred. She did not then know of the ratification of New Hampshire. If she thought it necessary to adopt, when only eight states had ratified, is it not much more necessary for us after the ratification by ten? I do not say that we ought servilely to imitate any example. But I may say, that the examples of wise men and intelligent nations are worthy of respect; and that, in general, we may be much safer in following than in departing from them. In my opinion, as many of the amendments proposed are similar to amendments recommended not only by Virginia, but by other states, there is great probability of their being obtained. All the amendments proposed, undoubtedly, will not be, nor I think ought to be; but such as tend to secure more effectually the liberties of the people against an abuse of the powers granted in all human probability, will; for in such amendments all the states are equally interested. The probability of such amendments being obtained is extremely great; for though three states ratified the Constitution unanimously, there has been a considerable opposition in the other states. In New Hampshire, the majority was small. In Massachusetts, there was a strong opposition. In Connecticut, the opposition was about one third: so it was in Pennsylvania. In Maryland, the minority was small, but very respectable. In Virginia, they had little more than a bare majority. There was a powerful minority in South Carolina. Can any man pretend to say that, thus circumstanced, the states would disapprove of amendments calculated to give satisfaction to the people at large? There is a very great probability, if not an absolute certainty, that amendments will be obtained. The interest of North Carolina would add greatly to the scale in their favor. If we do not accede, we may injure the states who wish for amendments, by withdrawing ourselves from their assistance. We are not, at any event, in a condition to stand alone. God forbid we should be a moment separated from our sister states! If we are, we shall be in great danger of a separation forever. I trust every gentleman will pause before he contributes to so awful an event.

We have been happy in our connection with the other states. Our freedom, independence, every thing dear to us, has been derived from that union we are now going rashly to dissolve. If we are to be separated, let every gentleman well weigh the ground he stands on before he votes for the separation. Let him not have to reproach himself, hereafter, that he voted without due consideration for a measure that proved the destruction of his country.

Mr. Iredell then observed that there were insinuations

thrown out, against those who favored the Constitution, that they had a view of getting offices and emoluments. He said, he hoped no man thought him so wicked as to sacrifice the interest of his country to private views. He declared, in the most solemn manner, the insinuation was unjust and ill-founded as to himself. He believed it was so with respect to the rest. The interest and happiness of his country solely governed him on that occasion. He could appeal to some members in the house, and particularly to those who knew him in the lower part of the country, that his disposition had never been pecuniary, and that he had never aspired to offices. At the beginning of the revolution, he said, he held one of the best offices in the state under the crown — an office on which he depended for his support. His relations were in Great Britain ; yet, though thus circumstanced, so far was he from being influenced by pecuniary motives, or emoluments of office, that, as soon as his situation would admit of it, he did not hesitate a moment to join the opposition to Great Britain ; nor would the richest office of America have tempted him to adhere to that unjust cause of the British government. He apologized for taking up the time of the committee ; but he observed, that reflections of that kind were considered as having applied, unless they were taken notice of. He attributed no unworthy motives to any gentleman in the house. He believed most of them wished to pursue the interest of their country according to their own ideas of it. He hoped other gentlemen would be equally liberal.

Mr. WILLIE JONES observed, that he assigned unworthy motives to no one. He thought a gentleman had insinuated that the opposition all acted from base motives. He was well assured that their motives were as good as those of the other party, and he thought he had a right to retort by showing that selfish views might influence as well on one side as the other. He intended, however, no particular reflection on those two gentlemen who had applied the observation to themselves — for whom, he said, he had the highest respect, and was sorry he had made the observation, as it had given them pain. But if they were conscious that the observation did not apply to them, they ought not to be offended at it. He then explained the nature of the resolutions he proposed ; and the plain question was, whether they

should adopt them or not.   He was not afraid that North
Carolina would not be admitted at any time hereafter
Maryland, he said, had not confederated for many years with
the other states; yet she was considered in the mean time
as a member of the Union, was allowed as such to send her
proportion of men and money, and was at length admitted
into the confederacy, in 1781.   This, he said, showed how
the adopting states would act on the present occasion.
North Carolina might come into the Union when she
pleased.

Gov. JOHNSTON made some observations as to the particular case of Maryland, but in too low a voice to be distinctly heard.

Mr. BLOODWORTH observed, that the first convention
which met to consult on the necessary alterations of the Confederation, so as to make it efficient, and put the commerce
of the United States on a better footing, not consisting of a
sufficient number from the different states, so as to authorize
them to proceed, returned without effecting any thing; but
proposed that another convention should be called, to have
more extensive powers to alter and amend the Confederation.   This proposition of that convention was warmly opposed in Congress.   Mr. King, from Massachusetts, insisted
on the impropriety of the measure, and that the existing
system ought to stand as it was.   His arguments, he said,
were, that it might destroy the Confederation to propose alterations; that the unanimous consent of all the states was
necessary to introduce those alterations, which could not possibly be obtained; and that it would, therefore, be in vain to
attempt it.   He wondered how gentlemen came to entertain different opinions now.   He declared he had listened
with attention to the arguments of the gentlemen on the
other side, and had endeavored to remove every kind of bias
from his mind; yet he had heard nothing of sufficient weight
to induce him to alter his opinion.   He was sorry that there
was any division on that important occasion, and wished they
could all go hand in hand.

As to the disadvantages of a temporary exclusion from the
Union, he thought them trifling.   He asked if a few political advantages could be put in competition with our liberties.   Gentlemen said that amendments would probably
be obtained.   He thought their arguments and reasons were

not so sure a method to obtain them as withholding their
consent would be.   He could not conceive that the adopting
states would take any measures to keep this state out of the
Union.   If a right view were taken of the subject, he said
they could not be blamed in staying out of the Union till
amendments were obtained.   The compact between the
states was violated by the other states, and not by North
Carolina.   Would the violating party blame the upright
party?   This determination would correspond with the opinion of the gentleman who had written from France on the
subject.   He would lay stress on no man's opinion, but the
opinion of that gentleman was very respectable.

Mr. DAVIE.   Mr. Chairman, it is said that there is a
great majority against the Constitution, and in favor of the
gentleman's proposition.   The object of the majority, I suppose, is to pursue the most probable method of obtaining
amendments.   The honorable gentleman from Halifax has
said this is the most eligible method of obtaining them.   My
opinion is the very reverse.   Let us weigh the probability
of both modes proposed, and determine with candor which
is the safest and surest method of obtaining the wished-for
alterations.   The honorable gentleman from Anson has said
that our conduct in adhering to these resolutions would be
modest.   What is his idea or definition of modesty?   The
term must be very equivocal.   So far from being modest, it
appears to me to be no less than an arrogant, dictatorial
proposal of a constitution to the United States of America.
We shall be no part of that confederacy, and yet attempt to
dictate to one of the most powerful confederacies in the
world.   It is also said to be most agreeable to *prudence*.   If
our real object be amendments, every man must agree that
the most likely means of obtaining them are the most prudent.
Four of the most respectable states have adopted the Constitution, and recommended amendments.   New York, (if she refuses to adopt,) Rhode Island, and North Carolina, will be the
only states out of the Union.   But if these three were added,
they would compose a majority in favor of amendments, and
might, by various means, compel the other states into the
measure.   It must be granted that there is no way of obtaining amendments but the mode prescribed in the Constitution ; two thirds of the legislatures of the states *in the
confederacy* may require Congress to call a convention to

propose amendments, or the same proportion of both houses may propose them. It will then be of no consequence that we stand out and propose amendments. Without adoption we are not a member of the confederacy, and, possessing no federal rights, can neither make any proposition nor require Congress to call a convention.

Is it not clear, however strange it may be, that we are withholding our weight from those states who are of our own opinion, and by a perverse obstinacy obstructing the very measure we wish to promote? If two thirds of both houses are necessary to send forward amendments to the states, would it not be prudent that we should be there, and add our vote to the number of those states who are of the same sentiment? The honorable member from Anson has likened this business to a copartnership, comparing small things to great. The comparison is only just in one respect: the dictatorial proposal of North Carolina to the American confederacy is like a beggarly bankrupt addressing an opulent company of merchants, and arrogantly telling them, "I wish to be in copartnership with you, but the terms must be such *as I please.*" What has North Carolina to put into the stock with the other states? Have we not felt our poverty? What was the language of Congress on their last requisition on this state? Surely gentlemen must remember the painful terms in which our delinquency was treated. The gentleman has also said that we shall still be a part of the Union, and if we be separated, it is not our fault. This is an obvious solecism. It is our *own fault*, sir, and the direct consequence of the means we are now pursuing. North Carolina stands foremost in the point of delinquency, and has repeatedly violated the Confederation. The conduct of this state has been among the principal causes which produced this revolution in our federal government. The honorable gentleman has also added, "that it was a rule in law that the same solemnities were necessary to annul, which were necessary to create or establish, a compact; and that, as thirteen states created, so thirteen states must concur in the dissolution of the Confederation." — This may be talking like a lawyer or a judge, but it is very *unlike* a politician. A majority is the rule of republican decisions. It was the voice of a majority of the people of America that gave that system validity, and the same authority can and will annul

it at any time. Every man of common sense knows that
political power is *political right.* Lawyers may cavil and
quibble about the necessity of unanimity, but the true principle is otherwise. In every republican community, the
majority binds the minority ; and whether confederated or separated, the principle will equally apply. We have no right
to come into the Union until we exercise the right of deciding on the question referred to us. Adoption places us in
the Union — rejection extinguishes the *right* forever. The
scheme proposed by these gentlemen will certainly be considered as an absolute rejection ; it may amuse the people,
and answer a purpose *here*, but will not answer any purpose
there.

The honorable gentleman from Halifax asserts, "We may
come in when we please." The gentleman from New
Hanover, on the same side of the question, endeavored to
alarm and frighten us about the dangerous influence of the
Eastern States. If he deserves any credit, can we expect
they will let us into the Union, until they have accomplished
their particular views, and then but on the most disadvantageous terms? Commercial regulations will be one of the
great objects of the first session of Congress, in which our
interests will be totally neglected. Every man must be convinced of the importance of the first acts and regulations,
as they will probably give a tone to the policy of ages yet to
come ; and this scheme will add greatly to the influence of
the Eastern States, and proportionably diminish the power
and interests of the Southern States.

The gentleman says he has a project in his pocket, which,
he risks his life, will induce the other states to give us a share
of the general impost. I am fully satisfied, sir, this project
will not answer the purpose, and the forfeiture of his life will
be no compensation for irretrievable public loss. Every
man who knows the resources of our commerce, and our
situation, will be clearly convinced that the project cannot
succeed. The whole produce of our duties, both by land and
water, is very trifling. For several years past, it has not exceeded £10,000 of our own paper money. It will not be
more — probably less — if we were out of the Union. The
whole proportion of this state of the public debts, except this
mere pittance, must be raised from the people by direct and
immediate taxation.

But the fact is, sir, it cannot be raised, because it cannot be paid; and without sharing in the general impost, we shall never discharge our quota of the federal debt. What does he offer the other states? The poor pittance I have mentioned. Can we suppose Congress so lost to every sense of duty, interest, and justice? Would their constituents permit them to put their hands into their pockets to pay *our debts?* We have no equivalent to give them for it. As several powerful states have proposed amendments, they will, no doubt, be supported with zeal and perseverance, so that it is not probable that the object of amendments will be lost. We may struggle on for a few years, and render ourselves wretched and contemptible; but we must at last come into the Union on their terms, however humiliating they may be. The project on the table is little better than an absolute rejection, and is neither rational nor politic, as it cannot promote the end proposed.

Mr. LOCKE, in reply to Mr. Davie, expressed some apprehensions that the Constitution, if adopted as it then stood, would render the people poor and miserable. He thought it would be very productive of expenses. The advantages of the impost he considered as of little consequence, as he thought all the money raised that way, and more, would be swept away by courtly parade — the emoluments of the President, and other members of the government, the Supreme Court, &c. These expenses would double the impost, in his opinion. They would render the states bankrupt. The imposts, he imagined, would be inconsiderable. The people of America began to import less foreign frippery. Every wise planter was fond of home manufacture. The Northern States manufactured considerably, and he thought manufactures would increase daily. He thought a previous ratification dangerous. The worst that could happen would be, that we should be thrown out of the Union. He would rather that should be the case, than embrace a tyrannical government, and give away our rights and privileges. He was therefore determined to vote for the resolutions of the gentleman from Halifax.

Mr. SPENCER observed that, if the conduct of North Carolina would be immodest and dictatorial in proposing amendments, and if it was proposing a constitution to the other states, he was sure the other states, who had proposed the same amendments, were equally guilty of immodesty and

dictating a constitution to the other states; the only difference being, that this state does not adopt previously. The
gentleman had objections to his legal maxims, and said they
were not politic. He would be extremely sorry, he said, if
the maxims of justice should not take place in politics.
Were this to be the case, there could be no faith put in any
compact. He thought the comparison of the state to a beggar was a degradation of it, and insisted on the propriety of
his own comparison, which he thought obvious to any one.
He acknowledged that an exclusion from the Union would
be a most unhappy circumstance; but he had no idea that
it would be the case. As this mode of proceeding would
hasten the amendments, he could not but vote for it.

Mr. JONES defined the word *modesty* by contrasting it
with its antagonist, *impudence*. The gentleman found fault
with the observation, that this was the most decent and best
way of obtaining amendments. If gentlemen would propose
a more eligible method, he would consent to that. He said
the gentleman had reviled the state by his comparison, and
must have hurt the feelings of every gentleman in the house.
He had no apprehension that the other states would refuse
to admit them into the Union, when they thought proper to
come in. It was their interest to admit them. He asked
if a beggar would refuse a boon, though it were but a shilling;
or if twelve men, struggling under a heavy load, would refuse
the assistance of a thirteenth man.

A desultory conversation now took place.

Mr. DAVIE hoped they would not take up the whole
collectively, but that the proposed amendments would be
considered one by one. Some other gentlemen expressed
the same desire.

Many other gentlemen thought the resolution very proper as it stood.

The question being put, the resolution was agreed to by a great majority of the committee.

It was then resolved that the committee should rise. Mr. President
resumed the chair, and Mr. Kenan reported, from the committee of the
whole Convention, that the committee had again had the Constitution
proposed for the future government of the United States under consideration, and had come to a resolution thereupon; which he read in his
place, and afterwards delivered in at the clerk's table.

Ordered, That the said report lie on the table until to-morrow morning, 9 o'clock; to which time the house adjourned.

FRIDAY, *August* 1, 1788

The Convention met according to adjournment.

Mr. IREDELL.   Mr. President: I believe, sir, all debate is now at an end.   It is useless to contend any longer against a majority that is irresistible.   We submit, with the deference that becomes us, to the decision of a majority; but my friends and myself are anxious that something may appear on the Journal to show our sentiments on the subject. I have therefore a resolution in my hand to offer, not with a view of creating any debate, (for I know it will be instantly rejected,) but merely that it may be entered on the Journal, with the yeas and nays taken upon it, in order that our constituents and the world may know what our opinions really were on this important occasion.   We prefer this to the exceptionable mode of a protest, which might increase the spirit of party animosity among the people of this country, which is an event we wish to prevent, if possible.   I therefore, sir, have the honor of moving—

"That the consideration of the report of the committee be postponed, in order to take up the consideration of the following resolution."

Mr. IREDELL then read the resolution in his place, and afterwards delivered it in at the clerk's table, and his motion was seconded by Mr. JOHN SKINNER.

Mr. JOSEPH M'DOWALL, and several other gentle men, most strongly objected against the propriety of this motion.   They thought it improper, unprecedented, and a great contempt of the voice of the majority.

Mr. IREDELL replied, that he thought it perfectly regular, and by no means a contempt of the majority.   The sole intention of it was to show the opinion of the minority, which could not, in any other manner, be so properly done. They wished to justify themselves to their constituents, and the people at large would judge between the merits of the two propositions.   They wished also to avoid, if possible, the disagreeable alternative of a protest.   This being the first time he ever had the honor of being a member of a representative body, he did not solely confide in his own judgment, as to the proper manner of bringing his resolution forward, but had consulted a very respectable and experienced member of that house, who recommended this method to him; and he well knew it was conformable to a frequent practice in Congress, as he had observed by their Journals. Each member had an equal right to make a motion, and if seconded, a vote ought to be taken upon it; and he trusted the majority would not be so arbitrary as to prevent them from taking this method to deliver their sentiments to the world.

He was supported by Mr. MACLAINE and Mr. SPAIGHT.

Mr. WILLIE JONES and Mr. SPENCER insisted on its being irregular, and said they might protest. Mr. Jones said, there never was an example of the kind before; that such a practice did not prevail in Congress when he was a member of it, and he well knew no such practice had ever prevailed in the Assembly.

Mr. DAVIE said, he was sorry that gentlemen should not deal fairly and liberally with one another. He declared it was perfectly parliamentary, and the usual practice in Congress. They were in possession of the motion, and could not get rid of it without taking a vote upon it. It was in the nature of a previous question. He declared that nothing hurt his feelings so much as the blind tyranny of a dead majority.

After a warm discussion on this point by several gentlemen on both sides of the house, it was at length intimated to Mr. Iredell, by Mr. Spaight, across the house, that Mr. Lenoir, and some other gentlemen of the majority, wished he would withdraw his motion for the present, on purpose that the resolution of the committee might be first entered on the Journal, which had not been done; and afterwards his motion might be renewed. Mr. Iredell declared he would readily agree to this, if the gentleman who had seconded him would, desiring the house to remember that he only withdrew his motion for that reason, and hoped he should have leave to introduce it afterwards; which seemed to be understood. He accordingly, with the consent of Mr. Skinner, withdrew his motion; and the resolution of the committee of the whole house was then read, and ordered to be entered on the Journal. The resolution was accordingly read and entered, as follows, viz.: —

"*Resolved*, That a declaration of rights, asserting and securing from encroachment the great principles of civil and religious liberty, and the unalienable rights of the people, together with amendments to the most ambiguous and exceptionable parts of the said Constitution of government, ought to be laid before Congress, and the convention of the states that shall or may be called for the purpose of amending the said Constitution, for their consideration, previous to the ratification of the Constitution aforesaid on the part of the state of North Carolina."

"DECLARATION OF RIGHTS.

"1. That there are certain natural rights, of which men, when they form a social compact, cannot deprive or divest their posterity, among which are the enjoyment of life and liberty, with the means of acquiring, possessing, and protecting property, and pursuing and obtaining happiness and safety.

"2. That all power is naturally vested in, and consequently derived from, the people; that magistrates, therefore, are their trustees and agents, and at all times amenable to them.

"3. That government ought to be instituted for the common benefit, protection, and security, of the people; and that the doctrine of non-resistance against arbitrary power and oppression is absurd, slavish, and destructive to the good and happiness of mankind.

"4. That no man or set of men are entitled to exclusive or separate public emoluments or privileges from the community, but in consideration of public services, which not being descendible, neither ought the offices of magistrate, legislator, or judge, or any other public office, to be hereditary.

"5. That the legislative, executive, and judiciary powers of government should be separate and distinct, and that the members of the two first may be restrained from oppression by feeling and participating the public burdens: they should, at fixed periods, be reduced to a private station, return into the mass of the people, and the vacancies be supplied by certain and regular elections, in which all or any part of the former members to be eligible or ineligible, as the rules of the constitution of government and the laws shall direct.

"6. That elections of representatives in the legislature ought to be free and frequent, and all men having sufficient evidence of permanent common interest with, and attachment to, the community, ought to have the right of suffrage; and no aid, charge, tax, or fee, can be set, rated, or levied, upon the people without their own consent, or that of their representatives so elected; nor can they be bound by any law to which they have not in like manner assented for the public good.

"7. That all power of suspending laws, or the execution of laws, by any authority, without the consent of the representatives of the people in the legislature, is injurious to their rights, and ought not to be exercised.

"8. That, in all capital and criminal prosecutions, a man hath a right to demand the cause and nature of his accusation, to be confronted with the accusers and witnesses, to call for evidence, and be allowed counsel in his favor, and a fair and speedy trial by an impartial jury of his vicinage, without whose unanimous consent he cannot be found guilty, (except in the government of the land and naval forces;) nor can he be compelled to give evidence against himself.

"9. That no freeman ought to be taken, imprisoned, or disseized of his freehold, liberties, privileges, or franchises, or outlawed or exiled, or in any manner destroyed, or deprived of his life, liberty, or property, but by the law of the land.

"10. That every freeman, restrained of his liberty, is entitled to a remedy to inquire into the lawfulness thereof, and to remove the same if unlawful; and that such remedy ought not to be denied nor delayed.

"11 That, in controversies respecting property, and in suits between man and man, the ancient trial by jury is one of the greatest securities to the rights of the people, and ought to remain sacred and inviolable.

" 12. That every freeman ought to find a certain remedy, by recourse to the laws, for all injuries and wrongs he may receive in his person, property, or character; he ought to obtain right and justice freely without sale, completely and without denial, promptly and without delay; and that all establishments or regulations contravening these rights are oppressive and unjust.

" 13. That excessive bail ought not to be required, nor excessive fines imposed, nor cruel and unusual punishments inflicted.

" 14. That every freeman has a right to be secure from all unreasonable searches and seizures of his person, his papers and property; all warrants, therefore, to search suspected places, or to apprehend any suspected person, without specially naming or describing the place or person, are dangerous, and ought not to be granted.

" 15. That the people have a right peaceably to assemble together, to consult for the common good, or to instruct their representatives; and that every freeman has a right to petition or apply to the legislature for redress of grievances.

" 16. That the people have a right to freedom of speech, and of writing and publishing their sentiments; that freedom of the press is one of the greatest bulwarks of liberty, and ought not to be violated.

" 17. That the people have a right to keep and bear arms; that a well-regulated militia, composed of the body of the people, trained to arms, is the proper, natural, and safe defence of a free state; that standing armies, in time of peace, are dangerous to liberty, and therefore ought to be avoided, as far as the circumstances and protection of the community will admit; and that, in all cases, the military should be under strict subordination to, and governed by, the civil power.

" 18. That no soldier, in time of peace, ought to be quartered in any house without the consent of the owner, and in time of war, in such manner only as the laws direct.

" 19. That any person religiously scrupulous of bearing arms ought to be exempted, upon payment of an equivalent to employ another to bear arms in his stead.

" 20. That religion, or the duty which we owe to our Creator, and the manner of discharging it, can be directed only by reason and conviction, not by force or violence; and therefore all men have an equal, natural, and unalienable right to the free exercise of religion, according to the dictates of conscience; and that no particular religious sect or society ought to be favored or established by law in preference to others."

" AMENDMENTS TO THE CONSTITUTION.

" 1. That each state in the Union shall respectively retain every power, jurisdiction, and right, which is not by this Constitution delegated to the Congress of the United States, or to the departments of the federal government.

" 2. That there shall be one representative for every thirty thousand, according to the enumeration or census mentioned in the Constitution, until the whole number of representatives amounts to two hundred; after which that number shall be continued or increased as Congress shall direct, upon the principles fixed in the Constitution, by apportioning the representatives of each state to some greater number of the people, from time to time, as the population increases.

" 3. When Congress shall lay direct taxes or excises, they shall immediately inform the executive power of each state of the quota of such state, according to the census herein directed, which is proposed to be thereby raised ; and if the legislature of any state shall pass any law which shall be effectual for raising such quota at the time required by Congress, the taxes and excises laid by Congress shall not be collected in such state.

" 4. That the members of the Senate and House of Representatives shall be ineligible to, and incapable of holding, any civil office under the authority of the United States, during the time for which they shall respectively be elected.

" 5. That the Journals of the proceedings of the Senate and House of Representatives shall be published at least once in every year, except such parts thereof relating to treaties, alliances, or military operations, as in their judgment require secrecy.

" 6. That a regular statement and account of receipts and expenditures of all public moneys shall be published at least once in every year.

" 7. That no commercial treaty shall be ratified without the concurrence of two thirds of the whole number of the members of the Senate. And no treaty, ceding, contracting, restraining, or suspending, the territorial rights or claims of the United States, or any of them, or their, or any of their, rights or claims of fishing in the American seas, or navigating the American rivers, shall be made, but in cases of the most urgent and extreme necessity ; nor shall any such treaty be ratified without the concurrence of three fourths of the whole number of the members of both houses respectively.

" 8. That no navigation law, or law regulating commerce, shall be passed without the consent of two thirds of the members present in both houses.

" 9. That no standing army or regular troops shall be raised or kept up in time of peace, without the consent of two thirds of the members present in both houses.

" 10. That no soldier shall be enlisted for any longer term than four years, except in time of war, and then for no longer term than the continuance of the war.

" 11. That each state respectively shall have the power to provide for organizing, arming, and disciplining its own militia, whensoever Congress shall omit or neglect to provide for the same ; that the militia shall not be subject to martial law, except when in actual service in time of war, invasion, or rebellion ; and when not in the actual service of the United States, shall be subject only to such fines, penalties, and punishments, as shall be directed or inflicted by the laws of its own state.

" 12. That Congress shall not declare any state to be in rebellion, without the consent of at least two thirds of all the members present in both houses.

" 13. That the exclusive power of legislation given to Congress over the federal town and its adjacent district, and other places purchased or to be purchased by Congress of any of the states, shall extend only to such regulations as respect the police and good government thereof.

" 14. That no person shall be capable of being President of the United States for more than eight years in any term of fifteen years.

"15. That the judicial power of the United States shall be vested in one Supreme Court, and in such courts of admiralty as Congress may from time to time ordain and establish in any of the different states. The judicial power shall extend to all cases in law and equity arising under treaties made, or which shall be made, under the authority of the United States; to all cases affecting ambassadors, other foreign ministers, and consuls; to all cases of admiralty and maritime jurisdiction; to controversies to which the United States shall be a party; to controversies between two or more states, and between parties claiming lands under the grants of different states. In all cases affecting ambassadors, other foreign ministers, and consuls, and those in which a state shall be a party, the Supreme Court shall have original jurisdiction. In all other cases before mentioned, the Supreme Court shall have appellate jurisdiction as to matters of law only, except in cases of equity, and of admiralty and maritime jurisdiction, in which the Supreme Court shall have appellate jurisdiction both as to law and fact, with such exceptions, and under such regulations, as the Congress shall make: but the judicial power of the United States shall extend to no case where the cause of action shall have originated before the ratification of this Constitution, except in disputes between states about their territory, disputes between persons claiming lands under the grants of different states, and suits for debts due to the United States.

"16. That, in criminal prosecutions, no man shall be restrained in the exercise of the usual and accustomed right of challenging or excepting to the jury.

"17. That Congress shall not alter, modify, or interfere in, the times, places, or manner, of holding elections for senators and representatives, or either of them, except when the legislature of any state shall neglect, refuse, or be disabled, by invasion or rebellion, to prescribe the same.

"18. That those clauses which declare that Congress shall not exercise certain powers be not interpreted in any manner whatsoever to extend the power of Congress; but that they be construed either as making exceptions to the specified powers, where this shall be the case, or otherwise as inserted merely for greater caution.

"19. That the laws ascertaining the compensation of senators and representatives for their services, be postponed in their operation until after the election of representatives immediately succeeding the passing thereof, that excepted which shall first be passed on the subject.

"20. That some tribunal other than the Senate be provided for trying impeachments of senators.

"21. That the salary of a judge shall not be increased or diminished during his continuance in office, otherwise than by general regulations of salary, which may take place on a revision of the subject at stated periods of not less than seven years, to commence from the time such salaries shall be first ascertained by Congress.

"22. That Congress erect no company of merchants with exclusive advantages of commerce.

"23. That no treaties which shall be directly opposed to the existing laws of the United States in Congress assembled shall be valid until such laws shall be repealed, or made conformable to such treaty; nor shall any treaty be valid which is contradictory to the Constitution of the United States.

"24. That the latter part of the 5th paragraph of the 9th section of the 1st article be altered to read thus: 'Nor shall vessels bound to a particu

lar state be obliged to enter or pay duties in any other ; nor, when bound
from any one of the states, be obliged to clear in another.'

" 25. That Congress shall not, directly or indirectly, either by themselves or through the judiciary, interfere with any one of the states in the
redemption of paper money already emitted and now in circulation, or in
liquidating and discharging the public securities of any one of the states,
but each and every state shall have the exclusive right of making such laws
and regulations, for the above purposes, as they shall think proper.

" 26. That Congress shall not introduce foreign troops into the United
States without the consent of two thirds of the members present of both
houses."

Mr. SPENCER then moved that the report of the committee be concurred with, and was seconded by Mr. J.
M'DOWALL.

Mr. IREDELL moved that the consideration of that motion be postponed, in order to take into consideration the following resolution :

[Which resolution was the same he introduced before, and
which he afterwards, in substance, moved by way of amendment.]

This gave rise to a very warm altercation on both sides,
during which the house was in great confusion.   Many gentlemen in the majority (particularly Mr. WILLIE JONES)
strongly contended against the propriety of the motion.
Several gentlemen in the minority resented, in strong terms,
the arbitrary attempt of the majority (as they termed it) to
suppress their sentiments ; and Mr. SPAIGHT, in particular, took notice, with great indignation, of the motion made
to concur with the committee, when the gentleman from
Edenton appeared in some measure to have had the faith of
the house that he should have an opportunity to renew his
motion, which he had withdrawn at the request of some of
the majority themselves.   Mr. WHITMILL HILL spoke
with great warmth, and declared that, in his opinion, if the
majority persevered in their tyrannical attempt, the minority
should secede.

Mr. WILLIE JONES still contended that the motion
was altogether irregular and improper, and made a motion
calculated to show that such a motion, made and seconded
under the circumstances in which it had been introduced,
was not entitled to be entered on the Journal.   His motion,
being seconded, was carried by a great majority.   The yeas
and nays were moved for, and were taking, when Mr. IRE-
DELL arose, and said he was sensible of the irregularity he

was guilty of, and hoped he should be excused for it, but it arose from his desire of saving the house trouble; that Mr. Jones (he begged pardon for naming him) had proposed an expedient to him, with which he should be perfectly satisfied, if the house approved of it, as it was indifferent to him what was the mode, if his object in substance was obtained. The method proposed was, that the motion for concurrence should be withdrawn, and his resolution should be moved by way of an amendment. If the house, therefore, approved of this method, and the gentlemen who had moved and seconded the motion would agree to withdraw it, he hoped it would be deemed unnecessary to proceed with the yeas and nays.

Mr. NATHAN BRYAN said, the gentleman treated the majority with contempt. Mr. IREDELL declared he had no such intention; but as the yeas and nays were taken on a difference between both sides of the house, which he hoped might be accommodated, he thought he might be excused for the liberty he had taken.

Mr. SPENCER and Mr. M'DOWALL, after some observations not distinctly heard, accordingly withdrew their motion; and it was agreed that the yeas and nays should not be taken, nor the motion which occasioned them entered on the Journal. Mr. IREDELL then moved as follows, viz.: —

That the report of the committee be amended, by striking out all the words of the said report except the two first, viz.: " Resolved, That," and that the following words be inserted in their room, viz.: — " this Convention, having fully deliberated on the Constitution proposed for the future government of the United States of America by the Federal Convention lately held, at Philadelphia, on the 17th day of September last, and having taken into their serious and solemn consideration the present critical situation of America, which induces them to be of opinion that, though certain amendments to the said Constitution may be wished for, yet that those amendments should be proposed subsequent to the ratification on the part of this state, and not previous to it: — they do, therefore, on behalf of the state of North Carolina, and the good people thereof, and by virtue of the authority to them delegated, ratify the said Constitution on the part of this state; and they do at the same time recommend that, as early as possible, the following amendments to the said

Constitution may be proposed for the consideration and adoption of the several states in the Union, in one of the modes prescribed by the 5th article thereof: " —

" AMENDMENTS.

" 1. Each state in the Union shall respectively retain every power, jurisdiction, and right, which is not by this Constitution delegated to the Congress of the United States, or to the departments of the general government; nor shall the said Congress, nor any department of the said government, exercise any act of authority over any individual in any of the said states, but such as can be justified under some power particularly given in this Constitution ; but the said Constitution shall be considered at all times a solemn instrument, defining the extent of their authority, and the limits of which they cannot rightfully in any instance exceed.

" 2. There shall be one representative for every thirty thousand, according to the enumeration or census mentioned in the Constitution, until the whole number of representatives amounts to two hundred ; after which, that number shall be continued or increased, as Congress shall direct, upon the principles fixed in the Constitution, by apportioning the representatives of each state to some greater number of people, from time to time, as the population increases.

" 3. Each state respectively shall have the power to provide for organizing, arming, and disciplining, its own militia, whensoever Congress shall omit or neglect to provide for the same. The militia shall not be subject to martial law, except when in actual service in time of war, invasion, or rebellion ; and when they are not in the actual service of the United States, they shall be subject only to such fines, penalties, and punishments, as shall be directed or inflicted by the laws of its own state.

" 4. The Congress shall not alter, modify, or interfere in the times, places, or manner, of holding elections for senators and representatives, or either of them, except when the legislature of any state shall neglect, refuse, or be disabled by invasion or rebellion, to prescribe the same.

" 5. The laws ascertaining the compensation of senators and representatives, for their services, shall be postponed in their operation until after the election of representatives immediately succeeding the passing thereof; that excepted which shall first be passed on the subject.

" 6. Instead of the following words in the 9th section of the 1st article, viz , ' Nor shall vessels bound to or from one state be obliged to enter, clear, or pay duties, in another,' [the meaning of which is by many deemed not sufficiently explicit,] it is proposed that the following shall be substituted : ' No vessel bound to one state shall be obliged to enter or pay duties, to which such vessel may be liable at any port of entry, in any other state than that to which such vessel is bound; nor shall any vessel bound from one state be obliged to clear, or pay duties to which such vessel shall be liable at any port of clearance, in any other state than that from which such vessel is bound.' "

He was seconded by Mr. JOHN SKINNER.

The question was then put, " Will the Convention adopt

that amendment or not?" and it was negatived; whereupon Mr. IREDELL moved that the yeas and nays should be taken, and he was seconded by Mr. STEELE. They were accordingly taken, and were as follows:—

YEAS.

His excellency, Samuel Johnston, *President.*

Messrs. Ja's Iredell,
Archibald Maclaine,
Nathan Keas,
John G. Blount,
Thomas Alderson,
John Johnson,
Andrew Oliver,
Goodwin Elliston,
Charles M'Dowall,
Richard D. Spaight,
William J. Dawson,
James Porterfield,
Wm. Barry Grove,
George Elliott,
Wallis Styron,
William Shepperd,
Carteret.
James Philips,
John Humphreys,
Michael Payne,
Charles Johnston,
Stephen Cabarrus,

Edmund Blount,
Chowan.
Henry Abbot,
Isaac Gregory,
Peter Dauge,
Charles Grandy,
Enoch Sawyer,
George Lucas,
John Willis,
John Cade,
Elias Barnes,
Neil Brown,
James Winchester,
William Stokes,
Thomas Stewart,
Josiah Collins,
Thomas Hines,
Nathaniel Jones,
John Steele,
William R. Davie,
Joseph Reddick,
James Gregory,

Thomas Hunter,
Gates.
Thomas Wyns,
Abraham Jones,
John Eborne,
James Jasper,
Caleb Forman,
Seth Hovey,
John Sloan,
John Moore,
William Maclaine,
Nathan Mayo,
William Slade,
William M'Kenzie,
Robert Erwin,
John Lane,
Thomas Reading,
Edward Everagain,
Enoch Rolfe,
Devotion Davis,
William Skinner,
Joshua Skinner,

Thomas Hervey,
John Skinner,
Samuel Harrel,
Joseph Leech,
Wm Bridges,
Wm. Burden,
Edmund Blount,
Tyrel.
Simeon Spruil,
David Tanner,
Whitmill Hill,
Benjamin Smith,
John Sitgreaves,
Nathaniel Allen,
Thomas Owen,
George Wyns,
David Perkins,
Joseph Ferebee,
Wm. Ferebee,
Wm. Baker,
Abner Neale.

84

NAYS.

Messrs. Willie Jones,
Samuel Spencer,
Lewis Lanier,
Thomas Wade,
Daniel Gould,
James Bonner,
Alexius M. Foster,
Lewis Dupree,
Thomas Brown,
James Greenlee,
Joseph M'Dowall,
Robert Miller,
Benjamin Williams,
Richard Nixon,
Thomas Armstrong,
Alex. M'Allister,
Robert Dickens,
George Roberts,
John Womack,
Ambrose Ramsey,
James Anderson,
Jos. Stewart,
Wm. Vestal,
Thomas Evans,
Thomas Hardiman,
Robert Weakly,
Wm. Donnelson,
Wm. Dobins,
Robert Diggs,
Bythel Bell,
Elisha Battle,

Wm. Fort,
Etheld. Gray,
Wm. Lancaster,
Thomas Sherrod,
John Norward,
Sterling Dupree,
Robert Williams,
Richard Moye,
Arthur Forbes,
David Caldwell,
Wm. Goudy,
Daniel Gillespie,
John Anderson,
John Hamilton,
Thomas Person,
Joseph Taylor,
Thornton Yancey,
Howell Lewis, Jun.,
E. Mitchell,
George Moore,
George Ledbetter,
Wm. Porter,
Zebedee Wood,
Edmund Waddell,
James Galloway,
J Regan,
Joseph Winston,
James Gains,
Charles M'Annelly,
Absalom Bostick,
John Scott,

John Dunkin,
David Dodd,
Curtis Ivey,
Lewis Holmes,
Richard Clinton,
H. Holmes,
Robert Alison,
James Stewart,
John Tipton,
John Macon,
Thomas Christmass,
H. Monfort,
Wm. Taylor,
James Hanley,
Britain Saunders,
Wm. Lenoir,
R. Allen,
John Brown,
Joseph Herndon,
James Fletcher,
Lemuel Burkit,
Wm. Little,
Thomas King,
Nathan Bryan,
John H. Bryan,
Edward Whitty,
Robert Alexander,
James Johnson,
John Cox,
John Carrel,
Cornelius Doud,

Thomas Tyson,
W. Martin,
Thomas Hunter
Martin.
John Graham,
Wm. Loftin,
Wm. Kindal,
Thomas Ussery,
Thomas Butler,
John Bentford,
James Vaughan,
Robert Prebles,
James Vinson,
Wm. S. Marnes,
Howell Ellin,
Redman Bunn,
John Bonds,
David Pridgen,
Daniel Yates,
Thomas Johnston,
John Spicer,
A Tatom,
Alex. Mebane,
Wm. Mebane,
Wm. M'Cauley,
Wm. Shepperd,
Orange.
Jonathan Linley,
Wyatt Hawkins,
James Payne,
John Graves.

John Blair,
Joseph Tipton,
Wm. Bethell,
Abraham Phillips,
John May,
Charles Galloway,
James Boswell,
John M'Allister,
David Looney,
John Sharpe,
Joseph Gaitier,
John A. Campbell,
John P. Williams,
Wm. Marshall,
Charles Robertson,
James Gillespie,

Charles Ward,
Wm. Randal,
Frederick Harget,
Richard M'Kinnie,
John Cains,
Jacob Leonard,
Thomas Carson,
Richard Singleton,
James Whitside,
Caleb Phifer,
Zachias Wilson,
Joseph Douglass,
Thomas Dougan,
James Kenan,
John Jones,
Egbert Haywood,

Wm. Wootten,
John Branch,
Henry Hill,
Andrew Bass,
Joseph Boon,
Wm. Farmer,
John Bryan,
Edward Williams,
Francis Oliver,
Matthew Brooks,
Griffith Rutherford,
Geo H Barringer,
Timo. Bloodworth,
Everet Pearce,
Asahel Rawlins,
James Wilson.

James Roddy,
Samuel Cain,
B. Covington,
J. M'Dowall, Jun.
Durham Hill,
Jas Bloodworth,
Joel Lane,
James Hinton,
Thomas Devane,
James Brandon,
Wm. Dickson,
Burwell Mooring,
Matthew Locke,
Stokely Donelson.
184.

SATURDAY, *August* 2, 1788.

The Convention met according to adjournment.

The report of the committee of the whole Convention, according to order, was taken up and read in the same words as on yesterday; when it was moved by Mr. PERSON, and seconded by Mr. MACON, that the Convention do concur therewith, which was objected to by Mr. A. MACLAINE.

The question being put, "Will the Convention concur with the report of the committee of the whole convention, or not?" it was carried in the affirmative; whereupon Mr. DAVIE moved for the yeas and nays, and was seconded by Mr. CABARRUS. They were accordingly taken; and those who voted yesterday *against* the amendment, voted for concurring with the report of the committee : those who voted *in favor* of the amendment, now voted *against* a concurrence with the report.

On motion of Mr. WILLIE JONES, and seconded by Mr. JAMES GALLOWAY, the following resolution was adopted by a large majority, viz. :—

"Whereas this Convention has thought proper neither to ratify nor reject the Constitution proposed for the government of the United States, and as Congress will proceed to act under the said Constitution, ten states having ratified the same, and probably lay an impost on goods imported into the said ratifying states, —

"*Resolved*, That it be recommended to the legislature of this state, that whenever Congress shall pass a law for collecting an impost in the states aforesaid, this state enact a law for collecting a similar impost on goods imported into this state, and appropriate the money arising therefrom to the use of Congress."

On the motion made by Mr. WILLIE JONES, and seconded by Mr. JAMES GALLOWAY, —

· *Resolved, unanimously*, That it be recommended to the General Assembly to take effectual measures for the redemption of the paper currency, as speedily as may be, consistent with the situation and circumstances of the people of this state."

On a motion made by Mr. WILLIE JONES, and seconded by Mr. JAMES GALLOWAY, —

" *Resolved, unanimously*, That the honorable the president be requested to transmit to Congress, and to the executives of New Hampshire, Massachusetts, Connecticut, Rhode Island, New York, New Jersey, Pennsylvania, Delaware, Maryland, Virginia, South Carolina, and Georgia, a copy of the resolution of the committee of the whole Convention on the subject of the Constitution proposed for the government of the United States, concurred with by this Convention, together with a copy of the resolutions on the subject of impost and paper money."

The Convention afterwards proceeded to the business of fixing the seat of government, and on Monday, the 4th of August, adjourned *sine die*.

DEBATES

IN THE

LEGISLATURE AND IN CONVENTION

OF THE

STATE OF SOUTH CAROLINA,

ON THE

ADOPTION OF THE FEDERAL CONSTITUTION.

House of Representatives. In the Legislature, Wednesday, *January* 16, 1788.

READ the proposed Federal Constitution, after which the house resolved itself into a committee of the whole. Hon. THOMAS BEE in the chair.

Hon. CHARLES PINCKNEY (one of the delegates of the Federal Convention) rose in his place, and said that, although the principles and expediency of the measures proposed by the late Convention will come more properly into discussion before another body, yet, as their appointment originated with them, and the legislatures must be the instrument of submitting the plan to the opinion of the people, it became a duty in their delegates to state with conciseness the motives which induced it.

It must be recollected that, upon the conclusion of the definitive treaty, great inconveniences were experienced, as resulting from the inefficacy of the Confederation. The one first and most sensibly felt was the destruction of our commerce, occasioned by the restrictions of other nations, whose policy it was not in the power of the general government to counteract. The loss of credit, the inability in our citizens to pay taxes, and languor of government, were, as they ever must be, the certain consequences of the decay of commerce. Frequent and unsuccessful attempts were made by Congress to obtain the necessary powers. The states, too, individually attempted, by navigation acts and other

22

commercial provisions, to remedy the evil. These, instead of correcting, served but to increase it ; their regulations interfered not only with each other, but, in almost every instance, with treaties existing under the authority of the Union. Hence arose the necessity of some general and permanent system, which should at once embrace all interests, and, by placing the states upon firm and united ground, enable them effectually to assert their commercial rights. Sensible that nothing but a concert of measures could effect this, Virginia proposed a meeting of commissioners at Annapolis, from the legislature of each state, who should be empowered to take into consideration the commerce of the Union ; to consider how far a uniform system in their commercial regulations might be necessary to their common interest ; and to report to the states such an act as, when unanimously ratified by them, would enable Congress effectually to provide for the same. In consequence of this, ten states appointed delegates. By accident, or otherwise, they did not attend, only five states being represented. The gentlemen present, not being a majority of the Union, did not conceive it advisable to proceed ; but in an address to their constituents, which was also transmitted to the other legislatures, acquainted them with the circumstances of their meeting ; that there appeared to them to be other and more material defects in the federal system than merely those of commercial powers. That these, upon examination, might be found greater than even the acts of their appointments implied, was at least so far probable, from the embarrassments which mark the present state of national affairs, foreign and domestic, as to merit, in their opinions, a deliberate and candid discussion in some mode which would unite the sentiments and councils of all the states. They therefore suggested the appointment of another convention, under more extensive powers, for the purpose of devising such further provisions as should appear to them necessary to render the federal government adequate to the exigencies of the Union.

Under this recommendation the late Convention assembled ; for most of the appointments had been made before the recommendation of Congress was formed or known. He thought proper concisely to mention the manner of the Convention's assembling, merely to obviate an objection which all the opposers of the federal system had used, viz., that, at the time the Convention met, no opinion was entertained of their departing from the Confederation — that merely the grant of commercial powers, and the establishment of a federal revenue, were in agitation ; whereas nothing can be more true, than that its promoters had for their object a firm national government.　Those who had seriously contemplated the subject were fully convinced that a total change of system was necessary — that, however the repair of the Confederation might for a time avert the inconveniences of a dissolution, it was impossible a government of that sort could long unite this growing and extensive country. They also thought that the public mind was fully prepared for the change, and that no time could be more proper for introducing it than the present — that the total want of government, the destruction of commerce, of public credit, private confidence, and national character, were surely sufficiently alarming to awaken their constituents to a true sense of their situation.

Under these momentous impressions the Convention met, when the first question that naturally presented itself to the view of almost every member, although it was never formally brought forward, was the formation of a new, or the amendment of the existing system.　Whatever might have been the opinions of a few speculative men, who either did, or pretended to, confide more in the virtue of the people than prudence warranted, Mr. Pinckney said he would venture to assert that the states were unanimous in preferring a change. They wisely considered that, though the Confederation might possess the great outlines of a general government, yet that it was, in fact, nothing more than a federal union ; or, strictly speaking, a league founded in paternal and persuasive principles, with nothing permanent and coercive in its construction, where the members might, or might not, comply with their federal engagements, as they thought proper — that no power existed of raising supplies but by the requisitions or quotas on the states — that this defect had been almost fatally evinced by the experience of the states for the last six or eight years, in which not one of them had completely complied ; but a few had even paid up their specie proportions ; others very partially ; and some, he had every reason to believe, had not to this day contributed a shilling to the common treasury since the Union was formed.　He should not go into a detail of the conduct of the states, or the unfortunate and embarrassing situation to which their inattention has reduced the Union; these have been so often and so strongly represented by Congress, that he was sure there could not be a member on the floor unacquainted with them. It was sufficient to remark that the Convention saw and felt the necessity of establishing a government upon different principles, which, instead of requiring the intervention of thirteen different legislatures between the demand and the compliance, should operate upon the people in the first instance.

He repeated, that the necessity of having a government which should at once operate upon the people, and not upon the states, was conceived to be indispensable by every delegation present; that, however they may have differed with respect to the quantum of power, no objection was made to the system itself. They considered it, however, highly necessary that, in the establishment of a constitution possessing extensive national authorities, a proper distribution of its powers should be attended to. Sensible of the danger of a single body, and that to such a council the states ought not to intrust important rights, they considered it their duty to divide the legislature into two branches, and, by a limited revisionary power, to mingle, in some degree, the executive in their proceedings — a provision that he was pleased to find meets with universal approbation. The degree of weight which each state was to have in the federal council became a question of much agitation. The larger states contended that no government could long exist whose principles were founded in injustice; that one of the most serious and unanswerable objections to the present system was the injustice of its tendency in allowing each state an equal vote, notwithstanding their striking disparity. The small ones replied, and perhaps with reason, that, as the states were the pillars upon which the general government must ever rest, their state governments must remain; that, however they may vary in point of territory or population, as political associations they were equal; that upon these terms they formally confederated, and that no inducement whatsoever should tempt them to unite upon others; that, if they did, it would amount to nothing less than throwing the whole government of the Union into the hands of three or four of the largest states.

After much anxious discussion, — for, had the Convention separated without determining upon a plan, it would have been on this point, — a compromise was effected, by which it was determined that the first branch be so chosen as to represent in due proportion the people of the Union ; that the Senate should be the representatives of the states, where each should have an equal weight. Though he was at first opposed to this compromise, yet he was far from thinking it an injudicious one. The different branches of the legislature being intended as checks upon each other, it appeared to him they would more effectually restrain their mutual intemperances under this mode of representation than they would have done if both houses had been so formed upon proportionable principles ; for, let us theorize as much as we will, it will be impossible so far to divest the majority of the federal representatives of their state views and policy, as to induce them always to act upon truly national principles. Men do not easily wean themselves of those preferences and attachments which country and connections invariably create ; and it must frequently have happened, had the larger states acquired that decided majority which a proportionable representation would have given them in both houses, that state views and policy would have influenced their deliberations. The ease with which they would, upon all occasions, have secured a majority in the legislature, might, in times less virtuous than the present, have operated as temptations to designing and ambitious men to sacrifice the public good to private views. This cannot be the case at present ; the different mode of representation for the Senate will, as has already been observed, most effectually prevent it. The purpose of establishing different houses of legislation was to introduce the influence of different interests and principles ; and he thought that we should derive, from this mode of separating the legislature into two branches, those benefits which a proper complication of principles is capable of producing, and which must, in his judgment, be greater than any evils that may arise from their temporary dissensions.

The judicial he conceived to be at once the most important and intricate part of the system. That a supreme federal jurisdiction was indispensable, cannot be denied. It is equally true that, in order to insure the administration of justice, it was necessary to give it all the powers, original as

well as appellate, the Constitution has enumerated ; without
it we could not expect a due observance of treaties — that
the state judiciary would confine themselves within their
proper sphere, or that general sense of justice pervade the
Union which this part of the Constitution is intended to
introduce and protect — that much, however, would depend
upon the wisdom of the legislatures who are to organize it
— that, from the extensiveness of its powers, it may be
easily seen that, under a wise management, this department
might be made the keystone of the arch, the means of connecting and binding the whole together, of preserving uniformity in all the judicial proceedings of the Union — that,
in republics, much more (in time of peace) would always
depend upon the energy and integrity of the judicial than
on any other part of the government — that, to insure these,
extensive authorities were necessary ; particularly so were
they in a tribunal constituted as this is, whose duty it would
be not only to decide all national questions which should
arise within the Union, but to control and keep the state
judicials within their proper limits whenever they shall attempt to interfere with its power.

And the executive, he said, though not constructed upon
those firm and permanent principles which he confessed
would have been pleasing to him, is still as much so as the
present temper and genius of the people will admit.   Though
many objections had been made to this part of the system,
he was always at a loss to account for them.   That there
can be nothing dangerous in its powers, even if he was
disposed to take undue advantages, must be easily discerned
from reviewing them.   He is commander-in-chief of the
land and naval forces of the Union, but he can neither raise
nor support forces by his own authority.   He has a revisionary power in the making of laws ; but if two thirds of both
houses afterwards agree notwithstanding his negative, the
law passes.   He cannot appoint to an office without the Senate concurs ; nor can he enter into treaties, or, in short, take a
single step in his government, without their advice.   He is,
also, to remain in office but four years.   He might ask, then,
From whence are the dangers of the executive to proceed ?
It may be said, From a combination of the executive and
the Senate, they might form a baneful aristocracy.

He had been opposed to connecting the executive and

the Senate in the discharge of those duties, because their
union, in his opinion, destroyed that responsibility which the
Constitution should, in this respect, have been careful to
establish; but he had no apprehensions of an aristocracy.
For his part, he confessed that he ever treated all fears of
aristocracies or despotisms, in the federal head, as the most
childish chimeras that could be conceived.   In a Union extensive as this is, composed of so many state governments,
and inhabited by a people characterized, as our citizens are, by
an impatience under any act which even looks like an infringement of their rights, an invasion of them by the federal
head appeared to him the most remote of all our public
dangers.   So far from supposing a change of this sort at all
probable, he confessed his apprehensions were of a different
kind : he rather feared that it was impossible, while the
state systems continue — and continue they must — to construct any government upon republican principles sufficiently
energetic to extend its influence through all its parts.   Near
the federal seat, its influence may have complete effect;
but he much doubted its efficacy in the more remote districts.
The state governments will too naturally slide into an opposition against the general one, and be easily induced to
consider themselves as rivals.   They will, after a time,
resist the collection of a revenue ; and if the general government is obliged to concede, in the smallest degree, on
this point, they will of course neglect their duties, and
despise its authority : a great degree of weight and energy
is necessary to enforce it ; nor is any thing to be apprehended
from them.   All power being immediately derived from the
people, and the state governments being the basis of the
general one, it will easily be in their power to interfere, and
to prevent its injuring or invading their rights.   Though at
first he considered some declaration on the subject of trial by
jury in civil causes, and the freedom of the press, necessary,
and still thinks it would have been as well to have had it
inserted, yet he fully acquiesced in the reasoning which was
used to show that the insertion of them was not essential.
The distinction which has been taken between the nature of
a federal and state government appeared to be conclusive —
that in the former, no powers could be executed, or assumed,
out such as were expressly delegated ; that in the latter, the
indefinite power was given to the government, except on

points that were by express compact reserved to the people.

On the subject of juries, in civil cases, the Convention were anxious to make some declaration; but when they reflected that all courts of admiralty and appeals, being governed in their propriety by the civil law and the laws of nations, never had, or ought to have, juries, they found it impossible to make any precise declaration upon the subject; they therefore left it as it was, trusting that the good sense of their constituents would never induce them to suppose that it could be the interest or intention of the general government to abuse one of the most invaluable privileges a free country can boast; in the loss of which, themselves, their fortunes and connections, must be so materially involved, and to the deprivation of which, except in the cases alluded to, the people of this country would never submit. When we reflect that the exigencies of the government require that a general government upon other principles than the present should be established, — when we contemplate the difference between a federal union and a government operating upon the people, and not upon the states, — we must at once see the necessity of giving to it the power of direct taxation. Without this, it must be impossible for them to raise such supplies as are necessary to discharge the debts, or support the expenses, of the Union — to provide against the common dangers, or afford that protection to its members which they have a right to expect from the federal head. But here he begged leave to observe that, so far from apprehending danger from the exercise of this power, few or no inconveniences are to be expected. He had not a doubt that, except in time of war, or pressing necessity, a sufficient sum would always be raised, by impost, to defray the general expenses. As to the power of raising troops, it was unnecessary to remark upon it further than merely to say, that this is a power the government at present possesses and exercises; a power so essential, that he should very much doubt the good sense or information of the man that should conceive it improper. It is guarded by a declaration that no grants for this purpose shall be longer than two years at a time. For his own part, notwithstanding all that had been said upon this popular topic, he could not conceive that either the dignity of a government could be maintained, its safety insured, or its laws administered, without a body of regular forces to aid the magistrate in the execution of his duty. All government is a kind of restraint. We may be told, a free government imposes no restraint upon the private wills of individuals which does not conduce in a greater degree to the public happiness; but all government is restraint, and founded in force. We are the first nation who have ever held a contrary opinion, or even attempted to maintain one without it. The experiment has been made, and he trusted there would hereafter be few men weak enough to suppose that some regular force ought not to be kept up, or that the militia ever can be depended upon as the support or protection of the Union.

Upon the whole, he could not but join those in opinion who have asserted that this is the best government that has ever yet been offered to the world, and that, instead of being alarmed at its consequences, we should be astonishingly pleased that one so perfect could have been formed from such discordant and unpromising materials. In a system founded upon republican principles, where the powers of government are properly distributed, and each confined to a separate body of magistracy, a greater degree of force and energy will always be found necessary than even in a monarchy. This arises from the national spirit of union being stronger in monarchies than in republics: it is said to be naturally strong in monarchies, because, in the absence both of manners and principles, the compelling power of the sovereign collects and draws every thing to a point; and thereby, in all common situations, effectually supplies their place. But in free countries it is naturally weak, unless supported by public spirit; for as, in most cases, a full spirit of national union will require that the separate and partial views of private interest be on every occasion sacrificed to the general welfare, so, when this principle prevails not, (and it will only prevail in moments of enthusiasm,) the national union must ever be destroyed by selfish views and private interest. He said that, with respect to the Union, this can only be remedied by a strong government, which, while it collects its powers to a point, will prevent that spirit of disunion from which the most serious consequences are to be apprehended. He begged leave, for a moment, to examine what effect this spirit of disunion must have upon us, as we may be affected by a foreign enemy. It weakens the consistency of all public measures, so that no extensive scheme of thought can be carried into action, if its accomplishment demand any long continuance of time. It weakens not only the consistency, but the vigor and expedition, of all public measures; so that, while a divided people are contending about the means of security or defence, a united enemy may surprise and invade them. These are the apparent consequences of disunion. Mr. Pinckney confessed, however, that, after all that had been said upon the subject, our Constitution was in some measure but an experiment; nor was it possible yet to form a just conclusion as to its practicability.

It had been an opinion long established, that a republican form of government suited only the affairs of a small state; which opinion is founded in the consideration, that unless the people in every district of the empire be admitted to a share in the national representation, the government is not to them as a republic; that in a democratic constitution, the mechanism is too complicated, the motions too slow, for the operations of a great empire, whose defence and government require execution and despatch in proportion to the magnitude, extent, and variety of its concerns. There was, no doubt, weight in these reasons; but much of the objection, he thought, would be done away by the continuance of a federal republic, which, distributing the country into districts, or states, of a commodious extent, and leaving to each state its internal legislation, reserves unto a superintending government the adjustment of their general claims, the complete direction of the common force and treasure of the empire. To what limits such a republic might extend, or how far it is capable of uniting the liberty of a small commonwealth with the safety of a peaceful empire; or whether, among coördinate powers, dissensions and jealousies would not arise, which, for want of a common superior, might proceed to fatal extremities, — are questions upon which he did not recollect the example of any nation to authorize us to decide, because the experiment has never been yet fairly made. We are now about to make it upon an extensive scale, and under circumstances so promising, that he considered it the fairest experiment that had been ever made in favor of human nature. He concluded with expressing a thorough conviction that the firm establishment of the present system is better calculated to answer the great ends of public happiness than any that has yet been devised.

A long debate arose on reading the Constitution in paragraphs; but, on a division, there appeared to be a majority against it.

Hon. ROBERT BARNWELL hoped gentlemen would confine themselves to the principles of this Constitution An honorable member had already given much valuable information as reasons that operated in the Convention, so that they were now able to lay before their constituents the necessity of bringing forward this Constitution.

Judge PENDLETON read a paragraph in the Constitution, which says "the Senate shall have the sole power of impeachment." In the British government, and all governments where power is given to make treaties of peace, or declare war, there had been found necessity to annex responsibility. In England, particularly, ministers that advised illegal measures were liable to impeachment, for advising the king. Now, if justice called for punishment of treachery in the Senate, on account of giving bad advice, before what tribunal could they be arraigned? Not surely before their house; that was absurd to suppose. Nor could the President be impeached for making treaties, he acting only under advice of the Senate, without a power of negativing.

Maj. PIERCE BUTLER (one of the delegates of the Federal Convention) was one of a committee that drew up this clause, and would endeavor to recollect those reasons by which they were guided. It was at first proposed to vest the sole power of making peace or war in the Senate; but this was objected to as inimical to the genius of a republic, by destroying the necessary balance they were anxious to preserve. Some gentlemen were inclined to give this power to the President; but it was objected to, as throwing into his hands the influence of a monarch, having an opportunity of involving his country in a war whenever he wished to promote her destruction. The House of Representatives was then named; but an insurmountable objection was made to this proposition — which was, that negotiations always required the greatest secrecy, which could not be expected in a large body. The honorable gentleman then gave a clear, concise opinion on the propriety of the proposed Constitution.

Gen. CHARLES COTESWORTH PINCKNEY (one

of the delegates of the Federal Convention) observed, that the honorable judge, from his great penetration, had hit upon one of those difficult points which for a long time occasioned much debate in the Convention. Indeed, this subject appeared to be of so much magnitude, that a committee consisting of one member from each state was appointed to consider and report upon it. His honorable friend (Major Butler) was on the committee for this state. Some members were for vesting the power for making treaties in the legislature; but the secrecy and despatch which are so frequently necessary in negotiations evinced the impropriety of vesting it there. The same reason showed the impropriety of placing it solely in the House of Representatives. A few members were desirous that the President alone might possess this power, and contended that it might safely be lodged with him, as he was to be responsible for his conduct, and therefore would not dare to make a treaty repugnant to the interest of his country; and from his situation he was more interested in making a good treaty than any other man in the United States. This doctrine General Pinckney said he could not acquiesce in. Kings, he admitted, were in general more interested in the welfare of their country than any other individual in it, because the prosperity of the country tended to increase the lustre of the crown, and a king never could receive a sufficient compensation for the sale of his kingdoms; for he could not enjoy in any other country so advantageous a situation as he permanently possessed in his own. Hence kings are less liable to foreign bribery and corruption than any other set of men, because no bribe that could be given them could compensate the loss they must necessarily sustain for injuring their dominions; indeed, he did not at present recollect any instance of a king who had received a bribe from a foreign power, except Charles II., who sold Dunkirk to Louis XIV. But the situation of a President would be very different from that of a king: he might withdraw himself from the United States, so that the states could receive no advantage from his responsibility; his office is not to be permanent, but temporary; and he might receive a bribe which would enable him to live in greater splendor in another country than his own; and when out of office, he was no more interested in the prosperity of his country than any other patriotic citizen: and in framing a treaty, he might perhaps show an improper partiality for the state to which he particularly belonged. The different propositions made on this subject, the general observed, occasioned much debate. At last it was agreed to give the President a power of proposing treaties, as he was the ostensible head of the Union, and to vest the Senate (where each state had an equal voice) with the power of agreeing or disagreeing to the terms proposed. This, in some measure, took away their responsibility, but not totally ; for, though the Senate were to be judges on impeachments, and the members of it would not probably condemn a measure they had agreed to confirm, yet, as they were not a permanent body, they might be tried hereafter by other senators, and condemned, if they deserved it. On the whole, a large majority of the Convention thought this power would be more safely lodged where they had finally vested it, than any where else. It was a power that must necessarily be lodged somewhere : political caution and republican jealousy rendered it improper for us to vest it in the President alone ; the nature of negotiation, and the frequent recess of the House of Representatives, rendered that body an improper depository of this prerogative. The President and Senate joined were, therefore, after much deliberation, deemed the most eligible corps in whom we could with safety vest the diplomatic authority of the Union.

Hon. RAWLINS LOWNDES could not consider the representation of two thirds in the Senate as equal to the old Confederation, which required nine states. By this new Constitution, a quorum in the Senate might consist only of fourteen ; two thirds of which were ten. Now, was this any thing like a check equal to the present ? Was it consistent with prudence to vest so much power in the hands of so small a body of men, who might supersede every existing law in the Union ? Here he read the 2d clause in the 6th article of the Constitution, viz. : " This Constitution, and the laws of the United States which shall be made in pursuance thereof, and all treaties made, or which shall be made, under the authority of the United States, shall be the supreme law of the land ; and the judges in every state shall be bound thereby — any thing in the Constitution or laws of any state to the contrary notwithstanding." Now, in the history of the known world, was there an instance of the

rulers of a republic being allowed to go so far? Even the
most arbitrary kings possessed nothing like it. The tyrannical Henry VIII. had power given him by Parliament to
issue proclamations that should have the same force as laws
of the land; but this unconstitutional privilege had been
justly reprobated and exploded. The king of France, though
a despotic prince, (he meant no reflection on that prince;
his opinion was very well known,) yet could not enforce his
edicts until they had been registered in Parliament. In
England, the ministers proceed with caution in making treaties: far from being considered as legal without parliamentary sanction, the preamble always stated that his majesty
would endeavor to get it ratified by his Parliament. He observed, that the clause entirely did away the instalment law;
for, when this Constitution came to be established, the treaty
of peace might be pleaded against the relief which that law
afforded. The honorable gentleman commented on the extensive powers given to the President, who was not, he believed, likely ever to be chosen from South Carolina or
Georgia.

Gen. CHARLES COTESWORTH PINCKNEY rose
to obviate some of the objections made by the honorable
gentleman who sat down, and whose arguments, he thought,
were calculated *ad captandum*, and did not coincide with
that ingenuous, fair mode of reasoning he in general made
use of. The treaty could not be construed to militate against
our laws now in existence; and while we did not make, by
law, any distinction between our citizens and foreigners,
foreigners would be content. The treaty had been enrolled
in the prothonotary's office by the express order of the judges.
It had been adjudged, in a variety of cases, to be part of the
law of the land, and had been admitted to be so whenever it
was pleaded. If this had not been the case, and any individual state possessed a right to disregard a treaty made by
Congress, no nation would have entered into a treaty with us.

The comparison made between kings and our President
was not a proper one. Kings are, in general, hereditary, in
whose appointment the people have no voice; whereas, in the
election of our President, the people have a voice, and the
state of South Carolina hath a thirteenth share in his appointment. In the election of senators, South Carolina has an
equal vote with any other state; so has Georgia; and if we

have a man as fit for the office of President in this state as in
others, he did not think the being a southern man could be an
objection.   More than one president of Congress had been
taken from this state.   If we should not be represented in
the Senate, it would be our own fault ; the mode of voting
in that body *per capita*, and not by states, as formerly, would
be a strong inducement to us to keep up a full representation : the alteration was approved by every one of the Convention who had been a member of Congress.   He then
mentioned several instances of difficulties which he had been
informed had occurred in Congress in determining questions
of vast importance to the Union, on account of the members
voting as states, and not individually.   He did not think the
Southern States would be remiss in keeping a full representation.   Experience proved that the Eastern and the Southern
States were most punctual in attendance.   He understood
that it was the Middle ones that principally neglected this
duty.

Hon. JOHN RUTLEDGE (one of the delegates of the
Federal Convention) thought the gentleman mistaken both
as to law and fact; for every treaty was law paramount, and
must operate.   [Read part of the 9th article of Confederation.]   In England, treaties are not necessarily ratified, as
was proved when the British Parliament took up the last
treaty of peace.   A vote of disapprobation dispossessed Lord
Shelburne, the minister, of his place ; the Commons only
addressed the king for having concluded a peace ; yet this
treaty is binding in our courts and in England.   In that
country, American citizens can recover debts due to them
under the treaty ; and in this, but for the treaty, what vio-
lences would have taken place !   What security had violent
tories, stealers of horses, and a number of lawless men, but a
law that we passed for recognizing the treaty ?   There might
have been some offenders punished ; but if they had obtained
a writ of *habeas corpus*, no doubt they would have been relieved.   There was an obvious difference between treaties
of peace and those of commerce, because commercial treaties
frequently clashed with the laws upon that subject ; so that
it was necessary to be ratified in Parliament.   As a proof
that our present Articles of Confederation were paramount,
it was there expressed that France should enjoy certain privileges.   Now, supposing any law had passed taking those

privileges away, would not the treaty be a sufficient bar to any local or municipal laws? What sort of power is that which leaves individuals in full power to reject or approve? Suppose a treaty was unexpectedly concluded between two nations at war; could individual subjects ravage and plunder under letters of marque and reprisal? Certainly not. The treaty concluded, even secretly, would be a sufficient bar to the establishment. Pray, what solid reasons could be urged to support gentlemen's fears that our new governors would wish to promote measures injurious to their native land? Was it not more reasonable that, if every state in the Union had a negative voice, a single state might be tampered with, and defeat every good intention? Adverting to the objection relative to the instalment law being done away, he asked, supposing a person gave security conformable to that law, whether, judging from precedent, the judges would permit any further proceedings contrary to it. He scouted the idea that only ten members would ever be left to manage the business of the Senate; yet, even if so, our delegates might be part of that ten, and consequently our interest secured. He described difficulties experienced in Congress in 1781 and 1782. In those times business of vast importance stood still because nine states could not be kept together. Having said that the laws would stand exactly as they did before, the chancellor asked whether gentlemen seriously could suppose that a President, who has a character at stake, would be such a fool and knave as to join with ten others to tear up liberty by the roots, when a full Senate were competent to impeach him.

Hon. RALPH IZARD gave a clear account of the manner in which edicts are registered in France, which, however, were legal without that ceremony. Even the kings of England had power to make treaties of peace or war. In the congress held at Utrecht, two treaties were agreed upon, one relative to peace, the other of commerce; the latter was not ratified, being found to clash with some laws in existence; yet the king's right to make it was never disputed.

Mr. SPEAKER (Hon. John Julius Pringle) said, that in general he paid great deference to the opinions of the gentleman, (Mr. Lowndes,) because they flowed from good natural sense, matured by much reflection and experience. On this occasion, he entirely disagreed with him. The gentleman

appeared extremely alarmed by a phantom of his own creation — a phantom, like every other, without body or substance, and which will vanish as soon as touched. If the
objections which we may have to other parts of the Constitution be no better founded than to this article, the Constitution will pass through the medium of this house, like gold
through the crucible, the purer, and with much greater lustre.
His objections will only serve to confirm the sentiments of those
who favor it.   All the gentleman's objections may be comprised in the following compass: By the article, the President, with ten senators, if only ten attend, may make
treaties to bind all the states — that the treaties have the
force of, and indeed are paramount to, the laws of the land
— therefore, the President and Senate have a legislative
power; and then he gives scope to a great deal of declamation on the vast danger of their having such legislative power,
and particularly that they might have a treaty which might
thus repeal the instalment law.   This is a greater power, he
says, than the king of France has; the king of Great Britain
has his ratified by Parliament — the treaties of the French
king must be registered.   But he conceived the gentleman
was mistaken as to those treaties made by these monarchs.
The king of France registers his edicts on some occasions, to
facilitate the execution, but not his treaties.   The king of
Great Britain's treaties are discussed by Parliament, not for
ratification, but to discover whether the ministers deserve
censure or approbation.   The making of treaties is justly a
part of their prerogative: it properly belongs to the executive part of government, because they must be conducted
with despatch and secrecy not to be expected in larger assemblies.   No such dangers as the gentleman apprehends
can ensue from vesting it with the President and Senate.
Although the treaties they make may have the force of laws
when made, they have not, therefore, legislative power.   It
would be dangerous, indeed, to trust them with the power
of making laws to affect the rights of individuals; for this
might tend to the oppression of individuals, who could not
obtain redress.   All the evils would, in that case, flow from
blending the legislative, executive, and judicial powers.
This would violate the soundest principles of policy and government.   It is not with regard to the power of making
treaties as of legislation in general.   The treaties will affect

all the individuals equally of all the states.   If the President
and Senate make such as violate the fundamental laws, and
subvert the Constitution, or tend to the destruction of the
happiness and liberty of the states, the evils, equally oppressing all, will be removed as soon as felt, as those who are
oppressed have the power and means of redress.   Such
treaties, not being made with good faith, and on the broad
basis of reciprocal interest and convenience, but by treachery
and a betraying of trust, and by exceeding the powers with
which the makers were intrusted, ought to be annulled.   No
nations would keep treaties thus made.   Indeed, it is too
much the practice for them to make mutual interest and convenience the rule of observation, or period of duration.   As
for the danger of repealing the instalment law, the gentleman has forgot that one article ordains that there shall be no
retrospective law.   The President and Senate will, therefore,
hardly ever make a treaty that would be of this kind.   After
other arguments to obviate the objections of the honorable
gentleman, Mr. Speaker concluded with saying, that it was
not necessary for him to urge what further occurred to him,
as he saw several of the honorable members of the Convention preparing, whose duty it more particularly was, and
who were more able to confute the honorable gentleman in
opposition.

Dr. DAVID RAMSAY asked if the gentleman meant us
ever to have any treaties at all.   If not superior to local laws,
who will trust them ?   Would not the question naturally be,
" Did you mean, when you made treaties, to fulfil them ?"
Establish once such a doctrine, and where will you find ambassadors ?   If gentlemen had been in the situation of
receiving similar information with himself, they would have
heard letters read from our ambassadors abroad, in which
loud complaints were made that America had become faithless and dishonest.   Was it not full time that such conduct
as this should be amended ?

Gen. CHARLES COTESWORTH PINCKNEY rose
to mention some instances he had omitted of the treaty with
Great Britain being considered in our courts as part of the
law of the land.   The judge who held the court at Ninety-
six discharged upwards of one hundred recognizances of persons committed for different crimes, which fell within the
meaning of this treaty.   A man named Love, accused of

murder, was liberated.   It is true, the people, enraged at the enormity of his conduct, hanged him soon after; but of this the judicial power knew nothing until after its perpetration. Another murderer was allowed to plead the treaty of peace in bar, that had conducted General Pickens's brother into the hands of the Indians, who soon after put him to death.

Hon. RAWLINS LOWNDES desired gentlemen to consider that his antagonists were mostly gentlemen of the law, who were capable of giving ingenious explanations to such points as they wished to have adopted.   He explained his opinion relative to treaties to be, that no treaty concluded contrary to the express laws of the land could be valid. The king of England, when he concluded one, did not think himself warranted to go further than to promise that he would endeavor to induce his Parliament to sanction it. The security of a republic is jealousy; for its ruin may be expected from unsuspecting security.   Let us not, therefore, receive this proffered system with implicit confidence, as carrying with it the stamp of superior perfection; rather let us compare what we already possess with what we are offered for it.   We are now under the government of a most excellent constitution, one that had stood the test of time, and carried us through difficulties generally supposed to be insurmountable; one that had raised us high in the eyes of all nations, and given to us the enviable blessings of liberty and independence; a constitution sent like a blessing from Heaven; yet we are impatient to change it for another, that vested power in a few men to pull down that fabric, which we had raised at the expense of our blood.   Charters ought to be considered as sacred things.   In England, an attempt was made to alter the charter of the East India Company; but they invoked heaven and earth in their cause; moved lords, nay, even the king, in their behalf, and thus averted the ruin with which they were threatened.

It has been said that this new government was to be considered as an experiment.   He really was afraid it would prove a fatal one to our peace and happiness.   An experiment!   What, risk the loss of political existence on experiment!   No, sir; if we are to make experiments, rather let them be such as may do good, but which cannot possibly do any injury to us or our posterity.   So far from having any expectation of success from such experiments, he sincerely believed that, when this new Constitution should be adopted, the sun of the Southern States would set, never to rise again.

To prove this, he observed, that six of the Eastern States formed a majority in the House of Representatives. In the enumeration he passed Rhode Island, and included Pennsylvania. Now, was it consonant with reason, with wisdom, with policy, to suppose, in a legislature where a majority of persons sat whose interests were greatly different from ours, that we had the smallest chance of receiving adequate advantages? Certainly not. He believed the gentlemen that went from this state, to represent us in Convention, possessed as much integrity, and stood as high in point of character, as any gentlemen that could have been selected; and he also believed that they had done every thing in their power to procure for us a proportionate share in this new government; but the very little they had gained proved what we may expect in future — that the interest of the Northern States would so predominate as to divest us of any pretensions to the title of a republic. In the first place, what cause was there for jealousy of our importing negroes? Why confine us to twenty years, or rather why limit us at all? For his part, he thought this trade could be justified on the principles of religion, humanity, and justice; for certainly to translate a set of human beings from a bad country to a better, was fulfilling every part of these principles. But they don't like our slaves, because they have none themselves, and therefore want to exclude us from this great advantage. Why should the Southern States allow of this, without the consent of nine states?

Judge PENDLETON observed, that only three states, Georgia, South Carolina, and North Carolina, allowed the importation of negroes. Virginia had a clause in her Constitution for this purpose, and Maryland, he believed, even before the war, prohibited them.

Mr. LOWNDES continued — that we had a law prohibiting the importation of negroes for three years, a law he greatly approved of; but there was no reason offered why the Southern States might not find it necessary to alter their conduct, and open their ports. Without negroes, this state would degenerate into one of the most contemptible in the Union; and he cited an expression that fell from General

Pinckney on a former debate, that whilst there remained one acre of swamp-land in South Carolina, he should raise his voice against restricting the importation of negroes. Even in granting the importation for twenty years, care had been taken to make us pay for this indulgence, each negro being liable, on importation, to pay a duty not exceeding ten dollars; and, in addition to this, they were liable to a capitation tax. Negroes were our wealth, our only natural resource; yet behold how our kind friends in the north were determined soon to tie up our hands, and drain us of what we had! The Eastern States drew their means of subsistence, in a great measure, from their shipping; and, on that head, they had been particularly careful not to allow of any burdens: they were not to pay tonnage or duties; no, not even the form of clearing out: all ports were free and open to them! Why, then, call this a reciprocal bargain, which took all from one party, to bestow it on the other!

Major BUTLER observed, that they were to pay five per cent. impost.

This, Mr. LOWNDES proved, must fall upon the consumer. They are to be the carriers; and, we being the consumers, therefore all expenses would fall upon us. A great number of gentlemen were captivated with this new Constitution, because those who were in debt would be compelled to pay; others pleased themselves with the reflection that no more confiscation laws would be passed; but those were small advantages, in proportion to the evils that might be apprehended from the laws that might be passed by Congress, whenever there was a majority of representatives from the Eastern States, who were governed by prejudices and ideas extremely different from ours. He was afraid, in the present instance, that so much partiality prevailed for this new Constitution, that opposition from him would be fruitless: however, he felt so much the importance of the subject, that he hoped the house would indulge him in a few words, to take a view, comparatively, of the old constitution and the new one, in point of modesty. Congress, laboring under many difficulties, asked to regulate commerce for twenty-one years, when the power reverted into the hands of those who originally gave it; but this infallible new Constitution eased us of any more trouble, for it was to regulate commerce *ad infinitum*; and thus called upon us to pledge ourselves and posterity, forever, in support of their measures ; so when our local legislature had dwindled down to the confined powers of a corporation, we should be liable to taxes and excise ; not, perhaps, payable in paper, but in specie. However, they need not be uneasy, since every thing would be managed in future by great men ; and great men, every body knew, were incapable of acting under mistake or prejudice : they were infallible ; so that if, at any future period, we should smart under laws which bore hard upon us, and think proper to remonstrate, the answer would probably be, "Go : you are totally incapable of managing for yourselves. Go : mind your private affairs ; trouble not yourselves with public concerns — 'Mind your business.'" The latter expression was already the motto of some coppers in circulation, and he thought it would soon be the style of language held out towards the Southern States. The honorable member apologized for going into the merits of this new Constitution, when it was ultimately to be decided on by another tribunal; but understanding that he differed in opinion with his constituents, who were opposed to electing any person as a member of the Convention that did not approve of the proposed plan of government, he should not therefore have an opportunity of expressing those sentiments which occurred to him on considering the plan for a new federal government. But if it was sanctioned by the people, it would have his hearty concurrence and support. He was very much, originally, against a declaration of independency ; he also opposed the instalment law ; but when they received the approbation of the people, it became his duty, as a good citizen, to promote their due observance.

Hon. E. RUTLEDGE was astonished to hear the honorable gentleman pass such eulogium on the old Confederation, and prefer it, as he had done, to the one before the house. For his part, he thought that Confederation so very weak, so very inadequate to the purposes of the Union, that, unless it was materially altered, the sun of American independence would indeed soon set — never to rise again. What could be effected for America under that highly-extolled constitution ? Could it obtain security for our commerce in any part of the world ? Could it force obedience to any one law of the Union ? Could it obtain one shilling of money for the discharge of the most honorable obligations ? The

honorable gentleman knew it could not.   Was there a single
power in Europe that would lend us a guinea on the faith
of that Confederation? or could we borrow one on the public faith of our own citizens?   The people of America had
seen these things; they had felt the consequences of this
feeble government, if that deserved the name of government
which had no power to enforce laws founded on solemn compact; and it was under the influence of those feelings that
with almost one voice, they had called for a different government.   But the honorable gentleman had said that this government had carried us gloriously through the last war.   Mr.
Rutledge denied the assertion.   It was true we had passed
gloriously through the war while the Confederation was in
existence; but that success was not to be attributed to the
Confederation; it was to be attributed to the firm and uncon-
querable spirit of the people, who were determined, at the
hazard of every consequence, to oppose a submission to British government; it was to be attributed to the armaments
of an ally, and the pecuniary assistance of our friends : these
were the wings on which we were carried so triumphantly
through the war; and not this wretched Confederation, which
is unable, by universal acknowledgment, to obtain a discharge of any part of our debts in the hour of the most
perfect domestic tranquillity.   What benefits, then, are to be
expected from such a constitution in the day of danger?
Without a ship, without a soldier, without a shilling in the
federal treasury, and without a nervous government to obtain
one, we hold the property that we now enjoy at the courtesy
of other powers.   Was this such a tenure as was suitable to
the inclinations of our constituents?   It certainly was not.
They had called upon us to change their situation, and we
should betray their interest, and our own honor, if we neglected it.   But the gentleman has said that there were
points in this new confederation which would endanger the
rights of the people — that the President and ten senators
may make treaties, and that the balance between the states
was not sufficiently preserved — that he is for limiting the
powers of Congress, so that they shall not be able to do
any harm; for, if they have the power to do any harm,
they may.   To this Mr. Rutledge observed, that the greatest
part of the honorable gentleman's objection was founded on
an opinion that the choice of the people would fall on the
most worthless and the most negligent part of the com-

munity; but if it was to be admitted, it would go to the withholding of all power from all public bodies. The gentleman would have done well to have defined the kind of power that could do no harm. The very idea of power included a possibility of doing harm; and if the gentleman would show the power that could do no harm, he would at once discover it to be a power which could do no good. To argue against the use of a thing from the abuse of it, had long since been exploded by all sensible people. It was true that the President, with the concurrence of two thirds of the Senate, might make treaties; and it was possible that ten senators *might* constitute the two thirds, but it was just within the reach of possibility, and a possibility from whence no danger could be apprehended. If the President or the senators abused their trust, they were liable to impeachment and punishment; and the fewer that were concerned in the abuse of the trust, the more certain would be the punishment. In the formation of this article, the delegates had done their duty fully; they had provided that two thirds of the Senate should concur in the making of treaties. If the states should be negligent in sending their senators, it would be their own fault, and the injury would be theirs, not the framers of the Constitution; but if they were not negligent, they would have more than their share. Is it not astonishing that the gentleman who is so strenuous an advocate for the powers of the people, should distrust the people the moment that power is given to them, and should found his objections to this article in the corruption of the representatives of the people, and in the negligence of the people themselves? If such objections as these have any weight, they tend to the destruction of all confidence — the withholding of all power — the annihilation of all government. Mr. Rutledge insisted that we had our full share in the House of Representatives, and that the gentleman's fears of the northern interest prevailing at all times were ill-founded. The Constitution had provided for a census of the people, and the number of representatives was to be directed by the number of the people in the several states; this clause was highly favorable to the southern interest. Several of the Northern States were already full of people: it was otherwise with us; the migrations to the south were immense, and we should, in the course of a few years, rise high in our representation, whilst other states would keep their present position.   Gentlemen should carry their views into futurity, and not confine themselves to the narrow limits of a day, when contemplating a subject of such vast importance.   The gentleman had complained of the inequality of the taxes between the Northern and Southern States ; that ten dollars a head was imposed on the importation of negroes ; and that those negroes were afterwards taxed.   To this it was answered, that the ten dollars per head was an equivalent to the five per cent. on imported articles ; and as to their being afterwards taxed, the advantage is on our side, or, at least, not against us.

In the Northern States the labor is performed by white people, in the Southern by black.   All the free people (and there are few others) in the Northern States are to be taxed by the new Constitution ; whereas only the free people, and two fifths of the slaves, in the Southern States, are to be rated, in the apportioning of taxes.   But the principal objection is, that no duties are laid on shipping ; that, in fact, the carrying trade was to be vested, in a great measure, in the Americans ; that the ship-building business was principally carried on in the Northern States.   When this subject is duly considered, the Southern States should be the last to object to it.   Mr. Rutledge then went into a consideration of the subject ; after which the house adjourned.

THURSDAY, *January* 17, 1788.

Gen. CHARLES COTESWORTH PINCKNEY observed, that the honorable gentleman (Mr. Lowndes) who opposed the new Constitution had asserted that treaties made under the old Confederation were not deemed paramount to the laws of the land, and that treaties made by the king of Great Britain required the ratification of Parliament to render them valid.   The honorable gentleman is surely mistaken in his assertion.   His honorable friend (Chancellor Rutledge) had clearly shown that, by the 6th, 9th, and 13th Articles of the old Confederation, Congress have a power to make treaties, and each state is pledged to observe them ; and it appears, from the debates of the English Parliament, that the House of Commons did not ratify, but actually censure, the peace made by the king of Great Britain with America ; yet the very members who censured it acknowledged it was binding on the nation.   [Here the general

24

read extracts from the parliamentary debates of the 17th and 21st of February, 1784.]   Indeed, the doctrine that the king of Great Britain may make a treaty with a foreign state, which shall irrevocably bind his subjects, is asserted by the best writers on the laws and constitution of England — particularly by Judge Blackstone, who, in the first book of his Commentaries, (ch. 7, p. 257,) declares " that it is the king's prerogative to make treaties, leagues, and alliances, with foreign states and princes, and that no other power in the kingdom can legally delay, resist, or annul them."   If treaties entered into by Congress are not to be held in the same sacred light in America, what foreign nation will have any confidence in us?   Shall we not be stigmatized as a faithless, unworthy people, if each member of the Union may, with impunity, violate the engagements entered into by the federal government?   Who will confide in us?   Who will treat with us if our practice should be conformable to this doctrine?   Have we not been deceiving all nations, by holding forth to the world, in the 9th Article of the old Confederation, that Congress may make treaties, if we, at the same time, entertain this improper tenet, that each state may violate them?   I contend that the article in the new Constitution, which says that treaties shall be paramount to the laws of the land, is only declaratory of what treaties were, in fact, under the old compact.   They were as much the law of the land under that Confederation, as they are under this Constitution; and we shall be unworthy to be ranked among civilized nations if we do not consider treaties in this view. Vattel, one of the best writers on the law of nations, says, " There would be no more security, no longer any commerce between mankind, did they not believe themselves obliged to preserve their faith, and to keep their word.   Nations, and their conductors, ought, then, to keep their promises and their treaties inviolable.   This great truth is acknowledged by all nations.   Nothing adds so great a glory to a prince and the nation he governs, as the reputation of an inviolable fidelity to his engagements.   By this, and their bravery, the Swiss have rendered themselves respectable throughout Europe.   This national greatness of soul is the source of immortal glory ; upon it is founded the confidence of nations, and it thus becomes a certain instrument of power and splendor."   Surely this doctrine is right ; it speaks to the heart , it impresses itself on the feelings of mankind, and convinces us that the tranquillity, happiness, and prosperity, of the human race, depend on inviolably preserving the faith of treaties.

Burlamaqui, another writer of great reputation on political law, says " that treaties are obligatory on the subjects of the powers who enter into treaties; they are obligatory as conventions between the contracting powers; but they have the force of law with respect to their subjects." These are his very words : " *Ils ont force de loi a l'égard des sujets, considérés comme tels*; and it is very manifest," continues he, " that two sovereigns, who enter into a treaty, impose, by such treaty, an obligation on their subjects to conform to it, and in no manner to contravene it." It is remarkable that the words made use of by Burlamaqui establish the doctrine, recognized by the Constitution, that treaties shall be considered as the law of the land ; and happy will it be for America if they shall be always so considered : we shall then avoid the disputes, the tumults, the frequent wars, we must inevitably be engaged in, if we violate treaties. By our treaty with France, we declare she shall have all the privileges, in matters of commerce, with the most favored nation. Suppose a particular state should think proper to grant a particular privilege to Holland, which she refuses to France ; would not this be a violation of the treaty with France ? It certainly would ; and we in this state would be answerable for the consequences attending such violation by another state ; for we do not enter into treaties as separate states, but as united states ; and all the members of the Union are answerable for the breach of a treaty by any one of them. South Carolina, therefore, considering its situation, and the valuable produce it has to export, is particularly interested in maintaining the sacredness of treaties, and the good faith with which they should be observed by every member of the Union. But the honorable gentleman complains that the power of making treaties is vested in the President and Senate, and thinks it is not placed so safely with them as with the Congress under the old Confederation. Let us examine this objection. By the old Confederation, each state had an equal vote in Congress, and no treaty could be made without the assent of the delegates from nine states. By the present Constitution, each state sends two members to the Senate, who vote *per capita ;* and the President has power, with advice and consent of the Senate, to make treaties, provided two thirds of the Senate present concur. This inconvenience attended the old method : it was frequently difficult to obtain a representation from nine states ; and if only nine states were present, they must all concur in making a treaty.   A single member would frequently prevent the business from being concluded ; and if he absented himself, Congress had no power to compel his attendance. This actually happened when a treaty of importance was about to be concluded with the Indians ; and several states, being satisfied, at particular junctures, that the nine states present would not concur in sentiments on the subject of a treaty, were indifferent whether their members attended or not.   But now that the senators vote individually, and not by states, each state will be anxious to keep a full representation in the Senate ; and the Senate has now power to compel the attendance of its own members.   We shall thus have no delay, and business will be conducted in a fuller representation of the states than it hitherto has been.   All the members of the Convention, who had served in Congress, were so sensible of the advantage attending this mode of voting, that the measure was adopted unanimously.   For my own part, I think it infinitely preferable to the old method. So much for the manner of voting.

Now let us consider whether the power of making treaties is not as securely placed as it was before.   It was formerly vested in Congress, who were a body constituted by the legislatures of the different states in equal proportions.   At present, it is vested in a President, who is chosen by the people of America, and in a Senate, whose members are chosen by the state legislatures, each legislature choosing two members.   Surely there is greater security in vesting this power as the present Constitution has vested it, than in any other body.   Would the gentleman vest it in the President alone ?   If he would, his assertion that the power we have granted was as dangerous as the power vested by Parliament in the proclamations of Henry VIII., might have been, perhaps, warranted.   Would he vest it in the House of Representatives ?   Can secrecy be expected in sixty-five members ? The idea is absurd.   Besides, their sessions will probably last only two or three months in the year ; therefore, on that

account, they would be a very unfit body for negotiation
whereas the Senate, from the smallness of its numbers, from
the equality of power which each state has in it, from the
length of time for which its members are elected, from the
long sessions they may have without any great inconveniency
to themselves or constituents, joined with the president, who
is the federal head of the United States, form together a
body in whom can be best and most safely vested the diplomatic power of the Union.

General Pinckney then observed, that the honorable
gentleman had not conducted his arguments with his usual
candor.   He had made use of many which were not well
founded, and were only thrown out *ad captandum*.   Why
say, upon this occasion, that every thing would, in future, be
managed by great men, and that great men could do no
wrong ?   Under the new Constitution, the abuse of power
was more effectually checked than under the old one.   A
proper body, immediately taken from the people, and return-
able to the people every second year, are to impeach those
who behave amiss, or betray their public trust ; another body,
taken from the state legislatures, are to try them.   No man,
however great, is exempt from impeachment and trial.   If
the representatives of the people think he ought to be impeached and tried, the President cannot pardon him ; and
this great man himself, whom the honorable gentleman pre-
tends to be so much afraid of, as well as the Vice-President,
and all civil officers of the United States, are to be removed
from office on impeachment and conviction of treason, bribery, or other high crimes and misdemeanors.   Then why
make use of arguments to occasion improper jealousies and
ill-founded fears ?   Why is the invidious distinction of " great
men " to be reiterated in the ears of the members ?   Is there
any thing in the Constitution which prevents the President
and senators from being taken from the poor as well as the
rich ?   Is there any pecuniary qualification necessary to the
holding of any office under the new Constitution ?   There
is not.   Merit and virtue, and federal principles, are the
qualifications which will prefer a poor man to office, before
a rich man who is destitute of them.   The gentleman has
made a warm panegyric on the old Confederation.   Can he
possibly be serious, and does he really think it can secure us
tranquillity at home, or respect abroad ?   Ask the citizens

of Massachusetts if the Confederation protected them during the insurrection of Shays. Ask the crews of our vessels captured by the Algerines if respect for our government hath softened the rigors of their captivity. Inquire of our delegates to Congress if all the despatches from your public ministers are not filled with lamentations of the imbecility of Congress; and whether foreign nations do not declare they can have no confidence in our government, because it has not power to enforce obedience to treaties. Go through each state in the Union, and be convinced that a disregard for law hath taken the place of order, and that Congress is so slighted by all of them that not one hath complied with her requisitions. Every state in the Union, except Rhode Island, was so thoroughly convinced that our government was inadequate to our situation, that all, except her, sent members to the Convention at Philadelphia. General Pinckney said, it had been alleged that, when there, they exceeded their powers. He thought not. They had a right, he apprehended, to propose any thing which they imagined would strengthen the Union, and be for the advantage of our country; but they did not pretend to a right to determine finally upon any thing. The present Constitution is but a proposition which the people may reject; but he conjured them to reflect seriously before they did reject it, as he did not think our state would obtain better terms by another convention, and the anarchy which would, in all probability, be the consequence of rejecting this Constitution, would encourage some daring despot to seize upon the government, and effectually deprive us of our liberties.

Every member who attended the Convention was, from the beginning, sensible of the necessity of giving greater powers to the federal government. This was the very purpose for which they were convened. The delegations of Jersey and Delaware were, at first, averse to this organization; but they afterwards acquiesced in it; and the conduct of their delegates has been so very agreeable to the people of these states, that their respective conventions have unanimously adopted the Constitution. As we have found it necessary to give very extensive powers to the federal government both over the persons and estates of the citizens, we thought it right to draw one branch of the legislature immediately from the people, and that both wealth and

numbers should be considered in the representation. We
were at a loss, for some time, for a rule to ascertain the
proportionate wealth of the states.   At last we thought that
the productive labor of the inhabitants was the best rule for
ascertaining their wealth.   In conformity to this rule, joined
to a spirit of concession, we determined that representatives
should be apportioned among the several states, by adding
to the whole number of free persons three fifths of the slaves.
We thus obtained a representation for our property ; and I
confess I did not expect that we had conceded too much to
the Eastern States, when they allowed us a representation
for a species of property which they have not among them.
    The numbers in the different states, according to the
most accurate accounts we could obtain, were —

In New Hampshire,	102,000
Massachusetts,	360,000
Rhode Island,	58,000
Connecticut,	202,000
New York,	233,000
New Jersey,	138,000
Pennsylvania,	360,000
Delaware,	37,000
Maryland, (including three fifths of 80,000 negroes,)	218,000
Virginia, (including three fifths of 280,000 negroes,)	420,000
N. Carolina, (including three fifths of 60,000 negroes,)	200,000
S. Carolina, (including three fifths of 80,000 negroes,)	150,000
Georgia, (including three fifths of 20,000 negroes,)	90,000

    The first House of Representatives will consist of sixty-
five members.   South Carolina will send five of them.   Each
state has the same representation in the Senate that she has
at present ; so that South Carolina will have, under the new
Constitution, a thirteenth share in the government, which is
the proportion she has under the old Confederation : and
when it is considered that the Eastern States are full of
men, and that we must necessarily increase rapidly to the
southward and south-westward, he did not think that the
Southern States will have an inadequate share in the representation.   The honorable gentleman alleges that the
Southern States are weak.   I sincerely agree with him.
We are so weak that by ourselves we could not form a union
strong enough for the purpose of effectually protecting each
other.   Without union with the other states, South Carolina
must soon fall.   Is there any one among us so much a

Quixote as to suppose that this state could long maintain her independence if she stood alone, or was only connected with the Southern States? I scarcely believe there is. Let an invading power send a naval force into the Chesapeake to keep Virginia in alarm, and attack South Carolina with such a naval and military force as Sir Henry Clinton brought here in 1780; and though they might not soon conquer us, they would certainly do us an infinite deal of mischief; and if they considerably increased their numbers, we should probably fall. As, from the nature of our climate and the fewness of our inhabitants, we are undoubtedly weak, should we not endeavor to form a close union with the Eastern States, who are strong? And ought we not to endeavor to increase that species of strength which will render them of most service to us both in peace and war? — I mean their navy. We certainly ought; and by doing this we render it their particular interest to afford us every assistance in their power, as every wound that we receive will eventually affect them. Reflect, for a moment, on the situation of the Eastern States; their country full of inhabitants, and so impracticable to an invading enemy by their numberless stone walls, and a variety of other circumstances, that they can be under no apprehension of danger from an attack. They can enjoy their independence without our assistance. If our government is to be founded on equal compact, what inducement can they possibly have to be united with us, if we do not grant them some privileges with regard to their shipping? Or, supposing they were to unite with us without having these privileges, can we flatter ourselves that such union would be lasting, or that they would afford us effectual assistance when invaded? Interest and policy both concurred in prevailing upon us to submit the regulation of commerce to the general government. But I will also add, justice and humanity require it likewise. For who have been the greatest sufferers in the Union, by our obtaining our independence? I answer, the Eastern States. They have lost every thing but their country and their freedom. It is notorious that some ports to the eastward. which used to fit out one hundred and fifty sail of vessels, do not now fit out thirty; that their trade of shipbuilding, which used to be very considerable, is now annihilated; that their fisheries are trifling, and their mariners in want of bread. Surely we are called upon by every tie o justice, friendship, and humanity, to relieve their distresses; and as, by their exertions, they have assisted us in establishing our freedom, we should let them, in some measure, partake of our prosperity. The general then said he would make a few observations on the objections which the gentleman had thrown out on the restrictions that might be laid on the African trade after the year 1808. On this point your delegates had to contend with the religious and political prejudices of the Eastern and Middle States, and with the interested and inconsistent opinion of Virginia, who was warmly opposed to our importing more slaves. I am of the same opinion now as I was two years ago, when I used the expressions the gentleman has quoted — that, while there remained one acre of swamp-land uncleared of South Carolina, I would raise my voice against restricting the importation of negroes. I am as thoroughly convinced as that gentleman is, that the nature of our climate, and the flat, swampy situation of our country, obliges us to cultivate our lands with negroes, and that without them South Carolina would soon be a desert waste.

You have so frequently heard my sentiments on this subject, that I need not now repeat them. It was alleged, by some of the members who opposed an unlimited importation, that slaves increased the weakness of any state who admitted them; that they were a dangerous species of property, which an invading enemy could easily turn against ourselves and the neighboring states; and that, as we were allowed a representation for them in the House of Representatives, our influence in government would be increased in proportion as we were less able to defend ourselves. "Show some period," said the members from the Eastern States, "when it may be in our power to put a stop, if we please, to the importation of this weakness, and we will endeavor, for your convenience, to restrain the religious and political prejudices of our people on this subject." The Middle States and Virginia made us no such proposition; they were for an immediate and total prohibition. We endeavored to obviate the objections that were made in the best manner we could, and assigned reasons for our insisting on the importation, which there is no occasion to repeat, as they must occur to every gentleman in the house: a committee of the states was appointed in order to accommodate this matter, and, after a great deal of difficulty, it was settled on the footing recited in the Constitution.

By this settlement we have secured an unlimited importation of negroes for twenty years. Nor is it declared that the importation shall be then stopped; it may be continued. We have a security that the general government can never emancipate them, for no such authority is granted; and it is admitted, on all hands, that the general government has no powers but what are expressly granted by the Constitution, and that all rights not expressed were reserved by the several states. We have obtained a right to recover our slaves in whatever part of America they may take refuge, which is a right we had not before. In short, considering all circumstances, we have made the best terms for the security of this species of property it was in our power to make. We would have made better if we could; but, on the whole, I do not think them bad.

Dr. DAVID RAMSAY thought our delegates had made a most excellent bargain for us, by transferring an immense sum of Continental debt, which we were pledged to pay, upon the Eastern States, some of whom (Connecticut, for instance) could not expect to receive any material advantage from us. He considered the old Confederation as dissolved.

Hon. JACOB READ looked on the boasted efficiency of Congress to be farcical, and instanced two cases in proof of his opinion. One was, that, when the treaty should have been ratified, a sufficient number of members could not be collected in Congress for that purpose; so that it was necessary to despatch a frigate, at the expense of four thousand dollars, with particular directions for Mr. Adams to use his endeavors to gain time. His application proved successful; otherwise, very disagreeable consequences must have ensued. The other case was, a party of Indians came to Princeton for the purpose of entering into an amicable treaty with Congress; before it could be concluded, a member went to Philadelphia to be married, and his secession had nearly involved the western country in all the miseries of war. Mr. Read urged a concurrence with those states that were in favor of the new Constitution.

Hon. CHARLES PINCKNEY observed, that the honorable gentleman was singular in his opposition to the new Constitution, and equally singular in his profuse praise of the

old one.   He described, with much good sense, the impracticability of annexing responsibility to the office of President
in a republican form of government ; the only remedy against
despotism being to form a party against those who were
obnoxious, and turn them out.   He observed that the President's powers did not permit him to declare war.

Hon. RAWLINS LOWNDES declared himself almost
willing to give up his post, finding he was opposed by such
a phalanx of able antagonists, any one of them possessing
sufficient abilities to contend with him ; but as a number of
respectable members, men of good sense, though not in the
habit of speaking in public, had requested that he would state
his sentiments, for the purpose of gaining information on
such points as seemed to require it, — rather in compliance,
therefore, with their wishes, than any inclination on his part,
he should make a few further observations on the subject.
Much had been said, from different parts of the house, against
the old Confederation — that it was such a futile, inefficient,
impolitic government as to render us the objects of ridicule
and contempt in the eyes of other nations.   He could not
agree to this, because there did not appear any evidence of
the fact, and because the names of those gentlemen who had
signed the old Confederation were eminent for patriotism,
virtue, and wisdom, — as much so as any set of men that
could be found in America, — and their prudence and wisdom
particularly appeared in the care which they had taken
sacredly to guaranty the sovereignty of each state.   The
treaty of peace expressly agreed to acknowledge us as free,
sovereign, and independent states, which privileges we lived
at present in the exercise of.   But this new Constitution at
once swept those privileges away, being sovereign over all ;
so that this state would dwindle into a mere skeleton of what
it was ; its legislative powers would be pared down to little
more than those now vested in the corporation ; and he
should value the honor of a seat in the legislature in no
higher estimation than a seat in the city council.   Adverting
to the powers given to the President, he considered them as
enormous, particularly in being allowed to interfere in the
election of members in the House of Representatives ; astonishing that we had not this reserved to us, when the senators
were to be chosen from that body : — thinks it might be so
managed that the different legislatures should be limited to
the passing a few laws for regulating ferries and roads.

The honorable gentleman went into an investigation of the weight of our representation in the proposed government, which he thought would be merely virtual, similar to what we were allowed in England, whilst under the British government. We were then told that we were represented in Parliament; and this would, in the event, prove just such another. The mode of choosing senators was exceedingly exceptionable. It had been the practice formerly to choose the Senate or council for this state from that house, which practice proved so inconvenient and oppressive, that, when we framed our present Constitution, great care was taken to vest the power of electing the Senate originally with the people, as the best plan for securing their rights and privileges. He wished to know in what manner it was proposed to elect the five representatives. Was it to be done in this city? or would some districts return one member, and others none at all?

Still greater difficulties would be found in the choice of a President, because he must have a majority of ninety-one votes in his favor. For the first President there was one man to whom all America looked up, (General Washington,) and for whom he most heartily would vote; but after that gentleman's administration ceased, where could they point out another so highly respected as to concentre a majority of ninety-one persons in his favor? and if no gentleman should be fully returned, then the government must stand still. He went over much of the ground which he had trod the preceding day, relative to the Eastern States having been so guarded in what they had conceded to gain the regulation of our commerce, which threw into their hands the carrying trade, and put it in their power to lay us under payment of whatever freightage they thought proper to impose. It was their interest to do so, and no person could doubt but they would promote it by every means in their power. He wished our delegates had sufficiently attended to this point in the Convention — had been more attentive to this object, and taken care to have it expressed, in this Constitution, that all our ports were open to all nations; instead of putting us in the power of a set of men who may fritter away the value of our produce to a little or nothing, by compelling payment of exorbitant freightage. Neither did he believe it was in the power of the Eastern States to furnish a sufficient number of ships to carry our produce. It was, indeed, a general way of talking, that the Eastern States had a great number of seamen, a vast number of ships; but where were they? Why did they not come here now, when ships are greatly wanted? He should always wish to give them a preference, and so, no doubt, would many other gentlemen; and yet very few ships come here from the Eastern States. Another exceptionable point was, that we were to give up the power of taxing ourselves. During our connection with Great Britain, she left us the power of raising money in any way most convenient : a certain sum was only required to defray the public wants, but no mode of collecting it ever prescribed. In this new Constitution, every thing is transferred, not so much power being left us as Lord North offered to guaranty to us in his conciliatory plan. Look at the articles of union ratified between England and Scotland. How cautiously had the latter taken care of her interest in reserving all the forms of law — her representation in Parliament — the right of taxation — the management of her revenue — and all her local and municipal interests! Why take from us the right of paying our delegates, and pay them from the federal treasury? He remembered formerly what a flame was raised in Massachusetts, on account of Great Britain assuming the payment of salaries to judges and other state officers; and that this conduct was considered as originating in a design to destroy the independence of their government. Our local expenses had been nearly defrayed by our impost duty; but now that this was given away, and thrown into a general fund, for the use of all the states indiscriminately, we should be obliged to augment our taxes to carry on our local government, notwithstanding we were to pay a poll tax for our negroes. Paper money, too, was another article of restraint, and a popular point with many; but what evils had we ever experienced by issuing a little paper money to relieve ourselves from any exigency that pressed us? We had now a circulating medium which every body took. We used formerly to issue paper bills every year, and recall them every five, with great convenience and advantage. Had not paper money carried us triumphantly through the war, extricated us from difficulties generally supposed to be insurmountable, and fully established us in our independence?

and now every thing is so changed that an entire stop must
be put to any more paper emissions, however great our distress may be. It was true, no article of the Constitution
declared there should not be jury trials in civil cases; yet
this must be implied, because it stated that all crimes, except in cases of impeachment, shall be tried by a jury. But
even if trials by jury were allowed, could any person rest
satisfied with a mode of trial which prevents the parties from
being obliged to bring a cause for discussion before a jury
of men chosen from the vicinage, in a manner conformable
to the present administration of justice, which had stood the
test of time and experience, and ever been highly approved
of? Mr. Lowndes expatiated some time on the nature of
compacts, the sacred light in which they were held by all
nations, and solemnly called on the house to consider whether it would not be better to add strength to the old Confederation, instead of hastily adopting another; asking whether
a man could be looked on as wise, who, possessing a magnificent building, upon discovering a flaw, instead of repairing the injury, should pull it down, and build another.
Indeed, he could not understand with what propriety the
Convention proceeded to change the Confederation; for
every person with whom he had conversed on this subject
concurred in opinion that the sole object of appointing a
convention was to inquire what alterations were necessary
in the Confederation, in order that it might answer those
salutary purposes for which it was originally intended.

He recommended that another convention should be called;
and as the general sense of America appeared now to be
known, every objection could be met on fair grounds, and
adequate remedies applied where necessary. This mode of
proceeding would conciliate all parties, because it was
candid, and had a more obvious tendency to do away all
inconveniences than the adoption of a government which
perhaps might require the bayonet to enforce it; for it
could not be expected that the people, who had disregarded
the requisitions of Congress, though expressed in language
the most elegant and forcible that he ever remembered to
have read, would be more obedient to the government
until an irresistible force compelled them to be so. Mr.
Lowndes concluded a long speech with a glowing eulogy on
the old Confederation, and challenged his opponents, whilst

one state objected, to get over that section which said, " The
Articles of this Confederation shall be inviolably observed
in every state, and the Union shall be perpetual ; nor shall
any alteration at any time hereafter be made in them, unless
such alteration be agreed to in a Congress of the United
States, and be afterwards confirmed by the legislature of
every state."

Hon. ROBERT BARNWELL said, although he had been
opposed to the investigation of the Federal Constitution at
that period, and in that house, and foretold the unnecessary expenditure of both time and treasure that would be
occasioned by it, yet he acknowledged that, if individual
information upon its principles could by any means be a
compensation for these wastes, he should be extremely
indebted to the honorable gentleman for the opposition
which he had given.   Mr. Barnwell was most decidedly in
favor of the Constitution as recommended by the Convention,
and viewed with pleasure the small sacrifices of interest,
which, in his opinion, have been made to effect it.   The
arguments which had been adduced by the honorable gentleman in opposition had riveted his affections still more
firmly to it, and had established in his mind, as conviction,
what was only approbation before.   If he did not view
some part of the Constitution through a medium different
from any of the gentlemen who had spoken before him, he
should not have troubled this house.   With this idea he rose,
and left it to the house to determine whether he had done
his duty as a member, or whether he had unnecessarily
contributed to the interruption of the business before them.
When he found that a gentleman of such acknowledged
abilities, and of so great experience, was opposed to the
Constitution, he expected a train of reasoning, and a power
of argument, that would have made the federal fabric totter
to its foundation.   But to him they rather appeared like
those storms which shake the edifice to fix it more strongly
on its basis.   To give his reasons for this opinion, he begged
the indulgence of the house while he made the following
observations upon the principles of the gentleman's opposition.   In the first instance, it appeared to him that the gentleman had established, as the basis of his objections, that
the Eastern States entertained the greatest aversion to those
which lay to the south, and would endeavor in every

instance to oppress them. This idea he considered as founded in prejudice, and unsupported by facts. To prove this assertion, Mr. B. requested gentlemen for a moment to turn their attention to the transactions which the late war has engraved upon the memory of every man. When the arm of oppression lay heavy on us, were they not the first to arouse themselves? When the sword of civil discord was drawn, were they not the first in the field? When war deluged their plains with blood, what was their language? Did they demand the southern troops to the defence of the north? No! Or, when war floated to the south, did they withhold their assistance? The answer was the same. When we stood with the spirit, but weakness, of youth, they supported us with the vigor and prudence of age. When our country was subdued, when our citizens submitted to superior power, it was then these states evinced their attachment. He saw not a man who did not know that the shackles of the south were broken asunder by the arms of the north. With the above-mentioned supposition of oppression, the gentleman had objected to the formation of the Senate; that the Confederation required nine states to ratify matters of importance, but by the Constitution a majority of fourteen can do almost any thing. That this was the case he did not deny; but the conclusions that he had drawn were by no means consequential. The seven Eastern States, the gentleman had said, whose interests were similar, will unite together, and, by having a majority in the Senate, will do what they please. If this was the case, it went against uniting at all; for, if he was not mistaken, the interests of nine of the United States are almost the same. New Hampshire, Massachusetts, Rhode Island, Connecticut, New York, New Jersey, Pennsylvania, and Delaware, are very similar in their interests. They are most of them entirely carriers for others; and those states which are exporting ones are very nearly equal to the carrying of their products themselves. Supposing, then, the desire of oppression to exist, he asked if they could not do it equally as well under the Confederation as the Constitution. He thought so; and, as the gentleman's arguments equally lay against every kind of coercive government, he was of opinion that the Senate, as established by this Constitution, was the most proper. Upon this head he begged permission to ask these questions : If the majority was in the Southern States, (which, as ten is a majority, might be the case,) would not objections, equally forcible as the gentleman's, lie on the side of the Eastern States ? and yet that, in all governments, a majority must be somewhere, is most evident : nothing would be more completely farcical than a government completely checked. Having commented thus far on the gentleman's opposition to the Federal Constitution, he proceeded, according to the order of his objections, to consider the presiding power. On this he would be extremely concise ; for, as the only objection which had fallen upon this head from the honorable gentleman was, that we had only a thirteenth part of him ; and as this might equally, and, in his opinion, with more justice, be the objection of many and almost every state, he considered it only as a weight thrown into the scale of other objections, and not a subject for discussion.

With respect to the President's responsibility, it could not be established more firmly than it is by the Constitution. When treaties are made, if in the time of prosperity, men seldom think they gain enough ; if in the day of adversity, they would be apt to make the President the pillow upon whom they would rest all their resentment. The Constitution had then wisely made him, as a man, responsible by the influence of fame, his character, and his feelings ; as a citizen, they have postponed the period at which he could be tried with propriety until the fervor of party and cool reflection can determine his fate. The gentleman had also objected to the power given to those two branches of making treaties, and that these treaties should become the law of the land. A number of gentlemen have proved this power to be in the possession of the head of every free nation, and that it is within the power of the present Congress. He should only, therefore, observe, that the most free and enlightened nations of the world had a federal head, in which this power was established — he meant the Amphictyonic council of the Greeks, which was the palladium of their united liberties, and, until destroyed by the ambition of a few of the states of Greece, was revered by that jealous people as the corner-stone of their federal union. Against the representation he generally objects, that they are too few, and not elected immediately by the people. The whole body consists of sixty five persons, in the proportion of one to thirty thousand. The British Parliament have one to fifteen thousand in the island of Great Britain, without considering her possessions elsewhere. The numbers of her Parliament are fixed; our congressional powers may be increased almost *ad infinitum*. Supposing, then, that a smaller apportionment had been made, in time we should have been oppressed with the number of legislators, and our government would be as languid and inoperative as it is at present; and he differed so much from the honorable gentleman, that he was apprehensive lest he should find that, by the Constitution, their numbers will be too great. As for their not being immediately elected by the people at large, the gentleman would please to observe, that, contradictory to their present method of electing delegates to Congress,—a method laid down by that Confederation which he admires,—all the representatives are elected by the people; so that, in this instance, the gentleman was very unfortunate in his objection. The gentleman also asked why we were deprived of the liberty of paying our own delegates? This is another of the gentleman's unfounded suspicions; for the reason is so evident, and the regulation so favorable, that he was astonished how it escaped the honorable gentleman's notice. Congress are to have the sole power of laying on imposts; and therefore, when that fund is given up by which we were enabled to pay our delegates, we are also eased of the burden of doing it. This is so evident, that the establishment of the objection takes not a little from the weight of the gentleman's other observations. Mr. Barnwell proceeded to say that the gentleman, upon the deprivation of the right to issue paper medium, has altogether made use of an argument *ad hominem*, calculated to seduce; and his eulogium upon it was, in his opinion, misapplied. However, supposing that to be the clew that led us to our liberty, yet the gentleman must acknowledge it was not the state, but the Continental money, that brought about the favorable termination of the war. If to strike off a paper medium becomes necessary, Congress, by the Constitution, still have that right, and may exercise it when they think proper.

The honorable gentleman asks why the trial by jury was not established in every instance. Mr. Barnwell considered this right of trial as the birthright of every American, and the basis of our civil liberty; but still most certainly particular circumstances may arise, which would induce even the greatest advocates for this right to yield it for a time. In his opinion, the circumstances that would lead to this point were those which are specified by the Constitution. Mr Barnwell said, Suffer me to state a case, and let every gentleman determine whether, in particular instances, he would not rather resign than retain this right of trial. A suit is depending between a citizen of Carolina and Georgia, and it becomes necessary to try it in Georgia. What is the consequence? Why, the citizen of this state must rest his cause upon the jury of his opponent's vicinage, where, unknown and unrelated, he stands a very poor chance for justice against one whose neighbors, whose friends and relations, compose the greater part of his judges. It is in this case, and only in cases of a similar nature with this, that the right of trial by jury is not established; and judging from myself, it is in this instance only that every man would wish to resign it, not to a jury with whom he is unacquainted, but to an impartial and responsible individual.

Mr. Barnwell then adverted to the parts of the Constitution which more immediately affected our state; namely, the right of establishing imposts and granting preferences, and the clause which respects the importation of negroes. Upon the first he premised, that, in the compacts which unite men into society, it always is necessary to give up a part of our natural rights to secure the remainder; and that, in every instance, if the latter could be maintained without giving up the former, every individual would be willing to keep back his share of those aggregate ties which then would bind the rest of the community; each individual would wish to retain his right to act as he pleases, whilst all but himself were restricted in their conduct. Let us, then, apply this to the United States; and yet the honorable gentleman supposes that South Carolina should be free herself. Surely this is not just, and cannot be admissible.

Mr. Chairman, suffer me to make this one other remark — that, when the distinctions occasioned by wealth take place, the desire of equality and the appetite for property soon render it necessary that the wealthy weak man should make greater sacrifices than the man who has nothing to lose, and consequently nothing to fear. This is the case with us. To secure our wealth, and establish our security, perhaps some little sacrifice was necessary; and what is this sacrifice? Why, that, generally, American vessels should have a preference in the carrying trade. The gentleman asserts that, by granting this preference, we, as a large importing state, will suffer greatly. Let us examine the truth of this position. By so doing, says the honorable gentleman, we shall destroy all competition, and the carrying states will establish what freight they please. I deny the declaration; and upon this principle: bounties act as encouragements; and this preference may, in a trifling degree, injure us for one or two years, but will throw so many capitals into this trade, that, even if the Eastern States should desire to oppress us, this would prevent them; for when this bounty takes place, our harbors will most indisputably reduce the freight. The gentleman will perhaps say that this is conjectural only. I appeal to every author, who has written upon the subject, for the certainty of this commercial maxim, and will ask the gentleman himself, whether an overstock of the market, in every instance, does not reduce the price of the commodity. Thus he had proved, he thought, that, should the Eastern States be desirous to take unfriendly advantages, their own interest would defeat their intention.

Mr. Barnwell continued to say, I now come to the last point for consideration, — I mean the clause relative to the negroes; and here I am particularly pleased with the Constitution. It has not left this matter, of so much importance to us, open to immediate investigation. No; it has declared that the United States shall not, at any rate, consider this matter for twenty-one years; and yet gentlemen are displeased with it. Congress has guarantied this right for that space of time, and at its expiration may continue it as long as they please. This question then arises — What will their interest lead them to do? The Eastern States, as the honorable gentleman says, will become the carriers of America. It will, therefore, certainly be their interest to encourage exportation to as great an extent as possible; and if the quantum of our products will be diminished by the prohibition of negroes, I appeal to the belief of every man, whether he thinks those very carriers will themselves dam up the sources from whence their profit is derived. To think so is so contradictory to the general conduct of mankind, that I am of opinion, that, without we ourselves put a stop to them, the traffic for negroes will continue forever.

Mr. Barnwell concluded by declaring that this Constitution was, in his opinion, like the laws of Solon, not the best possible to be formed, but the best that our situation will admit of. He considered it as the panacea of America, whose healing power will pervade the continent, and sincerely believed that its ratification is a consummation devoutly to be wished.

Commodore GILLON wished to know what reason the house had to suppose that, if another convention met, our interest would be better taken care of by men of equal abilities with those who went to the other; or if, when there, they could procure for us superior advantages to those already agreed on. Indeed, he could not but consider our negativing the proffered government as an oblique mode of reflecting on the conduct of our delegates, instead of giving them that praise they were so justly entitled to. He called the attention of the house to the late commotions that had happened in Holland, where one part of the citizens had called in the assistance of foreigners, for the sanguinary purpose of cutting the throats of the other. Are we more virtuous? If not, may it not happen that, if dissension unhappily prevail among us, foreign aid will be joined to those enemies already amongst us, and introduce the horrors of a civil war? He was warmly in favor of our sister states becoming the carriers of America; not that he wished to exclude our employing foreigners; at present two thirds of our produce was carried in American bottoms. The commodore hoped the gentleman who had approved of our state Constitution of 1778, would be, in time, equally pleased with the Federal Constitution proposed in 1787. He had represented our present situation to be calm and peaceable, but it was such a calm as mariners often experience at sea, after a storm, when one ship rolls against another, and they sink.

Hon. RAWLINS LOWNDES said, the honorable gentleman frequently thought proper to level his shot at him; but on the present occasion they were not well pointed. The reason why he assented unto the Constitution in 1778 was, because it had been approved of by the people. There had been something said about a ship: the Confederation was our old ship; it had cost us a great deal of money; and he hoped we should keep her at sea without having any new commanders.

Hon. JOHN MATHEWS, chancellor, confessed himself astonished at hearing such encomiums on the Articles of Confederation, as if they had carried us victoriously through the war, when, in fact, they were not ratified until the year 1781 ; and if the Confederation had been in force in 1776, this country would have inevitably been lost, because, under it, Congress had not authority to give General Washington the powers of a dictator at Valley Forge. Surely the honorable gentleman must be sensible that the success of Congress depended on the explicit confidence of the people ; the voice of Congress had the force of law, and was cheerfully and readily obeyed. With regard to the carrying trade, when the Convention was first appointed, he was afraid that, if a navigation act passed, the Northern States could not for some time furnish shipping sufficient for carrying the produce of America ; but on going, last year, to the northward, he was fully convinced to the contrary. At Rhode Island, he received information that they could immediately furnish 50,000 tons of shipping, and that in 1787 Massachusetts could furnish 150,000 tons. He then.went into a calculation of the produce of the Southern States. Virginia raised between 60,000 and 70,000 hogsheads annually ; South Carolina, he supposed, would raise nearly 150,000 barrels of rice ; Georgia about 40,000 ; which, making large allowances for other kind of produce, still left an excess of shipping. As to any fears that the Northern States would so far engross the navigation of America as to lay the Southern States under a kind of contribution, by charging excessive freightage, we must suppose that they and the Middle States would confederate for this purpose ; for, if they did not, a competition would naturally arise between them, and also between America and the European nations, which would always secure us against the payment of great and exorbitant freights. As to the idea that a Senate could overturn our liberties and establish tyranny, this evil never could take place whilst the President was an honest man, because he possessed the power of negativing any improper proceedings of the two other branches of government.

Hon. EDWARD RUTLEDGE proved, from the act passed last session, appointing delegates from the state to

meet those from other states, in Convention at Philadelphia,
that they had not exceeded their powers.   He then compared the powers given under the old and new constitutions.
and proved that they differed very little, except in that
essential point which gave the power to government of enforcing its engagements ; and surely no person could object
to this.   Mr. Rutledge thought very lightly of those fears
entertained about bayonets being necessary to enforce an
obedience in the people to the laws, when it became certain
that they could not be broken with impunity ; but if a spirit
of resistance should appear, surely it ought to be in the power
of government to compel a coercion in the people.   He then
took some notice of the union between Great Britain and
Scotland, showed the difference between the articles of
union and our Federal Constitution.   Great Britain reserved
to herself the power of passing navigation laws, regulating
the excise ; the rate of taxation was also proportionate ; for
every two millions of money raised in England, Scotland
engaged to raise £45,000 ; but in this country, we were to
be equally taxed ; no distinction had been made, and we
went on all-fours.   So far from not preferring Northern
States by a navigation act, it would be politic to increase
their strength by every means in our power ; for we had no
other resource, in the day of danger, than in the naval force
of our northern friends ; nor could we ever expect to become
a great nation until we were powerful on the waters.   Look
only at the partiality of an act passed in England last year,
in which we were excluded from trading in some parts of
the West Indies, whilst liberty was given to all European
powers.   In fact, we must hold our country by courtesy,
unless we have a navy ; for, if we are invaded, supposing in the
month of July, Congress could not send troops nine hundred
miles, in time to rescue us from danger, were we to run such
risk, because it was possible we should be charged a little
more freightage for our produce.   But if we are a great
maritime people, what have we to fear ?   Nothing ; because
European powers were so far removed from us that it would
be very dangerous to send a considerable force against us ;
besides, as the West India trade must pass near our coast, it
naturally lay at our mercy.   The honorable gentleman had
said a great deal about establishing an aristocracy, and yet
he wanted more power to the old constitution : now, did not

his own proposition, which tended to establish a precedent for slipping in, by degrees, additional power, appear as likely to promote what he dreaded, as to agree with a constitution that came sanctioned by the voice of the people?

Hon. ARTHUR SIMKINS, of *Ninety-six*, asked, for information, whether Congress had a right to interfere in religion.

Gen. CHARLES COTESWORTH PINCKNEY answered, they had no power at all, and explained this point to Mr. Simkins's satisfaction.

Hon. RAWLINS LOWNDES saying that he was much in arrear, the committee rose, reported some progress, and asked leave to sit again. Leave was given.

FRIDAY, *January* 18, 1788.

Maj. PIERCE BUTLER opened the debate (as we understand; the reporter of those debates unfortunately not being in the house) with several satisfactory answers to some points of objection the preceding day.

Gen. CHARLES COTESWORTH PINCKNEY, in answer to Mr. Lowndes, observed, that, though ready to pay every tribute of applause to the great characters whose names were subscribed to the old Confederation, yet his respect for them could not prevent him from being thoroughly sensible of the defects of the system they had established; sad experience had convinced him that it was weak, inefficient, and inadequate to the purposes of good government; and he understood that most of the framers of it were so thoroughly convinced of this truth, that they were eager to adopt the present Constitution. The friends of the new system do not mean to shelter it under the respectability of mere names; they wish every part of it may be examined with critical minuteness, convinced that the more thoroughly it is investigated, the better it will appear. The honorable gentleman, in the warmth of his encomiums on the old plan, had said that it had carried us with success through the war. In this it has been shown that he is mistaken, as it was not finally ratified till March, 1781, and, anterior to that ratification, Congress never acted under it, or considered it as binding. Our success, therefore, ought not to be imputed to the old Confederation; but to the vast abilities of a Washington, to the valor and enthusiasm of our people, to the cruelty of our enemies, and to the assistance of our friends. The gentleman had mentioned the treaty of peace in a manner as if our independence had been granted us by the king of Great Britain. But that was not the case ; we were independent before the treaty, which does not in fact grant, but acknowledges, our independence. We ought to date that invaluable blessing from a much older charter than the treaty of peace — from a charter which our babes should be taught to lisp in their cradles ; which our youth should learn as a *carmen necessarium*, or indispensable lesson ; which our young men should regard as their compact of freedom ; and which our old should repeat with ejaculations of gratitude for the bounties it is about to bestow on their posterity : I mean the Declaration of Independence, made in Congress the 4th of July, 1776. This admirable manifesto, which, for importance of matter and elegance of composition, stands unrivalled, sufficiently confutes the honorable gentleman's doctrine of the individual sovereignty and independence of the several states.

In that Declaration the several states are not even enumerated ; but after reciting, in nervous language, and with convincing arguments, our right to independence, and the tyranny which compelled us to assert it, the declaration is made in the following words : " We, therefore, the representatives of the United States of America in General Congress assembled, appealing to the Supreme Judge of the world for the rectitude of our intentions, do, in the name and by the authority of the good people of these colonies, solemnly publish and declare, that these United Colonies are, and of right ought to be, FREE AND INDEPENDENT STATES." The separate independence and individual sovereignty of the several states were never thought of by the enlightened band of patriots who framed this Declaration ; the several states are not even mentioned by name in any part of it, — as if it was intended to impress this maxim on America, that our freedom and independence arose from our union, and that without it we could neither be free nor independent. Let us, then, consider all attempts to weaken this Union, by maintaining that each state is separately and individually independent, as a species of political heresy, which

26

can never benefit us, but may bring on us the most serious distresses.

The general, then, in answer to Mr. Lowndes's objections, that the powers vested in the general government were too extensive, enumerated all the powers granted, and remarked particularly on each, showing that the general good of the Union required that all the powers specified ought necessarily to be vested where the Constitution had placed them; and that, as all the powers granted sprang from the people, and were to be exercised by persons frequently chosen, mediately or immediately, by the people; and that, as we had as great a share in the government, in proportion to our importance, as any other state had, — the assertion that our representation would be merely virtual, similar to what we possessed under the British government, was altogether unfounded; that there was no danger of the powers granted being abused while the people remained uncorrupt; and that corruption was more effectually guarded against, in the manner this government was constituted, than in any other that had ever been formed. From the number of electors who have a right to vote for a member of the House of Representatives, little danger can be apprehended of corruption or undue influence. If a small district sent a member, there would be frequent opportunities for cabal and intrigue; but if the sphere of election is enlarged, then opportunities must necessarily diminish. The little demagogue of a petty parish or county will find his importance annihilated, and his intrigues useless, when several counties join in an election; he probably would not be known, certainly not regarded, out of his own circle; while the man whose abilities and virtues had extended a fair reputation beyond the limits of his county, would, nine times out of ten, be the person who would be the choice of the people.

There will be no necessity, as the honorable gentleman has strangely supposed, for all the freeholders in the state to meet at Charleston to choose five members for the House of Representatives; for the state may be divided into five election districts, and the freeholders in each election district may choose one representative. These freeholders need not all meet at the same place in the district; they may ballot in their particular parishes and counties on the same day, and the ballots may be thence carried into a central part of the district, and opened at the same time ; and whoever shall appear to have a majority of the votes of the freeholders of the whole district will be one of the five representatives for this state. But if any state should attempt to fix a very in- convenient time for the election, and name (agreeably to the ideas of the honorable gentleman) only one place in the state, or even one place in one of the five election districts, for the freeholders to assemble to vote, and the people should dislike this arrangement, they can petition the general gov- ernment to redress this inconvenience, and to fix times and places of election of representatives in the state in a more convenient manner ; for, as this house has a right to fix the times and places of election, in each parish and county, for the members of the House of Representatives of this state, so the general government has a similar right to fix the times and places of election, in each state, for the members of the general House of Representatives. Nor is there any real danger to be apprehended from the exercise of this power, as it cannot be supposed that any state will consent to fix the election at inconvenient seasons and places in any other state, lest she herself should hereafter experience the same incon- venience ; but it is absolutely necessary that Congress should have this superintending power, lest, by the intrigues of a ruling faction in a state, the members of the House of Rep- resentatives should not really represent the people of the state, and lest the same faction, through partial state views, should altogether refuse to send representatives of the people to the general government. The general government has not the same authority with regard to the members of the Senate. It would have been improper to have intrusted them with it ; for such a power would, in some measure, have authorized them to fix the times and places when and where the state legislatures should convene, and would tend to destroy that necessary check which the general and state governments will have on each other. The honorable gentleman, as if he was determined to object to every part of the Constitution, though he does not approve of electing representatives im- mediately by the people, or at least cannot conceive how it is to be effected, yet objects to the constitution of the Senate, because the senators are to be elected by the state legislatures, and not immediately by the people. When the Constitu- tion says the people shall elect, the gentleman cries out. " It is chimerical!——the election will be merely virtual." When the Constitution determines that the state legislatures are to elect, he exclaims, "The people's rights are invaded!——the election should be immediately by them, and not by their representatives." How, then, can we satisfy him, as he is determined to censure, in this Constitution, that mode of election which he so highly approves in the old Confederation? The reason why our present state Constitution, made in 1778, changed the mode of electing senators from the mode prescribed by our first constitution, passed in 1776, was because, by the first, the senators were elected by this house, and therefore, being their mere creatures, they could not be supposed to have that freedom of will as to form a proper check on its proceedings; whereas, in the general Constitution, the House of Representatives will be elected immediately by the people, and represent them and their personal rights individually; the Senate will be elected by the state legislatures, and represent the states in their political capacity; and thus each branch will form a proper and independent check on the other, and the legislative powers will be advantageously balanced.

With regard to the objection that had been made to the mode of electing the President of the United States, General Pinckney asked what other mode would have been so proper. If he was to be elected by the House of Representatives and the Senate, as one of them have the power of impeaching and the other of trying him, he would be altogether their creature, and would not have independence enough to exercise with firmness the revisionary power and other authorities with which he is invested by the Constitution. This want of independence might influence his conduct, in some degree, if he was to be elected by one branch of the legislature alone; but as he is to be elected by the people, through the medium of electors chosen particularly for that purpose, and he is in some measure to be a check on the Senate and House of Representatives, the election, in my opinion, could not have been placed so well if it had been made in any other mode.

In all elections of a chief magistrate, foreign influence is to be guarded against. Here it is very carefully so; and it is almost impossible for any foreign power to influence thirteen different sets of electors, distributed throughout the states, from New Hampshire to Georgia. By this mode, also, and for the same reason, the dangers of intrigue and corruption are avoided, and a variety of other inconveniences, which must have arisen if the electors from the different states had been directed to assemble at one place, or if either branch of the legislature (in case the majority of electors did not fix upon the same person) might have chosen a President who had not been previously put in nomination by the people. I have before spoken of the policy and justice of vesting the majority of Congress with the power of making commercial regulations, and the necessity there is, in all well-constituted republics, that the majority should control the minority; and I should have had a very strong objection if it had contained the restrictive clause the honorable gentleman appears so anxious for, "that Congress should not have it in their power to prevent the ships of any nation from entering our ports." I cannot think it would have been prudent or fitting to have given the ships of all foreign nations a constitutional right to enter our ports whenever they pleased, and this, too, notwithstanding we might be at war with them; or they may have passed laws denying us the privileges they grant to all other commercial nations; or circumstances not now foreseen might render it necessary for us to prohibit them. Such a clause would have injured the Eastern States, would have been eventually detrimental to ourselves, and would have in fact amounted to a declaration that we were resolved never to have a navy. To such a clause the general declared he never would have consented, and desired the gentleman to produce an instance of any independent power who did not give exclusive advantages to their own shipping. He then took notice that Chancellor Matthews had fully answered what had been alleged concerning the exorbitant freights we should be obliged to pay, and had clearly shown that no danger was to be apprehended on that subject; and that the Eastern States could soon furnish us, and all the Southern States, with a sufficient number of ships to carry off our produce. With regard to the general government imposing internal taxes upon us, he contended that it was absolutely necessary they should have such a power: requisitions had been in vain tried every year since the ratification of the old Confederation, and not a single state had paid the quota required of her. The general government could not abuse this power, and favor one state and oppress another, as each state was to be taxed only in proportion to its representation; and as to excises, when it is considered how many more excisable articles are manufactured to the northward than there are to the southward, and the ease and convenience of raising a revenue by indirect taxation, and the necessity there is to obtain money for the payment of our debts, for our common defence, and for the general welfare, he thought every man would see the propriety, and even the necessity, of this clause. For his part, he knew of no sum that he would not sooner have consented to have paid, if he had had it, rather than have adopted Lord North's conciliatory plan, which seems, by the argument of the gentleman, to be in some respect preferable to the proposed Constitution; but in asserting this, the gentleman certainly cannot be serious. As to the payment of members of the legislature out of the federal treasury, General Pinckney contended it was right, and particularly beneficial to us, who were so distant from the seat of the federal government, as we at present paid our members not only while they were actually in Congress, but for all the time they were going there and returning home, which was an expense the Middle States felt but in a slight degree; but now that all the members are to be paid out of the public treasury, our remote situation will not be particularly expensive to us. The case of the payment of the Massachusetts judges under the royal government can by no ingenuity be made applicable to the payment of the members of the federal legislature. With regard to Mr. Lowndes's question, " What harm had paper money done?" General Pinckney answered, that he wondered that gentleman should ask such a question, as he had told the house that he had lost fifteen thousand guineas by depreciation; but he would tell the gentleman what further injuries it had done — it had corrupted the morals of the people; it had diverted them from the paths of honest industry to the ways of ruinous speculation; it had destroyed both public and private credit, and had brought total ruin on numberless widows and orphans.

As to the judiciary department, General Pinckney observed, that trial by jury was so deservedly esteemed by the people of America, that it is impossible for their representatives to omit introducing it whenever it can with propriety be done. In appeals from courts of chancery, it surely would be improper. In a dispute between a citizen of Carolina and a citizen of Georgia, if a jury was to try the case, from which state are they to be drawn? If from both or either, would the citizens of Carolina and Georgia choose to be summoned to attend on juries eight hundred miles from their home? and if the jury is to be drawn from the state in which Congress shall sit, would these citizens wish that a cause relative to negro property should be tried by the Quakers of Pennsylvania, or by the freeholders of those states that have not that species of property amongst them? Surely not. Yet it is necessary, when a citizen of one state cannot obtain an impartial trial in another, that, for the sake of justice, he should have a right to appeal to the supreme judiciary of the United States to obtain redress; and as this right of appeal does not extend to citizens of the same state, (unless they claim under grants of different states,) but only to the causes and persons particularly mentioned in the Constitution, and Congress have power to make such regulations and impose such restrictions relative to appeals as they think proper, it can hardly be supposed that they will exercise it in a manner injurious to their constituents.

Trials by jury are expressly secured in all criminal cases, and not excluded in any civil cases whatsoever. But experience had demonstrated that it was impossible to adhere to them in all civil cases: for instance, on the first establishment of the admiralty jurisdiction, Congress passed an ordinance requiring all causes of capture to be decided by juries: this was contrary to the practice of all nations, and we knew it; but still an attachment to a trial by jury induced the experiment. What was the consequence? The property of our friends was, at times, condemned indiscriminately with the property of our enemies, and the property of our citizens of one state by the juries of another. Some of our citizens have severely felt these inconveniences. Citizens of other states and other powers experienced similar misfortunes from this mode of trial. It was, therefore, by universal consent and approbation, laid aside in cases of capture. As the ordinance which regulated these trials was passed by Congress, they had the power of altering it, and they exercised that power · but had that ordinance been part of the Confedera-

tion, it could not then have been repealed in the then situation of America ; and had a clause of a similar tendency
been inserted in this Constitution, it could only be altered by
a convention of the different states.   This shows at once
how improper it would have been to have descended to
minutiæ in this particular ; and he trusted it was unnecessary, because the laws which are to regulate trials must be
made by the representatives of the people chosen as this
house are, and as amenable as they are for every part of
their conduct.   The honorable gentleman says, compacts
should be binding, and that the Confederation was a compact.   It was so ; but it was a compact that had been
repeatedly broken by every state in the Union ; and all the
writers on the laws of nations agree that, when the parties to a
treaty violate it, it is no longer binding.   This was the case
with the old Confederation ; it was virtually dissolved, and it
became necessary to form a new constitution, to render us
secure at home, respectable abroad, and to give us that station
among the nations of the world, to which, as free and independent people, we are justly entitled.

Hon. RAWLINS LOWNDES observed, that he had
been accused of obstinacy in standing out against such a
formidable opposition ; but he would sincerely assure the
house that he was as open to conviction as any gentleman
on the floor : yet he never would allow himself to be drawn
into the adoption of specious arguments ; for such he considered many of those now opposed against him to be.   Indeed, some gentlemen had departed from their usual candor
in giving an interpretation to his arguments which they did not
merit.   In one instance, it had been stated as if he was of
opinion that treaties had not the force of law.   This was
going too far.   He did not recollect that he had asserted any
more than that the king of Great Britain had not a legal power
to ratify any treaty which trenched on the fundamental laws
of the country.   He supposed a case, under the dispensing
act of William and Mary, asking, " If the king had made a
treaty with the Roman Catholics, could that which was
excepted by the laws ever be considered as paramount ? "
The honorable gentleman again took an ample view of the
old Confederation, on which he dwelt with fervency for some
time, and ridiculed the depraved inconsistency of those who
pant for the change.   Great stress was laid on the admirable

checks which guarded us, under the new Constitution, from
the encroachments of tyranny; but too many checks in a
political machine must produce the same mischief as in a
mechanical one — that of throwing all into confusion.   But
supposing we considered ourselves so much aggrieved as to
reduce us to the necessity of insisting on redress, what
probability had we of relief?   Very little indeed.   In the
revolving on misfortune, some little gleams of comfort
resulted from a hope of being able to resort to an impartial
tribunal for redress; but pray what reason was there for
expectancy that, in Congress, the interest of five Southern
States would be considered in a preferable point of view to
the nine Eastern ones?   With respect to migration from the
Eastern States to the Southern ones, he did not believe that
people would ever flock here in such considerable numbers,
because our country had generally proved so uncomfortable,
from the excessive heats, that our acquaintance, during the
heats, is rather shunned than solicited.   The honorable gentleman mentioned that he had sent for a person from Europe,
who did not long survive his introduction here, falling a
sacrifice to the baneful effects of fogs and swamps; so that,
from our limitation of importing negroes after the term of
twenty years, instead of rising in representation, we should
gradually degenerate.   He treated those fears of our falling
a prey to foreigners as one of those arguments tending to
precipitate us into measures inimical to our natural interest;
for was it to be supposed that the policy of France would
ever suffer America to become an appendage of the crown
of Great Britain; or that Great Britain, equally jealous of
France, would permit her to reduce us to subjection?   Our
danger of ruin should rather be apprehended from dissensions amongst ourselves — from our running into debt without any intention to pay: that was the rock on which we
might split, rather than foreign enemies; and, therefore, all
those arguments for establishing the necessity of a navy and
standing army were nugatory, and entitled to very little
attention.

It was urged that, until we had a navy powerful enough
to protect us, our liberties and property were held only on
courtesy; but if gentlemen adverted, where this navy, so
necessary, was to come from, — not from the Southern States,
but the Northern ones, — they would easily perceive to whom

this country would belong.   It was true, the old Confederation was a mere paper defence ; but then it was a good proof
on our behalf if we were overcome by unmerited wrongs.
Some had made this a question — " Will you join, or will
you be single ? "   For his part, he did not think matters had
come to such a crisis ; rather let us comply with our federal
connection, which, not yet being broken, admits of being
strengthened.   A gentleman had instanced Vattel in support
of his argument, and laid down, from that author, an opinion
that where parties engaged in the performance of an obligation, should any one of them fly off from his agreement, the
original was null and void.   He had ingeniously applied this
to our present Continental situation, and contended, as some
of the states acted in a refractory manner towards the Continental Union, and obstinately refused a compliance, on
their parts, with solemn obligations, that of course the Confederation was virtually dissolved.   But Vattel merely recited
such a case as where only a part of a confederation was
broken ; whereas ours was totally different, every state in the
Union having been uniform in refusing a compliance with
the requisitions of Congress.   Some gentlemen had advanced
a set of assertions to prove that the Eastern States had
greatly suffered in the war.   Pray, how had they suffered ?
Did they not draw from the Continental treasury large sums
of money ?   Was not every expense incurred by them
defrayed out of the Continental coffers ?   Another great advantage held out was, that we should be eased, in future, from
the obligation and difficulty of defraying the expenses of delegates.   Had we gained so much by this, when we had
given up the very means of furnishing this sort of supply,
formerly in our own option ?   As to the taxes, undoubtedly
they must be increased under this new government.   We
paid at present two dollars per head upon our negroes ; but
the expenses attending our pompous government might increase this expense into six dollars per head, and this enormous sum collected by a sort of foreign power ; for did any
man, that knew America, suppose such tax will be easily
paid ?   But if there was such a universal propensity to set up
this golden image, why delay its inauguration ?   Let us at
once go plump into the adoration of it ; let us at once surrender every right which we at present possess.   A material
objection of his to the offered plan was, that the President

would have power to call both houses at what time and place he thought proper. Suppose a political cause for partiality, might he not so arrange things, as to carry a favorite point, by assembling the federal government, to the ruin or detriment of those states he meant to crush, and laws be enacted before those in extreme parts of the country knew any thing of their tendency? Surely some restrictions, as to time of meeting, should have been specified. The President had also the power of adjourning to any day he thought proper. In our old constitution, no such power was given to the chief magistrate to adjourn or dissolve. On the whole, this was the best preparatory plan for a monarchical government he had read. The Constitution of Great Britain he considered as the best monarchical one he ever perused; and this new government came so near to it, that, as to our changing from a republic to a monarchy, it was what every body must naturally expect. How easy the transition! No difficulty occurred in finding a king: the President was the man proper for this appointment. The Senate, hailing him a king, (constituted, according to Mr. Adams's description, from the well-born,) will naturally say to one another, "You see how we are situated; certainly it is for our country's benefit that we should be all lords;" and lords they are.

Mr. Lowndes concluded his speech with thanking the house for their very great indulgence in permitting him to take up so much time. He hoped that the vast importance of the subject would plead his excuse. He also thanked those gentlemen on the other side of the question for the candid, fair manner in which they had answered his arguments. Popularity was what he never courted; but on this point he spoke merely to point out those dangers to which his fellow-citizens were exposed — dangers that were so evident, that, when he ceased to exist, he wished for no other epitaph, than to have inscribed on his tomb, "Here lies the man that opposed the Constitution, because it was ruinous to the liberty of America."

Hon. JOHN RUTLEDGE declared he had often heard the honorable gentleman with much pleasure; but on the present occasion, he was astonished at his perseverance. Well might he apologize for his taking up the time of gentlemen, when, in the very outset, he declared that this Constitution must necessarily be submitted to a future convention of the people.   Why, then, enter so largely in argument on its merits, when the ultimate decision depended on another body?   Mr. Rutledge then took up an argument relative to treaties not being paramount to the laws of the land.   Was not the last treaty contrary to the Declaratory Act, and a great number of other acts of Parliament? Yet who ever doubted its validity?   The gentleman had declared that his sentiments were so much in contradiction to the voice of his constituents, that he did not expect to be appointed a member of the Convention.   Mr. Rutledge hoped he would be appointed, and did not hesitate to pledge himself to prove, demonstrably, that all those grounds on which he dwelt so much amounted to nothing more than mere declamation; that his boasted Confederation was not worth a farthing; and that, if Mr. Chairman was intrenched in such instruments up to his chin, they would not shield him from one single national calamity.   So far from thinking that the sun of this country was obscured by the new Constitution, he did not doubt but that, whenever it was adopted, the sun of this state, united with twelve other suns, would exhibit a meridian radiance astonishing to the world.   The gentleman's obstinacy brought to his recollection a friend to this country, once a member of that house, who said, "It is generally imputed to me that I am obstinate.   This is a mistake. I am not so, but sometimes hard to be convinced."

Hon. PATRICK CALHOUN, of *Ninety-six*, made some observations on the too great latitude allowed in religion.

Hon. JAMES LINCOLN, of *Ninety-six*, declared, that if ever any person rose in a public assembly with diffidence, he then did ; if ever any person felt himself deeply interested in what he thought a good cause, and at the same time lamented the want of abilities to support it, it was he.   On a question on which gentlemen, whose abilities would do honor to the senate of ancient Rome, had enlarged with so much eloquence and learning, who could venture without anxiety and diffidence ?   He had not the vanity to oppose his opinion to such men ; he had not the vanity to suppose he could place this business in any new light ; but the justice he owed to his constituents — the justice he owed to his own feelings, which would perhaps upbraid him hereafter, if he indulged himself so far as to give merely a silent vote on this great question — impelled him, reluctantly impelled him, to intrude himself on the house. He had, for some years past, turned his thoughts towards the politics of this country; he long since perceived that not only the federal but the state Constitution required much the hand of correction and revision. They were both formed in times of confusion and distress, and it was a matter of wonder they were so free from defects as we found them. That they were imperfect, no one would deny; and that something must be done to remedy those imperfections, was also evident; but great care should be taken that, by endeavoring to do some good, we should not do an infinite deal of mischief. He had listened with eager attention to all the arguments in favor of the Constitution; but he solemnly declared that the more he heard, the more he was persuaded of its evil tendency. What does this proposed Constitution do? It changes, totally changes, the form of your present government. From a well-digested, well-formed democratic, you are at once rushing into an aristocratic government. What have you been contending for these ten years past? Liberty! What is liberty? The power of governing yourselves. If you adopt this Constitution, have you this power? No: you give it into the hands of a set of men who live one thousand miles distant from you. Let the people but once trust their liberties out of their own hands, and what will be the consequence? First, a haughty, imperious aristocracy; and ultimately, a tyrannical monarchy. No people on earth are, at this day, so free as the people of America. All other nations are, more or less, in a state of slavery. They owe their constitutions partly to chance, and partly to the sword; but that of America is the offspring of their choice — the darling of their bosom: and was there ever an instance in the world that a people in this situation, possessing all that Heaven could give on earth, all that human wisdom and valor could procure — was there ever a people so situated, as calmly and deliberately to convene themselves together for the express purpose of considering whether they should give away or retain those inestimable blessings? In the name of God, were we a parcel of children, who would cry and quarrel for a hobby-horse, which, when we were once in possession of, we quarrel with and throw it away? It is said this Constitution is an experiment; but all regular-bred physicians are cautious of experiments. If the constitution be crazed a little, or somewhat feeble, is it therefore necessary to kill it in order to cure it ? Surely not. There are many parts of this Constitution he objected to: some few of them had not been mentioned; he would therefore request some information thereon. The President holds his employment for four years; but he may hold it for fourteen times four years: in short, he may hold it so long that it will be impossible, without another revolution, to displace him. You do not put the same check on him that you do on your own state governor — a man born and bred among you; a man over whom you have a continual and watchful eye; a man who, from the very nature of his situation, it it almost impossible can do you any injury: this man, you say, shall not be elected for more than four years; and yet this mighty, this omnipotent governor-general may be elected for years and years.

He would be glad to know why, in this Constitution, there is a total silence with regard to the liberty of the press. Was it forgotten? Impossible! Then it must have been purposely omitted; and with what design, good or bad, he left the world to judge. The liberty of the press was the tyrant's scourge — it was the true friend and firmest supporter of civil liberty; therefore why pass it by in silence? He perceived that not till almost the very end of the Constitution was there any provision made for the nature or form of government we were to live under: he contended it should have been the very first article; it should have been, as it were, the groundwork or foundation on which it should have been built. But how is it? At the very end of the Constitution, there is a clause which says, — "The Congress of the United States shall guaranty to each state a republican form of government." But pray, who are the United States ? — A President and four or five senators ? Pray, sir, what security have we for a republican form of government, when it depends on the mere will and pleasure of a few men, who, with an army, navy, and rich treasury at their back, may change and alter it as they please ? It may be said they will be sworn. Sir, the king of Great Britain, at his coronation, swore to govern his subjects with justice and mercy. We were then his subjects, and continued so for a long time after. He would be glad to know how he observed his oath. If, then, the king of Great Britain forswore himself, what security have we that a future President and four or five

senators — men like himself — will think more solemnly of
so sacred an obligation than he did ?

Why was not this Constitution ushered in with the bill
of rights ? Are the people to have no rights ? Perhaps this
same President and Senate would, by and by, declare them.
He much feared they would. He concluded by returning
his hearty thanks to the gentleman who had so nobly opposed this Constitution : it was supporting the cause of the
people ; and if ever any one deserved the title of man of
the people, he, on this occasion, most certainly did.

Gen. CHARLES COTESWORTH PINCKNEY an-
swered Mr. Lincoln on his objections. He said, that the
time for which the President should hold his office, and
whether he should be reëligible, had been fully discussed in
the Convention. It had been once agreed to by a majority,
that he should hold his office for the term of seven years,
but should not be reëlected a second time. But upon re-
considering that article, it was thought that to cut off all
hopes from a man of serving again in that elevated station, might render him dangerous, or perhaps indifferent to
the faithful discharge of his duty. His term of service might
expire during the raging of war, when he might, perhaps,
be the most capable man in America to conduct it ; and
would it be wise and prudent to declare in our Constitution
that such a man should not again direct our military operations, though our success might be owing to his abilities ?
The mode of electing the President rendered undue influence
almost impossible ; and it would have been imprudent in us
to have put it out of our power to reëlect a man whose talents, abilities, and integrity, were such as to render him the
object of the general choice of his country. With regard to
the liberty of the press, the discussion of that matter was
not forgotten by the members of the Convention. It was
fully debated, and the impropriety of saying any thing about
it in the Constitution clearly evinced. The general government has no powers but what are expressly granted to it ;
it therefore has no power to take away the liberty of the
press. That invaluable blessing, which deserves all the encomiums the gentleman has justly bestowed upon it, is
secured by all our state constitutions ; and to have mentioned
it in our general Constitution would perhaps furnish an argument, hereafter, that the general government had a right

to exercise powers not expressly delegated to it.   For the
same reason, we had no bill of rights inserted in our Constitution ; for, as we might perhaps have omitted the enumeration of some of our rights, it might hereafter be said
we had delegated to the general government a power to
take away such of our rights as we had not enumerated ;
but by delegating express powers, we certainly reserve to
ourselves every power and right not mentioned in the Constitution.   Another reason weighed particularly, with the
members from this state, against the insertion of a bill of
rights.   Such bills generally begin with declaring that all
men are by nature born free.   Now, we should make that
declaration with a very.bad grace, when a large part of our
property consists in men who are actually born slaves.   As
to the clause guarantying to each state a republican form of
government being inserted near the end of the Constitution,
the general observed that it was as binding as if it had
been inserted in the first article.   The Constitution takes
its effect from the ratification, and every part of it is to be
ratified at the same time, and not one clause before the
other ; but he thought there was a peculiar propriety in
inserting it where it was, as it was necessary to form the
government before that government could guaranty any thing.

Col. MASON thanked Mr. Lowndes for his opposition,
by the desire of several gentlemen, members of that house.
It had drawn forth from the other side most valuable information, and he thanked those gentlemen for the willingness
with which they had given it, with so much good-nature.
Those gentlemen who lived in the country were now enabled to satisfy their constituents.

The question being put, that a convention of the people
should be called for the purpose of considering, and of ratifying or rejecting, the Constitution framed for the United
States by a Convention of delegates assembled at Philadelphia in May last, it was unanimously agreed to.

[*There will appear some omissions in what fell from Mr. Lowndes,
which could not be supplied, owing to the loss of a note-book in the fire
which consumed the State-House.*]

SATURDAY, *January* 19, 1788.

On the question being put for the Convention to assemble
in Charleston on Monday, the 12th day of May next, the
ayes and nays were as follows, viz. : —

For the Parishes of St. Philip and St. Michael, Charleston. — Ayes: Edward Rutledge, Dr. David Ramsay, William Johnson, C. C. Pinckney, Edward Darrell, Thomas Jones, Isaac Motte, John Mathews, Daniel Cannon, Daniel Stevens, John Blake, Anthony Toomer, John F. Grimke, Thomas Heywood, Jun., Richard Lushington, Francis Kinloch, Jacob Read, Edward Blake, John Budd, Rawlins Lowndes, Michael Kalteisen, Thomas Bee, Adanus Burke, Hugh Rutledge, Edward Lightwood. — Nays: none.

Christ Church. — Ayes: Charles Pinckney, Plowden Weston, Joseph Manigault, John Hutter. — Nays: none.

St. John's, Berkley County. — Ayes: Peter Fassoux, Theodore Gourdine, Thomas Simons. — Nays: Robert M'Kelvey, Gideon Kirke.

St. Andrew's. — Ayes: John Rivers, Glen Drayton, Thomas Farr, James Ladson, Charles Drayton. — Nay: William Scott.

St. George's, Dorchester. — Ayes: John Glaze, Walter Izard, William Postell, John Bell. — Nays: none.

St. James's, Goose Creek. — Ayes: Ralph Izard, Gabriel Manigault, William Smith, John Parker, Jun. — Nays: none.

St. Thomas, and St. Dennis. — Ayes: Thomas Screven, Robert Daniel, Thomas Shrubrick. — Nays: none.

St. Paul's. — Ayes: George Haig, William Washington, Paul Hamilton. — Nays: none.

St. Bartholomew's. — Ayes: William Furguson, Peter Youngblood, William C. Snipes, John North. — Nays: none.

St. Helena. — Ayes: William Haxard Wigg, John Joyner, John Jenkins, Robert Barnwell, Benjamin Reynolds, Bernard Elliott. — Nays: none.

St. James's, Santee. — Ayes: Thomas Horry, Jacob Bond, I'On, William Douxsaint, Lewis Miles. — Nays: none.

Prince George's, Winyaw. — Ayes: Thomas Waties, Matthew Irvine. — Nays James Withers, Thomas Dunbar.

All Saints. — Ayes: Robert Herriot, Daniel Morral — Nays: none.

Prince Frederick's. — Ayes: none. — Nays: John T. Green, John Dicky, Benjamin Porter, James Pettigrew.

St. John's, Colleton County. — Ayes: Isaac Je⬤ William Smelie. — Nays none.

St. Peter's. — Ayes: none. — Nays: James Thompson, John Chisholm, John Fenwick, Samuel Maner.

Prince William's. — Ayes: Pierce Butler, John Lightwood, John A. Cuthbert. — Nays: Stephen Bull, William Murray.

St. Stephen's. — Ayes: none. — Nays: Thomas Palmer, John Coutuier, T Cordes.

District to the Eastward of Wateree. — Ayes: none. — Nays: Isaac Alexander, Thomas Sumter, Andrew Baskins, Joseph Lee, Thomas M'Faddin, George Cooper, Benjamin Cudworth, Samuel Dunlap, Hugh White.

District of Ninety-six. — Ayes: Patrick Calhoun, John Purvis. — Nays: Arthur Simpkins, James Lincoln, Adam Crain Jones, William Butler.

District of Saxe-Gotha. — Ayes: none. — Nays: Joseph Culpeper, Henry Pendleton, John Threewits, Llewellen Threewits.

Lower Districts, between Broad and Saluda Rivers. — Ayes: none. Nays Philemon Waters, George Ruff, John Lindsay, William Wadlington.

Little River District. — Ayes: none. — Nays: John Hunter, Angus Campbel, Levi Casey, James Mason.

Upper, or Spartan District. — Ayes: none. — Nays: Thomas Brandon, S. M'Junkin Winn, James Craig, John Gray, James Knox, John Turner, Aromanus Lyles, John Cook, James Pedian.

District called the New Acquisition. — Ayes: none. — Nays: Andrew Love, James Powell, William Fergus, William Bratton, Robert Patton, James Ramsay, John Drennan, James Martin, Joseph Palmer, Alexander Moore.

St Matthew's. — Ayes: none. — Nays: Thomas Sabb, J. Frierson, Paul Warley

Orange Parish. — Ayes: none. — Nays: William Robinson, Lewis Lesterjette.

St. David's. — Ayes: none. — Nays: Calvin Spencer, Robert Baxwill, A. Hunter

District between Savannah River and the North Fork of Edisto. — Ayes: none. — Nays: William Davis, Isaac Cush, James Fair, Daniel Greene.

Ayes, - - - - - - - - - - 76. | Nays, - - - - - - - - - - 75

So it was resolved in the affirmative.

JOHN SANDFORD DART, C. H. R

DEBATES IN CONVENTION.

MONDAY, *May* 12, 1788.

This day being appointed for the meeting of the state Convention, (Mr. Thomas Bee, in the chair, *pro tem.*,) the returns were read, and there not being a majority, adjourned until Tuesday, the 13th.

TUESDAY, *May* 13, 1788.

On this day the Convention met, and the names being called over, there appeared to be present one hundred and seventy-three members; upon which they proceeded to ballot, when

His excellency, Governor THOMAS PINCKNEY, was elected *President.*

Colonel JOHN SANDFORD DART was elected *Secretary.*

Mr. Atmore, Messenger. Mr. Athwell, Door-keeper. Mr. John Bounetheau, Bar-keeper. Mr. Stevens, Cashier. Colonel Lushington, Assistant-Cashier.

WEDNESDAY, *May* 14, 1788.

Speech of Mr. CHARLES PINCKNEY, (*one of the delegates to the Federal Convention.*)

Mr. President, after so much has been said with respect to the powers possessed by the late Convention to form and propose a new system — after so many observations have been made on its leading principles, as well in the House of Representatives as in the conventions of other states, whose proceedings have been published — it will be as unnecessary for me again minutely to examine a subject which has been so thoroughly investigated, as it would be difficult to carry you into a field that has not been sufficiently explored.

Having, however, had the honor of being associated in the delegation from this state, and presuming upon the indulgence of the house, I shall proceed to make some observations which appear to me necessary to a full and candid discussion of the system now before us.

It seems to be generally confessed that, of all sciences, that of government, or politics, is the most difficult. In the old world, as far as the lights of history extend, from the earliest ages to our own, we find nations in the constant exercise of all the forms with which the world is at present furnished. We have seen among the ancients, as well as the moderns, monarchies, limited and absolute, aristocracies, republics of a single state, and federal unions. But notwithstanding all their experience, how confined and imperfect is their knowledge of government! how little is the true doctrine of representation understood! how few states enjoy what we call freedom! how few governments answer those great ends of public happiness which we seem to expect from our own!

In reviewing such of the European states as we are best acquainted with, we may with truth assert that there is but one among the most important which confirms to its citizens their civil liberties, or provides for the security of private rights. But as if it had been fated that we should be the first perfectly free people the world had ever seen, even the government I have alluded to withholds from a part of its subjects the equal enjoyment of their religious liberties. How many thousands of the subjects of Great Britain at this moment labor under civil disabilities, merely on account of their religious persuasions! To the liberal and enlightened mind, the rest of Europe affords a melancholy picture of the depravity of human nature, and of the total subversion of those rights, without which we should suppose no people could be happy or content.

We have been taught here to believe that all power of right belongs to the people; that it flows immediately from them, and is delegated to their officers for the public good; that our rulers are the servants of the people, amenable to their will, and created for their use. How different are the governments of Europe! There the people are the servants and subjects of their rulers; there merit and talents have little or no influence; but all the honors and offices of government are swallowed up by birth, by fortune, or by rank.

From the European world are no precedents to be drawn for a people who think they are capable of governing themselves. Instead of receiving instruction from them, we may, with pride, affirm that, new as this country is in point of settlement, inexperienced as she must be upon questions of government, she still has read more useful lessons to the old world, she has made them more acquainted with their own rights, than they had been otherwise for centuries. It is with pride I repeat that, old and experienced as they are, they are indebted to us for light and refinement upon points of all others the most interesting.

Had the American revolution not happened, would Ireland

enjoy her present rights of commerce and legislation ? Would
the subjects of the emperor in the Netherlands have presumed
to contend for, and ultimately to secure, the privileges they
demanded ? Would the parliaments of France have resisted
the edicts of their monarch, and justified in a language that
will do honor to the freest people ? Nay, I may add, would
a becoming sense of liberty, and of the rights of mankind,
have so generally pervaded that kingdom, had not their
knowledge of America led them to the investigation ? Undoubtedly not. Let it be therefore our boast that we have
already taught some of the oldest and wisest nations to ex-
plore their rights as men ; and let it be our prayer that the
effects of the revolution may never cease to operate until
they have unshackled all the nations that have firmness to
resist the fetters of despotism. Without a precedent, and
with the experience of but a few years, were the Convention
called upon to form a system for a people differing from all
others we are acquainted with.

The first knowledge necessary for us to acquire, was a
knowledge of the people for whom this system was to be
formed ; for unless we were acquainted with their situation,
their habits, opinions, and resources, it would be impossible
to form a government upon adequate or practicable principles.

If we examine the reasons which have given rise to the
distinctions of rank that at present prevail in Europe, we
shall find that none of them do, or in all probability ever
will, exist in the Union.

The only distinction that may take place is that of wealth.
Riches, no doubt, will ever have their influence ; and where
they are suffered to increase to large amounts in a few hands,
there they may become dangerous to the public — particularly when, from the cheapness of labor and the scarcity of
money, a great proportion of the people are poor. These,
however, are dangers that I think we have very little to
apprehend, for these reasons : One is from the destruction
of the right of primogeniture ; by which means, the estates
of intestates are equally to be divided among all their children — a provision no less consonant to the principles of
a republican government, than it is to those of general equity
and parental affection. To endeavor to raise a name by
accumulating property in one branch of a family, at the ex
pense of others equally related and deserving, is a vanity no

less unjust and cruel than dangerous to the interests of liberty
it is a practice no wise state will ever encourage or tolerate
In the Northern and Eastern States, such distinctions among
children are seldom heard of.   Laws have been long since
passed in all of them, destroying the right of primogeniture,
and as laws never fail to have a powerful influence upon the
manners of a people, we may suppose that, in future, an
equal division of property among children will, in general,
take place in all the states, and one means of amassing inor-
dinate wealth in the hands of individuals be, as it ought,
forever removed.

Another reason is that, in the Eastern and Northern States,
the landed property is nearly equally divided : very few have
large bodies, and there are few that have not small tracts.

The greater part of the people are employed in cultivating
their own lands ; the rest in handicraft and commerce.   They
are frugal in their manner of living.   Plain tables, clothing,
and furniture, prevail in their houses, and expensive appear-
ances are avoided.   Among the landed interest, it may be
truly said there are few of them rich, and few of them very
poor ; nor, while the states are capable of supporting so many
more inhabitants than they contain at present — while so vast
a territory on our frontier remains uncultivated and unexplored
— while the means of subsistence are so much within every
man's power — are those dangerous distinctions of fortune to
be expected which at present prevail in other countries.

The people of the Union may be classed as follows :
Commercial men, who will be of consequence or not, in the
political scale, as commerce may be made an object of the
attention of government.   As far as I am able to judge, and
presuming that proper sentiments will ultimately prevail upon
this subject, it does not appear to me that the commercial
line will ever have much influence in the politics of the
Union.   Foreign trade is one of the enemies against which
we must be extremely guarded — more so than against any
other, as none will ever have a more unfavorable operation.
I consider it as the root of our present public distress — as
the plentiful source from which our future national calamities
will flow, unless great care is taken to prevent it.   Divided
as we are from the old world, we should have nothing to do
with their politics, and as little as possible with their com-

merce : they can never improve, but must inevitably corrupt us.

Another class is that of professional men, who, from their
education and pursuits, must ever have a considerable influence, while your government retains the republican principle, and its affairs are agitated in assemblies of the people.

The third, with whom I will connect the mechanical, as
generally attached to them, are the landed interest — the
owners and cultivators of the soil — the men attached to the
truest interests of their country from those motives which
always bind and secure the affections of the nation.   In
these consists the great body of the people ; and here rests,
and I hope ever will continue, all the authority of the
government.

I remember once to have seen, in the writings of a very
celebrated author upon national wealth, the following remarks :   " Finally," says he, " there are but three ways for
a nation to acquire wealth.   The first is by war, as the
Romans did in plundering their conquered neighbors : this is
robbery.   The second is by commerce, which is generally
cheating.   The third is by agriculture, the only honest way,
wherein a man receives a real increase of the seed thrown
into the ground, in a kind of continual miracle wrought by
the hand of God in his favor, as a reward for his innocent
life and virtuous industry."

I do not agree with him so far as to suppose that commerce is generally cheating.   I think there are some kinds
of commerce not only fair and valuable, but such as ought to
be encouraged by government.   I agree with him in this
general principle — that all the great objects of government
should be subservient to the increase of agriculture and the
support of the landed interest, and that commerce should
only be so far attended to, as it may serve to improve and
strengthen them ; that the object of a republic is to render
its citizens virtuous and happy ; and that an unlimited
foreign commerce can seldom fail to have a contrary tendency.

These classes compose the people of the Union ; and,
fortunately for their harmony, they may be said in a great
measure to be connected with and dependent upon each
other.

The merchant is dependent upon the planter, as the pur-

chaser of his imports, and as furnishing him with the means
of his remittances.   The professional men depend upon both
for employment in their respective pursuits, and are, in their
turn, useful to both.   The landholder, though the most independent of the three, is still, in some measure, obliged to
the merchant for furnishing him at home with a ready sale
for his productions.

From this mutual dependence, and the statement I have
made respecting the situation of the people of the Union,
I am led to conclude that mediocrity of fortune is a leading
feature in our national character; that most of the causes
which lead to destructions of fortune among other nations
being removed, and causes of equality existing with us
which are not to be found among them, we may with safety
assert that the great body of national wealth is nearly
equally in the hands of the people, among whom there are
few dangerously rich or few miserably poor; that we may
congratulate ourselves with living under the blessings of a
mild and equal government, which knows no distinctions
but those of merits or talents — under a government whose
honors and offices are equally open to the exertions of all her
citizens, and which adopts virtue and worth for her own,
wheresoever she can find them.

Another distinguishing feature in our Union is its division
into individual states, differing in extent of territory, manners, population, and products.

Those who are acquainted with the Eastern States, the
reason of their original migration, and their pursuits, habits,
and principles, well know that they are essentially different
from those of the Middle and Southern States; that they
retain all those opinions respecting religion and government
which first induced their ancestors to cross the Atlantic; and
that they are, perhaps, more purely republican in habits and
sentiment than any other part of the Union.   The inhabitants of New York and the eastern part of New Jersey —
originally Dutch settlements — seem to have altered less than
might have been expected in the course of a century; indeed,
the greatest part of New York may still be considered as a
Dutch settlement, the people in the interior country generally using that language in their families, and having very
little varied their ancient customs.   Pennsylvania and Delaware are nearly one half inhabited by Quakers, whose

passive principles upon questions of government, and rigid
opinions in private, render them extremely different from the
citizens either of the Eastern or Southern States.   Maryland
was originally a Roman Catholic colony, and a great number
of their inhabitants, some of them the most wealthy and cultivated, are still of this persuasion.   It is unnecessary for me
to state the striking difference in sentiment and habit which
must always exist between the Independents of the East —
the Calvinists and Quakers of the Middle States, and the
Roman Catholics of Maryland; but striking as this is, it is
not to be compared with the difference that there is between
the inhabitants of the Northern and Southern States.   When
I say Southern, I mean Maryland, and the states to the southward of her.   Here we may truly observe, that Nature has
drawn as strong marks of distinction in the habits and manners of the people as she has in her climates and productions.
The southern citizen beholds, with a kind of surprise, the
simple manners of the east, and is too often induced to
entertain undeserved opinions of the apparent purity of the
Quaker; while they, in their turn, seem concerned at what
they term the extravagance and dissipation of their southern
friends, and reprobate, as unpardonable moral and political
evil, the dominion they hold over a part of the human race.
The inconveniences which too frequently attend these differences in habits and opinions among the citizens that compose
the Union, are not a little increased by the variety of their
state governments; for, as I have already observed, the constitution or laws under which a people live never fail to have
a powerful effect upon the manners.   We know that all the
states have adhered, in their forms, to the republican principle, though they have differed widely in their opinions of
the mode best calculated to preserve it.

· In Pennsylvania and Georgia, the whole powers of government are lodged in a legislative body, of a single branch,
over which there is no control; nor are their executives or judicials, from their connection and necessary dependence on
the legislature, capable of strictly executing their respective
offices.   In all the other states, except Maryland, Massachusetts, and New York, they are only so far improved as to
have a legislature with two branches, which completely
involve and swallow up all the powers of their government.
In neither of these are the judicial or executive placed in

that firm or independent situation which can alone secure the safety of the people or the just administration of the laws. In Maryland, one branch of their legislature is a Senate, chosen, for five years, by electors chosen by the people. The knowledge and firmness which this body have, upon all occasions, displayed, not only in the exercise of their legislative duties, but in withstanding and defeating such of the projects of the other house as appeared to them founded in local and personal motives, have long since convinced me that the Senate of Maryland is the best model of a senate that has yet been offered to the Union; that it is capable of correcting many of the vices of the other parts of their Constitution, and, in a great measure, atoning for those defects which, in common with the states I have mentioned, are but too evident in their execution — the want of stability and independence in the judicial and executive departments.

In Massachusetts, we find the principle of legislation more improved by the revisionary power which is given to their governor, and the independence of their judges.

In New York, the same improvement in legislation has taken place as in Massachusetts; but here, from the executive's being elected by the great body of the people; holding his office for three years, and being reëligible; from the appointment to offices being taken from the legislature and placed in a select council, — I think their Constitution is, upon the whole, the best in the Union. Its faults are the want of permanent salaries to their judges, and giving to their executive the nomination to offices, which is, in fact, giving him the appointment.

It does not, however, appear to me, that this can be called a vice of their system, as I have always been of opinion that the insisting upon the right to nominate was a usurpation of their executive's, not warranted by the letter or meaning of their Constitution.

These are the outlines of their various forms, in few of which are their executive or judicial departments wisely constructed, or that solid distinction adopted between the branches of their legislative which can alone provide for the influence of different principles in their operation.

Much difficulty was expected from the extent of country to be governed. All the republics we read of, either in the ancient or modern world, have been extremely limited in territory. We know of none a tenth part so large as the United States; indeed, we are hardly able to determine, from the lights we are furnished with, whether the governments we have heard of under the names of republics really deserved them, or whether the ancients ever had any just or proper ideas upon the subject. Of the doctrine of representation, the fundamental of a republic, they certainly were ignorant. If they were in possession of any other safe or practicable principles, they have long since been lost and forgotten to the world. Among the other honors, therefore, that have been reserved for the American Union, not the least considerable of them. is that of defining a mixed system, by which a people may govern themselves, possessing all the virtues and benefits, and avoiding all the dangers and inconveniences, of the three simple forms.

I have said that the ancient confederacies, as far as we are acquainted with them, covered up an inconsiderable territory.

Among the moderns, in our sense of the word, there is no such system as a confederate republic. There are, indeed, some small states whose interior governments are democratic; but these are too inconsiderable to afford information. The Swiss cantons are only connected by alliances; the Germanic body is merely an association of potentates, most of them absolute in their own dominions; and as to the United Netherlands, it is such a confusion of states and assemblies, that I have always been at loss what species of government to term it. According to my idea of the word, it is not a republic; for I conceive it as indispensable, in a republic, that all authority should flow from the people. In the United Netherlands, the people have no interference either in the election of their magistrate or in the affairs of government. From the experiment, therefore, never having been fairly made, opinions have been entertained, and sanctioned by high authorities, that republics are only suited to small societies. This opinion has its advocates among all those who, not having a sufficient share of industry or talents to investigate for themselves, easily adopt the opinions of such authors as are supposed to have written with ability upon the subject; but I am led to believe other opinions begin to prevail — opinions more to be depended upon, because they result from juster principles.

We begin now to suppose that the evils of a republic —

dissension, tumult, and faction — are more dangerous in small societies than in large confederate states.   In the first, the people are easily assembled and inflamed — are always exposed to those convulsive tumults of infatuation and enthusiasm which often overturn all public order.   In the latter. the multitude will be less imperious, and consequently less inconstant, because the extensive territory of each republic and the number of citizens, will not permit them all to be assembled at one time and in one place : the sphere of government being enlarged, it will not easily be in the power of factious and designing men to infect the whole people ; it will give an opportunity to the more temperate and prudent part of the society to correct the licentiousness and injustice of the rest.   We have strong proofs of the truth of this opinion in the examples of Rhode Island and Massachusetts — instances which have, perhaps, been critically afforded by an all-merciful Providence to evince the truth of a position extremely important to our present inquiries.   In the former, the most contracted society in the Union, we have seen their licentiousness so far prevail as to seize the reins of government, and oppress the people by laws the most infamous that have ever disgraced a civilized nation.   In the latter, where the sphere was enlarged, similar attempts have been rendered abortive by the zeal and activity of those who were opposed to them.

As the Constitution before you is intended to represent states as well as citizens, I have thought it necessary to make these remarks, because there are, no doubt, a great number of the members of this body, who, from their particular pursuits, have not had an opportunity of minutely investigating them, and because it will be impossible for the house fairly to determine whether the government is a proper one or not, unless they are in some degree acquainted with the people and the states, for whose use it is instituted.

For a people thus situated is a government to be formed — a people who have the justest opinion of their civil and religious rights, and who have risked every thing in asserting and defending them.

In every government there necessarily exists a power from which there is no appeal, and which, for that reason, may be formed absolute and uncontrollable.

The person or assembly in whom this power resides is

called the sovereign or supreme power of the state.   With us, the sovereignty of the Union is in the people.

One of the best political and moral writers (Paley, a deacon of Carlisle — vol. ii. 174, 175) I have met with, enumerates three principal forms of government, which, he says, are to be regarded rather as the simple forms, by some combination and intermixture of which all actual governments are composed, than as any where existing in a pure and elementary state.   These forms are, —

1st.   Despotism, or absolute monarchy, where the legislature is in a single person.

2d.   An aristocracy, where the legislature is in a select assembly, the members of which either fill up, by election, the vacancies in their own body, or succeed to it by inheritance, property, tenure of lands, or in respect of some personal right or qualification.

3d.   A republic, where the people at large, either collectively or by representation, form the legislature.

The separate advantages of monarchy are unity of council, decision, secrecy, and despatch; the military strength and energy resulting from these qualities of government; the exclusion of popular and aristocratical contentions; the preventing, by a known rule of succession, all competition for the supreme power, thereby repressing the dangerous hopes and intrigues of aspiring citizens.

The dangers of a monarchy are tyranny, expense, exactions, military dominations, unnecessary wars, ignorance, in the governors, of the interest and accommodation of all people, and a consequent deficiency of salutary regulations; want of constancy and uniformity in the rules of government, and, proceeding from thence, insecurity of persons and property.

The separate advantage of an aristocracy is the wisdom that may be expected from experience and education.   A permanent council naturally possesses experience, and the members will always be educated with a view to the stations they are destined by their birth to occupy.

The mischiefs of an aristocracy are dissensions in the ruling orders of the state; an oppression of the lower orders by the privilege of the higher, and by laws partial to the separate interests of the law-makers.

The advantages of a republic are liberty, exemption from needless restrictions, equal laws, public spirit, averseness to war, frugality, — above all, the opportunities afforded, to men of every description, of producing their abilities and counsels to public observation, and the exciting to the service of the commonwealth the faculties of its best citizens.

The evils of a republic are dissensions, tumults, faction, the attempts of ambitious citizens to possess power, the confusion and clamor which are the inevitable consequences of propounding questions of state to the discussion of large popular assemblies, the delay and disclosure of the public councils, and too often the imbecility of the laws.

A mixed government is composed by the combination of two or more of the simple forms above described ; and in whatever proportion each form enters into the constitution of government, in the same proportion may both the advantages and evils which have been attributed to that form be expected.

The citizens of the United States would reprobate, with indignation, the idea of a monarchy. But the essential qualities of a monarchy — unity of council, vigor, secrecy, and despatch — are qualities essential in every government.

While, therefore, we have reserved to the people, the fountain of all power, the periodical election of their first magistrate, — while we have defined his powers, and bound them to such limits as will effectually prevent his usurping authorities dangerous to the general welfare, — we have, at the same time, endeavored to infuse into this department that degree of vigor which will enable the President to execute the laws with energy and despatch.

By constructing the Senate upon rotative principles, we have removed, as will be shown upon another occasion, all danger of an aristocratic influence ; while, by electing the members for six years, we hope we have given to this part of the system all the advantages of an aristocracy — wisdom, experience, and a consistency of measures.

The House of Representatives, in which the people of the Union are proportionably represented, are to be biennially elected by them. Those appointments are sufficiently short to render the member as dependent as he ought to be upon his constituents.

They are the moving-spring of the system. With them all grants of money are to originate : on them depend the wars we shall be engaged in, the fleets and armies we shall raise and support, the salaries we shall pay; in short, on them depend the appropriations of money, and consequently all the arrangements of government. With this powerful influence of the purse, they will be always able to restrain the usurpations of the other departments, while their own licentiousness will, in its turn, be checked and corrected by them.

I trust that, when we proceed to review the system by sections, it will be found to contain all those necessary provisions and restraints, which, while they enable the general government to guard and protect our common rights as a nation, to restore to us those blessings of commerce and mutual confidence which have been so long removed and impaired, will secure to us those rights, which, as the citizens of a state, will make us happy and content at home — as the citizens of the Union, respectable abroad.

How different, Mr. President, is this government constructed from any we have known among us!

In their individual capacities as citizens, the people are proportionably represented in the House of Representatives. Here they who are to pay to support the expenses of government, have the purse-strings in their hands; here the people hold, and feel that they possess, an influence sufficiently powerful to prevent every undue attempt of the other branches, to maintain that weight in the political scale which, as the source of all authority, they should ever possess; here, too, the states, whose existence as such we have often heard predicted as precarious, will find, in the Senate, the guards of their rights as political associations.

On them (I mean the state systems) rests the general fabric: on their foundation is this magnificent structure of freedom erected, each depending upon, supporting, and protecting the other: nor — so intimate is the connection — can the one be removed without prostrating the other in ruin: like the head and the body, separate them and they die.

Far be it from me to suppose that such an attempt should ever be made the good sense and virtue of our country forbid the idea. To the Union we will look up, as to the temple of our freedom — a temple founded in the affections, and supported by the virtue, of the people. Here we will pour out our gratitude to the Author of all good, for suffering us to participate in the rights of a people who govern themselves.

Is there, at this moment, a nation upon earth that enjoys this right, where the true principles of representation are understood and practised, and where all authority flows from and returns at stated periods to, the people? I answer, there is not. Can a government be said to be free where these rights do not exist? It cannot. On what depends the enjoyment of these rare, these inestimable privileges? On the firmness, on the power, of the Union to protect and defend them.

How grateful, then, should we be, that, at this important period, — a period important, not to us alone, but to the general rights of mankind, — so much harmony and concession should prevail throughout the states; that the public opinion should be so much actuated by candor, and an attention to their general interests; that, disdaining to be governed by the narrow motives of state policy, they have liberally determined to dedicate a part of their advantages to the support of that government from which they received them! To fraud, to force, or accident, all the governments we know have owed their births. To the philosophic mind, how new and awful an instance do the United States at present exhibit in the political world! They exhibit, sir, the first instance of a people, who, being dissatisfied with their government, — unattacked by foreign force, and undisturbed by domestic uneasiness, — coolly and deliberately resort to the virtue and good sense of their country, for a correction of their public errors.

It must be obvious that, without a superintending government, it is impossible the liberties of this country can long be secured.

Single and unconnected, how weak and contemptible are the largest of our states! — how unable to protect themselves from external or domestic insult! How incompetent to national purposes would even partial union be! — how liable to intestine wars and confusion! — how little able to secure the blessings of peace!

Let us, therefore, be careful in strengthening the Union. Let us remember that we are bounded by vigilant and attentive neighbors, who view with a jealous eye our rise to empire.

Let us remember that we are bound, in gratitude to our northern brethren, to aid them in the recovery of those rights which they have lost in obtaining for us an extension of our commerce, and the security of our liberties. Let us not be unmindful that those who are weak, and may expect support, must, in their turn, be ready to afford it.

We are called upon to execute an important trust — to examine the principles of the Constitution now before you, and, in the name of the people, to receive or reject it.

I have no doubt we shall do this with attention and harmony ; and flatter myself that, at the conclusion of our discussion, we shall find that it is not only expedient, but safe and honorable, to adopt it.

TUESDAY, *May* 20, 1788.

This day the Convention went through the discussion of the Federal Constitution by paragraphs.

Mr. ALEXANDER TWEED, of Prince Frederick, said : Since I came to town, I have more than once heard it asserted, that the representatives of the parish of Prince Frederick were, prior to their election, put under promise to their constituents, that they should by no means give their sanction to the adoption of the new Constitution. Any such restriction, sir, on my own part, I deny. Had they taken upon them so far as to dictate for me, I should have spurned at the idea, and treated such proposals with that contempt they would have justly merited ; and I am clearly of opinion, and I think warranted to say, that these are the sentiments and situation of (at least) some others of my colleagues. Notwithstanding, sir, from all I have heard or can learn, the general voice of the people is against it. For my own part, Mr. President, I came not here to echo the voice of my constituents, nor determined to approve or put a negative upon the Constitution proposed. I came with a mind open to conviction, in order to hear what, in the course of the debates of this house, might be said for and against it. Much, very much, sir, has been advanced on both sides. The matter in hand I look upon to be the most important and momentous that ever came before the representatives of the people of South Carolina. We were told, sir, some days ago, by a learned and honorable gentleman now on the floor, that, as our case at present stood, we must adopt the Constitution proposed ; for, if we did not, in all probability some powerful despot might start up and seize the reins of government

Another learned and honorable gentleman on my left hand said, we must look up to it as the rock of our salvation. To make short, sir, *necessitas non habet legem* was the word.

Those gentlemen, Mr. President, and some others, members of this respectable Convention, — whose profound oratory and elocution would, on the journals of a British House of Commons, stand as lasting monuments of their great abilities, — a man of my circumscribed scale of talents is not adequate to the task of contending with ; nor have I a turn for embellishing my language, or bedecking it with all the flowers of rhetoric. In a word, Mr. President, my idea of the matter now under our consideration is, that we very much stand in need of a reform of government, as the very sinews of our present constitution are relaxed. But, sir, I would fondly hope that our case is not so bad as represented. Are we invaded by a foreign enemy ? Or are the bowels of our country torn to pieces by insurrections and intestine broils ? I answer, No.

Sir, admit but this, and then allow me to ask if history furnishes us with a single instance of any nation, state, or people, who had it more in their power than we at present have to frame for ourselves a perfect, permanent, free, and happy constitution. The Constitution, sir, now under consideration, was framed (I shall say) by the wisdom of a General Convention of the United States ; it now lies before us to wait our concurrence or disapprobation. We, sir, as citizens and freemen, have an undoubted right of judging for ourselves ; it therefore behoves us most seriously to consider, before we determine a matter of such vast magnitude. We are not acting for ourselves alone, but, to all appearance, for generations unborn.

Speech of Mr. CHARLES PINCKNEY, *on the 10th Section of Article 1st of the Federal Constitution.*

This section I consider as the soul of the Constitution, — as containing, in a few words, those restraints upon the states, which, while they keep them from interfering with the powers of the Union, will leave them always in a situation to comply with their federal duties — will teach them to cultivate those principles of public honor and private honesty which are the sure road to national character and happiness

The only parts of this section that are objected to are those which relate to the emission of paper money, and its consequences, tender-laws, and the impairing the obligation of contracts.

The other parts are supposed as exclusively belonging to, and such as ought to be vested in, the Union.

If we consider the situation of the United States as they are at present, either individually or as the members of a general confederacy, we shall find it extremely improper they should ever be intrusted with the power of emitting money, or interfering in private contracts ; or, by means of tender-laws, impairing the obligation of contracts.

I apprehend these general reasonings will be found true with respect to paper money : That experience has shown that, in every state where it has been practised since the revolution, it always carries the gold and silver out of the country, and impoverishes it — that, while it remains, all the foreign merchants, trading in America, must suffer and lose by it ; therefore, that it must ever be a discouragement to commerce — that every medium of trade should have an intrinsic value, which paper money has not ; gold and silver are therefore the fittest for this medium, as they are an equivalent, which paper can never be — that debtors in the assemblies will, whenever they can, make paper money with fraudulent views — that in those states where the credit of the paper money has been best supported, the bills have never kept to their nominal value in circulation, but have constantly depreciated to a certain degree.

I consider it as a granted position that, while the productions of a state are useful to other countries, and can find a ready sale at foreign markets, there can be no doubt of their always being able to command a sufficient sum in specie to answer as a medium for the purposes of carrying on this commerce ; provided there is no paper money, or other means of conducting it. This, I think, will be the case even in instances where the balance of trade is against a state ; but where the balance is in favor, or where there is nearly as much exported as imported, there can be no doubt that the products will be the means of always introducing a sufficient quantity of specie.

If we were to be governed by partial views, and each state was only to consider how far a general regulation suited her own interests, I think it can be proved there is no state in the Union which ought to be so anxious to have this part of the Constitution passed as ourselves.

We are to reflect that this Constitution is not framed to answer temporary purposes. We hope it will last for ages — that it will be the perpetual protector of our rights and properties.

This state is, perhaps, of all others, more blessed in point of soil and productions than any in the Union. Notwithstanding all her sufferings by the war, the great quantity of lands still uncultivated, and the little attention she pays to the improvement of agriculture, she already exports more than any state in the Union, (except Virginia,) and in a little time must exceed her.

Exports are a surer mode of determining the productive wealth of a country than any other, and particularly when these products are in great demand in foreign countries.

Thus circumstanced, where can be the necessity of paper money? Will you not have specie in sufficient quantities? Will you not have more money in circulation without paper money than with it?— I mean, without having only paper in such quantities as you are able to maintain the credit of, as at present. I aver you may, and appeal only to the experience of the last five or six years. Will it not be confessed that, in 1783 and 1784, we had more money than we have at present, and that the emission of your present paper banished double the amount out of circulation? Besides, if paper should become necessary, the general government still possess the power of emitting it, and Continental paper, well funded, must ever answer the purpose better than state paper.

How extremely useful and advantageous must this restraint be to those states which mean to be honest, and not to defraud their neighbors! Henceforth, the citizens of the states may trade with each other without fear of tender-laws or laws impairing the nature of contracts. The citizen of South Carolina will then be able to trade with those of Rhode Island, North Carolina, and Georgia, and be sure of receiving the value of his commodities. Can this be done at present? It cannot! However just the demand may be, yet still your honest, suffering citizen must be content to receive their depreciated paper, or give up the debt.

But above all, how much will this section tend· to restore your credit with foreigners — to rescue your national character from that contempt which must ever follow the most flagrant violations of public faith and private honesty! No more shall paper money, no more shall tender-laws, drive their commerce from our shores, and darken the American name in every country where it is known. No more shall our citizens conceal in their coffers those treasures which the weakness and dishonesty of our government have long hidden from the public eye. The firmness of a just and even system shall bring them into circulation, and honor and virtue shall be again known and countenanced among us. No more shall the widow, the orphan, and the stranger, become the miserable victims of unjust rulers. Your government shall now, indeed, be a government of laws. The arm of Justice shall be lifted on high; and the poor and the rich, the strong and the weak, shall be equally protected in their rights. Public as well as private confidence shall again be established; industry shall return among us; and the blessings of our government shall verify that old, but useful maxim, that with states, as well as individuals, honesty is the best policy.

Speech of Mr. PATRICK DOLLARD, of Prince Frederick's.

Mr. President, I rise, with the greatest diffidence, to speak on this occasion, not only knowing myself unequal to the task, but believing this to be the most important question that ever the good people of this state were called together to deliberate upon. This Constitution has been ably supported, and ingeniously glossed over by many able and respectable gentlemen in this house, whose reasoning, aided by the most accurate eloquence, might strike conviction even in the predetermined breast, had they a good cause to support. Conscious that they have not, and also conscious of my inability to point out the consequences of its defects, which have in some measure been defined by able gentlemen in this house, I shall therefore confine myself within narrow bounds; that is, concisely to make known the sense and language of my constituents. The people of Prince Frederick's Parish, whom I have the honor to represent, are a brave,

honest, and industrious people.   In the late bloody contest,
they bore a conspicuous part, when they fought, bled, and
conquered, in defence of their civil rights and privileges,
which they expected to transmit untainted to their posterity.
They are nearly all, to a man, opposed to this new Constitution, because, they say, they have omitted to insert a bill of
rights therein, ascertaining and fundamentally establishing,
the unalienable rights of men, without a full, free, and secure
enjoyment of which there can be no liberty, and over which
it is not necessary that a good government should have the
control.   They say that they are by no means against vesting Congress with ample and sufficient powers ; but to make
over to them, or any set of men, their birthright, comprised
in Magna Charta, which this new Constitution absolutely
does, they can never agree to.   Notwithstanding this, they
have the highest opinion of the virtues and abilities of the
honorable gentlemen from this state, who represented us in
the General Convention ; and also a few other distinguished
characters, whose names will be transmitted with honor to
future ages ; but I believe, at the same time, they are but
mortal, and, therefore, liable to err ; and as the virtue and
abilities of those gentlemen will consequently recommend
their being first employed in jointly conducting the reins of
this government, they are led to believe it will commence
in a moderate aristocracy : but, that it will, in its future operations, produce a monarchy, or a corrupt and oppressive aristocracy, they have no manner of doubt.   Lust of dominion
is natural in every soil, and the love of power and superiority
is as prevailing in the United States, at present, as in any part
of the earth ; yet in this country, depraved as it is, there still
remains a strong regard for liberty : an American bosom is
apt to glow at the sound of it, and the splendid merit of preserving that best gift of God, which is mostly expelled from
every country in Europe, might stimulate Indolence, and
animate even Luxury to consecrate herself at the altar of
freedom.

My constituents are highly alarmed at the large and rapid
strides which this new government has taken towards despotism.   They say it is big with political mischiefs, and pregnant with a greater variety of impending woes to the good
people of the Southern States, especially South Carolina,
than all the plagues supposed to issue from the poisonous

box of Pandora.   They say it is particularly calculated for
the meridian of despotic aristocracy ; that it evidently tends
to promote the ambitious views of a few able and designing
men, and enslave the rest ; that it carries with it the appearance of an old phrase, formerly made use of in despotic
reigns, and especially by Archbishop Laud, in the reign of
Charles I., that is, " non-resistance."   They say they will
resist against it ; that they will not accept of it unless compelled by force of arms, which this new Constitution plainly
threatens ; and then, they say, your standing army, like
Turkish janizaries enforcing despotic laws, must ram it down
their throats with the points of bayonets.   They warn the
gentlemen of this Convention, as the guardians of their liberty, to beware how they will be accessory to the disposal of,
or rather sacrificing, their dear-bought rights and privileges.
This is the sense and language, Mr. President, of the people ;
and it is an old saying, and I believe a very true one, that
the general voice of the people is the voice of God.   The
general voice of the people, to whom I am responsible, is
against it.   I shall never betray the trust resposed in me by
them ; therefore, shall give my hearty dissent.

WEDNESDAY, *May* 21, 1788.

Gen. SUMPTER, agreeably to notice given yesterday,
(Tuesday, 20th,) moved for an adjournment of the Convention to the (20th October) twentieth day of October next,
in order to give time for the *further consideration* of the
Federal Constitution.   After considerable debate, it was
rejected by a majority of (46) forty-six — yeas, eighty-nine,
(89 ;) nays, one hundred and thirty-five (135).

FRIDAY, *May* 23, 1788.

On motion, *Resolved,* That this Convention do assent to and ratify the
Constitution agreed to on the 17th day of September last, by the Convention
of the United States of America, held at Philadelphia.

On the question being put to agree to the same, the yeas and nays were
called for by the unanimous voice of the Convention, and are as follows : —

FOR THE PARISHES OF ST. PHILIP AND ST. MICHAEL, CHARLESTON. — *Yeas:*
His excel'ency, Governor Thomas Pinckney, did not vote.   Lieutenant-Governor
Thomas Gadsden, C. C. Pinckney, (general,) Christopher Gadsden, (general — mem-
ber of Congress of '65, at New York.) Edward Rutledge, (governor — one of the Con-
gress of '76,) David Ramsay, (Dr.,) Thomas Heyward, Jun., (judge — and one of the
Congress of '76,) Edward Darrell, Isaac Motte, John Mathews, (governor,) Edward
Blake, Thomas Bee, (judge,) Daniel De Soussure, Thomas Jones, John F. Grimke,
(judge,) William Johnson, John J. Pringle, (attorney-general,) John Blake, Daniel

Stevens, Daniel Cannon, Anthony Toomer, Hugh Rutledge, (judge,) John Budd, (Dr.,) Francis Kinloch, Thomas Sommersall, Michael Kalteisen, (captain of Fort Johnson,) Richard Lushington, (colonel,) Nathaniel Russel, Josiah Smith, Lewis Morris, Edward Lightwood, John Edwards. 31.

CHRIST CHURCH. — *Yeas:* Hon. Charles Pinckney, Hon. John Rutledge, Hon. A. Vanderhorst, William Read, Joseph Manigault, Jacob Read, Joshua Toomer. 7.

ST. JOHN'S, BERKLEY. — *Yeas:* Hon. Henry Laurens, Gen. William Moultrie, Henry Laurens, Jun. 3. — *Nays:* Peter Fayssoux, Keating Simons, Thomas Walter. 3. — *Absent:* Francis Marion. 1.

ST. ANDREW's. — *Yeas:* Glen Drayton, Hon. Richard Hutson, Thomas Fuller, James Ladson, Ralph Izard, Jun., Charles Drayton, Hon. William Scott. 7. — *Nays:* none.

ST. GEORGE'S, DORCHESTER. — *Yeas:* John Glaze, Morton Waring, Thomas Warring, Maj. J. Postell, William Postell, Mathias Hutchinson, John Dawson. 7. — *Nays:* none.

ST. JAMES'S, GOOSE CREEK. — *Yeas:* Hon. Ralph Izard, Peter Smith, Hon. Benjamin Smith, Gabriel Manigault, William Smith, J. Parker, Jun., J. Deas, Jun. 7. — *Nays:* none.

ST. THOMAS AND ST. DENNIS. — *Yeas:* Hon. John Huger, Thomas Karwon, Thomas Screven, Robert Daniel, Lewis Fogartie, Isaac Harleston, Isaac Parker. — *Nays:* none.

ST. PAUL's PARISH. — *Yeas:* Paul Hamilton, George Haig, Joseph Slann, Roger Parker Saunders, William Washington, (hero of Eutaw and Cowpens.) — *Nays:* John Wilson, Hon. Melcher Garner. 2.

ST. BARTHOLOMEW's. — *Yeas:* Hon. John Lloyd, John Crosskeys. — *Nays:* Benjamin Postell, William Clay Snipes, O'Brien Smith, Paul Walter, Edmund Bellinger. 5.

ST. HELENA's. — *Yeas:* Hon. John Barnwell, Hon. John Joyner, Hon. John Kean, Hon. William H Wigg, Hon. Robert Barnwell, Hon. William Elliott, Hon. James Stuart. 7. — *Nays:* none.

ST. JAMES's, SANTEE. — *Yeas:* Isaac Dubose, Lewis Miles, Samuel Warren, Richard Withers, John Mayrant, Thomas Horry. 6. — *Nay:* John Bowman. 1.

PRINCE GEORGE's, WINYAW. — *Yeas:* Hon. Thomas Waties, (judge of C. C. P., and chancellor,) Samuel Smith, Cleland Kinloch, Hon. William Allston, Jun. 4. — *Nays:* none. — *Absent:* Peter Horry. 1.

ALL SAINTS'. — *Yeas:* Daniel Morral, Thomas Allston. 2. — *Nays:* none.

PRINCE FREDERICK's. — *Yeas:* William Wilson, Alexander Tweed, William Frierson, James Pettigrew 4. — *Nays:* Patrick Dollard, William Read, J. Burges, Jun. 3.

ST. JOHN's, COLLETON COUNTY. — *Yeas:* Thomas Legare, Richard Muncreef, Jun., Hon. Daniel Jenkins, Hugh Wilson, Isaac Jenkins, Ephraim Mikel, William Smelie. — *Nays:* none.

ST. PETER's. — *Yeas:* John Fenwick, Joachin Hartstone, Seth Stafford, Rev. Henry Holcom. 4. — *Nays:* John Chisholm, John Lewis Bourjin, Jun. 2. — *Absent:* William Stafford. 1.

PRINCE WILLIAM's. — *Yeas:* Thomas Hutson, John M'Pherson, James Maine, John A. Cuthbert, John Lightwood, John Simmons, Stephen Devaux. 7. — *Nays:* none.

ST. STEPHEN's — *Yeas:* John Palmer, Hon. Hezekiah Mahams, Samuel Dubose, John Peyre. 4. — *Nays:* none. — *Absent:* Thomas Cooper, Thomas Palmer. 1 vacant.

DISTRICT EASTWARD OF THE WATEREE. — *Yea:* John Chesnut. 1. — *Nays:* Thomas Sumter, Andrew Baskins, John Lowry, Benjamin Cudworth, William Massay, Hugh White, Thomas Dunlap, Samuel Dunlap, John Montgomery. 9. — *Absent:* S. Boykin.

DISTRICT OF NINETY-SIX. — *Yea:* Dr. John Harris. 1. — *Nays:* James Lincoln, Adam Crain Jones, Edmond Martin, Andrew Hamilton, Joseph Calhoun, William Butler, John Bowie, Hon. John L. Gervais. 8. — *Absent:* John Ewing Calhoun, Charles Davenport. 2.

NORTH SIDE OF SALUDA. — *Yeas:* Samuel Earle, Lemuel J. Allstone, John Thomas, Jun. 3. — *Nays:* none.

SOUTH SIDE OF SALUDA. — *Yeas:* John Miller, William M'Caleb. 2. — *Nays:* none — *Absent:* Robert Anderson. 1.

DISTRICT OF SAXE-GOTHA. — *Yea:* Hon. Henry Pendleton. 1. — *Nays:* Hon. Richard Hampton, J. Culpeper, William Fitzpatrick, Llewellen Threewits, John Threewits, Wade Hampton. 6

LOWER DISTRICTS BETWEEN BROAD AND SALUDA RIVERS. — *Yeas:* none. — *Nays:* Hon. Edanus Burke, J. Lindsay, Philemon Waters, Robert Ruthford, Hon. J. Hampton. 5.

LITTLE RIVER DISTRICT. — *Yeas:* John Hunter, Thomas Wadsworth. 2. — *Nays:* Samuel Saxon, Joshua Saxon. 2. — *Absent:* James Mayson. 1.

UPPER OR SPARTAN DISTRICT. — *Yeas:* none. — *Nays:* William Kennedy, James Jourdon, Charles Sims, Thomas Brandon, Hon. Zacariah Bullock. 5.

DISTRICT BETWEEN BROAD AND CATAWBA RIVERS, RICHLAND COUNTY. — *Yeas:* none. — *Nays:* Hon. Thomas Taylor, William Meyer, Thomas Howell. 3.

FAIRFIELD COUNTY. — *Nays:* James Craig, Jacob Brown, John Gray, John Cook. 4.

CHESTER DISTRICT. — *Yeas:* none. — *Nays:* Edward Lacy, Joseph Brown, William Miles, James Knox. 4.

DISTRICT CALLED THE NEW ACQUISITION. — *Yea:* Rev. Francis Cummins. 1. — *Nays:* Hon. William Hill, Robert Patton, Samuel Watson, James Martin, James G. Hunt, Samuel Lowry, Andrew Love, John M'Caw, Adam Meek, Abraham Smith. 10.

ST. MATTHEW'S. — *Yeas:* Hon. William Thompson, Hon. Paul Warley. 2. — *Nay:* Hon. John Linton. 1.

ORANGE. — *Yeas:* Lewis Lesterjette, Jacob Rumph, Donald Bruce. 3. — *Nays:* none. — *Absent:* Lewis Golsan. 1.

ST. DAVID'S. — *Yeas:* Lemuel Benton, William Dewitt, Calvin Spencer, Samuel Taylor, R. Brownfield, Benjamin Hicks, Jun. 6. — *Nays:* none. — *Absent:* Trist. Thomas. 1.

DISTRICT BETWEEN SAVANNAH RIVER, AND THE NORTH FORK OF EDISTO. — *Yeas:* Stephen Smith, Hon. William Dunbar, Joseph Vince, William Robison, John Collins, Jonathan Clark. 6. — *Nays:* none. — *Absent:* William Buford. 1.

Yeas, - - 149. | *Nays,* - - 73. | *Majority,* - - 76. | *Absent,* - 15

So it was resolved in the affirmative.

JOHN S. DART, *Secretary of Convention*

	Yeas.	Nays.	Absent.
St. Philip and St. Michael,	31	0	0
Christ Church,	7	0	0
St. John's, Berkley County,	3	3	1
St. Andrew's,	7	0	0
St. George's, Dorchester,	7	0	0
St. James's, Goose Creek,	7	0	0
St. Thomas and St. Dennis,	7	0	0
St. Paul's Parish,	5	2	0
St Bartholomew's,	2	5	0
St. Helena's,	7	0	0
St. James's, Santee,	6	1	0
Prince George's, Winyaw,	4	0	1
All Saints',	2	0	0
Prince Frederick's,	4	3	0
St. John's, Colleton County,	7	0	0
St. Peter's,	4	2	1
Prince William's,	7	0	0
St. Stephen's,	4	0	3
District Eastward of the Wateree,	1	9	1
District of Ninety-six,	1	8	2
North side of the Saluda,	3	0	1
South side of the Saluda,	2	0	1
District of Saxe-Gotha,	1	6	0
Lower District, between Broad and Saluda Rivers,	0	5	0
Little River District,	2	2	1
Upper, or Spartan District,	0	5	0
District between Broad and Catawba Rivers, Richland County,	0	3	0
Fairfield County,	0	4	0
Chester County,	0	4	0
District called the New Acquisition,	1	10	0
St. Matthew's,	2	1	0
Orange,	3	0	1
St. David's,	6	0	1
District between Savannah River and the North Fork of Edisto,	6	0	1
	149	73	14

Two hundred and thirty-six members appointed to the Convention
Fourteen absent.
Two hundred and twenty-two attended, of which there were,

In favor of adoption,...	140
Against adoption,...	73
Majority,..	67

OVUM REIPUBLICÆ. — *The Congress of* 1765.

[From Garden's Anecdotes, Second Series.]

South Carolina is literally one of the Nine primitive Muses of American Liberty. "*Before the thirteen were — she is.*" We must never forget that the parent of the revolution, the very *Ovum Reipublicæ*, was the Congress which convened in New York, in 1765. But nine colonies were represented, as four were overpowered by the royal party. But South Carolina beat down the strong opposition of the crown, and was the only one, south of the Potomac, that sent a delegation. This was the achievement of General Gadsden. In this primeval council, our members were far from being insignificant. Three committees only were appointed, and of two the sons of Carolina were chairmen. Mr. Lynch (father of the patriot who signed the Declaration of Independence) was chairman of the one to prepare an address to the House of Commons, and John Rutledge (who was then but twenty-six years of age) of that for the house of lords This Convention of sages was the parent plant of our present confederacy of republics. Thus was South Carolina among the aboriginal founders of the Union.

Delegates to the Congress of 1765.

Massachusetts, 3 — James Otis, Oliver Partridge, Timothy Ruggles.
Rhode Island, 2 — Metcalf Bowler, Henry Ward.
Connecticut, 3 — Eliphalet Dyer, David Rowland, William S. Johnston.
New York, 5 — Robert R. Livingston, John Cruger, Philip Livingston, William Bayard, Leonard Lispenard
New Jersey, 3 — Robert Ogden. Hendrick Fisher, Joseph Borden.
Pennsy vania, 3 — John Dickinson, John Morton, George Bryan.
Delaware, 3 — Jacob Kollock, Thomas M'Kean, Cæsar Rodney.
Maryland, 3 — William Murdock. Edward Tilghman, Thomas Ringgold.
South Carolina, 3 — Thomas Lynch, Christopher Gadsden, John Rutledge.
Nine colonies, and twenty-eight delegates.

Extract from the official Journal of the Congress of 1765.

Met in New York, on Monday, 7th of October, 1765. After having examined and admitted the certificates of appointment of the above members, the said committees proceeded to choose a chairman by ballot; and Timothy Ruggles, Esq., of Massachusetts, on sorting and counting the votes, appeared to have a majority, and thereupon was placed in the chair.
Resolved, nem. con., That John Cotton be clerk to this Congress, during the continuance thereof.
Resolved, That the committee of each colony shall have one voice only, in determining any questions that shall arise in the Congress.

After meeting regularly every day, with the exception of the Sabbath, they concurred in a declaration of the rights and grievances of America, and appointed the following committees, on Saturday, 19th October, 1765 : —

Upon motion, *Voted*, That Robert R. Livingston, of New York, William Samuel Johnston, and William Murdock, Esqrs., be a committee to prepare an address to his majesty, and lay the same before the Congress on Monday next.

Voted also, That John Rutledge, of South Carolina, Edward Tilghman, and Philip Livingston, Esqrs., be a committee to prepare a memorial and petition to the Lords in Parliament, and lay the same before the Congress on Monday next.

Voted also, That Thomas Lynch, of South Carolina, James Otis, and Thomas M'Kean, Esqrs., be a committee to prepare a petition to the House of Commons of Great Britain, and lay the same before the Congress on Monday next. After having attended daily, the last meeting was held on Thursday, 24th October, 1765.

Voted, unanimously, That the clerk of this Congress sign the minutes of their proceedings, and deliver a copy for the use of each colony and province. — See " Principles and Acts of the Revolution."

It is to be regretted that the few speeches here published constitute all of the able debates in the South Carolina Convention which could be procured. The discussion commenced on the 14th of May, and, it is understood, was continued with brilliancy eight days ; Judge Burke, Mr. Bowman, Dr. Fayssoux, and others, disclosing the abuses and misconstructions of which the Constitution was susceptible ; Judge Pendleton, General Pinckney, and Hon. J. Pringle, among many other distinguished members, enforcing the expediency and necessity of its adoption.

" This acceptance and ratification was not without opposition. In addition to the common objections which had been urged against the Constitution, South Carolina had some local reasons for refusing, or at least delaying, a final vote on the question. Doubts were entertained of the acceptance of the Constitution by Virginia. To gain time till the determination of that leading state was known, a motion for postponement was brought forward. This, after an animated debate, was overruled by a majority of 46. The rejection of it was considered as decisive in favor of the Constitution. When the result of the vote was announced, an event unexampled in the annals of Carolina took place. Strong and involuntary expressions of applause and joy burst forth from the numerous transported spectators. The minority complained of disrespect ; unpleasant consequences were anticipated. The majority joined with the complaining members in clearing the house, and in the most delicate manner soothed their feelings. In the true style of republicanism, the minority not only acquiesced, but heartily joined in supporting the determination of the majority. The Constitution went into operation with general consent, and has ever since been strictly observed." — *Ramsay's History of South Carolina*, vol. ii. p. 432.

OPINIONS,

SELECTED FROM DEBATES IN CONGRESS,

FROM

1789 TO 1836,

INVOLVING

CONSTITUTIONAL PRINCIPLES.

Oath. — On a Bill prescribing the Oath to support the Constitution.

May 6, 1789.

Mr. GERRY said, he did not discover what part of the Constitution gave to Congress the power of making this provision, (for regulating the time and manner of administering certain oaths,) except so much of it as respects the form of the oath; it is not expressly given by any clause of the Constitution, and, if it does not exist, must arise from the *sweeping clause*, as it is frequently termed, in the 8th section of the 1st article of the Constitution, which authorizes Congress " to make all laws which shall be necessary and proper for carrying into execution the foregoing powers, and all other powers vested by this Constitution in the government of the United States, or in any department or officer thereof." To this clause there seems to be no limitation, so far as it applies to the extension of the powers vested by the Constitution; but even this clause gives no legislative authority to Congress to carry into effect any power not expressly vested by the Constitution. In the Constitution, which is the supreme law of the land, provision is made that the members of the legislatures of the several states, and all executive and judicial officers thereof, shall be bound by oath to support the Constitution. But there is no provision for empowering the government of the United States, or any officer or department thereof, to pass a law obligatory on the members of the legislatures of the several states, and other officers thereof, to take this oath. This is made their duty already by the Constitution, and no such law of Congress can add force to the obligation; but, on the other hand, if it is admitted that such a law is necessary, it tends to weaken the Constitution, which requires such aid: neither is any law, other than to prescribe the form of the oath, necessary or proper to carry this part of the Constitution into effect; for the oath required by the Constitution, being a necessary qualification for the state officers mentioned, cannot be dispensed with by any authority whatever, other than the people, and the judicial power of the United States, extending to all cases arising in law or equity under this Constitution.   The judges of the United States, who are bound to support the Constitution, may, in all cases within their jurisdiction, annul the official acts of state officers, and even the acts of the members of the state legislatures, if such members and officers were disqualified to do or pass such acts, by neglecting or refusing to take this oath.

Mr. BLAND had no doubt respecting the powers of Congress on this subject.   The evident meaning of the words of the Constitution implied that Congress should have the power to pass a law directing the time and manner of taking the oath prescribed for supporting the Constitution. There can be no hesitation respecting the power to direct their own officers, and the constituent parts of Congress : besides, if the state legislatures were to be left to direct and arrange this business, they would pass different laws, and the officers might be bound in different degrees to support the Constitution.   He not only thought Congress had the power to do what was proposed by the Senate, but he judged it expedient also.

Mr. JACKSON.   The states had better be left to regulate this matter among themselves ; for an oath that is not voluntary is seldom held sacred. Compelling people to swear to support the Constitution will be like the attempts of Britain, during the late revolution, to secure the fidelity of those who fell within the influence of her arms ; and like those attempts they will be frustrated.   The moment the party could get from under her wings, the oath of allegiance was disregarded.   If the state officers will not willingly pay this testimony of their attachment to the Constitution, what is extorted from them against their inclination is not much to be relied on.

Mr. LAWRENCE.   Only a few words will be necessary to convince us that Congress have this power.   It is declared by the Constitution, that its ordinances shall be the supreme law of the land.   If the Constitution is the supreme law of the land, every part of it must partake of this supremacy ; consequently, every general declaration it contains is the supreme law.   But then these general declarations cannot be carried into effect without particular regulations adapted to the circumstances : these particular regulations are to be made by Congress, who, by the Constitution, have power to make all laws necessary or proper to carry the declarations of the Constitution into effect.   The Constitution likewise declares that the members of the state legislatures, and all officers, executive and judicial, shall take an oath to support the Constitution.   This declaration is general, and it lies with the supreme legislature to detail and regulate it.

Mr. SHERMAN.   It appears necessary to point out the oath itself, as well as the time and manner of taking it.   No other legislature is competent to all these purposes ; but if they were, there is a propriety in the supreme legislature's doing it.   At the same time, if the state legislatures take it up, it cannot operate disagreeably upon them, to find all their neighboring states obliged to join them in supporting a measure they approve.   What a state legislature may do, will be good as far as it goes. On the same principle, the Constitution will apply to each individual of the state officers : they may go, without the direction of the state legislature, to a justice, and take the oath voluntarily.

This, I suppose, would be binding upon them ; but this is not satisfactory ; the government ought to know that the oath has been properly taken ; and this can only be done by a general regulation.   If it is in the discretion of the state legislatures to make laws to carry the declaration of the Constitution into execution, they have the power of refusing, and may avoid the positive injunctions of the Constitution. As the power of Congress, in this particular, extends over the whole Union, it is most proper for us to take the subject up, and make the proper provision for carrying it into execution, to the intention of the Constitution.

Duties. — *Bill laying Duties on Goods, &c.*

Mr. WHITE. The Constitution, having authorized the House of Representatives alone to originate money bills, places an important trust in our hands, which, as their protectors, we ought not to part with. I do not mean to imply that the Senate are less to be trusted than this house; but the Constitution, no doubt for wise purposes, has given the immediate representatives of the people a control over the whole government in this particular, which, for their interest, they ought not to let out of their hands.

Mr. MADISON. The Constitution places the power in the House of originating money bills. The principal reason why the Constitution had made this distinction was, because they were chosen by the people, and supposed to be the best acquainted with their interest and ability. In order to make them more particularly acquainted with these objects, the democratic branch of the legislature consisted of a greater number, and were chosen for a shorter period; that so they might revert more frequently to the mass of the people.

Mr. MADISON "moved to lay an impost of eight cents on all beer imported. He did not think this would be a monopoly, but he hoped it would be such an encouragement as to induce the manufacture to take deep root in every state in the Union." — *Lloyd's Debates of Congress,* vol. i. p. 65.

The same. "The states that are most advanced in population, and ripe for manufactures, ought to have their particular interests attended to in some degree. While these states retained the power of making regulations of trade, they had the power to protect and cherish such institutions. By adopting the present Constitution, they have thrown the exercise of this power into other hands. They must have done this with an expectation that those interests would not be neglected here." — *Idem,* p. 24.

The same. "There may be some manufactures which, being once formed, can advance towards perfection without any adventitious aid; while others, for want of the fostering hand of government, will be unable to go on at all. Legislative attention will therefore be necessary to collect the proper objects for this purpose." — *Idem,* p. 26.

Mr. CLYMER "did not object to this mode of encouraging manufactures, and obtaining revenues, by combining the two objects in one bill. He was satisfied that a political necessity existed for both the one and the other." — *Idem,* p. 31.

Mr. CLYMER "hoped gentlemen would be disposed to extend a degree of patronage to a manufacture [steel] which a moment's reflection would convince them was highly deserving protection." — *Idem,* p. 69.

Mr. CARROLL "moved to insert window and other glass. A manufacture of this article was begun in Maryland, and attended with consid erable success.   If the legislature was to grant a small encouragement, it would be permanently established." — *Idem*, p. 94.

Mr. WADSWORTH. " By moderating the duties, we shall obtain revenue, and give that encouragement to manufactures which is intended." — *Idem*, p. 128.

Mr. AMES " thought this a useful and accommodating manufacture, [nails,] which yielded a clear gain of all it sold for; but the cost of the material, the labor employed in it, would be thrown away probably in many instances. * * * He hoped the article would remain in the bill." — *Idem*, p. 81.

The same. " The committee were already informed of the flourishing situation of the manufacture, [nails,] but they ought not to join the gentleman from South Carolina, Mr. Tucker, in concluding that it did not, therefore, deserve legislative protection.   He had no doubt but the committee would concur in laying a small protecting duty in favor of this manufacture." — *Idem*, p. 82.

Mr. FITZSIMONS " was willing to allow a small duty, because it conformed to the policy of the states who thought it proper in this manner to protect their manufactures." — *Idem*, p. 83.

The same. " It being my opinion that an enumeration of articles will tend to clear away difficulties, I wish as many to be selected as possible. For this reason I have prepared myself with an additional number : among these are some calculated to encourage the productions of our country, and protect our infant manufactures."— *Idem*, p. 17.

Mr. HARTLEY. " If we consult the history of the ancient world, Europe, we shall see that they have thought proper, for a long time past, to give great encouragement to establish manufactures, by laying such partial duties on the importation of foreign goods, as to give the home manufactures a considerable advantage in the price when brought to market. * * * I think it both politic and just that the fostering hand of the general government should extend to all those manufactures which will tend to national utility.   Our stock of materials is, in many instances, equal to the greatest demand, and our artisans sufficient to work them up, even for exportation.   In those cases, I take it to be the policy of every enlightened nation to give their manufacturers that degree of encouragement necessary to perfect them, without oppressing the other parts of the community ; and, under this encouragement, the industry of the manufacturer will be employed to add to the wealth of the nation." — *Idem*, p. 22.

Mr. WHITE. " In order to charge specified articles of manufacture so as to encourage our domestic ones, it will be necessary to examine the present state of each throughout the Union." — *Idem*, p. 19.

Mr. BLAND (of Virginia) " thought that very little revenue was likely to be collected from the importation of this article, [beef;] and, as it was to be had in sufficient quantities within the United States, perhaps a tax amounting to a prohibition would be proper." — *Idem*, p. 66.

Mr. BLAND " informed the committee that there were mines opened in Virginia capable of supplying the whole of the United States ; and, if some restraint was laid on importation of foreign coals, those mines might be worked to advantage." — *Idem*, p. 97.

Mr. BOUDINOT. " I shall certainly move for it, [the article of glass,] as I suppose we are capable of manufacturing this as well as many of the others.   In fact, it is well known that we have and can do it as well as most nations, the materials being almost all produced in our country." — *Idem*, p. 28.

The same. " Let us take, then, the resolution of Congress in 1783, and make it the basis of our system, adding only such protecting duties as are necessary to support the manufactures established by the legislatures of the manufacturing states." — *Idem*, p. 34.

Mr. SINNICKSON " declared himself a friend to this manufacture, [beer,] and thought that, if the duty was laid high enough to effect a prohibition, the manufacture would increase, and of consequence the price would be lessened." — *Idem*, p. 65.

Mr. LAWRENCE " thought that if candles were an object of considerable importation, they ought to be taxed for the sake of obtaining revenue, and if they were not imported in considerable quantities, the burden upon the consumer would be small, while it tended to cherish a valuable manufacture." — *Idem*, p. 68.

Mr. FITZSIMONS " moved to lay a duty of two cents per pound on tallow candles. The manufacture of candles is an important manufacture, and far advanced towards perfection. I have no doubt but in a few years we shall be able to supply the consumption of every part of the continent." — *Idem*, p. 67.

The same. " Suppose 5s. cwt. were imposed, [on unwrought steel :] it might be, as stated, a partial duty; but would not the evil be soon overbalanced by the establishment of such an important manufacture ?" — *Idem*, p. 69.

The same. " The necessity of continuing those encouragements which the state legislatures have deemed proper, exists in a considerable degree. Therefore it will be politic in the government of the United States to continue such duties until their object is accomplished." — *Idem*, p. 67.

Mr. SMITH (of South Carolina.) " The people of South Carolina are willing to make sacrifices to encourage the manufacturing and maritime interests of their sister states " — *Idem*, p. 212.

Gen. Washington's Speech to Congress, of January 11, 1790, declares, " That the safety and interest of a free people require that Congress should promote such manufactures as tend to render them independent of others for essential, particularly military supplies.

" The advancement of agriculture, commerce, and manufactures, by all proper means, will not, I trust, need recommendation."

Extract from the reply of the Senate, to the speech of Gen. Washington, January, 1790. — " Agriculture, commerce, and manufactures, forming the basis of the wealth and strength of our confederated republic, must be the frequent subject of our deliberations, and shall be advanced by all the proper means in our power."

Extract from the reply of the House of Representatives. — " We concur with you in the sentiment that ' agriculture, commerce, and manufactures, are entitled to legislative protection.' "

His *speech of December,* 1796, holds out the same doctrine. — " Congress have repeatedly, and not without success, directed their attention to the encouragement of manufactures. The object is of too much importance not to insure a continuance of these efforts in every way which shall appear eligible."

Extract from the reply of the Senate to the speech of Gen. Washington, December, 1796. — " The necessity of accelerating the establishment of certain useful branches of manufactures, by the intervention of legislative aid and protection, and the encouragement due to agriculture by the creation of boards, (composed of intelligent individuals,) to patronize the primary pursuit of society, are subjects which will readily engage our most serious attention."

Mr. Jefferson, in his Message of 1802, states that — " To cultivate peace, maintain commerce and navigation, to foster our fisheries, and protect manufactures adapted to our circumstances, &c., are the landmarks by which to guide ourselves in all our relations."

From Mr. Jefferson's Message of 1808. — " The situation into which we have been thus forced has impelled us to apply a portion of our industry and capital to internal manufacturing improvements The extent of this conversion is daily increasing, and little doubt remains that the establishments formed and forming will, under the auspices of cheaper materials and subsistence, the freedom of labor from taxation with us, and protecting duties and prohibitions, become permanent."

Extract from the Message of Mr. Madison, December 5, 1815. — " Under circumstances giving powerful impulse to manufacturing industry, it has made among us a progress, and exhibited an efficiency, which justify the belief that, with a protection not more than is due to the enterprising citizens whose interests are now at stake, it will become, at an early day, not only safe against occasional competitions from abroad, but a source of domestic wealth, and even of external commerce.   *   *   *   *

In selecting the branches more especially entitled to public patronage, a preference is obviously claimed by such as will relieve the United States from a dependence on foreign supplies, ever subject to casual failures, for articles necessary for public defence, or connected with the primary wants of individuals. It will be an additional recommendation of particular manufactures, where the materials for them are extensively drawn from our agriculture, and consequently impart and insure to that great fund of national prosperity and independence an encouragement which cannot fail to be rewarded."

From the Message of President Monroe, December, 1818. — " It is deemed of importance to encourage our domestic manufactures. In what manner the evils which we have adverted to may be remedied, and how it may be practicable in other respects to afford them further encouragement, paying due regard to the other great interests of the nation, is submitted to the wisdom of Congress."

From the same, December 3, 1822. — " Satisfied I am, whatever may be the abstract doctrine in favor of unrestricted commerce, provided all nations would concur in it, and it was not liable to be interrupted by war, which has never occurred, and cannot be expected, that there are strong reasons applicable to our situation, and relations with other countries, which impose on us the obligation to cherish and sustain our manufactures."

From the same, December, 1823. — " Having communicated my views to Congress, at the commencement of the last session, respecting the encouragement which ought to be given to our manufactures, and the principle on which it should be founded, I have only to add that those views remain unchanged, and that the present state of those countries with which we have the most immediate political relations, and greatest commercial intercourse, tends to confirm them. Under this impression, I recommend a review of the tariff, for the purpose of affording such additional protection to those articles which we are prepared to manufacture, or which are more immediately connected with the defence and independence of the country."

Wm. H. Crawford, Secretary of the Treasury, in his report, December, 1819, says, — "It is believed that the present is a favorable moment for affording efficient protection to that increasing and important interest, if it can be done consistently with the general interest of the nation."

Extract from the Message of President Jefferson, December 2, 1806. — "The question now comes forward, To what objects shall *surpluses* be appropriated, and the whole surplus of impost, after the entire discharge of the public debt, and during those intervals when the purposes of war shall not call for them? Shall we suppress the impost, and give that advantage to foreign over domestic manufactures? On a few articles of a more general and necessary use, the suppression, in due season, will doubtless be right; but the great mass of the articles on which impost is paid are foreign luxuries, purchased only by those who are rich enough to afford themselves the use of them. Their patriotism would certainly prefer its continuance, and application to the great purposes of public education, roads, rivers, canals, and such other objects of public improvement as it may be thought proper to add to the constitutional enumeration of federal powers. By these operations, new channels of communication will be opened between the states; the lines of separation will disappear; their interests will be identified, and the union cemented by new and indissoluble ties. Education is here placed among the articles of public care. Not that it would be proposed to take its ordinary branches out of the hands of private enterprise, which manages so much better all the concerns to which it is equal; but a public institution alone can supply those sciences which, though rarely called for, are yet necessary to complete the circle, all the parts of which contribute to the improvement of the country, and some of them to its preservation. The subject is now proposed for the consideration of Congress, because, if approved, by the time the state legislatures shall have deliberated on this extension of the federal trusts, and the laws shall be passed, and other arrangements made for their execution, the necessary funds will be on hand and without employment. I suppose an amendment to the Constitution, by consent of the states, necessary, because the objects now recommended are not among those enumerated in the Constitution, and to which it permits the public money to be applied." * * *

From the same, Nov. 8, 1808. — "The probable accumulation of surpluses of revenue beyond what can be applied to the payment of the public debt, whenever the freedom and safety of our commerce shall be restored, merits the consideration of Congress. Shall it lie unproductive in the public vaults? Shall the revenue be reduced? Or shall it not rather be appropriated to the improvements of roads, canals, rivers, education, and other great foundations of prosperity and union, under the powers which Congress may already possess, or such amendment of the Constitution as may be approved by the states? While uncertain of the course of things, the time may be advantageously employed in obtaining the powers necessary for a system of improvement, should that be thought best." * * *

Removal by the President. — *On the Bill for establishing an executive Department, to be denominated the Department of Foreign Affairs.*

House of Representatives, *June* 16, 1789.

The first clause, after recapitulating the title of the officer and his duties, had these words : " to be *removable* from office by the President of the United States."

Mr. WHITE.   The Constitution gives the President the power of nominating, and by and with the advice and consent of the Senate, appointing to office.   As I conceive the power of appointing and dismissing to be united in their natures, and a principle that never was called in question in any government, I am adverse to that part of the clause which subjects the secretary of foreign affairs to be removed at the will of the President.   In the Constitution, special provision is made for the removal of the judges : that I acknowledge to be a deviation from my principle ; but as it is a constitutional provision, it is to be admitted.   In all cases not otherwise provided for in this Constitution, I take it that the principle I have laid down is the governing one.   Now, the Constitution has associated the Senate with the President in appointing the heads of department ; for the words of the law declare that there shall be a department established, at the head of which shall be an officer to be so denominated.   If, then, the Senate is associated with the President in the appointment, they ought also to be associated in the dismission from office.   Upon the justness of this construction, I take the liberty of reviving the motion made in the committee of the whole for striking out these words, " to be removable from office by the President of the United States."

Mr. SMITH, (of South Carolina.)   The gentleman has anticipated me in his motion.   I am clearly in sentiment with him that the words ought to go out.   It is in the recollection of the committee, that, when the subject was last before us, this power was excepted to ; and although the words were then allowed to stand, it was generally understood that it should be further debated.   I then was opposed to giving this power to the President, and am still of opinion that we ought not to make this declaration, even if he has the power by the Constitution.

I would premise, that one of these two ideas is just — either that the Constitution has given the President the power of removal, and therefore it is nugatory to make the declaration here, or it has not given the power to him, and therefore it is improper to make an attempt to confer it upon him.   If it be not given to him by the Constitution, but belongs conjointly to the President and Senate, we have no right to deprive the Senate of their constitutional prerogative ; and it has been the opinion of sensible men that the power was lodged in this manner.   A publication of no inconsiderable eminence, in the class of political writings on the Constitution, has advanced this sentiment.   The author, or authors, (for I have understood it to be the production of two gentlemen of great information,) of the work published under the signature of Publius, has these words : ——

" It has been mentioned as one of the advantages to be expected from the coöperation of the Senate in the business of appointments, that it would contribute to the stability of the administration.   The consent of that body would be necessary to displace as well as appoint.   A change of the chief magistrate, therefore, would not occasion so violent or so general a revolution in the offices of the government as might be expected if he were the sole disposer of offices. Where a man, in any station, has given satisfactory evidence of his fitness for it, a new President would be restrained from attempting a change, in favor of a person more agreeable to him, by the apprehension that the discountenance of the Senate might frustrate the attempt, and bring some degree of discredit upon himself. Those who can best estimate the value of a steady administration will be most disposed to prize a provision which connects the official existence of public men with the approbation or disapprobation of that body which, from the greater permanency of its own composition, will, in all probability, be less subject to inconstancy than any other member of the government."

Here this author lays it down, that there can be no doubt of the power of the Senate in the business of removal. Let this be as it may, I am clear that the President alone has not the power. Examine the Constitution; the powers of the several branches of government are there defined; the President has particular powers assigned him; the judicial have, in like manner, powers assigned them; but you will find no such power as removing from office given to the President. I call upon gentlemen to show me where it is said that the President shall remove from office. I know they cannot do it. Now I infer from this, as the Constitution has not given the President the power of removability, it meant that he should not have that power, and this inference is supported by that clause in the Constitution, which provides that all civil officers of the United States shall be removed from office on impeachment for and conviction of treason, bribery, or other high crimes and misdemeanors. Here is a particular mode prescribed for removing, and if there is no other mode directed, I contend that the Constitution contemplated only this mode. But let me ask gentlemen if any other mode is necessary. For what other cause should a man be removed from office? Do gentlemen contend that sickness or ignorance would be a sufficient cause? I believe, if they will reflect, they cannot instance any person who was removed from ignorance. I venture to say, there never was an instance of this nature in the United States. There have been instances where a person has been removed for offences: the same may again occur, and are therefore judiciously provided for in the Constitution. But in this case, is he removed from his ignorance, or his error, which is the consequence of his ignorance? I suppose it is for his error, because the public are injured by it, and not for incapacity. The President is to nominate the officer, and the Senate to approve: here is provision made against the appointment of ignorant officers. They cannot be removed for causes which subsisted before their coming into office. Their ignorance therefore must arise after they are appointed; but this is an unlikely case, and one that cannot be contemplated as probable.

I imagine, sir, we are declaring a power in the President which may hereafter be greatly abused, for we are not always to expect a chief magistrate in whom such entire confidence can be placed as in the present. Perhaps gentlemen are so much dazzled with the splendor of the virtues of the present President, as not to be able to see into futurity. The framers of the Constitution did not confine their views to the first person who was looked up to, to fill the presidential chair. If they had, they might have omitted those checks and guards with which the powers of the executive are surrounded. They knew, from the course of human events, that they could not expect to be so highly favored of Heaven, as to have the blessing of his administration more than seven or fourteen years; after which, they supposed a man might get into power, who, it was possible, might misbehave. We ought to follow their example, and contemplate this power in the hands of an ambitious man, who might apply it to dangerous purposes.   If we give this power to the President, he may, from caprice, remove the most worthy men from office : his will and pleasure will be the slight tenure by which an office is to be held ; and of consequence, you render the officer the mere state dependant, the abject slave, of a person who may be disposed to abuse the confidence his fellow-citizens have placed in him.

Another danger may result.   If you desire an officer to be a man of capacity and integrity, you may be disappointed.   A gentleman possessed of these qualities, knowing he may be removed at the pleasure of the President, will be loath to risk his reputation on such insecure ground.   As the matter stands in the Constitution, he knows, if he is suspected of doing any thing wrong, he shall have a fair trial, and the whole of his transactions developed by an impartial tribunal : he will have confidence in himself when he knows he can only be removed for improper behavior.   But if he is subjected to the whim of any man, it may deter him from entering into the service of his country ; because, if he is not subservient to that person's pleasure, he may be turned out, and the public may be led to suppose for improper behavior.   This impression cannot be removed, as a public inquiry cannot be obtained.   Beside this, it ought to be considered, that the person who is appointed will probably quit some other office or business in which he is occupied.   Ought he, after making this sacrifice in order to serve the public, to be turned out of place without even a reason being assigned for such behavior ?   Perhaps the President does not do this with an ill intention : he may have been misinformed, for it is presumable that a President may have round him men envious of the honors or emoluments of persons in office, who will insinuate suspicions into his honest breast, that may produce a removal : be this as it may, the event is still the same to the removed officer.   The public suppose him guilty of malpractices — hence his reputation is blasted, his property sacrificed.   I say his property is sacrificed, because I consider his office as his property : he is stripped of this, and left exposed to the malevolence of the world, contrary to the principles of the Constitution, and contrary to the principles of all free governments, which are, that no man shall be despoiled of his property but by a fair and impartial trial.

I have stated that, if the power is given by the Constitution, the declaration in the law is nugatory ; and I will add, if it is not given, it will be nugatory also to attempt to vest the power.   If the Senate participate, on any principle whatever, in the removal, they will never consent to transfer their power to another branch of the government ; therefore they will not pass a law with such a declaration in it.

Upon this consideration alone, if there was no other, the words should be struck out, and the question of right, if it is one, left to the decision of the judiciary.   It will be time enough to determine the question when the President shall remove an officer in this way.   I conceive it can properly be brought before that tribunal ; the officer will have a right to a *mandamus* to be restored to his office ; and the judges would determine whether the President exercised a constitutional authority or not.

Some gentlemen think the Constitution takes no notice of this officer, as the head of a department.   They suppose him an inferior officer in aid of the executive.   This, I think, is going too far ; because the Constitution, in the words authorizing the President to call on the heads of department for their opinions in writing, contemplates several departments.   It says, " the principal officer in each of the executive departments."

I have seriously reflected on this subject, and am convinced that the President has not this power by the Constitution, and that, if we had the right to invest him with it, it would be dangerous to do so.

Mr. HUNTINGDON. I think the clause ought not to stand. It was well observed, that the Constitution was silent respecting the removal, otherwise than by impeachment. I would likewise add, that it mentions no other cause of removal than treason, bribery, or other high crimes and misdemeanors. It does not, I apprehend, extend to cases of infirmity or incapacity. Indeed, it appears hard to me that, after an officer has become old in an honorable service, he should be impeached for this infirmity. The Constitution, I think, must be the only rule to guide us on this occasion. As it is silent with respect to the removal, Congress ought to say nothing about it, because it implies that we have a right to bestow it, and I believe this power is not to be found among the enumerated powers delegated by the Constitution to Congress.

It was said, if the President had this authority, it would make him more responsible for the conduct of the officer. But if we have a vicious President, who inclines to abuse this power, which God forbid! his responsibility will stand us in little stead : therefore that idea does not satisfy me that it is proper the President should have this power.

Mr. SEDGWICK. I wish the words to be struck out, because I conceive them to be unnecessary in this place. I do conceive, Mr. Speaker, that this officer will be the mere creature of the law, and that very little need be said to prove to you that of necessity this ought to be the case. I apprehend, likewise, that it requires but a small share of abilities to point out certain causes for which a person ought to be removed from office, without being guilty of treason, bribery, or malfeasance ; and the nature of things demands that it should be so. Suppose, sir, a man becomes insane by the visitation of God, and is likely to ruin our affairs ; are the hands of government to be confined from warding off the evil ? Suppose a person in office not possessing the talents he was judged to have at the time of the appointment ; is the error not to be corrected ? Suppose he acquires vicious habits, an incurable indolence, or total neglect of the duties of his office, which forebode mischief to the public welfare ; is there no way to arrest the threatened danger ? Suppose he becomes odious and unpopular by reason of the measures which he pursues, — and this he may do without committing any positive offence against the law, — must he preserve his office in despite of the public will ? Suppose him grasping at his own aggrandizement, and the elevation of his connections, by every means short of the treason defined by the Constitution, — hurrying your affairs to the precipice of destruction, endangering your domestic tranquillity, plundering you of the means of defence, by alienating the affections of your allies, and promoting the spirit of discord, — is there no way suddenly to seize the worthless wretch, and hurl him from the pinnacle of power ? Must the tardy, tedious, desultory road, by way of impeachment, be travelled to overtake the man who, barely confining himself within the letter of the law, is employed in drawing off the vital principle of the government ? Sir, the nature of things, the great objects of society, the express objects of this Constitution, require that this thing should be otherwise. Well, sir, this is admitted by gentlemen ; but they say the Senate is to be united with the President in the exercise of this power. I hope, sir, this is not the case, because it would involve us in the most serious difficulty. Suppose a discovery of any of those events which I have just enumerated were to take place when the Senate is not in session ; how is the remedy to be applied ?   This is a serious consideration, and the evil could be avoided no other way than by the Senate's sitting always.   Surely no gentleman of this house contemplates the necessity of incurring such an expense.   I am sure it will be very objectionable to our constituents ; and yet this must be done, or the public interest be endangered by keeping an unworthy officer in place until that body shall be assembled from the extremes of the Union.

It has been said that there is danger of this power being abused if exercised by one man.   Certainly, the danger is as great with respect to the Senate, who are assembled from various parts of the continent, with different impressions and opinions.   It appears to me that such a body is more likely to misuse this power than the man whom the united voice of America calls to the presidential chair.   As the nature of the government requires the power of removal, I think it is to be exercised in this way by a hand capable of exerting itself with effect ; and the power must be conferred on the President by the Constitution, as the executive officer of the government.

I believe some difficulty will result from determining this question by a *mandamus.*   A *mandamus* is issued to replace an officer who has been removed contrary to law.   Now, this officer being the creature of the law, we may declare that he shall be removed for incapacity ; and if so declared, the removal will be according to law.

Mr. MADISON.   If the construction of the Constitution is to be left to its natural course, with respect to the executive powers of this government, I own that the insertion of this sentiment in law may not be of material importance, though, if it is nothing more than a mere declaration of a clear grant made by the Constitution, it can do no harm ; but if it relates to a doubtful part of the Constitution, I suppose an exposition of the Constitution may come with as much propriety from the legislature as any other department of government.   If the power naturally belongs to the government, and the Constitution is undecided as to the body which is to exercise it, it is likely that it is submitted to the discretion of the legislatures, and the question will depend upon its own merits.

I am clearly of opinion with the gentleman from South Carolina, (Mr. Smith,) that we ought, in this and every other case, to adhere to the Constitution, so far as it will serve as a guide to us ; and that we ought not to be swayed in our decisions by the splendor of the character of our present chief magistrate, but consider it with respect to the merit of men who, in the ordinary course of things, may be supposed to fill the chair.   I believe the power here declared is a high one, and in some respects a dangerous one ; but, in order to come to a right decision on this point, we must consider both sides of the question — the possible abuses which may spring from the single will of the first magistrate, and the abuse which may spring from the combined will of the executive and the senatorial qualification.

When we consider that the first magistrate is to be appointed at present by the suffrages of three millions of people, and, in all human probability, in a few years' time, by double that number, it is not to be presumed that a vicious or bad character will be selected.   If the government of any country on the face of the earth was ever effectually guarded against the election of ambitious or designing characters to the first office of the state, I think it may with truth be said to be the case under the Constitution of the United States.   With all the infirmities incident to a popular election corrected by the particular mode of conducting it, as directed under the present system, I think we may fairly calculate that the instances will be very rare in which an unworthy man will receive that mark of public confidence which is required to designate the President of the United States. Where the people are disposed to give so great an elevation to one of their fellow-citizens, I own that I am not afraid to place my confidence in him; especially when I know he is impeachable, for any crime or misdemeanor, before the Senate at all times; and that, at all events, he is impeachable before the community at large every four years, and liable to be displaced if his conduct shall have given umbrage during the time he has been in office. Under these circumstances, although the trust is a high one, and in some degree, perhaps, a dangerous one, I am not sure but it will be safer here than in placed where some gentlemen suppose it ought to be.

It is evidently the intention of the Constitution that the first magistrate should be responsible for the executive department; so far, therefore, as we do not make the officers who are to aid him in the duties of that department responsible to him, he is not responsible to his country. Again: is there no danger that an officer, when he is appointed by the concurrence of the Senate, and has friends in that body, may choose rather to risk his establishment on the favor of that branch, than rest it upon the discharge of his duties to the satisfaction of the executive branch, which is constitutionally authorized to inspect and control his conduct? and if it should happen that the officers connect themselves with the Senate, they may mutually support each other, and, for want of efficacy, reduce the power of the President to a mere vapor, in which case his responsibility would be annihilated, and the expectation of it unjust. The high executive officers, joined in cabal with the Senate, would lay the foundation of discord, and end in an assumption of the executive power, only to be removed by a revolution in the government. I believe no principle is more clearly laid down in the Constitution than that of responsibility. After premising this, I will proceed to an investigation of the merits of the question upon constitutional ground.

I have, since the subject was last before the house, examined the Constitution with attention; and I acknowledge that it does not perfectly correspond with the ideas I entertained of it from the first glance. I am inclined to think that a free and systematic interpretation of the plan of government will leave us less at liberty to abate the responsibility than gentlemen imagine. I have already acknowledged that the powers of the government must remain as apportioned by the Constitution. But it may be contended that, where the Constitution is silent, it becomes a subject of legislative discretion. Perhaps, in the opinion of some, an argument in favor of the clause may be successfully brought forward on this ground. I, however, leave it for the present untouched.

By a strict examination of the Constitution on what appear to be its true principles, and considering the great departments of the government in the relation they have to each other, I have my doubts whether we are not absolutely tied down to the construction declared in the bill.

In the 1st section of the 1st article, it is said that all legislative powers herein granted shall be vested in a Congress of the United States. In the 2d article, it is affirmed that the executive power shall be vested in a President of the United States of America. In the 3d article, it is declared that the judicial power of the United States shall be vested in one Supreme Court, and in such inferior courts as Congress may from time to time or dain and establish. I suppose it would be readily admitted that, so far as the Constitution has separated the powers of these great departments, it would be improper to combine them together; and so far as it has left any particular department in the entire possession of the powers incident to that department, I conceive we ought not to qualify them further than they are qualified by the Constitution. The legislative powers are vested in Congress, and are to be exercised by them uncontrolled by any other department, except the Constitution has qualified it otherwise. The Constitution has qualified the legislative power by authorizing the President to object to any act it may pass — requiring, in this case, two thirds of both houses to concur in making a law; but still the absolute legislative power is vested in the Congress, with this qualification alone.

The Constitution affirms that the executive power shall be vested in the President. Are there exceptions to this proposition? Yes, there are. The Constitution says that, in appointing to office, the Senate shall be associated with the President, unless in the case of inferior officers, when the law shall otherwise direct. Have we a right to extend this exception? I believe not. If the Constitution has invested all executive power in the President, I venture to assert that the legislature has no right to diminish or modify his executive authority.

The question now resolves itself into this: Is the power of displacing an executive power? I conceive that, if any power whatsoever is in its nature executive, it is the power of appointing, overseeing, and controlling those who execute the laws. If the Constitution had not qualified the power of the President in appointing to office, by associating the Senate with him in that business, would it not be clear that he would have the right, by virtue of his executive power, to make such appointment? Should we be authorized, in defiance of that clause in the Constitution, — " The executive power shall be vested in a President," — to unite the Senate with the President in the appointment to office? I conceive not. If it is admitted we should not be authorized to do this, I think it may be disputed whether we have a right to associate them in removing persons from office, the one power being as much of an executive nature as the other; and the first only is authorized by being excepted out of the general rule established by the Constitution, in these words, " The executive power shall be vested in the President."

The judicial power is vested in a Supreme Court; but will gentlemen say the judicial power can be placed elsewhere, unless the Constitution has made an exception? The Constitution justifies the Senate in exercising a judiciary power in determining on impeachments. But can the judicial powers be further blended with the powers of that body? They cannot. I therefore say it is incontrovertible, if neither the legislative nor judicial powers are subjected to qualifications other than those demanded in the Constitution, that the executive powers are equally unabatable as either of the other; and inasmuch as the power of removal is of an executive nature, and not affected by any constitutional exception, it is beyond the reach of the legislative body.

If this is the true construction of this instrument, the clause in the bill is nothing more than explanatory of the meaning of the Constitution, and therefore not liable to any particular objection on that account. If the Constitution is silent, and it is a power the legislature have a right to confer, it will appear to the world, if we strike out the clause, as if we doubted the propriety of vesting it in the President of the United States. I therefore think it best to retain it in the bill.

Mr. WHITE. I have no doubt in my mind but an officer can be removed without a public trial. I think there are cases in which it would be improper that his misdemeanors should be publicly known; the tranquillity and harmony of the Union might be endangered if his guilt was not secreted from the world. I have therefore no hesitation in declaring, as my sentiment, that the President and Senate may dismiss him.

The Constitution contemplates a removal in some other way besides that by impeachment, or why is it declared, in favor of the judges only, that they shall hold their offices during good behavior? Does not this strongly imply that, without such an exception, there would have been a discretionary power in some branch of the government to dismiss even them?

Several objections have arisen from the inconvenience with which the power must be exercised, if the Senate is blended with the executive; and therefore it is inferred that the President ought exclusively to have this power. If we were framing a constitution, these arguments would have their proper weight, and I might approve such an arrangement. But at present, I do not consider we are at liberty to deliberate on that subject; the Constitution is already formed, and we can go no farther in distributing the powers than the Constitution warrants.

It was objected that the President could not remove an officer unless the Senate was in session; but yet the emergency of the case might demand an instant dismission. I should imagine that no inconvenience would result on this account; because, on my principle, the same power which can make a temporary appointment, can make an equal suspension: the powers are opposite to each other.

The gentleman says we ought not to blend the executive and legislative powers further than they are blended in the Constitution. I contend we do not. There is no expression in the Constitution which says that the President shall have the power of removal from office: but the contrary is strongly implied; for it is said that Congress may establish officers by law, and vest the appointment, and consequently the removal, in the President alone, in the courts of law, or heads of departments. Now, this shows that Congress are not at liberty to make any alteration by law in the mode of appointing superior officers, and consequently that they are not at liberty to alter the manner of removal.

Mr. BOUDINOT. This is a question, Mr. Speaker, that requires full consideration, and ought only to be settled on the most candid discussion. It certainly involves the right of the Senate to a very important power. At present, I am so impressed with the importance of the subject, that I dare not absolutely decide on any principle, although I am firmly persuaded we ought to retain the clause in the bill; and, so far as it has been examined, I agree that it is a legislative construction of the Constitution necessary to be settled for the direction of your officers. But if it is a deviation from the Constitution, or in the least degree an infringement upon the authority of the other branch of the legislature, I shall most decidedly be against it. But I think it will appear, on a full consideration of this business, that we can do no otherwise than agree to this construction, in order to preserve to each department the full exercise of its powers, and to give this house security for the proper conduct of the officers who are to execute the laws.

The arguments adduced are to show that the power of removal lies either in the President and the Senate, or the President alone, except in cases of removal by impeachment. There is nothing, I take it, in the Constitution, or the reason of the thing, that officers should be only removable by impeachment. Such a provision would be derogatory to the powers of government, and subversive of the rights of the people. What says the Constitution on this point? I fear, sir, it has not been rightly comprehended. That the House of Representatives shall have the sole power of impeachment; that the Senate shall have the sole power to try all impeachments; and judgment shall not extend further than to removal from office, and disqualification to hold it in future: then comes the clause declaring, absolutely, that he shall be removed from office on impeachment for and conviction of treason, bribery, or other high crimes or misdemeanors.

It is this clause which guards the right of the house, and enables them to pull down an improper officer, although he should be supported by all the power of the executive. This, then, is a necessary security to the people, and one that is wisely provided in the Constitution. But I believe it is nowhere said that officers shall never be removed but by impeachment; but it says they shall be removed on impeachment. Suppose the secretary of foreign affairs shall misbehave, and we impeach him; notwithstanding the clearest proof of guilt, the Senate might only impose some trifling punishment, and retain him in office, if it was not for this declaration in the Constitution.

Neither this clause nor any other goes so far as to say it shall be the only mode of removal: therefore we may proceed to inquire what the other is. Let us examine whether it belongs to the Senate and President. Certainly, sir, there is nothing that gives the Senate this right in express terms; but they are authorized in express words to be concerned in the appointment. And does this necessarily include the power of removal? If the President complains to the Senate of the misconduct of an officer, and desires their advice and consent to the removal, what are the Senate to do? Most certainly, they will inquire if the complaint is well founded. To do this, they must call the officer before them to answer. Who, then, are the parties? The supreme executive officer against his assistant; and then the Senate are to set judges to determine whether sufficient cause of removal exists. Does not this set the Senate over the head of the President? But suppose they shall decide in favor of the officer; what a situation is the President then in, surrounded by officers with whom, by his situation, he is compelled to act, but in whom he can have no confidence, reversing the privilege, given him by the Constitution, to prevent his having officers imposed upon him who do not meet his approbation!

But I have another more solid objection, which places the question in a more important point of view. The Constitution has placed the Senate as the only security and barrier between the House of Representatives and the President. Suppose the President has desired the Senate to concur in removing an officer, and they have declined; or suppose the House have applied to the President and Senate to remove an officer obnoxious to them, and they determine against the measure; the house can have recourse to nothing but an impeachment, if they suppose the criminality of the officer will warrant such procedure. Will the Senate, then, be that upright court which they ought, to appeal to on this occasion, when they have prejudged your cause? I conceive the Senate will be too much under the control of their former decision, to be a proper body for this house to apply to for impartial justice.

As the Senate are the *dernier ressort*, and the only court of judicature which can determine on cases of impeachment, I am for preserving them free and independent, both on account of the officer and this house. I therefore conceive that it was never the intention of the Constitution to vest the power of removal in the President and Senate; but as it must exist somewhere, it rests on the President alone. I conceive this point was made fully to appear by the honorable member from Virginia, (Mr. Madison ;) inasmuch as the President is the supreme executive officer of the United States.

It was asked if ever we knew a person removed from office by reason of sickness or ignorance. If there never was such a case, it is perhaps nevertheless proper that they should be removed for those reasons, and we shall do well to establish the principle.

Suppose your secretary of foreign affairs rendered incapable of thought or action by a paralytic stroke. I ask whether there would be any propriety in keeping such a person in office; and whether the *salus populi* — the first object of republican government — does not absolutely demand his dismission. Can it be expected that the President is responsible for an officer under these circumstances, although, when he went into office, he might have been a wise and virtuous man, and the President well inclined to risk his own reputation upon the integrity and abilities of the person ?

I conceive it will be improper to leave the determination of this question to the judges. There will be some indelicacy in subjecting the executive action in this particular to a suit at law ; and there may be much inconvenience if the President does not exercise this prerogative until it is decided by the courts of justice.

From these considerations, the safety of the people, the security of this house, and adherence to the spirit of the Constitution, I am disposed to think the clause proper ; and as some doubts respecting the construction of the Constitution have arisen, I think it also necessary ; therefore I hope it will remain.

Mr. SMITH, (of South Carolina.) The gentleman from Virginia has said that the power of removal is executive in its nature. I do not believe this to be the case. I have turned over the constitutions of most of the states, and I do not find that any of them have granted this power to the governor. — In some instances I find the executive magistrate suspends, but none of them have the right to remove, officers; and I take it that the Constitution of the United States has distributed the powers of government on the same principles which most of the state constitutions have adopted ; for it will not be contended but the state governments furnished the members of the late Convention with the skeleton of this Constitution.

The gentlemen have observed that it would be dangerous if the President had not this power. But is there not danger in making your secretary of foreign affairs dependent upon the will and pleasure of the President ? Can gentlemen see the danger on one side only ? Suppose the President averse to a just and honorable war which Congress have embarked in ; can he not countenance the secretary at war (for it is in contemplation to establish such an officer) in the waste of public stores, and misapplication of the supplies ? Nay, cannot he dragoon your officer into a compliance with his designs by threatening him with a removal, by which his reputation and property would be destroyed ? If the officer was established on a better tenure, he would dare to be honest ; he would know himself invulnerable in his integrity, and defy the shafts of malevolence, though aimed with Machiavellian policy. He would be a barrier to your executive officer, and save the state from ruin.

But, Mr. Chairman, the argument does not turn upon the expediency of the measure. The great question is with respect to its constitutionality; and as yet I have heard no argument advanced sufficiently cogent to prove to my mind that the Constitution warrants such a disposition of the power of removal; and until I am convinced that it is both expedient and constitutional, I cannot agree to it.

Mr. GERRY. Some gentlemen consider this as a question of policy; but to me it appears a question of constitutionality, and I presume it will be determined on that point alone. The best arguments I have heard urged on this occasion came from the honorable gentleman from Virginia, (Mr. Madison.) He says, the Constitution has vested the executive power in the President; and that he has a right to exercise it under the qualifications therein made. He lays it down as a maxim, that the Constitution, vesting in the President the executive power, naturally vests him with the power of appointment and removal. Now, I would be glad to know from that gentleman, by what means we are to decide this question. Is his maxim supported by precedent drawn from the practice of the individual states? The direct contrary is established. In many cases, the executives are not, in particular, vested with the power of appointment; nor do they exercise that power by virtue of their office. It will be found that other branches of the government make appointments. How, then, can gentlemen assert that the powers of appointment and removal are incident to the executive department of the government? To me it appears at best but problematical. Neither is it clear to me that the power that appoints naturally possesses the power of removal. As we have no certainty on either of these points, I think we must consider it, as established by the Constitution.

It has been argued that, if the power of removal vests in the President alone, it annuls or renders nugatory the clause in the Constitution which directs the concurrence of the Senate in the case of appointment: it behoves us not to adopt principles subversive of those established by the Constitution. It has been frequently asserted, on former occasions, that the Senate is a permanent body, and was so constructed in order to give durability to public measures. If they are not absolutely permanent, they are formed on a renovating principle which gives them a salutary stability. This is not the case either with the President or House of Representatives; nor is the judiciary equally lasting, because the officers are subject to natural dissolution. It appears to me that a permanency was expected in the magistracy; and therefore the Senate were combined in the appointment to office. But if the President alone has the power of removal, it is in his power at any time to destroy all that has been done. It appears to me that such a principle would be destructive of the intention of the Constitution expressed by giving the power of appointment to the Senate. It also subverts the clause which gives the Senate the sole power of trying impeachments; because the President may remove the officer, in order to screen him from the effects of their judgment on an impeachment. Why should we construe any part of the Constitution in such a manner as to destroy its essential principles, when a more consonant construction can be obtained?

It appears very clear to me that, however this power may be distributed by the Constitution, the House of Representatives have nothing to do with it.   Why, then, should we interfere in the business ?   Are we afraid the President and Senate are not sufficiently informed to know their respective duties ?   Our interposition argues that they want judgment, and are not able to adjust their powers without the wisdom of this house to assist them.   To say the least on this point, it must be deemed indelicate for us to intermeddle with them.   If the fact is, as we seem to suspect, that they do not understand the Constitution, let it go before the proper tribunal ; the judges are the constitutional umpires on such questions.   Why, let me ask, gentlemen, shall we commit an infraction of the Constitution, for fear the Senate or President should not comply with its directions?

It has been said, by my colleague, that these officers are the creatures of the law ; but it seems as if we were not content with that, — we are making them the mere creatures of the President.   They dare not exercise the privilege of their creation, if the President shall order them to forbear.   Because he holds their thread of life, his power will be sovereign over them, and will soon swallow up the small security we have in the Senate's concurrence to the appointment, and we shall shortly need no other than the authority of the supreme executive officer to nominate, appoint, continue, or remove.

Mr. AMES.   When this question was agitated at a former period, I took no part in the debate.   I believe it was then proposed without any idea or intention of drawing on a lengthy discussion, and to me it appeared to be well understood and settled by the house ; but since it has been reiterated and contested again, I feel it my bounden duty to deliver the reasons for voting in the manner I then did and shall do now.   Mr. Chairman, I look upon every question which touches the Constitution as serious and important, and therefore worthy of the fullest discussion and the most solemn decision.   I believe, on the present occasion, we may come to something near certainty, by attending to the leading principles of the Constitution.   In order that the good purposes of a federal government should be answered, it was necessary to delegate considerable powers; and the principle upon which the grant was made intended to give sufficient power to do all possible good, but to restrain the rulers from doing mischief.

The Constitution places all executive power in the hands of the President ; and could he personally execute all the laws, there would be no occasion for establishing auxiliaries ; but the circumscribed powers of human nature in one man demand the aid of others.   When the objects are widely stretched out, or greatly diversified, meandering through such an extent of territory as what the United States possess, a minister cannot see with his own eyes every transaction, or feel with his hands the *minutiæ* that pass through his department : he must therefore have assistants. But in order that he may be responsible to his country, he must have a choice in selecting his assistants, a control over them, with power to remove them when he finds the qualifications which induced their appointment cease to exist.   There are officers under the Constitution who hold their office by a different tenure : your judges are appointed during good behavior ; and from the delicacy and peculiar nature of their trust, it is right it should be so, in order that they may be independent and impartial in administering justice between the government and its citizens.   But the removability of the one class, or immovability of the other, is founded on the same principle — the security of the people against the abuse of power.   Does any gentleman imagine that an officer is entitled to his office as to an estate? Or does the legislature establish them for the convenience of an individual? For my part, I conceive it intended to carry into effect the purposes for which the Constitution was intended.

The executive powers are delegated to the President, with a view to have a responsible officer to superintend, control, inspect, and check, the officers necessarily employed in administering the laws. The only bond between him and those he employs is the confidence he has in their integrity and talents. When that confidence ceases, the principal ought to have the power to remove those whom he can no longer trust with safety. If an officer shall be guilty of neglect or infidelity, there can be no doubt but he ought to be removed; yet there may be numerous causes for removal which do not amount to a crime. He may propose to do a mischief, but I believe the mere intention would not be cause of impeachment: he may lose the confidence of the people upon suspicion, in which case it would be improper to retain him in service; he ought to be removed at any time, when, instead of doing the greatest possible good, he is likely to do an injury, to the public interest, by being combined in the administration.

I presume gentlemen will generally admit that officers ought to be removed when they become obnoxious; but the question is, How shall this power be exercised? It will not, I apprehend, be contended that all officers hold their offices during good behavior. If this is the case, it is a most singular government. I believe there is not another in the universe that bears the least semblance to it in this particular: such a principle, I take it, is contrary to the nature of things.

But the manner how to remove is the question. If the officer misbehaves, he can be removed by impeachment. But, in this case, is impeachment the only mode of removal? It would be found very inconvenient to have a man continued in office after being impeached, and when all confidence in him was suspended or lost. Would not the end of impeachment be defeated by this means? If Mr. Hastings, who was mentioned by the gentleman from Virginia, (Mr. Vining,) preserved his command in India, could he not defeat the impeachment now pending in Great Britain? If that doctrine obtains in America, we shall find impeachments come too late; while we are preparing the process, the mischief will be perpetrated, and the offender escape. I apprehend it will be as frequently necessary to prevent crimes as to punish them; and it may often happen that the only prevention is by removal. The superintending power possessed by the President will perhaps enable him to discover a base intention before it is ripe for execution. It may happen that the treasurer may be disposed to betray the public chest to the enemy, and so injure the government beyond the possibility of reparation. Should the President be restrained from removing so dangerous an officer until the slow formality of an impeachment was complied with, when the nature of the case rendered the application of a sudden and decisive remedy indispensable?

But it will, I say, be admitted that an officer may be removed: the question then is, by whom? Some gentlemen say, by the President alone; and others, by the President, by and with the advice of the Senate. By the advocates of the latter mode it is alleged that the Constitution is in the way of the power of removal being by the President alone. If this is absolutely the case, there is an end to all further inquiry. But before we suffer this to be considered an insuperable impediment, we ought to be clear that the Constitution prohibits him the exercise of what, on a first view, appears to be a power incident to the executive branch of the gov ernment. The gentleman from Virginia (Mr. Madison) has made so many observations to evince the constitutionality of the clause, that it is un necessary to go over the ground again. I shall therefore confine myself to answer only some remarks made by the gentleman from South Carolina, (Mr. Smith.) The powers of the President are defined in the Constitution; but it is said that he is not expressly authorized to remove from office. If the Constitution is silent also with respect to the Senate, the argument may be retorted. If this silence proves that the power cannot be exercised by the President, it certainly proves that it cannot be exercised by the President, by and with the advice and consent of the Senate. The power of removal is incident to government; but, not being distributed by the Constitution, it will come before the legislature, and, like every other omitted case, must be supplied by law.

Gentlemen have said, when the question was formerly before us, that all powers not intended to be given up to the general government were retained. I beg gentlemen, when they undertake to argue from implication, to be consistent, and admit the force of other arguments drawn from the same source. It is a leading principle in every free government — it is a prominent feature in this — that the legislative and executive powers should be kept distinct; yet the attempt to blend the executive and legislative departments, in exercising the power of removal, is such a maxim as ought not to be carried into practice on arguments grounded on implication. And the gentleman from Virginia's (Mr. White's) reasoning is wholly drawn from implication. He supposes, as the Constitution qualifies the President's power of appointing to office, by subjecting his nomination to the concurrence of the Senate, that the qualification follows of course in the removal.

If this is to be considered as a question undecided by the Constitution, and submitted on the footing of expediency, it will be well to consider where the power can be most usefully deposited, for the security and benefit of the people. It has been said by the gentleman on the other side of the house, (Mr. Smith,) that there is an impropriety in allowing the exercise of this power; that it is a dangerous authority, and much evil may result to the liberty and property of the officer who may be turned out of business without a moment's warning. I take it, the question is not whether such power shall be given or retained; because it is admitted, on all hands, that the officer may be removed; so that it is no grant of power — it raises no new danger. If we strike out the clause, we do not keep the power, nor prevent the exercise of it; so the gentleman will derive none of the security he contemplates by agreeing to the motion for striking out. It will be found that the nature of the business requires it to be conducted by the head of the executive; and I believe it will be found, even there, that more injury will arise from not removing improper officers, than from displacing good ones. I believe experience has convinced us that it is an irksome business; and officers are more frequently continued in one place after they become unfit to perform the duties, than turned out while their talents and integrity are useful. But advantages may result from keeping the power of removal, *in terrorem*, over the heads of the officers : they will be stimulated to do their duty to the satisfaction of the principal, who is to be responsible for the whole executive department.

The gentleman has supposed there will be great difficulty in getting officers of abilities to engage in the service of their country upon such terms. There has never yet been any scarcity of proper officers in any department of the government of the United States ; even during the war, when men risked their lives and property by engaging in such service, there were candidates enough.

But why should we connect the Senate in the removal? Their attention is taken up with other important business, and they have no constitutional authority to watch the conduct of the executive officers, and therefore cannot use such authority with advantage. If the President is inclined to shelter himself behind the Senate, with respect to having continued an improper person in office, we lose the responsibility which is our greatest security : the blame, amongst so many, will be lost. Another reason occurs to me against blending these powers. An officer who superintends the public revenue will naturally acquire a great influence. If he obtains support in the Senate, upon an attempt of the President to remove him, it will be out of the power of the house, when applied to by the first magistrate, to impeach him with success ; for the very means of proving charges of malconduct against him will be under the power of the officer : all the papers necessary to convict him may be withheld while the person continues in his office. Protection may be rendered for protection ; and, as this officer has such extensive influence, it may be exerted to procure the reëlection of his friends. These circumstances, in addition to those stated by the gentleman from New Jersey, (Mr. Boudinot,) must clearly evince to every gentleman the impropriety of connecting the Senate with the President, in removing from office.

I do not say these things will take effect now ; and if the question only related to what might take place in a few years, I should not be uneasy on this point, because I am sensible the gentlemen who form the present Senate are above corruption ; but in future ages, (and I hope this government may be perpetuated to the end of time,) such things may take place, and it is our duty to provide against evils which may be foreseen, but if now neglected, will be irremediable.

I beg to observe, further, that there are three opinions entertained by gentlemen on this subject. One is, that the power of removal is prohibited by the Constitution ; the next is, that it requires it by the President ; and the other is, that the Constitution is totally silent. It therefore appears to me proper for the house to declare what is their sense of the Constitution. If we declare justly on this point, it will serve for a rule of conduct to the executive magistrate : if we declare improperly, the judiciary will revise our decision ; so that, at all events, I think we ought to make the declaration.

Mr. LIVERMORE. I am for striking out this clause, Mr. Chairman, upon the principles of the Constitution, from which we are not at liberty to deviate. The honorable gentleman from Massachusetts (Mr. Sedgwick) calls the minister of foreign affairs the creature of the law, and that very properly ; because the law establishes the office, and has the power of creating him in what shape the legislature pleases. This being the case, we have a right to create the office under such limitations and restrictions as we think proper, provided we can obtain the consent of the Senate ; but it is very improper to draw, as a conclusion from having the power of giving birth to a creature, that we should therefore bring forth a monster, merely to show we had such power. I call that creature a monster that has not the proper limbs and features of its species. I think the creature we are forming is unnatural in its proportions It has been often said that the Constitution declares the President, by and with the advice and consent of the Senate, shall appoint this officer. This, to be sure is very true, and so is the conclusion which an honorable gentleman from Virginia (Mr. White) drew from it — that an officer must be discharged in the way he was appointed.

I believe, Mr. Chairman, this question depends upon a just construction of a short clause in the Constitution — "The President shall have power, by and with the advice and consent of the Senate, to appoint ambassadors, other public ministers, and consuls, judges of the Supreme Court, and all other officers of the United States." Here is no difference with respect to the power of the President to make treaties and appoint officers, only it requires in the one case a larger majority to concur than in the other. I will not, by any means, suppose that gentlemen mean, when they argue in favor of removal by the President alone, to contemplate the extension of the power to the repeal of treaties; because, if they do, there will be little occasion for us to sit here. But, let me ask these gentlemen — as there is no real or imaginary distinction between the appointment of ambassadors and ministers, or secretaries of foreign affairs — whether they mean that the President should have the power of recalling or discarding ambassadors and military officers, — for the words in the Constitution are, "all other officers," — as well as he can remove your secretary of foreign affairs. To be sure, they cannot extend it to the judges, because they are secured under a subsequent article, which declares they shall hold their offices during good behavior; they have an inheritance which they cannot be divested of but on conviction of some crime. But I presume gentlemen mean to apply it to all those who have not an inheritance in their offices. In this case, it takes the whole power of the President and Senate to create an officer; but half the power can uncreate him. Surely, a law passed by the whole legislature cannot be repealed by one branch of it; so, I conceive, in the case of appointments, it requires the same force to supersede an officer as to put him in office.

I acknowledge that the clause relative to impeachment is for the benefit of the people. It is intended to enable their representatives to bring a bad officer to justice, who is screened by the President. But I do not conceive, with the honorable gentleman from South Carolina, (Mr. Smith,) that it, by any means, excludes the usual ways of superseding officers. It is said, in the Constitution, that the house shall have the power of choosing their own officers. We have chosen a clerk, and, I am satisfied, a very capable one; but will any gentleman contend that we may not discharge him, and choose another, and another, as often as we see cause? And so it is in every other instance — where they have power to make, they have likewise the power to unmake. · It will be said, by gentlemen, that the power to make does not imply the power of unmaking; but I believe they will find very few exceptions in the United States.

Were I to speak of the expediency, every one of my observations would be against it. When an important and confidential trust is placed in a man, it is worse than death to him to be displaced without cause; his reputation depends upon the single will of the President, who may ruin him on bare suspicion. Nay, a new President may turn him out on mere caprice, or in order to make room for a favorite. This contradicts all my notions of propriety; every thing of this sort should be done with due deliberation; every person ought to have a hearing before they are punished. It is on these considerations that I wish the general principle laid down by the gentleman from Virginia (Mr. White) may be adhered to.

I will add one word more, and I have done. This seems, Mr. Chairman, altogether to be aimed at the Senate. What have they done to chagrin us? or why should we attempt to abridge their powers, because we can reach them by our regulations in the shape of a bill? I think we had better let it alone. If the Constitution has given them this power, they will reject this part of the bill, and they will exercise that one privilege judiciously, however they may the power of removal. If the Constitution has not given it to them, it has not vested it any where else; consequently, this house would have no right to confer it.

Mr. HARTLEY. I apprehend, Mr. Chairman, that this officer cannot be considered as appointed during good behavior, even in point of policy; but with respect to the constitutionality, I am pretty confident he cannot be viewed in that light. The Constitution declares the tenure of the officers it recognizes, and says one class of them shall hold their offices during good behavior; they are the judges of your Supreme and other courts; but as to any other officer being established on this firm tenure, the Constitution is silent. It, then, necessarily follows that we must consider every other according to its nature, and regulate it in a corresponding manner. The business of the secretary of foreign affairs is of an executive nature, and must consequently be attached to the executive department.

I think the gentleman from South Carolina goes too far, in saying that the clause respecting impeachments implies that there is no other mode of removing an officer. I think it does not follow that, because one mode is pointed out by the Constitution, there is no other, especially if that provision is intended for nothing more than a punishment for a crime. The 4th section of the 2d article says that all civil officers shall be removed on conviction of certain crimes. But it cannot be the intention of the Constitution to prevent, by this, a removal in any other way. Such a principle, if once admitted, would be attended with very inconvenient and mischievous consequences.

The gentleman further contends that every man has a property in his office, and ought not to be removed but for criminal conduct; he ought not to be removed for inability. I hope this doctrine will never be admitted in this country. A man, when in office, ought to have abilities to discharge the duties of it. If he is discovered to be unfit, he ought to be immediately removed; but not on principles like what that gentleman contends for. If he has an estate in his office, his right must be purchased, and a practice like what obtains in England will be adopted here. We shall be unable to dismiss an officer, without allowing him a pension for the interest he is deprived of. Such doctrine may suit a nation which is strong in proportion to the number of dependants upon the crown, but will be very pernicious in a republic like ours. When we have established an office, let the provision for the support of the officer be equal to compensate his services; but never let it be said that he has an estate in his office when he is found unfit to perform his duties. If offices are to be held during good behavior, it is easy to foresee that we shall have as many factions as heads of departments. The consequence would be, corruption in one of the great departments of government; and if the balance is once destroyed, the Constitution must fall amidst the ruins. From this view of the subject, I have no difficulty to declare that the secretary of foreign affairs is an officer during pleasure, and not during good behavior, as contended for.

One gentleman (Mr. White) holds the same principles, but differs with respect to the power which ought to exercise the privilege of removal. On this point we are reduced to a matter of construction ; but it is of high importance to the United States that a construction should be rightly made.   But gentlemen say it is inconsistent with the Constitution to make this declaration ; that, as the Constitution is silent, we ought not to be too explicit.   The Constitution has expressly pointed out several matters which we can do, and some which we cannot ; but in other matters it is silent, and leaves them to the discretion of the legislature.   If this is not the case, why was the last clause of the 8th section of the 1st article inserted ?   It gives power to Congress to make all laws necessary and proper to carry the government into effect.

I look upon it that the legislature have, therefore, a right to exercise their discretion on such questions ; and, however attentively gentlemen may have examined the Constitution on this point, I trust they have discovered no clause which forbids this house interfering in business necessary and proper to carry the government into effect.

The Constitution grants expressly to the President the power of filling all vacancies during the recess of the Senate.   This is a temporary power, like that of removal, and liable to very few of the objections which have been made.   When the President has removed an officer, another must be appointed ; but this cannot be done without the advice and consent of the Senate.   Where, then, is the danger of the system of favoritism ? The President, notwithstanding the supposed depravity of mankind, will hardly remove a worthy officer to make way for a person whom the Senate may reject.   Another reason why the power of removal should be lodged with the President, rather than with the Senate, arises from their connection with the people.   The President is the representative of the people ; in a near and equal manner, he is the guardian of his country.   The Senate are the representatives of the State legislatures ; but they are very unequal in that representation : each state sends two members to that house, although their proportions are as ten to one.   Hence arises a degree of insecurity to an impartial administration ; but if they possessed every advantage of equality, they cannot be the proper body to inspect into the behavior of officers, because they have no constitutional powers for this purpose.   It does not always imply criminality to be removed from office, because it may be proper to remove for other causes ; neither do I see any danger which can result from the exercise of this power by the President, because the Senate is to be consulted in the appointment which is afterwards to take place.   Under these circumstances, I repeat it, that I have no doubt, in my own mind, that this office is during pleasure ; and that the power of removal, which is a mere temporary one, ought to be in the President, whose powers, taken together, are not very numerous, and the success of this government depends upon their being unimpaired.

Mr. LAWRENCE.   It has been objected against this clause, that the granting of this power is unconstitutional.   It was also objected, if it is not unconstitutional, it is unnecessary ; that the Constitution must contain, in itself, the power of removal, and have given it to some body, or person, of the government, to be exercised ; that, therefore, the law could make no disposition of it, and the attempt to grant it was unconstitutional : or the law is unnecessary ; — for, if the power is granted in the way the clause supposes, the legislature can neither add to nor diminish the power by making the declaration.

With respect to the unconstitutionality of the measure, I observe, that, if it is so, the Constitution must have given the power expressly to some person or body other than the President ; otherwise, it cannot be said with certainty that it is unconstitutional in us to declare that he shall have the power of removal. I believe it is not contended that the Constitution expressly gives this power to any other person ; but it is contended that the objection is collected from the nature of the body which has the appointment, and the particular clause in the Constitution which declares, that all officers shall be removed on conviction. It will be necessary to examine the expressions of that clause ; but I believe it will be found not to comprehend the case we have under consideration. I suppose the Constitution contemplates somewhere the power of removal for other causes besides those expressed as causes of impeachment. I take it that the clause in the Constitution respecting impeachments is making a provision for removal against the will of the President ; because the house can carry the offender before a tribunal which shall remove him, notwithstanding the desire of the chief magistrate to keep him in office. If this is not to be the construction, then a particular clause in the Constitution will be nugatory. The Constitution declares that the judges shall hold their offices during good behavior. This implies that other officers shall hold their offices during a limited time, or according to the will of some persons ; because, if all persons are to hold their offices during good behavior, and to be removed only by impeachment, then this particular declaration in favor of the judges will be useless. We are told that an officer must misbehave before he can be removed. This is true with respect to those officers who hold their commissions during good behavior ; but it cannot be true of those who are appointed during pleasure : they may be removed for incapacity, or if their want of integrity is suspected ; but the question is, to find where this power of removal resides.

It has been argued that we are to find this in the construction arising from the nature of the authority which appoints. Here I would meet the gentleman, if it was necessary to rest it entirely on that ground. Let me ask the gentleman, who appoints? The Constitution gives an advisory power to the Senate ; but it is considered that the President makes the appointment. The appointment and responsibility are actually his ; for it is expressly declared that he shall nominate and appoint, though their advice is required to be taken. If, from the nature of the appointment, we are to collect the authority of removal, then I say the latter power is lodged in the President ; because, by the Constitution, he has the power of appointment : instantly as the Senate have advised the appointment, the act is required to be executed by the President. The language is explicit : " He shall nominate, and, by and with the advice and consent of the Senate, appoint ; " so that, if the gentleman's general principle, that the power appointing shall remove also, is true, it follows that the removal shall be by the President.

It has been stated, as an objection, that we should extend the powers of the President, if we give him the power of removal ; and we are not to construe the Constitution in such way as to enlarge the executive power to the injury of any other ; that, as he is limited in the power of appointment by the control of the Senate, he ought to be equally limited in the removal.

If there is any weight in this argument, it implies as forcibly against vesting the power conjointly in the President and Senate ; because, if we are not to extend the powers of the executive beyond the express detail of duties found in the Constitution, neither are we at liberty to extend the duties of the Senate beyond those precise points fixed in the same instrument : of course, if we cannot say the President alone shall remove, we cannot say the President and Senate may exercise such power.

It is admitted that the Constitution is silent on this subject; but it is also silent with respect to the appointments it has vested in the legislature. The Constitution declares that Congress may by law vest the appointment of such inferior officers as they think proper in the President alone, in the courts of law, or heads of departments; yet says nothing with respect to the removal. Now, let us suppose the legislature to have vested the power of appointment in the President in cases of inferior offices; can the intention of the Constitution in this, (contemplating this mode of appointment for the sake of convenience,) be ever carried into effect if we say nothing respecting the removal? What would be the consequence if the legislature should not make the declaration? Could it be supposed that he would not have the authority to dismiss the officer he has so appointed? To be sure he could. Then, of course, in those cases in which the Constitution has given the appointment to the President, he must have the power of removal, for the sake of consistency; for no person will say that, if the President should appoint an inferior officer, he should not have the power to remove him when he thought proper, if no particular limitation was determined by the law. Thus stands the matter with respect to the Constitution. There is no express prohibition of the power, nor positive grant. If, then, we collect the power by inference from the Constitution, we shall find it pointed strongly in favor of the President, much more so than in favor of the Senate combined with him.

This is a case omitted, or it is not; if it is omitted, and the power is necessary and essential to the government, and to the great interests of the United States, who are to make the provision and supply the defect? Certainly the legislature is the proper body. It is declared they shall establish offices by law. The establishment of an office implies every thing relative to its formation, constitution, and termination; consequently, the Congress are authorized to declare their judgment on each of these points. But if the arguments of the gentleman from South Carolina (Mr. Smith) prevail, that, as the Constitution has not meditated the removal of an officer in any other way than by impeachment, it would be an assumption in Congress to vest the President, courts of law, or heads of departments, with power to dismiss their officers in any other manner : — would a regulation of this kind be effectual to carry into effect the great objects of the Constitution? I contend it would not. Therefore, the principle which opposes the carrying of the Constitution into effect, must be rejected as dangerous and incompatible with the general welfare. Hence all those suppositions, that, because the Constitution is silent, the legislature must not supply the defect, are to be treated as chimeras and illusory inferences.

I believe it is possible that the Constitution may be misconstrued by the legislature; but will any gentleman contend that it is more probable that the Senate, one branch only of the legislature, should make a more upright decision on any point than the whole legislature, — especially on a point in which they are supposed by some gentlemen to be so immediately interested, even admitting that honorable body to have more wisdom and more integrity than this house? Such an inference can hardly be admitted. But I believe it seldom or never was so contended, that there was more wisdom or security in a part than in the whole.

But supposing the power to vest in the Senate, is it more safe in their hands than where we contend it should be? Would it be more satisfactory to our constituents for us to make such a declaration in their favor? I believe not.

With respect to this and every case omitted, but which can be collected from the other provisions made in the Constitution, the people look up to the legislature, the concurrent opinion of the two branches, for their construction; they conceive those cases proper subjects for legislative wisdom; they naturally suppose, where provisions are to be made, they ought to spring from this source, and this source alone.

From a view of these circumstances, we may be induced to meet the question in force. Shall we now venture to supply the defect? For my part, I have no hesitation. We should supply the defect; we should place the power of removal in the great executive officer of the government.

In the Constitution, the heads of departments are considered as the mere assistants of the President in the performance of his executive duties. He has the superintendence, the control, and the inspection, of their conduct; he has an intimate connection with them; they must receive from him his orders and directions; they must answer his inquiries in writing, when he requires it. Shall the person having these superior powers to govern — with such advantages of discovering and defeating the base intentions of his officers, their delinquencies, their defective abilities, or their negligence — be restrained from applying these advantages to the most useful, nay, in some cases, the only useful purpose which can be answered by them?

It appears to me that the power can be safely lodged here. But it has been said by some gentlemen, that if it is lodged here it will be subject to abuse; that there may be a change of officers, and a complete revolution throughout the whole executive department, upon the election of every new President. I admit that this may be the case, and contend that it should be the case if the President thinks it necessary. I contend that every President should have those men about him in whom he can place the most confidence, provided the Senate approve his choice. But we are not from hence to infer that changes will be made in a wanton manner, and from capricious motives; because the Presidents are checked and guarded in a very safe manner with respect to the appointment of their successors; from all which it may be fairly presumed that changes will be made on principles of policy and propriety only.

Will the man chosen by three millions of his fellow-citizens, be such a wretch as to abuse them in a wanton manner? For my part I should think, with the gentleman from Virginia, (Mr. Madison,) that a President, thus selected and honored by his country, is entitled to my confidence; and I see no reason why we should suppose he is more inclined to do harm than good. Elected as he is, I trust we are secure. I do not draw these observations from the safety I conceive under the present administration, or because our chief magistrate is possessed of irradiated virtues, whose lustre brightens this western hemisphere, and incites the admiration of the world! But I calculate upon what our mode of election is likely to bring forward, and the security which the Constitution affords. If the President abuses his trust, will he escape the popular censure when the period which terminates his elevation arrives? And would he not be liable to impeachment for displacing a worthy and able man who enjoyed the confidence of the people?

We ought not to consider one side alone ; we should consider the ben efit of such an arrangement, as well as the difficulties. We should also consider the difficulties arising from the exercise of the power of removing by the Senate. It was well observed by an honorable gentleman (Mr Sedgwick) on this point, that the Senate must continue in session the whole year, or be hastily assembled from the extremes and all parts of the continent, whenever the President thinks a removal necessary. Suppose an ambassador, or minister plenipotentiary, negotiating or intriguing contrary to his instructions, and to the injury of the United States ; before the Senate can be assembled to accede to his recall, the interest of his country may be betrayed, and the evil irrevocably perpetrated. A great number of such instances could be enumerated ; but I will not take up the time of the committee ; gentlemen may suggest them to their own minds ; and I imagine they will be sufficient to convince them that, with respect to the expediency, the power of removal ought not to be in the Senate.

I take it, Mr. Chairman, that it is proper for the legislature to speak their sense upon those points on which the Constitution is silent. I believe the judges will never decide that we are guilty of a breach of the Constitution, by declaring a legislative opinion in cases where the Constitution is silent. If the laws shall be in violation of any part of the Constitution, the judges will not hesitate to decide against them. Where the power is incident to the government, and the Constitution is silent, it can be no impediment to a legislative grant. I hold it necessary, in such cases, to make provision. In the case of removal, the Constitution is silent. The wisdom of the legislature should therefore declare in what place the power resides.

Mr. JACKSON. As a constitutional question, it is of great moment, and worthy of full discussion. I am, sir, a friend to the full exercise of all the powers of government, and deeply impressed with the necessity there exists of having an energetic executive. But, friend as I am to the efficient government, I value the liberties of my fellow-citizens beyond every other consideration ; and where I find them endangered, I am willing to forego every other blessing to secure them. I hold it as good a maxim as it is an old one — of two evils to choose the least.

It has been mentioned, that in all governments the executive magistrate had the power of dismissing officers under him. This may hold good in Europe, where monarchs claim their powers *jure divino ;* but it never can be admitted in America, under a Constitution delegating enumerated powers. It requires more than a mere *ipse dixit* to demonstrate that any power is in its nature executive, and consequently given to the President of the United States by the present Constitution. But if this power *is* incident to the executive branch of government, it does not follow that it vests in the President alone ; because he alone does not possess all executive powers. The Constitution has lodged the power of forming treaties, and all executive business, I presume, connected therewith, in the President ; but it is qualified by and with the advice and consent of the Senate — provided two thirds of the Senate agree therein. The same has taken place with respect to appointing officers. From this I infer that those arguments are done away which the gentleman from Virginia (Mr. Madison) used, to prove that it was contrary to the principles of the Constitution that we should blend the executive and legislative powers in the same body. It may be wrong that the great powers of government should be blended in this manner, but we cannot separate them : the error is adopted in the

Constitution, and can only be eradicated by weeding it out of that instrument. It may therefore be a proper subject for amendment, when we come to consider that business again.

It has been observed, that the President ought to have this power to remove a man when he becomes obnoxious to the people, or disagreeable to himself. Are we, then, to have all the officers the mere creatures of the President? This thirst of power will introduce a treasury bench into the house, and we shall have ministers obtrude upon us to govern and direct the measures of the legislature, and to support the influence of their master; and shall we establish a different influence between the people and the President? I suppose these circumstances must take place, because they have taken place in other countries. The executive power falls to the ground in England, if it cannot be supported by the Parliament; therefore a high game of corruption is played, and a majority secured to the ministry by the introduction of placemen and pensioners.

The gentlemen have brought forward arguments drawn from possibility. It is said that our secretary of foreign affairs may become unfit for his office by a fit of lunacy, and therefore a silent remedy should be applied. It is true such a case may happen; but it may also happen in cases where there is no power of removing. Suppose the President should be taken with a fit of lunacy; would it be possible by such arguments to remove him? I apprehend he must remain in office during his four years. Suppose the Senate should be seized with a fit of lunacy, and it was to extend to the House of Representatives; what could the people do but endure this mad Congress till the term of their election expired? We have seen a king of England in an absolute fit of lunacy, which produced an interregnum in the government. The same may happen here with respect to our President; and although it is improbable that the majority of both houses of Congress may be in that situation, yet it is by no means impossible. But gentlemen have brought forward another argument, with respect to the judges. It is said they are to hold their offices during good behavior. I agree that ought to be the case. But is not a judge liable to the act of God, as well as any other officer of government? However great his legal knowledge, his judgment and integrity, it may be taken from him at a stroke, and he rendered the most unfit of all men to fill such an important office. But can you remove him? Not for this cause: it is impossible; because madness is no treason, crime, or misdemeanor. If he does not choose to resign, like Lord Mansfield he may continue in office for ninety or one hundred years; for so long have some men retained their faculties.

But let me ask gentlemen if it is possible to place their officers in such a situation — to deprive them of their independency and firmness; for I apprehend it is not intended to stop with the secretary of foreign affairs. Let it be remembered that the Constitution gives the President the command of the military. If you give him complete power over the man with the strong box, he will have the liberty of America under his thumb. It is easy to see the evil which may result. If he wants to establish an arbitrary authority, and finds the secretary of finance not inclined to second his endeavors, he has nothing more to do than to remove him, and get one appointed of principles more congenial with his own. Then says he, "I have got the army; let me have but the money, and I will establish my throne upon the ruins of your visionary republic." Let no gentleman say I am contemplating imaginary dangers — the mere chimeras of a heated brain. Behold the baneful influence of the royal prerogative. All officers till lately held their commissions during the pleasure of the crown.

At this moment, see the king of Sweden aiming at arbitrary power, shutting the doors of his senate, and compelling, by the force of arms, his shuddering councillors to acquiesce in his despotic mandates. I agree that this is the hour in which we ought to establish our government; but it is an hour in which we should be wary and cautious, especially in what respects the executive magistrate. With him every power may be safely lodged. Black, indeed, is the heart of that man who even suspects him to be capable of abusing them. But alas! he cannot be with us forever : he is liable to the vicissitudes of life ; he is but mortal ; and though I contemplate it with great regret, yet I know the period must come which will separate him from his country ; and can we know the virtues or vices of his successor in a very few years? May not a man with a Pandora's box in his breast come into power, and give us sensible cause to lament our present confidence and want of foresight ?

A gentleman has declared that, as the Constitution has given the power of appointment, it has consequently given the power of removal. I agree with him in all that the Constitution expressly grants, but I must differ in the constructive reasoning. It was said by the advocates of this Constitution, that the powers not given up in that instrument were reserved to the people. Under this impression, it has been proposed, as a favorite amendment to the Constitution, that it should be declared that all powers not expressly given should be retained. As to what gentlemen have said of its giving satisfaction to the people, I deny it. They never can be pleased that we should give new and extraordinary powers to the executive. We must confine ourselves to the powers described in the Constitution ; and the moment we pass it, we take an arbitrary stride toward a despotic government.

The gentleman from New York (Mr. Lawrence) contends that the President appoints, and therefore he ought to remove. I shall agree to give him the same power, in cases of removal, as he has in appointing ; but nothing more. Upon this principle, I would agree to give him the power of suspension during the recess of the Senate. This, in my opinion, would effectually provide against those inconveniences which have been apprehended, and not expose the government to the abuses we have to dread from the wanton and uncontrolled authority of removing officers at pleasure. I am the friend of an energetic government ; but while we are giving vigor to the executive arm, we ought to be careful not to lay the foundation of future tyranny.

For my part, I must declare that I think this power too great to be safely trusted in the hands of a single man ; especially in the hands of a man who has so much constitutional power. I believe, if those powers had been more contracted, the system of government would have been more generally agreeable to our constituents ; that is, at present it would conform more to the popular opinion, at least. For my part, though I came from a state where the energy of government can be useful, and where it is at this moment wanting, I cannot agree to extend this power ; because I conceive it may, at some future period, be exercised in such a way as to subvert the liberties of my country ; and no consideration shall ever induce me to put them in jeopardy. It is under this impression that I shall vote decidedly against the clause.

Mr. CLYMER. If I was to give my vote merely on constitutional

32

ground, I should be totally indifferent whether the words were struck out or not; because I am clear that the executive has the power of removal, as incident to his department; and if the Constitution had been silent with respect to the appointment, he would have had that power also. The reason, perhaps, why it was mentioned in the Constitution, was to give some further security against the improper introduction of improper men into office. But in cases of removal there is not such necessity for this check. What great danger would arise from the removal of a worthy man, when the Senate must be consulted in the appointment of his successor? Is it likely that they will consent to advance an improper character? The presumption therefore is, that he would not abuse this power; or, if he did, only one good man would be changed for another.

If the President is divested of this power, his responsibility is destroyed; you prevent his efficiency, and disable him from affording that security to the people which the Constitution contemplates. What use will it be of, to call the citizens of the Union together every four years to obtain a purified choice of a representative, if he is to be a mere cipher in the government? The executive must act by others; but you reduce him to a mere shadow, when you control both the power of appointment and removal. If you take away the latter power, he ought to resign the power of superintending and directing the executive parts of government into the hands of the Senate at once; and then we become a dangerous aristocracy, or shall be more destitute of energy than any government on earth. These being my sentiments, I wish the clause to stand as a legislative declaration that the power of removal is constitutionally vested in the President.

Mr. PAGE. I venture to assert that this clause of the bill contains in it the seeds of royal prerogative. If gentlemen lay such stress on the energy of the government, I beg them to consider how far this doctrine may go. Every thing which has been said in favor of energy in the executive may go to the destruction of freedom, and establish despotism. This very energy, so much talked of, has led many patriots to the Bastile, to the block, and to the halter. If the chief magistrate can take a man away from the head of a department without assigning any reason, he may as well be invested with power, on certain occasions, to take away his existence. But will you contend that this idea is consonant with the principles of a free government, where no man ought to be condemned unheard, nor till after a solemn conviction of guilt on a fair and impartial trial? It would, in my opinion, be better to suffer, for a time, the mischief arising from the conduct of a bad officer, than admit principles which would lead to the establishment of despotic prerogatives.

There can be little occasion for the President to exercise this power, unless you suppose that the appointments will be made in a careless manner, which by no means is likely to be the case. If, then, you have a good officer, why should he be made dependent upon the will of a single man? Suppose a colonel in your army should disobey his orders, or cowardly flee before the enemy; what would the general do? Would he be at liberty to dismiss the officer? No; he would suspend him, until a court-martial was held to decide the degree of guilt. If gentlemen had been content to say that the President might suspend, I should second their motion, and afterward the officer might be removed by and with the advice and consent of the Senate; but to make every officer of the government dependent on the will and pleasure of one man, will be vesting

such arbitrary power in him as to occasion every friend to liberty to tremble for his country.   I confess it seems to me a matter of infinite concern, and I should feel very unhappy if I supposed the clause would remain in the bill.

Mr. SHERMAN.   I consider this as a very important subject in every
point of view, and therefore worthy of full discussion.   In my mind, it
involves three questions : First, whether the President has, by the Constitution, the right to remove an officer appointed by and with the advice and
consent of the Senate.   No gentleman contends but the advice and consent of the Senate are necessary to make the appointment in all cases, unless in inferior offices, where the contrary is established by law ; but then
they allege that, although the consent of the Senate is necessary to the
appointment, the President alone, by the nature of his office, has the power of removal.   Now, it appears to me that this opinion is ill founded,
because this provision was intended for some useful purpose, and by that
construction would answer none at all.   I think the concurrence of the
Senate as necessary to appoint an officer as the nomination of the President ; they are constituted as the mutual checks, each having a negative
upon the other.

I consider it as an established principle, that the power which appoints
can also remove, unless there are express exceptions made.   Now, the
power which appoints the judges cannot displace them, because there is
a constitutional restriction in their favor ; otherwise, the President, by and
with the advice and consent of the Senate, being the power which appointed them, would be sufficient to remove them.   This is the construction in England, where the king had the power of appointing judges ; it
was declared to be during pleasure, and they might be removed when
the monarch thought proper.   It is a general principle in law, as well as
reason, that there should be the same authority to remove as to establish.
It is so in legislation, where the several branches whose concurrence was
necessary to pass a law, must concur in repealing it.   Just so I take it
to be in cases of appointment ; and the President alone may remove
when he alone appoints, as in the case of inferior offices to be established
by law.

Here another question arises — whether this officer comes within the
description of inferior officers.   Some gentlemen think not, because he is
the head of the department for foreign affairs.   Others may perhaps think
that, as he is employed in the executive department in aid of the President, he is not such an officer as is understood by the term *heads of departments ;* because the President is the head of the executive department,
in which the secretary of foreign affairs serves.   If this is the construction
which gentlemen put upon the business, they may vest the appointment
in the President alone, and the removal will be in him of consequence.
But if this reasoning is not admitted, we can by no means vest the appointment or removal in the chief magistrate alone.   As the officer is the
mere creature of the legislature, we may form it under such regulations
as we please, with such powers and duration as we think good policy requires.   We may say he shall hold his office during good behavior, or that
he shall be annually elected ; we may say he shall be displaced for neglect
of duty, and point out how he should be convicted of it, without calling
upon the President or Senate.

The third question is, if the legislature has the power to authorize the
President alone to remove this officer, whether it is expedient to vest him

with it   I do not believe it is absolutely necessary that he should have such power, because the power of suspending would answer all the purposes which gentlemen have in view by giving the power of removal.   I do not think that the officer is only to be removed by impeachment, as is argued by the gentleman from South Carolina, (Mr. Smith;) because he is the mere creature of the law, and we can direct him to be removed on conviction of mismanagement or inability, without calling upon the Senate for their concurrence.   But I believe, if we make no such provision, he may constitutionally be removed by the President, by and with the advice and consent of the Senate; and I believe it would be most expedient for us to say nothing in the clause on the subject.

Mr. STONE.   I think it necessary, Mr. Chairman, to determine the question before us.   I do not think it would do to leave it to the determination of courts of law hereafter.   It should be our duty, in cases like the present, to give our opinion on the construction of the Constitution.

When the question was brought forward, I felt unhappy, because my mind was in doubt; but since then, I have deliberately reflected upon it, and have made up an opinion perfectly satisfactory to myself.   I consider that, in general, every officer who is appointed should be removed by the power that appoints him.   It is so in the nature of things.   The power of appointing an officer arises from the power over the subject on which the officer is to act.   It arises from the principal, who appoints, having an interest in, and a right to conduct, the business which he does by means of an agent; therefore this officer appears to be nothing more than an agent appointed for the convenient despatch of business.   This is my opinion on this subject, and the principle will operate from a minister of state down to a tide-waiter.   The Constitution, it is admitted by every gentleman, recognizes the principle; because it has not been denied, whenever general appointments are made under the Constitution, that they are to be at will and pleasure: that where an appointment is made during good behavior, it is an exception to the general rule; there you limit the exercise of the power which appoints: it is thus in the case of the judges.

Let us examine, then, whence originates the power of Congress with respect to the officer under consideration.   I presume it is expressly contained in the Constitution, or clearly deducible from that instrument, that we have a right to erect the department of foreign affairs.   No gentleman will consent to a reduction or relinquishment of that power.   The Constitution has given us the power of laying and collecting taxes, duties, imposts, and excises; this includes the power of organizing a revenue board.   It gives us power to regulate commerce; this includes the power of establishing a board of trade: to make war, and organize the militia; this enables us to establish a minister at war: and generally to make all laws necessary to carry these powers into effect.   Now, it appears to me, that the erection of this department is expressly within the Constitution. Therefore it seems to me, as Congress, in their legislative capacity, have an interest in, and power over, this whole transaction, that they consequently appoint and displace their officers.   But there is a provision in the Constitution which takes away from us the power of appointing officers of a certain description; they are to be appointed by the President, by and with the advice and consent of the Senate; then the Constitution limits the legislature in appointing certain officers, which would otherwise be within their power.

It will, then, become a considerable question, as it has been in my mind, that as, in the nature of things, the power which appoints removes also and as the power of appointment, by the Constitution, is placed in the President and Senate, whether the removal does not follow as incidental to that power. But I am averse to that construction, as the terms of the Constitution are sufficient to invest the legislature with complete power for performing its duties; and since it has given the power of making treaties, and judging of them, to the Senate and President, I should be inclined to believe that, as they have an immediate concern in, and control over this business, therefore they ought to have the power of removal. It may be said, with respect to some other officers, that, agreeably to this principle, the President alone ought to have the sole power of removal, because he is interested in it, and has the control over the business they manage; for example, the minister at war. The President is the commander-in-chief of the army and militia of the United States; but the ground is narrowed by the Senate being combined with him in making treaties; though even here the ground is reduced, because of the power combined in the whole legislature to declare war and grant supplies. If it is considered that Congress have a right to appoint these officers, or dictate the mode by which they shall be appointed, — and I calculate in my own opinion the manner of dismission from the mode of appointment, — I should have no doubt but we might make such regulations as we may judge proper. If the Constitution had given no rule by which officers were to be appointed, I should search for one in my own mind. But as the Constitution has laid down the rule, I consider the mode of removal as clearly defined as by implication it can be: it ought to be the same with that of the appointment. What quality of the human mind is necessary for the one that is not necessary for the other? Information, impartiality, and judgment in the business to be conducted, are necessary to make a good appointment. Are not the same properties requisite for a dismission? It appears so to me.

I cannot subscribe to the opinion, delivered by some gentlemen, that the executive in its nature implies the power to appoint the officers of government. Why does it imply it? The appointment of officers depends upon the qualities that are necessary for forming a judgment on the merits of men; and the displacing of them, instead of including the idea of what is necessary for an executive officer, includes the idea necessary for a judicial one; therefore it cannot exist, in the nature of things, that an executive power is either to appoint or displace the officers of government. Is it a political dogma? Is it founded in experience? If it is, I confess it has been very long wrapped up in mysterious darkness. As a political rule, it is not common in the world, excepting monarchies, where this principle is established, that the interest of the state is included in the interest of the prince; that whatever injures the state is an injury to the sovereign; because he has a property in the state and the government, and is to take care that nothing of that kind is to be injured or destroyed, he being so intimately connected with the well-being of the nation, it appears a point of justice only to suffer him to manage his own concerns. Our principles of government are different; and the President, instead of being master of the people of America, is only their great servant. But. if it arises from a political dogma, it must be subject to exceptions, which hold good as they are applied to governments which give greater or lesser proportions of power to their executive. I shall only remark that the Constitution in no one part of it, so far as I can see, supposes that the President is the sole judge of the merits of an appointment ; it is very forcible to my mind, that the Constitution has confined his sole appointment to the case of inferior officers. It also strikes me, from the clause that gives the President the power to grant reprieves and pardons for offences against the United States, except in cases of impeachment, that the Constitution reposes a confidence in the Senate which it has not done in this officer ; and therefore, there is no good reason for destroying that participation of power which the system of government has given to them.

Whether it would be expedient to give the power of removal to the President alone, depends on this consideration : — they are both bodies chosen with equal care and propriety ; the people show as much confidence in the one as in the other ; the best President and the best Senate, it is to be presumed, will always be chosen that they can get. All the difficulties and embarrassments that have been mentioned can be removed by giving to the President the power of suspension during the recess of the Senate ; and I think that an attention to the Constitution will lead us to decide that this is the only proper power to be vested in the President of the United States.

Mr. MADISON. I feel the importance of the question, and know that our decision will involve the decision of all similar cases. The decision that is at this time made will become the permanent exposition of the Constitution ; and on a permanent exposition of the Constitution will depend the genius and character of the whole government. It will depend, perhaps, on this decision, whether the government shall retain that equilibrium which the Constitution intended, or take a direction towards aristocracy, or anarchy, among the members of the government. Hence, how careful ought we to be to give a true direction to a power so critically circumstanced! It is incumbent on us to weigh, with particular attention, the arguments which have been advanced in support of the various opinions with cautious deliberation. I own to you, Mr. Chairman, that I feel great anxiety upon this question. I feel an anxiety, because I am called upon to give a decision in a case that may affect the fundamental principles of the government under which we act, and liberty itself. But all that I can do, on such an occasion, is to weigh well every thing advanced on both sides, with the purest desire to find out the true meaning of the Constitution, and to be guided by that, and an attachment to the true spirit of liberty, whose influence I believe strongly predominates here.

Several constructions have been put upon the Constitution relative to the point in question. The gentleman from Connecticut (Mr. Sherman) has advanced a doctrine which was not touched upon before. He seems to think (if I understood him right) that the power of displacing from office is subject to legislative discretion, because, it having a right to create, it may limit or modify, as is thought proper. I shall not say but at first view this doctrine may seem to have some plausibility. But when I consider that the Constitution clearly intended to maintain a marked distinction between the legislative, executive, and judicial powers of government; and when I consider that, if the legislature has a power such as contended for, they may subject, and transfer, at discretion, powers from one department of government to another ; they may, on that principle, exclude the President altogether from exercising any authority in the removal of officers ; they may give it to the Senate alone, or the President and Senate combined ; they may vest it in the whole Congress, or they may reserve it to be exercised by this house. When I consider the consequences of this doctrine, and compare them with the true principles of the Constitution, I own that I cannot subscribe to it.

Another doctrine, which has found very respectable friends, has been particularly advocated by the gentleman from South Carolina, (Mr. Smith.) It is this : When an officer is appointed by the President and Senate, he can only be displaced, from malfeasance in his office, by impeachment. I think this would give a stability to the executive department, so far as it may be described by the heads of departments, which is more incompatible with the genius of republican governments in general, and this Constitution in particular, than any doctrine which has yet been proposed. The danger to liberty — the danger of maladministration — has not yet been found to lie so much in the facility of introducing improper persons into office, as in the difficulty of displacing those who are unworthy of the public trust. If it is said that an officer once appointed shall not be displaced without the formality required by impeachment, I shall be glad to know what security we have for the faithful administration of the government. Every individual in the long chain, which extends from the highest to the lowest link of the executive magistracy, would find a security in his situation which would relax his fidelity and promptitude in the discharge of his duty.

The doctrine, however, which seems to stand most in opposition to the principles I contend for is, that the power to annul an appointment is, in the nature of things, incidental to the power which makes the appointment. I agree that, if nothing more was said in the Constitution than that the President, by and with the advice and consent of the Senate, should appoint to office, there would be great force in saying that the power of removal resulted, by a natural implication, from the power of appointing. But there is another part of the Constitution no less explicit than the one on which the gentleman's doctrine is founded ; it is that part which declares that the executive power shall be vested in a President of the United States. The association of the Senate with the President, in exercising that particular function, is an exception to this general rule ; and exceptions to general rules, I conceive, are ever to be taken strictly. But there is another part of the Constitution which inclines, in my judgment, to favor the construction I put upon it : the President is required to take care that the laws be faithfully executed. If the duty to see the laws faithfully executed be required at the hands of the executive magistrate, it would seem that it was generally intended he should have that species of power which is necessary to accomplish that end.

Now, if the officer, when once appointed, is not to depend upon the President for his official existence, but upon a distinct body, (for where there are two negatives required, either can prevent the removal,) I confess I do not see how the President can take care that the laws be faithfully executed. It is true, by a circuitous operation, he may obtain an impeachment, and even without this it is not impossible he may obtain the concurrence of the Senate, for the purpose of displacing an officer ; but would this give that species of control to the executive magistrate which seems to be required by the Constitution ? I own, if my opinion was not contrary to that entertained by what I suppose to be the minority on this question, I should be doubtful of being mistaken, when I discovered how inconsistent that construction would make the Constitution with itself. I can hardly bring myself to imagine, the wisdom of the Convention who framed the Constitution contemplated such incongruity.

There is another maxim which ought to direct us in expounding the Constitution, and is of great importance. It is laid down in most of the constitutions, or bills of rights, in the republics of America, — it is to be found in the political writings of the most celebrated civilians, and is every where held as essential to the preservation of liberty, — that the three great departments of government be kept separate and distinct; and if in any case they are blended, it is in order to admit a partial qualification, in order more effectually to guard against an entire consolidation. I think, therefore, when we review the several parts of this Constitution, — when it says that the legislative powers shall be vested in a Congress of the United States, under certain exceptions, and the executive power vested in the President, with certain exceptions, — we must suppose they were intended to be kept separate in all cases in which they are not blended, and ought, consequently, to expound the Constitution so as to blend them as little as possible.

Every thing relative to the merits of the question, as distinguished from a constitutional question, seems to turn on the danger of such a power vested in the President alone. But when I consider the checks under which he lies in the exercise of this power, I own to you I feel no apprehensions but what arise from the dangers incidental to the power itself; for dangers will be incidental to it, vest it where you please. I will not reiterate what was said before, with respect to the mode of election, and the extreme improbability that any citizen will be selected from the mass of citizens who is not highly distinguished by his abilities and worth : in this alone we have no small security for the faithful exercise of this power. But, throwing that out of the question, let us consider the restraints he will feel after he is placed in that elevated station. It is to be remarked that the power, in this case, will not consist so much in continuing a bad man in office as in the danger of displacing a good one. Perhaps the great danger, as has been observed, of abuse in the executive power, lies in the improper continuance of bad men in office. But the power we contend for will not enable him to do this; for if an unworthy man be continued in office by an unworthy President, the House of Representatives can at any time impeach him, and the Senate can remove him, whether the President chooses or not. The danger, then, consists merely in this — the President can displace from office a man whose merits require that he should be continued in it. What will be the motives which the President can feel for such abuse of his power, and the restraints that operate to prevent it? In the first place, he will be impeachable by this house, before the Senate, for such an act of maladministration; for I contend that the wanton removal of meritorious officers would subject him to impeachment and removal from his own high trust. But what can be his motives for displacing a worthy man? It must be, that he may fill the place with an unworthy creature of his own. Can he accomplish this end? No: he can place no man in the vacancy whom the Senate shall not approve; and if he could fill the vacancy with the man he might choose, I am sure he would have little inducement to make an improper removal.

Let us consider the consequences. The injured man will be supported by the popular opinion; the community will take sides with him against the President; it will facilitate those combinations, and give success to those exertions which will be pursued to prevent his reëlection. To displace a man of high merit, and who, from his station, may be supposed a man of extensive influence, are considerations which will excite serious reflections beforehand in the mind of any man who may fill the presiden tial chair: the friends of those individuals, and the public sympathy, wi. be against him. If this should not produce his impeachment before the Senate, it will amount to an impeachment before the community, who will have the power of punishment by refusing to reëlect him. But suppose this persecuted individual cannot obtain revenge in this mode : there are other modes in which he could make the situation of the President very inconvenient, if you suppose him resolutely bent on executing the dictates of resentment. If he had not influence enough to direct the vengeance of the whole community, he may probably be able to obtain an appoint- ment in one or other branch of the legislature ; and, being a man of weight, talents, and influence, in either case he may prove to the President trouble- some indeed. We have seen examples, in the history of other nations, which justify the remark I now have made : though the prerogatives of the British king are as great as his rank, and it is unquestionably known that he has a positive influence over both branches of the legislative body, yet there have been examples in which the appointment and removal of ministers has been found to be dictated by one or other of those branches. Now, if this is the case with an hereditary monarch, possessed of those high prerogatives, and furnished with so many means of influence, can we suppose a President, elected for four years only, dependent upon the pop- ular voice, impeachable by the legislature, little if at all distinguished, for wealth, personal talents, or influence, from the head of the department himself; — I say, will he bid defiance to all these considerations, and wantonly dismiss a meritorious and virtuous officer ? Such abuse of power exceeds my conception. If any thing takes place in the ordinary course of business of this kind, my imagination cannot extend to it on any rational principle.

But let us not consider the question on one side only : there are dan- gers to be contemplated on the other. Vest the power in the Senate jointly with the President, and you abolish at once the great principle of unity and responsibility in the executive department, which was intended for the security of liberty and the public good. If the President should possess alone the power of removal from office, those who are employed in the execution of the law will be in their proper situation, and the chain of dependence be preserved; the lowest officer, the middle grade, and the highest, will depend, as they ought, on the President, and the President on the community. The chain of dependence, therefore, terminates in the supreme body, namely, in the people ; who will possess besides, in aid of their original power, the decisive engine of impeachment. Take the other supposition — that the power should be vested in the Senate, on the principle that the power to displace is necessarily connected with the power to appoint. It is declared by the Constitution, that we may by law vest the appointment of inferior officers in the heads of departments, the power of removal being incidental, as stated by some gentlemen. Where does this terminate? If you begin with the subordinate officers, they are dependent on their superior, he on the next superior, and he, on whom ? — on the Senate, a permanent body, by its peculiar mode of election, in reality existing forever — a body possessing that proportion of aristocratic power which the Constitution no doubt thought wise to be established in the system, but which some have strongly excepted against. And, let me ask, gentlemen, is there equal security in this case as in the other ? Shall we trust the Senate, responsible to individual legislatures, rather than the person who is responsible to the whole community? It is true, the Senate do not hold their offices for life, like aristocracies recorded in the historic page; yet the fact is, they will not possess that responsibility for the exercise of executive powers which would render it safe for us to vest such powers in them. What an aspect will this give to the executive! Instead of keeping the departments of government distinct, you make an executive out of one branch of the legislature; you make the executive a two-headed monster, to use the expression of the gentleman from New Hampshire, (Mr. Livermore;) you destroy the great principle of responsibility, and perhaps have the creature divided in its will, defeating the very purposes for which a unity in the executive was instituted.

These objections do not lie against such an arrangement as the, bill establishes. I conceive that the President is sufficiently accountable to the community; and if this power is vested in him, it will be vested where its nature requires it should be vested : if any thing in its nature is executive, it must be that power which is employed in superintending, and seeing that the laws are faithfully executed ; the laws cannot be executed but by officers appointed for that purpose; therefore, those who are over such officers naturally possess the executive power. If any other doctrine be admitted, what is the consequence? You may set the Senate at the head of the executive department, or you may require that the officers hold their places during the pleasure of this branch of the legislature, if you cannot go so far as to say we shall appoint them; and by this means you link together two branches of the government which the preservation of liberty requires to be constantly separated.

Another species of argument has been urged against this clause. It is said that it is improper, or at least unnecessary, to come to any decision on this subject. It has been said by one gentleman that it would be officious in this branch of the legislature to expound the Constitution, so far as it relates to the division of power between the President and the Senate. It is incontrovertibly of as much importance to this branch of the government as to any other, that the Constitution be preserved entire. It is *our duty*, so far as it depends upon us, to take care that the powers of the Constitution be preserved entire to every department of government. The breach of the Constitution in one point will facilitate the breach in another : a breach in this point may destroy the equilibrium by which the house retains its consequence and share of power ; therefore we are not chargeable with an officious interference. Besides, the bill, before it can have effect, must be submitted to both those branches who are particularly interested in it ; the Senate may negative, or the President may object, if he thinks it unconstitutional.

But the great objection, drawn from the source to which the last arguments would lead us, is, that the legislature itself has no right to expound the Constitution; that wherever its meaning is doubtful, you must leave it to take its course, until the judiciary is called upon to declare its meaning. I acknowledge, in the ordinary course of government, that the exposition of the laws and Constitution devolves upon the judicial ; but I beg to know upon what principle it can be contended that any one department draws from the Constitution greater powers than another, in marking out the limits of the powers of the several departments. The Constitution is the charter of the people in the government ; it specifies certain great powers as absolutely granted, and marks out the departments to exercise them. If the constitutional boundary of either be brought into question, I do not see that any one of these independent departments has more right than another to declare their sentiments on that point.

Perhaps this is an admitted case.   There is not one government on the face of the earth, so far as I recollect — there is not one in the United States — in which provision is made for a particular authority to determine the limits of the constitutional division of power between the branches of the government.   In all systems, there are points which must be adjusted by the departments themselves, to which no one of them is competent.   If it cannot be determined in this way, there is no resource left but the will of the community, to be collected in some mode to be provided by the Constitution, or one dictated by the necessity of the case.   It is, therefore, a fair question, whether this great point may not as well be decided, at least by the whole legislature, as by part — by us, as well as by the executive or the judicial.   As I think it will be equally constitutional, I cannot imagine it will be less safe, that the exposition should issue from the legislative authority, than any other; and the more so, because it involves in the decision the opinions of both those departments whose powers are supposed to be affected by it.   Besides, I do not see in what way this question could come before the judges to obtain a fair and solemn decision; but even if it were the case that it could, I should suppose, at least while the government is not led by passion, disturbed by faction, or deceived by any discolored medium of sight, but while there is a desire in all to see and be guided by the benignant ray of truth, that the decision may be made with the most advantage by the legislature itself.

My conclusion from these reflections is, that it will be constitutional to retain the clause; that it expresses the meaning of the Constitution as it must be established by fair construction — and a construction which, upon the whole, not only consists with liberty, but is more favorable to it than any one of the interpretations that have been proposed.

Mr. GERRY.   I am clearly of opinion, with the gentleman last up, that it is of importance to decide this question on its true principles; and am free to declare that I shall be as ready to oppose every innovation or encroachment upon the rights of the executive, as upon those of the legislative.   I conceive myself bound to do this, not only by oath, but by an obligation equally strong — I mean the obligation of honor.

I wish, sir, to consider this question so far as to ascertain whether it is or is not unconstitutional.   I have listened with attention to the arguments which have been urged on both sides; and it does appear to me that the clause is as inconsistent with the Constitution as any set of words which could possibly be inserted in the bill.

.   There are two questions relative to this clause — the first, whether the sovereignty of the Union has delegated to the government the power of removal; and the second, to whom?   That they have delegated such power has been clearly proved by the gentlemen who advocate the clause — who justly say, if the power is not delegated, the clause in the Constitution, declaring the appointment of judges to be during good behavior, would be nugatory, unless some branch of government could otherwise have removed them from office.   As to the second question, it depends upon the first: if the power is delegated, it must vest in some part of the government.   The gentlemen will agree that this house has not the power of removal; they will also agree that it does not vest in the judicial: then it must vest in the President, or the President by and with the advice and consent of the Senate.   In either of these cases, the clause is altogether useless and nugatory.   It is useless if the power vests in the President; because, when the question comes before him, he will decide upon the provision made in the Constitution, and not on what is contained in this clause.   If the power er vests in the President and Senate, the Senate will not consent to pass the bill with this clause in it; therefore the attempt is nugatory: but if the Senate will assent to the exercise of the power of removal by the President alone, whenever he thinks proper to use it so, then, in that case, the clause is, as I said before, both useless and nugatory.

The second question which I proposed to examine is, to whom the power of removal is committed.   The gentlemen in favor of this clause have not shown that, if the construction that the power vests in the President and Senate is admitted, it will be an improper construction.   I call on gentlemen to point out the impropriety, if they discover any.   To me it appears to preserve the unity of the several clauses of the Constitution; while their construction produces a clashing of powers, and renders of none effect some powers the Senate by express grants possess.   What becomes of their power of appointing, when the President can remove at discretion?   Their power of judging is rendered vain by the President's dismission, for the power of judging implies the power of dismissing, which will be totally insignificant in its operation, if the President can immediately dismiss an officer whom they have judged and declared innocent.

It is said that the President will be subject to an impeachment for dismissing a good man.   This, in my mind, involves an absurdity.   How can the house impeach the President for doing an act which the legislature has submitted to his discretion?

But what consequence may result from giving the President the absolute control over all officers?   Among the rest, I presume he is to have an unlimited control over the officers of the treasury.   I think, if this is the case, you may as well give him at once the appropriation of the revenue; for of what use is it to make laws on this head, when the President, by looking at the officer, can make it his interest to break them?   We may expect to see institutions arising under the control of the revenue, and not of the law.

Little, then, will it answer to say that we can impeach the President, when he can cover all his crimes by an application of the revenue to those who are to try him.   This application would certainly be made in case of a corrupt President.   And it is against corruption in him that we must endeavor to guard.   Not that we fear any thing from the virtuous character who now fills the executive chair; he is perhaps to be safer trusted with such a power than any man on earth; but it is to secure us against those who may hereafter obtrude themselves into power.

But if we give the President the power to remove, (though I contend, if the Constitution has not given it him, there is no power on earth that can, — except the people, by an alteration of the Constitution, — though I will suppose it for argument's sake,) you virtually give him a considerable power over the appointment, independent of the Senate; for if the Senate should reject his first nomination, which will probably be his favorite, he must continue to nominate till the Senate concur: then, immediately after the recess of the Senate, he may remove the officer, and introduce his own creature, as he has this power expressly by the Constitution.   The influence created by this circumstance would prevent his removal from an office which he held by a temporary appointment from his patron.

This has been supposed by some gentlemen to be an omitted case, and that Congress have the power of supplying the defect. Let gentlemen consider the ground on which they tread. If it is an omitted case, an attempt in the legislature to supply the defect will be, in fact, an attempt to amend the Constitution. But this can only be done in the way pointed out by the fifth article of that instrument; and an attempt to amend it in any other way may be a high crime or misdemeanor, or perhaps something worse. From this view of our situation, gentlemen may perhaps be led to consent to strike out the clause.

In Great Britain there are three estates — King, Lords, and Commons. Neither of these can be represented by the other; but they conjointly can form constructions upon the rights of the people, which have been obtained, sword in hand, from the crown. These, with the legislative acts, form the British constitution; and if there is an omitted case, Parliament has a right to make provision for it. But this is not the case in America, consisting of a single estate. The people have expressly granted certain powers to Congress, and they alone had the right to form the Constitution. In doing so, they directed a particular mode of making amendments, which we are not at liberty to depart from.

The system, it cannot be denied, is in many parts obscure. If Congress are to explain and declare what it shall be, they certainly will have it in their power to make it what they please. It has been a strong objection to the Constitution, that it was remarkably obscure; nay, some have gone so far as to assert that it was studiously obscure — that it might be applied to every purpose by Congress. By this very act, the house are assuming a power to alter the Constitution. The people of America can never be safe, if Congress have a right to exercise the power of giving constructions to the Constitution different from the original instrument. Such a power would render the most important clause in the Constitution nugatory; and one without which, I will be bold to say, this system of government never would have been ratified. If the people were to find that Congress meant to alter it in this way, they would revolt at the idea: it would be repugnant to the principles of the revolution, and to the feelings of every freeman in the United States.

It is said that the power to advise the President in appointing officers is an exception to a general rule. To what general rule? That the President, being an executive officer, has the right of appointing. From whence is this general rule drawn? Not from the Constitution, nor from custom, because the state governments are generally against it. Before the gentleman had reasoned from this general rule, he ought to have demonstrated that it was one. He ought to have shown that the President, *ex officio*, had the power to appoint and remove from office; that it was necessarily vested in the executive branch of the government.

It is said to be the duty of the President to see the laws faithfully executed, and he could not discharge this trust without the power of removal. I ask the gentleman if the power of suspension, which we are willing to give, is not sufficient for that purpose? In case the Senate should not be sitting, the officer could be suspended; and at their next session the causes which require his removal might be inquired into.

It is said to be incumbent on us to keep the departments distinct. I agree to this; but, then, I ask, what department is the Senate of, when it exercises its power of appointment or removal? If legislative, it shows that the power of appointment is not an executive power; but if it exercises the power as an executive branch of government, there is no mixing of the departments; and therefore the gentleman's objections fall to the ground.

The dangers which lie against investing this power jointly in the Senate and President, have been pointed out; but I think them more than counterbalanced by the dangers arising from investing it in the President alone. It was said that the community would take part with the injured officer against the President, and prevent his reëlection. I admit that the injured officer may be a man of influence and talents; yet it is fifty to one against him, when he is opposed by such a powerful antagonist. It is said that, if the Senate should have this power, the government would contain a two-headed monster; but it appears to me, that if it consists in blending the power of making treaties and appointing officers, — as executive officers, with their legislative powers, the Senate is already a two-headed monster. If it is a two-headed monster, let us preserve it a consistent one; for surely it will be a very inconsistent monster, while it has the power of appointing, if you deprive it of the power of removing. It was said that the judges could not have the power of deciding on this subject, because the Constitution was silent; but I may ask if the judges are, *ex officio*, judges of the law; and whether they would not be bound to declare the law a nullity, if this clause is continued in it, and is inconsistent with the Constitution. There is a clause in this system of government that makes it their duty: I allude to that which authorizes the President to obtain the opinions of the heads of departments in writing; so the President and Senate may require the opinion of the judges respecting this power, if they have any doubts concerning it.

View the matter in any point of light, and it is utterly impossible to admit this clause. It is both useless and unnecessary; it is inconsistent with the Constitution, and is an officious interference of the house in a business which does not properly come before them. We expose ourselves to most dangerous innovations by future legislatures, which may finally overturn the Constitution itself.

Mr. BENSON. I will not repeat what has been said to prove that the true construction is, that the President alone has the power of removal, but will state a case to show the embarrassment which must arise by a combination of the senatorial and legislative authority in this particular. I will instance the officer to which the bill relates. To him will necessarily be committed negotiations with the ministers of foreign courts. This is a very delicate trust. The supreme executive officer, in superintending this department, may be entangled with suspicions of a very delicate nature, relative to the transactions of the officer, and such as, from circumstances, would be injurious to name: indeed, he may be so situated, that he will not, cannot, give the evidence of his suspicion. Now, thus circumstanced. suppose he should propose to the Senate to remove the secretary of foreign affairs: are we to expect the Senate will, without any reason being assigned, implicitly submit to his proposition? They will not.

Suppose he should say he suspected the man's fidelity: they would say, "We must proceed farther, and know the reasons for this suspicion;" they would insist on a full communication. Is it to be supposed that this man will not have a single friend in the Senate who will contend for a fair trial and full hearing? The President, then, becomes the plaintiff, and the secretary the defendant. The Senate are sitting in judgment between the chief magistrate of the United States and a subordinate officer. Now, I submit to the candor of the gentlemen, whether this looks like good government.

Yet, in every instance when the President thinks proper to have an officer removed, this absurd scene must be displayed. How much better, even on principles of expediency, will it be that the President alone have the power of removal!

But suppose the Senate to be joined with the President in the exercise of the power of removal; what mode will they proceed in? Shall the President always propose the removal, or shall the Senate undertake this part of the business? If so, how are they to act? There is no part of the Constitution which obliges the President to meet them, to state his reasons for any measure he may recommend. Are they to wait upon the President? In short, it appears to me that introducing this clashing of the powers, which the Constitution has given to the executive, will be destructive of the great end of the government. So far will restraining the powers of that department be from producing security to the liberties of the people, that they would inevitably be swallowed up by an aristocratic body.

Mr. SEDGWICK. It will be agreed, on all hands, that this officer, without observing on the subject at large, is merely to supply a natural incompetency in man: in other words, if we could find a President capable of executing this and all other business assigned him, it would be unnecessary to introduce any other officer to aid him. It is then merely from necessity that we institute such an office; because all the duties detailed in the bill are, by the Constitution, pertaining to the department of the executive magistrate. If the question respected the expediency, I should be content to advocate it on that ground, if expediency is at all to be considered. Gentlemen will perceive that this man is as much an instrument, in the hands of the President, as the pen is the instrument of the secretary in corresponding with foreign courts. If, then, the secretary of foreign affairs is the mere instrument of the President, one would suppose, on the principle of expediency, this officer should be dependent upon him. It would seem incongruous and absurd, that an officer who, in the reason and nature of things, was dependent on his principal, and appointed merely to execute such business as was committed to the charge of his superior, (for this business, I contend, is committed solely to his charge,) — I say it would be absurd, in the highest degree, to continue such a person in office contrary to the will of the President, who is responsible that the business be conducted with propriety, and for the general interest of the nation. The President is made responsible, and shall he not judge of the talents, abilities, and integrity of his instruments?

Will you depend on a man who has imposed upon the President, and continue him in office when he is evidently disqualified, unless he can be removed by impeachment? If this idea should prevail, — which God forbid! — what would be the result? Suppose even that he should be removable by and with the advice and consent of the Senate; what a wretched situation might not our public councils be involved in! Suppose the President has a secretary in whom he discovers a great degree of ignorance, or a total incapacity to conduct the business he has assigned him; suppose him inimical to the President; or suppose any of the great variety of cases which would be good cause for removal, and impress the propriety of such a measure strongly on the mind of the President, without any other evidence than what exists in his own ideas from a contemplation of the man's conduct and character day by day; what, let me ask, is to be the consequence if the Senate are to be applied to? If they are to do any thing in this business, I presume they are to deliberate, because they are to advise and consent; if they are to deliberate, you put them between the officer and the President; they are then to inquire into the causes of removal; the President must produce his testimony. How is the question to be investigated? — because, I presume, there must be some rational rule for conducting this business.

Is the President to be sworn to declare the whole truth, and to bring forward facts? or are they to admit suspicion as testimony? or is the word of the President to be taken at all events? If so, this check is not of the least efficacy in nature. But if proof is necessary, what is then the consequence? Why, in nine cases out of ten, where the case is very clear to the mind of the President that the man ought to be removed, the effect cannot be produced; because it is absolutely impossible to produce the necessary evidence. Are the Senate to proceed without evidence? Some gentlemen contend not; then the object will be lost. Shall a man, under these circumstances, be saddled upon the President, who has been appointed for no other purpose, in the creation, but to aid the President in performing certain duties? Shall he be continued, I ask again, against the will of the President? If he is, where is the responsibility? Are you to look for it in the President, who has no control over the officer, no power to remove him if he acts unfeelingly or unfaithfully? Without you make him responsible, you weaken and destroy the strength and beauty of your system. What is to be done in cases which can only be known from a long acquaintance with the conduct of an officer? But so much has been said on this subject, that I will add no further observations upon it.

Let me ask, what will be the consequence of striking out these words? Is the officer to be continued during an indefinite time? for it has been contended that he cannot be removed but by impeachment. Others have contended that he is always in the power of them who appoint him. But who will undertake to remove him? Will the President undertake to exercise an authority which has been so much doubted here, and which will appear to be determined against him if we consent to strike out the words? Will the Senate undertake to exercise this power? I apprehend they will not. But if they should, would they not also be brought before the judges, to show by what authority they did it? because it is supposed by one gentleman, that the case might go before that tribunal, if the President alone removed the officer. But how is this to be done? Gentlemen tell you, the man who is displaced must apply for a *mandamus* to admit him to his office. I doubt much if this would be adequate to the purpose. It would be difficult to say whether the *mandamus* should be directed to the President, to the President and Senate, to the legislature, or to the people. Could the President be compelled to answer to a civil suit, for exercising the power vested in him by law and by the Constitution? The question upon either of those points would be involved in doubts and difficulties.

If these observations strike the committee in the same point of light, and with the same force, as they have struck my mind, they will proceed to determine the present question; and I have no doubt but they will determine right.

Mr. LEE. I contend we have the power to modify the establishment of offices. So ought we, Mr. Chairman, to modify them in such a way as to promote the general welfare, which can only be done by keeping the three branches distinct; by informing the people where to look, in order to guard against improper executive acts. It is our duty, therefore, to vest all executive power, belonging to the government, where the Convention intended it should be placed.   It adds to the responsibility of the most responsible branch of the government; and without responsibility, we should have little security against the depred itions and gigantic strides of arbitrary power.   I say it is necessary, sir, to hold up a single and specific object to the public jealousy to watch ; therefore it is necessary to connect the power of removal with the President.   The executive is the source of all appointments : is his responsibility complete unless he has the power of removal ?   If he has this power, it will be his fault if any wicked or mischievous act is committed ; and he will hardly expose himself to the resentment of three millions of people, of whom he holds his power, and to whom he is accountable every four years.

If the power of removal is vested in the Senate, it is evident, at a single view, that the responsibility is dissipated, because the fault cannot be fixed on any individual : besides, the members of the Senate are not accountable to the people ; they are the representatives of the state legislatures ; but even if they were, they have no powers to enable them to decide with propriety in the case of removals, and therefore are improper persons to exercise such authority.

Mr. BOUDINOT.   Sir, the efficacy of your government may depend upon the determination of this house respecting the present question.   For my part, I shall certainly attend to the terms of the Constitution in making a decision ; indeed, I never wish to see them departed from or construed, if the government can possibly be carried into effect in any other manner. But I d > not agree with the gentleman, that Congress have no right to modify principles established by the Constitution ; for, if this doctrine be true, we have no bus ness here.   Can the Constitution be executed, if its principles are not modified by the legislature ?   A Supreme Court is established by the Constitution ; but do gentlemen contend that we cannot modify that court, direct the manner in which its functions shall be performed, and assign and limit its jurisdiction ?   I conceive, notwithstanding the ingenious arguments of the gentleman from Virginia, (Mr. White,) and the ingenious arguments of the gentleman from South Carolina, (Mr Smith,) that there has not been, nor can be, any solid reason adduced to prove that this house has not power to modify the principles of the Constitution.   But is the principle now in dispute to be found in the Constitution ?   If it is to be found there, it will serve as a line to direct the modification by Congress.   But we are told that the members of this house appear to be afraid to carry the principles of the Constitution into effect.   I believe, sir, we were not sent here to carry into effect every principle of the Constitution ; but I hope, whenever we are convinced it is for the benefit of the United States to carry any of them into effect, we shall not hesitate.

The principle of the Constitution is, generally, to vest the government in three branches.   I conceive this to be completely done, if we allow for one or two instances, where the executive and legislative powers are intermixed, and the case of impeachment.   These cases I take to be exceptions to a principle which is highly esteemed in America.   Let gentlemen attend to what was said by some of the conventions when they ratified the Constitution.   One great objection was, that the powers were not totally separated.   The same objection is, I believe, to be found among the amendments proposed by the state of North Carolina.   Now, I conceive. if we do any thing to conciliate the minds of people to the Constitution, we ought not to modify the principle of the government so as to increase the evil complained of, by a further blending of the executive and legislative powers, and that too upon construction, when gentlemen deny that we ought to use construction in any case.

Now, let us take up the Constitution, and consider, from the terms and principles of it, in whom this power is vested. It is said by some gentlemen to be an omitted case. I shall take up the other principle, which is easier to be maintained, — that it is not an omitted case, — and say the power of removal is vested in the President. I shall also take up the principle laid down by the gentleman from Virginia, (Mr. White,) at the beginning of this argument, that, agreeably to the nature of all executive powers, it is right and proper that the person who appoints should remove. This leads me to consider in whom the appointment is vested by the Constitution. The President nominates and appoints: he is further expressly authorized to commission all officers. Now, does it appear, from this distribution of power, that the Senate appoints? Does an officer exercise powers by authority of the Senate? No. I believe the President is the person from whom he derives his authority. He appoints, but under a check. It is necessary to obtain the consent of the Senate; but after that is obtained, I ask, who appoints? who vests the officer with authority? who commissions him? The President does these acts by his sole power; but they are exercised in consequence of the advice of another branch of government. If, therefore, the officer receives his authority and commission from the President, surely the removal follows as co-incident.

Now, let us examine whether this construction consists with the true interest of the United States and the general principles of the Constitution. It consists with the general principles of the Constitution, because the executive power is given to the President, and it is by reason of his incapacity that we are called upon to appoint assistants. Mention, to be sure, is made of principal officers in departments; out it is from construction only that we derive our power to constitute this particular office. If we were not at liberty to modify the principles of the Constitution, I do not see how we could erect an office of foreign affairs. If we establish an office avowedly to aid the President, we leave the conduct of it to his discretion. Hence the whole executive is to be left with him, agreeably to this maxim — All executive power shall be vested in a President. But how does this comport with the true interest of the United States? Let me ask gentlemen where they suspect danger. Is it not made expressly the duty of the secretary of foreign affairs to obey such orders as shall be given to him by the President? And would you keep in office a man who should refuse or neglect to do the duties assigned him? Is not the President responsible for the administration? He certainly is. How, then, can the public interest suffer?

Then, if we find it to be naturally inferred, from the principles of the Constitution, coincident with the nature of his duty, that this officer should be dependent upon him, and to the benefit of the United States, for what purpose shall Congress refuse a legislative declaration of the Constitution, and leave it to remain a doubtful point? Because, if Congress refuses to determine, we cannot conceive that others will be more entitled to decide upon it than we are. This will appear to give ground for what the gentlemen have asserted — that we are afraid to carry the Constitution into effect. This, I apprehend, would not be doing our duty.

Gentlemen say they have a sufficient remedy for every evil likely to re
sult from connecting the Senate with the President.   This they propose to
do by allowing the power of suspension.   This, in the first place, does not
answer the end ; because there is a possibility that the officer may not be
displaced after a hearing before the Senate; and in the second place, it
is entirely inconsistent with the whole course of reasoning pursued by the
gentlemen in opposition.   I would ask them, if the Constitution does not
give to the President the power of removal, what part is it that gives the
power of suspension ?   If you will in one case construe the Constitution,
you may do it in another; for I look upon it as dangerous to give the power
of suspension, by implication, as to give the full power of removal.   Gentlemen, observe that I take it for granted that the President has no express
right to the power of suspension; and that, if he is to exercise it, it must
be drawn, by constructive reasoning alone, from the Constitution.   If we
are to exercise our authority, we had better at once give a power that
would answer two valuable purposes, than one altogether nugatory.   In
the first place, it would entirely separate the legislative and executive departments, conformably to the great principles of the Constitution ; and,
in the second place, it would answer the end of government better, and
secure real benefits to the Union.

The great evil, as was stated by the gentleman from Virginia, (Mr.
Madison,) yesterday, is, that bad officers shall continue in office, and not
that good ones be removed ; yet this last is all that is in the power of the
President.   If he removes a good officer, he cannot appoint his successor
without the consent of the Senate ; and it is fairly to be presumed, that,
if at any time he should be guilty of such an oversight as to remove a
useful and valuable officer, the evil will be small, because another as valuable will be placed in his stead.   If it is said that this is an injury to the
individual, I confess that it is possible that it may be so.   But ought we
not, in the first place, to consult the public good ?   But, on mature consideration, I do not apprehend any very great injury will result to the
individual from this practice ; because, when he accepts of the office, he
knows the tenure by which he is to hold it, and ought to be prepared
against every contingency.

These being the principles on which I have formed my opinion, in
addition to what was stated, I do conceive that I am perfectly justified to
my constituents, and to my oath, to support this construction.   And when
I give my vote that the President ought to have the power of removal from
office, I do it on principle ; and gentlemen in the opposition will leave us
to the operation of our judgments on this as well as every other question
that comes before us.   For my part, I conceive it is impossible to carry
into execution the powers of the President, in a salutary manner, unless he
has the power of removal vested in him.   I do not mean that, if it was not
vested in him by the Constitution, it would be proper for Congress to
confer it, though I do believe the government would otherwise be very
defective ; yet we would have to bear this inconvenience until it was rec-
tified by an amendment of the Constitution.

Mr. GERRY.   The Parliament of England is one of the most important bodies on earth; but they can do nothing without the concurrence of
the executive magistrate.   The Congress of the United States are likely
to become a more important body ; the executive magistrate has but a
qualified negative over them.   The Parliament of England, with the consent of the king, can expound their constitution ; in fact, they are the

constitu ion itself.   But Congress may, if once the doctrine of construction is established, make the Constitution what they please, and the President can have no control over them.

It has been said by my colleague, (Mr. Sedgwick,) that the President not only nominates, but appoints, the officers; and he infers from hence, that, as the power of removal is incidental to the power of appointing, the President has the power of removal also.   But I should be glad to know how it can with justice be said that the President appoints.   The Constitution requires the consent of the Senate; therefore they are two distinct bodies, and intended to check each other.   If my colleague's is a true construction, it may be extended farther, and said, that, in the act of nominating, the assent of the Senate is virtually given, and therefore he has a right to make the whole appointment himself, without any interference on the part of the Senate.   I contend, sir, that there is just as much propriety in the one construction as in the other.   If we observe the enacting style of the statutes of Great Britain, we shall find pretty near the same words as what are used in the Constitution with respect to appointments : — " Be it enacted by the king's most excellent majesty, by and with the advice and consent of Parliament."   Here it might be said the king enacts all laws; but I believe the truth of this fact will be disputed in that country. I believe no one will pretend to say that the king is the three branches of Parliament; and unless my colleague will do all this, I never can admit that the President, in himself, has the power of appointment.

My colleague has gone farther, to show the dependence of this officer on the President.   He says the necessity of appointing a secretary of foreign affairs arises from a natural defect in man; that if the President was able to administer all these departments, there would be no occasion of making provision by law.   If the President had power superior to the limits of humanity, he might render his country great services; but we are not likely to have any such Presidents; the Constitution itself contemplates none; it makes provision for the infirmities of human nature; it authorizes us to establish offices by law; and this is the ground upon which we stand; indeed, this is the ground that was assumed yesterday by my colleague, when he said that this officer was the creature of the law. If he is the creature of the law, let him conduct according to law; and let it not be contended that he is the creature of the President, because he is no further the creature of the President than that he is obliged to give his opinion in writing when required.   But it is said the President is responsible for the conduct of this officer.   I wish to know what this responsibility is.   Does it mean, if a subordinate executive officer commits treason, that the President is to suffer for it?   This is a strange kind of responsibility.   Suppose, in the case of the secretary of the treasury, there should be a defalcation of the public revenue; is he to make good the loss?   Or, if the head of the army should betray his trust, and sacrifice the liberties of his country, is the President's head to be the devoted sacrifice?   The Constitution shows the contrary, by the provision made for impeachment; and this I take to be one of the strongest arguments against the President's having the power of removing one of the principal officers of government — that he is to bear his own responsibility.

The question before the committee must be decided on one of these two grounds.   Either they must suppose this power is delegated particularly to the President by the Constitution, or it is not.   Let us examine these two cases.   If gentleman say that it is delegated by the Constitution, then there is no use for the clause : but if it is not particularly delegated to the President by the Constitution, and we are inclined to authorize him to exercise this power, I would ask gentlemen whether this is the proper way to do it ; whether a little clause hid in the body of a bill can be called a declaratory act. I think it cannot. It looks as if we were afraid of avowing our intentions. If we are determined upon making a declaratory act, let us do it in such a manner as to indicate our intention. But perhaps gentlemen may think we have no authority to make declaratory acts. They may be right in this opinion ; for though I have examined the Constitution with attention, I have not been able to discover any clause which vests Congress with that power. But if the power of making declaratory acts really vests in Congress, and the judges are bound by our decisions, we may alter that part of the Constitution which is secured from being amended by the 5th article ; we may say, that the 9th section of the Constitution, respecting the migration or importation of persons, does not extend to negroes ; that the word *persons* means only white men and women. We then proceed to lay a duty of twenty or thirty dollars per head on the importation of negroes. The merchant does not construe the Constitution in the manner that we have done. He therefore institutes a suit, and brings it before the supreme judicature of the United States for trial. The judges, who are bound by oath to support the Constitution, declare against this law ; they would therefore give judgment in favor of the merchant.

But, say Congress, we are the constitutional expounders of this clause, and your decision in this case has been improper. Shall the judges, because Congress have usurped power, and made a law founded in construction, be impeached by one branch, and convicted by the other, for doing a meritorious act, and standing in opposition to their usurpation of power ? If this is the meaning of the Constitution, it was hardly worth while to have had so much bustle and uneasiness about it. I would ask gentlemen, if the Constitution has given us power to make declaratory acts, where is the necessity of inserting the 5th article for the purpose of obtaining amendments ? The word *amendment* implies a defect ; a declaratory act conceives one. Where, then, is the difference between an amendment and a declaratory act ? I call upon the gentleman to point out what part of the Constitution says we shall correct that instrument by a declaratory act. If gentlemen once break through the constitutional limits of their authority, they will find it very difficult to draw a boundary which will secure to themselves and their posterity that liberty which they have so well contended for.

Mr. SHERMAN. The Convention, who formed this Constitution, thought it would tend to secure the liberties of the people, if they prohibited the President from the sole appointment of all officers. They knew that the crown of Great Britain, by having that prerogative, has been enabled to swallow up the whole administration ; the influence of the crown upon the legislature subjects both houses to its will and pleasure. Perhaps it may be thought, by the people of that kingdom, that it is best for the executive magistrate to have such kind of influence ; if so, it is very well, and we have no right to complain that it is injurious to them, while they themselves consider it beneficial. But this government is different, and intended by the people to be different. I have not heard any gentleman produce an authority from law or history which proves, where two branches are interested in the appointment, that one of them has the power of removal. I remember that the gentleman from Massachusetts (Mr. Sedgwick) told us that the two houses, notwithstanding the partial negative of the President, possessed the whole legislative power; but will the gentleman infer from that, because the concurrence of both branches is necessary to pass a law, that a less authority can repeal it? This is all we contend for.

Some gentlemen suppose, if the President has not the power by the Constitution, we ought to vest it in him by law. For my part, I very much doubt if we have the power to do this. I take it we would be placing the heads of departments in a situation inferior to what the Constitution contemplates; but if we have the power, it will be better to exercise it than attempt to construe the Constitution. But it appears to me, that the best way will be to leave the Constitution to speak for itself whenever occasion demands.

It has been said, that the Senate are merely an advisory body. I am not of this opinion, because their consent is expressly required; if this is not obtained, an appointment cannot be made. Upon the whole, I look upon it as necessary, in order to preserve that security which the Constitution affords to the liberty of the people, that we avoid making this declaration, especially in favor of the President; as I do not believe the Constitution vests the authority in him alone.

Mr. AMES. I believe there are very few gentlemen on this floor who have not made up their opinions; therefore it is particularly disagreeable to solicit their attention, especially when their patience is already exhausted, and their curiosity sated; but still I hope to be of some use in collecting the various arguments, and bringing them to a point. I shall rather confine myself to this task, than attempt to offer any thing that is new. I shall just observe, that the arguments of the gentleman from Pennsylvania, (Mr. Scott,) which are complained of as being ridiculous, were arguments addressed to the understandings of the committee; my own understanding was enlightened by them, although they wore the garb of pleasantry. But to proceed to my main object.

The question, so far as it relates to the Constitution, is this — whether it has vested the sole power of removing in the President alone, or whether it is to take place by and with the advice and consent of the Senate. If the question of constitutionality was once despatched, we should be left to consider of the expediency of the measure. I take it to be admitted on all hands, though it was at first objected to by a worthy gentleman from South Carolina, that the power of removal from office, at pleasure, resides somewhere in the government. If it does not reside in the President, or the President and Senate, or if the Constitution has not vested it in any particular body, it must be in the legislature; for it is absurd to suppose that officers once appointed cannot be removed. The argument tending to prove that the power is in the President alone, by an express declaration, may not be satisfactory to the minds of those gentlemen who deem the Constitution to be silent on that head. But let those gentlemen revert to the principles, spirit, and tendency, of the Constitution, and they will be compelled to acknowledge that there is the highest degree of probability that the power does vest in the President of the United States. I shall not undertake to say that the arguments are conclusive on this point. I do not suppose it is necessary that they should be so; for I believe nearly as good conclusions may be drawn from the refutations of an argument as from any other proof; for it is well said, that *destructio unius est generatio alterius.*

It has been said, and addressed with solemnity to our consciences, that we ought not to destroy the Constitution, to change, or modify it; nay, it has been inferred that it is unnecessary and dangerous for us to proceed in this inquiry. It is true, we may decide wrong, and therefore there may be danger; but it is not unnecessary: we have entered too far into the discussion to retreat with honor to ourselves or security to our country: we are sworn as much to exercise constitutional authority, for the general good, as to refrain from assuming powers that are not given to us: we are as responsible for forbearing to act, as we are for acting. Are we to leave this question undetermined, to be contended between the President and Senate? Are we to say that the question to us is indissoluble, and therefore throw it upon the shoulders of the President to determine? If it is complex and difficult, it is certainly disingenuous in us to throw off the decision: besides, after so long a debate has been had, a decision must be made; for it never would do to strike out the words, as that would be deciding, and deciding against the power of the President.

It must be admitted that the Constitution is not explicit on the point in contest; yet the Constitution strongly infers that the power is in the President alone. It is declared that the executive power shall be vested in the President. Under these terms, all the powers properly belonging to the executive department of the government are given, and such only taken away as are expressly excepted. If the Constitution had stopped here, and the duties had not been defined, either the President had no powers at all, or he would acquire from that general expression all the powers properly belonging to the executive department. In the Constitution, the President is required to see the laws faithfully executed. He cannot do this without he has a control over officers appointed to aid him in the performance of his duty. Take this power out of his hands, and you virtually strip him of his authority; you virtually destroy his responsibility, the great security which this Constitution holds out to the people of America.

Gentlemen will say that, as the Constitution is not explicit, it must be matter of doubt where the power vests. If gentlemen's consciences will not let them agree with us, they ought to permit us to exercise the like liberty on our part. But they tell us we must meet them on the ground of accommodation, and give up a declaration that the power of removal is in the President, and they will acquiesce in declaring him to have the power of suspension; but they should recollect that, in so doing, we sacrifice the principles of the Constitution.

It has been frequently said, that the power of removing is incidental to the power of appointing: as the Constitution implies that all officers, except the judges, are appointed during pleasure, so the power of removal may, in all cases, be exercised. But suppose this general principle true; yet it is an arbitrary principle, I take it, and one that cannot be proved: if it was denied, it could not be established; and if it was established, it is still doubtful whether it would make for the adverse side of this question or not, because it is dubious whether the Senate do actually appoint or not. It is admitted that they may check and regulate the appointment by the President; but they can do nothing more; they are merely an advisory body, and do not secure any degree of responsibility, which is one great object of the present Constitution: they are not answerable for their secret advice; but if they were, the blame, divided among so many, would fall upon none.

Certainly this assumed principle is very often untrue; but if it is true, it is not favorable to the gentlemen's doctrine. The President, I contend, has expressly the power of nominating and appointing, though he must obtain the consent of the Senate. He is the agent: the Senate may prevent his acting, but cannot act themselves. It may be difficult to illustrate this point by examples which will exactly correspond: but suppose the case of an executor, to whom is devised lands, to be sold with the advice of a certain person, on certain conditions; the executor sells with the consent, and upon the conditions, required in the will: the conditions are broken; may the executor reënter for the breach of them? or has the person whom he was obliged to consult with in the sale any power to restrain him? The executor may remove the wrongful possessor from the land, though, perhaps, by the will, he may hold it in trust for another person's benefit. In this manner, the President may remove from office, though, when vacant, he cannot fill it without the advice of the Senate. We are told it is dangerous to adopt constructions; and that what is not expressly given is retained. Surely it is as improper in this way to confer power upon the Senate as upon the President; for if the power is not in the President solely by the Constitution, it never can be in the President and Senate by any grant of that instrument: any arguments, therefore, that tend to make the first doubtful, operate against the other, and make it absurd. If gentlemen, therefore, doubt with respect to the first point, they will certainly hesitate with respect to the other. If the Senate have not the power, — and it is proved that they have it not, by the arguments on both sides, — the power either vests with the President or the legislature. If it is in the disposal of the latter, and merely a matter of choice with us, clearly we ought not to bestow it on the Senate; for the doubt, whether the President is not already entitled to it, is an argument against placing it in other hands: besides, the exercise of it by the Senate would be inconvenient; they are not always sitting: it would be insecure, because they are not responsible: it would be subversive of the great principles of the Constitution, and destructive to liberty, because it tends to intermingle executive and legislative powers in one body of men, and this blending of powers ever forms a tyranny. The Senate are not to accuse offenders; they are to try them: they are not to give orders; but, on complaint, to judge of the breach of them. We are warned against betraying the liberties of our country: we are told that all powers tend to abuse: it is our duty, therefore, to keep them single and distinct. Where the executive swallows up the legislature, it becomes a despotism; where the legislature trenches upon the executive, it approaches towards despotism; and where they have less than is necessary, it approximates towards anarchy.

We should be careful, therefore, to preserve the limits of each authority, in the present question. As it respects the power of the people, it is but of little importance; it is not pretended that the people have reserved the power of removing bad officers. It is admitted, on all hands, that the government is possessed of such power; consequently, the people can neither lose nor gain power by it. We are the servants of the people; we are the watchmen; and we should be unfaithful, in both characters, if we should so administer the government as to destroy its great principles and most essential advantages. The question now among us is, which of these servants shall exercise a power already granted. Wise and virtuous as the Senate may be, such a power lodged in their hands will not only tend to abuse, but cannot tend to any thing else. Need I repeat the inconveniences which will result from vesting it in the Senate? No. I appeal to that maxim which has the sanction of experience, and is authorized by the decision of the wisest men : to prevent an abuse of power, it must be distributed into three branches, who must be made independent, to watch and check each other : the people are to watch them all. While these maxims are pursued, our liberties will be preserved. It was from neglecting or despising these maxims, the ancient commonwealths were destroyed. A voice issues from the tomb which covers their ruins, and proclaims to mankind the sacredness of the truths that are at this moment in controversy.

It is said that the Constitution has blended these powers which we advise to keep separate, and, therefore, we ought to follow in completing similar regulations ; but gentlemen ought to recollect, that has been an objection against the Constitution ; and if it is a well-founded one, we ought to endeavor, all that is in our power, to restrain the evil, rather than to increase it. But, perhaps, with the sole power of removal in the President, the check of the Senate in appointments may have a salutary tendency : in removing from office, their advice and consent are liable to all the objections that have been stated. It is very proper to guard the introduction of a man into office by every check that can properly be applied ; but after he is appointed, there can be no use in exercising a judgment upon events which have heretofore taken place. If the Senate are to possess the power of removal, they will be enabled to hold the person in office, let the circumstances be what they may, that point out the necessity or propriety of his removal ; it creates a permanent connection ; it will nurse faction ; it will promote intrigue to obtain protectors, and to shelter tools. Sir, it is infusing poison into the Constitution ; it is an impure and unchaste connection : there is ruin in it : it is tempting the Senate with forbidden fruit : it ought not to be possible for a branch of the legislature even to hope for a share of the executive power ; for they may be tempted to increase it, by a hope to share the exercise of it. People are seldom jealous of their own power ; and if the Senate become part of the executive, they will be very improper persons to watch that department : so far from being champions for liberty, they will become conspirators against it.

The executive department should ever be independent, and sufficiently energetic to defeat the attempts of either branch of the legislature to usurp its prerogative. But the proposed control of the Senate is setting that body above the President : it tends to establish an aristocracy. And at the moment we are endangering the principles of our free and excellent Constitution, gentlemen are undertaking to amuse the people with the sound of liberty. If their ideas should succeed, a principle of mortality will be infused into a government which the lovers of mankind have wished might last to the end of the world. With a mixture of the executive and legislative powers in one body, no government can long remain uncorrupt. With a corrupt executive, liberty may long retain a trembling existence. With a corrupt legislature, it is impossible : the vitals of the Constitution would be mortified, and death must follow in every step. A government thus formed would be the most formidable curse that could befall this country. Perhaps an enlightened people might timely foresee and correct the error ; but if a season was allowed for such a compound to grow and produce its natural fruit, it would either banish liberty, or the people would be driven to exercise their unalienable right, the right of uncivilized nature, and

34

destroy a monster whose voracious and capacious jaws could crush and swallow up themselves and their posterity.

The principles of this Constitution, while they are adhered to, will perpetuate that liberty which it is the honor of Americans to have well contended for. The clause in the bill is calculated to support those principles; and for this, if there was no other reason, I should be inclined to give it my support.

Mr. LIVERMORE. The decision of this question depends upon the construction of a short clause in the Constitution, in which is designated the power of the President. It is said he shall have power, by and with the advice and consent of the Senate, to make treaties, provided two thirds of the senators present concur. He shall nominate, and, by and with the advice and consent of the Senate, appoint ambassadors, other public ministers, and consuls, justices of the Supreme Court, and all other officers of the United States. Such strange constructions have been given to this advice and consent of the Senate, which, if agreed to, will make the whole Constitution nothing, or any thing, just as we please. If we can deprive the Senate of their powers in making treaties, and say, with truth, that they have no authority in the business, the legislature will become a dangerous branch of the government. So, in the case of appointing officers, if it can be truly said that these heads of departments are the servants of the President alone, we shall make the executive department a dangerous one.

I do not admit that any man has an estate in his office. I conceive all officers to be appointed during pleasure, except where the Constitution stipulates for a different tenure — unless, indeed, the law should create the office, or officer, for a term of years. After observing this, I must contend that the power of removal is incidental to the power of appointment. If it was the President alone that appointed, he alone could displace. If the President and Senate, by a joint agreement, appoint an officer, they alone have the power to supersede him; and however any gentleman may say he doubts, or does not understand, the force of this principle, yet to me it appears as clear and demonstrable as any principle of law or justice that I am acquainted with. There is another method to displace officers expressly pointed out by the Constitution; and this implies, in the clearest manner, that in all other cases officers may be removed at pleasure; and if removed at pleasure, it must be at the pleasure of the parties who appointed them.

Congress are enabled, by the Constitution, to establish offices by law. In many cases they will, no doubt, vest the power of appointing inferior officers in the President alone. They have no express right, by the Constitution, to vest in him the power of removing these at pleasure; yet no gentleman will contend but inferior officers ought to be removable at pleasure. How, then, can the President acquire this authority, unless it be on the principle that the power of removal is incidental, and the natural consequence of the power of appointing. If gentlemen will maintain consistency, they will be compelled to acknowledge the force of this principle and if they acknowledge the principle, they must agree to strike out the words.

Mr. MADISON The question now seems to be brought to this — whether it is proper or improper to retain these words in the clause, provided they are explanatory of the Constitution. I think this branch of the legislature is as much interested in the establishment of the true meaning of the Constitution, as either the President or Senate; and when the Constitution submits it to us to establish offices by law, we ought to know by what tenure the office should be held, and whether it should depend upon the concurrence of the Senate with the President, or upon the will of the President alone, because gentlemen may hesitate, in either case, whether they will make it for an indefinite or precise time. If the officer can be removed at discretion by the President, there may be safety in letting it be for an indefinite period. If he cannot exert his prerogative, there is no security, even by the mode of impeachment; because the officer may intrench himself behind the authority of the Senate, and bid defiance to every other department of government. In this case, the question of duration would take a different turn. Hence it is highly proper that we and our constituents should know the tenure of the office. And have we not as good a right as any branch of the government to declare our sense of the meaning of the Constitution?

Nothing has yet been offered to invalidate the doctrine, that the meaning of the Constitution may as well be ascertained by the legislative as by the judicial authority. When a question emerges, as it does in this bill, — and much seems to depend upon it, — I should conceive it highly proper to make a legislative construction. In another point of view, it is proper that this interpretation should now take place, rather than at a time when the exigency of the case may require the exercise of the power of removal. At present, the disposition of every gentleman is to seek the truth, and abide by its guidance when it is discovered. I have reason to believe the same disposition prevails in the Senate. But will this be the case when some individual officer of high rank draws into question the capacity of the President, with the Senate, to effect his removal? If we leave the Constitution to take this course, it can never be expounded until the President shall think it expedient to exercise the right of removal, if he supposes he has it. Then the Senate may be induced to set up their pretensions; and will they decide so calmly as at this time, when no important officer in any of the great departments is appointed to influence their judgments? The imagination of no member here, or of the Senate, or of the President himself, is heated or disturbed by faction. If ever a proper moment for decision should offer, it must be one like the present.

I do not conceive that this question has been truly stated by some gentlemen. In my opinion, it is not whether we shall take the power from one branch of the government, and give it to another; but the question is, to which branch has the Constitution given it? Some gentlemen have said that it resides in the people at large, and that, if it is necessary to the government, we must apply to the people for it, and obtain it by way of amendment to the Constitution. Some gentlemen contend, that although it is given in the Constitution as a necessary power to carry into execution the other powers vested by the Constitution, yet it is vested in the legislature. I cannot admit this doctrine either, because it is setting the legislature at the head of the executive branch of the government. If we take the other construction, of the gentleman from South Carolina, that all officers hold their places by the firm tenure of good behavior, we shall find it still more improper. I think gentlemen will see, upon reflection, that this doctrine is incompatible with the principles of free government. If there is no removability but by way of impeachment, then all the executive officers of government hold their offices by the firm tenure of good behavior, from the chief justice down to the tide-waiter.

[Mr. SMITH interrupted Mr. Madison, and said, that he had admitted that inferior officers might be removed, because the Constitution had left it in the power of the legislature to establish them on what terms they pleased; consequently, to direct their appointment and removal]

Mr. MADISON had understood the gentleman as he now explained himself. But still he contended that the consequences he had drawn would necessarily follow; because there was no express authority given to the legislature, in the Constitution, to enable the President, the courts of law, or heads of departments, to remove an inferior officer. All that was said on that head was confined solely to the power of appointing them. If the gentleman admits, says he, that the legislature may vest the power of removal, with respect to inferior officers, he must also admit that the Constitution vests the President with the power of removal in the case of superior officers, because both powers are implied in the same words; the President may appoint the one class, and the legislature may authorize the courts of law or heads of departments to appoint in the other case. If, then, it is admitted that the power of removal vests in the President, or President and Senate, the arguments which I urged yesterday, and those which have been urged by honorable gentlemen on this side of the question for these three days past, will fully evince the truth of the construction which we give, — that the power is in the President alone. I will not repeat them, because they must have full possession of every gentleman's mind. I am willing, therefore, to rest the decision here, and hope that it will be made in such a manner as to perpetuate the blessings which this Constitution was intended to embrace.

Mr. BALDWIN. I have felt an unusual anxiety during the debate upon this question. I have attentively listened to the arguments which have been brought forward, and have weighed them in my mind with great deliberation; and as I consider a proper decision upon it of almost infinite importance to the government, I must beg the indulgence of the house while I submit a few observations.

The main ground on which the question is made to rest is, that if we adopt this clause, we violate the Constitution. Many of the gentlemen who advocate the present motion for striking out, would, if they could do it with consistency to the Constitution, be in favor of the clause. We have been reminded of our oaths, and warned not to violate the solemn obligation. This injunction has come from so many parts of the house, that it arrested my whole attention for a few minutes; and then they produced us the clause in the Constitution which directed that officers should be appointed by and with the advice and consent of the Senate. They then tell us that he should be removable in the same manner. We see the clause by which it is directed that they should be appointed in that manner, but we do not see the clause respecting their removal in the same way. Gentlemen have only drawn it as an inference from the former: they construe that to be the meaning of the Constitution, as we construe the reverse. I hope, therefore, gentlemen will change their expression, and say, we shall violate their construction of the Constitution, and not the Constitution itself. This will be a very different charge! unless the gentlemen pretend to support the doctrine of infallibility, as it respects their decisions; and that would perhaps be more than the house are willing to admit, and more than the people in this country are accustomed to believe.

I have said the gentlemen rest their principal opposition on this point — that the Constitution plainly means that the officers must be removed in the way they are appointed. Now, when gentlemen tell me that I was going to construe the Constitution, and many interpret it in a manner which was never intended, I am very cautious how I proceed. I do not like to construe over much.   It is a very delicate and critical branch of our duty; and there is not, perhaps, any part of the Constitution on which we should be more cautious and circumspect than on the present.

I am well authorized to say, that the mingling the powers of the President and Senate was strongly opposed in the Convention which had the honor to submit to the consideration of the United States, and the different states, the present system for the government of the Union.   Some gentlemen opposed it to the last; and finally it was the principal ground on which they refused to give it their signature and assent.   One gentleman called it a monstrous and unnatural connection, and did not hesitate to affirm it would bring on convulsions in the government.   This objection was not confined to the walls of the Convention; it has been the subject of newspaper declamation, and perhaps justly so.   Ought not we, therefore, to be careful not to extend this unchaste connection any farther?

Gentlemen who undertake to construe, say that they see clearly that the power which appoints must also remove.   Now, I have reviewed this subject with all the application and discernment my mind is capable of, and have not been able to see any such thing.   There is an agency given to the President, in making appointments, to which the Senate are connected.   But how it follows that the connection extends to the removal, positively I cannot see.   They say that it follows as a natural, inseparable consequence.   This sounds like logic.   But if we consult the premises, perhaps the conclusion may not follow.   The Constitution opposes this maxim more than it supports it.   The President is appointed by electors chosen by the people themselves, or by the state legislatures.   Can the state legislatures, either combined or separate, effect his removal?   No.   But the Senate may, on impeachment by this house.   The judges are appointed by the President, by and with the advice and consent of the Senate; but they are only removable by impeachment; the President has no agency in the removal.   Hence, I say, it is not a natural consequence that the power which appoints should have the power of removal also.

We may find it necessary that subordinate officers should be appointed, in the first instance, by the President and Senate.   I hope it will not be contended that the President and Senate shall be applied to in all cases when their removal may be necessary.   This principle, sir, is not pursued by the Senate themselves, in the very bill that is now before this house, sent down by the Senate, to establish the judicial courts of the United States   It is directed that a marshal shall be appointed for each district, who shall have power to appoint one or more deputies; and these deputies are to be removable from office by the judge of the District Court, or the Circuit Court sitting within the district, at the pleasure of either.   It is not said they shall be appointed by the marshal, who may remove them at pleasure; which ought to be the case, if the maxim is true, that the power which appoints necessarily has the power of removal.   But I dispute the maxim altogether; for though it is sometimes true, it is often fallacious; but by no means is it that kind of conclusive argument which they contend for.

Gentlemen proceed in their constructions, and they ask, "Why did not the Convention insert a clause in the Constitution. declaring the removal to be in a manner different from the appointment?"   They tell us 'hat it must naturally have occurred to them, and that here and there was the proper place to insert such a clause. Now, let me ask them, also, if theirs is the natural construction, why the Convention, after declaring that officers should be appointed by and with the advice and consent of the Senate, did not add, to be removed in like manner. It must have as naturally occurred to insert the one as the other. It is very possible that such a clause might have been moved and contended for; but it is hardly probable it would meet with success from those who opposed giving the Senate any check or control whatsoever over the powers of the President; much less was it probable that those gentlemen who opposed it there should wish to enlarge it by construction: for my part, I hope never to see it increased in this way. What of this nature is brought in by the letter of the Constitution, let it be there; but let us never increase evils of which we have some right to complain. A gentleman asks, " Where is the danger of mixing these powers, if the Constitution has already done it ?" That gentleman knows that it has always been viewed as an evil, and an association of the legislative and executive powers in one body has been found to produce tyranny. It is a maxim among the wisest legislators not to blend the branches of government further than is necessary to carry their separate powers into more complete operation. It was found necessary to blend the powers to a certain degree; so far we must acquiesce. The Senate must concur with the President in making appointments; but with respect to the removal, they are not associated; no such clause is in the Constitution; and, therefore, I should conclude that the Convention did not choose they should have the power. But what need was there that such a clause should be there? What is the evil it was intended to guard against? Why, we are afraid the President will unnecessarily remove a worthy man from office; and we say it is a pity the poor man should be turned out of service without a hearing; it is injurious to his reputation; it is his life, says the gentleman from New Hampshire, (Mr. Livermore;) it is cruelty in the extreme. But why are we to suppose this? I do not see any well-grounded apprehension for such an abuse of power. Let us attend to the operation of this business. The Constitution provides for what? That no bad man should come into office: this is the first evil. Hence we have nothing to dread from a system of favoritism; the public are well secured against that great evil; therefore the President cannot be influenced by a desire to get his own creatures into office; for it is fairly presumable that they will be rejected by the Senate. But suppose that one such could be got in; he can be got out again, in spite of the President: we can impeach him, and drag him from his place; and then there will be some other person appointed.

Some gentlemen seem to think there should be another clause in the Constitution, providing that the President should not turn out a good officer, and then they would not apprehend so much danger from that quarter. There are other evils which might have been provided against, and other things which might have been regulated: but if the Convention had undertaken to have done them, the Constitution, instead of being contained in a sheet of paper, would have swelled to the size of a folio volume. But what is the evil of the President's being at liberty to exercise this power of removal? Why, we fear that he will displace, not one good officer only, but, in a fit of passion, all the good officers of the government, by which, to be sure, the public would suffer: but I venture to say he would suffer himself more than any other man. But I trust there is no dearth of good men. I believe he could not turn out so many, but that the

Senate would still have some choice, out of which to supply a good one. But, even if he was to do this, what would be the consequence? He would be obliged to do the duties himself; or, if he did not, we would impeach him, and turn him out of office, as he had done others. I must admit, though, that there is a possibility of such an evil, but it is a remote possibility indeed.

I think gentlemen must concede that, if there should be such a passion, — such resentment as I have supposed between the President and the heads of departments, — the one or the other ought to be removed; they must not go on pulling different ways, for the public will receive most manifest injury: therefore it mitigates the appearance of the evil by suffering the public business to go on, which, from their irreconcilable difference, would otherwise be at a stand.

Mr. GERRY. The judges are the expositors of the Constitution and the acts of Congress. Our exposition, therefore, would be subject to their revisal. In this way the constitutional balance would be destroyed. The legislature, with the judicial, might remove the head of the executive branch. But a further reason why we are not the expositors, is, that the judiciary may disagree with us, and undo what all our efforts have labored to accomplish. A law is a nullity, unless it can be carried into execution: in this case, our law will be suspended. Hence all construction of the meaning of the Constitution is dangerous, or unnatural, and therefore ought to be avoided.

This is our doctrine, that no power of this kind ought to be exercised by the legislature. But, we say, if we must give a construction to the Constitution, it is more natural to give the construction in favor of the power of removal vesting in the President, by and with the advice and consent of the Senate, because it is in the nature of things that the power which appoints removes also. If there are deviations from this general rule, the instances are few, and not sufficient to warrant our departure on this occasion. We say our construction is superior also, because it does not militate against any clause of the Constitution; whilst their construction militates against several, and, in some respects, renders them mere nullities.

There is a consistency, under a monarchy, of the king's exercising the power of appointment and removal at pleasure. In Great Britain this is the prerogative of the throne; where it is likewise held a maxim, that the king can do no wrong. The chief magistrate under this Constitution is a different character. There is a constitutional tribunal, where he may be arraigned, condemned, and punished, if he does wrong. The reason of this distinction I take to be this: the majesty of the people receives an injury when the President commits an improper act, for which they are to receive satisfaction. Kings have a property in government; and when a monarch acts unwisely he injures his own interest, but is accountable to none, because satisfaction is due to himself alone. He is established in his office for life; it is an estate to him which he is interested to transmit to his posterity unimpaired: the good of the people, upon principles of interest, will be his peculiar study; he ought, therefore, to have power to act in such a manner as is most likely to secure to him this object; then, necessarily, he must have the right of choosing or displacing his agents. There can be no difficulty on this point. But in a confederated republic the chief magistrate has no such trust; he is elected but for four years; after which the government goes into other hands; he is not stimulated to improve a patrimony, and therefore has no occasion for complete power over the officers of the government.   If he has such power, it can only be made useful to him by being the means of procuring him a reëlection, but can never be useful to the people by inducing him to appoint good officers or remove bad ones.   It appears to me that such unbounded power vitiates the principles of the Constitution; and the officers, instead of being the machinery of the government, moving in regular order prescribed by the legislature, will be the mere puppets of the President, to be employed or thrown aside as useless lumber, according to his prevailing fancy.

If gentlemen will take this step, they must take another, and secure the public good by making it the interest of the President to consult it; they must elect him for life, or, what will be more consistent still, they must make his office hereditary.   Then gentlemen may say, with some degree of truth, that he ought to have the power of removal, to secure in his hands a balance in the government.   But if gentlemen are willing to remain where they are, and abide by the Constitution, regarding its true principles, they will not contend that there is a necessity, or even a propriety, in vesting this power in the President alone.

Gentlemen tell us they are willing to consider this as a constitutional question; and yet the bill shows that they consider the Constitution silent, for the clause grants the power in express terms: this also implies that the legislature have a right to interfere with the executive power contrary to their avowed principles.   If the legislature has not the power of removal, they cannot confer it upon others; if they have it, it is a legislative power, and they have no right to transfer the exercise of it to any other body; so, view this question in whatever point of light you please, it is clear the words ought to be struck out.

The call for *the question* being now very general, it was put — Shall the words " to be removable by the President " be struck out?

It was determined in *the negative ;* being yeas 20, nays 34.

Amendments to the Constitution.

HOUSE OF REPRESENTATIVES, *August* 13, 1789.

Mr. GERRY.   The Constitution of the United States was proposed by a Convention met at Philadelphia; but with all its importance, it did not possess as high authority as the President, Senate, and House of Representatives of the Union; for that Convention was not convened in consequence of any express will of the people, but an implied one, through their members in the state legislatures.   The Constitution derived no authority from the first Convention; it was concurred in by conventions of the people, and that concurrence armed it with power, and invested it with dignity.   Now, the Congress of the United States are expressly authorized, by the sovereign and uncontrollable voice of the people, to propose amendments whenever two thirds of both houses shall think fit.   Now, if this is the fact, the propositions of amendment will be found to originate with a higher authority than the original system.   The conventions of the states respectively have agreed, for the people, that the state legislatures shall be authorized to decide upon these amendments in the manner of a convention.   If these acts of the state legislatures are not good, because they are not specifically instructed by their constituents, neither were the acts calling the first and subsequent conventions.

Mr. AMES.   It is not necessary to increase the representation, in ordeto guard against corruption ; because no one will presume to think that a body composed like this, and increased in a ratio of 4 to 3, will be much less exposed to sale than we are.   Nor is a greater number necessary to secure the rights and liberties of the people, for the representative of a great body of people is likely to be more watchful of its interests than the representative of a lesser body.

Mr. MADISON.   Suppose they, the people, instruct a representative by his vote to violate the Constitution ; is he at liberty to obey such instructions ?   Suppose he is instructed to patronize certain measures, and from circumstances known to him, but not to his constituents, he is convinced that they will endanger the public good ; is he obliged to sacrifice his own judgment to them ?   Is he absolutely bound to perform what he is instructed to do ?   Suppose he refuses ; will his vote be the less valid, or the community be disengaged from that obedience which is due, from the laws of the Union ?   If his vote must inevitably have the same effect, what sort of a right is this, in the Constitution, to instruct a representative who has a right to disregard the order, if he pleases ?   In this sense, the right does not exist; in the other sense, it does exist, and is provided largely for.

Domestic Debt.

House of Representatives, *February* 22, 1790.

Mr. SMITH, (of South Carolina.)   The Constitution itself was opposed to the measure, (discrimination of the domestic debt;) for it was an *ex post facto* law, which was prohibited in express terms.   The transference of public securities was lawful at the time these alienations were made ; an attempt therefore to punish the transferees, is an attempt to make an *ex post facto* law, by making that unlawful which was lawful at the time it was done ; it alters the nature of the transaction, and annexes the idea of guilt to that which, at the moment of commission, was not only perfectly innocent, but was explicitly authorized and encouraged by a public act of Congress.   By that act, those who had money were invited to purchase of those who held securities; and now they were called upon to punish the purchasers who bought under that invitation.   The Constitution restrains the states from passing any law impairing the force of contracts : *a fortiori*, is the legislature of the Union restrained ?   What an example to hold up to the judiciary of the United States !   How could they annul a state law, when the state would be able to plead a precedent on the part of Congress ?   The right of property was a sacred right ; no tribunal on earth, nor even legislative body, could deprive a citizen of his property, unless by a fair equivalent, for the public welfare.   The purchaser was vested, by the sale, with an absolute right to the full amount of the security, and it was beyond their authority to divest him of it.   They might, indeed, by an act of power, declare that he should be paid only half; but his right to the other moiety would not be extinguished.

The present Constitution, which is a mild one, met with considerable opposition.   Had it been rejected, the public securities would never have been paid.

It was the surest policy of governments to adhere strictly to their plighted faith, when it was in their power to do so, even should such strict adherence work an injury to some part of the community.   This was the practice of nations in the case of a treaty, which, when made by competent authority they considered themselves bound to observe, although they deemed it disadvantageous to them, lest a refusal should deter other nations from treating with them in future. It is by this line of conduct that public credit can alone be supported.

Mr. MADISON. The constitutionality of the proposition had been drawn into question. He (Mr. Madison) asked whether words could be devised that would place the new government more precisely in the same relation to the real creditors with the old. The power was the same; the objection was the same: the means only were varied.

If the gentlemen persisted, however, in demanding precedents, he was happy in being able to gratify them with two, which, though not exactly parallel, were, on that account, of the greater force, since the interposition of government had taken place where the emergencies could less require them. The first was the case of the Canada bill. During the war which ended in 1763, and which was attended with a revolution in the government of Canada, the supplies obtained for the French army in that province were paid for in bills of exchange and certificates. This paper depreciated, and was bought up chiefly by British merchants. The sum and the depreciations were so considerable as to become a subject of negotiation between France and Great Britain at the peace. The negotiation produced a particular article, by which it was agreed by France that the paper ought to be redeemed, and admitted by Great Britain that it should be redeemed, at a stipulated value. In the year 1766, this article was accordingly carried into effect by ministers from the two courts, who reduced the paper, in the hands of the British holders, in some instances as much as seventy-five per cent. below its nominal value. It was stated, indeed, by the reporter of the case, that the holders of the paper had themselves concurred in the liquidation; but it was not probable that the concurrence was voluntary. If it was voluntary, it shows that they themselves were sensible of the equity of the sacrifice.

The other case was of still greater weight, as it had no relation to war or to treaty, and took place in the nation which had been held up as a model with respect to public credit. In the year 1715, the civil list of Great Britain had fallen in arrears to the amount of £500,000. The creditors who had furnished supplies to the government, had, instead of money, received debentures only from respectable officers. These had depreciated. In that state they were assigned in some instances; in others, covenanted to be assigned. When the Parliament appropriated funds for satisfying these arrears, they inserted an express provision in the act, that the creditors who had been obliged, by the defaults of government, to dispose of their paper at a loss, might redeem it from the assignees by repaying the actual price, with an interest of six per cent., and that all agreements and covenants to assign should be absolutely void. Here, then, was an interposition on the very principle that a government ought to redress the wrongs sustained by its default, and on an occasion trivial when compared with that under consideration; yet it does not appear that the public credit of its nation was injured by it.

Slave Trade. — *On committing the Memorial of the Quakers on the Slave Trade.*

House of Representatives, *March,* 1790.

Mr. TUCKER said, he conceived the memorial to be so glaring an interference with the Constitution, that he had hoped the house would not have given so much countenance to a request so improper in itself. He was sorry that the society had discovered so little prudence in their memorial, as to wish that Congress should intermeddle in the internal regulations of the particular states. He hoped the petition would not be committed, as it would operate directly against the interest of those it was designed to benefit. This is a business that may be attended with the most serious consequences; it may end in a subversion of the government, being a direct attack on the rights and property of the Southern States. He then inquired what satisfaction was to be made to the proprietors of slaves. He believed it was not in the power of the states to make indemnification for the loss that would attend emancipation. He reprobated the interposition of the society, and denied that they possessed any more humanity than other denominations.

Mr. GERRY replied to Mr. Tucker, and desired the gentleman to point out any part of the memorial which proposed that the legislature should infringe on the Constitution. For his part, he heard nothing read that had such a tendency. Its only object was, that Congress should exert their constitutional authority to abate the horrors of slavery so far as they could. He hoped the petition would be committed. Indeed, he considered that all altercation on the subject of commitment was at an end, as the house had essentially determined that it should be committed.

Mr. BURKE reprobated the commitment, as subversive of the Constitution, as sounding an alarm, and blowing the trumpet of sedition in the Southern States. He should oppose the business totally; and if chosen on the committee, he should decline serving.

Mr. SCOTT was in favor of the commitment.

Mr. JACKSON was opposed to it, and painted in strong colors the alarming consequences to be apprehended from taking up the business, — revolt, insurrection, and devastation, — and concluded by an observation similar to Mr. Burke's.

Mr. SHERMAN could see no difficulty in committing the memorial; the committee may bring in such a report as may prove satisfactory to gentlemen on all sides.

Mr. BALDWIN referred to the principles of accommodation which prevailed at the time of forming the government. Those mutual concessions which then took place gave us a Constitution which was to insure the peace and the equal rights and properties of the various states: and to prevent all infraction of the rights in this particular instance, they precluded themselves, by an express stipulation, from all interposition in the slave trade. Congress are not called upon to declare their sentiments upon this occasion; they cannot constitutionally interfere in the business. He deprecated the consequences of such a measure in very forcible terms, and hoped the house would proceed no farther in the investigation of the subject.

Mr. SMITH, (of South Carolina,) recurring to the memorial, observed, that Congress could not constitutionally interfere in the business, upon the prayer of the memorialists, as that went to an entire abolition of slavery; it could not, therefore, with propriety, be referred to a committee.

In the Southern States, difficulties on this account had arisen in respect to the ratification of the Constitution; and, except their apprehensions on this head had been dissipated by their property being secured and guarantied to them by the Constitution itself, they never could have adopted it.

He then depicted the miseries that would result from the interference of Congress in the southern governments. He asserted, as his opinion, that if there were no slaves in the Southern States, they would be entirely depopulated; from the nature of the country, it could not be cultivated without them. Their proprietors are persons of as much humanity as the inhabitants of any part of the continent: they are as conspicuous for their morals as any of their neighbors.

He then asserted that the Quakers are a society not known to the laws; that they stand in exactly the same situation with other religious societies. Their memorial relates to a matter in which they are no more interested than any other sect whatever; and it must therefore be considered in the light of advice; and is it customary to refer a piece of advice to a committee? He then contrasted this memorial with one which might be presented from the sect called Shaking Quakers, whose principles and practices are represented in a very exceptionable point of light; and asked whether Congress would pay any attention to such a memorial. He hoped the memorial would not be committed.

Mr. PAGE was in favor of the commitment. He hoped that the benevolent designs of the respectable memorialists would not be frustrated at the threshold, so far as to preclude a fair discussion of the prayer of their memorial. He observed that they do not apply for a total abolition of slavery. They only request that such measures may be taken, consistent with the Constitution, as may finally issue in the total abolition of the slave trade. He could not conceive that the apprehensions entertained by the gentlemen from Georgia and South Carolina were well founded, as they respected the proposed interference of Congress.

Mr. MADISON observed, that it was his opinion, yesterday, that the best way to proceed in the business was to commit the memorial, without any debate on the subject. From what has taken place, he was more convinced of the propriety of the idea; but, as the business has engaged the attention of many members, and much has been said by gentlemen, he would offer a few observations for the consideration of the house. He then entered into a critical review of the circumstances respecting the adoption of the Constitution; the ideas upon the limitation of the powers of Congress to interfere in the regulation of the commerce in slaves, and showing that they undeniably were not precluded from interposing in their importation; and generally, to regulate the mode in which every species of business shall be transacted. He adverted to the western country, and the cession of Georgia, in which Congress have certainly the power to regulate the subject of slavery; which shows that gentlemen are mistaken in supposing that Congress cannot constitutionally interfere in the business in any degree whatever. He was in favor of committing the petitions, and justified the measure, by repeated precedents in the proceedings of the house.

Mr. GERRY entered into a justification of the interference of Congress, as being fully compatible with the Constitution. He descanted on the miseries to which the Africans are subjected by this traffic, and said that he never contemplated this subject without reflecting what his own feelings would be, in case himself, his children, or friends, were placed in the same deplorable circumstances. He then adverted to the flagrant acts of cruelty which are committed in carrying on that traffic, and asked whether it can be supposed that Congress has no power to prevent such transactions as far as possible. He then referred to the Constitution, and pointed out the restrictions laid on the general government respecting the importation of slaves.   It is not, he presumed, in the contemplation of any gentleman in this house to violate that part of the Constitution; but that we have a right to regulate this business is as clear as that we have any rights whatever; nor has the contrary been shown by any person who has spoken on the occasion.   Congress can, agreeably to the Constitution, lay a duty of ten dollars a head on slaves : they may do this immediately. He made a calculation of the value of the slaves in the Southern States. He supposed they might be worth about ten million of dollars.   Congress have a right, if they see proper to make a proposal to the Southern States, to purchase the whole of them; and their resources in the western country may furnish them with means.   He did not mean to suggest a measure of this kind : he only instanced these particulars to show that Congress certainly have a right to intermeddle in this business.   He thought that no objections had been offered of any force to prevent the committing of the memorial.

Mr. BOUDINOT was in favor of the commitment, enlarged on the idea suggested by Mr. Gerry, and observed that the memorial contained only a request that Congress would interfere their authority in the cause of humanity and mercy.

Mr. GERRY and Mr. STONE severally spoke again on the subject. The latter gentleman, in opposition to the commitment, said, that this memorial was a thing of course ; for there never was a society of any considerable extent which did not interfere with the concerns of other people; and this interference has at one time or other deluged the world with blood. On this principle he was opposed to the commitment.

Mr. TUCKER moved to modify the first paragraph by striking out all the words after the word *opinion*, and to insert the following : "that the several memorials proposed to the consideration of this house a subject on which its interference would be unconstitutional, and even its deliberations highly injurious to some of the states of the Union."

Mr. JACKSON rose, and observed, that he had been silent on the subject of the reports coming before the committee, because he wished the principles of the resolutions to be examined fairly, and to be decided on their true grounds.   He was against the propositions generally, and would examine the policy, the justice, and use of them ; and he hoped, if he could make them appear in the same light to others as they did to him by fair argument, that the gentlemen in opposition were not so determined in their opinions as not to give up their present sentiments.

With respect to the policy of the measure, — the situation of the slaves here, their situation in their native states, and the disposal of them in case of emancipation, should be considered.   That slavery was an evil habit he did not mean to controvert ; but that habit was already established, and there were peculiar situations in countries which rendered that habit necessary.   Such situations the states of South Carolina and Georgia were in : large tracts of the most fertile lands on the continent remained uncultivated for the want of population.   It was frequently advanced on the floor of Congress how unhealthy those climates were, and how impossible it was for northern constitutions to exist there.   What, he asked, is to be done with this uncultivated territory ?   Is it to remain a waste?   Is the rice trade to be banished from our coasts ?   Are Congress willing to deprive themselves of the revenue arising from that trade, and which is daily increasing, and to throw this great advantage into the hands of other countries?

Let us examine the use or the benefit of the resolutions contained in the report. I call upon gentlemen to give me one single instance in which they can be of service. They are of no use to Congress. The powers of that body are already defined, and those powers cannot be amended, confirmed, or diminished, by ten thousand resolutions. Is not the first proposition of the report fully contained in the Constitution? Is not that the guide and rule of this legislature? A multiplicity of laws is reprobated in any society, and tends but to confound and to perplex. How strange would a law appear which was to confirm a law! and how much more strange must it appear for this body to pass resolutions to confirm the Constitution under which they sit! This is the case with others of the resolutions.

A gentleman from Maryland (Mr. STONE) very properly observed that the Union had received the different states with all their ill habits about them. This was one of these habits established long before the Constitution, and could not now be remedied. He begged Congress to reflect on the number on the continent who were opposed to this Constitution, and on the number which yet remained in the Southern States. The violation of this compact they would seize on with avidity; they would make a handle of it to cover their designs against the government; and many good federalists, who would be injured by the measure, would be induced to join them. His heart was truly federal, and it had always been so, and he wished those designs frustrated. He begged Congress to beware, before they went too far. He called on them to attend to the interest of two whole states, as well as to the memorials of a society of Quakers, who came forward to blow the trumpet of sedition, and to destroy that Constitution which they had not in the least contributed by personal service or supply to establish.

He seconded Mr. Tucker's motion.

Mr. SMITH (of South Carolina) said, the gentleman from Massachusetts (Mr. GERRY) had declared that it was the opinion of the select committee, of which he was a member, that the memorial from the Pennsylvania society required Congress to violate the Constitution. It was not less astonishing to see Dr. Franklin taking the lead in a business which looks so much like a persecution of the southern inhabitants, when he recollected the parable he had written some time ago, with a view of showing the impropriety of one set of men persecuting others for a difference of opinion. The parable was to this effect: "An old traveller, hungry and weary, applied to the patriarch Abraham for a night's lodging. In conversation, Abraham discovered that the stranger differed with him on religious points, and turned him out of doors. In the night, God appeared unto Abraham, and said, Where is the stranger? Abraham answered, I found that he did not worship the true God, and so I turned him out of doors. The Almighty thus rebuked the patriarch: Have I borne with him three-score and ten years, and couldst thou not bear with him one night?" Has not the Almighty, said Mr. Smith, borne with us for more than threescore years and ten? He has even made our country opulent, and shed the blessings of affluence and prosperity on our land, notwithstanding all its slaves; and must we now be ruined on account of the tender consciences of a few scrupulous individuals, who differ from us on this point?

Mr. BOUDINOT agreed with the general doctrines of Mr. S., but could not agree that the clause in the Constitution relating to the want of power in Congress to prohibit the importation of such persons as any of the states, *now existing*, shall think proper to admit, prior to the year 1808, and authorizing a tax or duty on such importation, not exceeding ten dollars for each person, did not extend to negro slaves. Candor required that he should acknowledge that this was the express design of the Constitution; and therefore Congress could not interfere in prohibiting the importation or promoting the emancipation of them prior to that period. Mr. Boudinot observed, that he was well informed that the tax or duty of ten dollars was provided, instead of the five per cent. ad valorem, and was so expressly understood by all parties in the Convention; that, therefore, it was the interest and duty of Congress to impose this tax, or it would not be doing justice to the states, or equalizing the duties throughout the Union. If this was not done, merchants might bring their whole capitals into this branch of trade, and save paying any duties whatever. Mr. Boudinot observed, that the gentleman had overlooked the prophecy of St. Peter, where he foretells that, among other damnable heresies, " through covetousness shall they with feigned words make merchandise of you."

[Nᴏᴛᴇ. — In the first edition, p. 211, vol. iv., this head terminated, " *Memorial rejected* " — a mistake, which the editor in the present edition corrects, by stating that with other petitions of a similar object, it was committed to a select committee : that committee made a report; the report was referred to a committee of the whole house, and discussed on four successive days : it was then reported to the house with amendments, and by the house ordered to be inscribed in its Journals, and then *laid on the table.*

That report, as amended in committee, is in the following words : " The committee to whom were referred sundry memorials from the people called Quakers, and also a memorial from the Pennsylvania Society for promoting the Abolition of Slavery, submit the following report, (as amended in committee of the whole :) —

" First That the migration or importation of such persons, as any of the states now existing shall think proper to admit, cannot be prohibited by Congress prior to the year 1808.

" Secondly. That Congress have no power to interfere in the emancipation of slaves, or in the treatment of them, within any of the states; it remaining with the several states alone to provide any regulation therein which humanity and true policy may require.

" Thirdly. That Congress have authority to restrain the citizens of the United States from carrying on the African slave trade, for the purpose of supplying foreigners with slaves, and of providing, by proper regulations, for the humane treatment, during their passage, of slaves imported by the said citizens into the states admitting such importations.

" Fourthly. That Congress have also authority to prohibit foreigners from fitting out vessels in any part of the United States for transporting persons from Africa to any foreign port."]

On the Establishment of a National Bank.

Hᴏᴜsᴇ ᴏғ Rᴇᴘʀᴇsᴇɴᴛᴀᴛɪᴠᴇs, *February* 2, 1791.

Mr. GILES said he was disposed to consider the plan as containing a principle not agreeable to the Constitution, and in itself not altogether expedient.

To show its unconstitutionality, he read the 1st section of the bill which established the subscribers of the bank into a corporation, to do which, he conceived the Constitution had given Congress no power. He read the clause in the Constitution which had been adduced as sanctioning the exercise of such a power. This clause only respects, he said, all the necessary powers to carry into effect such as were expressly delegated; that of forming corporations was not expressly granted. He then adverted o the power of borrowing money, vested in Congress by the Constitution, and controverted the idea that a bank was necessary to carry it into execution. It might, he granted, conduce to a greater facility in exercising that power; but that it was expedient or necessary he denied, either to effect loans or establish the government.

If Congress, in this instance, he observed, exercised the power of erecting corporations, it was nowhere limited, and they might, if they thought fit, extend it to every object, and, in consequence thereof, monopolies of the East and West India trade be established; and this would place us, he said, in the precise situation of a nation without a free constitution.

He referred to the clause in the Constitution which prohibits Congress from giving a preference to one part of the United States over another. This he considered, together with his other objections, fully sufficient to justify a rejection of the plan.

He then offered some observations relative to the expediency of the measure. If it is problematical only, whether the establishment of this national bank is agreeable to the Constitution, this ought to be, he thought, sufficient to prevent an adoption of the system. He showed the consequences which will result from a doubt of the legality of the measure. He noticed the objection which had been originally made by the people to the Constitution, and the pains which were taken to obviate their fears and apprehensions. The adoption of this plan, he said, would realize many of their disagreeable anticipations. He denied the *necessity* of a bank for the *preservation* of government. The only object, as the subject struck his mind, was to raise stock; but it was certainly not expedient, he conceived, to kindle the flame of discontent, and rouse the fears and jealousies of the people, in many states, to raise stock.

He took notice of some observations which had fallen from a gentleman from Connecticut, respecting incidental powers, and denied that Congress possessed those powers. The general government, he said, was not a consolidated government, but a federal government, possessed of such powers as the states or the people had expressly delegated; but to support these incidental powers, ceded to Congress, was to make it, not a federal, not even a republican consolidated government, but a despotic one. If this idea was contemplated, the people would be alarmed, they would be justly alarmed, and he hoped they would be alarmed.

Mr. VINING observed, that he had endeavored to give the subject a full and dispassionate consideration; and, so far from thinking the plan contrary to the Constitution, he considered it perfectly consonant to it.

He adverted to the principles, design, and operations of the bank systems. Their usefulness he deduced from the experience of those countries which had been the longest in the use of those institutions. The constitutionality of the measure he urged from a fair construction of those powers, expressly delegated, and from a necessary implication; for he insisted that the Constitution was a dead letter, if implied powers were not to be exercised.

Mr MADISON did not oppose all the banking systems, but did not approve of the plan now under consideration.

Upon the general view of banks, he recapitulated the several advantages which may be derived from them. The public credit, he granted, might be raised for a time, but only partially. Banks, he conceived, tended to diminish the quantity of precious metals in a country; and the articles received in lieu of a portion of them, which was banished, conferred no substantial benefit on the country. He dwelt on the casualties that banks are subject to.

To be essentially useful in so extensive a country, banks, he said, should be fixed in different parts of the United States; and in this view, the local banks of the several states, he said, could be employed with more advantage than if any other banking system was substituted. Circumstances, in Great Britain, he observed, required that there should be one bank, as the object there is to concentrate the wealth of the country to a point, as the interest of their public debt is all paid in one place. Here a difference in circumstances called for another kind of policy: the public debt is paid in all the different states.

He then expressly denied the power of Congress to establish banks. And this, he said, was not a novel opinion; he had long entertained it. All power, he said, had its limits; those of the general government were ceded from the mass of general power inherent in the people, and were consequently confined within the bounds fixed by their act of cession. The Constitution was this act; and to warrant Congress in exercising the power, the grant of it should be pointed out in that instrument. This, he said, had not been done; he presumed it could not be done. If we ventured to construe the Constitution, such construction only was admissible, as it carefully preserved entire the idea on which that Constitution is founded.

He adverted to the clauses in the Constitution which had been adduced as conveying this power of incorporation. He said he could not find it in that of laying taxes. He presumed it was impossible to deduce it from the power given to Congress to provide for the general welfare. If it is admitted that the right exists there, every guard set to the powers of the Constitution is broken down, and the limitations become nugatory.

The present Congress, it was said, had all the powers of the old Confederation, and more. Under the old government a bank had been established; and thence it was deduced that the present legislature had indubitably that power. The exigencies of government were such, he answered, under the old Confederation, as to justify almost any infraction of parchment rights; but the old Congress were conscious they had not every power necessary for the complete establishment of a bank, and recommended to the individual states to make sundry regulations for the complete establishment of the institution.

To exercise the power included in the bill was an infringement on the rights of the several states; for they could establish banks within their respective jurisdictions, and prohibit the establishment of any others. A law existed in one of the states prohibitory of cash notes of hand, payable on demand. The power of making such a law could not, he presumed, be denied to the states; and if this was granted, and such laws were in force, it certainly would effectually exclude the establishment of a bank.

This power of establishing a bank had been, he said, deduced from the right, granted in the Constitution, of borrowing money; but this, he conceived, was not a bill to borrow money. It was said that Congress had not only this power to borrow money, but to enable people to lend. In answer to this, he observed that, if Congress had a right to enable those people to lend, who are willing, but not able, it might be said that they have a right to compel those to lend, who were able, and not willing.

He adverted to that clause in the Constitution which empowers Congress to pass all the laws necessary to carry its powers into execution, and, observing on the diffusive and ductile interpretation of these words, and the boundless latitude of construction given them by the friends of the bank, said that, by their construction, every possible power might be exercised.

The government would then be paramount in all public cases: charters, incorporations, and monopolies, might be given, and every limitation effectually swept away, and could supersede the establishment of every bank in the several states. The doctrine of implication, he warned the friends to this system, was a dangerous one, which, multiplied and combined in the manner some gentlemen appeared to contemplate, would form a chain reaching every object of legislation of the United States. This power to incorporate, he contended, was of primary importance, and could by no means be viewed as a subaltern, and therefore ought to be laid down in the Constitution, to warrant Congress in the exercise of it, and ought not to be considered as resulting from any other power.

Incorporation, he said, is important as the power of naturalization; and Congress, he presumed, would not exercise the power of naturalizing a foreigner, unless expressly authorized by the Constitution. He read a sentence in the bill respecting the power of making such regulations as were not contrary to law. What law? Was it the law of the United States? There were so few, that this allowed a very considerable latitude to the power of making regulations, and more than any member, he conceived, would wish to grant. Were the laws of the individual states contemplated by this provision? Then it would be in the power of the separate states to defeat an institution of the Union. He asked by what authority Congress empowered a corporation to possess real estate. He reprobated this idea. To establish this bank was, he said, establishing a monopoly guarantied in such a manner that no similar privilege could be granted to any other number of persons whatever. He denied the necessity of instituting a bank at the present time. The Constitution ought not to be violated without urgent necessity indeed. There were banks, in several of the states, from which some advantages could be derived which could not be gained from an institution on the plan proposed.

In confirmation of his sentiments, he adduced certain passages from *speeches* made in several of the *state conventions* by those in favor of adopting the Constitution. These passages were fully in favor of this idea — that the general government could *not* exceed the *expressly*-delegated powers. In confirmation also of this sentiment, he adduced the amendments proposed by Congress to the Constitution.

He urged, from a variety of considerations, the postponement of the buisness to the next session of Congress.

Mr. AMES. For his own part, he never doubted the constitutionality of the plan; and if the public sense was to be regarded on the occasion, their approbation of the measures taken by the old Confederation, respecting the Bank of North America, and their total silence on the constitutionality of the plan before Congress at this day, were to him sufficient proofs of their opinions on the subject.

The first question that occurred on this subject was, whether the powers of the house were confined to those expressly granted by the letter of the Constitution, or whether the doctrine of implication was safe ground to proceed upon. If the letter of the Constitution was to be adhered to, the question he deemed determined; but if a more rational plan was adopted, and the sense of the Constitution, upon strict examination, appeared even doubtful, every member must then appeal to his conscience and understanding. If the powers of the house were circumscribed by the letter of the Constitution, much expense might have been saved to the public, as their hands would have been completely tied. But, by the very nature of government, the legislature had an implied power of using every means, not positively prohibited by the Constitution, to execute the ends for which that government was instituted. Every constitutional right should be so liberally construed as to effect the public good. This, it has been said, was taking too great a latitude; but certainly to promote the ends of government was the end of its existence; and by the ties of conscience, each member was bound to exercise every lawful power which could have a tendency to promote the general welfare. It had been said that the doctrine of implication was dangerous, and would alarm the people. He thought it would not, unless the alarm was founded.

Suppose, he said, the power of raising armies was not expressly granted to the general government; would it be inferred from hence, that the power of declaring war, without the means of carrying it on, had been ceded to them? Would it be said that the blood of fellow-citizens was crying for vengeance, though their lives and property called for protection from the hand of government? Would it be said that they had not a constitutional right to be protected? Would it be urged that the Constitution, by not expressly granting to the general government the power of levying armies, had put it out of their power to protect its citizens? This, he conceived, would be a very dangerous doctrine.

Suppose the power of borrowing money had not been expressly given to the federal government; would it not, in emergencies, be inferred from the nature of the general powers granted to it? Suppose the power to lend had not been mentioned, and a *surplus of revenue* in the public coffers; should it not be distributed among the people, but locked up and suffered to remain unproductive in the treasury? He imagined not. Suppose the question of redeeming the prisoners in captivity at Algiers was before the house; would it be urged that nothing could be done in their favor by the general government, because no power was specially granted? No. Every person, he conceived, that felt as a man, would not think his hands tied when they were to be extended to the relief of suffering fellow-citizens. The power of buying certificates was not particularly mentioned in the Constitution; yet it had been exercised by the general government, and was inferred from that of paying the public debt, and from the reason of the case. The power of establishing banks, he conceived, could be deduced from the same source — from their utility in the ordinary operations of government, and their indispensable necessity in cases of sudden emergencies. It was said that the state banks would serve all these purposes; but why deprive the general government, he asked, of the power of self-defence?

Mr. Ames proceeded to prove that the power of incorporating the subscribers to the bank could be deduced from that clause in the Constitution which had been termed the *sweeping clause.* Unless a reasonable latitude of construction of this part of the Constitution was allowed, he did not see upon what authority several acts of Congress would rest. Whence did the general government draw the authority they had exercised over the western territory? That authority, he answered, must of necessity belong to Congress: it could not rest with the individual states

The power here was derived by implication, and was deduced from the reason and necessity of the case; and the power contended for in the present case might, for the same reasons, be exercised, and was drawn from the same source. The government of the western territory was a species of corporation — a corporation in its nature the most important; and would it be said that Congress had acted unconstitutionally when they established it? And would the territory be left under the control of the individual states? He presumed not.

By the Constitution, a power of regulating trade was specially given to Congress; and under this clause they had established regulations affecting ships, seamen, lighthouses, &c. By parity of reasoning, he conceived that, as the power of collecting taxes was specified among the rights granted by the Constitution to Congress, they undoubtedly were entitled to make regulations affecting the instruments by means of which those taxes were to be collected.

Some opposition to the system arose from the idea that it was an infringement on the rights of the individual states. This objection he answered. It could not be denied, he said, that Congress had the right to exercise complete and exclusive jurisdiction over the district of ten miles square, ceded for the seat of permanent residence, and over such spots as were ceded for the establishment of lighthouses, &c. In these places, then, it must be granted that Congress had authority to establish a bank. If this was allowed, (and he could not see how it could be denied,) then the question became a question of place, and not of principle. He adverted to the preamble of the Constitution, which declares that it is established for the general welfare of the Union. This vested Congress with the authority over all objects of national concern, or of a general nature. A national bank undoubtedly came under this idea; and though not specially mentioned, yet the general design and tendency of the Constitution proved more evidently the constitutionality of the system, than its silence in this particular could be construed to express the contrary. He deduced the power also from those clauses in the Constitution which authorize Congress to lay and collect taxes. This, he said, could not be done from every corner of so extended an empire without the assistance of paper. In the power of borrowing money, he saw that of providing the means, by the establishment of a bank. But it has been said that, if Congress could exercise the power of making those who were willing, able to lend, they might carry their authority to creating the will in those who were able. This would be, he said, an abuse of power, and reasonings drawn from it could not be just.

Gentlemen had noticed the amendment proposed by Congress to the Constitution, as conveying the sense of the legislature on the nature of the powers vested by that instrument. The amendment stated, that it should be declared, that the powers not expressly delegated to the general government, and such as could be exercised by the states, should be considered as belonging to the states. But the power of establishing a national bank, he said, could not be exercised by the states, and therefore rested nowhere but in the federal legislature.

The doctrine of implication, it had been said, would excite alarms. It had been resorted to, and alarms had not been excited. He conceived it a necessary doctrine in many cases.

He had no desire to extend the powers granted by the Constitution beyond the limits prescribed by them. But in cases where there was doubt as to its meaning and intention, he thought it his duty to consult his conscience and judgment to solve them; and even if doubts did still remain on two different interpretations of it, he would constantly embrace that the least involved in doubt.

Mr. SEDGWICK expressed his surprise at the objections made to the constitutionality of the bill.

A gentleman from Virginia (Mr. Madison) had taken some pains to convince the house that he had uniformly been opposed to seeing the general government exercise the power of establishing banks. He did not wish to dispute with the honorable member the merit of consistency, but only begged leave to remark that the same gentleman had not always been averse to the exercise of power by implication. Witness the proceedings on the propriety of vesting the President of the United States with the authority of removing officers. But in this case, he was willing to take up the question solely on its own merits, without reference to former opinions.

In the present case, he conceived the determination of the question rested, in a great measure, on the meaning of the words *necessary* and *proper.*

Mr. MADISON. Those two words had been, by some, taken in a very limited sense, and were thought only to extend to the passing of such laws as were indispensably necessary to the very existence of the government. He was disposed to think that a more liberal construction should be put on them, — indeed, the conduct of the legislature had allowed them a fuller meaning, — for very few acts of the legislature could be proved essentially necessary to the absolute existence of government. He wished the words understood so as to permit the adoption of measures the best calculated to attain the ends of government, and produce the greatest *quantum* of public utility.

In the Constitution, the great ends of government were particularly enumerated; but all the means were not, nor could they all be, pointed out, without making the Constitution a complete code of laws: some discretionary power, and reasonable latitude, must be left to the judgment of the legislature. The Constitution, he said, had given power to Congress to lay and collect taxes; but the quantum, nature, means of collecting, &c., were of necessity left to the honest and sober discretion of the legislature.

It authorized Congress to borrow money; but of whom, on what terms, and in what manner, it had not ventured to determine; these points of secondary importance were also left to the wisdom of the legislature. The more important powers are specially granted; but the choice from the known and useful means of carrying the power into effect, is left to the decision of the legislature. He enumerated some other powers which are specified in the Constitution as belonging to Congress, and of which the means of execution are not mentioned; and concluded this part of his argument by observing that, if the bank which it was proposed to establish by the bill before the house could be proven necessary and proper to carry into execution any one of the powers given to Congress by the Constitution, this would at once determine the constitutionality of the measure.

He would not, he said, dwell any longer on the constitutionality of the plan under consideration, but would only observe that no power could be exercised by Congress, if the letter of the Constitution was strictly adhered to, and no latitude of construction allowed, and all the good that might be reasonably expected from an efficient government entirely frustrated.

Mr. LAWRENCE. The principles of the government, and ends of the Constitution, he remarked, were expressed in its preamble. It is established for the common defence and general welfare. The body of that instrument contained provisions the best adapted to the intention of those principles and attainment of those ends. To these ends, principles, and provisions, Congress was to have, he conceived, a constant eye; and then, by the sweeping clause, they were vested with the powers to carry the ends into execution.

Mr. JACKSON. From the power given the general government of making all necessary laws concerning the property of the United States, a right to establish a national bank had been deduced; and it was asked if bank notes were not property. He said they were a property of a peculiar nature. They were not property as well as an ox or an ass; so they could not be taxed.

It had been asked whether Congress could not establish a bank within the ten miles square, granted to the general government for the permanent residence of the federal legislature. Congress could not, because they had no authority to force the circulation of this paper beyond the limits of the ten miles. The fiscal administration of the Union was said to be vested in Congress. But this did not authorize their adoption of any measures they should think fit for the regulation of the finances. The very Constitution which granted these fiscal powers restricted them by particular clauses; for example, Congress could not without control lay a poll tax, and could not, in any shape, impose duties on exports; yet they were undoubtedly fiscal operations.

Gentlemen, he said, had deduced this power from various parts of the Constitution. The preamble and context had been mentioned; the clause that provides for laying taxes had been particularly dwelt upon; but surely the bill before the house did neither lay an excise, direct tax, or any other, and could, therefore, not come within the meaning of the clause.

Mr. BOUDINOT. But gentlemen say that the Constitution does not expressly warrant the establishment of such a corporation. If, by *expressly*, express words are meant, it is agreed that there are no express words; and this is the case with most of the powers exercised by Congress; for if the doctrine of necessary implication is rejected, he did not see what the supreme legislature of the Union could do in that character; if this power is not clearly given in the Constitution by necessary implication, then it is a necessary end proposed and directed, while the common and useful necessary means to attain that end are refused, or at least not granted. Mr. Boudinot was firmly of opinion that the national bank was the necessary means, without which the end could not be obtained.

Mr. STONE thought that the friends of the bill were not willing to confine themselves to such means as were *necessary* and *proper*, but had extended their views to those *convenient* and *agreeable*. If, in the plan before the house, he said, a provision had been made to secure a certainty that money could be procured by the government on loan from this bank, there would be more plausibility, he thought, in urging its establishment by a construction of the power of borrowing money. But the bank could, and, whenever it was their interest, certainly would, refuse lending to government. If the power, in this case, was deduced by implication, and was exercised because it was thought *necessary* and *proper*, it might be the opinion of a future Congress that monopolies, in certain cases, might be useful, and a door would then be open for their establishment.

February 7, 1791.

Mr. GERRY. The gentlemen on different sides of the question do not disagree with respect to the meaning of the terms *taxes, duties, imposts, excises,* &c., and of *borrowing money,* but of the word *necessary ;* and the question is, What is the general and popular meaning of the term ? Perhaps the answer to the question will be truly this — That, in a general and popular one, the word does not admit of a definite meaning, but that this varies according to the *subject* and *circumstances.* With respect to the subject, for instance ; if the people, speaking of a garrison besieged by a superior force, and without provisions or a prospect of relief, should say it was under the *necessity* of surrendering, they would mean a physical necessity ; for troops cannot subsist long without provisions. But if, speaking of a debtor, the people should say he was frightened by his creditor, and then reduced to the necessity of paying his debts, they would mean a *legal,* which is very different from a physical necessity ; for although the debtor, by refusing payment, might be confined, he would be allowed sustenance ; and the necessity he was under to pay his debts would not extend beyond his confinement. Again, if it should be said that a *client* is under the necessity of giving to his lawyer more than legal fees, the general and popular meaning of *necessity* would in this case be very different from that in the other cases. The necessity would neither be physical nor legal, but *artificial,* or, if I may be allowed the expression, a *long-robed* necessity. The meaning of the word "*necessary*" varies, also, according to circumstances : for, although Congress have power to levy and collect taxes, duties, &c. ; to borrow money ; and to determine the time, quantum, mode, and every regulation *necessary* and proper for supplying the treasury, — yet the people would apply a different meaning to the word *necessary* under different circumstances. For instance, without a sufficiency of precious metals for a medium, laws creating an artificial medium would be generally thought necessary for carrying into effect the power to levy and collect taxes ; but if there was a sufficiency of such metals, those laws would not generally be thought necessary. Again, if specie was scarce, and the credit of the government low, collateral measures would be by the people thought necessary for obtaining public loans ; but not so if the case was reversed. Or, if parts of the states should be invaded and overrun by an enemy, it would be thought necessary to levy on the rest heavy taxes, and collect them in a short period, and to take stock, grain, and other articles, from the citizens, without their consent, for common defence ; but in a time of peace and safety such measures would be generally supposed unnecessary. Instances may be multiplied in other respects, but it is conceived that these are sufficient to show that the popular and general meaning of the word " necessary " varies according to the subject and circumstances.

The Constitution, in the present case, is the great law of the people, who are themselves the sovereign legislature ; and the preamble is in these words — " We, the people of the United States, in order to form a more perfect union, establish justice, insure domestic tranquillity, provide for the common defence, promote the general welfare, and secure the blessing of liberty to ourselves and our posterity, *do* ordain and establish this *Constitution* for the United States of America."

These are the great objects for which the Constitution was established; and in administering it, we should always keep them in view. And here it is remarkable, that, although common defence and general welfare are held up, in the preamble, amongst the primary objects of attention, they are again mentioned in the 8th section of the 1st article, whereby we are enjoined, in laying taxes, duties, &c., particularly to regard the common defence and general welfare. Indeed, common sense dictates the measure; for the security of our property, families, and liberties — of every thing dear to us — depends on our ability to defend them. The means, therefore, for attaining this object, we ought not to omit a year, a month, or even a day, if we could avoid it; and we are never provided for defence unless prepared for sudden emergencies.

In the present case, the gentlemen in the opposition generally, as well as the gentleman first up, from Virginia, give the whole clause by which Congress are authorized " to make all laws necessary and proper," &c., no meaning whatever; for they say the former Congress had the same power under the Confederation, without this clause, as the present Congress have with it. The "Federalist" is quoted on this occasion; but, although the author of it discovered great ingenuity, this part of his performance I consider as a political heresy. His doctrine, indeed, was calculated to lull the consciences of those who differed in opinion with him at that time; and, having accomplished his object, he is probably desirous that it may die with the opposition itself. The rule in this case says, that where the words bear no signification, we must deviate a little; and as this deviation cannot be made by giving the words less than no meaning, it must be made by a more liberal construction than is given by gentlemen in the opposition. Thus their artillery is turned against themselves; for their own interpretation is an argument against itself.

The last rule mentioned relates to the spirit and reason of the law; and the judge is of opinion " that the most universal and effectual way of discovering the true meaning of a law, when the words are dubious, is by considering the reason and spirit of it — of the cause which moved the legislature to enact it." The causes which produced the Constitution were an imperfect union, want of public and private confidence, internal commotions, a defenceless community, neglect of the public welfare, and danger to our liberties. These are known to be the causes, not only by the preamble of the Constitution, but also from our own knowledge of the history of the times which preceded the establishment of it. If these weighty causes produced the Constitution, and it not only gives power for removing them, but also authorizes Congress to make all laws necessary and proper for carrying these powers into effect, shall we listen to assertions, that these words have no meaning, and that the new Constitution has not more energy than the old? Shall we thus unnerve the government, leave the Union as it was under the Confederation, — defenceless against a banditti of Creek Indians, — and thus relinquish the protection of its citizens? Or shall we, by a candid and liberal construction of the powers expressed in the Constitution, promote the great and important objects thereof? Each member must determine for himself. I shall, without hesitation, choose the latter, and leave the people and states to determine whether or not I am pursuing their true interest. If it is inquired where we are to draw the line of a liberal construction, I would also inquire, Where is the line of restriction to be drawn?

The interpretation of the Constitution, like the prerogative of a sovereign, may be abused; but from hence the disabuse of either cannot be inferred. In the exercise of prerogative, the minister is responsible for his advice to his sovereign, and the members of either house are responsible to their constituents for their conduct in construing the Constitution. We act at our peril : if our conduct is directed to the attainment of the great objects of government, it will be approved, and not otherwise. But this cannot operate as a reason to prevent our discharging the trusts reposed in us.

Let us now compare the different modes of reasoning on this subject, and determine which is right — for both cannot be.

The gentleman from Virginia (Mr. Madison) has urged the dangerous tendency of a liberal construction; but which is most dangerous, a *liberal* or a *destructive* interpretation ? The liberty we have taken in interpreting the Constitution, we conceive to be *necessary*, and it cannot be denied to be *useful* in attaining the objects of it ; but whilst he denies us this liberty, he grants to himself a right to annul part, and a very important p rt, of the Constitution. The same principle that will authorize a destruction of part, will authorize the destruction of the whole, of the Constitution; and if gentlemen have a right to make such rules, they have an equal right to make others for enlarging the powers of the Constitution, and indeed of forming a despotism. Thus, if we take the gentleman for our pilot, we shall be wrecked on the reef which he cautions us to avoid.

The gentleman has referred us to the last article of the amendment proposed to the Constitution by Congress, which provides that the powers not delegated to Congress, or prohibited to the states, shall rest in them or the people ; and the question is, What powers are *delegated?* Does the gentleman conceive that such only are delegated as are *expressed ?* If so, he must admit that our whole code of laws are unconstitutional. This he disavows, and yields to the necessity of interpretation, which, by a fair and candid application of established rules of construction to the Constitution, authorize, as has been shown, the measure under consideration.

The *usage* of Congress has also been referred to; and if we look at their acts under the existing Constitution, we shall find they are generally the result of a liberal construction. I will mention but two. The first relates to the establishment of the executive departments, and gives to the President the power of removing officers. As the Constitution is silent on this subject, the power mentioned, by the gentleman's own reasoning, is vested in the states or the people. He, however, contended for an *assumption* of the power, and, when assumed, urged that it should be vested in the President, although, like the power of appointment, it was, by a respectable minority in both houses, conceived that it should have been vested in the President and Senate. His rule of interpretation *then* was, therefore, more liberal than it is *now.* In the other case, Congress determined by law, with the sanction of the President, when and where they should hold their next session, although the Constitution provides that this power shall rest solely in the two houses. The gentleman also advocated this measure, and yet appears to be apprehensive of the consequences that *may* result from a construction of the Constitution which admits of a national bank. But from which of these measures is danger to be apprehended ? The *only* danger from our interpretation would be the exercise by Congress of a general power to form corporations ; but the dangers resulting from the gentleman's interpretation are very different ; for what *may* we not apprehend from the precedent of having *assumed* a power on which the Constitution was silent, and from having annexed it to the supreme executive ? If we have this right in one instance, we may extend it to others, and make him a despot.

Militia Bill.

Mr. BLOODWORTH moved to strike out the words in the 1st section, "except as herein exempted," and to insert, in lieu thereof, "except such as shall be exempted by *the legislatures* of the particular states."

Mr. SHERMAN wished the gentleman would consent to alter his motion, and let it be all between certain ages, and who are not exempted from militia duty by the respective states.

Mr. MADISON said, the motion ought to go still farther, and exempt the judges of the federal courts ; because some states, having no militia laws, could not have exempted them, and the propriety of exonerating them from militia duty was too apparent to need any arguments to prove it.

Mr. SHERMAN thought the motion was simple as it stood, and would decide a question upon which the house seemed to be divided. It would afterwards be open for amendment, so far as to add the exemptions.

Mr. MADISON said, if the gentleman would vary his motion, so as to embrace his idea, he would have no objection to the adoption of that part which was first moved.

Mr. LIVERMORE declared, that he had several objections. The first was, that the expression in the motion was of a doubtful import. It could not be readily ascertained, whether it had relation to the militia laws at this time existing in the several states, or to the existing and future laws. If it opens a door to future laws, it is impossible for us to foresee where it will end. It destroys that certainty which is necessary in a government of laws, and renders us incapable of judging of the propriety of our own act. Some states may exempt all persons above thirty years of age ; some may exempt all mechanics ; and others all husbandmen, or any general description of persons ; and this uncertainty will be productive of inconceivable inconveniences. Hence it will be improper to adopt the amendment in the present form.

Mr. SHERMAN observed, that most of the powers delegated to the government of the United States, by the Constitution, were altogether distinct from the local powers retained by the individual states. But in the case of the militia it was different. Both governments are combined in the authority necessary to regulate that body. The national government is to provide for organizing, arming, and disciplining the militia, and for governing such part of them as may be employed in the service of the United States. But, then, it is to be observed, that the states do, respectively and expressly, reserve out of such power the right of appointing officers, and the authority of training the militia; so that the concurrence of both governments is evidently necessary, in order to form and train them. Now, in governing the militia, the states have, at times other than when they are in the actual service of the United States, an indisputable title to act as their discretion shall dictate. And here it was an allowable supposition, that the particular states would have the greatest advantage of judging of the disposition of their own citizens. and who are the most proper characters to be exempted from their gov

ernment. He admitted, however, that the general government had (under
that clause of the Constitution which gave the authority to exercise all
powers necessary to carry the particularly enumerated powers into effect)
a right to make exemptions of such officers of the government whose
duties were incompatible with those of militiamen. Every thing, besides
this, he believed, was vested in the particular states ; and he would ask
the gentleman whether it was not a desirable thing to give satisfaction on
these points ; and whether they ought not to avoid stretching the general
power, which he had mentioned, beyond what was absolutely necessary to
answer the end designed.

An accommodation (continues Mr. Sherman) on this point took place
between the gentlemen, and the two motions were blended and made into
one ; whereupon Mr. GILES rose and said, he had now greater objections
to the motion than before, and was well persuaded that if the gentleman
(Mr. Sherman) attended to its consequences, he would find that it was
not only extremely dissimilar in its principles, but tended to overthrow the
very doctrine laid down in the first proposition, which was intended to
decide whether, under the division of the authority for forming and raising
the militia, the power of making *exemptions* remained in the state governments, or was granted by the Constitution to the government of the
United States. Now, in the compromised proposition, there appears to
be a mixture of power ; the first part seems to declare that the states
ought to make the exemptions ; yet the subsequent absolutely exercises it
on the part of the United States. If, then, the power of exemption be
either ceded to the general government, or reserved to the state governments, the amendment must fall to the ground.

But this was not his only objection. He conceived that, whether the
power of exemption was in the state or federal government, there was one
description of men mentioned in the proposition which could not be exempted or further privileged by the house. He alluded to the members
of the legislature of the United States. The privilege of these persons
was taken up and duly considered by the Convention, who then decided
what privileges they were entitled to. It is under this clause, said he, that
every thing necessary or proper to be done for members of Congress was
done. "The senators and representatives shall receive a compensation
for their services, to be ascertained by law, and paid out of the treasury of
the United States. They shall in all cases, except treason, felony, and
breach of peace, be privileged from arrest during their attendance at the
session of their respective houses, and in going to and returning from the
same ; and for any speech or debate in either house, they shall not be
questioned in any other place." Now, if the Convention took up this subject, (as it is plain from the foregoing clause that they did,) it is reason
able to presume that they made a full declaration of all our privileges ; and
it is improper to suppose that we are possessed of similar powers with the
Convention, and able to extend our own privileges. I conceive that every
inconvenience which would attend the want of an exemption in the bill, is
completely remedied by the Constitution ; and therefore it is impolitic to
make a useless regulation.

Mr. WILLIAMSON. When we departed from the straight line of
duty marked out for us by the first principles of the social compact, we
found ourselves involved in difficulty. The burden of militia duty lies
equally upon all persons ; and when we contemplate a departure from this
principle, by making exemptions, it involves us in our present embarrassment. I wish, therefore, that, before we proceed any farther in consider

ing the propriety of the amendment, we should consider the intention of the Constitution. When it speaks of regulating the militia, was it for organizing, arming, and disciplining, the militia of the several states, that Congress ought to provide? I think it was not the militia of the nation, but that which existed in the several states. It is impossible the Convention could have had any thing else in contemplation; because the Constitution says that Congress shall have the power of such parts of them as may be employed in the service of the United States. If we are, then, to govern the militia, it must be such men as the particular states have declared to be militia.

Mr. BOUDINOT. With respect to the power of exempting from militia duty, I believe little doubt will remain on the mind of any gentleman, after a candid examination of the Constitution, but that it is vested in Congress. This, then, reduces the question to the doctrine of expediency. Is it more expedient that the general government should make the exemptions, or leave it to the state legislatures? For my part, I think we ought to exercise the power ourselves; because I can see neither necessity, propriety, nor expediency, in leaving that to be done by others which we ourselves can do without inconvenience.

Mr. JACKSON, (a gentleman of superior talents, who had been an active member of the Federal Convention, in framing the general Constitution, and who is one of the judges of the Supreme Court of the United States; was likewise a member of the late Convention of Pennsylvania; and it is in evidence that he gave his assent to the present Constitution of that state, one article of which declared that persons conscientiously scrupulous of bearing arms shall be exempted from performing militia duty, upon the condition of their paying an equivalent.) Is not this a declaration of the sense of the people of Pennsylvania, that they, and they only, had the right to determine exemptions so far as relates to their own citizens? And it is observable that this Constitution has been framed whilst the federal government was in full operation. If this privilege belongs to the state, as they have declared it does, why shall Congress attempt to wrest it from them, first by undertaking exemptions for them, and then depriving them of a tax, which they contemplate to receive into the state treasury, as an equivalent for such exemption? Certainly such conduct must excite alarm, and occasion no inconsiderable degree of jealousy. These circumstances and considerations are forcible arguments with me to desist.

December 24, 1790.

Mr. LIVERMORE. He saw no reason why Congress should grant an exemption to those who are conscientiously scrupulous of bearing arms, more than to any other description of men. They ought, in his opinion, to be exempted by the state legislatures. As to the money accruing from such exemptions, he could not conceive that Congress was authorized to raise a revenue for the United States by the militia bill; nor was any such thing ever intended by the Constitution.

Bill to determine the Time when the Electors of President and Vice-President shall be chosen.

House of Representatives, *January* 14, 1791.

Mr. SHERMAN showed, from the Constitution, that Congress possess the power of appointing the time of choosing the electors, and the time when they should meet to give in their votes. He was in favor of Congress exercising this power, in order to guard against all intrigue; and this, he conceived, was agreeable to the people; for in none of the conventions was an amendment of this article ever moved for.

On the Post-Office Bill. — On a Motion to authorize the President to choose the Mail Route.

HOUSE OF REPRESENTATIVES, *December* 6, 1791.

Mr. SEDGWICK. As to the constitutionality of this delegation, (of power to establish post-roads,) it was admitted by the committee themselves, who brought in the bill; for, if the power was altogether indelegable, no part of it could be delegated; and if a part of it could, he saw no reason why the whole could not. The 2d section was as unconstitutional as the 1st; for it is there said, that "it shall be lawful for the postmaster-general to establish such other roads, or post-roads, as to him may seem necessary."

Congress, he observed, are authorized not only to establish post-offices and post-roads, but also to borrow money. But is it understood that Congress are to go, in a body, to borrow every sum that may be requisite? Is it not rather their office to determine the principle on which the business is to be conducted, and then delegate the power of carrying their resolves into execution?

Mr. GERRY observed, that, since the words of the Constitution expressly vested in Congress the power of establishing post-offices and post-roads, and since the establishing of post-roads cannot possibly mean any thing else but to point out what roads the post shall follow, the proposed amendment cannot take effect without altering the Constitution. The house could not transfer the power which the Constitution had vested in them. Supposing even they could; still it must be allowed that they, assembled from every quarter of the Union, must collectively possess more of that kind of information which the present subject required, than could be obtained by any executive officer. If it was thought necessary, in the present instance, to transfer the power from their own to other hands, with what degree of propriety could they be said to have undertaken to determine the ports of entry throughout the United States, since the Constitution mentions nothing further on that subject than the power of laying *duties, imposts,* and *excises?* According to the arguments now advanced, the legislature might have contented themselves with simply determining the amount of the duties and excises, and left the rest to the executive. But if such conduct would have been improper in that instance, much more so would it appear in the present case; since, on the one hand, there is no provision in Congress that should establish ports of entry, whereas there is no other for the establishment of post-roads.

Mr. B. BOURNE was in favor of the amendment, which he thought both expedient and constitutional. In speaking of *post-offices and post-roads,* the Constitution, he observed, speaks in general terms, as it does of a *mint, excises,* &c. In passing the excise law, the house, not thinking themselves possessed of sufficient information, empowered the President to mark out the districts and surveys; and if they had a right to delegate such power to the executive, the further delegation of the power of marking out the roads for the conveyance of the mail could hardly be thought dangerous. The Constitution meant no more than that Congress should possess the exclusive right of doing that by themselves, or by any other person, which amounts to the same thing: the business he thought much more likely to be well executed by the President, or the postmaster-general, than by Congress.

Post-Offices and Post-Roads.

On a motion of Mr. FITZSIMONS, to allow stage proprietors, who transport the mail, to carry passengers also, it was argued —

That clause of the Constitution which empowers the federal government to establish post-offices and post-roads, cannot (it was said) be understood to extend farther than the conveyance of intelligence, which is the proper subject of the post-office establishment: it gives no power to send men and baggage by post. The state governments have always possessed the power of stopping or taxing passengers. That power they have never given up; and the proposition now made to wrest it from them might be viewed as an attempt to lay the state legislatures prostrate at the feet of the general government, and will give a shock to every state in the Union.

If, by the construction of that clause of the Constitution which authorizes Congress to make all laws necessary for carrying into execution the several powers vested in them, they should establish the proposed regulations for the conveyance of the mail, they may proceed farther, and so regulate the post-roads as to prevent passengers from travelling on them; they may say what weights shall be carried on those roads, and at what seasons of the year; they may remove every thing that stands in the way; they may level buildings to the ground, under the pretence of making more convenient roads; they may abolish tolls and turnpikes; they may, where an established ferry has been kept for a hundred years past in the most convenient place for crossing a river, give the post-rider authority to set up a new one beside it, and ruin the old establishment; they may say, that the person who carries the mail shall participate in every privilege that is now exclusively enjoyed by any man or body of men; — and allege, as a reason for these encroachments, that they are only necessary encouragements to carry the mail of the United States: in short, the ingenuity of man cannot devise any new proposition so strange and inconsistent, as not to be reducible within the pale of the Constitution, by such a mode of construction. If this were once admitted, the Constitution would be a useless and dead letter; and it would be to no purpose that the states, in convention assembled, had framed that instrument, to guide the steps of Congress. As well might they at once have said, "There shall be a Congress who shall have full power and authority to make all laws which to their wisdom will seem meet and proper."

On the Cod Fishery Bill, granting Bounties.

Mr. GILES. The present section of the bill (he continued) appears to contain a direct bounty on occupations; and if that be its object, it is the *first* attempt as yet made by this government to exercise such authority; — and its constitutionality struck him in a doubtful point of view; for in no part of the Constitution could he, in express terms, find a power given o Congress to grant bounties on occupations: the power is neither directly granted, nor (by any reasonable construction that he could give) annexed to any other specified in the Constitution.

February 7, 1792.

Mr. WILLIAMSON. In the Constitution of this government, there are two or three remarkable provisions which seem to be in point. It is provided that direct taxes shall be apportioned among the several states according to their respective numbers. It is also provided that " all duties, imposts, and excises, shall be uniform throughout the United States; " and it is provided that no preference shall be given, by any regulation of commercial revenue, to the ports of one state over those of another. The clear and obvious intention of the articles mentioned was, that Congress might not have the power of imposing unequal burdens — that it might not be in their power to gratify one part of the Union by oppressing another. It appeared possible, and not very improbable, that the time might come, when, by greater cohesion, by more unanimity, by more address, the representatives of one part of the Union might attempt to impose unequal taxes, or to relieve their constituents at the expense of the people. To prevent the possibility of such a combination, the articles that I have mentioned were inserted in the Constitution.

I do not hazard much in saying that the present Constitution had never been adopted without those preliminary guards on the Constitution. Establish the general doctrine of bounties, and all the provisions I have mentioned become useless. They vanish into air, and, like the baseless fabric of a vision, leave not a trace behind. The common defence and general welfare, in the hands of a good politician, may supersede every part of our Constitution, and leave us in the hands of time and chance. Manufactures in general are useful to the nation; they prescribe the public good and general welfare. How many of them are springing up in the Northern States! Let them be properly supported by bounties, and you will find no occasion for unequal taxes. The tax may be equal in the beginning; it will be sufficiently unequal in the end.

The object of the bounty, and the amount of it, are equally to be disregarded in the present case. We are simply to consider whether bounties may safely be given under the present Constitution. For myself, I would rather begin with a bounty of one million per annum, than one thousand. I wish that my constituents may know whether they are to put any confidence in that paper called the Constitution.

Unless the Southern States are protected by the Constitution, their valuable staple, and their visionary wealth, must occasion their destruction. Three short years has this government existed; it is not three years; but we have already given serious alarms to many of our fellow-citizens. Establish the doctrine of bounties; set aside that part of the Constitution which requires equal taxes, and demands similar distributions; destroy this barrier; — and it is not a few fishermen that will enter, claiming ten or twelve thousand dollars, but all manner of persons; people of every trade and occupation may enter in at the breach, until they have eaten up the bread of our children.

Mr. MADISON. It is supposed, by some gentlemen, that Congress have authority not only to grant bounties in the sense here used, merely as a commutation for drawback, but even to grant them under a power by virtue of which they may do any thing which they may think conducive to the general welfare! This, sir, in my mind, raises the important and fundamental question, whether the general terms which have been cited are to be considered as a sort of caption, or general description of the specified powers; and as having no further meaning, and giving no further powers, than what is found in that specification, or as an abstract and indefinite delegation of power extending to all cases whatever — to all such, at least, as will admit the application of money — which is giving as much latitude as any government could well desire.

I, sir, have always conceived — I believe those who proposed the Constitution conceived — it is still more fully known, and more material to observe, that those who ratified the Constitution conceived — that this is not an indefinite government, deriving its powers from the general terms prefixed to the specified powers — but a limited government, tied down to the specified powers, which explain and define the general terms.

It is to be recollected that the terms " common defence and general welfare," as here used, are not novel terms, first introduced into this Constitution. They are terms familiar in their construction, and well known to the people of America. They are repeatedly found in the old Articles of Confederation, where, although they are susceptible of as great a latitude as can be given them by the context here, it was never supposed or pretended that they conveyed any such power as is now assigned to them. On the contrary, it was always considered clear and certain that the old Congress was limited to the enumerated powers, and that the enumeration limited and explained the general terms. I ask the gentlemen themselves, whether it was ever supposed or suspected that the old Congress could give away the money of the states to bounties to encourage agriculture, or for any other purpose they pleased. If such a power had been possessed by that body, it would have been much less impotent, or have borne a very different character from that universally ascribed to it.

The novel idea now annexed to those terms, and never before entertained by the friends or enemies of the government, will have a further consequence, which cannot have been taken into the view of the gentlemen. Their construction would not only give Congress the complete legislative power I have stated, — it would do more; it would supersede all the restrictions understood at present to lie, in their power with respect to a judiciary. It would put it in the power of Congress to establish courts throughout the United States, with cognizance of suits between citizen and citizen, and in all cases whatsoever.

This, sir, seems to be demonstrable; for if the clause in question really authorizes Congress to do whatever they think fit, provided it be for the general welfare, of which they are to judge, and money can be applied to it, Congress must have power to create and support a judiciary establishment, with a jurisdiction extending to all cases favorable, in their opinion, to the general welfare, in the same manner as they have power to pass laws, and apply money providing in any other way for the general welfare. I shall be reminded, perhaps, that, according to the terms of the Constitution, the judicial power is to extend to certain cases only, not to all cases. But this circumstance can have no effect in the argument, it being presupposed by the gentlemen, that the specification of certain objects does not limit the import of the general terms. Taking these terms as an abstract and indefinite grant of power, they comprise all the objects of legislative regulations — as well such as fall under the judiciary article in the Constitution as those falling immediately under the legislative article; and if the partial enumeration of objects in the legislative article does not, as these gentlemen contend, limit the general power, neither will it be limited by the partial enumeration of objects in the judiciary article.

There are consequences, sir, still more extensive, which, as they follow clearly from the doctrine combated, mus. either be admitted, or the doctrine must be given up. If Congress can employ money indefinitely to the general welfare, and are the sole and supreme judges of the general welfare, they may take the care of religion into their own hands: they may appoint teachers in every state, county, and parish, and pay them out of their public treasury; they may take into their own hands the education of children, establishing in like manner schools throughout the Union; they may assume the provision for the poor; they may undertake the regulation of all roads other than post-roads; in short, every thing, from the highest object of state legislation down to the most minute object of police, would be thrown under the power of Congress; for every object I have mentioned would admit of the application of money, and might be called, if Congress pleased, provisions for the general welfare.

The language held in various discussions of this house is a proof that the doctrine in question was never entertained by this body. Arguments, wherever the subject would permit, have constantly been drawn from the peculiar nature of this government, as limited to certain enumerated powers, instead of extending, like other governments, to all cases not particularly excepted. In a very late instance — I mean the debate on the representation bill — it must be remembered that an argument much used, particularly by gentlemen from Massachusetts, against the ratio of 1 for 30,000, was, that this government was unlike the state governments, which had an indefinite variety of objects within their power; that it had a small number of objects only to attend to; and therefore, that a smaller number of representatives would be sufficient to administer it.

Arguments have been advanced to show that because, in the regulation of trade, indirect and eventual encouragement is given to manufactures, therefore Congress have power to give money in direct bounties, or to grant it in any other way that would answer the same purpose. But surely, sir, there is a great and obvious difference, which it cannot be necessary to enlarge upon. A duty laid on imported implements of husbandry would, in its operation, be an indirect tax on exported produce; but will any one say that, by virtue of a mere power to lay duties on imports, Congress might go directly to the produce or implements of agriculture, or to the articles exported? It is true, duties on exports are expressly prohibited; but if there were no article forbidding them, a power directly to tax exports could never be deduced from a power to tax imports, although such a power might indirectly and incidentally affect exports.

In short, sir, without going farther into the subject, which I should not have here touched at all but for the reasons already mentioned, I venture to declare it as my opinion, that, were the power of Congress to be established in the latitude contended for, it would subvert the very foundations, and transmute the very nature of the limited government established by the people of America; and what inferences might be drawn, or what consequences ensue, from such a step, it is incumbent on us all to consider.

On the Proposition introduced by Mr. Fitzsimons, that Provision should be made for the Reduction of the Public Debt.

HOUSE OF REPRESENTATIVES, *November* 20, 1792.

Mr. MERCER. The Constitution permits the head of the treasury to propose plans. It may be proper, then, that the different secretaries may prepare such plans as are within their respective departments, which the chief magistrate may propose to the legislatures, if he sees fit; and when so done, it is constitutional, and the legislature may or may not, at their discretion, take them up; any other exposition is unconstitutional and idle. This is also the exposition of the documents and information that arise in the administration of government, which this house may require of the executive magistrate, and which he will communicate as he sees fit.   The house may go too far in asking information.   He may constitutionally deny such information of facts there deputed as are unfit to be communicated, and may assist in the legislation I always wish for.   But I want no *opinions* resulting from them.   If they are to influence us, they are wrong; if not to influence, they are useless.   This mode of procedure, of *originating* laws with the secretary, destroys the responsibility; it throws it on a man not elected by the people, and over whom they have no control.

November 21, 1792.

Mr. AMES.   What is the clause of the Constitution, opposed to the receiving a plan of a sinking fund from the secretary?   Bills for raising revenue shall originate in this house.   I verily believe the members of this house, and the citizens at large, would be very much surprised to hear this clause of the Constitution formally and gravely stated as repugnant to the reference to the treasury department for a plan, if they and we had not been long used to hear it.

To determine the force of this amazing constitutional objection, it will be sufficient to define terms.   .

What is a bill?   It is a term of technical import, and surely it cannot need a definition: it is an act of an inchoate state, having the form but not the authority of the law.

What is originating a bill?   Our rules decide it.   Every bill shall be introduced by a motion for leave, or by a committee.

It may be said, the plan of a sinking fund, reported by the secretary, is not, in technical, or even in popular language, a bill — nor, by the rules of the house or those of common sense, is this motion the originating a bill.   By resorting to the spirit of the Constitution, or by adopting any reasonable construction of the clause, is it possible to make it appear repugnant to the proposition for referring to the secretary?   The opposers of this proposition surely will not adopt a construction of the Constitution. They have often told us, we are to be guided by a strict adherence to the letter; that there is no end to the danger of constructions.

The letter is not repugnant; and will it be seriously affirmed that, according to the spirit and natural meaning of the Constitution, the report of the secretary will be a revenue bill, or any other bill, and that this proposition is originating such a bill?   If it be, where shall we stop?   If the idea of such a measure, which first passes through the mind, be confounded with the measure subsequent to it, what confusion will ensue! The President, by suggesting the proposition, may as well be pretended to originate a revenue bill; even a newspaper plan would be a breach of the exclusive privilege of this house, and the liberty of the press, so justly dear to us, would be found unconstitutional.   Yet if, without any order of the house, the draft of an act were printed, and a copy laid before every member in his seat, no person will venture to say that it is a bill — that it is originated, or can be brought under cognizance of the house, unless by a motion

I reply upon it, that neither the letter of the Constitution, nor any meaning that it can be tortured into, will support the objection which has so often been urged with solemn emphasis and persevering zeal.

We may repeat it, what color is there for saying that the secretary *legislates?* Neither my memory nor my understanding can discern any. I am well aware that no topic is better calculated to make popular impressions; but I cannot persuade myself that they will charge us with neglect or violation of duty, for putting ourselves into a situation to discharge it in the best and most circumspect manner.

Mr. MADISON. I insisted that a reference to the secretary of the treasury on subjects of loans, taxes, and provisions for loans, &c., was in fact a delegation of the authority of the legislature, although it would admit of much sophistical argument on the contrary.

On the Memorial of the Relief Committee of Baltimore, for the Relief of St. Domingo Refugees.

HOUSE OF REPRESENTATIVES, *January* 10, 1794.

Mr. MADISON remarked, that the government of the United States is a definite government, confined to specified objects. It is not like the state governments, whose powers are more general. Charity is no part of the legislative duty of the government. It would puzzle any gentleman to lay his finger on any part of the Constitution which would authorize the government to interpose in the relief of the St. Domingo sufferers. The report of the committee, he observed, involved this constitutional question — whether the money of our constituents can be appropriated to any other than specific purposes. Though he was of opinion that the relief contemplated could not be granted in the way proposed, yet he supposed a mode might be adopted which would answer the purpose without infringing the Constitution.

Mr. NICHOLAS concurred in the sentiment with Mr. Madison. He considered the Constitution as defining the duty of the legislature so expressly, as that it left them no option in the present case.

Mr. BOUDINOT supported the question on constitutional grounds. He instanced several cases, which had occurred and might occur, in which relief must necessarily be granted, and that without occasioning any doubt of the constitutionality of the business; such as granting pensions, affording relief to the Indians, supporting prisoners, &c. He alluded to the circumstance of the alliance between the United States and France, the connection between the citizens of the United States and that country, &c.

Mr. DEXTER stated sundry objections from the Constitution. · It will not be pretended, he supposed, that the grant of moneys, on this occasion, was for the general welfare; it is merely a private charity. He was in favor of going into a committee on the subject, but wished a short delay, that he might revolve the question more fully in his own mind.

Mr. MADISON, in reply to Mr. Boudinot, who had stated several cases as in point, observed, that those cases came within the law of nations, of which this government has express cognizance; the support of prisoners is a case provided for by the laws of nations; but the present question, he remarked, could not be considered in any such point of view. (*Motion lost.*)

[*Note.* In May, 1812, "An Act for *the relief* of the citizens of Venezuela " was passed, authorizing the President to expend $50,000 to purchase provisions for that object. The motion to fill the blank with that amount was moved by Mr. Calhoun, and carried by ayes, 45 ; noes, 29.]

Commercial Restrictions.

HOUSE OF REPRESENTATIVES, *January* 31, 1794.

Mr. MADISON insisted that trade ought to be left free to find its proper channels, under the conduct of merchants; that the mercantile opinion was the best guide in the case now depending; and that that opinion was against the resolutions.

In answer to this objection, he said it was obvious to remark that, in the very terms of the proposition, trade ought to be *free* before it could find its proper *channel.* It was not free at present : it could not, therefore, find the channels in which it would most advantageously flow. The dikes must be thrown down, before the waters could pursue their natural course. Who would pretend that the trade with the British West Indies, or even with Great Britain herself, was carried on, under the present restrictions, as it would go on of itself, if unfettered from restrictions on her part, as it is on ours? Who would pretend that the supplies to the West Indies, for example, would not flow thither in American bottoms, if they flowed freely? Who would pretend that our wheat, our flour, our fish, &c., would not find their way to the British market, if the channels to it were open for them?

It seemed to have been forgotten that the principle of this objection struck at every regulation in favor of manufactures, as much, or even more, than at regulations on the subject of commerce. It required that every species of business ought to be left to the sagacity and interest of those carrying it on, without any interference whatever of the public authority.

The interest of the mercantile class may happen to differ from that of the whole community. For example; it is, generally speaking, the interest of the merchant to import and export every thing; the interest of manufacturers to lessen imports in order to raise the price of domestic fabrics, and to check exports, where they may enhance the price of raw materials. In this case, it would be as improper to allow the one for the other as to allow either to judge for the whole.

It may be the interest of the merchant, under particular circumstances, to confine the trade to its established channels, when the national interest would require those channels to be enlarged or changed. The best writers on political economy have observed, that the regulations most unfriendly to the national wealth of Great Britain have owed their birth to mercantile counsels. It is well known that, in France, the greatest opposition to that liberal policy which was as favorable to the true interest of that country as of this, proceeded from the interests which merchants had in keeping the trade in its former course.

If, in any country, the mercantile opinion ought not to be implicitly followed, there were the strongest reasons why it ought not in this. The body of merchants who carry on the American commerce is well known to be composed of so great a proportion of individuals who are either British subjects, or trading on British capital, or enjoying the profits of British consignments, that the mercantile opinion here might not be an American opinion; nay, it might be the opinion of the very country of which, in the present instance at least, we ought not to take counsel. What the genuine mercantile American opinion would be, if it could be collected apart from the general one, Mr. M. said he did not undertake positively to decide. His belief was, that it would be in favor of the resolutions.

Direct Taxes.

May 6, 1794.

Mr. SEDGWICK said, that, in forming a constitution for a national government, to which was intrusted the preservation of that government, and of the existence of society itself, it was reasonable to suppose that every mean necessary to those important ends should be granted.   This was in fact the case in the Constitution of the United States.   To Congress it was expressly granted to impose "taxes, duties, imposts, and excises."   It had been universally concluded, and never, to his knowledge, denied, but that the legislature, by those comprehensive words, had authority to impose taxes on every subject of revenue.   If this position was just, a construction which limited their operation of this power (in its nature and by the Constitution illimitable) could not be the just construction.

He observed that, to obviate certain mischief, the Constitution had provided that capitation and other *direct* taxes should be proportioned according to the ratio prescribed in it.   If, then, the legislature was authorized to impose a tax on every subject of revenue, (and surely pleasure carriages, as an object of luxury, and in general owned by those to whom contributions would not be inconvenient, were fair and proper subjects of taxation,) and a tax on them could not be proportioned by the constitutional ratio, it would follow, irresistibly, that such a tax, in this sense of the Constitution, was not "direct."   On this idea he enlarged his reasoning, and showed that such a tax was incapable of apportionment.

He said that, so far as he had been able to form an opinion, there had been a general concurrence in a belief that the ultimate sources of public contributions were labor, and the subjects and effects of labor ; that taxes, being permanent, had a tendency to equalize, and to diffuse themselves through a community.   According to these opinions, a capitation tax, and taxes on land, and on property and income generally, were a direct charge, as well in the immediate as ultimate sources of contribution.   He had considered those, and those only, as direct taxes in their operation and effects.   On the other hand, a tax imposed on a specific article of personal property, and particularly of objects of luxury, as in the case under consideration, he had never supposed had been considered a direct tax within the meaning of the Constitution.   The exaction was indeed directly of the owner ; but by the equalizing operation, of which all taxes more or less partook, it created an indirect charge on others besides the owners.

The Bill for authorizing the President to lay, regulate, and revoke Embargoes.

HOUSE OF REPRESENTATIVES, *May* 29, 1794.

Mr. MADISON did not accede to the principle of the bill.   He did not see any such immediate prospect of a war as could induce the house to violate the Constitution.   He thought that it was a wise principle in the Constitution to make one branch of the government raise an army, and another conduct it.   If the legislature had the power to conduct an army, they might imbody it for that end.   On the other hand, if the President was empowered to raise an army, as he is to direct its motions when raised, he might wish to assemble it for the sake of the influence to be acquired by the command.   The Constitution had wisely guarded against the danger on either side.   Upon the whole, he could not venture to give his consent for violating so salutary a principle of the Constitution as that upon which this bill encroached.

On the Motion of Mr. Tazewell to strike out a complimentary Reply to the French Republic.

Mr. ELLSWORTH combated the resolution, as originally offered, as unconstitutional.   Nothing, he contended, could be found in the Constitution to authorize *either* branch of the legislature to keep up any kind of correspondence with a foreign nation.   To Congress were given the powers of legislation, and the right of declaring war.   If authority beyond this is assumed, however trifling the encroachment at first, where will it stop?

Mr. BUTLER.   There was nothing in the Constitution, he contended, that could prevent the legislature from expressing their sentiments.   It was not an executive act, but a mere complimentary reply to a complimentary presentation.   If this right was denied them, where would the principle stop?   The Senate might be made in time mere automata.

Internal Improvement.

Mr. MADISON moved that the resolution laid on the table some days ago be taken up, relative to the survey of the post-roads between the province of Maine and Georgia; which being read, he observed that two good effects would arise from carrying this resolution into effect: the shortest route from one place to another would be determined upon, and persons having a stability of the roads would not hesitate to make improvements upon them.

Mr. BALDWIN was glad to see this business brought forward; the sooner it could be carried into effect the better.   In many parts of the country, he said, there were no improved roads, nothing better than the original Indian track.   Bridges and other improvements are always made with reluctance whilst roads remain in this state; because it is known, as the country increases in population and wealth, better and shorter roads will be made.   All expense of this sort, indeed, is lost.   It was properly the *business of the general government*, he said, *to undertake the improvement of the roads;* for the different states are incompetent to the business, their different designs clashing with each other.   It is enough for them to make good roads to the different seaports; the cross-roads should be left to the government of the whole.   The expense, he thought, would not be very great.   Let a surveyor point out the shortest and best track, and the money will soon be raised.   There was nothing in this country, he said, of which we ought to be more ashamed than our public roads.

Mr. BOURNE thought very valuable effects would arise from the carrying of this resolution into effect.   The present may be much shortened, he observed.   The Eastern States, he said, had made great improvement in their roads; and he trusted the best effects would arise from having regular mails from one end of the Union to the other.

Mr. WILLIAMS did not think it right for the revenues of the post-office to be applied to this end.   He acknowledged the propriety of extending the post-roads to every part of the Union.   He thought the house had better wait for the report of the committee, to which business relative to the post-office had been referred, which was preparing to be laid before the house.

Mr. MADISON explained the nature and object of the resolution He said it was the commencement of an important work.   He wished not to extend it at present.   The expenses of the survey would be great. The post-office, he believed, would have no objection to the intended regulation.

After some observations from Mr. THACHER, on the obtaining of the shortest distance from one place to another, and the comparing old with new roads, so as to come at the shortest and best, the resolution was agreed to, and referred to a committee of five, to prepare and bring in a bill.

Treaty-Making   Power. — [*Jay's   Treaty.*]

HOUSE OF REPRESENTATIVES, *March* 23, 1796.

Mr. MURRAY said, in construing our Constitution, in ascertaining the metes and bounds of its various grants of power, nothing, at the present day, is left for expedience or sophistry to new-model or to mistake.   The explicitness of the instrument itself; the contemporaneous opinions, still fresh from the recency of its adoption; the journals of that Convention which formed it, still existing, though not public, — all tend to put this question, in particular, beyond the reach of mistake.   Many who are now present were in the Convention; and on this question, he learned a vote was actually taken.

That the paper upon the table, issued by the President's proclamation, as a treaty, was a treaty in the eye of the Constitution, and the law of nations; that, as a treaty, it is the supreme law of the land, agreeably to the Constitution; that, if it is a treaty, nothing that we can rightfully do, or refuse to do, will add or diminish its validity, under the Constitution and law of nations.

March 24, 1796.

Mr. GALLATIN said, the only contemporaneous opinions which could have any weight in favor of the omnipotence of the treaty-making power, were those of gentlemen who had advocated the adoption of the Constitution; and recourse had been had to the debates of the state conventions in order to show that such gentlemen had conceded that doctrine.   The debates of Virginia had first been partially quoted for that purpose; yet when the whole was read and examined, it had clearly appeared that, on the contrary, the general sense of the advocates of the Constitution there was similar to that now contended for by the supporters of the motion. The debates of the North Carolina Convention had also been partially quoted; and it was not a little remarkable that, whilst gentlemen from that state had declared, on that floor, during the present debate, that they were members of the Convention which *ratified and adopted* the Constitution, that they had voted for it, and that their own and the general impression of that Convention was, that the treaty-making power was limited by the other parts of the Constitution, in the manner now mentioned, — it was not a little remarkable, that, in opposition to those declarations, a gentleman from Rhode Island had quoted partial extracts of the debates of a Convention in North Carolina which *rejected* the Constitution.

A gentleman from New York (Mr. Williams) had read to them an amendment proposed in the Convention of that state, by which it was required that a treaty should not abrogate a law of the United States; from whence he inferred that that Convention understood the treaty-making powers would have that effect, unless the amendment was introduced.

The gentleman, however, forgot to inform the committee that the amendment did not obtain; and, therefore, that the inference was the reverse of what he stated. Leaving, however, to other gentlemen, to make further remarks on the debates of the Conventions of their respective states, he would conclude what he had to say on that ground, by adverting to the debates of the Pennsylvania Convention.

The only part of those debates which had been printed contained the speeches of the advocates of the Constitution; and although the subject was but slightly touched, yet what was said on the subject by the ablest advocate of the Constitution in Pennsylvania, by the man who had been most efficient to enforce its adoption in that state, would be found to be in point. He then read the following extracts from Judge Wilson's speech, (page 468, Debates of the Pennsylvania Convention:) "There is no doubt but, under this Constitution, treaties will become the supreme law of the land; nor is there doubt but the Senate and President possess the power of making them."

Mr. Wilson then proceeds to show the propriety of that provision, and how unfit the legislature were to conduct the negotiations; and then expresses himself in the following words: "It well deserves to be remarked that, though the House of Representatives possess no active part in making treaties, yet their legislative authority will be found to have strong restraining influence upon both President and Senate. In England, if the king and his ministers find themselves, during their negotiation, to be embarrassed because an existing law is not repealed, or a new law enacted, they give notice to the legislature of their situation, and inform them that it will be necessary, before the treaty can operate, that some law be repealed, or some be made. And will not the same thing take place here?"

April 15, 1796.

Mr. MADISON. The proposition immediately before the committee was, that the treaty with Great Britain ought to be carried into effect by such provisions as depended on the House of Representatives. This was the point immediately in question.

If the propositions for carrying the treaty into effect be agreed to, it must be from one of three considerations: either that the legislature is bound by a constitutional necessity to pass the requisite laws, without examining the merits of the treaty; or that, on such examination, the treaty is deemed in itself a good one; or that there are good extraneous reasons for putting it into force, although it be in itself a bad treaty.

The first consideration being excluded by the decision of the house that they have a right to judge of the expediency or inexpediency of passing laws relative to treaties, the question first to be examined must relate to the merits of the treaty.

He mentioned the permission to aliens to hold lands in perpetuity, as a very extraordinary feature in this part of the treaty. He would not inquire how far this might be authorized by constitutional principles; but he would continue to say, that no example of such a stipulation was to be found in any treaty that ever was made, either where territory was ceded, or where it was acknowledged by one nation or another. Although it was common and right, in such regulation, in favor of the property of the inhabitants, yet he believed that, in every case that ever had happened, the owners of landed property were universally required to swear allegiance to the new sovereign, or to dispose of their landed property within a reasonable time. With respect to the great points in the law of nations, comprehended in the stipulations of the treaty, the same want of real reciprocity, and the same sacrifice of the interests of the United States, were conspicuous.

It is well known to have been a great and favorite object with the United States, " that free ships make free goods." They had established the principle in their other treaties. They had witnessed, with anxiety, the general efforts, and the successful advances, towards incorporating this principle into the law of nations — a principle friendly to all neutral nations, and particularly interesting to the United States. He knew that, at a former period, it had been conceded, on the part of the United States, that the law of nations stood as the present treaty regulates it. But it did not follow, that more than acquiescence in that doctrine was proper. There was an evident distinction between silently acquiescing in it, and giving it the support of a formal and positive stipulation. The former was all that could have been required, and the latter was more than ought to have been unnecessarily yielded.

Mr. LYMAN. I have no doubt of its constitutionality, notwithstanding all the arguments which I have either seen or heard. Many arguments might be adduced in support of this opinion ; but I will dispense with all but one, and that I consider as conclusive ; and that is this : The stipulations in this treaty are nearly all of such nature as not to respect objects of legislation. They respect objects which lie beyond the bounds of our sovereignty ; and beyond these limits our laws cannot extend, as rules to regulate the conduct of subjects of foreign powers ; and although some of these stipulations respect objects which are within the reach of our sovereignty, yet it is in such manner as to be not only pertinent, but perhaps absolutely necessary in forming the treaty. This conclusion, I think, is the natural and necessary result of a fair construction of the principles of the Constitution, and especially of that paragraph which vests the power of making treaties in the supreme executive, with the advice of the Senate.

In acts of the smallest importance, we see, daily, that, after they have undergone any possible chance of fair and impartial discussion in this house, they are transmitted to another, who equally proceed to correct and amend them ; and even this not being deemed sufficient to secure, as it were, against all possibility of danger, they are sent to the President, who has ten days to consider, and who may return them with his objections. These we are bound respectfully to inscribe on our Journals, and if we disagree in opinion with the President, the majority of two thirds of both branches is requisite to give validity to the law. Do we not discover in all this infinite caution a wish rather not to act at all, by the difference of the branches among each other, than to act imprudently or precipitately ? and can we imagine that a Constitution thus guarded with respect to laws of little consequence, hath left without check the immense power of making treaties — embracing, as in the instrument before us, all our greatest interests, whether they be of territory, of agriculture, commerce, naviga tion, or manufactures, and this for an indefinite length of time? No. By one of the guards of that Constitution, relative to appropriations of money, this treaty hath, in the last stage of its progress, come before us.

"We have resolved," according to our best judgment of the Constitution, and, as we have seen above, according to the meaning of it, that we have a right to judge of the expediency or inexpediency of carrying it into effect. This will depend on its merits; and this is the discussion that is now before us.

Our duty requires of us, before we vote 90,000 dollars of the people's money, — the sum required to carry this treaty into effect, — to pause, and inquire as to the why and wherefore. But is it merely the sum of 90,000 dollars that is in question? If it was, we ought to proceed slowly and cautiously to vote away the money of our constituents. But it is in truth a sum indefinite, for British debts, the amount of which we know not; and we are to grant this in the moment our treasury is empty; when we are called upon to pay five millions to the bank, and when no gentleman hath resources to suggest, but those of borrowing, at a time when borrowing is unusually difficult and expensive. But is it merely a question of money? No. It is the regulation of our commerce; the adjustment of our limits; the restraint, in many respects, of our own faculties of obtaining good or avoiding bad terms with other nations. In short, it is all our greatest and most interesting concerns that are more or less involved in this question.

I must confess, Mr. Chairman, that the first point of view in which this treaty struck me with surprise, was the attitude Great Britain assumes in it of dictating laws and usages of reception and conduct different towards us, in every different part of her empire, while the surface of our country is entirely laid open to her in one general and advantageous point of admission. In Europe, we are told, we may freely enter her ports. In the West Indies we were to sail in canoes of seventy tons burden. In the East Indies we are not to settle or reside without leave of the local government. In the seaports of Canada and Nova Scotia we are not to be admitted at all : — while all our rivers and countries are opened without the least reserve; yet surely our all was as dear to us as the all of any other nation, and ought not to have been parted with but on equivalent terms.

On the Bill for organizing, arming, and disciplining, the Militia of the United States.

HOUSE OF REPRESENTATIVES, *December*, 1796.

Mr. RUTHERFORD said, he believed the government of the United States had nothing to do with the militia of the several sovereign states. This was his opinion, and it was the opinion of the people at large — however, of nine tenths of them. The Constitution is express upon this subject. It says, when the militia is called into actual service, it shall be under the direction of the general government, but not until that takes place; the several states shall have command over their own children — their own families. If the United States take it up, they will defeat the end in view — they grasp too much.

With respect to the unconstitutionality, Mr. R. joined in opinion with the gentleman from New Jersey, (Mr. Henderson.) This law would tend to alienate the minds of the people of the Eastern States, whose militia were already well disciplined.

He hoped nothing more would be done, in that house, than to advise those states who had neglected their militia to revise and amend their laws, and make them more effectual. This is all this house can do — all they have a right to do.

Appropriations of Money for fitting out Vessels of War.

HOUSE OF REPRESENTATIVES, *February* 25, 1797.

Mr. GALLATIN conceived the power of granting money to be vested solely in the legislature, and though, according to the opinion of some gentlemen, (though not in his,) the President and Senate could so bind the nation as to oblige the legislature to appropriate money to carry a treaty into effect, yet, in all other cases, he did not suppose there had been any doubt with respect to the powers *of the legislature in this respect.*

March 2, 1797.

Mr. NICHOLAS. The power of this house to control appropriations has been settled. It was indeed an absurdity to call a body a legislature, and at the same time deny them a control over the public purse. If it were not so, where would be the use of going through the forms of that house with a money bill? The executive might as well draw upon the treasury at once for whatever sums he might stand in need of. A doctrine like this would be scouted even in despotic countries.

Patronage. — During the Discussion of the Foreign Intercourse Bill.

HOUSE OF REPRESENTATIVES, *January* 18, 1798.

Mr. GALLATIN said, he believed, upon the whole, our government was in a great degree pure. Patronage was not very extensive, nor had it any material effect upon the house, or any other part of the government; yet he could suppose our government to be liable to abuse in this way. By the nature of the government, the different powers were divided; the power of giving offices was placed in the executive — an influence which neither of the other branches possessed; and if too large grants of money were made, it might give to that power an improper weight.

Our government, he said, was in its childhood; and if patronage had any existence, it could not, of course, be as yet alarming; but he desired gentlemen to look at all governments where this power was placed in the executive, and see if the greatest evil of the government was not the excessive influence of that department. Did not this corruption exist, in the government which was constituted most similar to ours, to such a degree as to have become a part of the system itself, and without which, it is said, the government could not go on? Was it not, therefore, prudent to keep a watchful eye in this respect?

He did not, however, speak against the power itself: it was necessary to be placed somewhere. The Constitution had fixed it in the executive. If the same power had been placed in the legislature, he believed they would have been more corrupt than the executive. He thought, therefore, the trust was wisely placed in the executive.

January 19, 1798.

On the same occasion, Mr. PINCKNEY said, all commercial regulations might as well be carried on by consuls as by ministers; and if any differences should arise betwixt this country and any of the European governments, special envoys might be sent to settle them, as heretofore.

January 22, 1798.

Mr. BAYARD. It had been supposed, by gentlemen, that he might appoint an indefinite number of ministers; and were the house, in that case, he asked, blindly to appropriate for them? This question was predicated upon an abuse of power, whilst the Constitution supposed it would be executed with fidelity. Suppose he were to state the question in an opposite light. Let it be imagined that this country has a misunderstanding with a foreign power, and that the executive should appoint a minister, but the house, in the plenitude of its power, should refuse an appropriation. What might be the consequence? Would not the house have contravened the Constitution by taking from the President the power which by it is placed in him? It certainly would. So that this supposition of the abuse of power would go to the destruction of all authority. The legislature was bound to appropriate for the salary of the chief justice of the United States; and though the President might appoint a *chimney-sweeper* to the office, they would still be bound. The Constitution had trusted the President, as well as it had trusted that house. Indeed, it was not conceivable that the house could act upon the subject of foreign ministers. Our interests with foreign countries came wholly under the jurisdiction of the executive. The duties of that house related to the internal affairs of the country; but what related to foreign countries and foreign agents was vested in the executive. The President was responsible for the manner in which this business was conducted. He was bound to communicate, from time to time, our situation with foreign powers; and if plans were carried on abroad for dividing or subjugating us, if he were not to make due communication of the design, he would be answerable for the neglect.

Retaliation for Aggressions.

May 23, 1798.

Mr. SITGREAVES said, it is a principle as well settled as any in the law of nations, that, when a nation has received aggressions from another nation, it is competent for the injured nation to pursue its remedy by reprisal before a declaration of war takes place; and these reprisals shall be perfectly warrantable whilst they are commensurate only with the injuries received; and are not, under such circumstances, justifiable cause of war. It is even clear that these reprisals may be made during the pendency of a negotiation, and cannot, according to the law of nations, be justifiable ground for the rupture of any such negotiations.

Alien and Sedition Laws.

June, 1798.

Mr. LIVINGSTON. By this act the President alone is empowered to make the law; to fix in his own mind what acts, what words, what thoughts, or looks, shall constitute the crime contemplated by the bill; that is, the crime of being "suspected to be dangerous to the peace and safety of the United States." This comes completely within the definition of despotism — a union of legislative, executive, and judicial powers. My opinions on this subject are explicit: they are, that wherever our laws manifestly infringe the Constitution under which they were made, the people ought not to hesitate which to obey. If we exceed our powers, we become tyrants, and our acts have no effect.

Mr. TAZEWELL opposed the bill. He knew but of one power, given to Congress by the Constitution, which could exclusively apply to aliens: and that was the power of naturalization. Whether this was a power which excluded the states from its exercise, or gave to Congress only a concurrent authority over the subjects, he would not now pretend to say. It neither authorized Congress to prohibit the migration of foreigners to any state, nor to banish them when admitted. It was a power which could only authorize Congress to give or withhold citizenship. The states, notwithstanding this power of naturalization, could impart to aliens the rights of suffrage, the right to purchase and hold lands. There were, in this respect, no restraints upon the states. The states, Mr. T. said, had not parted from their power of admitting foreigners to their society, nor with that of preserving the benefit which their admission gave them in the general government, otherwise than that by which they would be deprived of a citizen. [The bill passed the Senate by yeas, 16; nays, 7.]

On the same Subject. — 1799.

From a Report of Congress. — "The right of removing aliens, as incident to the power of war and peace, according to the theory of the Constitution, belongs to the government of the United States. By the 4th section of the 4th article of the Constitution, Congress is required to protect each state from invasion; and is vested by the 8th section of the 5th article with powers to make all laws which shall be proper to carry into effect all powers vested by the Constitution in the government of the United States, or any department or officer thereof; and, to remove from the country, in times of hostility, dangerous aliens, who may be employed in preparing the way for invasion, is a measure necessary for the purpose of preventing invasion, and, of course, a measure it is empowered to adopt."

In relation to the sedition act, the committee report that "a law to punish false, scandalous, and malicious writings against the government, with intent to stir up sedition, is a law necessary for carrying into effect the power vested by the Constitution in the government of the United States, and in the officers and departments thereof, and, consequently, such a law as Congress may pass."

Further — "Although the committee believe that each of the measures [alien and sedition laws] adopted by Congress is susceptible of an analytical justification, on the principles of the Constitution and national policy, yet they prefer to rest their vindication on the same ground of considering them as parts of a general system of defence, adapted to a crisis of extraordinary difficulty and danger."

[See Virginia and Kentucky Resolutions of '98, at the end of this volume.]

Reduction of the Standing Army.

HOUSE OF REPRESENTATIVES, *January* 5, 1800.

Mr. RANDOLPH. I suppose the establishment of a standing army in the country not only a useless and enormous expense, but, upon the ground of the Constitution, the spirit of that instrument and the genius of a free people are equally hostile to this dangerous institution, which ought to be resorted to (if it all) only in extreme cases of difficulty and danger, yet let it be remembered that usage, that immemorial custom, is paramount in every written obligation; and let us beware of engrafting this abuse upon the Constitution. A people who mean to continue free must be prepared to meet danger in person, not to rely upon the fallacious protection of mercenary armies.

Amendment to the Constitution. — *Election of President of the United States.*

SENATE, January 23, 1800.

Mr. C. PINCKNEY (of South Carolina) thought it a very dangerous practice to endeavor to amend the Constitution by making laws for the purpose. The Constitution was a sacred deposit put into their hands; they ought to take great care not to violate or destroy the essential provisions made by this instrument. He remembered very well that, *in the Federal Convention, great care was used to provide for the election of the President of the United States independently of Congress, and to take the business, as far as possible, out of* THEIR *hands.*

On an Act laying Duties on Licenses, &c.

HOUSE OF REPRESENTATIVES, December 31, 1800.

Mr. BIRD said, that he considered Congress as incompetent to transfuse into the state governments the right of judging on cases that occurred under the Constitution and laws of the federal government, as they were to transfuse executive or legislative power, derived from that Constitution, into the hands of the executive and legislative organs of the state governments.

Judiciary. — *On Mr. Breckenridge's Motion to repeal the Act passed for a new Organization of the Judiciary System.*

SENATE, January 8, 1800.

Mr. J. MASON. It will be found that the people, in forming their Constitution, meant to make the judges as independent of the legislature as of the executive; because the duties they have to perform call upon them to expound not only the laws, but the Constitution also; in which is involved the power of checking the legislature, in case it should pass any laws in violation of the Constitution. For this reason, it was more important that the judges in this country should be placed beyond the control of the legislature, than in other countries, where no such power attaches to them.

Mr. Mason knew that a legislative body was occasionally subject to the dominance of violent passions. He knew that they might pass unconstitutional laws; and that the judges, sworn to support the Constitution, would refuse to carry them into effect; and he knew that the legislature might contend for the execution of their statutes. Hence the necessity of placing the judges above the influence of these passions; and for these reasons the Constitution had put them out of the power of the legislature.

January 13, 1802.

Mr MASON, (of Virginia.) When I view the provisions of the Constitution on this subject, I observe a clear distinction between the Supreme

Court and other courts.   With regard to the institution of the Supreme
Court, the words are imperative; while with regard to inferior tribunals
they are discretionary.   The first *shall*, the last *may*, be established
And surely we are to infer, from the wise sages that formed that Constitution, that nothing was introduced into it in vain.   Not only sentences,
but words, and even points, elucidate its meaning.   When, therefore, the
Constitution, using this language, says a Supreme Court *shall* be established, are we not justified in considering it a constitutional creation?
and on the other, from the language applied to inferior courts, are we not
equally justified in considering their establishment as dependent upon the
legislature, who *may*, from time to time, ordain them, as the public good
requires?   Can any other meaning be applied to the words " from time to
time"?   And nothing can be more important on this subject than that
the legislature should have power, from time to time, to create, to annul, or
to modify, the courts, as the public good may require — not merely to-day,
but forever, and whenever a change of circumstances may suggest the
propriety of a different organization.   On this point, there is great force
in the remark, that, among the enumerated powers given to Congress,
while there is no mention made of the Supreme Court, the power of establishing inferior courts is expressly given.   Why this difference, but
that the Supreme Court was considered by the framers of the Constitution
as established by the Constitution? while they considered the inferior
courts as dependent upon the will of the legislature.

January 13, 1802.

    Mr. STONE, (of North Carolina.)   No part of the Constitution ex-
pressly gives the power of removal to the President; but a construction
has been adopted, and practised upon from necessity, giving him that
power in all cases in which he is not expressly restrained from the exercise
of it.   The judges afford an instance in which he is expressly restrained
from removal — it being declared, by the 1st section of the 3d article of
the Constitution, that the judges, both of the supreme and inferior courts,
shall hold their offices during good behavior.   They doubtless shall, (as
against the President's power to retain them in office,) in common with
other officers of his appointment, be removed from office by impeachment and conviction; but it does not follow that they may not be removed
by other means.   They shall hold their offices during good behavior, and
they shall be removed from office upon impeachment and conviction of
treason, bribery, and other high crimes and misdemeanors.   If the words
impeachment of high crimes and misdemeanors be understood according
to any construction of them hitherto received and established, it will be
found that, although a judge, guilty of high crimes and misdemeanors, is
always guilty of misbehavior in office; yet that, of the various species
of misbehavior in office which may render it exceedingly improper that a
judge should continue in office, many of them are neither treason nor
bribery; nor can they properly be dignified by the appellation of high
crimes and misdemeanors; and for impeachment of which no precedent
can be found, nor would the words of the Constitution justify such
impeachment.

    To what source, then, shall we resort for a knowledge of what consti-
tutes this thing called misbehavior in office?   The Constitution did not intend that a circumstance, as a tenure by which the judges hold their offices,
should be incapable of being ascertained.   *Their misbehavior* certainly is

not an impeachable offence ; still it is the ground by which the judges are to be removed from office. The process of impeachment, therefore, cannot be the only one by which the judges may be removed from office, under and according to the Constitution. I take it, therefore, to be a thing undeniable, that there resides somewhere in the government a power that shall amount to define misbehavior in office by the judges, and to remove them from office for the same without impeachment. The Constitution does not prohibit their removal by the legislature, who have the power to make all laws necessary and proper for carrying into execution the powers vested by the Constitution in the government of the United States.

Mr. BRECKENRIDGE. To make the Constitution a practical system, the power of the courts to annul the laws of Congress cannot possibly exist. My idea of the subject, in a few words, is — That the Constitution intended a separation only of the powers vested in the three great departments, giving to each the exclusive authority of acting on the subjects committed to each ; that each are intended to revolve within the sphere of their own orbits, are responsible for their own motion only, and are not to direct or control the course of others ; that those, for example, who make the laws, are presumed to have an equal attachment to, and interest in, the Constitution, are equally bound by oath to support it, and have an equal right to give a construction to it ; that the construction of one department, of the powers particularly vested in that department, is of as high authority, at least, as the construction given to it by any other department ; that it is, in fact, more competent to that department, to which powers are exclusively confided, to decide upon the proper exercise of those powers, than any other department, to which such powers are not intrusted, and who are not consequently under such high and responsible obligations for their constitutional exercise ; and that, therefore, the legislature would have an equal right to annul the decisions of the courts, founded on their construction of the Constitution, as the courts would have to annul the acts of the legislature founded on their construction.

Although, therefore, the courts may take upon them to give decisions which go to impeach the constitutionality of a law, and which, for a time, may obstruct its operation, yet I contend that such law is not the less obligatory because the organ through which it is to be executed has refused its aid. A pertinacious adherence of both departments to their opinions would soon bring the question to an issue, which would decide in whom the sovereign power of legislation resided, and whose construction of the Constitution as to the law-making power ought to prevail.

Mr. HEMPHILL. I have ever understood that there was difference in opinion on this point : that the general opinion was, that the words in the Constitution rendered the judges independent of both the other branches of the government. This appears, from the debates in the Convention in Virginia, to have been their opinion ; it appears also, from the strongest implication, to have been the opinion of the author of the Notes on Virginia.

What is the meaning of the words *from time to time ?* They are used but in three other parts of the Constitution, and, when used, they do not convey the idea of what may be done. Indeed, they are used in cases where it is impracticable to undo what shall have been done. [Mr. Hemphill here read 5th sec. 1st art. No. 3, 9th sec. 1st art. No. 6, and 3d sec. 2d art.] What do these words mean in that part of the Constitution under discussion ? The Supreme Court had been mentioned in 2d and 3d art.

— *the* Supreme Court, which implies that there should be but one. They were not used to give Congress power to constitute inferior courts, for that power had been previously given; and if the inferior courts, together with the offices of the judges, are, as is contended, subjects of ordinary .egislation, these words were unnecessary to enlarge the powers of Congress on them : for, on all subjects of ordinary legislation, Congress have an unquestionable right to enact and repeal at pleasure.

It is not said, in the 8th section, 1st article, that Congress shall have the power to borrow money from time to time, to regulate commerce from time to time, or to establish post-offices and post-roads from time to time; yet nobody doubts that Congress have a right to enact and repeal laws on these subjects when it may appear expedient; and the same power would have extended to the clause giving power to constitute inferior tribunals, if there had been no restriction in any other part of the Constitution. As these words are unnecessary to give the power contended for, they must have some other meaning. The plain meaning is this — that these words, together with the first part of the section, were not used to give a power to constitute courts; for that power had been expressly given: they were merely introduced to dispose of judiciary power, and to declare where it should reside. The judiciary power of the United States shall be vested in one Supreme Court, and in such inferior courts as the Congress may, from time to time, ordain and establish; meaning the power before given, which was discretionary as to number. The clause in the 8th section of the 1st article is brought here into view; and in the very next sentence, the offices are positively fixèd and limited. Here, then, is an express and positive provision, uncontradicted by any express declaration, or by any violent implication.

Mr. BAYARD. The 2d section of the 3d article of the Constitution expressly extends the judicial power to all cases arising under the Constitution, the laws, &c. The provision in the 2d clause of the 6th article leaves nothing to doubt. This Constitution, and the laws of the United States which shall be made in pursuance thereof, &c., shall be the supreme law of the land. The Constitution is absolutely the supreme law. Not so of the acts of the legislature. Such only are the laws of the land as are made in pursuance of the Constitution.

Mr. RUTLEDGE. Taught by examples the value of a good judiciary, the patriots who met at Philadelphia determined to establish one which should be independent of the executive and legislature, and possess the power of deciding rightfully and finally on conflicting claims between them. The Convention laid their hand upon this invaluable and protecting principle : in it they discovered what was essential to the security and duration of free states; what would prove the shield and palladium of our liberties; and they boldly said, notwithstanding the discouragement in other countries, in past times, to efforts in favor of republicanism, our experiment shall not miscarry, for we will establish an independent judiciary; we will create an asylum to secure the government and protect the people in all the revolutions of opinion, and struggles of ambition and faction. They did establish an independent judiciary. There is nothing, I think, more demonstrable than that the Convention meant the judiciary to be a coördinate, and not a subordinate branch of the government. This is my settled opinion. But on a subject so momentous as this is, I am unwilling to be directed by the feeble lights of my own understanding; and as my judgment, at all times very fallible, is liable to err much where

38

my anx.t ties are much excited, I have had recourse to other sources for the true meaning of this Constitution. During the throes and spasms, as they have been termed, which convulsed this nation prior to the late presidential election, strong doubts were very strongly expressed whether the gentleman who now administers this government was attached to it *as it is.* Shortly after his election, the legislature of Rhode Island presented a congratulatory address which our chief magistrate considered as soliciting some declaration of his opinions of the Federal Constitution ; and in his answer deeming it fit to give them, he said, " the Constitution *shall* be administered by me according to the safe and *honest* meaning contemplated by the *plain understanding of the people at the time of its adoption* — a meaning to be found in the explanations of those who advocated, not those who opposed it. These explanations are preserved in the *publications of the time.*" To this high authority I appeal — to the honest meaning of the instrument, the plain understanding of its framers. I, like Mr. Jefferson, appeal to the opinions of those who were the friends of the Constitution at the time it was submitted to the states. Three of our most distinguished statesmen, who had much agency in framing this Constitution, finding that objections had been raised against its adoption, and that much of the hostility produced against it had resulted from a misunderstanding of some of its provisions, united in the patriotic work of explaining the true meaning of its framers. They published a series of papers, under the signature of Publius, which were afterwards republished in a book called the Federalist. This contemporaneous exposition is what Mr. Jefferson must have adverted to when he speaks of the publication of the time. From this very valuable work, for which we are indebted to Messrs. Hamilton, Madison, and King, I will take the liberty of reading some extracts, to which I solicit the attention of the committee. In the seventy-eighth number we read, " *Good behavior* for the continuance in office of the judicial magistracy, is the most valuable of the modern improvements in the practice of government. In a republic, it is a barrier to the encroachments and oppressions of the representative body ; and it is the best expedient that can be devised in any government to secure a steady, upright, and impartial administration of the laws. The *judiciary*, in a government where the departments of power are separate from each other, from the nature of its functions, will always be the least dangerous to the political rights of the Constitution. It has no influence over the sword or the purse, and may be truly said to have neither *force* nor *will*, but merely judgment. The complete independence of the courts of justice is essential in a limited constitution ; one containing specified exceptions to the legislative authority ; such as that it shall pass no *ex post facto* law, no bill of attainder, &c. Such limitations can be preserved in practice no other way than through the courts of justice, whose duty it must be to declare all acts manifestly contrary to the Constitution *void*. Without this, all the reservations of particular rights or privileges of the states or the people *would amount to nothing*. Where the will of the legislature, declared in its statutes, stands in opposition to that of the people, declared in the Constitution, the courts, designed to be an intermediate body between the people and the legislature, are to keep the latter within the limits assigned to their authority. The Convention acted wisely in establishing *good behavior* as the tenure of judicial offices. Their plan would have been inexcusably defective had it wanted this important feature of good government." The authority I have read proves to demonstration what was the intention of the Convention on this subject — that it was to establish a judiciary completely independent of the executive and legislature, and to have judges removable only by impeachment.   This was not only the intention of the General Convention, but of the state conventions when they adopted this Constitution.   Nay, sir, had they not considered the judicial power to be coördinate with the other two great departments of government, they never would have adopted the Constitution.   I feel myself justified in making this declaration by the debates in the different state conventions. From those of the Virginia Convention I will read some extracts, to show what were there the opinions of the speakers of both political parties.

General Marshall, the present chief justice, says, " Can the government of the United States go beyond those delegated powers?   If they were to make a law not warranted by any of the powers enumerated, it would be considered as an infringement of the Constitution, *which they are to guard:* they would not consider such a law as coming under their jurisdiction . *they would declare it void.*"   Mr. Grayson, who opposed the Constitution, we find saying, " The judges will not be independent, because their salaries *may be augmented.*   This is left open.   What if you give £600 or £1000 annually to a judge?   'Tis but a trifling object, when, by that little money, you purchase the most invaluable blessing that any country can enjoy.   The judges are to defend the Constitution."   Mr. Madison, in answer, says, " I wished to insert a restraint on the augmentation as well as diminution of the compensation of the judges ; but I was overruled.   The business of the courts must increase.   If there was no power to increase their pay, according to the increase of business, *during the life of the judges,* it might happen that there would be such an accumulation of business as would reduce the pay to a most trivial consideration." Here we find Mr. Madison not using the words *good behavior,* but saying, (what we say was meant by *good behavior,*) *during the life of the judges.* The opinions of Mr. Madison I deem conclusive as to the meaning of the words *good behavior.*   Let us now see what was the opinion on this subject of the first Congress under the Constitution, when the first judiciary bill was debated.   Mr. Stone says, " The establishment of the courts is *immutable.*"   Mr. Madison says, " The judges are to be removed only on impeachment and conviction before Congress."   Mr. Gerry, who had been a member of the General Convention, expresses himself in this strong and unequivocal manner : " The judges will be independent, and no power can remove them : they will be beyond the reach of the other powers of the government ; they will be unassailable, and cannot be affected but by the united voice of America, and that only by a change of government." Here it is evident Mr. Gerry supposed a project like the present could only be effected by the people, through the medium of a convention ; he did not suppose it possible for Congress ever to grasp at this power.   The same opinions were held by Mr. Lawrence and Mr. Smith.

As early as the year 1789, among the first acts of the government, the legislature explicitly recognized the right of a state court to declare a treaty, a statute, and an authority exercised under the United States, void, subject to the revision of the Supreme Court of the United States; and it has expressly given the final power to the Supreme Court to affirm a judgment which is against the validity either of a treaty, statute, or an authority of the government.

Louisiana   Treaty.

HOUSE OF REPRESENTATIVES, *October* 25, 1803.

Mr. ELLIOT.   The Constitution is silent on the subject of the acquisition of territory; therefore the treaty is unconstitutional.   This question is not to be determined from a mere view of the Constitution itself, although it may be considered as admitted that it does not prohibit, in express terms, the acquisition of territory.   It is a rule of law that, in order to ascertain the import of a contract, the evident intention of the parties, at the time of forming it, is principally to be regarded.   Previous to the formation of this Constitution, there existed certain principles of the law of nature and nations, consecrated by time and experience, in conformity to which the Constitution was formed.   The question before us, I have always believed, must be decided upon the law of nations alone.

Dr. MITCHELL.   The people, in forming their Constitution, had an eye to that law of nations which is deducible by natural reason, and established by common consent, to regulate the intercourse and concerns of nations.   With a view to this law the treaty-making power was constituted, and, by virtue of this law, the government and people of the United States, in common with all other nations, possess the power and right of making acquisitions of territory by conquest, cession, or purchase.

Mr. SMILIE.   We are obliged to admit the inhabitants according to the principles of the Constitution.   Suppose those principles forbid their admission; then we are not obliged to admit them.   This followed as an absolute consequence from the premises.   There, however, existed a remedy for this case, if it should occur; for, if the prevailing opinion shal. be, that the inhabitants of the ceded territory cannot be admitted under the Constitution, as it now stands, the people of the United States can, if they see fit, apply a remedy, by amending the Constitution so as to authorize their admission.   And if they do not choose to do this, the inhabitants may remain in a colonial state.

Mr. RODNEY.   In the view of the Constitution, the Union is composed of two corporate bodies — of states and territories.   A recurrence to the Constitution will show that it is predicated on the principle of the United States' territory, either by war, treaty, or purchase.   There was one part of that instrument within whose capacious grasp all these modes of acquisition were embraced.   By the Constitution, Congress have power to " lay and collect taxes, duties, imposts, and excises ; to pay the debts and provide for the common defence and general welfare of the United States." To provide for the general welfare.   The import of these terms is very comprehensive indeed.   If this general delegation of authority be not at variance with other particular powers specially granted, nor restricted by them, — if it be not in any degree comprehended in those subsequently delegated, — I cannot perceive why, within the fair meaning of these general provisions, is not included the power of increasing our territory, if necessary for the general welfare or common defence.

Mr. TRACY, among other objections, said that the 7th article admits, for twelve years, the ships of France and Spain into the ceded territory, free of foreign duty.   This is giving a commercial preference to those ports over the other ports of the United States, because it is well known that a duty of forty-four cents on tonnage, and ten per cent. on duties, are paid by all foreign vessels in all the ports of the United States.   If it be said we must repeal those laws, and then the preference will cease, the answer is, that this 7th article gives the exclusive right of entering the ports of Louisiana to the ships of France and Spain; and if our discriminating duties were repealed this day, the preference would be given to the ports of the United States to those of Louisiana; so that the preference, by any regulation of commerce or revenue, which the Constitution expressly forbids from being given to the ports of one state over those of another, would be given by this treaty, in violation of the Constitution.

We can hold territory; but to admit the inhabitants into the Union, to make citizens of them, and states, by treaty, we cannot constitutionally do, and no subsequent act of legislation, or even ordinary amendment to our Constitution, can legalize such measures.

Mr. ADAMS. It has been argued that the bill ought not to pass, because the treaty itself is an unconstitutional, or, to use the words of the gentleman from Connecticut, (Mr. Tracy,) an extra-constitutional act, because it contains engagements which the powers of the Senate were not competent to ratify, the powers of Congress not competent to confirm; and, as two of the gentlemen have contended, not even the legislatures of the number of states requisite to effect an amendment of the Constitution, are adequate to sanction. It is, therefore, they say, a nullity. We cannot fulfil our part of its conditions; and on our failure in the performance of any one stipulation, France may consider herself as absolved from the obligations of the whole treaty on hers. I do not conceive it necessary to enter into the merits of the treaty at this time. The proper occasion for that discussion is past. But allowing even that this is a case for which the Constitution has not provided, it does not, in my mind, follow that the treaty is a nullity, or that its obligations, either on us or on France, must necessarily be cancelled. For my own part, I am free to confess, that the 3d article, and more especially the 7th, contain engagements placing us in a dilemma, from which I see no possible mode of extricating ourselves but by an amendment, or rather an addition, to the Constitution.

The gentleman from Connecticut, (Mr. Tracy,) both on a former occasion and in this day's debate, appears to me to have shown this to demonstration. But what is this more than saying that the President and Senate have bound the nation to engagements which require the coöperation of more extensive powers than theirs to carry them into execution? Nothing is more common, in the negotiations between nation and nation, than for a minister to agree to and sign articles beyond the extent of his powers. This is what your ministers, in the very case before you, have confessedly done. It is well known that their powers did not authorize them to conclude this treaty; but they acted for the benefit of their country, and this house, by a large majority, has advised to the ratification of their proceedings. Suppose, then, not only that the ministers who signed, but the President and Senate who ratified, this compact, have exceeded their powers; suppose that the other house of Congress, who have given their assent by passing this and other bills for the fulfilment of the obligations it imposes on us, have exceeded their powers; nay, suppose even that the majority of the states competent to amend the Constitution in other cases, could not amend it in this, without exceeding their powers, — and this is the extremest point to which any gentleman on this floor has extended his scruples; — suppose all this, and there still remains in the country a power competent to adopt and sanction every part of our engagements, and to carry them entirely into execution; for, notwithstanding the objections and apprehensions of many individuals, of many wise, able, and excellent men, in various parts of the Union, yet, such is the public favor attending the transaction which commenced by the negotiation of this treaty, and which I hope will terminate in our full, undisturbed, and undisputed possession of the ceded territory, that I firmly believe, if an amendment to the Constitution, amply sufficient for the accomplishment of every thing for which we have contracted, shall be proposed, as I think it ought, it will be adopted by the legislature of every state in the Union.   We can, therefore, fulfil our part of the convention, and this is all that France has a right to require of us.   France can never have a right to come and say, " I am discharged from the obligation of this treaty, because your President and Senate, in ratifying, exceeded their powers ; " for this would be interfering in the internal arrangements of our government.   It would be intermeddling in questions with which she has no concern, and which must be settled altogether by ourselves. The only question for France is, whether she has contracted with the department of our government authorized to make treaties ; and this being clear, her only right is to require that the conditions stipulated in our name be punctually and faithfully performed.   I trust they will be so performed, and will cheerfully lend my hand to every act necessary to the purpose; for I consider the object as of the highest advantage to us: and the gentleman from Kentucky himself, who has displayed, with so much eloquence, the immense importance, to this Union, of the possession of the ceded country, cannot carry his ideas farther on the subject than I do.

With these impressions, sir, perceiving in the first objection no substantial reason requiring the postponement, and in the second no adequate argument for the rejection, of this bill, I shall give my vote in its favor.

Mr. TRACY.   It is unreasonable to suppose that Congress should, by a majority only, admit new foreign states, and swallow up, by it, the old partners, when two thirds of all the members are made requisite for the least alteration in the Constitution.

Dr MITCHELL.   The 3d section of the 4th article of the Constitution contemplates that territory and other property may belong to the United States.   By a treaty with France, the nation has lately acquired title to a new territory, with various kinds of public property on it and annexed to it.   By the same section of the Constitution, Congress is so clothed with the power to dispose of such territory and property, and to make all needful rules and regulations respecting it.   This is as fair an exercise of constitutional authority as that by which we assemble and hold our seats in this house.   To the title thus obtained, we wish now to add the possession ; and it is proposed, for this important purpose, the President shall be empowered.

[*Note.* Jefferson himself (under whose auspices the treaty was made) was of opinion that the measure was unconstitutional, and required an amendment of the Constitution to justify it. He accordingly urged his friends strenuously to that course ; at the same time he added, " that it will be desirable for Congress to do what is necessary in silence : " " whatever Congress shall think necessary to do, should be done with as little debate as possible, and particularly so far as respects the constitutional difficulty ; " " I confess, then, I think it important, in the present case, to set an example against broad construction by appealing for new power to the people. If, however, our friends shall think differently, certainly I shall acquiesce with satisfaction, confiding that the good sense of our country will correct the evil of construction, when it shall produce ill effects."

His letter to Dr. Sibley, (in June, 1803,) recently published, is decisive that he thought an amendment of the Constitution necessary. Yet he did not hesitate, without such amendment, to give effect to every measure to carry the treaty into effect during his administration. See *Jefferson's Corresp.*, ii. pp. 1, 2, 3; *Story's Comm*]

District of Columbia. — *On the Report of the Committee of Elections, on the Case of John P. Van Ness.*

HOUSE OF REPRESENTATIVES, *January* 17, 1803.

Mr. VAN NESS said, the reasons he should offer to the committee for retaining his seat were few and simple. He thought the fair, liberal, and sound construction did not affect his case; that the incapacitating provision only applied to civil offices. The Constitution was only a digest of the most approved principles of the constitutions of the several states, in which the spirit of those constitutions was combined. Not one of those constitutions excluded from office those who had accepted military appointments, except in the regular service. He, therefore, felt a full conviction that it never was the intention of the framers of the Constitution of the United States to exclude militia officers from holding a seat in Congress. And however important it might be to adhere to the letter of the Constitution, yet, when the spirit of it was so clear as it appeared to him, it ought to have weight in the decision of the question before the committee which might affect objects of great importance. The right of every portion of the Union to a representation in that house was very important, and ought to be respected in all cases which may either directly or indirectly affect it.

Mr. BACON observed, though the first part of the section of the Constitution referred to *civil* offices, yet the latter part used the expression *any office*, which was more comprehensive, and appeared to them to have been intended to have a universal effect.

The question was then taken on the report of the committee of elections, which was agreed to without a division.

On Mr. Bacon's Resolution to re-cede the District of Columbia.

HOUSE OF REPRESENTATIVES, *February* 9, 1803.

Mr. BAYARD. Now, the states of Maryland and Virginia have made this cession, with the consent and approbation of the people in the ceded territory, and Congress has accepted the cession, and assumed the jurisdiction. Are they, then, at liberty, or can they relinquish it, without the consent of the other parties? It is presumed they cannot. In his opinion, they were constitutionally and morally bound to proceed in the exercise of that power regularly assumed, either immediately by themselves, or by the intervention of a territorial legislature, chosen and acting under a special act of Congress for that purpose. To relinquish the jurisdiction at this time, and re-cede the territory, would, in his view, exhibit a surprising inconsistency of conduct in the legislature; it would discover such a versatility, such a disposition to change, as could not fail to unsettle the minds of the people, and shake their confidence in the government.

Duelling. — *On a Resolution for rendering all Persons concerned in a Duel incapable of holding an Office under the General Government of the United States.*

HOUSE OF REPRESENTATIVES, *December* 31, 1803.

Mr. DAVIS said, if the house could be made sensible that the resolution embraced a subject on which it could not constitutionally act, they would reject it. To him it was plain that, if the house pursued the object of the resolution, it led them on forbidden ground. In the first place, it took from the citizens a right which, by their Constitution, they had secured themselves, — to wit, the right of free elections. Do what the resolution contemplates, and no man can hold a seat here who ever fought a duel, or gave or carried a challenge, although he may be the choice of the people. No such thing is said in the Constitution. The people, in that instrument, have already defined the disqualifications to office ; that charter of their rights declares that no person who has been impeached and found guilty shall hold an office ; and I contend that Congress cannot impeach a person for any offence done by him as an individual. Two things are requisite to ground an impeachment. First, the person must be an officer of the United States : secondly, he must have been guilty of some malfeasance in the discharge of the duties imposed on him by that office. If an individual who does not hold an office under the United States commits murder, I deny the right of Congress to impeach him. He is made amenable to the state laws. While we were busy in impeaching him, he might be executed by the statute laws of the states. My observations disclaim the right we have to act on it.

The resolution was negatived.

On the Amendment to the Constitution.

HOUSE OF REPRESENTATIVES, *December* 9, 1804.

Mr. JACKSON. The fate of the other little republics warranted the idea that the smaller members would be swallowed up by the larger ones, who would, in turn, attack each other ; and thus the liberty achieved by the blood of some of the bravest men that ever lived would pass away without leaving a trace behind it. They, therefore, yielded every thing to the little states, knowing they were not numerous, and naturally jealous of the large ones. If we examine the Constitution, we shall find the whole of the great powers of the government centred in the Senate.

On the Impeachment of Judge Chase.

HOUSE OF REPRESENTATIVES, *February* 21, 1805.

Mr. HOPKINSON. What part of the Constitution declares any of the acts charged and proved upon Judge Chase, even in the worst aspect, to be impeachable ? He has not been guilty of bribery or corruption ; he is not charged with them. Has he, then, been guilty of " other high crimes and misdemeanors " ? In an instrument so sacred as the Constitution, I presume every word must have its full and fair meaning. It is not, then, only for crimes and misdemeanors that a judge is impeachable, but it must be for *high* crimes and misdemeanors. Although this qualifying adjective " *high* " immediately precedes, and is directly attached to the word " crimes," yet, from the evident intention of the Constitution, and upon a just grammatical construction, it must also be applied to " *misdemeanors.*" If my construction of this part of the Constitution be not admitted, and the adjective " high " be given exclusively to " crimes," and denied to " misdemeanors," this strange absurdity must ensue — that when an officer of the government is impeached for a crime, he cannot be convicted, unless it proves to be a high crime ; but he may, nevertheless, be convicted of a misdemeanor of the most petty grade. Observe, sir the

crimes with which these "other high crimes" are classed in the Constitution, and we may learn something of their character.   They stand in connection with " *bribery and corruption*" — tried in the same manner, and
subject to the same penalties.   But, if we are to lose the force and meaning
of the word " *high*," in relation to misdemeanors, and this description of
offences must be governed by the mere meaning of the term " misdemeanors," without deriving any grade from the adjective, still my position remains unimpaired — that the offence, whatever it is, which is the ground
of impeachment, must be such a one as would support an indictment.
" Misdemeanor " is a legal and technical term, well understood and defined
in law ; and in the construction of a legal instrument, we must give words
their legal significations.   A misdemeanor, or a crime, — for in their just
and proper acceptation they are synonymous, — is an act committed,
or omitted, in the violation of a *public* law, either forbidding or commanding it.

[*Note.*   In the few cases of *impeachment* which have hitherto been tried, no one of
the charges has rested upon any suitable misdemeanors.   It seems to be the settled
doctrine of the high court of impeachment, (the Senate,) that though the common
law cannot be a foundation of a jurisdiction not given by the Constitution or laws,
that jurisdiction, when given, attaches, and is to be exercised according to the rules
of the common law ; and that what are, and what are not, high crimes and *misdemeanors*, is to be ascertained by a recurrence to the great basis of American jurisprudence. — *Story's Comm.*]

Mr. Madison's Motion for Commercial Restrictions.

HOUSE OF REPRESENTATIVES, *February* 14, 1806.

Resolved, As the opinion of this committee, that the interest of the
United States would be promoted by further restrictions and higher duties,
in certain cases, on the manufactures and navigation of foreign nations
employed in the commerce of the United States, than those now imposed.

1. *Resolved,* As the opinion of this committee, that an additional duty
ought to be laid on the following articles, manufactured by European nations having no commercial treaty with the United States : —

On articles of which leather is the material of chief value, an additional duty of   per cent. ad valorem.

On all manufactured iron, steel, tin, pewter, copper, brass, or other articles, of which either of these metals is the material of chief value, an
additional duty of   per cent. ad valorem.

On all articles of which cotton is the material of chief value, an additional duty of   per cent. ad valorem.

On all cloths of which wool is the material of chief value, where the
estimated value on which the duty is payable is above   , an additional
duty of   per cent. ad valorem ; where such value is below   , an
additional duty of   per cent. ad valorem.

On all other articles of which wool is the material of chief value, an
additional duty of   per cent. ad valorem.

On all cloths of which hemp or flax is the article of chief value, and of
which the estimated value on which the duty is payable is below   , an
additional duty of   per cent. ad valorem.

On all manufactures of which silk is the article of chief value, an additional duty of   per cent. ad valorem.

2. *Resolved,* As the opinion of this committee, that an additional duty

of   per ton ought to be laid on the vessels belonging to nations having no commercial treaty with the United States.

  3. *Resolved*, As the opinion of this committee, that the duty on vessels belonging to nations having commercial treaties with the United States, ought to be reduced to   per ton.

  4. *Resolved*, As the opinion of this committee, that where any nation may refuse to consider as vessels of the United States any vessels not built within the United States, the foreign-built vessels of such nation ought to be subjected to a like refusal, unless built within the United States.

  5. *Resolved*, As the opinion of this committee, that where any nation may refuse to admit the produce and manufactures of the United States, unless in vessels belonging to the United States, or to admit them in vessels of the United States if last imported from any place not within the United States, a like restriction ought, after the   day of   , to be extended to the produce and manufactures of such nation ; and that, in the mean time, a duty of   per ton, extraordinary, ought to be imposed on vessels so importing any such produce or manufacture.

  6. *Resolved*, As the opinion of this committee, that where any nation may refuse to the vessels of the United States a carriage of the produce and manufactures thereof, while such produce or manufactures are admitted by it in its own vessels, it would be just to make the restriction reciprocal ; but, inasmuch as such a measure, if suddenly adopted, might be particularly distressing in cases which merit the benevolent intention of the United States, it is expedient, for the present, that a tonnage extraordinary only of   be imposed on the vessels so employed ; and that all distilled spirits imported therein shall be subject to an additional duty of one   part of the existing duty.

  7. *Resolved*, As the opinion of this committee, that provision ought to be made for liquidating and ascertaining the losses, sustained by citizens of the United States, from the operation of particular regulations of any country, contravening the law of nations : and that such losses be reimbursed, in the first instance, out of the additional duties on manufactures, productions, and vessels of the nation establishing such unlawful regulations.

Contractors.

March 23, 1806.

Resolved, That a *contractor*, under the government of the United States, is an *officer* within the purview and meaning of the Constitution, and, as such, is incapable of holding a seat in this house.

Mr. EPPES. I do not believe Congress have power to pass this resolution. The words of the Constitution are, " No person holding an office under the United States shall be a member of either house during his continuance in office "

These words are plain and clear. Their obvious intention was, to have officers excluded, and officers only. It would certainly have been equally wise to have excluded contractors, because the reason for excluding officers applies to them with equal force. We are not, however, to inquire what the Constitution ought to have been, but what it is. We cannot legislate on its spirit against the strict letter of the instrument. Our inquiry must be, *is* he an officer ? If an officer, under the words of the Constitution, he is excluded. If not an officer, we cannot exclude him by law.

An extensive meaning has been given to the word *office*. How far such a construction of the meaning of this word is warranted, I leave for others to decide. That all contractors are not officers I am certain. A man, for instance, makes a contract with government to furnish supplies. He certainly is not an officer, according to the common and known acceptation of that word. He is, however, a contractor, and, under this resolution, excluded from a seat here. A carrier of the mail approaches very near an officer. The person takes an oath, is subject to penalties, the remission of which depends on the executive.

Public Lands. — *On the Resolution for investing a certain Portion of the Public Lands in Shares of the Chesapeake Canal.*

SENATE, *February* 13, 1807.

Mr. BAYARD. It is admitted that the Constitution does not expressly give the power to cut canals; but we possess, and are in the daily exercise of, the power to provide for the protection and safety of commerce, and the defence of the nation. It has never been contended that no power exists which has not been expressly delegated.

There is no express power given to erect a fort or magazine, though it is recognized in the delegation of exclusive legislative powers in certain cases. The power to erect lighthouses and piers, to survey and take the soundings on the coast, or to erect public buildings, is neither expressly given nor recognized in the Constitution; but it is embraced by a liberal and just interpretation of the clause in the Constitution, which legitimates all laws necessary and proper for carrying into execution the powers expressly delegated. On a like principle, the Bank of the United States was incorporated. Having a power to provide for the safety of commerce and the defence of the nation, we may fairly infer a power to cut a canal — a measure unquestionably proper with a view to either subject.

To suspend the Embargo.

HOUSE OF REPRESENTATIVES, *April* 19, 1808.

Mr. QUINCY. The Constitution of the United States, as I understand it, has in every part reference to the nature of things and necessities of society. No portion of it was intended as a mere ground for the trial of technical skill, or of verbal ingenuity. The direct, express powers with which it invests Congress are always to be so construed as to enable the people to attain the end for which they were given. This is to be gathered from the nature of those powers, compared with the known exigencies of society, and the other provisions of the Constitution. If a question arise, as in this case, concerning the extent of the incidental and implied powers vested in us by the Constitution, the instrument itself contains the criterion by which it is to be decided. We have authority to make "laws necessary and proper for carrying into execution" powers unquestionably vested. Reference must be had to the nature of these powers to know what is necessary and proper for their wise execution. When this necessity and propriety appear, the Constitution has enabled us to make the correspondent provisions. To the execution of many of the powers vested in us by the Constitution, a discretion is necessarily and properly incident; and when this appears from the nature of any particular power, it is certainly competent for us to provide, by law, that such discretion shall be exercised.

Mr. KEY said, all the respective representatives of the people, of the states at large, and the sovereignty in a political capacity of each state, must concur to enact a law.   An honorable gentleman from Tennessee (Mr. Campbell) admitted that the power to repeal must be coëxtensive with the power to make.   If this be admitted, I will not fail to convince you that, in the manner in which this law is worded, we cannot constitutionally assent to it.   What does it propose?   To give the President of the United States power to repeal an existing law now in force : — upon what?   Upon the happening of certain contingencies in Europe?   No. But in those contingencies which they suppose in his judgment shall render it safe to repeal the law, a discretion is committed to him — upon the happening of those events — to suspend the law.   It is that discretion to which I object.   I do not say it will be improperly placed at all; but the power and discretion to judge of the safety of the United States, is a power legislative in its nature and effects, and as such, under the Constitution, cannot be exercised by one branch of the legislature.   I pray gentlemen to note this distinction, that whenever the events happen, if the President exercise his judgment upon those events, and suspend the law, it is the exercise of a legislative power : the people, by the Constitution of the country, never meant to confide to any one man the power of legislating for it.

Renewal of the Charter of the United States Bank.

HOUSE OF REPRESENTATIVES, *April* 13, 1810.

Mr. LOVE.   The question of the constitutionality of the bank solely depends on the question, whether it is necessary and proper for conducting the moneyed operations of government.   So great a change has taken place on that subject within twenty years past, that it is supposed the question is now settled.   Not only the moneyed transactions of the United States, but, it is believed, of all the state governments, are carried on through the state banks, as well as commercial transactions, and other moneyed negotiations.

Mr. TROUP said, gentlemen might pass the bill but for the constitutional question.   If they did pass it, he hoped they would not permit themselves to become the retailing hucksters of the community, for the sale of bank charters.   There is a power in the Constitution to sell the public property ; but there is certainly no power to sell privileges of any kind.   I, therefore, move to strike out the bribe, the *douceur*, the bonus, as gentlemen call it, of 1,250,000 dollars.

Mr. KEY said, to him it clearly appeared within the power and limit of the Constitution to establish a bank, if necessary, for the collection of the revenue.

Mr. TROUP observed, that some gentlemen had said that the power to incorporate a bank was derived from the power to lay and collect revenue ; and that the power ought to be exercised, because banks give a facility to the collection of the revenue.   If the power be exercised, it must be necessary and proper.   If it be necessary to the collection of the revenue, the revenue cannot be collected without it.   The gentleman from Maryland might say a bank institution was useful.   He might say it would give facility to the collection of the revenue ; but facility and necessity are wholly different, and the Constitution says that a power, to be incidental, must be necessary and proper.

Mr. ALSTON.   In the 10th article, 1st section, of the Constitution, it is said, "No state shall coin money, emit bills of credit, or make any thing but gold and silver coin a legal tender in payment of debts." The interpretation which I give to it is, that the United States possess power to make any thing, besides gold and silver, a legal tender. If what I conceive to be a fair interpretation be admitted, it must follow that they have a right to make bank paper a legal tender. Much more, then, sir, have they the power of causing it to be received by themselves, in payment of taxes.

January 16, 1811.

Mr. BURWELL. It is my most deliberate conviction, that the Constitution of the country gives no authority to Congress to incorporate a bank, and endow the stockholders with chartered immunities.

The power to establish a bank cannot be deduced from the general phrases, "to provide for the common defence and general welfare," because they merely announce the object for which the general government was instituted. The only means by which this object is to be attained are specifically enumerated in the Constitution; and if they are not ample, it is a defect which Congress are incompetent to supply.

P. B. PORTER. The Constitution is a specification of the powers, or means, themselves, by which certain objects are to be accomplished. The powers of the Constitution, carried into execution according to the strict terms and import of them, are the appropriate means, and the only means, within the reach of this government, for the attainment of its ends. It is true, as the Constitution declares, — and it would be equally true if the Constitution did not declare it, — that Congress have a right to pass all laws necessary and proper for executing the delegated powers; but this gives no latitude of discretion in the selection of means or powers.

Mr. KEY. The end, or power given, is to lay and collect taxes, and pay the public debt. The power to make laws necessary and proper to effect that end is also given, and consists in devising and establishing the means of accomplishing it. The means to accomplish the end are nowhere restricted.

If a bank is useful and necessary in the collection of taxes and imposts, and payment of the public debt, and is the best mode of effecting it, the creation of a bank for such purposes is definitely within the power of Congress; and more, it is the bounden duty of Congress to establish it, because they are bound to adopt the best practicable, or, in other words, necessary and proper means to collect the tax and imposts.

Mr. EPPES. The Constitution of the United States has universally been considered as a grant of particular, and not of general, powers. Those powers are the primary or expressly delegated, and the derivative or implied. The character of the instrument precluded the necessity of a "bill of rights," because the question never could arise, what was reserved, but what was granted. The framers of the Constitution were well aware of this, and so were the people who adopted it. It is, therefore, fairly to be inferred that, whenever there appears a limitation or restriction, in the shape of a negative clause, Congress might have exercised the power interdicted had such clause not been made part of the instrument.

Mr CRAWFORD. If the state governments are restrained from exercising this right to incorporate a bank, it would appear, *ex necessitate rei*, that this right is vested in the government of the United States. The entire sove reignty of this nation is vested in the state governments, and in the federal government, except that part of it which is restrained by the people, which is solely the right of electing their public functionaries.

The right to create a corporation is a right inherent in every sovereignty. The people of the United States cannot exercise this right. If, then, the states are restrained from creating a bank with authority to emit bills of credit, it appears to be established that the federal government does possess this right. If, however, it is still believed that the law by which this bank has been created was the result of a forced construction, yet I must contend that that construction is entitled to some weight in the decision of this question. The time and state of the public mind, when this construction was given, gives it a strong claim to consideration upon this occasion. This construction was given shortly after the government was organized, when first impressions had not been effaced by lapse of time, or distorted by party feelings or individual animosity. The parties which then existed were literally federal and anti-federal. Those who were friendly to the Federal Constitution, and those who were inimical to it, formed the only parties then known in this nation.

Mr. CLAY. What is the nature of this government? It is emphatically federal; vested with an aggregate of specified powers for general purposes, conceded by existing sovereignties, who have themselves retained what is not so conceded. It is said there are cases in which it must act on implied powers. This is not controverted; but the implication must be necessary, and obviously flow from the enumerated powers with which it is allied. The power to charter companies is not specified in the grant, and, I contend, is of a nature not transferable by mere implication. It is one of the most exalted attributes of sovereignty.

Is it to be imagined that a power so vast would have been left by the wisdom of the Constitution to doubtful inference? It has been alleged that there are many instances, in the Constitution, where powers in their nature incidental, and which would have necessarily been vested along with the principal, are nevertheless expressly enumerated; and the power " to make rules and regulations for the government of the land and naval forces," which, it is said, is incidental to the power to raise armies, and provide a navy, is given as an example. What does this prove? How extremely cautious the Convention were to leave as little as possible to implication! In all cases where incidental powers are acted upon, the principal and incidental ought to be congenial with each other, and partake of a common nature. The incidental power ought to be strictly subordinate, and limited to the end proposed to be attained by the specified power. In other words, — under the name of accomplishing one object which is specified, the power implied ought not to be made to embrace other objects, which are not specified in the Constitution. If, then, you could establish a bank to collect and distribute the revenue, it ought to be expressly restricted to the purpose of such collection and distribution.

I contend that the states have the exclusive power to regulate contracts, to declare the capacities and incapacities to contract, and to provide as to the extent of responsibility of debtors to their creditors. If Congress have the power to erect an artificial body, and say it shall be endowed with the attributes of an individual, — if you can bestow on this object of your own creation the ability to contract, — may you not, in contravention of state rights, confer upon slaves, infants, and femes covert, the ability to contract? And if you have the power to say that an association of individuals shall be responsible for their debts only in a certain limited degree, what is to prevent an extension of a similar exemption to individuals? Where is the limitation upon this power to set up corporations? You establish one in the heart of a state, the basis of whose capital is money. You may erect others, whose capital shall consist of land, slaves, and personal estates; and thus the whole property within the jurisdiction of a state might be absorbed by these political bodies. The existing bank contends that it is beyond the power of a state to tax it; and if this pretension be well founded, it is in the power of Congress, by chartering companies, to dry up all the sources of state revenue.

On the Bill for raising a Volunteer Corps.

HOUSE OF REPRESENTATIVES, *January* 12, 1812.

Mr. POINDEXTER. Can we constitutionally employ volunteer militia, without the jurisdiction of the United States, in the prosecution of hostilities, in the enemy's country? He was of opinion, that no legislative act of Congress could confer such a power on the President.

Mr. GRUNDY. If the Constitution forbids the President from sending the militia out of the United States, how can we authorize him to do so by law? We cannot: we should legislate to no purpose. Whether he had the authority or not, would depend upon the construction the President himself shall give to the Constitution. Nor could he see how this proposition gets over the difficulty.

It provides that a militiaman may authorize the President to send him beyond the limits of the United States. He had always understood that, in framing the Constitution of this government, there was great jealousy exhibited lest the general government should swallow up the powers of the state governments; and when the power of making war and raising armies was given to Congress, the militia was retained by the states, except in cases mentioned by the Constitution. How, then, can you permit militiamen to engage in the service of the United States, contrary to the provisions of the Constitution, and by that means leave the state unprotected?

Mr. PORTER. He did not agree with the gentleman, (Mr. Poindexter,) that the militia could in no case be employed without the limits of the United States. He did not think their services were to be confined by geographical limits. If it became necessary for the executive to call out the militia to repel invasion, he thought they might pursue the enemy beyond the limits, until the invaders were effectually dispersed.

Mr. CHEVES. Though the gentleman from New York says the service of the militia is not to be bounded by geographical limits, I cannot, said Mr. C., discover the premises by which he comes to this conclusion, if the general government has no other power over the militia than is given to it in this clause of the Constitution. If they may cross the line, why not go to the walls of Quebec? The principle is trampled upon the instant they pass beyond the territorial limits of the United States; nor, if this be a correct construction, said he, can the consent of the individual add any thing to the powers or the rights of the general government, while he remains a member of the militia of the state.

Mr. CLAY. In one of the amendments, it is declared that a well-regulated militia is necessary to the security of a free state. But if you limit the use of the militia to executing the laws, suppressing insurrections, and repelling invasions, — if you deny the use of the militia to make

war, — can you say they are "the security of a state"? He thought
not.

Mr. CHEVES. It is said that the powers of the general government
were not sovereign, but limited. This was to deny the existence of any
sovereignty which was limited as to its objects, than which nothing is,
however, more common. But there is an authority on this point which
Mr. C. supposed would not be controverted. He meant Mr. Hamilton's
argument on the constitutionality of the Bank of the United States.

[Here Mr. C. read the following extract from that work : " The circumstance that
the powers of the sovereignty are, in this country, between the national and state
governments, does not afford the distinction required. It does not follow from this
that each of the portions of power, delegated to the one or the other, is not sovereign
with regard to its proper objects. It will only follow from it that each has sovereign
power with regard to *certain things*, and not as to other things. To deny that the government of the United States has sovereign power as to its declared purposes and
trusts, because its power does not extend to all laws, would be equally to deny that
state governments have sovereign power in *any* case, because their power does not
extend to *every* case."]

It was said, by the same gentleman, that the writers contemporaneous
with the adoption, and the debates of the several conventions on the
adoption of the Constitution, repelled the construction now contended for ;
but that gentleman had not produced, nor had any other gentleman produced, a sentence to that effect, except the gentleman from Tennessee,
(Mr. Grundy,) who read from the Virginia debates, in the argument of
Mr. Nicholas, a detached sentence, in which, speaking of that article of
the Constitution which gives power to Congress " to provide for calling
forth the militia to execute the laws of the Union, suppress insurrections,
and repel invasions," he says they cannot call them forth for any other
purpose than to execute the laws, suppress insurrections, and repel invasions. But Mr. Madison, in the same debate, says, " The most effectual
way to render it unnecessary, is to give the general government full power
to call forth the militia, and exert the whole natural strength of the Union,
when necessary." He (Mr. C.) was opposed to the latitude of the bill.

Seamen's Bill. — *For the Regulation of Seamen on Board
the Public Vessels, and in the Merchant Service of the
United States.*

Hᴏᴜsᴇ ᴏғ Rᴇᴘʀᴇsᴇɴᴛᴀᴛɪᴠᴇs, *February*, 1813.

Mr. SEYBERT. The Constitution of the United States declares,
Congress shall have power " to establish a *uniform* rule of naturalization,
and *uniform laws* on the subject of bankruptcies, throughout the United
States." Sir, the *rule* only relates to the *mode ;* it is only operative during
the *nascent state* of the political conversion, and it ceases to have effect
the moment after the process has been completed. Your Constitution
only recognizes the highest grade of citizenship that can be conferred.
The *alien* is thus made a *native*, as it were, and is fully vested with every
right and privilege attached to the native, with the exception impressed on
the Constitution. Your statutes cannot deprive any particular species of
citizens of the right of personal liberty, or the locomotive faculty, because the Constitution does not characterize the citizens of the United
States as native and naturalized. Our great family is composed of a class
of men forming a single *genus*, who, to all intents and purposes, are equal,
except in the instance specified — that of not being eligible to the presidency of the United States. The only exception to the rule is expressed

in the Constitution. If other exceptions had been contemplated by the framers of that instrument, they would also have been expressed. None other having been expressed, he said, it followed that your legislative acts could not make individual exceptions touching the occupation of a citizen. All freemen, citizens of the United States, may pursue their happiness in any manner and in any situation they please, provided they do not violate the rights of others. You cannot deny to any portion of your citizens, who desire to plough the deep, the right to do so, whilst you permit another portion of them the enjoyment of that right.

Mr. ARCHER. The framers of our Constitution did not intend to confine Congress to the technical meaning of the word *naturalization*, in the exercise of that power — the more especially when the comprehensive word *rule* was made use of. The principle upon which the power was to be exercised was left to the judicious exercise of Congress; all that was required was, that the *rule* should be uniform throughout the states. In the grant there is no other specification, as to the exercise of it, than that of its uniformity. The term *naturalization* was borrowed from England. It must be understood here in the sense and meaning which was there attached to it. Whether it was absolute or qualified, it was still a naturalization. But the grant of a power in general terms necessarily implied the right to exercise that power in all its gradations. It was in the political as it was in the natural world : the genus included the species. Besides, the power to naturalize was an attribute to sovereignty. It was either absolute or qualified; and if the grant to Congress only implied a power of unlimited naturalization, the power to qualify existed in the states or in the people, for what was not specifically granted was reserved.

In treating of the executive power, the Constitution defines the qualifications of the President. It declares that he should be a natural-born citizen, or a citizen at the adoption of the Constitution. This article is unquestionably no limitation of the power of Congress upon the subject of naturalization. It was impossible to abridge a specific grant of power without a specific limitation, and the article alluded to could not be tortured, by the most ingenious mind, to diminish, even by implication, the authority of Congress upon a subject to which it was totally irrelevant

Internal Improvement. — *Extract from Mr. Madison's Message to Congress.*

December 5, 1815.

Among the means of advancing the public interest, the occasion is a proper one for recalling the attention of Congress to the great importance of establishing throughout our country the roads and canals which can best be executed under the national authority. No objects within the circle of political economy so richly repay the expense bestowed on them ; there are none the utility of which is more universally ascertained and acknowledged ; none that do more honor to the government, whose wise and enlarged patriotism duly appreciates them. Nor is there any country which presents a field where Nature invites more the art of man to complete her own work for their accommodation and benefit. These considerations are strengthened, moreover, by the political effect of these facilities for intercommunication, in bringing and binding more closely together the various parts of our extended confederacy.

Whilst the states, individually, with a laudable enterprise and emulation, avail themselves of their local advantages, by new roads, by navigable canals, and by improving the streams susceptible of navigation, the general government is the more urged to similar undertakings, requiring a national jurisdiction, and national means, by the prospect of thus systematically completing so inestimable a work. And it is a happy reflection, that any defect of constitutional authority which may be encountered, can be supplied in a mode which the Constitution itself has providently pointed out.

On the Commercial Treaty with Great Britain.

HOUSE OF REPRESENTATIVES, *January* 8, 1816.

Mr. HOPKINSON. In the nature of things, there cannot exist, at the same time, under the same authority, two contradictory, inconsistent laws, and rules of action. One or the other must give way ; both cannot be obeyed ; and if, in this case, this [commercial] treaty has no constitutional supremacy over an ordinary act of legislation, it, at least, has the admitted advantages of being earlier in point of time, of being the last constitutional expression of the will of the nation on this subject. It is worthy of remark, that the general power of legislation is given to Congress in one part of the Constitution ; the special power of making treaties, to the President and Senate, in another part; and then the acts of both, if done constitutionally, are declared, in the same sentence, in another part of the Constitution, to be the supreme law of the land, and placed upon the same footing of authority.

Mr. CALHOUN. From the whole complexion of the case, said Mr. C., the bill before the house was mere form, and not supposed to be necessary to the validity of the treaty. It would be proper, however, he observed, to reply to the arguments which have been urged on the general nature of the treaty-making power ; and as it was a subject of great importance, he solicited the attentive hearing of the house.

It is not denied, he believed, that the President, with the concurrence of two thirds of the Senate, has a right to make commercial treaties ; it is not asserted that this treaty is couched in such general terms as to require a law to carry the details into execution. Why, then, is this bill necessary ? Because, say gentlemen, that the treaty of itself, without the aid of this bill, cannot exempt British tonnage, and goods imported in their bottoms, from the operation of the law laying additional duties on foreign tonnage and goods imported in foreign vessels; or, giving the question a more general form, because a treaty cannot annul a law. The gentleman from Virginia, (Mr. Barbour) who argued this point very distinctly, though not satisfactorily, took as his general position, that to repeal a law is a legislative act, and can only be done by law; that, in the distribution of the legislative and treaty-making power, the right to repeal a law fell exclusively under the former.

How does this comport with the admission immediately made by him, that the treaty of peace repealed the act declaring war ? If he admits the fact in a single case, what becomes of his exclusive legislative right? He indeed felt that his rule failed him, and in explanation assumed a position entirely new; for he admitted that, when the treaty did that which was not authorized to be done by law, it did not require the sanction of Congress, and might in its operation repeal a law inconsistent with it. He said, Congress is not authorized to make peace; and for this reason a treaty of peace repeals the act declaring war. In this position, he understood his colleague substantially to concur. He hoped to make it appear that, in taking this ground, they have both yielded to the point in discussion. He would establish, he trusted, to the satisfaction of the house, that the treaty-making power, when it was legitimately exercised, always did that which could not be done by law; and that the reasons advanced to prove that the treaty of peace repealed the act making war, so far from being peculiar to that case, apply to all treaties. They do not form an exception, but in fact constitute the rule. Why, then, he asked, cannot Congress make peace? They have the power to declare war. All acknowledge this power. Peace and war are opposite. They are the positive and negative terms of the same proposition; and what rule of construction more clear than that, when a power is given to do an act, the power is also given to repeal it? By what right do you repeal taxes, reduce your army, lay up your navy, or repeal any law, but by the force of this plain rule of construction? Why cannot Congress then repeal the act declaring war? He acknowledged, with the gentleman, they cannot, consistently with reason. The solution of this question explained the whole difficulty. The reason is plain; one power may make war; it requires two to make peace. It is a state of mutual amity succeeding hostility; it is a state that cannot be created but with the consent of both parties. It required a contract or a treaty between the nations at war. Is this peculiar to a treaty of peace? No; it is common to all treaties. It arises out of their nature, and not from any incidental circumstance attaching itself to a particular class. It is no more or less than that Congress cannot make a contract with a foreign nation. Let us apply it to a treaty of commerce — to this very case. Can Congress do what this treaty has done? It has repealed the discriminating duties between this country and England. Either could by law repeal its own. But by law they could go no further; and for the same reason, that peace cannot be made by law. Whenever, then, an ordinary subject of legislation can only be regulated by contract, it passes from the sphere of the ordinary power of making law, and attaches itself to that of making treaties, wherever it is lodged.

*   *   *   *   *

The treaty-making power has many and powerful limits; and it will be found, when he came to discuss what those limits are, that it cannot destroy the Constitution, or personal liberty; involve us, without the assent of this house, in war; or grant away our money. The limits he proposed to this power are not the same, it is true; but they appeared to him much more rational and powerful than those which were supposed to present effectual guards for its abuse. Let us now consider what they are.

The grant of the power to make treaties is couched in the most general terms. The words of the Constitution are, that the President shall have power, by and with the advice and consent of the Senate, to make treaties, provided two thirds of the senators present concur.

In a subsequent part of the Constitution, treaties are declared to be the supreme law of the land. Whatever limits are imposed on these general terms, ought to be the result of the sound construction of the instrument. There appeared to him but two restrictions on its exercise — the one derived from the nature of our government, and the other from that of the power itself. Most certainly all grants of power under the Constitution must be controlled by the instrument; for, having their existence from it, they must of necessity assume that form which the Constitution has imposed. This is acknowledged to be the true source of the legislative power, and it is doubtless equally so of the power to make treaties. The limits of the former are exactly marked; it was necessary to prevent collision with similar coëxisting state powers. This country within is divided into two distinct sovereignties. Exact enumeration here is necessary to prevent the most dangerous consequences. The enumeration of legislative powers in the Constitution has relation, then, not to the treaty-making power, but to the powers of the states. In our relation to the rest of the world, the case is reversed. Here the states disappear. Divided within, we present, without, the exterior of undivided sovereignty. The wisdom of the Constitution appears conspicuous. When enumeration was needed, there we find the powers enumerated and exactly defined; when not, we do not find what would be vain and pernicious to attempt. Whatever, then, concerns our foreign relations, whatever requires the consent of another nation, belongs to the treaty power — can only be regulated by it; and it is competent to regulate all such subjects, provided — and here are its true limits — such regulations are not inconsistent with the Constitution. If so, they are void. No treaty can alter the fabric of our government; nor can it do that which the Constitution has expressly forbidden to be done; nor can it do that differently which is directed to be done in a given mode, and all other modes prohibited.

For instance, the Constitution says no money "shall be drawn out of the treasury, but by an appropriation made by law." Of course no subsidy can be granted without an act of law; and a treaty of alliance could not involve the country in war without the consent of this house. Besides these constitutional limits, the treaty power, like all others, has other limits, derived from its object and nature. It has for its object contracts with foreign nations, as the powers of Congress have for their object whatever can be done in relation to the powers delegated to it without the consent of foreign nations. Each, in its proper sphere, operates with genial influence : but when they become erratic, then they are portentous and dangerous A treaty never can legitimately do that which can be done by law; and the converse is also true. Suppose the discriminating duties repealed on both sides by law; yet what is effected by this treaty would not even then be done: the plighted faith would be wanting; either side might repeal its law, without a breach of contract. It appeared to him that gentlemen are too much influenced on this subject by the example of Great Britain. Instead of looking to the nature of our government, they have been swayed in their opinion by the practice of that government, to which we are but too much in the habit of looking for precedents.

January 10, 1816.

Mr. TUCKER. It is contended by the gentleman from South Carolina (Mr. Calhoun) that a treaty is superior to the law, because it is a contract between one nation and another power. I am ready to admit, Mr. Speaker, the ingenuity of the gentleman in drawing this distinction. It is what may well be expected from his ingenious and active mind. But I think it will appear that it is more ingenious than solid, more true than applicable to the subject.

I admit that, where a contract has been entered into and completed by all the necessary powers under our Constitution, it is binding upon the nation. But the question still recurs, *When* is it complete? In the case of a treaty containing stipulations merely executive, it is complete when the ratifications are exchanged. In the case of a treaty which requires a legislative act to give it operation, we contend that the legislative sanction must be given before it is complete. Until then it is not a binding contract, and the rights of the third party (the foreign power) do not exist. Is it not the *petitio principii*, or — if the gentleman will permit me to use the vulgar translation — is it not begging the question, to contend that *before* the legislative sanction the contract is binding, when the very question before us is, whether that sanction *be* necessary to make it binding?

Mr. PINCKNEY. I lay it down as an incontrovertible truth, that the Constitution has assumed, (and indeed how could it do otherwise?) that the government of the United States might and would have occasion, like the other governments of the civilized world, to enter into treaties with foreign powers, upon the various subjects involved in their mutual relations; and further, that it might be and was proper to designate the department of the government in which the capacity to make such treaties should be lodged. It has said, accordingly, that the President, with the concurrence of the Senate, shall possess this part of the national sovereignty. It has, furthermore, given to the same magistrate, with the same concurrence, the exclusive creation and control of the whole machinery of diplomacy. He only, with the approbation of the Senate, can appoint a negotiator, or take any step towards a negotiation. The Constitution does not, in any part of it, even intimate that any other department shall possess either a constant or an occasional right to interpose in the preparation of any treaty, or in the final perfection of it. The President and the Senate are explicitly pointed out as the sole actors in that sort of transaction.

The prescribed concurrence of the *Senate* — and that, too, by a majority greater than the ordinary legislative majority — plainly excludes the necessity of congressional concurrence. If the consent of Congress to any treaty had been intended, the Constitution would not have been guilty of the absurdity of putting a treaty for ratification to the President and Senate exclusively, and again to the same President and Senate as portions of the legislature. It would have submitted the whole matter at once to Congress; and the more especially as the ratification of a treaty by the Senate, as a branch of the legislature, may be by a smaller number than a ratification of it by the same body as a branch of the executive government. If the ratification of any treaty by the President, with the consent of the Senate, must be followed by a legislative ratification, it is a mere nonentity. It is good for all purposes, or for none. And if it be nothing, in effect, it is a mockery by which nobody would be bound. The President and Senate would not themselves be bound by it; and the ratification would at last depend, not upon the will of the President and two thirds of the Senate, but upon the will of a bare majority of the two branches of the legislature, subject to the qualified legislative control of the President.

Upon the power of the President and Senate, therefore, there can be no doubt. The only question is as to the extent of it; or, in other words, as to the subject upon which it may be exerted. The *effect* of the power, when exerted within its lawful sphere, is beyond the reach of controversy. The Constitution has declared that whatsoever amounts to a treaty made under the authority of the United States, shall immediately be supreme law. It has contradistinguished a *treaty* as law, from an *act of Congress* as law. It has erected treaties, so contradistinguished, into a binding judicial rule. It has given them to our courts of justice, in defining the jurisdiction, as a portion of the *lex terræ*, which they are to interpret and enforce. In a word, it has communicated to them, if ratified by the department which it has specially provided for the making of them, the rank of law -- or it has spoken without meaning. And if it has elevated them to that rank, it is idle to attempt to raise them to it by ordinary legislation.

It is clear that the power of Congress, as to foreign commerce, is only what it professes to be in the Constitution, a legislative power — to be exerted municipally, without consultation or agreement with those with whom we have an intercourse of trade. It is undeniable that the Constitution meant to provide for the exercise of another power, relatively to commerce, which should exert itself in concert with the analogous power in other countries, and should bring about its results, not by statute enacted by itself, but by an international compact called a *treaty;* that it is manifest that this other power is vested by the Constitution in the President and Senate, the only department of the government which it authorizes to make any treaty, and which it enables to make all treaties; that, if it be so vested, its regular exercise must result in that which, as far as it reaches, is law in itself, and, consequently, repeals such municipal regulations as stand in its way; since it is expressly declared by the Constitution, that treaties regularly made shall have, as they ought to have, the force of law.

Mr. PICKERING. To a just understanding of the question before the house, a distinction should be taken; that is, between the *validity* and the *execution* of a treaty. While gentlemen on the other side (with a single exception) admit that some treaties made by the President and Senate are valid without any act to be done on the part of this house, such as simple treaties of peace, and even of alliance, — seeing no special power is granted to Congress, by the Constitution, to make peace and form alliances, — yet it is said that, when the intervention of this house is necessary, as in providing and making appropriations of money to carry treaties into execution, then the sanction of this house is requisite, to give them a binding force.

But shall treaties operate a repeal of a law of the United States? Yes; because treaties being, equally with acts of Congress, the law of the land, they must repeal all the provisions of prior laws contravening their stipulations — according to the well-known maxim, that the latter laws repeal all antecedent laws containing contrary provisions; and so long as treaties exist, so long the government and nation are bound to observe them, and the decision of the judges must conform to their stipulations. But as treaties may thus annul the laws of Congress, so may these laws annul treaties; and when Congress shall, by a formal act, declare a treaty no longer obligatory on the United States, the judges must abandon the treaty, and obey the law. And why? Because the *whole authority*, on our part, which gave *existence and force* to the treaty, is *withdrawn* by the annulling act.

Mr. PINCKNEY. Such is the effect of a law of Congress declaring war against a nation between whom and the United States any treaties had been made. Take, fo. example, the case of France, with whom we had a treaty of amity and commerce, a treaty of alliance, and consular convention. These treaties having been repeatedly violated on the part of the French government, and the just claims of the United States for repairing the injuries so committed having been refused, and their attempts to negotiate an amicable adjustment of all complaints between the two nations having been repelled with indignity, — and as the French persisted in their system of predatory violence, infracting those treaties, and hostile to the rights of a free and independent nation, — for these causes, explicitly, Congress, in July, 1798, passed a law, enacting that those treaties should not, thenceforth, be regarded as legally obligatory on the government or citizens of the United States.   And two days afterwards, Congress passed another law, authorizing the capture of all French armed vessels, to which the commerce of the United States long had been, and continued to be, a prey.   And as in this, so in every other case, in which Congress shall judge there existed good and sufficient cause for declaring a treaty void, they will so pronounce ; either because they intend to declare war, or because they are willing the United States should meet a war, to be declared on the other side, as less injurious to the country than an adherence to the treaty.   But should Congress, without adequate cause, declare a treaty no longer obligatory, they must be prepared to meet the reproach of perfidy, besides exposing the United States to the evils of war, should the offended nation think fit to avenge the wrong by making war upon them.

Internal Improvement. — Bonus Bill.

House of Representatives, *February*, 1817.

Mr. PICKERING.   He remembered that the supposition that Congress might, under that clause, exercise the power of making roads in any state, and where they pleased, was offered as a serious objection to the adoption of the Constitution, in the Convention of Pennsylvania, of which Mr. P. (then living in that state) was a member.   And his recollection was probably the more perfect because he answered the objection, observing, that the power " to establish post-offices and post-roads" could intend no more than the power to direct where post-offices should be kept, and on what roads the mails should be carried and this answer appeared, then, to be entirely satisfactory.

Mr. CLAY.   As to the constitutional point which had been made, he had not a doubt on his mind.   It was a sufficient answer to say, that the power was not now to be exercised.   It was proposed merely to designate the fund, and, from time to time, as the proceeds of it came in, to invest them in the funded debt of the United States.   It would thus be accumulating, and Congress could, at some future day, examine into the constitutionality of the question ; and if it has the power, it would exercise it ; if it has not, the Constitution, there could be very little doubt, would be so amended as to confer it.   It was quite obvious, however, that Congress might so direct the application of the fund, as not to interfere with the jurisdiction of the several states, and thus avoid the difficulty which had been started.   It might distribute it among those objects of private enterprise which called for national patronage, in the form of subscriptions to the capital stock of incorporated companies, such as that of the Delaware and Chesapeake Canal, and other similar institutions.   Perhaps that might be the best way to employ the fund : but he repeated that this was not the time to go into that inquiry.

Mr. PICKERING.   It has been said that the last clause but one, in the 8th section of the 1st article, expressly mentions " the erection of forts, arsenals, dock-yards, magazines, and other needful buildings ; " but whoever will examine that clause, will perceive that it does not give Congress any power to erect those works, but simply to exercise exclusive legislation over the places where they are erected, such place having been previously purchased with the consent of the states in which the same shall be.   The power to erect such works and buildings is nowhere expressed in the Constitution.   It is, then, an implied power, whose existence is recognized by the Constitution itself.   But where can it be found, unless it is involved in the express powers to regulate commerce, and provide for the common defence?   Without navigation, without commerce by sea, we should need no lighthouses, beacons, or piers.

If, then, it was constitutional to erect the works which have been mentioned, to give facility, safety, and expedition to commerce by sea, will any one deny the constitutional power of Congress to erect similar works on our interior waters on the great lakes?

Internal Improvements.

SENATE, *February* 27, 1817.

A Bill to set apart and pledge, as a permanent Fund for Internal Improvements, the Bonus of the National Bank, and the United States' Share of its Dividends.

Be it enacted, &c., That the bonus secured to the United States by the "act to incorporate the subscribers to the Bank of the United States," and the dividends which shall arise from their shares in its capital stock, during the present term of twenty years, for which the proprietors thereof have been incorporated, be, and the same is hereby, set apart and pledged, as a fund for constructing roads and canals, and improving the navigation of watercourses, in order to facilitate, promote, and give security to internal commerce among the several states, and to render more easy and less expensive the means and provisions necessary for their common defence.

Sect. 2. *And be it further enacted,* That the moneys constituting the said fund shall, from time to time, be applied in constructing such roads or canals, or in improving the navigation of such watercourses, or both, in each state, as Congress, with the assent of such state, shall by law direct, and in the manner most conducive to the general welfare; and the proportion of the said money to be expended on the objects aforesaid, in each state, shall be in the ratio of its representation, at the time of such expenditure, in the most numerous branch of the national legislature.

Sect. 3. *And be it further enacted,* That the said fund be put under the care of the secretary of the treasury for the time being; and that it shall be his duty, unless otherwise directed, to vest the said dividend, if not specifically appropriated by Congress, in the stock of the United States, which stock shall accrue to, and is hereby constituted a part of, the said fund.

Sect. 4. *And be it further enacted,* That it shall also be the duty of the said secretary, unless otherwise directed, to vest the bonus for the charter of said bank, as it may fall due, in the stock of the United States, and also to lay before Congress, at their usual session, the condition of the said fund.

Message of the President, transmitting to the House of Representatives his Objections to the [above] Bank Bonus Bill.

To the House of Representatives of the United States:

Having considered the bill this day presented to me, entitled "An Act to set apart and pledge certain funds for internal improvements;" and which sets and pledges funds "for constructing roads and canals, and improving the navigation of watercourses, in order to facilitate, promote, and give security to, internal commerce among the several states, and to render more easy and less expensive the means and provisions for the common defence," I am constrained, by the insuperable difficulty I feel in reconciling the bill with the Constitution of the United States, to return it, with *that objection,* to the House of Representatives, in which it originated.

The legislative powers vested in Congress are specified and enumerated in the 8th section of the 1st article of the Constitution; and it does not appear that the power, proposed to be exercised by the bill, is among the enumerated powers; or that it falls, by any just interpretation, within the power to make laws necessary and proper for carrying into execution those or other powers vested by the Constitution in the government of the United States.

The power to regulate commerce among the several states cannot include a power to construct roads and canals, and to improve the navigation of watercourses, in order to facilitate, promote, and secure, such a commerce, without a latitude of construction departing from the ordinary import of the terms, strengthened by the known inconveniences which doubtless led to the grant of this remedial power to Congress. To refer the power in question to the clause "to provide for the common defence and general welfare," would be contrary to the established and consistent rules of interpretation, as rendering the special and careful enumeration of powers which follow the clause nugatory and improper. Such a view of the Constitution would have the effect of giving to Congress a general power or legislation, instead of the defined and limited one hitherto understood to belong to them — the terms, " the common defence and general welfare," embracing every object and act within the purview of the legislative trust. It would have the effect of subjecting both the Constitution and laws of the several states, in all cases not specifically exempted, to be superseded by laws of Congress; it being expressly declared, " that the Constitution of the United States, and laws made in pursuance thereof, shall be the supreme law of the land; and the judges of every state shall be bound thereby, any thing in the Constitution or laws of any state to the contrary notwithstanding." Such a view of the Constitution, finally, would have the effect of excluding the judicial authority of the United States from its participation in guarding the boundary between the legislative powers of the general and the state governments; inasmuch as questions relating to the general welfare, being questions of policy and expediency, are unsusceptible of judicial cognizance and decision.

A restriction of the power " to provide for the common defence and general welfare " to cases which are to be provided for by the expenditure of money, would still leave within the legislative power of Congress all the great and most important measures of government; money being the ordinary and necessary means of carrying them into execution.

If a general power to construct roads and canals, to improve the navigation of watercourses, with the train of powers incident thereto, be not possessed by Congress, the assent of the states, in the mode provided in the bill, cannot confer the power. The only cases in which the consent and cession of particular states can extend the power of Congress, are those specified and provided for in the Constitution.

I am not unaware of the great importance of roads and canals, and the improved navigation of watercourses, and that a power in the national legislature to provide for them might be exercised with signal advantage to the general prosperity; but, seeing that such a power is not expressly given to the Constitution, and believing that it cannot be deduced from any part of it without an inadmissible latitude of construction, and a reliance on insufficient precedents; believing, also, that the permanent success of the Constitution depends on a definitive partition of powers

40

between the general and state governments, and that no adequate land-marks would be left by the constructive extension of the powers of Congress, as proposed in the bill, — I have no option but to withhold my signature from it; cherishing the hope that its beneficial objects may be obtained by a resort, for the necessary powers, to the same wisdom and virtue in the nation which established the Constitution in its actual form, and providently marked out, in the instrument itself, a safe and practicable mode of improving it, as experience might suggest.

JAMES MADISON.

March 3, 1817.

[It is understood that Mr. Calhoun, who reported the *Bonus* bill, did not touch the constitutional question involved in it, as he did not propose to make an appropriation, but simply to set aside the bonus as a fund for internal improvement, leaving it to a future Congress to determine the extent of its powers; or, if it should be determined that it did not possess power over the subject, to obtain an amendment of the Constitution, as recommended by Mr. Madison in his message at the opening of the session. Under these impressions, Mr. C. declined arguing the constitutional question in his speech on the bill, and limited his objections to the question of expediency.]

Bankrupt Bill.

HOUSE OF REPRESENTATIVES, February 16, 1818.

Mr. HOPKINSON. The subject seems to have been considered in this light by the framers of the Constitution, who have, therefore, among the enumerated powers of Congress, expressly granted the power " to establish uniform laws on the subject of bankruptcies."

Mr. H. said he considered this as a declaration of the will of the people, that Congress should act on this subject — at least, so far as to establish a uniform rule. It binds us to no particular system, it is true; but it does enjoin on us most impressively to provide some one which shall be uniform in its operations on the different states, giving a certain known rule, and preventing those numerous and obvious evils that must arise from various and conflicting systems in the different states, by which the relation between debtor and creditor, so interesting to all classes of our citizens, must forever be changing, be imperfectly understood, and be daily producing inequality and injustice between the creditors and debtors residing in the different states. Mr. H. insisted that, when the several states parted with this power, it was only to attain that uniformity of system which could be established only by the general government; and that the states, having surrendered the power for this purpose, had a fair claim on the general government not to disappoint this expectation, but to apply the power to the uses intended by the grant of it.

February 17, 1818.

Mr. TYLER, (of Virginia) The honorable gentleman yesterday demanded of this house to carry all the powers of the government; and represented it as our bounden duty, in every instance, in which the Constitution gave power, to exercise it. The gentleman's position leaves us no alternative. Our discretion is taken from us — our volition is gone. If the gentleman be correct, we are stopped at the threshold of this inquiry; for inasmuch as the Constitution confers on Congress the power to adopt a uniform system of bankruptcy, — according to his doctrine, we are not to inquire into the expediency of adopting such system, but must yield it our support. Here, sir, I join issue with that gentleman. What, sir, is the end of all legislation? Is it not the public good? Do we come here to legislate away the rights and happiness of our constituents, or to advance and secure them? Suppose, then, by carrying into effect a specified power in the Constitution, we inflict serious injury upon the political body; will gentlemen contend that we are bound by a blind fatality, and compelled to act? Sir, such a doctrine cannot be supported even by the distinguished talents of that gentleman. The powers of this Constitution are all addressed to the sound discretion of Congress. You are not imperatively commanded, but authorized to act, if by so acting the good of the country will be promoted.

Mr. SERGEANT, (of Pennsylvania.) Why, it is said, why not extend the provisions to all classes of the community? Why confine them to a single class? The answer is a very plain one. The design of the Constitution was to vest in the government of the United States such powers as were necessary for national purposes, and to leave to the states all other powers. Trade, commercial credit, and public or national credit, which is intimately allied to it, were deemed, and rightly deemed, to be national concerns of the highest importance. In the adjustment of our government, at once national and federal, they were intended to be confided, and were confided, to the care of the public authority of the nation.

It does not appear to me that we need inquire, whether the term "bankruptcy" had a definite meaning, to which we are limited, nor whether we are bound to follow the model of the statutes of England, or any state bankrupt laws that may have existed here before the Constitution was formed. For the present purpose, the general spirit and scope of the Constitution furnish a sufficient guide. The design of that instrument was to occupy national ground, and leave the rest to the states.

February 19, 1818.

Mr. MILLS, (of Massachusetts.) Once establish the principle that the situation of the country is such as to require the exercise of that power with which the Constitution has vested you upon this subject, — and whether the prominent features of your system shall be drawn from the commercial code of Napoleon, or the acts of the British Parliament, will be a mere question of expediency, to be determined by their relative merits, and their analogy to your habits and institutions. Sir, I shall not stop here to inquire into the extent of the obligation imposed on you by the Constitution. It is enough for me to find the power " to establish uniform laws on the subject of bankruptcies throughout the United States" expressly delegated to Congress by that instrument, and to satisfy myself that the exigencies of the country require its exercise, to appreciate the weight of this obligation. Too long already has this delegation of authority remained a mere dead letter in that compact; and too long have those, for whose benefit it was introduced, called upon you to give it life, and energy, and action.

Are you sure that, since the adoption of the Federal Constitution, the state legislatures have any legitimate authority to pass those laws? By that instrument, it is contended, Congress alone have power to establish a uniform system of bankruptcy, and the states are expressly prohibited from passing " any laws impairing the obligation of contracts." So far, therefore, as these laws impugn either of those provisions, so far they transcend the powers retained by the states. Upon this subject, however, I wish not to be understood as giving an opinion, or attempting to sustain an argument.

Mr. HOPKINSON. I have never contended that there is an absolute, indisputable, constitutional obligation on Congress to pass a bankrupt law; but I do contend that it comes so recommended by the Constitution, and by the people who speak in and by that Constitution, that we may not disregard it; that it is our duty to exercise that power, to execute the trust, — unless, on a full and fair investigation of the subject, it shall be unwise, and injurious to the nation, to do so. I do contend that this high and general duty ought not to be dispensed with on doubtful reasons, on hypothetical arguments, drawn altogether from a presumed abuse of the law; much less from an indulgence of old prejudices or local views and interests. It is a great national object of legislation; it should be decided on national principles; it is deeply interesting to a vast and valuable portion of the people of this country; it should, therefore, be considered in relation to those interests, and determined on a fair comparison between the good it will certainly produce to this class, and the evil it may inflict, if any, on the rest of the community. This government is founded on a compromise of interests, and every one has a fair claim to attention and regard.

Military Appropriation Bill.

House of Representatives, *January 4*, 1819.

Mr. LOWNDES. He thought there was no inconsistency in denying the general power of constructing internal improvements, and yet voting an appropriation for making any road where there should be a temporary encampment, &c. There was, he conceived, no inconsistency between the expressed opinion of the executive respecting the general power, and the conduct of the executive on this subject. The propriety of making specific appropriations for all objects, where it could well be done, he did not deny; but he was also apprehensive that it might be pushed to an improper extent. All appropriations could not be specific; but, after making them as minute as possible, and limiting the executive to a certain extent, there would be always some discretion left him. It was proper, also, he admitted, where it could be done, to designate and fix the place where the public money is to be applied; but this could not in all cases be done, and he mentioned instances in which this was left by law to the discretion of the executive; and the present was one of those cases in which this must necessarily be done.

Seminole War.

House of Representatives, *January 21*, 1819.

Mr. R. M. JOHNSON, (of Kentucky.) As early as 1787, and farther back, if it were necessary to trace, provisions of the same nature as those now existing were enacted by the venerable Congress of the Confederation. By various statutes, the same provisions had been continued to the present day. The statute gave to the President a discretionary power to employ the forces of the United States, and to call forth the militia to repress Indian hostility; and gave it to him properly on the principles of the Constitution. By the Constitution, the President is made commander-in-chief of the army; and it is made his duty to take care that the laws are executed, to suppress insurrections, and repel invasions; and by the same instrument it is made our duty to provide for calling forth the militia, to be employed in these objects. That power has been exercised

in the manner which will be shown by the laws of the United States.
[Mr. J. here requested the clerk to read the statute to which he alluded
and it was read accordingly.]   Now, Mr. J. said, he thought this was a
declaration of war of at least equal dignity to the manner in which the
savages make war against us, and to the light in which we view them.
We treat them, it is true, and we ought to treat them, with humanity;
we have given them privileges beyond all other nations; but we reserve
the right to repel their invasions, and to put to death murderers and vio-
lators of our peace, whether Indians or white men.

Tariff.

House of Representatives, *April* 26, 1820.

Mr. CLAY.   Sir, friendly as I am to the existence of domestic manufactures, I would not give them unreasonable encouragement by protecting duties.   Their growth ought to be gradual, but sure.   I believe all
the circumstances of the present period highly favorable to their success.
But they are the youngest and the weakest interest of the state.   Agriculture wants but little or no protection against the regulations of foreign
powers.   The advantages of our position, and the cheapness, and abundance, and fertility of our land, afford to that greatest interest of the state
almost all the protection it wants.   As it should be, it is strong and flourishing; or, if it be not at this moment prosperous, it is not because its
produce is not ample, but because, depending, as we do, altogether upon
a foreign market for the sale of the surplus of that produce, the foreign
market is glutted.   Our foreign trade, having almost exclusively engrossed
the protecting care of government, wants no further legislative aid; and
whatever depression it may now experience, it is attributable to causes
beyond the control of this government.   The abundance of capital, indicated by the avidity with which loans are sought, at the reduced rate of
five per centum; the reduction in the wages of labor; and the decline in
the price of property of every kind, as well as that of agricultural produce, — all concur favorably for domestic manufactures.   Now, as when
we arranged the existing tariff, is the auspicious moment for government
to step in and cheer and countenance them.   We did too little then, and
I endeavored to warn this house of the effects of inadequate protection.
We were called upon, at that time, by the previous pledges we had given,
by the inundation of foreign fabrics, which was to be anticipated from
their free admission after the termination of the war, and by the lasting
interests of this country, to give them efficient support.   We did not do
it; but let us not now repeat the error.   Our great mistake has been in
the irregularity of the action of the measures of this government upon
manufacturing industry.   At one period it is stimulated too high, and
then, by an opposite course of policy, it is precipitated into a condition
of depression too low.   First, there came the embargo; then non-intercourse, and other restrictive measures followed; and finally, that greatest
of all *stimuli* to domestic fabrication, war.   During all that long period,
we were adding to the positive effect of the measures of government all
the moral encouragement which results from popular resolves, legislative
resolves, and other manifestations of the public will, and the public wish
to foster our home manufactures, and to render our confederacy independent of foreign powers.   The peace ensued, and the country was flooded
with the fabrics of other countries; and we, forgetting all our promises,

coolly and philosophically talk of leaving things to themselves; making up our deficiency of practical good sense by the stores of learning which we collect from theoretical writers. I, too, sometimes amuse myself with the visions of these writers; and, if I do not forget, one of the best among them enjoins it upon a country to protect its industry against the influence of the prohibitions and restrictions of foreign countries, which operate upon it.

Let us manifest, by the passage of this bill, that Congress does not deserve the reproaches, which have been cast on it, of insensibility to the wants and the sufferings of the people.

The Petition of Matthew Lyon.

SENATE, *March*, 1821.

Mr. SMITH, (of South Carolina.) The Constitution of the United States is not the production of Congress; it is not the property of Congress. It is the production of the people, and the property of the people. It is their shield against the abuse of powers, as well as against the usurpation of powers, both by Congress and the judges. Your powers are limited. All legislative powers are granted to Congress, and all judicial powers are granted to the judges. You have, therefore, the power to enact laws, but no power to sit in judgment upon those laws. It is expressly and exclusively given to the judges to construe the laws, and to decide upon their constitutionality. The judges are an independent and coördinate branch of the government, deriving their authority from the Constitution, and not from Congress. They are accountable to the sovereign people; and if guilty of malpractice in administering the laws, they can and ought to be impeached; and you are the tribunal before which they are to answer, but there your powers cease. You have powers to punish judges for corruption, but none to revise or correct their decisions.

Mr. S. added, within three years after the adoption of the Federal Constitution, Mr. President Madison, in debate upon a proposition to incorporate the former Bank of the United States, opposed it, on the ground of its being unconstitutional. He said, —

" In making these remarks on the merits of the bill, he had reserved to himself the right to deny the authority of Congress to pass it. He had entertained this opinion from the date of the Constitution. His impression might, perhaps, be the stronger, because he well recollected that a power to grant charters to incorporations had been proposed in the General Convention, and rejected."

But when a bill to incorporate the present United States' Bank was submitted for his approval, and when he could have put it down forever, he found means to get over all his constitutional scruples, and approved the act.

Missouri Question.

HOUSE OF REPRESENTATIVES, *December* 13, 1821.

Mr. LOWNDES. The Constitution gives to Congress the power to admit states in the broadest terms. The high privileges which it is authorized to impart may commence instantly, and extend through all future time. When the convenience of a territory required that it should become a member of the Union at a future day, what principle of the Constitution was opposed to this prospective admission? Congress may raise armies: has any man ever suspected that this power could not be executed by giving a prospective, and even a contingent authority? Congress may lay

taxes : may they not be limited to take effect some time after the passage
of the law? Congress may institute inferior courts : would such an act
be void, because its operation was to commence from a future day? void
because it was not inconvenient and absurd? Run your eye along the
whole list of powers which are given to the federal legislature, and you will
find no countenance for the doctrine which would require that, at the very
moment when their will is pronounced, the object which they are empowered to effect should be instantly executed. The power of making treaties,
too, although given to another depository, is supposed to be pursued,
although the convention with a foreign state may take effect from a future
day. There is nothing plausible in the assertion which denies to Congress
the power of admitting states by an act which shall not go into operation
for some time after its passage. The house would see, in his subsequent
observations, the importance of determining whether Congress had the
constitutional right of admitting states by a prospective law. He need
not say that this question of right was distinct from that of expediency.

Bankrupt Bill.

HOUSE OF REPRESENTATIVES, *March* 12, 1822.

Mr. BUCHANAN, (of Pennsylvania.) It has been urged that, as the
powers of the Constitution gave to Congress the power of passing a bankrupt law, we are bound to put that power into practical operation, and not
to suffer it to remain dormant.

In answer to this argument I would reply, that power and duty are very
different in their nature. Power is optional ; duty is imperative. The
language of power is, that you may ; that of duty, you must. The Constitution has, in the same section and in the same terms, given to Congress
the power to declare war, to borrow money, to raise and support armies,
&c. Will any gentleman, however, undertake to say we are under an
obligation to give life and energy to these powers, by bringing them into
action ? Will it be contended, because we possess the power of declaring
war and of borrowing money, that we are under a moral obligation to em-
broil ourselves with foreign powers, or load the country with a national
debt ? Should any individual act upon the principle, that it is his duty to
do every thing which he has the legal power of doing, he would soon make
himself a fit citizen for a madhouse.

Power, whether vested in Congress or in an individual, necessarily implies the power of exercising the right of a sound discretion. The Constitution was intended not only for us, and for those who have gone before us,
but for generations yet to come. It has vested in Congress ample powers,
to be called into action whenever, in their sound discretion, they believe
the interest or the happiness of the people require their exertion. We
are, therefore, left to exercise our judgment on this subject, entirely
untrammelled by any constitutional injunction.

On the Constitutionality of the Tariff.

SENATE, *April*, 1824.

Mr. HAYNE. Will gentlemen suffer me to ask them to point out to
me, if they can, the power which this government possesses to adopt a
system for the avowed purpose of encouraging particular branches of industry ? The power to declare war may involve the right of bringing into
existence the means of national defence. But to tell us we have a right

to resort to theoretical speculations, as to the most convenient or profitable employments of industry, and that you can, by law, encourage certain pursuits and prohibit others, is to make this not merely a consolidated, but an unlimited government.   If you can control and direct any, why not all the pursuits of your citizens?   And if all, where is the limitation to your authority?   Gentlemen surely forget that the supreme power is not in the government of the United States.   They do not remember that the several states are free and independent sovereignties, and that all power not expressly granted to the federal government is reserved to the people of those sovereignties.   When I say expressly delegated, I wish to be understood that no power can be exercised by Congress which is not expressly granted, or which is not clearly incident to such a grant.   Now, when we call upon gentlemen to show their authority, they tell us it is derived from the authority to " regulate commerce."   But are *regulation* and *annihilation* synonymous terms?   Does one include the other?   Or are they not rather opposites, and does not the very idea of regulation exclude that of destruction?   I rejoice, sir, to find that gentlemen refer us to commerce; for the very clause which expressly confers the right to regulate commerce, by saying nothing of the regulation of manufactures, or of agriculture, or home industry, seems to demonstrate that they were intended to be put beyond our control, and to be reserved to the people of the states respectively.

But our opponents gravely inform us that this is a bill to levy imposts, and that it is, therefore, within the *very letter* of the Constitution.   True sir, if *imposts* were the end and aim of the bill.   But, surely, gentlemen will not attempt to justify a departure from the *spirit*, by an adherence to the *letter*, of the Constitution.   Will they contend that we could, by law, adopt and enforce the *Chinese policy*, and, by virtue of our authority to regulate commerce, interdict all intercourse with foreign nations?   And if you could not do that directly, can you accomplish the same thing indirectly, by levying such imposts as will produce the same result?   It may be difficult to draw the exact line which divides the lawful exercise from the abuse of authority — where regulation ceases, and unconstitutional prohibition begins.   But it is certain, if you have a right to prohibit the importation of cottons, and woollens, and cotton bagging, for the encouragement of domestic manufactures, you may, whenever you please, prohibit importations, and shut up your ports entirely.   An embargo can only be justified as a branch of the war power, and I think no one will contend, at this day, that a *general and perpetual embargo* could be lawfully laid.   If it be sufficient to adhere to the letter without regard to the spirit and intent of the Constitution, if we may use a power granted for one purpose for the accomplishment of another and very different purpose, it is easy to show that a constitution on parchment is worth nothing.

Orders of nobility, and a church establishment, might be created even under the power to raise armies.   We are informed that in Russia military titles alone confer civil rank, and all the departments of the government are filled with generals and colonels, entitled to rank, and to pay, without actual command or liability to service.   Now, suppose we were to follow the example of Russia, and should give rank and pay to a certain number of *generals* and CHAPLAINS, with total or qualified exemption from service; might we not easily build up orders of nobility, and a church establishment?   Sir, this government was never established for the purpose of divesting the states of their sovereignty; and I fear it cannot long exist, if the system, of which this bill is the foundation, shall be steadily pursued to the total destruction of foreign commerce, and the ruin of all who are connected with it.   Sir, it is my most sober and deliberate opinion, that the Congress of the United States have no more power to pass laws, for the purpose of directly or indirectly compelling any portion of the people to engage in manufactures, than they have to abolish trial by jury, or to establish the inquisition.   I will invoke gentlemen on the other side, while we yet pause on the brink of this mighty danger, in the name of Liberty and the Constitution, to examine this question, carefully and candidly; and if they shall search in vain, in our great charter, for power to pass this bill, they must surely suffer it to perish.

I must be permitted, while on this topic, to declare that, however this bill may be modified, still the system is one against which we feel ourselves constrained, in behalf of those we represent, to enter our most solemn protest.   Considering this scheme of promoting certain employments, at the expense of others, as unequal, oppressive, and unjust, — viewing prohibition as the *means*, and the destruction of all foreign commerce the *end* of this policy, — I take this occasion to declare, that we shall feel ourselves fully justified in embracing the very first opportunity of repealing all such laws as may be passed for the promotion of these objects.   Whatever interests may grow up under this bill, and whatever capital may be invested, I wish it to be distinctly understood, that we will not hold ourselves bound to maintain the system ; and if capitalists will, in the face of our protests, and in defiance of our solemn warnings, invest their fortunes in pursuits made profitable at our expense, on their own heads be the consequences of their folly.   This system is in its very nature PROGRESSIVE.   Grant what you may now, the manufacturers will never be satisfied ; do what you may for them, the advocates of home industry will never be content, until every article imported from abroad, which comes into competition with any thing made at home, shall be prohibited — until, in short, foreign commerce shall be entirely cut off.

Internal Improvement. — *Dismal Swamp Canal.*

Senate, *May,* 1824.

Mr. VAN BUREN.   He would not vote for the bill, for he did not believe that this government possessed the constitutional power to make these canals, or to grant money to make them.   * * *   If he believed in the power of the government to grant money for this purpose, the present mode would be the last one he should think of adopting.   If there was any grant of money, at all, for this purpose, it should be direct.   Where aid was granted in the mode now proposed, abuses would creep in, and, in nine cases out of ten, deception would be practised.   In the state of New York, Mr. Van Buren said, they had had full experience of this, in the application for charters for banks.   Plausible pretences were set up, that the state would be thereby benefited, till these practices became so numerous, that, in the end, public opinion was decidedly against them ; and the last legislature, to their honor, had refused all applications of this description.   * * *   As to the question (of constitutionality) being settled, he should protest against the admission of such a doctrine ; and he should resist, to all intents and purposes, the idea that the acts of this Congress were to bind him and his constituents hereafter.

Note. — Mr. Van Buren is by no means certain that, in this respect, he

himself has been altogether without fault.   At the very first session after
he came into the Senate, the knowledge of the perpetual drain that the
Cumberland road was destined to prove upon the public treasury unless
some means were taken to prevent it, and a sincere desire to go, at all
times, as far as he could consistently with the Constitution, to aid in the
improvement, and promote the prosperity, of the western country, had induced him, without full examination, to vote for a provision authorizing
the collection of toll on this road.   The affair of the Cumberland road, in
respect to its reference to the constitutional powers of this government, is
a matter entirely *sui generis.*   It was authorized during the administration
of Mr. Jefferson, and grew out of the disposition of the territory of the
United States through which it passed.   He has never heard an explanation
of the subject (although it has been a matter of constant reference) that
has been satisfactory to his mind.   All that he can say is, that, if the
question were again presented to him, he would vote against it, and that
his regret for having done otherwise would be greater, had not Mr. Monroe — much to his credit — put his veto upon the bill, and were it not the
only vote, in the course of a seven years' service, which the most fastidi-
ous critic can torture into an inconsistency with the principles which Mr.
Van Buren professed to maintain, and in the justice of which he is every
day more and more confirmed.

Judiciary.

Mr. WEBSTER.   In defining the power of Congress, the Constitution
says, it shall extend to the defining and punishing of piracies and felonies
upon the high seas, and offences against the law of nations.   Whether the
Constitution uses the term "high seas" in its strictly technical sense, or
in a sense more enlarged, is not material.   The Constitution throughout,
in distributing legislative power, has reference to its judicial exercise, and
so, in distributing judicial power, has respect to the legislature.   Congress
may provide by law for the punishment, but it cannot punish.   Now, it
says that the judicial power shall extend to all cases of maritime jurisdiction; and it has lately been argued that, as soon as a judicial system
is organized, it had maritime jurisdiction at once, by the Constitution,
without any law to that effect; but I do not agree to this doctrine, and I
am very sure that such has not been the practice of our government, from
its origin, in 1789, till now.

The Constitution defines what shall be the objects of judicial power,
and it establishes only a Supreme Court; but in the subordinate courts,
the jurisdiction they shall exercise must be defined by Congress: the defining of it is essential to the creation of those courts.   The judicial
power is indeed *granted* by the Constitution; but it is not, and cannot be,
exercised till Congress establishes the courts by which it is to be so exercised.   And I hold there is still a *residuum* of judicial power, which
has been granted by the Constitution, and is not yet exercised, viz., for the
punishment of crimes committed within the admiralty jurisdiction of the
United States' courts, and yet not without the jurisdiction of the particular
states.   So the Constitution says that the federal courts shall have jurisdiction of all civil cases between citizens of different states; and yet
the law restricts this jurisdiction in many respects — as to the amount sued
for, &c.   There is a mass of power intrusted to Congress; but Congress

has not granted it all to specific courts, and therefore the courts do not exercise it.   The Constitution gives to Congress legislative power in all cases of admiralty jurisdiction, from whence has occurred one of the most extraordinary of all circumstances — that causes of revenue have become cases of admiralty jurisdiction.   * * *

Many things are directed to be punished, in the act of 1800, on the high seas, which are neither piracies nor felonies, although the Constitution, speaking of the judicial power, restricts it to piracies and felonies, which would infer that the Constitution was then held to grant larger power by the other clause.

Internal Improvement.

January 18, 1825.

Mr. CAMBRELENG said he had hitherto uniformly, but silently, opposed measures of this character, only from a doubt of the constitutional power of the federal government.   He had, however, devoted much attention to the question ; and, after mature deliberation, he had been led to the conclusion that, if a government, enjoying the entire post-road and military powers of this Union, could not constitutionally construct a road or a canal, then it had no incidental power whatever.   He had, accordingly, for the first time, given his vote in favor of a subscription to the Chesapeake and Delaware Canal.

February 13, 1826.

Mr. BERRIEN said, as to the general right, asserted for the Union, to make roads through all the Indian countries, against such a doctrine he should desire to protest.   He would draw a distinction between those lands of Indians living within limits of the states which came into the confederation, with certain chartered limits, and those living within states who, at the time of the formation of the Constitution, had no limits, and whose limits were only defined by the laws regulating their admission into the Union.

Bankruptcy.

Senate, *January*, 1826.

Mr. VAN BUREN.   At the time of the adoption of the Constitution, they [bankruptcy and insolvent laws] were known and distinguished, both in England and in this country, as distinct systems — the one having for its object to afford a summary and speedy remedy for creditors against fraudulent or failing traders ; the other affording relief to insolvent debtors of all denominations.   The Constitution of the United States, he said, had clothed the national legislature with power to establish the former, and had left the right to pass, and the duty of establishing, the latter, upon the state governments.   The 93d section of this bill, he said, was, upon any definition that might be given of the different terms, an insolvent law.   If it passed, — that is, if Congress had the constitutional power to pass it, — the states had no right to pass any law upon the subject of insolvency ; not even to authorize the discharge of debtors imprisoned upon a process issuing out of their own courts, otherwise than as it might suit the pleasure or convenience of Congress to permit.   There was, he said, no middle ground.   If the partition wall between bankruptcy and insolvency was once broken down, all state legislation was subjected to the absolute and arbitrary supervision of Congress.   He did not believe that such was the design of the framers of the Constitution.   He did not believe that such was the Constitution. He therefore objected to the constitutional power of Congress to pass the section referred to. He had before said that he rose to explain, not to discuss, and he would not depart from the course he had marked out for himself. He would therefore only add, that, in his judgment, the provision contained in the 93d section was not within the reasons which induced the framers of the Constitution to vest this power of establishing uniform laws on the subject of bankruptcies in Congress; that it was a power which never ought to be, or to have been, vested in Congress; that it could only be well and successfully executed by the states, where those who made the Constitution had left it; that its exercise would operate most injuriously upon the system which governed the Union and the states separately: those mischiefs would, among other things, consist in an injurious extension of the patronage of the federal government, and an insupportable enlargement of the range of its judicial power.

Florida Canal.

February 14, 1826.

Mr. BRANCH perfectly coincided with the gentleman from Tennessee, (Mr. White.) Doubting of the constitutional right of the United States to cut roads and canals through the states, he had hitherto abstained from exercising it; but as regarded the territory, the objection did not seem to exist; for not only had Congress the right to make this appropriation for a road through the Indian country, acquired by treaty before it came into the Union, but it was an obligation on the general government to complete the work it had commenced, and he had therefore voted for it.

Mr. ROWAN. In the general government, they were, Mr. R. said, to look into the Constitution for all the power they possessed. There was no such power given in the Constitution; and he believed, with deference to the opinion entertained, that to convey the exercise of such a power was incompatible with what was the acknowledged power of the states. There was no power given to expend money in roads and canals in the states; there was no such power specifically given to the United States; and when once it was settled in this house that power could be derived to this government by construction, you have discovered the means by which the whole power of a state might be frittered down and annihilated.

On the Constitutional Power of the President to originate the Appointment of a Foreign Minister.

SENATE, *March*, 1826.

Mr. BERRIEN. By the Constitution, the President is authorized to nominate, and, by and with the advice and consent of the Senate, to appoint, ambassadors, and other public ministers and consuls, judges of the supreme courts, and all other officers of the United States, whose appointments are not therein otherwise provided for, and which shall be established by law. Now, it is plain that the appointing power does not include the power to create the office; in other words, that the office to which the appointee is nominated must be previously created by law. If an appointment be to an office to be exercised within the limits of the United States or its territories, it must be to one which exists, and has been created by the municipal laws of the United States. If to an office which is to be exercised without the limits of the United States, within the dominions of a foreign sovereign, it must be to one which exists, and is recognized by the general principles of international law, or which is specially created by positive and particular pacts and conventions. The limitation in the latter case results not only from the fundamental law of this government, but from the exclusive dominion, within his own territories, of the sovereign within whose territories this minister is to exercise his functions. That sovereign is bound, as a member of the great family of nations, to recognize as legitimate an appointment which is consonant to the code of international law, and of course to acknowledge one which, by express convention, he has stipulated ; but this is the extent of his obligation, and consequently the limit of the appointing power under our Constitution.

Let us look to the first of these propositions. Is it within the " constitutional competency " of the President to appoint to an office the functions of which are to be exercised within the limits of the United States, which office has not been created by the laws of the United States ? Take an example. The President deems it expedient to establish a home department. Is there any one sufficiently absurd to assert that he has a right, *ex mero motu*, or even with the assent of a majority of the Senate, to appoint a secretary for that department — to assign to him certain specific duties, and then to call on Congress for the requisite appropriation, to compensate his services ? — to imagine that the acts of such an officer would be valid, or that his attestations would be respected by our judicial tribunals ?

Before the passing of an act of Congress for the organization of a newly-acquired territory, and the creation, by that act, of the legislative, executive, and judicial officers deemed necessary for its government, is it within the " constitutional competency " of the President, aided even, as before, by a majority of the Senate, to appoint an officer or officers to exercise all or either of these functions ? The proposition is believed to be too clear for argument.

Within the United States, the office must be created by law before the appointing power can be called into action. Why should a different rule prevail without ? The law of nations operates on this government, in its intercourse with other sovereignties, as the municipal law does in its action on its own citizens. In this case, then, the law of nations, as in the other the municipal law, must have created the office, before the power of appointment can exist. Now, the law of nations does recognize ambassadors and other ministers, in the intercourse between sovereigns. But this law does no where recognize the right of a congress of ministers to receive an embassy. The right to receive, and the right to send, a minister, are co-relative. The one does not exist without the other. A congress of ministers is not authorized to receive an ambassador, unless it is authorized to send one. Who will assert, for the congress of Panama, the right to exercise the latter power?

A sovereign cannot, then, be represented in a congress of ministers, otherwise than by a deputy, who becomes a member of that congress. He is not an ambassador to that congress, but is himself a constituent part of it. He is not accredited to any particular power, but is commissioned as one of a number of deputies who are collectively to compose the congress. How are these deputies created ? The answer is obvious. From the necessity of the thing, it must be by conventions or treaties between the respective powers who are to be represented by those deputies. In this manner the congress at Verona was created by the treaty of Paris. The deputies who appeared there were called into existence by the express stipulations of that treaty. So, too, in the congress of Panama, the office of deputy to that congress is created by the special provisions of the treaties between the several powers who are to be represented there.

The result of what has been said is this: The office of a deputy to an international congress does not exist permanently under the law of nations, but is the offspring of particular convention — and this of necessity, because the congress itself is not preëxisting, but is the creature of treaty; and the treaty which creates the congress stipulates also for the appointment of the deputies of whom it is to be composed. Then the clause of the Constitution which authorizes the appointment of ambassadors, or other ministers, cannot be invoked to sustain this nomination, because a deputy to a congress is not a minister existing by force of the law of nations, but created by particular conventions between the powers represented in that congress; and we have no such conventions with the powers represented in the congress of Panama. Consequently, as to us, the office of minister or deputy to that congress does not exist, not being derived from the law of nations, nor provided for by any convention. A very simple view of the subject seems to be decisive. Could the President have sent ministers to the congress of Panama uninvited by the powers represented there? Could he, without such invitation, have required such ministers to be accredited by that congress? Would a refusal to receive them have furnished just ground of complaint? If these questions are answered in the negative, as I presume they must be, the conclusion is obvious: the office exists only by force of the invitation.

Unless, then, the mere invitation of a foreign nation is competent to create an office, and thus to call into action the appointing power of the President, — unless this appointing power includes the power to create the office, which we have seen that it does not, — the appointment by the President of ministers to the congress of Panama cannot be valid, nor can it be rendered so by the advice and consent of a majority of the Senate, nor by any power short of that which is competent to create the office; and that, we have seen, is the treaty-making power. The President can appoint a minister to the republic of Colombia, because such an office exists under the law of nations, and is, therefore, a legitimate object of the appointing power; and he may instruct such minister to communicate with the congress of Panama; but he cannot appoint a minister to take a seat in that congress, because we have no conventions with the powers represented there, by which, as to us, the office is created; nor can he send a minister, as an ambassador or legate, to that congress, because the congress, as such, has not the rights of embassy   If it be said that this is mere form, the answer is obvious: form becomes substance in this case, by force of the constitutional provision which requires the assent of two thirds of the Senate to the ratification of a treaty, while a bare majority is sufficient to give effect to an exercise of the appointing power.

Let us consider this question, for a moment, freed from the prejudices which operate in favor of the Spanish American republics   If the states represented in the congress of Vienna or Verona, or the Holy Alliance, had given us an invitation to be represented there, apart from the expediency of the measure, could it have been within the "constitutional competency" of the President to have sent ministers to take their seats in either of those assemblies ? If the nations of Europe should, by treaties, provide for a congress to devise the means of abolishing the slave trade, of resisting the extortions of the Barbary powers, or of suppressing the piracies of the West Indian seas, could the President, the United States not being parties to those treaties, of his own mere will, make us members of that congress, by sending deputies to represent us there ? The question is proposed in this form, because our ministers would, of necessity, if received at all, be members, and not ambassadors, since such a congress is neither competent to send or to receive an embassy.

Why, then, in the creation of this office of deputy or minister to the congress of Panama, was not the constitutional organ, the treaty-making power, resorted to ? What would have been the result of such a course is obvious, I think, in the recorded votes of the Senate, on the preliminary questions which have arisen. The object could not have been effected. Two thirds of the Senate could not have been obtained. The office would not have had existence; or the Senate, in the exercise of their legitimate powers, would have so modified the treaty, as to have limited the functions of the ministers to those objects of which they would have approved.

Mr. ROBBINS. The theory of our Constitution charges the executive with the care of our foreign relations, and of the public interest connected therewith : it supposes him intimately acquainted with all those interests, and therefore possessed of the means of forming a correct opinion of the measures conducive to their advancement. This opinion, though not binding as authority, is yet, I think, entitled to much weight, as well as to much respect, in our deliberations. We have the executive opinion in this case, under circumstances that entitle it to peculiar consideration. The credit of the government, in the estimation of all those nations, is in a degree connected with the adoption of this measure; and that estimation ought not, in my opinion, lightly to be forfeited, nor unnecessarily impaired.

On Slavery, [*Panama Mission.*]

Senate, *March*, 1826.

Mr. HAYNE. The question of slavery is one, in all its bearings, of extreme delicacy ; and concerning which I know of but a single wise and safe rule, either for the states in which it exists or for the Union. It must be considered and treated entirely as a DOMESTIC QUESTION. With respect to foreign nations, the language of the United States ought to be, that it concerns the peace of our own political family, and therefore we cannot permit it to be touched ; and in respect to the slave-holding states, the only safe and constitutional ground on which they can stand, is, that they will not permit it to be brought into question, either by their sister states or by the federal government. It is a matter for ourselves. To touch it at all, is to violate our most sacred rights — to put in jeopardy our dearest interests — the peace of our country — the safety of our families, our altars, and our firesides. Sir, on the question of our slave institutions, so often incidentally mentioned, I will take this opportunity, once for all, to declare, in a few words, my own feelings and opinions. It is a subject to which I always advert with extreme reluctance, and never except when it is forced upon me. On the present occasion, the subject has been forced upon our consideration ; and when called upon to give my sanction to the discussion, by our ministers, (in connection with a foreign congress,) of questions so intimately connected with the welfare of those whom I represent, I cannot consent to be silent. On the slave question, my opinion is this: I consider our rights in that species of property as not even open to discussion, either here or elsewhere; and in respect to our duties, (imposed by our situation,) we are not to be taught them by fanatics, religious or political. To call into question our rights, is grossly to violate them; to attempt to instruct us on this subject, is to insult us; to dare to assail our institutions, is wantonly to invade our peace. Let me solemnly declare, once for all, that the Southern States never will permit, and never can permit, any interference whatever in their domestic concerns; and that the very day on which the unhallowed attempt shall be made by the authorities of the federal government, we will consider ourselves as driven from the Union. Let the consequences be what they may, they never can be worse than such as must inevitably result from suffering a rash and ignorant interference with our domestic peace and tranquillity. But while I make these declarations, I must be permitted to add, that I apprehend no such violation of our constitutional rights. I believe that this house is not disposed, and that the great body of our intelligent and patriotic fellow-citizens in the other states have no inclination whatever, to interfere with us. There are parties, indeed, composed, some of them, of fanatics, and others of political aspirants, who are attempting, vainly I hope, to turn the current of popular opinion against us. These men have done us much harm already, and seem still fatally bent upon mischief. But if we are true to ourselves, we shall have nothing to fear. Now, sir, if it is the policy of the states not to suffer this great question to be touched by the federal government, surely it must be the policy of this government, exercising a paternal care over every member of the political family, not to suffer foreign nations to interfere with it. It is their imperative duty to shun discussion with them, and to avoid all treaty stipulations whatever, on any point connected, directly or remotely, with this great question. It is a subject of too delicate a nature — too vitally interesting to us — to be discussed abroad. On this subject, we committed an error when we entered into treaties with Great Britain and Colombia for the suppression of the slave trade. That error has been happily corrected.

The first treaty has failed, and the second was nearly unanimously rejected by this body. Our policy, then, is now firmly fixed — our course is marked out. With nothing connected with slavery, can we consent to treat with other nations? — and, least of all, ought we to touch the question of the independence of Hayti, in conjunction with revolutionary governments, whose own history affords an example scarcely less fatal to our repose. Those governments have proclaimed the principles of "liberty and equality," and have marched to victory under the banner of "universal emancipation." You find men of color at the head of their armies, in their halls, and in their executive departments. They are looking to Hayti even now with feelings of the strongest confraternity; and show, by the very documents before us, that they acknowledge her to be independent, at the very moment when it is manifest to all the world beside, that she has resumed her colonial subjection to France. Sir, it is altogether hopeless that we could, if we would, prevent the acknowledgment of Haytien independence by the Spanish American states; and I am constrained to add, that I must doubt, from the instruments to be employed by our government, whether they mean to attempt to do so. We are to send, it seems, an honest and respectable man, but a distinguished advocate of the

Missouri restriction — an acknowledged abolitionist — to plead the cause of the south at the congress of Panama. Our policy with regard to Hayti is plain. We never can acknowledge her independence. Other states will do as they please; but let us take the high ground, that these questions belong to a class which the peace and safety of a large portion of our Union forbid us even to discuss. Let our government direct all our ministers in South America and Mexico to *protest* against the independence of Hayti. But let us not go into council on the slave trade and Hayti. These are subjects not to be discussed any where. There is not a nation on the globe with whom I would consult on that subject; and least of all, the new republics.

Judicial System.

Mr. VAN BUREN. It has been justly observed that " there exists not upon this earth, and there never did exist, a judicial tribunal clothed with powers so various and so important " as the Supreme Court.

By it, treaties and laws made *pursuant* to the Constitution are declared to be the supreme law of the land. So far, at least, as the acts of Congress depend upon the courts for their execution, the Supreme Court is the judge whether or no such acts are *pursuant to the Constitution*, and from its judgment there is no appeal. Its veto, therefore, may absolutely suspend nine tenths of the acts of the national legislature. Although this branch of its jurisdiction is not that which has been most exercised, still instances are not wanting in which it has disregarded acts of Congress, in passing upon the rights of others, and in refusing to perform duties required of it by the legislature, on the ground that the legislature had no right to impose them.

Not only are the acts of the national legislature subject to its review, but it stands as the umpire between the conflicting powers of the general and state governments. That wide field of debatable ground between those rival powers is claimed to be subject to the exclusive and absolute dominion of the Supreme Court. The discharge of this solemn duty has not been unfrequent, and certainly not uninteresting. In virtue of this power, we have seen it holding for nought the statutes of powerful states, which had received the deliberate sanction, not only of their legislatures, but of their highest judicatories, composed of men venerable in years, of unsullied purity, and unrivalled talents — statutes, on the faith of which immense estates had been invested, and the inheritance of the widow and the orphan were suspended. You have seen such statutes abrogated by the decision of this court, and those who had confided in the wisdom and power of the state authorities plunged in irremediable ruin — decisions final in their effect, and ruinous in their consequences. I speak of the power of the court, not of the correctness or incorrectness of its decisions. With that we have here nothing to do.

But this is not all. It not only sits in final judgment upon our acts, as the highest legislative body known to the country, — it not only claims to be the absolute arbiter between the federal and state governments, — but it exercises the same great power between the respective *states* forming this great confederacy, and *their own citizens*. By the Constitution of the United States, the states are prohibited from passing " any law *impairing the obligation of contracts*." This brief provision has given to the jurisdiction of the Supreme Court a tremendous sweep. Before I proceed to delineate its tendency and character, I will take leave to remark upon some extraordinary circumstances in relation to it. We all know the severe scrutiny to which the Constitution was exposed — some from their own knowledge, others from different sources. We know with what jealousy, with what watchfulness, with what scrupulous care, its minutest provisions were examined, discussed, resisted, and supported, by those who opposed and those who advocated its ratification. But of this highly consequential provision, this provision which carries so great a portion of all that is valuable in state legislation to the feet of the federal judiciary, no complaints were heard, no explanation asked, no remonstrances made. If they were, they have escaped my researches. It is most mysterious, if the Constitution was then understood as it now is, that this was so. An explanation of it has been given — how correct I know not.

The difficulties which existed between us and Great Britain, relative to the execution of the treaty of peace, are known to all. Upon the avowed ground of retaliation for the refusal of England to comply with the stipulation on her part, laws were passed, between the years 1783 and 1788, by the states of Virginia, South Carolina, Rhode Island, New Jersey, and Georgia, delaying execution, liberating the body from imprisonment on the delivery of property, and admitting executions to be discharged in paper money. Although those laws were general in their terms, applicable as well to natives as to foreigners, their chief operation was upon the British creditors ; and such was the leading design of their enactment. England remonstrated against them as infractions of the stipulations in the treaty, that creditors, on either side, should meet with no impediments to the recovery of the full value, in sterling money, of all debts previously contracted, and attempted to justify the glaring violations of the treaty, on her part, on that ground. An animated discussion took place between the federal government and Great Britain, and between the former and the states in question, upon the subject of the laws referred to, their character and effect. It was during this time that the Constitution was formed and ratified. It is supposed that the difficulties, thus thrown in the way of adjustment with England, through the acts of the state governments, suggested the insertion in the Constitution of *the provision in question,* and that it was under a belief that its chief application would be to the evil then felt, that so little notice was taken of the subject.

If it be true that such was its object, and such its supposed effect, it adds another and a solemn proof to that which all experience has testified, of the danger of adapting general provisions for the redress of particular and partial evils. But whatever the motive that led to its insertion, or the cause that induced so little observation on its tendency, the fact of its extensive operation is known and acknowledged. The prohibition is not confined to express contracts, but includes such as are implied by law, from the nature of the transaction. Any one conversant with the usual range of state legislation, will at once see how small a portion of it is exempt, under this provision, from the supervision of the seven judges of the Supreme Court. The practice under it has been in accordance with what should have been anticipated.

There are few states in the Union, upon whose acts the seal of condemnation has not, from time to time, been placed by the Supreme Court. The sovereign authorities of Vermont, New Hampshire, New York, New Jersey, Pennsylvania, Maryland, Virginia, North Carolina, Missouri, Kentucky, and Ohio, have, in turn, been rebuked and silenced, by the overruling authority of this court.   I must not be understood, si:, as com plaining of the exercise of this jurisdiction by the Supreme Court, or to pass upon the correctness of their decisions.   The authority has been given to them, and this is not the place to question its exercise.   But this I will say — that, if the question of conferring it was now presented for the first time, I should unhesitatingly say, that the people of the states might with safety be left to their own legislatures, and the protection of their own courts.

Add to the immense powers of which I have spoken those of expounding treaties, so far, at least, as they bear upon individuals, citizens or aliens, — of deciding controversies between the states of the confederacy themselves, and between the citizens of the different states; and the justice of the remark will not be questioned, that there is no known judicial power so transcendently omnipotent as that of the Supreme Court of the United States.

Let us now consider the influence which this ought to have upon our legislation.   It would not be in accordance with the common course of nature, to expect that such mighty powers can long continue to be exercised, without accumulating a weight of prejudice that may, one day, become dangerous to an institution which all admit to be of inestimable value.   It is true, as has elsewhere been said, with apparent triumph, that the states whose legislative acts have successively fallen under the interdiction of the court have excited little or no sympathy on the part of their sister states, and, after struggling with the giant strength of the court, have submitted to their fate.   But, sir, it is feared that this will not always be the case.   Those who are most ardent in their devotion to this branch of the government, knowing the feelings produced by these decisions in those states affected by them, — sensible that those feelings are rather smothered, than abandoned upon conviction of their injustice, — fear that, by adding another and another state to the ranks of those who think they have reason to complain, an accumulation of prejudice may be produced, that will threaten, if not endanger, the safety of the institution.

April 11, 1826.

Mr. WOODBURY.   The proposed bill not only alters the system for local purposes, by requiring the attendance of an additional judge at the Circuit Court in regions of country not so populous as those where the judges of the Supreme Court now attend, but it alters the system for general purposes, by enlarging the Supreme Court itself one half its whole original number; by leaving its quorum so that contradictory decisions may constantly be made without any change in the court itself; and by increasing it to as great an extent as a majority of its present quorum, — so that new results may possibly be produced in all its grand supervising powers over each state, and over the whole confederation.

It is thus that a principle lurks in the last effect of this great alteration, which, in the opinion of many, should carry anxiety and dismay into every heart; because, among other objections, it places at the mercy of legislative breath, in any moment of overheated excitement, all that is valuable in any constitutional judgment on its records.   We have only, as in this case, to add a number to any court sufficient to balance a majority of its quorum, and, by a union of feeling with the appointing power, secure judges of certain desirable opinions; and any political or constitutional decision can, in the next case which arises, be overturned.   Every security is thus prostrated. The system is not extended, but is, in principle, destroyed; for thus does this increase open an avenue to a radical change in the highest functions of one great department of our government, and a department, too, of all others the most endangered by any change, because, in its very nature, designed for permanency, independence, and firmness, amidst those tempests which at times convulse most of the elements of society.

Gentlemen must perceive that I speak only of the general tendency and alarming character of such an increase, without reference to the motives which have now recommended it. They are doubtless pure. But its propriety is to be tried by the reasons for it, and not by motives.   *   *   *

If this system is to be extended to the six new states, because most excellent, without regard to the effect of such an extension on the Supreme Court itself, and without regard to population or expense, then why not extend it to every part of the Union now destitute of it? When gentlemen talk of equality and broad American grounds, — when they, with indignation and justice, disdain sectional views and favoritism, — why create new circuits for the people in these new states, and not, at the same time, create them for more than three times as many people, now destitute of such circuits, in Western New York, Pennsylvania, and Virginia? For, if the circuit system of itself be superior, and therefore, without regard to other circumstances, is to be extended to the west and south-west, for the safety and advantage of about half a million of people now destitute, then, surely, a million and a half of people, in the three great Atlantic states, are equally entitled to its security and blessings.

Disposal of the Public Lands.

SENATE, *May*, 1826.

Mr. VAN BUREN said, the subject of the public lands was becoming daily more and more interesting, and would occupy much time in legislation. It extended the patronage of the government over the states in which they were situated to a great extent; it subjected them to an unwise and unprofitable dependence on the federal government.   *   *   * No man could render the country a greater service than he who should devise some plan by which the United States might be relieved from the ownership of this property, by some equitable mode. He would vote for a proposition to vest the lands in the states in which they stood, on some just and equitable terms, as related to the other states in the confederacy. He hoped that, after having full information on the subject, they would be able to effect that great object. He believed that, if those lands were disposed of at once to the several states, it would be satisfactory to all.

Presidential Election.

SENATE, 1826.

Mr. VAN BUREN. Under the Articles of Confederation, the representation of each state in the general government was equal. The Union was in all respects purely federal, a league of sovereign states upon equal terms. To remedy certain defects, by supplying certain powers, the Convention which framed the present Constitution was called. That Convention, it is now well known, was immediately divided into parties, on the interesting question of the extent of power to be given to the new government — whether it should be *federal* or *national;* whether *dependent* upon or *independent* of the *state governments.* It is equally well known that that point, after having several times arrested the proceedings of the Convention, and threatened a dissolution of the Confederation, subsequently divided the people of the states on the question of ratification. He might add that, with the superadded question of what powers have been given by the Constitution to the federal government, to the agitation of which the feelings which sprang out in the Convention greatly contributed, it had continued to divide the people of this country down to the present period. The party in the Convention in favor of a more energetic government, being unable to carry, or, if able, unwilling to hazard the success of the plan with the states, a middle course was agreed upon. That was, that the government should be neither federal nor national, but a mixture of both; that of the legislative department, one branch — the power of representation — should be wholly national, and the other — the Senate — wholly federal; that, in the choice of the executive, both interests should be regarded, and that the judicial should be organized by the other two. But, to quiet effectually the apprehensions of the advocates for the rights and interest of the states, it was provided that the general government should be made entirely dependent, for its continuance, on the will and pleasure of the state governments. Hence it was decided that the House of Representatives should be apportioned among the states, with reference to their population, and chosen by the people; and power was given to Congress to regulate and secure their choice, independent of and beyond the control of the state governments. That the Senate should be chosen exclusively by the state legislatures; and that the choice of the electors of President and Vice-President, although the principle of their apportionment was established by the Constitution, should, in all respects, except the time of their appointment and of their meeting, be under the exclusive control of the legislatures of the several states.

On reference to the proceedings of the state conventions, it will be seen that, in several of the states, the control by Congress over the choice of representatives merely, was strongly remonstrated against; that amendments were proposed for its qualification by the states of South Carolina, North Carolina, Virginia, Massachusetts, New Hampshire, Rhode Island, and New York; that most of them resolved that it should be a standing instruction to their delegates in Congress, to endeavor to effect that and other amendments proposed. The proposition of the gentleman from New Jersey, to which Mr. Van Buren had alluded, would, if adopted, break an important link in the chain of dependency of the general upon the state governments. It would surrender to the general government all control over the election of President and Vice-President, by placing the choice of electors on the same footing with that of representatives. It would at this time be premature to go into a minute examination of the provisions of the resolution alluded to, to show that such would be its effects. Upon examination, it will be found that such would be its construction; that it does in substance what another proposition upon their table, originating in the other house, does in words. But even were there doubt upon that subject, that doubt should be removed by an express provision, reserving to the states their present control over the election, except as to what is particularly provided for in the resolution now proposed. If it is fit to take from the states their control over the choice of electors of President and Vice-President, and give it to the federal government, it would he equally proper, under the popular idea of giving their election to the people, to divide the states into districts for the choice of senators, as was proposed in the Convention, and give to Congress the control over their election also.   If the system be once broken in upon in this respect, the other measure will naturally follow, and we shall then have what was so much dreaded by those who have gone before us, and what he feared would be so much regretted by those who come after, — a completely consolidated government, a government in which the state governments would be no otherwise known or felt than as it became necessary to control them.   To all this Mr. Van Buren was opposed.

At the time of the adoption of the Federal Constitution, it was a question of much speculation and discussion, which of the two governments would be most in danger from the accumulation of influence by the operation of the powers distributed by the Constitution.   That discussion was founded on the assumption that they were, in several respects, rival powers, and that such powers would always be found in collision.   The best lights which could be thrown upon the subject were derived from the examples afforded by the fates of several of the governments of the old world, which were deemed to be, in some respects, similar to ours.   But the governments in question having operated upon, and been administered by, people whose habits, characters, tempers, and conditions, were essentially different from ours, the inferences to be derived from that source were, at best, unsatisfactory.   Mr. Van Buren thought that experience — the only unerring criterion by which matters of this description could be tested — had settled for us the general point of the operation of the powers conferred by the Constitution upon the relative strength and influence of the respective governments.   It was, in his judgment, susceptible of entire demonstration, that the Federal Constitution had worked a gradual, if not an undue, increase of the strength and control of the general government, and a correspondent reduction of the influence, and, consequently, of the respectability, of the state governments.

On the Bankrupt Law.

SENATE, *May* 1, 1826.

Mr. HAYNE.   The first question which presents itself for consideration is, *the necessity of a bankrupt law.*   It is asked " whether the laws of the states, on this subject, are not adequate to the object."   I answer, decidedly and unequivocally, that there exists the most pressing necessity for now establishing " uniform laws on the subject of bankruptcy throughout the United States;" and that the laws of the states, on this subject, are inefficient, unjust, and ruinous in their operation.   In the remarks I am about to make on this branch of the subject, I wish to be distinctly understood as confining my observations to the effect of the state insolvent laws *on persons concerned in trade.*   It is from the operation of these laws on the commerce of the country that those evils flow which demand a speedy and effectual remedy.

There now exist, in the several states of this Union, upwards of *twenty distinct systems of bankruptcy,* or insolvency, each differing from all the rest in almost every provision intended to give security to the creditor or relief to the debtor; differing in every thing which touches the rights and remedies of the one, or the duties and liabilities of the other.

By the laws of some of the states, debtors cannot be arrested either on *mesne or final process;* by others, personal property may be held in defiance of creditors; while, by others, real estate cannot be touched In some inst uces, executions are suspended; in others, the courts of justice are closed, or, which is the same thing, delays are sanctioned which amount to a denial of justice. In some states, a few creditors in the immediate neighborhood are suffered, by attachment, or other legal proceedings, (often the re-ult of collusion with the debtor,) to secure to themselves the whole estate of an insolvent. In several states, persons arrested for debt are permitted to "swear out," as it is called, after a notice of a few days; while in other states, they are required to lie in jail for three or four months. In some instances, the relief extended is confined to the discharge of the debtor from arrest in the particular suit; in others, from arrest in all suits; and in some few cases, the attempt has been made to release him from all future liability on existing *contracts.* These various systems, unequal and inconsistent as they must be admitted to be, are rendered still more objectionable by being perpetually *fluctuating.* It was the opinion of one of the ablest judges that ever sat on the English bench, or any other bench, that it was better for the community "that a rule should be certain than that it should be just;" for the obvious reason, that we can shape our conduct, or our contracts, in reference to any known and settled rule, so as to avoid its injurious effects; but when the rule is uncertain, we cannot avoid falling under its operation.

We are told that it was felt as a grievance by the Roman people, that the tyrant should write his laws "in a small character, and hang them up on high pillars," so that it was difficult to read them; but that grievance would have been rendered still more intolerable, if the inscriptions had been varied with the rising and setting of the sun.

Not a year, hardly a month passes by, which does not witness numerous, and, in many instances, radical changes in the insolvent systems of the several states. It is found utterly impracticable to conform to them, or to guard against them. It defies the wisdom of the bench, or the learning of the bar, to give certainty or consistency to a system of laws, upon which twenty-four different legislatures are constantly acting, and almost daily innovating — a system which changes with a rapidity that deceives the mental vision, and leaves us in the grossest ignorance.

It is manifest, Mr. President, that the states are now reduced to the necessity of entering into a competition with each other, in restricting the rights of creditors, and impairing the liabilities of debtors; and this, too, in a matter in which, as it is impossible to mark the exact line of equality, there must be great danger of their advancing, step by step, until every thing is unsettled. I am persuaded that nothing but the constitutional prohibition on the states, against "impairing the obligation of contracts," and the general — I might almost say the universal — belief that they have no right to pass an efficient bankrupt law, have hitherto prevented such an interference between debtor and creditor, as would have given a fatal blow to commercial credit and enterprise.

Sir, this whole country is filled with unfortunate debtors, who owe their failure to such causes. I have no hesitation in declaring it to be my firm belief, and settled conviction, founded on some personal knowledge, and information derived from those well acquainted with the subject, and worthy of entire confidence, that, from those causes, there is a mass of talent, industry — ay, sir, and virtue too — in our country, idle and useless; and that their number is daily and rapidly increasing. Thousands of individuals, who, in the commercial vicissitudes of the last twenty years, have become bankrupt, — sometimes from fraud, oftener from imprudence, but most frequently from misfortune, — are now struggling out a miserable existence, a burden to their friends and to their country. They live without hope, and will die without regret.

If we look into the proceedings of the Convention, or examine the commentaries on the Constitution by the great men who framed it, we shall find abundant reason to believe that the article which gives to Congress power over this subject, was designed *to prevent frauds.* The Journals of the Convention show that, on the 29th August, 1787, it was moved to commit the following proposition, to wit, " to establish uniform laws on the subject of bankruptcy, and respecting the damages arising from the protest of foreign bills of exchange ;" which passed in the affirmative by a vote of nine states against two — Connecticut, New Jersey, Pennsylvania, Delaware, Maryland, Virginia, North Carolina, South Carolina, and Georgia, voting in the affirmative, and New Hampshire and Massachusetts in the negative. On the 1st of September following, Mr. Rutledge, of South Carolina, (from the committee,) reported and recommended the insertion of the following words, viz. : " to establish uniform laws on the subject of bankruptcies ;" which, on the 3d of September, was agreed to by yeas and nays, every state voting in the affirmative, except Connecticut.

I confess I felt my confidence in the wisdom of this provision of the Constitution strengthened and confirmed, when I discovered that it had been introduced by John Rutledge, and had received the *unequivocal sanction* of James Madison. In a number of the Federalist, written by that distinguished statesman, speaking of this particular provision of the Constitution, he says, " Uniform laws on the subject of bankruptcy *will prevent so many frauds*, that the expediency of it seems not likely to be called in question." Sir, we are wiser than our ancestors ; that which they designed to " prevent frauds " we pronounce to be the most fruitful source of frauds. A proposition which seemed to them so clear that it was " not likely to be called in question," we have for twenty years rejected as unworthy even of a trial. It may be, Mr. President, that I am bigoted in my reverence for the authors of this Constitution ; but I am free to confess that I distrust my own judgment when I find it leading me to discard their precepts, or to reject their injunctions.

In relation to bankruptcy, it is the federal government only that ever *will* enact a wise and judicious system, and no power but Congress *can* establish UNIFORMITY. This is the great *desideratum.* This is the true, the only remedy for the evils which I have pointed out. The wise man now at the head of the Supreme Court of the United States (whose character has been drawn with a master's hand by the gentleman from Virginia, in a finished picture that I cannot venture to touch, lest I should impair its beauty) has given us his opinion on this clause of the Constitution in terms worthy of consideration : —

" The peculiar terms of the grant (says Chief Justice Marshall) certainly deserve notice. Congress is not authorized merely to pass laws, the operation of which shall be uniform, but to establish uniform laws on the subject throughout the United States. This *establishment of uniformity* is, perhaps, incompatible with state legislation on that part of the subject to which the acts of Congress may extend."

Now, let it be remembered, that while, on the one hand, the power is expressly conferred on the federal government of acting efficiently on this subject, the right has been taken away from the states. This the Supreme

Court of the United States have decided in the cases of Sturges and Crowninshield, and M'Millan and M'Neill, (4 Wheat. 122, 209.) A discharge under the bankrupt or insolvent law of a state is, in these cases, declared to be invalid, in consequence of the constitutional prohibition on the states of passing any law "impairing the obligation of contracts." Now, prior to the adoption of the Constitution, the states possessed this right, and, in some instances, exercised it to the most unlimited extent It is a right essential to commercial credit and prosperity. It has been taken from the states, and vested in us; and if proper to be exercised at all, can only be exerted by us. I am aware, sir, that there are cases still pending before the Supreme Court, in which the question is involved, whether a state bankrupt law may not be enforced, in such state, on parties residing there, and contracting in reference to that law. This question has remained for several years undecided; but, whatever may be the final decision, it is obvious that it will not restore to the states the power of acting on the subject matter in the only way at all adequate to the exigencies of the country. The application of the *lex loci contractus* would be but a miserable substitute or a general bankrupt law. And even if it were possible that the case of Sturges and Crowninshield could be reversed, and the power be restored to the states of passing bankrupt laws, without restriction or limitation, I should consider twenty-four different bankrupt laws as infinitely worse than none.

In this bill the committee have framed a system of bankruptcy, which will, in their opinion, greatly contribute to give security to creditors, and relief to debtors, within the sphere of its operation. It is believed that it offers the strongest inducements to debtors for honest dealing; that it holds out a temptation to insolvent traders to make a timely surrender of their effects to their creditors; and that, thus, it will have a powerful tendency to prevent over-trading and desperate adventures. This bill gives power to creditors to arrest the fraudulent career of their debtors, furnishes a prompt remedy for the recovery of debts, and time and means for thorough investigations; it prevents all unjust preferences, and secures an impartial distribution of insolvent estates: it puts citizens of different states on an equal footing, and gives a certain, a just rule for commercial contracts; it puts our own citizens on a footing with foreigners; and, lastly, it will restore to society, to honor, and usefulness, a mass of industry and talent which, under the present system, is irretrievably lost — thus " paying a just tribute to the rights of humanity, by depriving the creditor of the power he now has over the whole life of his debtor."

January 24, 1827.

Mr. WOODBURY. The gentleman on his right (Mr. Berrien) had said that Congress might legislate without limitation as to the objects or manner of a bankrupt system, because no limitation as to them had been expressed in the Constitution. But the limitation existed in the subject matter of the grant. The grant was not to legislate on the subject of contracts generally, of descents, of suits at law, but on the subject of bankruptcy. To bankruptcies, and to bankruptcies alone, then, was the power confined. And the word *bankruptcies*, as used in the Constitution, was never, in his apprehension, intended to extend beyond embarrassments and failures among mercantile men.

The bankrupt system had been limited essentially to persons more or less engaged in trade. The word itself, as remarked last year by the gen tleman from South Carolina, had been derived from the circumstance that the person coming within its operation had his bench ruptured or broken up. The bench of whom? Not of the farmer — not of the mechanic — but the bench of the money-dealer, and the bench, or counter, of the merchant. Grant that some persons, not strictly traders, may, at times, have been included in the provisions of some laws on the subject of bankruptcies; yet this was where the power of legislation was unlimited — where all legislation, as to all creditors and debtors, was invested in one body. It has but seldom occurred any where, and existed nowhere at the time of this grant of power to Congress.

That laws on the subject of bankruptcies were then deemed commercial only, is further manifest from the fact that when, late in the session of the Convention which framed the Constitution, this clause was introduced, it was coupled with a clause regulating the rate of damages, &c., on bills of exchange. It was well known to our fathers, that, in thirteen distinct sovereignties, the laws as to debtors and creditors were, and must always be, in many respects, very various, to meet their different usages, pursuits, prejudices, and educations; but that the merchants, throughout the confederacy, must carry on their business in other and remote states from those where they resided; and hence, as to their debts, their failures, and their adjustment of their affairs, it might be highly convenient and salutary to have similar rules and laws. In a Constitution, therefore, created, in a great degree, throughout, to benefit commerce, it was natural to confer power to make uniformity, or uniform laws, on a commercial subject.

It was impossible that Congress could, constitutionally, bring farmers and mechanics, by their individual consent, within the provisions of this act, where they would not be compelled to come without consent. It was no question between Congress and those individuals; it was solely a question between the general government and the individual states. He was opposed to this feature of the act; because to pass it would be to bring subjects and citizens within the scope of the general government, never contemplated by our fathers.

The question lay in a very narrow compass. It was, whether Congress had been clothed with power to pass laws regulating the insolvencies of persons not traders, and making their operation upon such persons dependent on their consent. The solution of this question rested mainly on the meaning of the word *bankruptcies,* as used in the grant of power on this subject, by the states, to the general government, in the 8th section of the 1st article of the Constitution. It thus became a momentous question of state rights, and hence deserved most deliberate consideration

Amendment to the Constitution.

SENATE, *March,* 1826.

Mr. DICKERSON. If, by our Constitution, the President of the United States was elected to hold his office during good behavior, our government would be, by whatever name it might be called, an elective monarchy, limited in its powers, but with sufficient inherent energy to break down, in time, any barriers that a written constitution could present against the encroachment of arbitrary power. If, under our Constitution, we adopt the practice of electing our Presidents from period to period until the infirmities of age admonish them to retire, our system will soon become that of an elective monarchy. That the want of the limitation now proposed has not been practically felt, must be attributed, not to any corrective principle in our Constitution, nor to any rigid adherence to the jealous maxims of democracy on the part of the people, but to the motives of action which have governed our chief magistrates. As yet, there has been nothing to excite alarm upon this subject.

The limitation proposed has not yet been wanted, and probably will not be for many years to come; but it is the dictate of prudence to provide for the danger while it is yet remote.

Although this question excites but little feeling at present, it once created more agitation than any other subject that came before them, as will appear by a few extracts from the Journal of that Convention : —

On the 1st of June, 1787, in the Federal Convention, Mr. Randolph introduced a resolution, that the national executive should not be eligible a second time, (p. 191;) and the next day it was agreed to, eight states being for the resolution, one against it, and one divided. (p. 191.) Seven years was the term then in contemplation.

On the 15th of June, Mr. Patterson submitted a proposition, that the United States in Congress be authorized to elect a federal executive for —— years, to be ineligible a second time. (p. 208.) The term in contemplation then was also seven years.

On the 18th of June, Colonel Hamilton submitted resolutions, that the President and Senate should be elected to serve during good behavior; that is, for life, with powers nearly as extensive as those of the King and House of Lords of Great Britain. (p. 212.)

Colonel Hamilton was one of the greatest men in this country, and, without doubt, believed that his plan was well calculated to promote the happiness and prosperity of the Union. Many of our distinguished citizens thought with him then, who afterwards changed their opinions, on witnessing the success of our present system.

On the 19th of June, the resolutions of Mr. Randolph, as altered and agreed to in the committee of the whole, were submitted, of which the 8th resolution was, " that a national executive be instituted, to consist of a single person, to be chosen by the national legislature, for the term of seven years, to be ineligible a second time." (pp. 75, 214.) July 17th, it was moved to strike out the words " to be ineligible a second time," which passed in the affirmative, — yeas, Massachusetts, Connecticut, New Jersey, Pennsylvania, Maryland, and Georgia; nays, Delaware, Virginia, North Carolina, and South Carolina. (p. 215.) On this occasion, Massachusetts, Maryland, and Georgia, changed their votes, which were first in favor of the limitation. Pennsylvania, which was divided before, now voted against the limitation. Delaware, Virginia, North Carolina, and South Carolina, maintained their ground. New Jersey did not vote on the first question.

It was moved to strike out " seven years," and insert " good behavior; " which passed in the negative — yeas, 4; nays, 6. It would seem that four states, at this time, preferred an executive for life.

A motion was made to reconsider, and passed in the affirmative.

On the 19th July, a motion was made to restore the words " to be ineligible a second time." It passed in the negative. (p. 242.)

July 25th, it was moved that no person should be capable of holding the office of President more than six years in any twelve; which passed in the negative — yeas, 5; nays, 6.

The next day, it was moved to amend the resolution, so as to read, " for the term of seven years, to be ineligible a second time." It passed in the affirmative, — yeas, New Hampshire, New Jersey, Maryland, Virginia, North Carolina, South Carolina; nays, Connecticut and Delaware. (p. 243.)

The same day, it was reported to the Convention as one of the resolutions agreed to

This resolution, together with those offered by Mr. Pinckney, and those offered by Mr. Patterson, were referred to a committee, who, on the 6th of August, reported a draft of a constitution, the 1st section of the 10th article of which was, " The President shall be elected by the legislature. He shall hold his office during seven years, but shall not be elected a second time." (p. 255.)

The friends of this limitation now considered the question at rest; but they were deceived : it was too important in the eyes of the friends to an executive for life to be given up yet.

On the 24th August, a motion was made to postpone the consideration of the two last clauses of the 1st section of article 10, to wit, the term of years and the limitation. It passed in the negative. It was moved to refer them to a committee of a member from each state. It passed in the negative.

August 31, it was agreed to refer such parts of the plan of a constitution as had been postponed, and such reports as had been acted on, to a committee of one member from each state. (p. 307.)

On the 4th of September, Mr. Brearly reported certain alterations, &c, the fourth of which was, " The President shall hold his office for four years." In this the limitation was omitted. (p. 312.)

On the 5th of September, it was moved to postpone the report, and take up the following : " The President shall be elected by joint ballot of the legislature. He shall hold his office during seven years, but shall not be elected a second time." This was decided in the negative, and seems to have been the last effort in the Convention in favor of limitation.

On the ratification of the Constitution, several states proposed amendments.

Virginia proposed that no person should be capable of being President more than eight years in sixteen ; North Carolina, the same.

New York proposed, that no person should be elected President a third time — exactly what is now proposed.

Although the principle of hereditary succession has gained no force in our presidential elections, the principle of a different succession has already become almost irresistible. It is, that the President shall designate his successor, by placing him in the most important office in his gift, and clothing him with such a degree of patronage and power, as to make him an overmatch for any competitor in the walks of private life, whatever may be his merits or his services. The Federal Convention could not have foreseen the operation of this principle as we now see it, or they would have adopted some rule analogous to that most important provision of the Roman law, that no one could be a candidate for the consulship, unless he presented himself in a private station. As no President has yet discovered a disposition to hold the office more than eight years, it may be considered by some as having grown into a law, that no one shall hold the office for a longer period.

State Rights. — *Foote's Resolutions.*

SENATE, *January*, 1830.

Mr. WEBSTER. There remains to be performed by far the most grave and important duty, which I feel to be devolved on me by this occasion. It is to state, and to defend, what I conceive to be the true principles of the Constitution under which we are here assembled.

I understand the honorable gentleman from South Carolina [Mr. Hayne] to maintain that it is a right of the state legislatures to interfere, whenever, in their judgment, this government transcends its constitutional limits, and to arrest the operations of its laws.

I understand him to maintain this right, as a right existing *under* the Constitution ; not as a right to overthrow it, on the ground of extreme necessity, such as would justify violent revolution.

I understand him to maintain an authority, on the part of the states, thus to interfere, for the purpose of correcting the exercise of power by the general government, of checking it, and of compelling it to conform to their opinion of the extent of its powers.

I understand him to maintain that the ultimate power of judging of the constitutional extent of its own authority is not lodged exclusively in the general government, or any branch of it ; but that, on the contrary, the states may lawfully decide for themselves, and each state for itself, whether, in a given case, the act of the general government transcends its power.

I understand him to insist that, if the exigency of the case, in the opinion of any state government, require it, such state government may, by its own sovereign authority, annul an act of the general government, which it deems plainly and palpably unconstitutional.

This is the sum of what I understand from him to be the South Carolina doctrine, and the doctrine which he maintains. I propose to consider

it, and to compare it with the Constitution.   Allow me to say, as a pre
liminary remark, that I call this the South Carolina doctrine only because
the gentleman himself has so denominated it.   I do not feel at liberty to
say that South Carolina, as a state, has ever advanced these sentiments.
I hope she has not, and never may.   That a great majority of her people
are opposed to the tariff laws is doubtless true.   That a majority, somewhat less than that just mentioned, conscientiously believe those laws unconstitutional, may probably also be true.   But that any majority holds to
the right of direct state interference, at state discretion, — the right of
nullifying acts of Congress by acts of state legislation, — is more than I
know, and what I shall be slow to believe.

That there are individuals, besides the honorable gentleman, who do
maintain these opinions, is quite certain.   I recollect the recent expression of a sentiment which circumstances attending its utterance and publication justify us in supposing was not unpremeditated — "The sovereignty of the state — never to be controlled, construed, or decided on,
but by her own feelings of honorable justice."

[Mr. HAYNE here rose, and said that, for the purpose of being clearly understood,
he would state that his proposition was in the words of the Virginia resolution, as
follows : " That this Assembly doth explicitly and peremptorily declare, that it views
the powers of the federal government, as resulting from the compact to which the
states are parties, as limited by the plain sense and intention of the instrument constituting that compact; as no further valid than they are authorized by the grants
enumerated in that compact; and that, in case of a deliberate, palpable, and dangerous exercise of other powers, not granted by the said compact, the states who are
parties thereto have the right, and are in duty bound, to interpose, for arresting the
progress of the evil, and for maintaining, within their respective limits, the authorities, rights, and liberties, appertaining to them."]

Mr. WEBSTER resumed : I am quite aware of the existence of the
resolution which the gentleman read, and has now repeated, and that he
relies on it as his authority.   I know the source, too, from which it is
understood to have proceeded.   I need not say that I have much respect
for the constitutional opinions of Mr. Madison ; they would weigh greatly
with me, always.   But, before the authority of his opinion be vouched for
the gentleman's proposition, it will be proper to consider what is the fair
interpretation of that resolution, to which Mr. Madison is understood to
have given his sanction.   As the gentleman construes it, it is an authority
for him.   Possibly he may not have adopted the right construction.   That
resolution declares that, in the case of the dangerous exercise of powers
not granted by the general government, the states may interpose to arrest
the progress of the evil.   But *how* interpose? and what does this declaration purport?   Does it mean no more than that there may be extreme
cases, in which the people, in any mode of assembling, may resist usurpation, and relieve themselves from a tyrannical government?   No one will
deny this.   Such resistance is not only acknowledged to be just in America, but in England, also.   Blackstone admits as much, in the theory, and
practice, too, of the English constitution   We, sir, who oppose the Carolina doctrine, do not deny that the people may, if they choose, throw off any
government, when it becomes oppressive and intolerable, and erect a better in its stead.   We all know that civil institutions are established for the
public benefit, and that when they cease to answer the ends of their existence, they may be changed.   But I do not understand the doctrine now
contended for to be that which, for the sake of distinctness, we may call
the right of revolution.   I understand the gentleman to maintain that,
without revolution, without civil commotion, without rebellion, a remedy

for supposed abuse and transgression of the powers of the general government lies in a direct appeal to the interference of the state government. [Mr. Hayne here rose.   He did not contend, he said, for the mere right of revolution, but for the right of constitutional resistance.   What he maintained was, that, in case of plain, palpable violation of the Constitution, by the general government, a state may interpose; and that this interposition is constitutional.]   Mr. Webster resumed: So, sir, I understood the gentleman, and am happy to find that I did not misunderstand him.   What he contends for is, that it is constitutional to interrupt the administration of the Constitution itself, in the hands of those who are chosen and sworn to administer it, by the direct interference, in form of law, of the states, in virtue of their sovereign capacity.   The inherent right in the people to reform their government, I do not deny; and they have another right, and that is, to resist unconstitutional laws, without overturning the government.   It is no doctrine of mine, that unconstitutional laws bind the people.   The great question is, Whose prerogative is it to decide on the constitutionality or unconstitutionality of the laws? On that the main debate hinges.   The proposition, that, in case of a supposed violation of the Constitution by Congress, the states have a constitutional right to interfere, and annul the law of Congress, is the proposition of the gentleman.   I do not admit it.   If the gentleman had intended no more than to assert the right of revolution, for justifiable cause, he would have said only what all agree to.   But I cannot conceive that there can be a middle course between submission to the laws, when regularly pronounced constitutional, on the one hand, and open resistance, which is revolution, or rebellion, on the other.   I say, the right of a state to annul a law of Congress cannot be maintained but on the ground of the unalienable right of man to resist oppression; that is to say, upon the ground of revolution.   I admit that there is an ultimate violent remedy, above the Constitution, and in defiance of the Constitution, which may be resorted to, when a revolution is to be justified.   But I do not admit that, under the Constitution, and in conformity with it, there is any mode in which a state government, as a member of the Union, can interfere and stop the progress of the general government, by force of her own laws, under any circumstances whatever.

This leads us to inquire into the origin of this government, and the source of its power.   Whose agent is it?   Is it the creature of the state legislatures, or the creature of the people?   If the government of the United States be the agent of the state governments, then they may control it, provided they can agree in the manner of controlling it; if it be the agent of the people, then the people alone can control it, restrain it, modify, or reform it.   It is observable enough, that the doctrine for which the honorable gentleman contends leads him to the necessity of maintaining, not only that this general government is the creature of the states, but that it is the creature of each of the states severally; so that each may assert the power, for itself, of determining whether it acts within the limits of its authority.   It is the servant of four-and-twenty masters, of different wills and different purposes, and yet bound to obey all.   This absurdity (for it seems no less) arises from a misconception as to the origin of this government, and its true character.   It is, sir, the people's Constitution, the people's government — made for the people, made by the people, and answerable to the people.   The people of the United States have declared that this Constitution shall be the supreme law.   We must either admit the proposition, or dispute their authority. The states are, unquestionably, sovereign, so far as their sovereignty is not affected by this supreme law. But the state legislatures, as political bodies, however sovereign, are yet not sovereign over the people. So far as the people have given power to the general government, so far the grants are unquestionably good, and the government holds of the people, and not of the state governments. We are all agents of the same supreme power, the people. The general government and the state governments derive their authority from the same source. Neither can, in relation to the other, be called primary, though one is definite and restricted, and the other general and residuary. The national government possesses those powers which it can be shown the people have conferred on it, and no more. All the rest belongs to the state governments or to the people themselves. So far as the people have restrained state sovereignty, by the expression of their will, in the Constitution of the United States, so far, it must be admitted, state sovereignty is effectually controlled. I do not contend that it is, or ought to be, controlled further. The sentiment to which I have referred propounds that state sovereignty is only to be controlled by its own " feeling of justice ; " that is to say, it is not to be controlled at all ; for one who is to follow his own feelings is under no legal control. Now, however men may think this ought to be, the fact is, that the people of the United States have chosen to impose control on state sovereignties. There are those, doubtless, who wish they had been left without restraint ; but the Constitution has ordered the matter differently. To make war, for instance, is an exercise of sovereignty ; but the Constitution declares that no state shall make war. To coin money is another exercise of sovereign power ; but no state is at liberty to coin money. Again, the Constitution says that no sovereign state shall be so sovereign as to make a treaty. These prohibitions, it must be confessed, are a control on the state sovereignty of South Carolina, as well as of the other states, which does not arise " from her own feelings of honorable justice." Such an opinion, therefore, is in defiance of the plainest provisions of the Constitution.

There are other proceedings of public bodies, which have already been alluded to, and to which I refer again, for the purpose of ascertaining more fully what is the length and breadth of that doctrine, denominated the *Carolina doctrine*, which the honorable member has now stood up on this floor to maintain. In one of them I find it resolved, that " the tariff of 1828, and every other tariff designed to promote one branch of industry at the expense of others, is contrary to the meaning and intention of the federal compact, and such a dangerous, palpable, and deliberate usurpation of power, by a determined majority, wielding the general government beyond the limits of its delegated powers, as calls upon the states which compose the suffering minority, in their sovereign capacity, to exercise the powers which, as sovereigns, necessarily devolve upon them, when their compact is violated."

Observe, sir, that this resolution holds the tariff of 1828, and every other tariff designed to promote one branch of industry at the expense of another, to be such a dangerous, palpable, and deliberate usurpation of power, as calls upon the states, in their sovereign capacity, to interfere by their own authority. This denunciation, Mr. President, you will please to observe, includes our old tariff of 1816, as well as all others ; because that was established to promote the interest of the manufacturers of cotton, to the manifest and admitted injury of the Calcutta cotton trade.

Observe, again, that all the qualifications are here rehearsed and charged upon the tariff, which are necessary to bring the case within the gentleman's proposition. The tariff is a usurpation; it is a dangerous usurpation; it is a palpable usurpation; it is a deliberate usurpation. It is such a usurpation, therefore, as calls upon the states to exercise their right of interference. Here is a case, then, within the gentleman's principles, and all his qualifications of his principles. It is a case for action. The Constitution is plainly, dangerously, palpably, and deliberately violated; and the states must interpose their own authority to arrest the law. Let us suppose the state of South Carolina to express this same opinion, by the voice of her legislature. That would be very imposing. But what then? Is the voice of one state conclusive? It so happens, at the very moment when South Carolina resolves that the tariff laws are unconstitutional, Pennsylvania and Kentucky resolve exactly the reverse. They hold those laws to be both highly proper and strictly constitutional. And now, sir, how does the honorable member propose to deal with this case? How does he relieve us from this difficulty, upon any principle of his? His construction gets us into it; how does he propose to get us out?

In Carolina, the tariff is a palpable, deliberate usurpation; Carolina, therefore, may *nullify* it, and refuse to pay the duties. In Pennsylvania, it is both clearly constitutional and highly expedient; and there the duties are to be paid. And yet we live under a government of uniform laws, and under a Constitution, too, which contains an express provision, as it happens, that all duties shall be equal in all the states! Does not this approach absurdity?

If there be no power to settle such questions, independent of either of the states, is not the whole Union a rope of sand? Are we not thrown again, precisely, upon the old Confederation?

It is too plain to be argued. Four-and-twenty interpreters of constitutional law, each with a power to decide for itself, and none with authority to bind any body else, and this constitutional law the only bond of their union! What is such a state of things but a mere connection during pleasure, or, to use the phraseology of the times, *during feeling?* — and that feeling, too, not the feeling of the people, who established the Constitution, but the feeling of the state governments.

In another of the South Carolina addresses, having premised that the crisis requires " all the concentrated energy of passion," an attitude of open resistance to the laws of the Union is advised. Open resistance to the laws, then, is the constitutional remedy, the conservative power of the state, which the South Carolina doctrine teaches for the redress of political evils, real or imaginary. And its authors further say, that, appealing with confidence to the Constitution itself to justify their opinions, they cannot consent to try their accuracy by the courts of justice. In one sense, indeed, sir, this is assuming an attitude of open resistance in favor of liberty. But what sort of liberty? The liberty of establishing their own opinions, in defiance of the opinions of all others; the liberty of judging and of deciding exclusively themselves, in a matter in which others have as much right to judge and decide as they; the liberty of placing their own opinions above the judgment of all others, above the laws, and above the Constitution. This is their liberty, and this is the fair result of the proposition contended for by the honorable gentleman. Or it may be more properly said, it is identical with it, rather than a result from it.

In the same publication, we find the following: " Previously to our revolution, when the arm of oppression was stretched over New England, where did our northern brethren meet with a braver sympathy than that which sprang from the bosoms of Carolinians? We had no extortion, no oppression, no collision with the king's ministers, no navigation interests springing up in envious rivalry of England."

This seems extraordinary language. South Carolina no collision with the king's ministers in 1775! No extortion! No oppression! But, sir, it is most significant language. Does any man doubt the purpose for which it was penned? Can any one fail to see that it was designed to raise in the reader's mind the question, whether, at this time, — that is to say, in 1828, — South Carolina has any collision with the king's ministers, any oppression, or extortion, to fear from England? — whether, in short, England is not as naturally the friend of South Carolina, as New England, with her navigation interests springing up in envious rivalry of England?

Is it not strange, sir, that an intelligent man in South Carolina, in 1828, should thus labor to prove, that, in 1775, there was no hostility, no cause of war, between South Carolina and England? — that she had no occasion, in reference to her own interest, or from a regard to her own welfare, to take up arms in the revolutionary contest? Can any one account for the expression of such strange sentiments, and their circulation through the state, otherwise than by supposing the object to be, what I have already intimated, to raise the question, if they had no "*collision*" (mark the expression) with the ministers of King George III., in 1775, what *collision* have they, in 1828, with the ministers of King George IV.? What is there now, in the existing state of things, to separate Carolina from *Old*, more, or rather, than from *New* England?

Resolutions, sir, have been recently passed by the legislature of South Carolina. I need not refer to them; they go no farther than the honorable gentleman himself has gone; and, I hope, not so far. I content myself, therefore, with debating the matter with him.

And now, sir, what I have first to say on this subject is, that at no time, and under no circumstances, has New England, or any state in New England, or any respectable body of persons in New England, or any public man of standing in New England, put forth such a doctrine as this Carolina doctrine.

The gentleman has found no case — he can find none — to support his own opinions by New England authority. New England has studied the Constitution in other schools, and under other teachers. She looks upon it with other regards, and deems more highly and reverently both of its just authority and its utility and excellence. The history of her legislative proceedings may be traced; the ephemeral effusions of temporary bodies, called together by the excitement of the occasion, may be hunted up; they have been hunted up. The opinions and votes of her public men, in and out of Congress, may be explored. It will all be vain. The Carolina doctrine can derive from her neither countenance nor support. She rejects it now: she always did reject it; and till she loses her senses, she always will reject it. The honorable member has referred to expressions on the subject of the embargo law, made in this place by an honorable and venerable gentleman (Mr. Hillhouse) now favoring us with his presence. He quotes that distinguished senator as saying, that, in his judgment, the embargo law was unconstitutional, and that, therefore in his opinion, the people were not bound to obey it. That, sir, is perfectly constitutional language. An unconstitutional law is not binding but, then, it does not rest with a resolution, or a law of a state legislature, to decide whether an act of Congress be, or be not, constitutional. An unconstitutional act of Congress would not bind the people of this district, although they have no legislature to interfere in their behalf; and, on the other hand, a constitutional law of Congress does bind the citizens of every state, although all their legislatures should undertake to annul it, by act or resolution. The venerable Connecticut senator is a constitutional lawyer, of sound principles and enlarged knowledge — a statesman, practised and experienced, bred in the company of Washington, and holding just views upon the na ure of our governments. He believed the embargo unconstitutional, and so did others. But what then? Who did he suppose was to decide that question? The state legislatures? Certainly not. No such sentiment ever escaped his lips. Let us follow up, sir, this New England opposition to the embargo laws; let us trace it till we discern the principle which controlled and governed New England, throughout the whole course of that opposition. We shall then see what similarity there is between the New England school of constitutional opinions and this modern Carolina school. The gentleman, I think, read a petition from some single individual, addressed to the legislature of Massachusetts, asserting the Carolina doctrine; that is, the right of state interference to arrest the laws of the Union. The fate of that petition shows the sentiment of the legislature. It met no favor. The opinions of Massachusetts were otherwise. They had been expressed in 1798, in answer to the resolutions of Virginia; and she did not depart from them, nor bend them to the times. Misgoverned, wronged, oppressed, as she felt herself to be, she still held fast her integrity to the Union. The gentleman may find in her proceedings much evidence of dissatisfaction with the measures of the government, and great and deep dislike to the embargo: all this makes the case so much the stronger for her; for, notwithstanding all this dissatisfaction and dislike, she claimed no right, still, to sever asunder the bonds of union. There was heat, and there was anger, in her political feeling. Be it so. Her heat or her anger did not, nevertheless, betray her into infidelity to the government. The gentleman labors to prove that she disliked the embargo as much as South Carolina dislikes the tariff, and expressed her dislike as strongly. Be it so. But did she propose the Carolina remedy? Did she threaten to interfere, by state authority, to annul the laws of the Union? That is the question for the gentleman's consideration.

No doubt, sir, a great majority of the people of New England conscientiously believe the embargo law of 1807 unconstitutional; as conscientiously, certainly, as the people of South Carolina hold that opinion of the tariff. They reasoned thus: " Congress has power to regulate commerce; but here is a law," they said, " stopping all commerce, and stopping it indefinitely. The law is perpetual; that is, it is not limited in point of time, and must, of course, continue until it shall be repealed by some other law. It is as perpetual, therefore, as the law against treason or murder. Now, is this regulating commerce, or destroying it? Is it guiding, controlling, giving the rule to commerce, as a subsisting thing, or is it putting an end to it altogether?" Nothing is more certain, than that a majority in New England deemed this law a violation of the Constitution. The very case required by the gentleman to justify state interference, had then arisen. Massachusetts believed this law to be " a deliberate, palpable, and dangerous exercise of a power not granted by the Constitution." Deliberate it was, for it was long continued; palpable she thought it, as no words in the Constitution gave the power, and only a construction, in her opinion most violent, raised it; dangerous it was, since it threatened utter ruin to her most important interests.   Here, then, was a Carolina case.   How did Massachusetts deal with it?   It was, as she thought, a plain, manifest, palpable violation of the Constitution; and it brought ruin to her doors. Thousands of families, and hundreds of thousands of individuals, were beggared by it.   While she saw and felt all this, she saw and felt, also, that, as a measure of national policy, it was perfectly futile; that the country was no way benefited by that which caused so much individual distress; that it was efficient only for the production of evil, and all that evil inflicted upon ourselves.   In such a case, under such circumstances, how did Massachusetts demean herself?   Sir, she remonstrated, she memorialized, she addressed herself to the general government, not exactly " with the concentrated energy of passion," but with her own strong sense, and the energy of sober conviction.   But she did not interpose the arm of her own power to arrest the law, and break the embargo.   Far from it.   Her principles bound her to two things; and she followed her principles, lead where they might.   First, to submit to every constitutional law of Congress; and, secondly, if the constitutional validity of the law be doubted, to refer that question to the decision of the proper tribunals. The first principle is vain and ineffectual without the second.   A majority of us in New England believed the embargo law unconstitutional; but the great question was, and always will be, in such cases, who is to decide this?   Who is to judge between the people and the government?   And, sir, it is quite plain that the Constitution of the United States confers on the government itself, to be exercised by its appropriate department, and under its own responsibility to the people, this power of deciding, ultimately and conclusively, upon the just extent of its own authority.   If this had not been done, we should not have advanced a single step beyond the old Confederation.

Being fully of opinion that the embargo law was unconstitutional, the people of New England were yet equally clear in the opinion — it was a matter they did not doubt upon — that the question, after all, must be decided by the judicial tribunals of the United States.   Before those tribunals, therefore, they brought the question.   Under the provisions of the law, they had given bonds, to millions in amount, and which were alleged to be forfeited.   They suffered the bonds to be sued, and thus raised the question.   In the old-fashioned way of settling disputes, they went to law. The case came to hearing, and solemn argument; and he who espoused their cause, and stood up for them against the validity of the embargo act, was none other than that great man of whom the gentleman has made honorable mention, Samuel Dexter.   He was then, sir, in the fulness of his knowledge, and the maturity of his strength.   He had retired from long and distinguished public service here, to the renewed pursuit of professional duties; carrying with him all that enlargement and expansion, all the new strength and force, which an acquaintance with the more general subjects discussed in the national councils is capable of adding to professional attainment, in a mind of true greatness and comprehension. He was a lawyer, and he was also a statesman.   He had studied the Constitution, when he filled a public station, that he might defend it; he had examined its principles, that he might maintain them.   More than all men, or at least as much as any man, he was attached to the general government, and to the union of the states.   His feelings and opinions all ran in that direction. A question of constitutional law, too, was, of all subjects, that one which was best suited to his talents and learning. Aloof from technicality, and unfettered by artificial rules, such a question gave opportunity for that deep and clear analysis, that mighty grasp of principle, which so much distinguished his higher efforts. His very statement was argument; his inference seemed demonstration. The earnestness of his own conviction wrought conviction in others. One was convinced, and believed, and assented, because it was gratifying, delightful to think, and feel, and believe, in unison with an intellect of such evident superiority.

Mr. Dexter, sir, such as I have described him, argued the New England cause. He put into his effort his whole heart, as well as all the powers of his understanding; for he had avowed, in the most public manner, his entire concurrence with his neighbors on the point in dispute. He argued the cause; it was lost, and New England submitted. The established tribunals pronounced the law constitutional, and New England acquiesced. Now, sir, is not this the exact opposite of the doctrine of the gentleman from South Carolina? According to him, instead of referring to the judicial tribunals, we should have broken up the embargo by laws of our own: we should have repealed it, *quoad* New England; for we had a strong, palpable, and oppressive case. Sir, we believed the embargo unconstitutional; but still, that was matter of opinion, and who was to decide it? We thought it a clear case; but, nevertheless, we did not take the law into our own hands, because we did not wish to bring about a revolution, nor to break up the Union; for I maintain that, between submission to the decision of the constituted tribunals, and revolution or disunion, there is no middle ground — there is no ambiguous condition, half allegiance and half rebellion. And, sir, how futile, how very futile, it is, to admit the right of state interference, and then attempt to save it from the character of unlawful resistance, by adding terms of qualification to the causes and occasions, leaving all these qualifications, like the case itself, in the discretion of the state governments! It must be a clear case, it is said; a deliberate case, a palpable case, a dangerous case. But then the state is still left at liberty to decide for herself what is clear, what is deliberate, what is palpable, what is dangerous. Do adjectives and epithets avail any thing? Sir, the human mind is so constituted, that the merits of both sides of a controversy appear very clear and very palpable to those who respectively espouse them; and both sides usually grow clearer as the controversy advances. South Carolina sees unconstitutionality in the tariff; she sees oppression there, also; and she sees danger. Pennsylvania, with a vision not less sharp, looks at the same tariff, and sees no such thing in it; she sees it all constitutional, all useful, all safe. The faith of South Carolina is strengthened by opposition, and she now not only sees, but *resolves*, that the tariff is palpably unconstitutional, oppressive, and dangerous; but Pennsylvania, not to be behind her neighbors, and equally willing to strengthen her own faith by a confident asseveration, *resolves*, also, and gives to every warm affirmative of South Carolina a plain, downright, Pennsylvania negative. South Carolina, to show the strength and unity of her opinion, brings her Assembly to a unanimity, within seven voices; Pennsylvania, not to be outdone in this respect more than others, reduces her dissentient fraction to a single vote. Now, sir, again I ask the gentleman, what is to be done? Are these states both right? Is he bound to consider them both right? If not, which is in the wrong? or, rather, which has the best right to decide?

And if he, and if I, are not to know what the Constitution means, and what it is, till those two state legislatures, and the twenty-two others, shall agree in its construction, what have we sworn to, when we have sworn to maintain it ? I was forcibly struck with one reflection, as the gentleman (Mr. Hayne) went on in his speech. He quoted Mr. Madison's resolutions to prove that a state may interfere, in a case of deliberate, palpable, and dangerous exercise of a power not granted. The honorable gentleman supposes the tariff law to be such an exercise of power ; and that, consequently, a case has arisen in which the state may, if they see fit, interfere by its own law. Now, it so happens, nevertheless, that Mr. Madison himself deems this same tariff law quite constitutional. Instead of a clear and palpable violation, it is, in his judgment, no violation at all. So that, while they use his authority for a hypothetical case, they reject it in the very case before them. All this, sir, shows the inherent — futility — I had almost used a stronger word — of conceding this power of interference to the states, and then attempting to secure it from abuse by imposing qualifications, of which the states themselves are to judge. One of two things is true — either the laws or the Union are beyond the discretion, and beyond the control, of the states ; or else we have no constitution of general government, and are thrust back again to the days of the confederacy.

Let me here say, sir, that if the gentleman's doctrine had been received and acted upon in New England, in the times of the embargo and non-intercourse, we should probably now not have been here. The government would, very likely, have gone to pieces, and crumbled into dust. No stronger case can ever arise than existed under those laws ; no states can ever entertain a clearer conviction than the New England States then entertained ; and if they had been under the influence of that heresy of opinion, as I must call it, which the honorable member espouses, this Union would, in all probability, have been scattered to the four winds. I ask the gentleman, therefore, to apply his principles to that case. I ask him to come forth and declare, whether, in his opinion, the New England States would have been justified in interfering to break up the embargo system, under the conscientious opinions which they held upon it. Had they a right to annul that law? Does he admit, or deny? If that which is thought palpably unconstitutional in South Carolina justifies that state in arresting the progress of the law, tell me, whether that which was thought palpably unconstitutional, also, in Massachusetts, would have justified her in doing the same thing? Sir, I deny the whole doctrine. It has not a foot of ground in the Constitution to stand on. No public man of reputation ever advanced it in Massachusetts, in the warmest times, or could maintain himself upon it there at any time.

I wish now, sir, to make a remark upon the Virginia resolutions of 1798. I cannot undertake to say how these resolutions were understood by those who passed them. Their language is not a little indefinite. In the case of the exercise, by Congress, of a dangerous power, not granted to them, the resolutions assert the right, on the part of the state, to interfere and arrest the progress of the evil. This is susceptible of more than one interpretation. It may mean no more than that the states may interfere by complaint and remonstrance ; or by proposing to the people an alteration of the Federal Constitution. This would be all quite unobjectionable ; or it may be, that no more is meant than to assert the general right of revolution, as against all governments, in cases of intolerable oppression

This no one doubts; and this, in my opinion, is all that he who framed the resolutions could have meant by it; for I shall not readily believe, that he was ever of opinion that a state, under the Constitution, and in conformity with it, could, upon the ground of her own opinion of its unconstitutionality, however clear and palpable she might think the case, annul a law of Congress, so far as it should operate on herself, by her own legislative power.

I must now beg to ask, sir, whence is this supposed right of the states derived? — where do they find the power to interfere with the laws of the Union? Sir, the opinion which the honorable gentleman maintains is a notion founded in a total misapprehension, in my judgment, of the origin of this government, and of the foundation on which it stands. I hold it to be a popular government, erected by the people; those who administer it responsible to the people; and itself capable of being amended and modified, just as the people may choose it should be. It is as popular, just as truly emanating from the people, as the state governments. It is created for one purpose, the state governments for another. It has its own powers, they have theirs. There is no more authority with them to arrest the operation of a law of Congress, than with Congress to arrest the operation of their laws. We are here to administer a Constitution emanating immediately from the people, and trusted by them to our administration. It is not the creature of the state governments. It is of no moment to the argument that certain acts of the state legislatures are necessary to fill our seats in this body. That is not one of their original state powers, a part of the sovereignty of the state. It is a duty which the people, by the Constitution itself, have imposed on the state legislatures, and which they might have left to be performed elsewhere, if they had seen fit. So they have left the choice of President with electors; but all this does not affect the proposition, that this whole government — President, Senate, and House of Representatives — is a popular government. It leaves it still all its popular character. The governor of a state (in some of the states) is chosen, not directly by the people, but by those who are chosen by the people, for the purpose of performing, among other duties, that of electing a governor. Is the government of a state, on that account, not a popular government? This government, sir, is the independent offspring of the popular will. It is not the creature of state legislatures; nay, more, if the whole truth must be told, the people brought it into existence, established it, and have hitherto supported it, for the very purpose, amongst others, of imposing certain salutary restraints on state sovereignties. The states cannot now make war; they cannot contract alliances; they cannot make, each for itself, separate regulations of commerce; they cannot lay imposts; they cannot coin money. If this Constitution, sir, be the creature of state legislatures, it must be admitted that it has obtained a strange control over the volition of its creators.

The people, then, sir, erected this government. They gave it a Constitution, and in that Constitution they have enumerated the powers which they bestow on it. They have made it a limited government. They have defined its authority. They have restrained it to the exercise of such powers as are granted; and all others, they declare, are reserved to the states or the people. But, sir, they have not stopped here. If they had, they would have accomplished but half their work. No definition can be so clear as to avoid possibility of doubt; no limitation so precise as to exclude all uncertainty. Who, then, shall construe this grant of the people? Who shall interpret their will, where it may be supposed they have left it doubtful? With whom do they repose this ultimate right of deciding on the powers of the government? Sir, they have settled all this in the fullest manner. They have left it, with the government itself, in its appropriate branches. Sir, the very chief end, the main design for which the whole Constitution was framed and adopted, was to establish a government that should not be obliged to act through state agency, depend on state opinion and state discretion.

But who shall decide on the question of interference? To whom lies the last appeal? This, sir, the Constitution itself decides, also, by declaring, "that the judicial power shall extend to all cases arising under the Constitution and laws of the United States." These two provisions, sir, cover the whole ground. They are, in truth, the keystone of the arch. With these, it is a constitution; without them, it is a confederacy. In pursuance of these clear and express provisions, Congress established, at its very first session, in the judicial act, a mode for carrying them into full effect, and for bringing all questions of constitutional power to the final decision of the Supreme Court. It then, sir, became a government. It then had the means of self-protection; and, but for this, it would in all probability have been now among things which are past. Having constituted the government, and declared its powers, the people have further said, that, since somebody must decide on the extent of these powers, the government shall itself decide — subject, always, like other popular governments, to its responsibility to the people. And now, sir, I repeat, how is it that a state legislature acquires any power to interfere? Who, or what, gives them the right to say to the people, "We, who are your agents and servants for one purpose, will undertake to decide that your other agents and servants, appointed by you for another purpose, have transcended the authority you gave them?" The reply would be, I think, not impertinent — "Who made you a judge over another's servants? To their own masters they stand or fall."

Sir, I deny this power of state legislatures altogether. It cannot stand the test of examination. Gentlemen may say, that, in an extreme case, a state government might protect the people from intolerable oppression. Sir, in such a case, the people might protect themselves, without the aid of the state governments. Such a case warrants revolution. It must make, when it comes, a law for itself. A nullifying act of a state legislature cannot alter the case, nor make resistance any more lawful. In maintaining these sentiments, sir, I am but asserting the rights of the people. I state what they have declared, and insist on their right to declare it. They have chosen to repose this power in the general government, and I think it my duty to support it, like other constitutional powers.

For myself, sir, I do not admit the jurisdiction of South Carolina, or any other state, to prescribe my constitutional duty, or to settle, between me and the people, the validity of laws of Congress for which I have voted. I decline her umpirage. I have not sworn to support the Constitution according to her construction of its clauses. I have not stipulated, by my oath of office, or otherwise, to come under any responsibility, except to the people, and those whom they have appointed to pass upon the question, whether laws, supported by my votes, conform to the Constitution of the country. And, sir, if we look to the general nature of the case, could any thing have been more preposterous than to make a government for the whole Union, and yet leave its powers subject, not to one interpretation but to thirteen, or twenty-four, interpretations? Instead of one tribunal, established by all, responsible to all, with power to decide for all, — shall constitutional questions be left to four-and-twenty popular bodies, each at liberty to decide for itself, and none bound to respect the decisions of others; and each at liberty, too, to give a new construction on every new election of its own members? Would any thing, with such a principle in it, or rather with such a destitution of all principle, be fit to be called a government? No, sir, it should not be denominated a constitution. It should be called, rather, a collection of topics for everlasting controversy — heads of debate for a disputatious people. It would not be a government. It would not be adequate to any practical good, nor fit for any country to live under. To avoid all possibility of being misunderstood, allow me to repeat again, in the fullest manner, that I claim no powers for the government by forced or unfair construction. I admit that it is a government of strictly limited powers, — of enumerated, specified, and particularized powers, — and that whatsoever is not granted is withheld. But notwithstanding all this, and however the grant of powers may be expressed, its limits and extent may yet, in some cases, admit of doubt; and the general government would be good for nothing — it would be incapable of long existing — if some mode had not been provided, in which these doubts, as they should arise, might be peaceably, but authoritatively, solved.

Let it be remembered that the Constitution of the United States is not unalterable. It is to continue in its present form no longer than the people, who established it, shall choose to continue it. If they shall become convinced that they have made an injudicious or inexpedient partition and distribution of power between the state governments and the general government, they can alter that distribution at will.

If any thing be found in the national Constitution, either by original provisions, or subsequent interpretation, which ought not to be in it, the people know how to get rid of it. If any construction be established, unacceptable to them, so as to become practically a part of the Constitution, they will amend it at their own sovereign pleasure. But while the people choose to maintain it as it is — while they are satisfied with it, and refuse to change it — who has given, or who can give, to the state legislatures a right to alter it, either by interference, construction, or otherwise? Gentlemen do not seem to recollect that the people have any power to do any thing for themselves: they imagine there is no safety for them, any longer than they are under the close guardianship of the state legislatures. Sir, the people have not trusted their safety, in regard to the general Constitution, to these hands. They have required other security, and taken other bonds. They have chosen to trust themselves, first, to the plain words of the instrument, and to such construction as the government itself, in doubtful cases, should put on its own powers, under their oaths of office, and subject to their responsibility to them, just as the people of a state trusts their own state governments with a similar power. Secondly, they have reposed their trust in the efficacy of frequent elections, and in their own power to remove their own servants and agents, whenever they see cause. Thirdly, they have reposed trust in the judicial power, which, in order that it might be trustworthy, they have made as respectable, as disinterested, and as independent, as was practicable. Fourthly, they have seen fit to rely, in case of necessity, or high expediency, on their known and admitted power to alter or amend the Constitution, peaceably and quietly, whenever experience shall point out defects or imperfections.   And, finally, the people of the United States have at no time, in no way, directly or indirectly, authorized any state legislatures to construe or interpret their high instrument of government, much less to interfere, by their own power, to arrest its course and operation.

Mr. Hayne's Reply to Mr. Webster, abridged by himself.

SENATE, *January 27,* 1830.

Mr. HAYNE.   The proposition which I laid down, and from which the gentleman dissents, is taken from the Virginia resolutions of '98, and is in these words — "that, in case of a deliberate, palpable, and dangerous exercise, by the federal government, of powers not granted by the compact, (the Constitution,) the states who are parties thereto *have a right to interpose*, for arresting the progress of the evil, and for maintaining, within their respective limits, the authorities, rights, and liberties, appertaining to them."   The gentleman insists that the states have no right to decide whether the Constitution has been violated by acts of Congress or not; but that the federal government is the exclusive judge of the extent of its own powers; and that, in case of a violation of the Constitution, however " deliberate, palpable, and dangerous," a state has no constitutional redress, except where the matter can be brought before the Supreme Court, whose decision must be final and conclusive on the subject.   Having thus distinctly stated the points in dispute between the gentleman and myself, I proceed to examine them.   And here it will be necessary to go back to the origin of the federal government.   It cannot be doubted, and is not denied, that before the Constitution, each state was an independent sovereignty, possessing all the rights and powers appertaining to independent nations; nor can it be denied, that, after the Constitution was formed, they remained equally sovereign and independent, as to all powers not expressly delegated to the federal government.   This would have been the case even if no positive provisions to that effect had been inserted in that instrument.   But to remove all doubt, it is expressly declared, by the 10th article of the amendment of the Constitution, " that the powers not delegated to the states, by the Constitution, nor prohibited by it to the states, are reserved to the states respectively, or to the people." The true nature of the Federal Constitution, therefore, is (in the language of Mr. Madison) " a compact to which the states are parties," — a compact by which each state, acting in its sovereign capacity, has entered into an agreement with the other states, by which they have consented that certain designated powers shall be exercised by the United States, in the manner prescribed in the instrument.   Nothing can be clearer than that, under such a system, the federal government, exercising strictly delegated powers, can have no right to act beyond the pale of its authority, and that all such acts are void.   A state, on the contrary, retaining all powers not expressly given away, may lawfully act in all cases where she has not voluntarily imposed restrictions on herself.   Here, then, is a case of a compact between sovereigns; and the question arises, what is the remedy for a clear violation of its express terms by one of the parties? And here the plain, obvious dictate of common sense is in strict conformity with the understanding of mankind and the practice of nations in all analogous cases — " that, where resort can be had to no common superior the parties to the compact must themselves be the rightful judges whether the bargain has been pursued or violated." (Madison's *Report*, p. 20.) When it is insisted by the gentleman that one of the parties "has the power of deciding ultimately and conclusively upon the extent of its own authority," I ask for the grant of such a power. I call upon the gentleman to show it to me in the Constitution. It is not to be found there.

But if there be no common superior, it results, from the very nature of things, that the parties *must be their own judges.* This is admitted to be the case where treaties are formed between independent nations; and if the same rule does not apply to the federal compact, it must be because the federal is superior to the state government, or because the states have surrendered their sovereignty. Neither branch of this proposition can be maintained for a moment.

Here, however, we are met by the argument that the Constitution was not formed by *the states* in their sovereign capacity, but by *the people ;* and it is therefore inferred that the federal government, being created by all the people, must be supreme; and though it is not contended that the Constitution may be rightfully violated, yet it is insisted that from the decision of the federal government there can be no appeal.

I deny that the Constitution was framed by the people in the sense in which that word is used on the other side, and insist that it was framed by the states, acting in their sovereign capacity. When, in the preamble of the Constitution, we find the words, "We, the people of the United States," it is clear they can only relate to the people as citizens of the several states, because the federal government was not then in existence.

We accordingly find, in every part of that instrument, that the people are always spoken of in that sense. Thus, in the 2d section of the 1st article, it is declared, "that the House of Representatives shall be composed of members chosen every second year by the people of the several states." To show that, in entering into this compact, the states acted in their sovereign capacity, and not merely as parts of one great community, what can be more conclusive than the historical fact, that when every state had consented to it except one, she was not held to be bound. A majority of the people in any state bound that state; but nine tenths of all the people of the United States could not bind the people of Rhode Island, until Rhode Island, as a state, had consented to the compact.

I am not disposed to dwell longer on this point, which does appear to my mind to be too clear to admit of controversy. But I will quote from Mr. Madison's Report, which goes the whole length in support of the doctrines for which I have contended.

Having now established the position that the Constitution was a compact between sovereign and independent states, having no common superior, "it follows of necessity" (to borrow the language of Mr. Madison) "that there can be no tribunal above their authority, to decide, in the last resort, whether the compact made by them be violated; and consequently that, as the parties to it, they must themselves decide, in the last resort, such questions as may be of sufficient magnitude to require their interposition."

But the gentleman insists that the tribunal provided by the Constitution, for the decisions of controversies between the states and the federal government, is the Supreme Court.

It is clear that questions of sovereignty are not the proper subjects of judicial investigation. They are much too large, and of too delicate a nature, to be brought within the jurisdiction of a court of justice. Courts whether supreme or subordinate, are the mere creatures of the sovereign power, designed to expound and carry into effect its sovereign will. No independent state ever yet submitted to a judge on the bench the true construction of a compact between itself and another sovereign. All courts may incidentally take cognizance of treaties, where rights are claimed under them ; but who ever heard of a court making an inquiry into the authority of the agents of the high contracting parties to make the treaty — whether its terms had been fulfilled, or whether it had become void on account of a breach of its conditions on either side ? All these are political and not judicial questions. Some reliance has been placed on those provisions of the Constitution which constitute " one Supreme Court," which provide " that the judicial power shall extend to all cases in law and equity arising under this Constitution, the laws of the United States, and treaties," and which declare " that the Constitution, and the laws of the United States which shall be made in pursuance thereof, and all treaties, &c., shall be the supreme law of the land," &c. Now, as to the name of the Supreme Court, it is clear that the term has relation only to its supremacy over the inferior courts provided for by the Constitution, and has no reference whatever to any supremacy over the sovereign states. The words are, " The judicial power of the United States shall be vested in one Supreme Court, and such inferior courts as Congress may, from time to time, establish," &c. Though jurisdiction is given " in cases arising under the Constitution," yet it is expressly limited to "cases in law and equity," showing conclusively that this jurisdiction was incidental merely to the ordinary administration of justice, and not intended to touch high questions of conflicting sovereignty. When it is declared that the " Constitution, and the laws of the United States made in pursuance thereof, shall be the supreme law of the land," it is manifest that no indication is given, either as to the power of the Supreme Court to bind the states by its decisions, or as to the course to be pursued in the event of laws being passed not in pursuance to the Constitution. And I beg leave to call gentlemen's attention to the striking fact, that the powers of the Supreme Court, in relation to questions arising under " the laws and the Constitution," are coëxtensive with those arising under treaties. In all of these cases, the power is limited to questions arising in law and equity ; that is to say, to cases where jurisdiction is incidentally acquired in the ordinary administration of justice. But as, with regard to treaties, the Supreme Court has never assumed jurisdiction over questions arising between the sovereigns who are parties to them, so, under the Constitution, they cannot assume jurisdiction over questions arising between individual states and the United States.

But to prove, as I think conclusively, that the judiciary were not designed to act as umpires, it is only necessary to observe that, in a great majority of cases, that court could manifestly not take jurisdiction of the matters in dispute. Whenever it may be designed by the federal government to commit a violation of the Constitution, it can be done, and always will be done, in such a manner as to deprive the court of all jurisdiction over the subject. Take the case of the tariff and internal improvements ; whether constitutional or unconstitutional, it is admitted that the Supreme Court have no jurisdiction. Suppose Congress should, for the acknowledged purpose of making an equal distribution of the property of the country among states or individuals, proceed to lay taxes to the amount of $50,000,000 a year. Could the Supreme Court take cognizance of the act laying the tax, or making the distribution ? Certainly not

Take another case, which is very likely to occur. Congress have the unlimited power of taxation. Suppose them also to assume an unlimited power of appropriation. Appropriations of money are made to establish presses, promote education, build and support churches, create an order of nobility, or for any other unconstitutional object; it is manifest that in none of these cases could the constitutionality of the laws making those grants be tested before the Supreme Court.

It would be in vain that a state should come before the judges with an act appropriating money to any of these objects, and ask of the court to decide whether these grants were constitutional. They could not even be heard; the court would say they had nothing to do with it; and they would say rightly. It is idle, therefore, to talk of the Supreme Court affording any security to the states, in cases where their rights may be violated by the exercise of unconstitutional powers on the part of the federal government. On this subject Mr. Madison, in his Report, says: " But it is objected that the judicial authority is to be regarded as the sole expositor of the Constitution in the last resort; and it may be asked, for what reason the declaration by the General Assembly, supposing it to be theoretically true, could be required at the present day, and in so solemn a manner.

" On this objection it might be observed, first, that there may be instances of usurped power which the forms of the Constitution would never draw within the control of the judicial department."

" But the proper answer to the objection is, that the resolution of the General Assembly relates to those great and extraordinary cases in which all the forms of the Constitution may prove ineffectual against infractions dangerous to the essential rights of the parties to it.

" However true, therefore, it may be, that the judicial department is, in all questions submitted to it by the forms of the Constitution, to decide in the last resort, this resort must necessarily be deemed the last in relation to the authorities of the other departments of the government; not in relation to the rights of the parties to the constitutional compact, from which the judicial, as well as the other departments, hold their delegated trusts. On any other hypothesis, the delegation of judicial power would annul the authority delegating it; and the concurrence of this department with the others in usurped powers might subvert forever, and beyond the possible reach of any rightful remedy, the very Constitution which all were instituted to preserve."

If, then, the Supreme Court are not, and, from their organization, cannot be, the umpires in questions of conflicting sovereignty, the next point to be considered is, whether Congress themselves possess the right of deciding conclusively on the extent of their own powers. This, I know, is a popular notion, and it is founded on the idea that, as all the states are represented here, nothing can prevail which is not in conformity with the will of the majority; and it is supposed to be a republican maxim, " that the majority must govern."

Now, will any one contend that it is the true spirit of this government, that the will of a majority of Congress should, in all cases, be the supreme law? If no security was intended to be provided for the rights of the states, and the liberty of the citizens, beyond the mere organization of the federal government, we should have had no written constitution, but Congress would have been authorized to legislate for us in all cases whatsoever, and the acts of our state legislatures, like those of the present legislative councils in the territories, would have been subjected to the revision and control of Congress. If the will of a majority of Congress is to be the supreme law of the land, it is clear the Constitution is a dead letter, and has utterly failed of the very object for which it was designed — the protection of the rights of the minority. But when, by the very terms of the compact, strict limitations are imposed on every branch of the federal government, and it is, moreover, expressly declared that all powers not granted to them " are reserved to the states or the people," with what show of reason can it be contended that the federal government is to be the exclusive judge of the extent of its own powers? A written constitution was resorted to in this country, as a great experiment, for the purpose of ascertaining how far the rights of a minority could be secured against the encroachments of majorities — often acting under party excitement, and not unfrequently under the influence of strong interests. The moment that Constitution was formed, the will of the majority ceased to be the law, except in cases that should be acknowledged by the parties to be within the Constitution, and to have been thereby submitted to their will. But when Congress (exercising a delegated and strictly limited authority) pass beyond these limits, their acts become null and void, and must be declared to be so by the courts, in cases within their jurisdiction; and may be pronounced to be so by the states themselves, in cases not within the jurisdiction of the courts, of sufficient importance to justify such an interference.

But what then? asks the gentleman. A state is brought into collision with the United States, in relation to the exercise of unconstitutional powers; who is to decide between them? Sir, it is the common case of difference of opinion between sovereigns, as to the true construction of a compact. Does such a difference of opinion necessarily produce war? No. And if not among rival nations, why should it do so among friendly states? In all such cases, some mode must be devised, by mutual agreement, for settling the difficulty; and, most happily for us, that mode is clearly indicated in the Constitution itself, and results, indeed, from the very form and structure of the government. The creating power is three fourths of the states. By their decision, the parties to the compact have agreed to be bound, even to the extent of changing the entire form of the government itself; and it follows of necessity, that, in case of a deliberate and settled difference of opinion between the parties to the compact, as to the extent of the powers of either, resort must be had to their common superior, (that power which may give any character to the Constitution they may think proper,) viz., three fourths of the states.

But, it has been asked, why not compel a state objecting to the constitutionality of a law to appeal to her sister states by a proposition to amend the Constitution? I answer, because such a course would, in the first instance, admit the exercise of an unconstitutional authority, which the states are not bound to submit to, even for a day; and because it would be absurd to suppose that any redress would ever be obtained by such an appeal, even if a state were at liberty to make it. If a majority of both houses of Congress should, from any motive, be induced deliberately to exercise " powers not granted," what prospect would there be of " arresting the progress of the evil," by a vote of three fourths? But the Constitution does not permit a minority to submit to the people a proposition for an amendment of the Constitution. Such a proposition can only come from " two thirds of the two houses of Congress, or the legislatures of two thirds of the states." It will be seen, therefore, at once, that a minority, whose constitutional rights are violated, can have no redress by an amendment of the Constitution. When any state is brought into direct collision with the federal government, in the case of an attempt, by the latter, to exercise unconstitutional powers, the appeal must be made by Congress, (the party proposing to exert the disputed powers,) in order to have it expressly conferred; and until so conferred, the exercise of such authority must be suspended. Even in case of doubt, such an appeal is due to the peace and harmony of the government. On this subject our present chief magistrate, in his opening message to Congress, says, " I regard an appeal to the source of power, in cases of real doubt, and where its exercise is deemed indispensable to the general welfare, as among the most sacred of all our obligations. Upon this country, more than any other, has, in the providence of God, been cast the special guardianship of the great principle of adherence to *written constitutions.* If it fail here, all hope in regard to it will be extinguished. That this was intended to be a government of limited and specific, and not general powers, must be admitted by all; and it is our duty to preserve for it the character intended by its framers. The scheme has worked well. It has exceeded the hopes of those who devised it, and become an object of admiration to the world. Nothing is clearer, in my view, than that we are chiefly indebted for the success of the Constitution, under which we are now acting, to the watchful and auxiliary operation of the state authorities. This is not the reflection of a day, but belongs to the most deeply-rooted convictions of my mind. I cannot, therefore, too strongly or too earnestly, for my own sense of its importance, warn you against all encroachments upon the legitimate sphere of state sovereignty. Sustained by its healthful and invigorating influence, the federal system can never fail."

I have already shown, that it has been fully recognized by the Virginia resolutions of '98, and by Mr. Madison's report on these resolutions, that it is not only " the right but the duty of the states " to "judge of infractions of the Constitution," and to interpose for maintaining within their limits the authorities, rights, and liberties, appertaining to them.

Mr. Jefferson, on various occasions, expressed himself in language equally strong. In the Kentucky resolutions of '98, prepared by him, it is declared that the federal government " was not made the exclusive and final judge of the extent of the powers delegated to itself, since that would have made its discretion, and not the Constitution, the measure of its powers; but that, as in all other cases of compact among parties having no common judge, each party has an equal right to judge for itself, as well of infractions as the mode and measure of redress."

In the Kentucky resolutions of '99, it is even more explicitly declared ' that the several states which formed the Constitution, being sovereign and independent, have the unquestionable right to judge of its infraction, and that nullification by those sovereignties of all unauthorized acts done under color of that instrument is the rightful remedy."

But the gentleman says, this right will be dangerous. Sir, I insist that, of all the checks that have been provided by the Constitution, this is by far the safest, and the least liable to abuse.

But there is one point of view in which this matter presents itself to my mind with irresistible force. The Supreme Court, it is admitted, may nullify an act of Congress, by declaring it to be unconstitutional. Can Congress, after such a nullification, proceed to enforce the law, even if they should differ in opinion from the court? What, then, would be the effect of such a decision? And what would be the remedy in such a case? Congress would be arrested in the exercise of the disputed power, and the only remedy would be, an appeal to the creating power — three fourths of the states — for an amendment to the Constitution. And by whom must such an appeal be made? It must be made by the party proposing to exercise the disputed power. Now, I will ask whether a sovereign state may not be safely intrusted with the exercise of a power, operating merely as a check, which is admitted to belong to the Supreme Court, and which may be exercised every day by any three of its members. Sir, no idea that can be formed of arbitrary power on the one hand, and abject dependence on the other, can be carried farther than to suppose that three individuals, mere men, " subject to like passions with ourselves," may be safely intrusted with the power to nullify an act of Congress, because they conceive it to be unconstitutional ; but that a sovereign and independent state — even the great state of New York — is bound, implicitly, to submit to its operation, even where it violates, in the grossest manner, her own rights, or the liberties of her citizens. But we do not contend that a common case would justify the interposition.

This is the "extreme medicine of the state," and cannot become our daily bread.

Mr. Madison, in his Report, says, " It does not follow, however, that because the states, as sovereign parties to their constitutional compact, must ultimately decide whether it has been violated, that such a decision ought to be interposed, either in a hasty manner, or on doubtful and inferior occasions.

" The resolution has, accordingly, guarded against any misapprehensions of its object, by expressly requiring, for such an interposition, ' the case of a deliberate, palpable, and dangerous breach of the Constitution, by the exercise of powers not granted by it.'

" But the resolution has done more than guard against misconstruction, by expressly referring to cases of a deliberate, palpable, and dangerous nature. It specifies the object of the interposition, which it contemplates to be solely that of arresting the progress of the evil of usurpation, and of maintaining the authorities, rights, and liberties, appertaining to the states, as parties to the Constitution."

No one can read this without perceiving that Mr. Madison goes the whole length, in support of the principles for which I have been contending.

The gentleman has called upon us to carry out our scheme *practically.* Now, sir, if I am correct in my view of this matter, then it follows, of course, that, the right of a state being established, the federal government is bound to acquiesce in a solemn decision of a state, acting in its sovereign capacity, at least so far as to make an appeal to the people for an amendment of the Constitution. This solemn decision of a state (made either through its legislature or a convention, as may be supposed to be the proper organ of its sovereign will — a point I do not propose now to discuss) binds the federal government, under the highest constitutional obligation, not to resort to any means of coercion against the citizens of the dissenting state. How, then, can any collision ensue between the federal and state governments — unless, indeed, the former should determine to enforce the law by unconstitutional means?

Sir, I will put the case home to the gentleman. Is there any violation of the constitutional rights of the states, and the liberties of the citizen, (sanctioned by Congress and the Supreme Court,) which he would believe it to be the right and duty of a state to resist? Does he contend for the doctrine " of passive obedience and non-resistance ? " Would he justify an open resistance to an act of Congress, sanctioned by the courts, which should abolish the trial by jury, or destroy the freedom of religion, or the freedom of the press? Yes, sir, he would advocate resistance in such cases; and so would I, and so would all of us. But such resistance would, according to this doctrine, be revolution : it would be rebellion. According to my opinion, it would be just, legal, and constitutional resistance. The whole difference between us, then, consists in this : the gentleman would make force the only arbiter in all cases of collision between the states and the federal government; I would resort to a peaceful remedy — the interposition of the state to " arrest the progress of the evil," until such times as " a convention (assembled at the call of Congress or two thirds of the states) shall decide to which they mean to give an authority claimed by two of their organs." Sir, I say, with Mr. Jefferson, (whose words I have here borrowed,) that " it is the peculiar wisdom and felicity of our Constitution to have provided this peaceable appeal, where that of other nations" (and I may add that of the gentleman) " is at once to force."

Mr. WEBSTER, in some closing remarks, said a few words on the constitutional argument, which the honorable gentleman (Mr. Hayne) labored to reconstruct.

His argument consists of two propositions, and an inference. His propositions are —

1. That the Constitution is a compact between the states.

2. That a compact between two, with authority reserved to one to interpret its terms, would be a surrender, to that one, of all power whatever

3. Therefore (such is his inference) the general government does not possess the authority to construe its own powers.

Now, sir, who does not see, without the aid of exposition or detection, the utter confusion of ideas involved in this so elaborate and systematic argument ?

The Constitution, it is said, is a compact between states : the states, then, and the states only, are parties to the compact. How comes the general government itself a party? Upon the honorable gentleman's hypothesis, the general government is the result of the compact, the creature of the compact, not one of the parties to it. Yet the argument, as the gentleman has now stated it, makes the government itself one of its own creators. It makes it a party to that compact to which it owes its own existence.

For the purpose of erecting the Constitution on the basis of a compact, the gentleman considers the states as parties to that compact; but as soon as his compact is made, then he chooses to consider the general government, which is the offspring of that compact, not its offspring, but one of its parties; and so, being a party, has not the power of judging on the terms of compact.

If the whole of the gentleman's main proposition were conceded to him — that is to say, if I admit, for the sake of the argument, that the Constitution is a compact between states, — the inferences which he draws from that proposition are warranted by no just reason; because, if the

Constitution be a compact between states, still that Constitution, or that compact, has established a government with certain powers; and whether it be one of those powers, that it shall construe and interpret for itself the terms of the compact in doubtful cases, can only be decided by looking to the compact, and inquiring what provisions it contains on this point. Without any inconsistency with natural reason, the government, even thus created, might be trusted with this power of construction. The extent of its powers, therefore, must still be sought for in the instrument itself.

If the old Confederation had contained a clause, declaring that resolutions of the Congress should be the supreme law of the land, any state law or constitution to the contrary notwithstanding, and that a committee of Congress, or any other body created by it, should possess judicial powers, extending to all cases arising under resolutions of Congress, then the power of ultimate decision would have been vested in Congress under the Confederation, although that Confederation was a compact between states; and for this plain reason — that it would have been competent to the states, who alone were parties to the compact, to agree who should decide in cases of dispute arising on the construction of the compact.

For the same reason, sir, if I were now to concede to the gentleman his principal proposition, viz., that the Constitution is a compact between states, the question would still be, what provision is made, in this compact, to settle points of disputed construction, or contested power, that shall come into controversy; and this question would still be answered, and conclusively answered, by the Constitution itself. While the gentleman is contending against construction, he himself is setting up the most loose and dangerous construction. The Constitution declares that the laws of Congress shall be the supreme law of the land. No construction is necessary here. It declares, also, with equal plainness and precision, that the judicial power of the United States shall extend to every case arising under the laws of Congress. This needs no construction. Here is a law, then, which is declared to be supreme; and here is a power established which is to interpret that law. Now, sir, how has the gentleman met this? Suppose the Constitution to be a compact; yet here are its terms; and how does the gentleman get rid of them? He cannot argue the seal off the bond, nor the words out of the instrument. Here they are. What answer does he give to them? None in the world, sir, except that the effect of this would be to place the states in a condition of inferiority; and because it results, from the very nature of things, there being no superior, that the parties must be their own judges! Thus closely and cogently does the honorable gentleman reason on the words of the Constitution. The gentleman says, if there be such a power of final decisions in the general government, he asks for the grant of that power. Well, sir, I show him the grant — I turn him to the very words — I show him that the laws of Congress are made supreme, and that the judicial power extends, by express words, to the interpretation of these laws. Instead of answering this, he retreats into the general reflection, that it must result from the nature of things that the states, being the parties, must judge for themselves.

I have admitted, that, if the Constitution were to be considered as the creature of the state governments, it might be modified, interpreted, or construed, according to their pleasure. But, even in that case, it would be necessary that they should agree. One, alone, could not interpret it conclusively; one, alone, could not construe it; one, alone, could not modify it. Yet the gentleman's doctrine is, that Carolina, alone, may

44

construe and interpret that compact which equally binds all, and gives equal rights to all.

So then, sir, even supposing the Constitution to be a compact between the states, the gentleman's doctrine, nevertheless, is not maintainable; because, first, the general government is not a party to that compact, but a government established by it, and vested by it with the powers of trying and deciding doubtful questions; and, secondly, because, if the Constitution be regarded as a compact, not one state only, but all the states, are parties to that compact, and one can have no right to fix upon it her own peculiar construction.

So much, sir, for the argument, even if the premises of the gentleman were granted, or could be proved. But, sir, the gentleman has failed to maintain his leading proposition. He has not shown — it cannot be shown — that the Constitution is a compact between state governments. The Constitution itself, in its very front, refutes that proposition; it declares that it is ordained and established by the people of the United States. So far from saying that it is established by the governments of the several states, it does not even say that it is established by the people of the several states; but it pronounces that it is established by the people of the United States, in the aggregate. The gentleman says, it must mean no more than that the people of the several states, taken collectively, constitute the people of the United States. Be it so; but it is in this their collective capacity, it is as all the people of the United States, that they establish the Constitution. So they declare; and words cannot be plainer than the words used.

When the gentleman says, the Constitution is a compact between the states, he uses language exactly applicable to the old Confederation. He speaks as if he were in Congress before 1789. He describes fully that old state of things then existing. The Confederation was, in strictness, a compact; the states, as states, were parties to it. We had no other general government. But that was found insufficient, and inadequate to the public exigencies. The people were not satisfied with it, and undertook to establish a better. They undertook to form a general government which should stand on a new basis — not a confederacy, not a league, not a compact between states, but a constitution; a popular government, founded in popular election, directly responsible to the people themselves, and divided into branches, with prescribed limits of power, and prescribed duties. They ordained such a government; they gave it the name of a constitution; and therein they established a distribution of powers between this, their general government, and their several state governments. When they shall become dissatisfied with this distribution, they can alter it. Their own power over their own instrument remains. But until they shall alter it, it must stand as their will, and is equally binding on the general government and on the states.

The gentleman, sir, finds analogy where I see none. He likens it to the case of a treaty, in which, there being no common superior, each party must interpret for itself, under its own obligation of good faith. But this is not a treaty, but a constitution of government, with powers to execute itself, and fulfil its duties.

I admit, sir, that this government is a government of checks and balances; that is, the House of Representatives is a check on the Senate, and the Senate is a check on the House, and the President is a check on both. But I cannot comprehend him — or if I do, I totally differ from him — when he applies the notion of checks and balances to the interference of different governments.   He argues that, if we transgress, each state, as a state, has a right to check us.   Does he admit the converse of the proposition — that we have a right to check the states?   The gentleman's doctrines would give us a strange jumble of authorities and powers, instead of governments of separate and defined powers.   It is the part of wisdom, [1] think, to avoid this; and to keep the general government and the state governments each in its proper sphere — avoiding, as carefully as possible, every kind of interference.

Finally, sir, the honorable gentleman says that the states will only interfere, by their power, to preserve the Constitution.   They will not destroy it, they will not impair it — they will only save, they will only preserve, they will only strengthen it !   All regulated governments, all free governments, have been broken up by similar disinterested and well-disposed interference !

Mr. EDWARD LIVINGSTON.   I think that the Constitution is the result of a compact entered into by the several states, by which they surrendered a part of their sovereignty to the Union, and vested the part so surrendered in a general government.

That this government is partly popular, acting directly on the citizens of the several states ; partly federative, depending for its existence and action on the existence and action of the several states.

That, by the institution of this government, the states have unequivocally surrendered every constitutional right of impeding or resisting the execution of any decree or judgment of the Supreme Court, in any case of law or equity between persons or on matters, of whom or on which that court has jurisdiction, even if such decree or judgment should, in the opinion of the states, be unconstitutional.

That, in cases in which a law of the United States may infringe the constitutional right of a state, but which, in its operation, cannot be brought before the Supreme Court, under the terms of the jurisdiction expressly given to it over particular persons or matters, that court is not created the umpire between a state that may deem itself aggrieved and the general government.

That, among the attributes of sovereignty retained by the states, is that of watching over the operations of the general government, and protecting its citizens against their unconstitutional abuse ; and that this can be legally done —

First, in the case of an act, in the opinion of the state palpably unconstitutional, but affirmed in the Supreme Court in the legal exercise of its functions ;

By remonstrating against it to Congress ;

By an address to the people, in their elective functions, to change or instruct their representatives ;

By a similar address to the other states, in which they will have a right to declare that they consider the act as unconstitutional, and therefore void ;

By proposing amendments to the Constitution in the manner pointed out by that instrument ;

And, finally, if the act be intolerably oppressive, and they find the general government persevere in enforcing it, by a resort to the natural right which every people have to resist extreme oppression.

Secondly, if the act be one of the few which, in its operation, cannot be submitted to the Supreme Court, and be one that will, in the opinion of the state, justify the risk of a withdrawal from the Union, that this last extreme remedy may at once be resorted to.

That the right of resistance to the operation of an act of Congress, in the extreme cases above alluded to, is not a right derived from the Constitution, but can be justified only on the supposition that the Constitution has been broken, and the state absolved from its obligation ; and that, whenever resorted to, it must be at the risk of all the penalties attached to an unsuccessful resistance to established authority.

That the alleged right of a state to put a *veto* on the execution of a law of the United States, which such state may declare to be unconstitutional, attended (as, if it exist, it must be) with a correlative obligation, on the part of the general government, to refrain from executing it ; and the further alleged obligation, on the part of that government, to submit the question to the states, by proposing amendments, are not given by the Constitution, nor do they grow out of any of the reserved powers.

That the exercise of the powers last mentioned would introduce a feature in our government not expressed in the Constitution ; not implied from any right of sovereignty reserved to the states ; not suspected to exist, by the friends or enemies of the Constitution, when it was framed or adopted ; not warranted by practice or contemporaneous exposition, nor implied by the true construction of the Virginia resolutions in '98.

That the introduction of this feature in our government would totally change its nature, make it inefficient, invite to dissension, and end, at no distant period, in separation ; and that, if it had been proposed in the form of an explicit provision in the Constitution, it would have been unanimously rejected, both in the Convention which framed that instrument and in those which adopted it.

That the theory of the federal government being the result of the general will of the people of the United States in their aggregate capacity, and founded in no degree on compact between the states, would tend to the most disastrous practical results ; that it would place three fourths of the states at the mercy of one fourth, and lead inevitably to a consolidated government, and finally to monarchy, if the doctrine were generally admitted ; and if partially so, and opposed, to civil dissensions.

Mr. WOODBURY.   From the very fact of there being two parties in the federal government, it would seem a necessary inference that the agents of each party, on proper occasions, must be allowed, and are required by an official oath, to conform to the Constitution, and to decide on the extent of its provisions, so far as is necessary for the expression of their own views, and for the performance of their own duties.   This being, to my mind, the *rationale* of the case, I look on the express words of the Constitution as conforming to it, by limiting the grant of judicial jurisdiction to the Supreme Court, both by the Constitution and by the acts of Congress, to specify enumerated objects.   In the same way, there are limited grants of judicial jurisdiction to state courts, under most of the state constitutions.   When cases present themselves within these grants, the judges, whether of the state or United States, must decide, and enforce their decision with such means as are confided to them by the laws and the constitutions.   But, when questions arise, not confided to the judiciary of the states, or United States, the officers concerned in those questions must themselves decide them ; and, in the end, must pursue such course as their views of the Constitution dictate. In such instances, they have the same authority to make this decision as the Supreme Court itself has in other instances.

On Powers of the State and Federal Governments.

February 29.

Mr. GRUNDY. I will proceed to an examination of a subject upon which a great diversity of opinion seems to prevail. I mean the powers of the state and federal governments. As to the true division or distribution of their powers, no difficulty exists so long as we speak in general terms; differences of opinion arise when we come to an act on particular cases. At present, we have no case before the Senate, and are only discussing the subject for the purpose of ascertaining the true rule by which to test cases as they arise; and in the event Congress should transcend the limits or boundaries of its constitutional powers, to ascertain where we are to look for the ultimate corrective tribunal.

The states existed prior to this government. Each of them possessed all the rights and powers which appertain to sovereign and independent nations. For all the purposes of self-government, no want of power, or the means of using it, was felt by any of these communities. Life, liberty, reputation, and property, all found an ample protection in the state governments. If any internal improvement were necessary, within its limits, the sovereign power of the state, having entire and uncontrolled jurisdiction, could cause it to be undertaken and effected. For none of these purposes or objects was there a defect of competency in the state governments. There were objects, however, of high importance, to which the states, separately, were not equal or adequate to provide. These are specified in the recommendatory letter by the Convention, and signed by General Washington, which accompanied the Constitution, when presented to the old Congress for its consideration. The language is, "The friends of our country have long seen and desired, that the power of making war, peace, and treaties; that of levying money and regulating commerce; and the correspondent executive and judicial authorities, should be fully and effectually vested in the general government of the Union." Here is an enumeration of the objects which made it necessary to establish this government; and when we are called on to decide whether a subject be within our powers, we ought not to lose sight of the purposes for which the government was created. When it is recollected that all the powers now possessed by the general and state governments belonged originally to the latter, and that the former is constructed from grants of power yielded up by the state governments, the fair and just conclusion would be, that no other power was conferred except what was plainly and expressly given. But if doubt could exist, the 10th article in the amendments to the Constitution settles this question. It declares that "the powers not delegated to the United States by the Constitution, nor prohibited by it to the states, are reserved to the states, respectively, or to the people." The conclusion hence arises, that this government is one of limited, delegated powers, and can only act on subjects expressly placed under its control by he Constitution, and upon such other matters as may be necessarily and properly within the sphere of its action, to enable it to carry the enumerated and specified powers into execution, and without which the powers granted would be inoperative.

VOL. IV.   66

Public Lands.

Mr. WOODBURY. Not examining the particular kind of sales the government can make for the common benefit, such as grants to the new states for such schools, receiving virtual compensation therefor, by having the rest of the land freed from taxation, I merely lay down what I suppose to be the general principle.

On that principle, no reasoning has been offered which convinces me that lands can be legally appropriated to any object for which we might not legally appropriate money. The lands are as much the property of the Union as its money in the treasury. The cessions and purchases of them were as much for the benefit of all as the collection of the money. The Constitution, as well as common sense, seems to recognize no difference; and if the money can only be appropriated to specified objects, it follows that the land can only be so appropriated. Within those specified objects I have ever been, and ever shall be, as ready to give lands or money to the west as to the east; but beyond them, I never have been ready to give either to either. Towards certain enumerated objects, Congress have authority to devote the common funds — the land or the money; because those objects were supposed to be better managed under their control than under that of the states; but the care of the other objects is reserved to the states themselves, and can only be promoted by the common funds, in a return or division of these funds to proprietors, to be expended as they may deem judicious.

The whole debate on these points goes to satisfy my mind of the correctness of that construction of the Constitution, which holds no grants of money or lands valid, unless to advance some of the enumerated objects intrusted to Congress. When we once depart from that great landmark on the appropriation of lands or money, and wander into indefinite notions of " common good " or of the " general welfare," we are, in my opinion, at sea without compass or rudder; and in a government of acknowledged limitations, we put every thing at the caprice of a fluctuating majority here; pronouncing that to be for the general welfare to-day, which tomorrow may be denounced as a general curse. Were the government not limited, this broad discretion would, of course, be necessary and right. But here every grant of power is defined. Many powers are not ceded to the general government, but are expressly withheld to the states and people; and right is, in my opinion, given to promote the " general welfare," by granting money or lands, but in the exercise of specific powers granted, and in the modes prescribed, by the Constitution.

In fine, if the government, and the principles of strict construction of the Constitution, cannot be prosperously administered, it requires no spirit of prophecy to foresee, that, in a few brief years, in a new crisis approaching, and before indicated, it must, as a confederation, probably cease to be administered at all. It will, in my judgment, become a government of usurped, alarming, undefined powers; and the sacred rights of the states will become overshadowed in total eclipse. When that catastrophe more nearly approaches, unless the great parties to the government shall arouse, and in some way interfere and rescue it from consolidation, it will follow as darkness does the day, that the government ends, like all republics of olden times, either in anarchy or despotism.

Nullification.

SENATE, *April* 2, 1830.

Mr. JOHNSTON. The right of a state to annul a law of Congress must depend on their showing that this is a mere confederation of states: which has not been done, and cannot be said to be true, although it should not appear to be absolutely a government of the people. It is by no means necessary to push the argument, as to the character of the government, to its utmost limit; the ground has been taken, and maintained with great force of reasoning, that this government is the agent of the supreme power, the people. It is sufficient for the argument, that this is not a compact of states. It may be assumed that it is neither strictly a confederation nor a national government: it is compounded of both: it is an anomaly in the political world; an experiment growing out of our peculiar circumstances; a compromise of principles and opinions: it is partly federal, partly national.

"The proposed Constitution is, in strictness, neither national nor federal; it is a composition of both; in its foundation it is federal, not national; in the sources from which the ordinary powers of the government are drawn, it is partly federal, partly national; in the operation of these powers, it is national, not federal; in the mode for amendment, it is neither wholly federal nor wholly national." — *Federalist.*

The following list will exhibit the nature and number of the causes decided, [in the Supreme Court.] The same case is sometimes counted under different heads:

1. Declaring acts of Congress unconstitutional,	2	8. Acquiescing in appeal jurisdiction,	21
2. Constitutional,		9. States parties, really and nominally,	6
3. Declaring state laws constitutional,	9	10. States parties, incidentally,	4
4. Declaring state laws unconstitutional,	26	11. Opinions against the President,	2
5. Affirming judgments of state courts,	14	12. Opinions in favor of the President,	2
6. Annulling judgments of state courts	14	13. Opinions against the Secretary of State,	2
7. Assenting to appeal jurisdiction,	7		

They have decided twenty-six state laws to be unconstitutional; that is, interfering with the rights of the general government; which, considering these as twenty-four states, are not equal to the number of decisions against the acts of Congress. * * *

The [Supreme] Court has annulled the judgments of state courts in fourteen cases, which drew in question the Constitution, laws, or treaties of the United States; but has affirmed as many; which shows they have no bearing against the rights of states, and which, if it has had no other effect, has preserved the uniformity so essential to the administration of justice under them. * * *

Indian " Treaties."

SENATE, *May,* 1830.

Mr. SPRAGUE. These contracts with aboriginal communities have been denominated *treaties* from the first settlement of this country. It has been their peculiar and appropriate name without even an *alias dictus.* Great Britain made *treaties* with the Indians; the several colonies formed many, and gave them the same appellation. The Continental Congress, from the time it first assembled until it was merged in the present national government, uniformly called them treaties. They did so in 1775, 1776, 1778, 1783, 1784, 1785, 1786, 1787, 1788, and even to the day of the formation and adoption of the Constitution. We find them repeatedly and particularly mentioned in July, August, and October, 1787, the Constitution being formed in September of the same year.

United States Bank.

House of Representatives, *April* 13, 1830.

Mr. M'DUFFIE. It remains for the committee to show that the Bank of the United States is a " necessary and proper," or, in other words, a natural and appropriate, means of executing the powers vested in the fed eral government. In the discussion of 1791, and also in that before the Supreme Court, the powers of raising, collecting, and disbursing, the public revenue, of borrowing money on the credit of the United States, and paying the public debt, were those which were supposed most clearly to carry with them the incidental right of incorporating a bank, to facilitate these operations. There can be no doubt that these fiscal operations are greatly facilitated by a bank, and it is confidently believed that no person has presided twelve months over the treasury, from its first organization to the present time, without coming to the conclusion that such an institution is exceedingly useful to the public finances in time of peace, but indispensable in time of war. But as this view of the question has been fully unfolded in former discussions familiar to the house, the committee will proceed to examine the relation which the Bank of the United States bears to another of the powers of the federal government, but slightly adverted to in former discussions of the subject.

The power to " coin money and fix the value thereof" is expressly and exclusively vested in Congress. This grant was evidently intended to invest Congress with the power of regulating the circulating medium. " Coin " was regarded, at the period of framing the Constitution, as synonymous with " currency," as it was then generally believed that bank notes could only be maintained in circulation by being the true representative of the precious metals. The word " coin," therefore, must be regarded as a particular term, standing as the representative of a general idea. No principle of sound construction will justify a rigid adherence to the letter, in opposition to the plain intention of the clause. If, for example, the gold bars of Ricardo should be substituted for our present coins, by the general consent of the commercial world, could it be maintained that Congress would not have the power to *make* such money, and fix its value, because it is not " coined "? This would be sacrificing sense to sound, and substance to mere form. This clause of the Constitution is analogous to that which gives Congress the power " to establish post-roads." Giving to the word " establish " its restricted interpretation, as being equivalent to " fix " or " prescribe," can it be doubted that Congress has the power to establish a canal, or a river, as a post-route, as well as a road? Roads were the ordinary channels of conveyance, and the term was, therefore, used as synonymous with " routes," whatever might be the channel of transportation; and, in like manner, " coin " being the ordinary and most known form of a circulating medium, that term was used as synonymous with currency.

An argument in favor of the view just taken may be fairly deduced from the fact, that the states are expressly prohibited from " coining money, or emitting bills of credit," and from " making any thing but gold and silver a lawful tender in payment of debts." This strongly confirms the idea, that the subject of regulating the circulating medium, whether consisting of coin or paper, was, at the same time that it was taken from the control of the states, vested in the only depository in which it could be placed, consistently with the obvious design of having a common measure of value throughout the Union.

MR. MONROE'S OBJECTIONS

TO

'AN ACT FOR THE PRESERVATION AND REPAIR OF THE CUMBERLAND ROAD."

Having duly considered the bill, entitled " An Act for the Preservation and Repair of the Cumberland Road," it is with deep regret, approving as I do the policy, that I am compelled to object to its passage, and to return it to the House of Representatives, in which it originated, under a conviction that Congress do not possess the power, under the Constitution, to pass such a law.

A power to establish turnpikes with gates and tolls, and to enforce the collection of tolls by penalties, implies a power to adopt and execute a system of internal improvement. A right to impose duties, to be paid by all persons passing a certain road, and on horses and carriages, as is done by this bill, involves the right to take land from the proprietor, on a valuation, and to pass laws for the protection of the road from injuries; and if it exist as to one road, it exists as to any other, and to as many roads as Congress may think proper to establish. A right to legislate for one of these purposes, is a right to legislate for the others. It is a complete right of jurisdiction and sovereignty, for all the purposes of internal improvement, and not merely the right of appropriating money, under the power vested in Congress to make appropriations, — under which power, with the consent of the states through which the road passes, the work was originally commenced, and has been so far executed. I am of opinion that Congress do not possess this power; that the states, individually, cannot grant it; for, although they may assent to the appropriation of money within their limits for such purposes, they can grant no power of jurisdiction or sovereignty by special compacts with the United States. This power can be granted only by an amendment to the Constitution, and in the mode prescribed by it.

If the power exist, it must, either because it has been specifically granted to the United States, or that which is incidental to some power which has been specifically granted. If we examine the specific grants of power, we do not find it among them; nor is it incidental to any power which has been specifically granted.

It never has been contended that the power was specifically granted. It is claimed only as being incidental to one or more of the powers which are specifically granted. The following are the powers from which it is said to be derived: —

1st, from the right to establish post-offices and post-roads; 2d, from the right to declare war; 3d, to regulate commerce; 4th, to pay the debts and provide for the common defence and general welfare; 5th, from the power to make all laws necessary and proper for carrying into execution all the powers vested by the Constitution in the government of the United States, or in any department or officer thereof; 6th, and lastly, from the power to dispose of, and make all needful rules and regulations respecting, the territory and other property of the United States.

According to my judgment, it cannot be derived from either of those powers, nor from all of them united; and, in consequence, does not exist. * * *

JAMES MONROE.

Washington, *May* 4, 1822.

On the evening of the 24th, President Monroe also transmitted his "*views*," in support of his *veto*, in an elaborate argument, which is the exposition quoted in President Jackson's objections.

———◆———

OBJECTIONS OF THE PRESIDENT OF THE UNITED STATES

ON RETURNING TO THE HOUSE OF REPRESENTATIVES THE ENROLLED BILL, ENTITLED

"AN ACT AUTHORIZING A SUBSCRIPTION OF STOCK IN THE MAYSVILLE, WASHINGTON, PARIS, AND LEXINGTON TURNPIKE ROAD COMPANY."

The constitutional power of the federal government to construct or promote works of internal improvement presents itself in two points of view — the first, as bearing upon the sovereignty of the states within whose limits their execution is contemplated, if jurisdiction of the territory which they may occupy be claimed as necessary to then preservation and use ; the second, as asserting the simple right to appropriate money from the national treasury in aid of such works when undertaken by state authority, surrendering the claim of jurisdiction. In the first view, the question of power is an open one, and can be decided without the embarrassment attending the other, arising from the practice of the government.

Although frequently and strenuously attempted, the power, to this extent, has never been exercised by the government in a single instance. It does not, in my opinion, possess it, and no bill, therefore, which admits it, can receive my official sanction.

But, in the other view of the power, the question is differently situated. The ground taken at an early period of the government was, " that, whenever money has been raised by the general authority, and is to be applied to a particular measure, a question arises whether the particular measure be within the enumerated authorities vested in Congress. If it be, the money requisite for it may be applied to it ; if not, no such application can be made." The document in which this principle was first advanced is of deservedly high authority, and should be held in grateful remembrance for its immediate agency in rescuing the country from much existing abuse, and for its conservative effect upon some of the most valuable principles of the Constitution. The symmetry and purity of the government would, doubtless, have been better preserved, if this restriction of the power of appropriation could have been maintained without weakening its ability to fulfil the general objects of its institution — an effect so likely to attend its admission, notwithstanding its apparent fitness, that every subsequent administration of the government, embracing a period of thirty out of the forty-two years of its existence, has adopted a more enlarged construction of the power.

In the administration of Mr. Jefferson, we have two examples of the exercise of the right of appropriation, which, in the consideration that led to their adoption, and in their effects upon the public mind, have had a greater agency in marking the character of the power, than any subsequent events. I allude to the payment of fifteen millions of dollars for the purchase of Louisiana, and to the original appropriation for the construction of the Cumberland Road ; the latter act deriving much weight from the acquiescence and approbation of three of the most powerful of the original members of the confederacy, expressed through their respective legislatures. Although the circumstances of the latter case may be such as to deprive so much of it as relates to the actual construction of the road of the force of an obligatory exposition of the Constitution, it must, nevertheless, be admitted that, so far as the mere appropriation of money is concerned, they present the principle in its most imposing aspect. No less than twenty-three different laws have been passed through all the forms of the Constitution, appropriating upwards of two millions of dollars out of the national treasury in support of that improvement, with the approbation of every President of the United States, including my predecessor, since its commencement.

Independently of the sanction given to appropriations for the Cumberland and other roads and objects, under this power, the administration of Mr. Madison was characterized by an act which furnishes the strongest evidence of his opinion extant. A bill was passed through both houses of Congress, and presented for his approval, " setting apart and pledging certain funds for constructing roads and canals, and improving the navigation of watercourses, in order to facilitate, promote, and give security to internal commerce among the several states ; and to render more easy, and less expensive, the means and provision for the common defence." Regarding the bill as asserting a power in the federal government to construct roads and canals within the limits of the states in which they were made, he objected to its passage, on the ground of its unconstitutionality, declaring that the assent of the respective states, in the mode provided by the bill, could not confer the powers in question ; that the only cases in which the consent and cession of particular states can extend the power of Congress are those specified and provided for in the Constitution ; and superadding to this avowal his opinion, that " a restriction of the power ' to provide for the common defence and general welfare,' to cases which are to be provided for by the expenditure of money, would still leave within the legislative power of Congress all the great and most important measures of government, money being the ordinary and necessary means of carrying them into execution." I have not been able to consider these declarations in any other point of view than as a concession that the right of appropriation is not limited by the power to carry into effect the measure for which the money is asked, as was formerly contended.

The views of Mr. Monroe upon this subject were not left to inference. During his administration, a bill was passed through both houses of Congress, conferring the jurisdiction, and prescribing the mode by which the federal government should exercise it in the case of the Cumberland road. He returned it, with objections to its passage, and, in assigning them, took occasion to say that, in the early stages of the government, he had inclined to the construction that it had no right to expend money except in the performance of acts authorized by the other specific grants of power, according to a strict construction of them ; but that, on further reflection and observation, his mind had undergone a change ; that his opinion then was, "that Congress have unlimited power to raise money, and that, in its appropriation, they have a discretionary power, restricted only by the duty to appropriate it to purposes of common defence, and of general, national, not local, or state, benefit ; " and this was avowed to be the governing principle through the residue of his administration. The views of the last administration are of such recent date as to render a particular reference to them unnecessary. It is well known that the appropriating power, to the utmost extent which had been claimed for it, in relation to internal improvements, was fully recognized and exercised by it.

This brief reference to known facts will be sufficient to show the difficulty, if not impracticability, of bringing back the operation of the government to the construction of the Constitution set up in 1798, assuming that to be its true reading, in relation to the power under consideration ; thus giving an admonitory proof of the force of implication, and the necessity of guarding the Constitution, with sleepless vigilance, against the authority of precedents which have not the sanction of its most plainly-defined powers ; for, although it is the duty of all to look to that sacred instrument, instead of the statute-book, — to repudiate, at all times, encroachments upon its spirit, which are too apt to be effected by the conjuncture of peculiar and facilitating circumstances, — it is not less true that the public good and the nature of our political institutions require that individual differences should yield to a well-settled acquiescence of the people and confederated authorities, in particular constructions of the Constitution, on doubtful points. Not to concede this much to the spirit of our institutions would impair their stability, and defeat the objects of the Constitution itself.

The only remaining view which it is my intention to present at this time, involves the expediency of embarking in a system of internal improvement, without a previous amendment of the Constitution, explaining and defining the precise powers of the federal government over it. Assuming the right to appropriate money, to aid in the construction of national works, to be warranted by the contemporaneous and continued exposition of the Constitution, its insufficiency for the successful prosecution of them must be admitted by all candid minds. If we look to usage to define the extent of the right, that will be found so variant, and embracing so much that has been overruled, as to involve the whole subject in great uncertainty, and to render the execution of our respective duties in relation to it replete with difficulty and embarrassment. It is in regard to such works, and the acquisition of additional territory, that the practice obtained its first footing. In most, if not all, other disputed questions of appropriation, the construction of the Constitution may be regarded as unsettled, if the right to apply money, in the enumerated cases, is placed on the ground of usage.

If it be the desire of the people that the agency of the federal government should be confined to the appropriation of money, in aid of such undertakings, in virtue of the state authorities, then the occasion, the manner, and the extent of the appropriations, should be made the subject of constitutional regulation. This is the more necessary, in order that they may be equitable among the several states ; promote harmony between sections of the Union and their representatives ; preserve other parts of the Constitution from being undermined by the exercise of doubtful powers, or the too great extension of those which are not so ; and protect the whole subject against the deleterious influence of combinations to carry, by concert, measures which, considered by themselves, might meet but little countenance.

That a constitutional adjustment of this power, upon equitable principles, is, in the highest degree, desirable, can scarcely be doubted ; nor can it fail to be promoted by every sincere friend to the success of our political institutions. In no government are appeals to the source of power, in cases of real doubt, more suitable than in ours. No good motive can be assigned for the exercise of power by the constituted authorities ; while those, for whose benefit it is to be exercised, have not conferred it, and may not be willing to confer it. It would seem to me that an honest application of the conceded powers of the general government to the advancement of the common weal presents a sufficient scope to satisfy a reasonable ambition. The difficulty and supposed impracticability of obtaining an amendment of the Constitution, in this respect, is, I firmly believe, in a great degree, unfounded.

In presenting these opinions, I have spoken with the freedom and candor which I thought the occasion for their expression called for ; and now respectfully *return* the bill which has been under consideration, for your further deliberation and judgment.

ANDREW JACKSON.

[General Jackson, in addition to the above, has exercised the veto power on several bills. — See APPENDIX.]

VIRGINIA RESOLUTIONS OF 1798,

PRONOUNCING THE ALIEN AND SEDITION LAWS TO BE UNCONSTITU-
TIONAL, AND DEFINING THE RIGHTS OF THE STATES.

DRAWN BY MR. MADISON.

In the Virginia House of Delegates,
Friday, *December* 21, 1798.

Resolved, That the General Assembly of Virginia doth unequivocally express a firm resolution to maintain and defend the Constitution of the United States, and the Constitution of this state, against every aggression, either foreign or domestic ; and that they will support the government of the United States in all measures warranted by the former.

That this Assembly most solemnly declares a warm attachment to the union of the states, to maintain which it pledges its powers : and that, for this end, it is their duty to watch over and oppose every infraction of those principles which constitute the only basis of that union, because a faithful observance of them can alone secure its existence and the public happiness.

That this Assembly doth explicitly and peremptorily declare, that it views the powers of the federal government as resulting from the compact to which the states are parties, as limited by the plain sense and intention of the instrument constituting that compact, as no further valid than they are authorized by the grants enumerated in that compact ; and that, in case of a deliberate, palpable, and dangerous exercise of other powers, not granted by the said compact, the states, who are parties thereto, have the right, and are in duty bound, to interpose, for arresting the progress of the evil, and for maintaining, within their respective limits, the authorities, rights, and liberties, appertaining to them.

That the General Assembly doth also express its deep regret, that a spirit has, in sundry instances, been manifested by the federal government to enlarge its powers by forced constructions of the constitutional charter which defines them ; and that indications have appeared of a design to expound certain general phrases (which, having been copied from the very lim-
ited grant of powers in the former Articles of Confederation, were the less liable to be misconstrued) so as to destroy the meaning and effect of the partic-
ular enumeration which necessarily explains and limits the general phrases, and so as to consolidate the states, by degrees, into one sovereignty, the obvious tendency and inevitable result of which would be, to transform the present republican system of the United States into an absolute, or, at best, a mixed monarchy.

That the General Assembly doth particularly PROTEST against the palpable and alarming infractions of the Constitution, in the two late cases of the "Alien and Sedition Acts," passed at the last session of Congress ; the first of which exercises a power nowhere delegated to the federal government, and which, by uniting legislative and judicial powers to those of executive, subverts the general principles of free government, as well as the particular organization and positive provisions of the Federal Constitution ; and the other of which acts exercises, in like manner, a power not delegated by the Constitution, but, on the contrary, expressly and positively forbidden by one of the amendments thereto, — a power which,

more than any other, ought to produce universal alarm, because it is levelled against the right of freely examining public characters and measures, ana of free communication among the people thereon, which has ever been justly deemed the only effectual guardian of every other right.

That this state having, by its Convention, which ratified the Federal Constitution, expressly declared that, among other essential rights, "the liberty of conscience and the press cannot be cancelled, abridged, restrained, or modified, by any authority of the United States," and from its extreme anxiety to guard these rights from every possible attack of sophistry and ambition, having, with other states, recommended an amendment for that purpose, which amendment was, in due time, annexed to the Constitution, — it would mark a reproachful inconsistency, and criminal degeneracy, if an indifference were now shown to the most palpable violation of one of the rights thus declared and secured, and to the establishment of a precedent which may be fatal to the other.

That the good people of this commonwealth, having ever felt, and continuing to feel, the most sincere affection for their brethren of the other states; the truest anxiety for establishing and perpetuating the union of all; and the most scrupulous fidelity to that Constitution, which is the pledge of mutual friendship, and the instrument of mutual happiness, — the General Assembly doth solemnly appeal to the like dispositions in the other states, in confidence that they will concur with this commonwealth in declaring, as it does hereby declare, that the acts aforesaid are unconstitutional; and that the necessary and proper measures will be taken *by each* for coöperating with this state, in maintaining unimpaired the authorities, rights, and liberties, reserved to the states respectively, or to the people.

That the governor be desired to transmit a copy of the foreging resolutions to the executive authority of each of the other states, with a request that the same may be communicated to the legislature thereof, and that a copy be furnished to each of the senators and representatives representing this state in the Congress of the United States.

Attest,   JOHN STEWART.

1798, December 24.   Agreed to by the Senate.

H. BROOKE.

A true copy from the original deposited in the office of the General Assembly.   JOHN STEWART, *Keeper of Rolls*

EXTRACTS FROM THE ADDRESS TO THE PEOPLE,

WHICH ACCOMPANIED THE FOREGOING RESOLUTIONS.

Fellow-citizens: Unwilling to shrink from our representative responsibilities, conscious of the purity of our motives, but acknowledging your right to supervise our conduct, we invite your serious attention to the emergency which dictated the subjoined resolutions. Whilst we disdain to alarm you by ill-founded jealousies, we recommend an investigation guided by the coolness of wisdom, and a decision bottomed on firmness, but tempered with moderation.

It would be perfidious in those intrusted with the GUARDIANSHIP OF THE STATE SOVEREIGNTY, and acting under the solemn obligation of the following oath, — "I do swear that I will support the Constitution of the United States," — not to warn you of encroachments, which, though clothed with the pretext of necessity, or disguised by arguments of expediency, may yet establish precedents which may ultimately devote a generous and unsuspicious people to all the consequences of usurped power.

Encroachments springing from a government WHOSE ORGANIZATION CANNOT BE MAINTAINED WITHOUT THE CO-OPERATION OF THE STATES, furnish the strongest excitements upon the state legislatures to watchfulness, and impose upon them the strongest obligation TO PRESERVE UNIMPAIRED THE LINE OF PARTITION.

The acquiescence of the states, under infractions of the federal compact, would either beget a speedy consolidation, by precipitating the state governments into impotency and contempt, or prepare the way for a revolution, by a repetition of these infractions until the people are aroused to appear in the majesty of their strength. It is to avoid these calamities that we exhibit to the people the momentous question, whether the Constitution of the United States shall yield to a construction which defies every restraint, and overwhelms the best hopes of republicanism.

Exhortations to disregard domestic usurpation, until foreign danger shall have passed, is an artifice which may be forever used; because the possessors of power, who are the advocates for its extension, can ever create national embarrassments, to be successively employed to soothe the people into sleep, whilst that power is swelling, silently, secretly, and fatally. Of the same character are insinuations of a foreign influence, which seize upon a laudable enthusiasm against danger from abroad, and distort it by an unnatural application, so as to blind your eyes against danger at home.

The Sedition Act presents a scene which was never expected by the early friends of the Constitution. It was then admitted that the state sovereignties were only diminished by powers specifically enumerated, or necessary to carry the specified powers into effect. Now, federal authority is deduced from implication; and from the existence of state law, it is inferred that Congress possess a similar power of legislation; whence Congress will be endowed with a power of legislation in all cases whatsoever, and the states will be stripped of every right reserved, by the concurrent claims of a paramount legislature.

The Sedition Act is the offspring of these tremendous pretensions, which inflict a death-wound on the sovereignty of the states.

For the honor of American understanding, we will not believe that the people have been allured into the adoption of the Constitution by an affectation of defining powers, whilst the *preamble* would admit a construction which would erect the will of Congress into a power paramount in all cases, and therefore limited in none. On the contrary, it is evident that the objects for which the Constitution was formed were deemed attainable only by a particular enumeration and specification of each power granted to the federal government; reserving all others to the people, or to the states. And yet it is in vain we search for any specified power embracing the right of legislation against the freedom of the press

Had the states been despoiled of their sovereignty by the generality of the preamble, and had the federal government been endowed with whatever they should judge to be instrumental towards the union, justice, tranquillity, common defence, general welfare, and the preservation of liberty, nothing could have been more frivolous than an enumeration of powers.

All the preceding arguments, arising from a deficiency of constitutional power in Congress, apply to the Alien Act ; and this act is liable to other objections peculiar to itself. If a suspicion that aliens are dangerous, constitutes the justification of that power exercised over them by Congress, then a similar suspicion will justify the exercise of a similar power over natives ; because there is nothing in the Constitution distinguishing between the power of a state to permit the residence of natives and aliens. It is, therefore, a right originally possessed, and never surrendered, by the respective states, and which is rendered dear and valuable to Virginia, because it is assailed through the bosom of the Constitution, and because her peculiar situation renders the easy admission of artisans and laborers an interest of vast importance.

But this bill contains other features, still more alarming and dangerous. It dispenses with the trial by jury ; it violates the judicial system ; it confounds legislative, executive, and judicial powers ; it punishes without trial ; and it bestows upon the President despotic power over a numerous class of men. Are such measures consistent with our constitutional principles ? And will an accumulation of power so extensive in the hands of the executive, over aliens, secure to natives the blessings of republican liberty ?

If measures can mould governments, and if an uncontrolled power of construction is surrendered to those who administer them, their progress may be easily foreseen, and their end easily foretold. A lover of monarchy, who opens the treasures of corruption by distributing emolument among devoted partisans, may at the same time be approaching his object and deluding the people with professions of republicanism. He may confound monarchy and republicanism, by the art of definition. He may varnish over the dexterity which ambition never fails to display, with the pliancy of language, the seduction of expediency, or the prejudices of the times ; and he may come at length to avow, that so extensive a territory as that of the United States can only be governed by the energies of monarchy ; that it cannot be defended, except by standing armies ; and that it cannot be united, except by consolidation.

Measures have already been adopted which may lead to these consequences. They consist —

In fiscal systems and arrangements, which keep a host of commercial and wealthy individuals imbodied, and obedient to the mandates of the treasury ; —

In armies and navies, which will, on the one hand, enlist the tendency of man to pay homage to his fellow-creature who can feed or honor him ; and on the other, employ the principle of fear, by punishing imaginary insurrections, under the pretext of preventive justice ; —

In swarms of officers, civil and military, who can inculcate political tenets tending to consolidation and monarchy, both by indulgences and severities, and can act as spies over the free exercise of human reason ; —

In restraining the freedom of the press, and investing the executive with legislative, executive, and judicial powers, over a numerous body of men —

Ar.d, t.at we may shorten the catalogue, in establishing, by successive precedents, such a mode of construing the Constitution as will rapidly remove every restraint upon federal power.

Let history be consulted; let the man of experience reflect; nay, let the artificers of monarchy be asked what further materials they can need for building up their favorite system.

These are solemn but painful truths; and yet we recommend it to you not to forget the possibility of danger from without, although danger threatens us from within. Usurpation is indeed dreadful; but against foreign invasion, if that should happen, let us rise with hearts and hands united, and repel the attack with the zeal of freemen who will strengthen their title to examine and correct domestic measures, by having defended their country against foreign aggression.

Pledged as we are, fellow-citizens, to these sacred engagements, we yet humbly, fervently implore the Almighty Disposer of events to avert from our land war and usurpation, the scourges of mankind; to permit our fields to be cultivated in peace; to instil into nations the love of friendly intercourse; to suffer our youth to be educated in virtue, and to preserve our morality from the pollution invariably incident to habits of war; to prevent the laborer and husbandman from being harassed by taxes and imposts; to remove from ambition the means of disturbing the commonwealth; to annihilate all pretexts for power afforded by war; to maintain the Constitution; and to bless our nation with tranquillity, under whose benign influence we may reach the summit of happiness and glory, to which we are destined by *nature* and *nature's God.*

Attest,   JOHN STEWART, *C. H. D.*

1799, January 23d.   Agreed to by the Senate.   H. BROOKE, *C. S.*

A true copy from the original deposited in the office of the General Assembly.   JOHN STEWART, *Keeper of Rolls.*

ANSWERS

OF THE SEVERAL STATE LEGISLATURES.

STATE OF DELAWARE.

IN THE HOUSE OF REPRESENTATIVES, *February* 1, 1799.

Resolved, By the Senate and House of Representatives of the state of Delaware, in General Assembly met, that they consider the resolutions from the state of Virginia as a very unjustifiable interference with the general government and constituted authorities of the United States, and of dangerous tendency, and therefore not fit subject for the further consideration of the General Assembly.

ISAAC DAVIS, *Speaker of the Senate.*

STEPHEN LEWIS, *Speaker of the House of Representatives.*

Test, JOHN FISHER, *C. S.* — JOHN CALDWELL, *C. H. R.*

STATE OF RHODE ISLAND AND PROVIDENCE PLANTATIONS.

In General Assembly, *February, A. D.* 1799.

Certain resolutions of the legislature of Virginia, passed on 21st of December last, being communicated to this Assembly, —

1. *Resolved,* That, in the opinion of this legislature, the second section of third article of the Constitution of the United States, in these words, to wit, — " The judicial power shall extend to all cases arising under the laws of the United States," — vests in the federal courts, exclusively, and in the Supreme Court of the United States, ultimately, the authority of deciding on the constitutionality of any act or law of the Congress of the United States.

2. *Resolved,* That for any state legislature to assume that authority would be —

1st.   Blending together legislative and judicial powers ;

2d.   Hazarding an interruption of the peace of the states by civil discord, in case of a diversity of opinions among the state legislatures ; each state having, in that case, no resort, for vindicating its own opinions, but the strength of its own arm ; —

3d.   Submitting most important questions of law to less competent tribunals ; and,

4th.   An infraction of the Constitution of the United States, expressed in plain terms.

3. *Resolved,* That, although, for the above reasons, this legislature, in their public capacity, do not feel themselves authorized to consider and decide on the constitutionality of the Sedition and Alien laws, (so called,) yet they are called upon, by the exigency of this occasion, to declare that, in their private opinions, these laws are within the powers delegated to Congress, and promotive of the welfare of the United States.

4. *Resolved,* That the governor communicate these resolutions to the supreme executive of the state of Virginia, and at the same time express to him that this legislature cannot contemplate, without extreme concern and regret, the many evil and fatal consequences which may flow from the very unwarrantable resolutions aforesaid of the legislature of Virginia, passed on the twenty-first day of December last.

A true copy,   SAMUEL EDDY, *Secretary,*

———

COMMONWEALTH OF MASSACHUSETTS.

In Senate, *February* 9, 1799.

The legislature of Massachusetts, having taken into serious consideration the resolutions of the state of Virginia, passed the 21st day of December last, and communicated by his excellency the governor, relative to certain supposed infractions of the Constitution of the United States, by the government thereof ; and being convinced that the Federal Constitution is calculated to promote the happiness, prosperity, and safety, of the people of these United States, and to maintain that union of the several states so essential to the welfare of the whole ; and being bound by solemn oath to support and defend that Constitution, — feel it unnecessary to make any professions of their attachment to it, or of their firm determination to support it against every aggression, foreign or domestic

But they deem it their duty solemnly to declare that, while they hold sacred the principle, that consent of the people is the only pure source of just and legitimate power, they cannot admit the right of the state legislatures to denounce the administration of that government to which the people themselves, by a solemn compact, have exclusively committed their national concerns. That, although a liberal and enlightened vigilance among the people is always to be cherished, yet an unreasonable jealousy of the men of their choice, and a recurrence to measures of extremity upon groundless or trivial pretexts, have a strong tendency to destroy all rational liberty at home, and to deprive the United States of the most essential advantages in relations abroad. That this legislature are persuaded that the decision of all cases in law and equity arising under the Constitution of the United States, and the construction of all laws made in pursuance thereof, are exclusively vested by the people in the judicial courts of the United States.

That the people, in that solemn compact which is declared to be the supreme law of the land, have not constituted the state legislatures the judges of the acts or measures of the federal government, but have confided to them the power of proposing such amendments of the Constitution as shall appear to them necessary to the interests, or conformable to the wishes, of the people whom they represent.

That, by this construction of the Constitution, an amicable and dispassionate remedy is pointed out for any evil which experience may prove to exist, and the peace and prosperity of the United States may be preserved without interruption.

But, should the respectable state of Virginia persist in the assumption of the right to declare the acts of the national government unconstitutional, and should she oppose successfully her force and will to those of the nation, the Constitution would be reduced to a mere cipher, to the form and pageantry of authority, without the energy of power; every act of the federal government which thwarted the views or checked the ambitious projects of a particular state, or of its leading and influential members, would be the object of opposition and of remonstrance; while the people, convulsed and confused by the conflict between two hostile jurisdictions, enjoying the protection of neither, would be wearied into a submission to some bold leader, who would establish himself on the ruins of both.

The legislature of Massachusetts, although they do not themselves claim the right, nor admit the authority of any of the state governments, to decide upon the constitutionality of the acts of the federal government, still, lest their silence should be construed into disapprobation, or at best into a doubt as to the constitutionality of the acts referred to by the state of Virginia; and as the General Assembly of Virginia has called for an expression of their sentiments, — do explicitly declare, that they consider the acts of Congress, commonly called " the Alien and Sedition Acts," not only constitutional, but expedient and necessary : That the former act respects a description of persons whose rights were not particularly contemplated in the Constitution of the United States, who are entitled only to a temporary protection while they yield a temporary allegiance — a protection which ought to be withdrawn whenever they become " dangerous to the public safety," or are found guilty of " treasonable machination " against the government : That Congress, having been especially intrusted by the people with the general defence of the nation, had not only the right, but were bound, to protect it against internal as well as external foes: That the United States, at the time of passing the *Act concerning Aliens*, were threatened with actual invasion ; had been driven, by the unjust and ambitious conduct of the French government, into warlike preparations, expensive and burdensome ; and had then, within the bosom of the country, thousands of aliens, who, we doubt not, were ready to coöperate in any external attack.

It cannot be seriously believed that the United States should have waited till the poniard had in fact been plunged. The removal of aliens is the usual preliminary of hostility, and is justified by the invariable usages of nations. Actual hostility had unhappily long been experienced, and a formal declaration of it the government had reason daily to expect. The law, therefore, was just and salutary ; and no officer could with so much propriety be intrusted with the execution of it, as the one in whom the Constitution has reposed the executive power of the United States.

The *Sedition Act*, so called, is, in the opinion of this legislature, equally defensible. The General Assembly of Virginia, in their resolve under consideration, observe, that when that state, by its Convention, ratified the Federal Constitution, it expressly declared, "that, among other essential rights, the liberty of conscience and of the press cannot be cancelled, abridged, restrained, or modified, by any authority of the United States," and, from its extreme anxiety to guard these rights from every possible attack of sophistry or ambition, with other states, recommended an amendment for that purpose ; which amendment was, in due time, annexed to the Constitution ; but they did not surely expect that the proceedings of their state Convention were to explain the amendment adopted by the Union. The words of that amendment, on this subject, are, " Congress shall make no law abridging the freedom of speech or of the press."

The act complained of is no abridgment of the freedom of either. The genuine liberty of speech and the press is the liberty to utter and publish the truth ; but the constitutional right of the citizen to utter and publish the truth is not to be confounded with the licentiousness, in speaking and writing, that is only employed in propagating falsehood and slander. This freedom of the press has been explicitly secured by most, if not all the state constitutions ; and of this provision there has been generally but one construction among enlightened men — that it is a security for the rational use, and not the abuse of the press ; of which the courts of law, the juries and people will judge : this right is not infringed, but confirmed and established, by the late act of Congress.

By the Constitution, the legislative, executive, and judicial departments of government are ordained and established ; and general enumerated powers vested in them respectively, including those which are prohibited to the several states. Certain powers are granted, in general terms, by the people, to their general government, for the purposes of their safety and protection. The government is not only empowered, but it is made their duty, to repel invasions and suppress insurrections ; to guaranty to the several states a republican form of government ; to protect each state against invasion, and, when applied to, against domestic violence : to hear and decide all cases in law and equity arising under the Constitution, and under any treaty or law made in pursuance thereof ; and all cases of admiralty and maritime jurisdiction, and relating to the law of nations. Whenever, therefore, it becomes necessary to effect any of the objects designated, it is perfectly consonant to all just rules of construction to infer that the usual means and powers necessary to the attainment of that object are also granted.   But the Constitution has left no occasion to resort to implication for these powers ; it has made an express grant of them, in the 8th section of the 1st article, which ordains, "that Congress shall have power to make all laws which shall be necessary and proper for carrying into execution the foregoing powers, and all other powers vested by the Constitution in the government of the United States, or in any department or officer thereof."

This Constitution has established a Supreme Court of the United States, but has made no provision for its protection, even against such improper conduct in its presence, as might disturb its proceedings, unless expressed in the section before recited.   But as no statute has been passed on this subject, this protection is, and has been for nine years past, uniformly found in the application of the principles and usages of the common law. The same protection may unquestionably be afforded by a statute passed in virtue of the before-mentioned section, as necessary and proper for carrying into execution the powers vested in that department.   A construction of the different parts of the Constitution, perfectly just and fair, will, on analogous principles, extend protection and security, against the offences in question, to the other departments of government, in discharge of their respective trusts.

The President of the United States is bound by his oath " to preserve, protect, and defend, the Constitution;" and it is expressly made his duty " to take care that the laws be faithfully executed."   But this would be impracticable by any created being, if there could be no legal restraint of those scandalous misrepresentations of his measures and motives which directly tend to rob him of the public confidence ; and equally impotent would be every other public officer, if thus left to the mercy of the seditious.

It is holden to be a truth most clear, that the important trusts before enumerated cannot be discharged by the government to which they are committed, without the power to restrain seditious practices and unlawful combinations against itself, and to protect the officers thereof from abusive misrepresentations.   Had the Constitution withheld this power, it would have made the government responsible for the effects, without any control over the causes which naturally produce them, and would have essentially failed of answering the great ends for which the people of the United States declare, in the first clause of that instrument, that they establish the same — viz., " to form a more perfect union, establish justice, insure domestic tranquillity, provide for the common defence, promote the general welfare, and secure the blessings of liberty to ourselves and posterity."

Seditious practices and unlawful combinations against the federal government, or any officer thereof, in the performance of his duty, as well as licentiousness of speech and of the press, were punishable, on the principles of common law, in the courts of the United States, before the act in question was passed.   This act, then, is an amelioration of that law in favor of the party accused, as it mitigates the punishment which that authorizes, and admits of any investigation of public men and measures which is regulated by truth.   It is not intended to protect men in office, only as they are agents of the people.   Its object is to afford legal security to public offices and trusts created for the safety and happiness of the people, and therefore the security derived from it is for the benefit of the people, and is their right.

This construction of the Constitution, and of the existing law of the land, as well as the act complained of, the legislature of Massachusetts most deliberately and firmly believe, results from a just and full view of the several parts of the Constitution ; and they consider that act to be wise and necessary, as an audacious and unprincipled spirit of falsehood and abuse had been too long unremittingly exerted for the purpose of perverting public opinion, and threatened to undermine and destroy the whole fabric of government.

The legislature further declare, that in the foregoing sentiments they have expressed the general opinion of their constituents, who have not only acquiesced without complaint in those particular measures of the federal government, but have given their explicit approbation by reëlecting those men who voted for the adoption of them. Nor is it apprehended that the citizens of this state will be accused of supineness, or of an indifference to their constitutional rights ; for while, on the one hand, they regard with due vigilance the conduct of the government, on the other, their freedom, safety, and happiness require that they should defend that government and its constitutional measures against the open or insidious attacks of any foe, whether foreign or domestic.

And, lastly, that the legislature of Massachusetts feel a strong conviction, that the several United States are connected by a common interest, which ought to render their union indissoluble ; and that this state will always coöperate with its confederate states in rendering that union productive of mutual security, freedom, and happiness.

Sent down for concurrence.   SAMUEL PHILLIPS, *President.*

In the House of Representatives, February 13, 1799.

Read and concurred.   EDWARD H. ROBBINS, *Speaker.*

A true copy.   Attest,   JOHN AVERY, *Secretary.*

STATE OF NEW YORK.

In SENATE, *March* 5, 1799.

Whereas the people of the United States have established for themselves a free and independent national government : And whereas it is essential to the existence of every government, that it have authority to defend and preserve its constitutional powers inviolate, inasmuch as every infringement thereof tends to its subversion : And whereas the judicial power extends expressly to all cases of law and equity arising under the Constitution and the laws of the United States, whereby the interference of the legislatures of the particular states in those cases is manifestly excluded : And whereas our peace, prosperity, and happiness, eminently depend on the preservation of the Union, in order to which a reasonable confidence in the constituted authorities and chosen representatives of the people is indispensable : And whereas every measure calculated to weaken that confidence has a tendency to destroy the usefulness of our public functionaries, and to excite jealousies equally hostile to rational liberty, and the principles of a good republican government : And whereas the Senate, not perceiving that the rights of the particular states have been violated, nor any unconstitutional powers assumed by the general government, cannot forbear to express the anxiety and regret with which they observe the inflammatory and pernicious sentiments and doctrines which are contained in the resolutions of the legislatures of Virginia and Kentucky — sentiments and doctrines no less repugnant to the Constitution of the United States, and the principles of their union, than destructive to the federal government, and unjust to those whom the people have elected to administer it; — wherefore

Resolved, That while the Senate feel themselves constrained to bear unequivocal testimony against such sentiments and doctrines, they deem it a duty no less indispensable explicitly to declare their incompetency, as a branch of the legislature of this state, to supervise the acts of the general government.

Resolved, That his excellency, the governor, be, and he is hereby, requested to transmit a copy of the foregoing resolution to the executives of the states of Virginia and Kentucky, to the end that the same may be communicated to the legislatures thereof.

A true copy.   ABM. B. BAUCKER, *Clerk.*

STATE OF CONNECTICUT.

At a General Assembly of the state of Connecticut, holden at Hartford, in the said state, on the second Thursday of May, Anno Domini 1799, his excellency, the governor, having communicated to this Assembly sundry resolutions of the legislature of Virginia, adopted in December, 1798, which relate to the measures of the general government, and the said resolutions having been considered, it is

Resolved, That this Assembly views with deep regret, and explicitly disavows, the principles contained in the aforesaid resolutions, and particularly the opposition to the " Alien and Sedition Acts " — acts which the Constitution authorized, which the exigency of the country rendered necessary, which the constituted authorities have enacted, and which merit the entire approbation of this Assembly. They, therefore, decidedly refuse to concur with the legislature of Virginia in promoting any of the objects attempted in the aforesaid resolutions.

And it is further resolved, That his excellency, the governor, be requested to transmit a copy of the foregoing resolution to the governor of Virginia, that it may be communicated to the legislature of that state.

Passed in the House of Representatives unanimously.

Attest,   JOHN C. SMITH, *Clerk.*

Concurred, unanimously, in the Upper House.

Teste,   SAMUEL WYLLYS, *Secretary.*

STATE OF NEW HAMPSHIRE.

IN THE HOUSE OF REPRESENTATIVES, *June* 14, 1799.

The committee to take into consideration the resolutions of the General Assembly of Virginia, dated December 21, 1798 ; also certain resolutions of the legislature of Kentucky, of the 10th November, 1798, report as follows : —

The legislature of New Hampshire, having taken into consideration certain resolutions of the General Assembly of Virginia, dated December

2!, 179?; also certain resolutions of the legislature of Kentucky, of the 1)th of November, 1798 : —

Resolved, That the legislature of New Hampshire unequivocally express a firm resolution to maintain and defend the Constitution of the United States, and the Constitution of this state, against every aggression, either foreign or domestic, and that they will support the government of the United States in all measures warranted by the former.

That the state legislatures are not the proper tribunals to determine the constitutionality of the laws of the general government; that the duty of such decision is properly and exclusively confided to the judicial department.

That, if the legislature of New Hampshire, for mere speculative purposes, were to express an opinion on the acts of the general government, commonly called " the Alien and Sedition Bills," that opinion would unreservedly be, that those acts are constitutional, and, in the present critical situation of our country, highly expedient.

That the constitutionality and expediency of the acts aforesaid have been very ably advocated and clearly demonstrated by many citizens of the United States, more especially by the minority of the General Assembly of Virginia. The legislature of New Hampshire, therefore, deem it unnecessary, by any train of arguments, to attempt further illustration of the propositions, the truth of which, it is confidently believed, at this day, is very generally seen and acknowledged.

Which report, being read and considered, was unanimously received and accepted, one hundred and thirty-seven members being present.

Sent up for concurrence.   JOHN PRENTICE, *Speaker.*

In Senate, same day, read and concurred unanimously.

AMOS SHEPARD, *President*

Approved, June 15, 1799.   J. T. GILMAN, *Governor.*

A true copy.   Attest,   JOSEPH PEARSON, *Secretary.*

STATE OF VERMONT.

In the House of Representatives, *October* 30, *A. D.* 1799.

The house proceeded to take under their consideration the resolutions of the General Assembly of Virginia, relative to certain measures of the general government, transmitted to the legislature of this state, for their consideration :   Whereupon, —

Resolved, That the General Assembly of the state of Vermont do highly disapprove of the resolutions of the General Assembly of Virginia, as being unconstitutional in their nature, and dangerous in their tendency It belongs not to state legislatures to decide on the constitutionality of 'aws made by the general government; this power being exclusively vested in the judiciary courts of the Union. That his excellency, the governor, be requested to transmit a copy of this resolution to the executive of Virginia, to be communicated to the General Assembly of that state: And that the same be sent to the governor and council for their concurrence.

SAMUEL C. CRAFTS, *Clerk.*

In Council, October 30, 1799.   Read and concurred unanimously.

RICHARD WHITNEY, *Secretary.*

KENTUCKY RESOLUTIONS OF 1798 AND 1799.

[THE ORIGINAL DRAFT PREPARED BY THOMAS JEFFERSON.]

[The following Resolutions passed the House of Representatives of Kentucky, Nov 10, 1798. On the passage of the 1st Resolution, one dissentient; 2d, 3d, 4th, 5th, 6th, 7th, 8th, two dissentients; 9th, three dissentients.]

1. *Resolved*, That the several states composing the United States of America are not united on the principle of unlimited submission to their general government; but that, by compact, under the style and title of a Constitution for the United States, and of amendments thereto, they constituted a general government for special purposes, delegated to that government certain definite powers, reserving, each state to itself, the residuary mass of right to their own self-government; and that whensoever the general government assumes undelegated powers, its acts are unauthoritative, void, and of no force; that to this compact each state acceded as a state, and is an integral party; that this government, created by this compact, was not made the exclusive or final judge of the extent of the powers delegated to itself, since that would have made its discretion, and not the Constitution, the measure of its powers; but that, as in all other cases of compact among parties having no common judge, *each party has an equal right to judge for itself, as well of infractions as of the mode and measure of redress.*

2. *Resolved*, That the Constitution of the United States having delegated to Congress a power to punish treason, counterfeiting the securities and current coin of the United States, piracies and felonies committed on the high seas, and offences against the laws of nations, and no other crimes whatever; and it being true, as a general principle, and one of the amendments to the Constitution having also declared " that the powers not delegated to the United States by the Constitution, nor prohibited by it to the states, are reserved to the states respectively, or to the people," — therefore, also, the same act of Congress, passed on the 14th day of July, 1798, and entitled " An Act in Addition to the Act entitled ' An Act for the Punishment of certain Crimes against the United States;'" as also the act passed by them on the 27th day of June, 1798, entitled " An Act to punish Frauds committed on the Bank of the United States," (and all other their acts which assume to create, define, or punish crimes other than those enumerated in the Constitution,) are altogether void, and of no force; and that the power to create, define, and punish, such other crimes is reserved, and of right appertains, solely and exclusively, to the respective states, each within its own territory.

3. *Resolved*, That it is true, as a general principle, and is also expressly declared by one of the amendments to the Constitution, that " the powers not delegated to the United States by the Constitution, nor prohibited by it to the states, are reserved to the states respectively, or to the people; " and that, no power over the freedom of religion, freedom of speech, or freedom of the press, being delegated to the United States by the Constitution, nor prohibited by it to the states, all lawful powers respecting the same did of right remain, and were reserved to the states, or to the people; that thus was manifested their determination to retain to themselves the right of

judging how far the licentiousness of speech, and of the press, may be abridged without lessening their useful freedom, and how far those abuses which cannot be separated from their use, should be tolerated rather than the use be destroyed; and thus also they guarded against all abridgment, by the United States, of the freedom of religious principles and exercises, and retained to themselves the right of protecting the same, as this, stated by a law passed on the general demand of its citizens, had already protected them from all human restraint or interference; and that, in addition to this general principle and express declaration, another and more special provision has been made by one of the amendments to the Constitution, which expressly declares, that "Congress shall make no laws respecting an establishment of religion, or prohibiting the free exercise thereof, or abridging the freedom of speech, or of the press," thereby guarding, in the same sentence, and under the same words, the freedom of religion, of speech, and of the press, insomuch that whatever violates either throws down the sanctuary which covers the others, — and that libels, falsehood, and defamation, equally with heresy and false religion, are withheld from the cognizance of federal tribunals. That therefore the act of the Congress of the United States, passed on the 14th of July, 1798, entitled " An Act in Addition to the Act entitled ' An Act for the Punishment of certain Crimes against the United States,' " which does abridge the freedom of the press, is not law, but is altogether void, and of no force.

4. *Resolved*, That alien friends are under the jurisdiction and protection of the laws of the state wherein they are; that no power over them has been delegated to the United States, nor prohibited to the individual states, distinct from their power over citizens; and it being true, as a general principle, and one of the amendments to the Constitution having also declared, that " the powers not delegated to the United States by the Constitution, nor prohibited to the states, are reserved to the states, respectively, or to the people," the act of the Congress of the United States, passed the 22d day of June, 1798, entitled " An Act concerning Aliens," which assumes power over alien friends not delegated by the Constitution, is not law, but is altogether void and of no force.

5. *Resolved*, That, in addition to the general principle, as well as the express declaration, that powers not delegated are reserved, another and more special provision inserted in the Constitution from abundant caution, has declared, " that the migration or importation of such persons as any of the states now existing shall think proper to admit, shall not be prohibited by the Congress prior to the year 1808." That this commonwealth does admit the migration of alien friends described as the subject of the said act concerning aliens; that a provision against prohibiting their migration is a provision against all acts equivalent thereto, or it would be nugatory; that to remove them, when migrated, is equivalent to a prohibition of their migration, and is, therefore, contrary to the said provision of the Constitution, and *void*.

6. *Resolved*, That the imprisonment of a person under the protection of the laws of this commonwealth, on his failure to obey the simple order of the President to depart out of the United States, as is undertaken by the said act, entitled, " An Act concerning Aliens," is contrary to the Constitution, one amendment in which has provided, that " no person shall be deprived of liberty without due process of law ;" and that another having provided, " that, in all criminal prosecutions, the accused shall enjoy the right of a public trial by an impartial jury, to be informed as to

46

the nature and cause of the accusation, to be confronted with the witnesses against him, to have compulsory process for obtaining witnesses in his favor, and to have assistance of counsel for his defence," the same act undertaking to authorize the President to remove a person out of the United States who is under the protection of the law, on his own suspicion, without jury, without public trial, without confrontation of the witnesses against him, without having witnesses in his favor, without defence, without counsel — contrary to these provisions also of the Constitution — is therefore not law, but utterly void, and of no force.

That transferring the power of judging any person who is under the protection of the laws, from the courts to the President of the United States, as is undertaken by the same act concerning aliens, is against the article of the Constitution which provides, that " the judicial power of the United States shall be vested in the courts, the judges of which shall hold their office during good behavior," and that the said act is void for that reason also; and it is further to be noted that this transfer of judiciary power is to that magistrate of the general government who already possesses all the executive, and a qualified negative in all the legislative powers.

7. *Resolved,* That the construction applied by the general government (as is evident by sundry of their proceedings) to those parts of the Constitution of the United States which delegate to Congress power to lay and collect taxes, duties, imposts, excises ; to pay the debts, and provide for the common defence and general welfare, of the United States, and to make all laws which shall be necessary and proper for carrying into execution the powers vested by the Constitution in the government of the United States, or any department thereof, goes to the destruction of all the limits prescribed to their power by the Constitution ; that words meant by that instrument to be subsidiary only to the execution of the limited powers, ought not to be so construed as themselves to give unlimited powers, nor a part so to be taken as to destroy the whole residue of the instrument ; that the proceedings of the general government, under color of those articles, will be a fit and necessary subject for revisal and correction at a time of greater tranquillity, while those specified in the preceding resolutions call for immediate redress.

8. *Resolved,* That the preceding resolutions be transmitted to the senators and representatives in Congress from this commonwealth, who are enjoined to present the same to their respective houses, and to use their best endeavors to procure, at the next session of Congress, a repeal of the aforesaid unconstitutional and obnoxious acts.

9. *Resolved,* lastly, That the governor of this commonwealth be, and is, authorized and requested to communicate the preceding resolutions to the legislatures of the several states, to assure them that this commonwealth considers union for special national purposes, and particularly for those specified in their late federal compact, to be friendly to the peace, happiness, and prosperity, of all the states : that, faithful to that compact, according to the plain intent and meaning in which it was understood and acceded to by the several parties, it is sincerely anxious for its preservation ; that it does also believe, that, to take from the states all the powers of self-government, and transfer them to a general and consolidated government, without regard to the special government, and reservations solemnly agreed to in that compact, is not for the peace, happiness, or prosperity of these states ; and that, therefore, this commonwealth is

determined, as it doubts not its co-states are, to submit to undelegated and consequently unlimited powers in no man, or body of men, on earth ; that, if the acts before specified should stand, these conclusions would flow from them — that the general government may place any act they think proper on the list of crimes, and punish it themselves, whether enumerated or not enumerated by the Constitution as cognizable by them ; that they may transfer its cognizance to the President, or any other person, who may himself be the accuser, counsel, judge, and jury, whose suspicions may be the evidence, his order the sentence, his officer the executioner, and his breast the sole record of the transaction ; that a very numerous and valuable description of the inhabitants of these states, being, by this precedent, reduced, as outlaws, to absolute dominion of one man, and the barriers of the Constitution thus swept from us all, no rampart now remains against the passions and the power of a majority of Congress, to protect from a like exportation, or other grievous punishment, the minority of the same body, the legislatures, judges, governors, and counsellors of the states, nor their other peaceable inhabitants, who may venture to reclaim the constitutional rights and liberties of the states and people, or who, for other causes, good or bad, may be obnoxious to the view, or marked by the suspicions, of the President, or be thought dangerous to his or their elections, or other interests, public or personal ; that the friendless alien has been selected as the safest subject of a first experiment ; but the citizen will soon follow, or rather has already followed ; for already has a Sedition Act marked him as a prey : That these and successive acts of the same character, unless arrested on the threshold, may tend to drive these states into revolution and blood, and will furnish new calumnies against republican governments, and new pretexts for those who wish it to be believed that man cannot be governed but by a rod of iron ; that it would be a dangerous delusion were a confidence in the men of our choice to silence our fears for the safety of our rights ; that confidence is every where the parent of despotism ; free government is founded in jealousy, and not in confidence ; it is jealousy, and not confidence, which prescribes limited constitutions to bind down those whom we are obliged to trust with power ; that our Constitution has accordingly fixed the limits to which, and no farther, our confidence may go ; and let the honest advocate of confidence read the Alien and Sedition Acts, and say if the Constitution has not been wise in fixing limits to the government it created, and whether we should be wise in destroying those limits : let him say what the government is, if it be not a tyranny, which the men of our choice have conferred on the President, and the President of our choice has assented to and accepted, over the friendly strangers, to whom the mild spirit of our country and its laws had pledged hospitality and protection ; that the men of our choice have more respected the bare suspicions of the President than the solid rights of innocence, the claims of justification, the sacred force of truth, and the forms and substance of law and justice.

In questions of power, then, let no more be said of confidence in man, but bind him down from mischief by the chains of the Constitution. That this commonwealth does therefore call on its co-states for an expression of their sentiments on the acts concerning aliens, and for the punishment of certain crimes herein before specified, plainly declaring whether these acts are or are not authorized by the federal compact. And it doubts not that their sense will be so announced as to prove their attachment to lim ated government, whether general or particular, and that the rights and liberties of their co-states will be exposed to no dangers by remaining embarked on a common bottom with their own ; but they will concur with this commonwealth in considering the said acts as so palpably against the Constitution as to amount to an undisguised declaration, that the compact is not meant to be the measure of the powers of the general government, but that it will proceed in the exercise over these states of all powers whatsoever. That they will view this as seizing the rights of the states, and consolidating them in the hands of the general government, with a power assumed to bind the states, not merely in cases made federal, but in all cases whatsoever, by laws made, not with their consent, but by others against their consent ; that this would be to surrender the form of government we have chosen, and live under one deriving its powers from its own will, and not from our authority; and that the co-states, recurring to their natural rights not made federal, will concur in declaring these void and of no force, and will each unite with this commonwealth in requesting their repeal at the next session of Congress.

EDMUND BULLOCK, *S. H. R.*
JOHN CAMPBELL, *S. S. P. T.*
Passed the House of Representatives, Nov. 10, 1798.
Attest,   THO'S. TODD, *C. H. R.*
In Senate, Nov. 13, 1798 — Unanimously concurred in.
Attest,   B. THURSTON, *C. S.*
Approved, November 19, 1798.
JAMES GARRARD, *Governor of Kentucky.*
By the Governor,   HARRY TOULMIN, *Secretary of State.*

HOUSE OF REPRESENTATIVES, *Thursday, Nov. 14, 1799.*

The house, according to the standing order of the day, resolved itself into a committee of the whole house, on the state of the commonwealth, (Mr. Desha in the chair,) and, after some time spent therein, the speaker resumed the chair, and Mr. Desha reported, that the committee had taken under consideration sundry resolutions passed by several state legislatures, on the subject of the Alien and Sedition Laws, and had come to a resolution thereupon, which he delivered in at the clerk's table, where it was read and *unanimously* agreed to by the house, as follows : —

The representatives of the good people of this commonwealth, in General Assembly convened, having maturely considered the answers of sundry states in the Union to their resolutions, passed the last session, respecting certain unconstitutional laws of Congress, commonly called the Alien and Sedition Laws, would be faithless, indeed, to themselves, and to those they represent, were they silently to acquiesce in the principles and doctrines attempted to be maintained in all those answers, that of Virginia only excepted. To again enter the field of argument, and attempt more fully or forcibly to expose the unconstitutionality of those obnoxious laws, would, it is apprehended, be as unnecessary as unavailing. We cannot, however, but lament that, in the discussion of those interesting subjects by sundry of the legislatures of our sister states, unfounded suggestions and uncandid insinuations, derogatory to the true character and principles of this commonwealth, have been substituted in place of fair reasoning and sound argument. Our opinions of these alarming measures of the general government, together with our reasons for those opinions, were detailed with decency and with temper, and submitted to the discussion and judgment of our fellow-citizens throughout the Union. Whether the like decency and temper have been observed in the answers of most of those states who have denied, or attempted to obviate, the great truths contained in those resolutions, we have now only to submit to a candid world. Faithful to the true principles of the federal Union, unconscious of any designs to disturb the harmony of that Union, and anxious only to escape the fangs of despotism, the good people of this commonwealth are regardless of censure or calumniation. Lest, however, the silence of this commonwealth should be construed into an acquiescence in the doctrines and principles advanced, and attempted to be maintained, by the said answers; or at least those of our fellow-citizens, throughout the Union, who so widely differ from us on those important subjects, should be deluded by the expectation that we shall be deterred from what we conceive our duty, or shrink from the principles contained in those resolutions, — therefore,

Resolved, That this commonwealth considers the federal Union, upon the terms and for the purposes specified in the late compact, conducive to the liberty and happiness of the several states: That it does now unequivocally declare its attachment to the Union, and to that compact, agreeably to its obvious and real intention, and will be among the last to seek its dissolution: That, if those who administer the general government be permitted to transgress the limits fixed by that compact, by a total disregard to the special delegations of power therein contained, an annihilation of the state governments, and the creation, upon their ruins, of a general consolidated government, will be the inevitable consequence: That the principle and construction, contended for by sundry of the state legislatures, that the general government is the exclusive judge of the extent of the powers delegated to it, stop not short of *despotism* — since the discretion of those who administer the government, and not the *Constitution*, would be the measure of their powers: That the several states who formed that instrument, being sovereign and independent, have the unquestionable right to judge of the infraction: and, *That a nullification, by those sovereignties, of all unauthorized acts done under color of that instrument, is the rightful remedy:* That this commonwealth does, under the most deliberate reconsideration, declare, that the said Alien and Sedition Laws are, in their opinion, palpable violations of the said Constitution; and, however cheerfully it may be disposed to surrender its opinion to a majority of its sister states, in matters of ordinary or doubtful policy, yet, in momentous regulations like the present, which so vitally wound the best rights of the citizen, it would consider a silent acquiescence as highly criminal: That, although this commonwealth, as a party to the federal compact, will bow to the laws of the Union, yet it does, at the same time, declare, that it will not now, or ever hereafter, cease to oppose, in a constitutional manner, every attempt, at what quarter soever offered, to violate that compact: And finally, in order that no pretext or arguments may be drawn from a supposed acquiescence, on the part of this commonwealth, in the constitutionality of those laws, and be thereby used as precedents for similar future violations of the federal compact, this commonwealth does now enter against them its solemn PROTEST.

Extract, &c. Attest, THOMAS TODD, *C. H. R.*
In Senate, *Nov.* 22, 1799. — Read and concurred in.
Attest, B. THURSTON, *C. S.*

MADISON'S REPORT on the VIRGINIA RESOLUTIONS.

HOUSE OF DELEGATES, Session of 1799—1800.

Report of the Committee to whom were referred the Communications of various States, relative to the Resolutions of the last General Assembly of this State, concerning the Alien and Sedition Laws.

Whatever room might be found in the proceedings of some of the states, who have disapproved of the resolutions of the General Assembly of this commonwealth, passed on the 21st day of December, 1798, for painful remarks on the spirit and manner of those proceedings, it appears to the committee most consistent with the duty, as well as dignity, of the General Assembly, to hasten an oblivion of every circumstance which might be construed into a diminution of mutual respect, confidence, and affection, among the members of the Union.

The committee have deemed it a more useful task to revise, with a critical eye, the resolutions which have met with their disapprobation ; to examine fully the several objections and arguments which have appeared against them ; and to inquire whether there can be any errors of fact, of principle, or of reasoning, which the candor of the General Assembly ought to acknowledge and correct.

The *first* of the resolutions is in the words following : —

" *Resolved*, That the General Assembly of Virginia doth unequivocally express a firm resolution to maintain and defend the Constitution of the United States, and the Constitution of this state, against every aggression, either foreign or domestic ; and that they will support the government of the United States in all measures warranted by the former."

No unfavorable comment can have been made on the sentiments here expressed. To maintain and defend the Constitution of the United States, and of their own state, against every aggression, both foreign and domestic, and to support the government of the United States in all measures warranted by their Constitution, are duties which the General Assembly ought always to feel, and to which, on such an occasion, it was evidently proper to express their sincere and firm adherence.

In their *next* resolution —

" The General Assembly most solemnly declares a warm attachment to the union of the states, to maintain which it pledges all its powers ; and that, for this end, it is their duty to watch over and oppose every infraction of those principles which constitute the only basis of that Union, because a faithful observance of them can alone secure its existence and the public happiness "

The observation just made is equally applicable to this solemn declaration of warm attachment to the Union, and this solemn pledge to maintain it ; nor can any question arise among enlightened friends of the Union, as to the duty of watching over and opposing every infraction of those principles which constitute its basis, and a faithful observance of which can alone secure its existence, and the public happiness thereon depending.

The *third* resolution is in the words following : —

" That this Assembly doth explicitly and peremptorily declare, that it views the powers of the federal government, as resulting from the compact to which the states are parties, as limited by the plain sense and intention of the instrument constituting that compact — as no further valid than they are authorized by the grants enumerated in that compact; and that, in case of a deliberate, palpable, and dangerous exercise of other powers, not granted by the said compact, the states who are parties thereto have the right, and are in duty bound, to interpose, for arresting the progress of the evil and for maintaining, within their respective limits, the authorities, rights, and liberties, appertaining to them."

On this resolution the committee have bestowed all the attention which its importance merits. They have *scanned* it not merely with a strict, but with a severe eye; and they feel confidence in pronouncing that, in its just and fair construction, it is unexceptionably true in its several positions, as well as constitutional and conclusive in its inferences.

The resolution declares, *first,* that "it views the powers of the federal government as resulting from the compact to which the states are parties;" in other words, that the federal powers are derived from the Constitution; and that the Constitution is a compact to which the states are parties.

Clear as the position must seem, that the federal powers are derived from the Constitution, and from that alone, the committee are not unapprized of a late doctrine which opens another source of federal powers, not less extensive and important than it is new and unexpected. The examination of this doctrine will be most conveniently connected with a review of a succeeding resolution. The committee satisfy themselves here with briefly remarking that, in all the contemporary discussions and comments which the Constitution underwent, it was constantly justified and recommended on the ground that the powers not given to the government were withheld from it; and that, if any doubt could have existed on this subject, under the original text of the Constitution, it is removed, as far as words could remove it, by the 12th amendment, now a part of the Constitution, which expressly declares, " that the powers not delegated to the United States by the Constitution, nor prohibited by it to the states, are reserved to the states respectively, or to the people."

The other position involved in this branch of the resolution, namely, "that the states are parties to the Constitution," or compact, is, in the judgment of the committee, equally free from objection. It is indeed true that the term "states" is sometimes used in a vague sense, and sometimes in different senses, according to the subject to which it is applied. Thus it sometimes means the separate sections of territory occupied by the political societies within each; sometimes the particular governments established by those societies; sometimes those societies as organized into those particular governments; and lastly, it means the people composing those political societies, in their highest sovereign capacity. Although it might be wished that the perfection of language admitted less diversity in the signification of the same words, yet little inconvenience is produced by it, where the true sense can be collected with certainty from the different applications. In the present instance, whatever different construction of the term "states," in the resolution, may have been entertained, all will at least concur in that last mentioned; because in that sense the Constitution was submitted to the "states;" in that sense the "states" ratified it; and in that sense of the term "states," they are consequently parties to the compact from which the powers of the federal government result.

The next position is, that the General Assembly views the powers of the federal government "as limited by the plain sense and intention of the instrument constituting that compact," and "as no further valid than they are authorized by the grants therein enumerated." It does not seem possible that any just objection can lie against either of these clauses

The first amounts merely to a declaration that the compact ought to have the interpretation plainly intended by the parties to it; the other, to a declaration that it ought to have the execution and effect intended by them. If the powers granted be valid, it is solely because they are granted; and if the granted powers are valid because granted, all other powers not granted must not be valid.

The resolution, having taken this view of the federal compact, proceeds to infer, "That, in case of a deliberate, palpable, and dangerous exercise of other powers, not granted by the said compact, the states, who are parties thereto, have the right, and are in duty bound, to interpose for arresting the progress of the evil, and for maintaining, within their respective limits, the authorities, rights, and liberties, appertaining to them."

It appears to your committee to be a plain principle, founded in common sense, illustrated by common practice, and essential to the nature of compacts, that, where resort can be had to no tribunal superior to the authority of the parties, the parties themselves must be the rightful judges, in the last resort, whether the bargain made has been pursued or violated. The Constitution of the United States was formed by the sanction of the states, given by each in its sovereign capacity. It adds to the stability and dignity, as well as to the authority, of the Constitution, that it rests on this legitimate and solid foundation. The states, then, being the parties to the constitutional compact, and in their sovereign capacity, it follows of necessity that there can be no tribunal, above their authority, to decide, in the last resort, whether the compact made by them be violated; and consequently, that, as the parties to it, they must themselves decide, in the last resort, such questions as may be of sufficient magnitude to require their interposition.

It does not follow, however, because the states, as sovereign parties to their constitutional compact, must ultimately decide whether it has been violated, that such a decision ought to be interposed either in a hasty manner or on doubtful and inferior occasions. Even in the case of ordinary conventions between different nations, where, by the strict rule of interpretation, a breach of a part may be deemed a breach of the whole, — every part being deemed a condition of every other part, and of the whole, — it is always laid down that the breach must be both wilful and material, to justify an application of the rule. But in the case of an intimate and constitutional union, like that of the United States, it is evident that the interposition of the parties, in their sovereign capacity, can be called for by occasions only deeply and essentially affecting the vital principles of their political system.

The resolution has, accordingly, guarded against any misapprehension of its object, by expressly requiring, for such an interposition, "the case of a deliberate, palpable, and dangerous breach of the Constitution, by the exercise of powers not granted by it." It must be a case not of a light and transient nature, but of a nature dangerous to the great purposes for which the Constitution was established. It must be a case, moreover, not obscure or doubtful in its construction, but plain and palpable. Lastly, it must be a case not resulting from a partial consideration or hasty determination, but a case stamped with a final consideration and deliberate adherence. It is not necessary, because the resolution does not require, that the question should be discussed, how far the exercise of any particular power, ungranted by the Constitution, would justify the interposition of the parties to it. As cases might easily be stated, which none would contend ought to fall within that description, — cases, on the other hand, might, with equal ease, be stated, so flagrant and so fatal as to unite every opinion in placing them within the description.

But the resolution has done more than guard against misconstruction, by expressly referring to cases of a deliberate, palpable, and dangerous nature. It specifies the object of the interposition, which it contemplates to be solely that of arresting the progress of the evil of usurpation, and of maintaining the authorities, rights, and liberties, appertaining to the states as parties to the Constitution.

From this view of the resolution, it would seem inconceivable that it can incur any just disapprobation from those who, laying aside all momentary impressions, and recollecting the genuine source and object of the Federal Constitution, shall candidly and accurately interpret the meaning of the General Assembly. If the deliberate exercise of dangerous powers, palpably withheld by the Constitution, could not justify the parties to it in interposing even so far as to arrest the progress of the evil, and thereby to preserve the Constitution itself, as well as to provide for the safety of the parties to it, there would be an end to all relief from usurped power, and a direct subversion of the rights specified or recognized under all the state constitutions, as well as a plain denial of the fundamental principle on which our independence itself was declared.

But it is objected, that the judicial authority is to be regarded as the sole expositor of the Constitution in the last resort; and it may be asked for what reason the declaration by the General Assembly, supposing it to be theoretically true, could be required at the present day, and in so solemn a manner.

On this objection it might be observed, first, that there may be instances of usurped power, which the forms of the Constitution would never draw within the control of the judicial department; secondly, that, if the decision of the judiciary be raised above the authority of the sovereign parties to the Constitution, the decisions of the other departments, not carried by the forms of the Constitution before the judiciary, must be equally authoritative and final with the decisions of that department. But the proper answer to the objection is, that the resolution of the General Assembly relates to those great and extraordinary cases, in which all the forms of the Constitution may prove ineffectual against infractions dangerous to the essential rights of the parties to it. The resolution supposes that dangerous powers, not delegated, may not only be usurped and executed by the other departments, but that the judicial department, also, may exercise or sanction dangerous powers beyond the grant of the Constitution; and, consequently, that the ultimate right of the parties to the Constitution, to judge whether the compact has been dangerously violated, must extend to violations by one delegated authority as well as by another — by the judiciary as well as by the executive, or the legislature.

However true, therefore, it may be, that the judicial department is, in all questions submitted to it by the forms of the Constitution, to decide in the last resort, this resort must necessarily be deemed the last in relation to the authorities of the other departments of the government; not in relation to the rights of the parties to the constitutional compact, from which the judicial, as well as the other departments, hold their delegated trusts. On any other hypothesis, the delegation of judicial power would annul the authority delegating it; and the concurrence of this department with the others in usurped powers, might subvert forever, and beyond the possible

reach of any rightful remedy, the very Constitution which all were instituted to preserve.

The truth declared in the resolution being established, the expediency
of making the declaration at the present day may safely be left to the temperate consideration and candid judgment of the American public.   It
will be remembered, that a frequent recurrence to fundamental principles
is solemnly enjoined by most of the state constitutions, and particularly
by our own, as a necessary safeguard against the danger of degeneracy, to
which republics are liable, as well as other governments, though in a less
degree than others.   And a fair comparison of the political doctrines not
unfrequent at the present day, with those which characterized the epoch
of our revolution, and which form the basis of our republican constitutions, will best determine whether the declaratory recurrence here made
to those principles ought to be viewed as unseasonable and improper, or
as a vigilant discharge of an important duty.   The authority of constitutions over governments, and of the sovereignty of the people over constitutions, are truths which are at all times necessary to be kept in mind;
and at no time, perhaps, more necessary than at present.

The fourth resolution stands as follows: —

" That the General Assembly doth also express its deep regret, that a spirit has, in
sundry instances, been manifested by the federal government, to enlarge its powers by
forced constructions of the constitutional charter which defines them; and that indications have appeared of a design to expound certain general phrases (which having
been copied from the very limited grant of powers in the former Articles of Confed-
ation, were the less liable to be misconstrued) so as to destroy the meaning and effect
of the particular enumeration which necessarily explains and limits the general
phrases, and so as to consolidate the states, by degrees, into one sovereignty, the obvious tendency and inevitable result of which would be to transform the present republican system of the United States into an absolute, or at best a mixed monarchy."

The *first* question here to be considered is, whether a spirit has, in sundry instances, been manifested by the federal government to enlarge its
powers by forced constructions of the constitutional charter.

The General Assembly having declared their opinion, merely, by regret-
ting, in general terms, that forced constructions for enlarging the federal
powers have taken place, it does not appear to the committee necessary to
go into a specification of every instance to which the resolution may allude.
The Alien and Sedition Acts, being particularly named in a succeeding
resolution, are of course to be understood as included in the allusion.
Omitting others which have less occupied public attention, or been less
extensively regarded as unconstitutional, the resolution may be presumed
to refer particularly to the bank law, which, from the circumstances of its
passage, as well as the latitude of construction on which it is founded,
strikes the attention with singular force, and the carriage tax, distinguished
also by circumstances in its history having a similar tendency.   Those
instances alone, if resulting from forced construction, and calculated to
enlarge the powers of the federal government, — as the committee cannot
but conceive to be the case, — sufficiently warrant this part of the resolution.   The committee have not thought it incumbent on them to extend
their attention to laws which have been objected to rather as varying the
constitutional distribution of powers in the federal government, than as an
absolute enlargement of them; because instances of this sort, however
important in their principles and tendencies, do not appear to fall strictly
within the text under view.

The other questions presenting themselves are, ¹ Whether indications have appeared of a design to expound certain general phrases, copied from the " Articles of Confederation," so as to destroy the effect of the particular enumeration explaining and limiting their meaning ; 2. Whether this exposition would, by degrees, consolidate the states into one sovereignty ; 3. Whether the tendency and result of this consolidation would be to transform the republican system of the United States into a monarchy.

1. The general phrases here meant must be those " of providing for the common defence and general welfare."

In the " Articles of Confederation," the phrases are used as follows, in Art. VIII. : " All charges of war, and all other expenses that shall be incurred for the common defence and general welfare, and allowed by the United States in Congress assembled, shall be defrayed out of a common treasury, which shall be supplied by the several states, in proportion to the value of all land within each state, granted to or surveyed for any person, as such land, and the buildings and improvements thereon, shall be estimated, according to such mode as the United States in Congress assembled shall, from time to time, direct and appoint."

In the existing Constitution, they make the following part of sect. 8 : " The Congress shall have power to lay and collect taxes, duties, imposts, and excises ; to pay the debts, and provide for the common defence and general welfare, of the United States."

This similarity in the use of these phrases, in the two great federal charters, might well be considered as rendering their meaning less liable to be misconstrued in the latter ; because it will scarcely be said, that in the former they were ever understood to be either a general grant of power, or to authorize the requisition or application of money, by the old Congress, to the common defence and general welfare, except in cases afterwards enumerated, which explained and limited their meaning ; and if such was the limited meaning attached to these phrases in the .very instrument revised and remodelled by the present Constitution, it can never be supposed that, when copied into this Constitution, a different meaning ought to be attached to them.

That, notwithstanding this remarkable security against misconstruction, a design has been indicated to expound these phrases, in the Constitution, so as to destroy the effect of the particular enumeration of powers by which it explains and limits them, must have fallen under the observation of those who have attended to the course of public transactions. Not to multiply proofs on this subject, it will suffice to refer to the debates of the federal legislature, in which arguments have, on different occasions, been drawn, with apparent effect, from these phrases, in their indefinite meaning.

To these indications might be added, without looking farther, the official report on manufacutures by the late secretary of the treasury, made on the 5th of December, 1791, and the report of a committee of Congress, in January, 1797, on the promotion of agriculture. In the first of these it is expressly contended to belong " to the discretion of the national legislature to pronounce upon the objects which concern the general welfare, and for which, under that description, an appropriation of money is requisite and proper. And there seems to be no room for a doubt, that whatever concerns the general interests of learning, of agriculture, of manufactures, and of commerce, is within the sphere of national councils as far as regards an application of money." The latter report assumes the same latitude of power in the national councils, and applies it to the encouragement of agriculture, by means of a society to be established at the seat of government.   Although neither of these reports may have received the sanction of a law carrying it into effect, yet, on the other hand, the extraordinary doctrine contained in both has passed without the slightest positive mark of disapprobation from the authority to which it was addressed.

Now, whether the phrases in question be construed to authorize every measure relating to the common defence and general welfare, as contended by some, or every measure only in which there might be an application of money, as suggested by the caution of others, — the effect must substantially be the same, in destroying the import and force of the particular enumeration of powers which follows these general phrases in the Constitution; for it is evident that there is not a single power whatever which may not have some reference to the common defence or the general welfare; nor a power of any magnitude which, in its exercise, does not involve, or admit, an application of money.   The government, therefore, which possesses power in either one or other of these extents, is a government without the limitations formed by a particular enumeration of powers; and, consequently, the meaning and effect of this particular enumeration is destroyed by the exposition given to these general phrases.

This conclusion will not be affected by an attempt to qualify the power over the "general welfare," by referring it to cases where the general welfare is beyond the reach of the separate provisions by the individual states, and leaving to these their jurisdiction in cases to which their separate provisions may be competent; for, as the authority of the individual states must in all cases be incompetent to general regulations operating through the whole, the authority of the United States would be extended to every object relating to the general welfare, which might, by any possibility, be provided for by the general authority.   This qualifying construction, therefore, would have little, if any, tendency to circumscribe the power claimed under the latitude of the term "general welfare."

The true and fair construction of this expression, both in the original and existing federal compacts, appears to the committee too obvious to be mistaken.   In both, the Congress is authorized to provide money for the common defence and general welfare.   In both is subjoined to this authority an enumeration of the cases to which their powers shall extend.   Money cannot be applied to the general welfare, otherwise than by an application of it to some particular measure, conducive to the general welfare.   Whenever, therefore, money has been raised by the general authority, and is to be applied to a particular measure, a question arises whether the particular measure be within the enumerated authorities vested in Congress.   If it be, the money requisite for it may be applied to it.   If it be not, no such application can be made.   This fair and obvious interpretation coincides with, and is enforced by, the clause in the Constitution which declares that "no money shall be drawn from the treasury but in consequence of appropriations made by law."   An appropriation of money to the general welfare would be deemed rather a mockery than an observance of this constitutional injunction.

2. Whether the exposition of the general phrases here combated would not, by degrees, consolidate the states into one sovereignty, is a question concerning which the committee can perceive little room for difference of opinion.   To consolidate the states into one sovereignty nothing more

can be wanted than to supersede their respective sovereignties, in the cases reserved to them, by extending the sovereignty of the United States to all cases of the "general welfare"—that is to say, to all cases whatever.

3. That the obvious tendency, and inevitable result, of a consolidation of the states into one sovereignty, would be to transform the republican system of the United States into a monarchy, is a point which seems to have been sufficiently decided by the general sentiment of America. In almost every instance of discussion relating to the consolidation in question, its certain tendency to pave the way to monarchy seems not to have been contested. The prospect of such a consolidation has formed the only topic of controversy. It would be unnecessary, therefore, for the committee to dwell long on the reasons which support the position of the General Assembly. It may not be improper, however, to remark two consequences, evidently flowing from an extension of the federal power to every subject falling within the idea of the "general welfare."

One consequence must be, to enlarge the sphere of discretion allotted to the executive magistrate. Even within the legislative limits properly defined by the Constitution, the difficulty of accommodating legal regulations to a country so great in extent, and so various in its circumstances, had been much felt, and has led to occasional investments of power in the executive, which involve perhaps as large a portion of discretion as can be deemed consistent with the nature of the executive trust. In proportion as the objects of legislative care might be multiplied, would the time allowed for each be diminished, and the difficulty of providing uniform and particular regulations for all be increased. From these sources would necessarily ensue a greater latitude to the agency of that department which is always in existence, and which could best mould regulations of a general nature, so as to suit them to the diversity of particular situations. And it is in this latitude, as a supplement to the deficiency of the laws, that the degree of executive prerogative materially consists.

The other consequence would be, that of an excessive augmentation of the offices, honors, and emoluments, depending on the executive will. Add to the present legitimate stock all those, of every description, which a consolidation of the states would take from them, and turn over to the federal government, and the patronage of the executive would necessarily be as much swelled, in this case, as its prerogative would be in the other.

This disproportionate increase of prerogative and patronage must evidently either enable the chief magistrate of the Union, by quiet means, to secure his reëlection from time to time, and finally to regulate the succession as he might please; or, by giving so transcendent an importance to the office, would render the election to it so violent and corrupt, that the public voice itself might call for an hereditary in place of an elective succession. Whichever of these events might follow, the transformation of the republican system of the United States into a monarchy, anticipated by the General Assembly from a consolidation of the states into one sovereignty, would be equally accomplished; and whether it would be into a mixed or an absolute monarchy, might depend on too many contingencies to admit of any certain foresight.

The resolution next in order is contained in the following terms:—

"That the General Assembly doth particularly protest against the palpable and alarming infractions of the Constitution, in the two late cases of the ' Alien and Sedition Acts,' passed at the last session of Congress; the first of which exercises a power nowhere delegated to the federal government; and which, by uniting legislative and judicial powers to those of the executive, subverts the general principles of free government, as well as the particular organization and positive provisions of the Federal Constitution; and the other of which acts exercises, in like manner, a power not delegated by the Constitution, but, on the contrary, expressly and positively forbidden by one of the amendments thereto — a power which, more than any other, ought to produce universal alarm, because it is levelled against the right of freely examining public characters and measures, and of free communication among the people thereon, which has ever been justly deemed the only effectual guardian of every other right."

The subject of this resolution having, it is presumed, more particularly led the General Assembly into the proceedings which they communicated to the other states, and being in itself of peculiar importance, it deserves the most critical and faithful investigation; for the length of which no apology will be necessary.

The subject divides itself into, —

First, the "Alien Act."

Secondly, the "Sedition Act."

Of the "Alien Act," it is affirmed by the resolution — 1. That it exercises a power nowhere delegated to the federal government; 2. That it unites legislative and judicial powers to those of the executive; 3. That this union of powers subverts the general principles of free government; 4. That it subverts the particular organization and positive provisions of the Federal Constitution.

In order to clear the way for a correct view of the first position, several observations will be premised.

In the first place, it is to be borne in mind, that, it being a characteristic feature of the Federal Constitution, as it was originally ratified, and an amendment thereto having precisely declared, "that the powers not delegated to the United States by the Constitution, nor prohibited by it to the states, are reserved to the states respectively, or to the people," it is incumbent in this, as in every other exercise of power by the federal government, to prove, from the Constitution, that it grants the particular power exercised.

The next observation to be made is, that much confusion and fallacy have been thrown into the question, by blending the two cases of *aliens, members of a hostile nation; and aliens, members of friendly nations.* These two cases are so obviously and so essentially distinct, that it occasions no little surprise that the distinction should have been disregarded · and the surprise is so much the greater, as it appears that the two cases are actually distinguished by two separate acts of Congress, passed at the same session, and comprised in the same publication; the one providing for the case of "alien enemies;" the other "concerning aliens" indiscriminately and consequently extending to aliens of every nation in peace and amity with the United States. With respect to alien enemies, no doubt has been intimated as to the federal authority over them; the Constitution having expressly delegated to Congress the power to declare war against any nation, and of course to treat it and all its members as enemies. With respect to aliens who are not enemies, but members of nations in peace and amity with the United States, the power assumed by the act of Congress is denied to be constitutional; and it is accordingly against this act that the protest of the General Assembly is expressly and exclusively directed.

A third observation is that, were it admitted, as is contended that the "act concerning aliens" has for its object, not a *penal*, but a *preventive* justice, it would still remain to be proved that it comes within the constitutional power of the federal legislature ; and, if within its power, that the legislature has exercised it in a constitutional manner.

In the administration of preventive justice, the following principles have been held sacred: that some probable ground of suspicion be exhibited before some judicial authority ; that it be supported by oath or affirmation ; that the party may avoid being thrown into confinement, by finding pledges or sureties for his legal conduct sufficient in the judgment of some judicial authority ; that he may have the benefit of a writ of *habeas corpus*, and thus obtain his release if wrongfully confined ; and that he may at any time be discharged from his recognizance, or his confinement, and restored to his former liberty and rights, on the order of the proper judicial authority, if it shall see sufficient cause.

All these principles of the only preventive justice known to American jurisprudence are violated by the Alien Act. The ground of suspicion is to be judged of, not by any judicial authority, but by the executive magistrate alone. No oath or affirmation is required. If the suspicion be held reasonable by the President, he may order the suspected alien to depart from the territory of the United States, without the opportunity of avoiding the sentence by finding pledges for his future good conduct. As the President may limit the time of departure as he pleases, the benefit of the writ of *habeas corpus* may be suspended with respect to the party, although the Constitution ordains that it shall not be suspended unless when the public safety may require it, in case of rebellion or invasion, — neither of which existed at the passage of the act ; and the party being, under the sentence of the President, either removed from the United States, or being punished by imprisonment, or disqualification ever to become a citizen, on conviction of not obeying the order of removal, he cannot be discharged from the proceedings against him, and restored to the benefits of his former situation, although the *highest judicial authority* should see the most sufficient cause for it.

But, in the last place, it can never be admitted that the removal of aliens, authorized by the act, is to be considered, not as punishment for an offence, but as a measure of precaution and prevention. If the banishment of an alien from a country into which he has been invited as the asylum most auspicious to his happiness, — a country where he may have formed the most tender connections ; where he may have invested his entire property, and acquired property of the real and permanent, as well as the movable and temporary kind ; where he enjoys, under the laws, a greater share of the blessings of personal security, and personal liberty, than he can elsewhere hope for ; and where he may have nearly completed his probationary title to citizenship ; if, moreover, in the execution of the sentence against him, he is to be exposed, not only to the ordinary dangers of the sea, but to the peculiar casualties incident to a crisis of war and of unusual licentiousness on that element, and possibly to vindictive purposes, which his emigration itself may have provoked ; — if a banishment of this sort be not a punishment, and among the severest of punishments, it will be difficult to imagine a doom to which the name can be applied. And if it be a punishment, it will remain to be inquired, whether it can be constitutionally inflicted, on mere suspicion, by the single will of the executive magistrate, on persons convicted of no personal offence against the laws of the land, nor involved in any offence against the law of nations, charged on the foreign state of which they are members.

One argument offered in justification of this power exercised over aliens is, that the admission of them into the country being of favor, not of right, the favor is at all times revocable.

To this argument it might be answered, that, allowing the truth of the inference, it would be no proof of what is required. A question would still occur, whether the Constitution had vested the discretionary power of admitting aliens in the federal government or in the state governments.

But it cannot be a true inference, that, because the admission of an alien is a favor, the favor may be revoked at pleasure. A grant of land to an individual may be of favor, not of right; but the moment the grant is made, the favor becomes a right, and must be forfeited before it can be taken away. To pardon a malefactor may be a favor, but the pardon is not, on that account, the less irrevocable. To admit an alien to naturalization, is as much a favor as to admit him to reside in the country; yet it cannot be pretended that a person naturalized can be deprived of the benefits, any more than a native citizen can be disfranchised.

Again, it is said that, aliens not being parties to the Constitution, the rights and privileges which it secures cannot be at all claimed by them

To this reasoning, also, it might be answered that, although aliens are not parties to the Constitution, it does not follow that the Constitution has vested in Congress an absolute power over them. The parties to the Constitution may have granted, or retained, or modified, the power over aliens, without regard to that particular consideration.

But a more direct reply is, that it does not follow, because aliens are not parties to the Constitution, as citizens are parties to it, that, whilst they actually conform to it, they have no right to its protection. Aliens are not more parties to the laws than they are parties to the Constitution; yet it will not be disputed that, as they owe, on one hand, a temporary obedience, they are entitled, in return, to their protection and advantage.

If aliens had no rights under the Constitution, they might not only be banished, but even capitally punished, without a jury or the other incidents to a fair trial. But so far has a contrary principle been carried, in every part of the United States, that, except on charges of treason, an alien has, besides all the common privileges, the special one of being tried by a jury, of which one half may be also aliens.

It is said, further, that, by the law and practice of nations, aliens may be removed, at discretion, for offences against the law of nations; that Congress are authorized to define and punish such offences; and that to be dangerous to the peace of society is, in aliens, one of those offences.

The distinction between alien enemies and alien friends is a clear and conclusive answer to this argument. Alien enemies are under the law of nations, and liable to be punished for offences against it. Alien friends, except in the single case of public ministers, are under the municipal law, and must be tried and punished according to that law only.

This argument also, by referring the alien act to the power of Congress to define and *punish* offences against the law of nations, yields the point that the act is of a *penal*, not merely of a preventive operation. It must, in truth, be so considered. And if it be a penal act, the punishment it inflicts must be justified by some offence that deserves it.

Offences for which aliens, within the jurisdiction of a country, are punishable, are — first, offences committed by the nation of which they make a part, and in whose offences they are involved; secondly, offences committed by themselves alone, without any charge against the nation to which they belong. The first is the case of alien enemies; the second, the case of alien friends. In the first case, the offending nation can no otherwise be punished than by war, one of the laws of which authorizes the expulsion of such of its members as may be found within the country against which the offence has been committed. In the second case, — the offence being committed by the individual, not by his nation, and against the municipal law, not against the law of nations, — the individual only, and not the nation, is punishable; and the punishment must be conducted according to the municipal law, not according to the law of nations. Under this view of the subject, the act of Congress for the removal of alien enemies, being conformable to the law of nations, is justified by the Constitution; and the "act" for the removal of alien friends, being repugnant to the constitutional principles of municipal law, is unjustifiable.

Nor is the act of Congress for the removal of alien friends more agreeable to the general practice of nations than it is within the purview of the law of nations. The general practice of nations distinguishes between alien friends and alien enemies. The latter it has proceeded against, according to the law of nations, by expelling them as enemies. The former it has considered as under a local and temporary allegiance, and entitled to a correspondent protection. If contrary instances are to be found in barbarous countries, under undefined prerogatives, or amid revolutionary dangers, they will not be deemed fit precedents for the government of the United States, even if not beyond its constitutional authority.

It is said that Congress may grant letters of marque and reprisal; that reprisals may be made on persons as well as property; and that the removal of aliens may be considered as the exercise, in an inferior degree, of the general power of reprisal on persons.

Without entering minutely into a question that does not seem to require it, it may be remarked that reprisal is a seizure of foreign persons or property, with a view to obtain that justice for injuries done by one state, or its members, to another state, or its members, for which a refusal of the aggressors requires such a resort to force, under the law of nations. It must be considered as an abuse of words, to call the removal of persons from a country a seizure, or a reprisal on them; nor is the distinction to be overlooked between reprisals on persons within the country, and under the faith of its laws, and on persons out of the country. But, laying aside these considerations, it is evidently impossible to bring the alien act within the power of granting reprisals; since it does not allege or imply any injury received from any particular nation, for which this proceeding against its members was intended as a reparation.

The proceeding is authorized against aliens *of every nation;* of nations charged neither with any similar proceedings against American citizens, nor with any injuries for which justice might be sought, in the mode prescribed by the act. Were it true, therefore, that good causes existed for reprisals against one or more foreign nations, and that neither the persons nor property of its members, under the faith of our laws, could plead an exemption, the operation of the act ought to have been limited to the aliens among us belonging to such nations. To license reprisals against all nations, for aggressions charged on one only, would be a measure as contrary to every principle of justice and public law, as to a wise policy, and the universal practice of nations.

It is said that the right of removing aliens is an incident to the power of war, vested in Congress by the Constitution.

This is a former argument in a new shape only, and is answered by repeating, that the removal of alien enemies is an incident to the power of war; that the removal of alien friends is not an incident to the power of war.

It is said that Congress are, by the Constitution, to protect each state against invasion; and that the means of *preventing* invasion are included in the power of protection against it.

The power of war, in general, having been before granted by the Constitution, this clause must either be a mere specification for greater caution and certainty, of which there are other examples in the instrument, or be the injunction of a duty, superadded to a grant of the power. Under either explanation, it cannot enlarge the powers of Congress on the subject. The power and the duty to protect each state against an invading enemy would be the same under the general power, if this regard to the greater caution had been omitted.

Invasion is an operation of war. To protect against invasion is an exercise of the power of war. A power, therefore, not incident to war, cannot be incident to a particular modification of war; and as the removal of alien friends has appeared to be no incident to a general state of war, it cannot be incident to a partial state, or a particular modification of war.

Nor can it ever be granted, that a power to act on a case, when it actually occurs, includes a power over all the means that may *tend to prevent* the occurrence of the case. Such a latitude of construction would render unavailing every practical definition of particular and limited powers. Under the idea of preventing war in general, as well as invasion in particular, not only an indiscriminate removal of all aliens might be enforced, but a thousand other things, still more remote from the operations and precautions appurtenant to war, might take place. A bigoted or tyrannical nation might threaten us with war, unless certain religious or political regulations were adopted by us; yet it never could be inferred, if the regulations which would prevent war were such as Congress had otherwise no power to make, that the power to make them would grow out of the purpose they were to answer. Congress have power to suppress insurrections; yet it would not be allowed to follow, that they might employ all the means tending to prevent them; of which a system of moral instruction for the ignorant, and of provident support for the poor, might be regarded as among the most efficacious.

One argument for the power of the general government to remove aliens would have been passed in silence, if it had appeared under any authority inferior to that of a report made, during the last session of Congress, to the House of Representatives, by a committee, and approved by the house. The doctrine on which this argument is founded is of so new and so extraordinary a character, and strikes so radically at the political system of America, that it is proper to state it in the very words of the report.

"The act (concerning aliens) is said to be unconstitutional, because to remove aliens is a direct breach of the Constitution, which provides, by the 9th section of the 1st article, that the migration or importation of such persons as any of the states shall think proper to admit, shall not be prohibited by the Congress prior to the year 1808."

Among the answers given to this objection to the constitutionality of the act, the following very remarkable one is extracted: —

"Thirdly, That, as the Constitution has *given to the states* no power o remove aliens, during the period of the limitation under consideration, in the mean time, on the construction assumed, there would be no authority in the country empowered to send away dangerous aliens; which cannot be admitted."

The reasoning here used would not, in any view, be conclusive; because there are powers exercised by most other governments, which, in the United States, are withheld by the people both from the general government and from the state governments. Of this sort are many of the powers prohibited by the declarations of rights prefixed to the constitutions, or by the clauses, in the constitutions, in the nature of such declarations. Nay, so far is the political system of the United States distinguishable from that of other countries, by the caution with which powers are delegated and defined, that, in one very important case, even of commercial regulation and revenue, the power is absolutely locked up against the hands of both governments. A tax on exports can be laid by no constitutional authority whatever. Under a system thus peculiarly guarded, there could surely be no absurdity in supposing that alien friends — who, if guilty of treasonable machinations, may be punished, or, if suspected on probable grounds, may be secured by pledges or imprisonment, in like manner with permanent citizens — were never meant to be subjected to banishment by an arbitrary and unusual process, either under the one government or the other.

But it is not the inconclusiveness of the general reasoning, in this passage, which chiefly calls the attention to it. It is the principle assumed by it, that the powers held by the states are given to them by the Constitution of the United States; and the inference from this principle, that the powers supposed to be necessary, which are not so given to the state governments, must reside in this government of the United States.

The respect which is felt for every portion of the constituted authorities forbids some of the reflections which this singular paragraph might excite; and they are the more readily suppressed, as it may be presumed, with justice perhaps as well as candor, that inadvertence may have had its share in the error. It would be unjustifiable delicacy, nevertheless, to pass by so portentous a claim, proceeding from so high an authority, without a monitory notice of the fatal tendencies with which it would be pregnant.

Lastly, it is said that a law on the same subject with the alien act, passed by this state originally in 1785, and reënacted in 1792, is a proof that a summary removal of suspected aliens was not heretofore regarded, by the Virginia legislature, as liable to the objections now urged against such a measure.

This charge against Virginia vanishes before the simple remark, that the law of Virginia relates to "suspicious persons, being the subjects of any foreign power or state who shall have *made a declaration of war*, or actually *commenced hostilities*, or from whom the President shall apprehend *hostile designs;*" whereas the act of Congress relates to aliens, being the subjects of foreign powers and states, who have *neither declared war, nor commenced hostilities, nor from whom hostile dangers are apprehended.*

2. It is next affirmed of the Alien Act, that it unites legislative, judicial, and executive powers, in the hands of the President.

However difficult it may be to mark, in every case, with clearness and certainty, the line which divides legislative power from the other departments of power, all will agree that the powers referred to these departments may be so general and undefined, as to be of a legislative, not of an executive or judicial nature, and may for that reason be unconstitutional. Details, to a certain degree, are essential to the nature and character of a law; and on criminal subjects, it is proper that details should leave as little as possible to the discretion of those who are to apply and execute the law. If nothing more were required, in exercising a legislative trust, than a general conveyance of authority — without laying down any precise rules by which the authority conveyed should be carried into effect — it would follow that the whole power of legislation might be transferred by the legislature from itself, and proclamations might become substitutes for law. A delegation of power in this latitude would not be denied to be a union of the different powers.

To determine, then, whether the appropriate powers of the distinct departments are united by the act authorizing the executive to remove aliens, it must be inquired whether it contains such details, definitions, and rules, as appertain to the true character of a law; especially a law by which personal liberty is invaded, property deprived of its value to the owner, and life itself indirectly exposed to danger.

The Alien Act declares "that it shall be lawful for the President to order all such aliens as he shall judge *dangerous* to the peace and safety of the United States, or shall have reasonable ground to *suspect* are concerned in any treasonable or *secret machinations* against the government thereof, to depart," &c.

Could a power be well given in terms less definite, less particular, and less precise? To be *dangerous to the public safety* — to be *suspected of secret machination* against the government; these can never be mistaken for legal rules or certain definitions. They leave every thing to the President. His will is the law.

But it is not a legislative power only that is given to the President. He is to stand in the place of the judiciary also. His suspicion is the only evidence which is to convict; his order, the only judgment which is to be executed.

Thus it is the President whose will is to designate the offensive conduct; it is his will that is to ascertain the individuals on whom it is charged; and it is his will that is to cause the sentence to be executed. It is rightly affirmed, therefore, that the act unites legislative and judicial powers to those of the executive.

3. It is affirmed that this union of power subverts the general principle of free government.

It has become an axiom in the science of government, that a separation of the legislative, executive, and judicial departments is necessary to the preservation of public liberty. Nowhere has this axiom been better understood in theory, or more carefully pursued in practice, than in the United States.

4. It is affirmed that such a union of power subverts the particular organization and positive provision of the Federal Constitution.

According to the particular organization of the Constitution, its legislative powers are vested in the Congress, its executive powers in the President, and its judicial powers in a supreme and inferior tribunals. The union of any of these powers, and still more of all three, in any one of these departments, as has been shown to be done by the Alien Act, must, consequently, subvert the constitutional organization of them.

That positive provisions, in the Constitution, securing to individuals the benefits of fair trial, are also violated by the union of powers in the Alien Act, necessarily results from the two facts, that the act relates to alien friends, and that alien friends, being under the municipal law only, are entitled to its protection.

The *second* object, against which the resolution protests, is the Sedition Act.

Of this act it is affirmed — 1. That it exercises, in like manner, a power not delegated by the Constitution ; 2. That the power, on the contrary, is expressly and positively forbidden by one of the amendments to the Constitution ; 3. That this is a power which, more than any other, ought to produce universal alarm, because it is levelled against that right of freely examining public characters and measures, and of free communication thereon, which has ever been justly deemed the only effectual guardian of every other right.

1. That it exercises a power not delegated by the Constitution.

Here, again, it will be proper to recollect that, the federal government being composed of powers specifically granted, with reservation of all others to the states or to the people, the positive authority under which the Sedition Act could be passed must be produced by those who assert its constitutionality.   In what part of the Constitution, then, is this authority to be found ?

Several attempts have been made to answer this question, which will be examined in their order.   The committee will begin with one which has filled them with equal astonishment and apprehension ; and which, they cannot but persuade themselves, must have the same effect on all who will consider it with coolness and impartiality, and with a reverence for our Constitution, in the true character in which it issued from the sovereign authority of the people.   The committee refer to the doctrine lately advanced, as a sanction to the Sedition Act, " that the common or unwritten law " — a law of vast extent and complexity, and embracing almost every possible subject of legislation, both civil and criminal — makes a part of the law of these states, in their united and national capacity.

The novelty, and, in the judgment of the committee, the extravagance of this pretension, would have consigned it to the silence in which they have passed by other arguments which an extraordinary zeal for the act has drawn into the discussion ; but the auspices under which this innovation presents itself have constrained the committee to bestow on it an attention which other considerations might have forbidden.

In executing the task, it may be of use to look back to the colonial state of this country prior to the revolution ; to trace the effect of the revolution which converted the colonies into independent states ; to inquire into the import of the Articles of Confederation, the first instrument by which the union of the states was regularly established ; and, finally, to consult the Constitution of 1787, which is the oracle that must decide the important question.

In the state prior to the revolution, it is certain that the common law, under different limitations, made a part of the colonial codes.   But, whether it be understood that the original colonists brought the law with them, or made it their law by adoption, it is equally certain that it was the separate law of each colony within its respective limits, and was unknown to them as a law pervading and operating through the whole, as one society.

It could not possibly be otherwise.   The common law was not the same in any two of the colonies ; in some, the modifications were materially and extensively different.   There was no common legislature, by which a common will could be expressed in the form of a law ; nor any common magistracy, by which such a law could be carried into practice.   The will of each colony, alone and separately, had its organs for these purposes.

This stage of our political history furnishes no foothold for the patrons of this new doctrine.

Did, then, the principle or operation of the great event which made the colonies independent states, imply or introduce the common law, as a law of the Union ?

The fundamental principle of the revolution was, that the colonies were coördinate members with each other, and with Great Britain, of an empire united by a common executive sovereign, but not united by any common legislative sovereign.   The legislative power was maintained to be as complete in each American Parliament, as in the British Parliament.   And the royal prerogative was in force, in each colony, by virtue of its acknowledging the king for its executive magistrate, as it was in Great Britain, by virtue of a like acknowledgment there.   A denial of these principles by Great Britain, and the assertion of them by America, produced the revolution.

There was a time, indeed, when an exception to the legislative separation of the several component and coëqual parts of the empire obtained a degree of acquiescence.   The British Parliament was allowed to regulate the trade with foreign nations, and between the different parts of the empire.   This was, however, mere practice without right, and contrary to the true theory of the Constitution.   The convenience of some regulations, in both cases, was apparent ; and, as there was no legislature with power over the whole, nor any constitutional preëminence among the legislatures of the several parts, it was natural for the legislature of that particular part which was the eldest and the largest, to assume this function, and for the others to acquiesce in it.   This tacit arrangement was the less criticised, as the regulations established by the British Parliament operated in favor of that part of the empire which seemed to bear the principal share of the public burdens, and were regarded as an indemnification of its advances for the other parts.   As long as this regulating power was confined to the two objects of conveniency and equity, it was not complained of, nor much inquired into.   But no sooner was it perverted to the selfish views of the party assuming it, than the injured parties began to feel and to reflect ; and the moment the claim to a direct and indefinite power was ingrafted on the precedent of the regulating power, the whole charm was dissolved, and every eye opened to the usurpation.   The assertion by Great Britain of a power to make laws for the other members of the empire, in all cases whatsoever, ended in the discovery that she had a right to make laws for them in no cases whatsoever.

Such being the ground of our revolution, no support or color can be drawn from it for the doctrine that the common law is binding on these states as one society.   The doctrine, on the contrary, is evidently repugnant to the fundamental principle of the revolution.

The Articles of Confederation are the next source of information on this subject.

In the interval between the commencement of the revolution and the final ratification of these Articles, the nature and extent of the Union was determined by the circumstances of the crisis, rather than by any accurate delineation of the general authority. It will not be alleged that the " common law " could have any legitimate birth, as a law of the United States, during that state of things. If it came, as such, into existence at all, the charter of confederation must have been its parent.

Here, again, however, its pretensions are absolutely destitute of foundation. This instrument does not contain a sentence or a syllable that can be tortured into a countenance of the idea that the parties to it were, with respect to the objects of the common law, to form one community. No such law is named, or implied, or alluded to, as being in force, or as brought into force by that compact. No provision is made by which such a law could be carried into operation; whilst, on the other hand, every such inference or pretext is absolutely precluded by art. 2, which declares " that each state retains its sovereignty, freedom, and independence, and every power, jurisdiction, and right, which is not by this Confederation expressly delegated to the United States in Congress assembled."

Thus far it appears that not a vestige of this extraordinary doctrine can be found in the origin or progress of American institutions. The evidence against it has, on the contrary, grown stronger at every step, till it has amounted to a formal and positive exclusion, by written articles of compact among the parties concerned.

Is this exclusion revoked, and the common law introduced as national law, by the present Constitution of the United States? This is the final question to be examined.

It is readily admitted that particular parts of the common law may have a sanction from the Constitution, so far as they are necessarily comprehended in the technical phrases which express the powers delegated to the government; and so far, also, as such other parts may be adopted by Congress, as necessary and proper for carrying into execution the powers expressly delegated. But the question does not relate to either of these portions of the common law. It relates to the common law beyond these limitations.

The only part of the Constitution which seems to have been relied on in this case, is the 2d section of art. 3: — " The judicial power shall extend to all cases, in law and equity, arising under this Constitution, the laws of the United States, and treaties made, or which shall be made, under their authority."

It has been asked what cases, distinct from those arising under the laws and treaties of the United States, can arise under the Constitution, other than those arising under the common law; and it is inferred that the common law is, accordingly, adopted or recognized by the Constitution.

Never, perhaps, was so broad a construction applied to a text so clearly unsusceptible of it. If any color for the inference could be found, it must be in the impossibility of finding any other cases, in law and equity, within the provisions of the Constitution, to satisfy the expression ; and rather than resort to a construction affecting so essentially the whole character of the government, it would perhaps be more rational to consider the expression as a mere pleonasm or inadvertence. But it is not necessary to decide on such a dilemma. The expression is fully satisfied, and its accuracy justified, by two descriptions of cases, to which the judicial authority is extended, and neither of which implies that the common law is the law of the United States. One of these descriptions comprehends the cases growing out of the restrictions on the legislative power of the states. For example, it is provided that "no state shall emit bills of credit," or "make any thing but gold and silver coin a tender for the payment of debts." Should this prohibition be violated, and a suit between citizens of the same state be the consequence, this would be a case arising under the Constitution before the judicial power of the United States. A second description comprehends suits between citizens and foreigners, of citizens of different states, to be decided according to the state or foreign laws, but submitted by the Constitution to the judicial power of the United States; the judicial power being, in several instances, extended beyond the legislative power of the United States.

To this explanation of the text, the following observations may be added : —

The expression " cases in law and equity " is manifestly confined to cases of a civil nature, and would exclude cases of criminal jurisdiction. Criminal cases in law and equity would be a language unknown to the law.

The succeeding paragraph in the same section is in harmony with this construction. It is in these words: " In all cases affecting ambassadors, or other public ministers, and consuls, and those in which a state shall be a party, the Supreme Court shall have original jurisdiction. *In all* the other cases, [including cases of law and equity arising under the Constitution,] the Supreme Court shall have *appellate* jurisdiction, both as to law and *fact*, with such exceptions, and under such regulations, as Congress shall make."

This paragraph, by expressly giving an *appellate* jurisdiction, in cases of law and equity arising under the Constitution, to *fact*, as well as to law, clearly excludes criminal cases, where the trial by jury is secured — because the fact, in such cases, is not a subject of appeal : and, although the appeal is liable to such *exceptions* and regulations as Congress may adopt, yet it is not to be supposed that an *exception* of *all* criminal cases could be contemplated, as well because a discretion in Congress to make or omit the exception would be improper, as because it would have been unnecessary. The exception could as easily have been made by the Constitution itself, as referred to the Congress.

Once more : The amendment last added to the Constitution deserves attention as throwing light on this subject. " The judicial power of the United States shall not be construed to extend to any suit in *law* or *equity*, commenced or prosecuted against one of the United States, by citizens of another state, or by citizens or subjects of any foreign power." As it will not be pretended that any criminal proceeding could take place against a state, the terms *law or equity* must be understood as appropriate to *civil*, in exclusion of *criminal* cases.

From these considerations, it is evident that this part of the Constitution, even if it could be applied at all to the purpose for which it has been cited, would not include any cases whatever of a criminal nature, and consequently would not authorize the inference from it, that the judicial authority extends to *offences* against the common law, as offences arising under the Constitution.

It is further to be considered that, even if this part of the Constitution could be strained into an application to every common-law case, criminal as well as civil, it could have no effect in justifying the Sedition Act, which is an act of legislative, and not of judicial power : and it is the judicial power only of which the extent is defined in this part of the Constitution.

There are two passages in the Constitution, in which a description of the law of the United States is found. The first is contained in art. 3, sect. 3, in the words following: "This Constitution, the laws of the United States, and treaties made, or which shall be made, under this authority." The second is contained in the second paragraph of art. 6, as follows: "This Constitution, and the laws of the United States which shall be made in pursuance thereof, and all treaties made, or which shall be made, under the authority of the United States, shall be the supreme law of the land." The first of these descriptions was meant as a guide to the judges of the United States; the second, as a guide to the judges of the several states. Both of them consist of an enumeration, which was evidently meant to be precise and complete. If the common law had been understood to be a law of the United States, it is not possible to assign a satisfactory reason why it was not expressed in the enumeration.

In aid of these objections, the difficulties and confusion inseparable from a constructive introduction of the common law would afford powerful reasons against it.

Is it to be the common law with or without the British statutes?

If without the statutory amendments, the vices of the code would be insupportable.

If with these amendments, what period is to be fixed for limiting the British authority over our laws?

Is it to be the date of the eldest, or the youngest, of the colonies?

Or are the dates to be thrown together, and a medium deduced?

Or is our independence to be taken for the date?

Is, again, regard to be had to the various changes in the common law made by the local codes of America?

Is regard to be had to such changes subsequent as well as prior to the establishment of the Constitution?

Is regard to be had to future as well as past changes?

Is the law to be different in every state, as differently modified by its code; or are the modifications of any particular state to be applied to all?

And on the latter supposition, which among the state codes forms the standard?

Questions of this sort might be multiplied with as much ease as there would be difficulty in answering them.

These consequences, flowing from the proposed construction, furnish other objections equally conclusive; unless the text were peremptory in its meaning, and consistent with other parts of the instrument.

These consequences may be in relation to the legislative authority of the United States; to the executive authority; to the judicial authority: and to the governments of the several states.

If it be understood that the common law is established by the Constitution, it follows that no part of the law can be altered by the legislature. Such of the statutes already passed as may be repugnant thereto, would be nullified; particularly the Sedition Act itself, which boasts of being a melioration of the common law; and the whole code, with all its incongruities, barbarisms, and bloody maxims, would be inviolably saddled on the good people of the United States.

Should this consequence be rejected, and the common law be held, like

48

other laws, liable to revision and alteration by the authority of Congress, it then follows that the authority of Congress is coëxtensive with the objects of common law; that is to say, with every object of legislation; for to every such object does some branch or other of the common law extend. The authority of Congress would, therefore, be no longer under the limitations marked out in the Constitution. They would be authorized to legislate in all cases whatsoever.

In the next place, as the President possesses the executive powers of the Constitution, and is to see that the laws be faithfully executed, his authority also must be coëxtensive with every branch of the common law The additions which this would make to his power, though not readily to be estimated, claim the most serious attention.

This is not all: it will merit the most profound consideration, how far an indefinite admission of the common law, with a latitude in construing it equal to the construction by which it is deduced from the Constitution, might draw after it the various prerogatives, making part of the unwritten law of England. The English constitution itself is nothing more than a composition of unwritten laws and maxims.

In the third place, whether the common law be admitted as of legal or of constitutional obligation, it would confer on the judicial department a discretion little short of a legislative power.

On the supposition of its having a constitutional obligation, this power in the judges would be permanent and irremediable by the legislature. On the other supposition, the power would not expire until the legislature should have introduced a full system of statutory provisions. Let it be observed, too, that, besides all the uncertainties above enumerated, and which present an immense field for judicial discretion, it would remain with the same department to decide what parts of the common law would, and what would not, be properly applicable to the circumstances of the United States.

A discretion of this sort has always been lamented as incongruous and dangerous, even in the colonial and state courts, although so much narrowed by positive provisions in the local codes on all the principal subjects embraced by the common law. Under the United States, where so few laws exist on those subjects, and where so great a lapse of time must happen before the vast chasm could be supplied, it is manifest that the power of the judges over the law would, in fact, erect them into legislators, and that, for a long time, it would be impossible for the citizens to conjecture either what was, or would be, law.

In the last place, the consequence of admitting the common law as the law of the United States, on the authority of the individual states, is as obvious as it would be fatal. As this law relates to every subject of legislation, and would be paramount to the constitutions and laws of the states, the admission of it would overwhelm the residuary sovereignty of the states, and, by one constructive operation, new-model the whole political fabric of the country.

From the review thus taken of the situation of the American colonies prior to their independence; of the effect of this event on their situation; of the nature and import of the Articles of Confederation; of the true meaning of the passage in the existing Constitution from which the common law has been deduced; of the difficulties and uncertainties incident to the doctrine; and of its vast consequences in extending the powers of the federal government, and in superseding the authorities of the state governments, — the committee feel the utmost confidence in concluding that the common law never was, nor by any fair construction ever can be, deemed a law for the American people as one community ; and they indulge the strongest expectation that the same conclusion will be finally drawn by all candid and accurate inquirers into the subject. It is, indeed, distressing to reflect that it ever should have been made a question, whether the Constitution, on the whole face of which is seen so much labor to enumerate and define the several objects of federal power, could intend to introduce in the lump, in an indirect manner, and by a forced construction of a few phrases, the vast and multifarious jurisdiction involved in the common law — a law filling so many ample volumes ; a law overspreading the entire field of legislation ; and a law that would sap the foundation of the Constitution as a system of limited and specified powers. A severer reproach could not, in the opinion of the committee, be thrown on the Constitution, on those who framed, or on those who established it, than such a supposition would throw on them.

The argument, then, drawn from the common law, on the ground of its being adopted or recognized by the Constitution, being inapplicable to the Sedition Act, the committee will proceed to examine the other arguments which have been founded on the Constitution.

They will waste but little time on the attempt to cover the act by the preamble to the Constitution, it being contrary to every acknowledged rule of construction to set up this part of an instrument in opposition to the plain meaning expressed in the body of the instrument. A preamble usually contains the general motives or reason for the particular regulations or measures which follow it, and is always understood to be explained and limited by them. In the present instance, a contrary interpretation would have the inadmissible effect of rendering nugatory or improper every part of the Constitution which succeeds the preamble.

The paragraph in art. 1, sect. 8, which contains the power to lay and collect taxes, duties, imposts, and excises, to pay the debts, and provide for the common defence and general welfare, having been already examined, will also require no particular attention in this place. It will have been seen that, in its fair and consistent meaning, it cannot enlarge the enumerated powers vested in Congress.

The part of the Constitution which seems most to be recurred to, in defence of the Sedition Act, is the last clause of the above section, empowering Congress to make all laws which shall be necessary and proper for carrying into execution the foregoing powers, and all other powers vested by this Constitution in the government of the United States, or in any department or officer thereof."

The plain import of this clause is, that Congress shall have all the incidental or instrumental powers necessary and proper for carrying into execution all the express powers, whether they be vested in the government of the United States, more collectively, or in the several departments or officers thereof.

It is not a grant of new powers to Congress, but merely a declaration, or the removal of all uncertainty, that the means of carrying into execution those otherwise granted are included in the grant.

Whenever, therefore, a question arises concerning the constitutionality of a particular power, the first question is, whether the power be expressed in the Constitution. If it be, the question is decided. If it be not expressed, the next inquiry must be, whether it is properly an incident to an express power, and necessary to its execution. If it be, it may be exercised by Congress. If it be not, Congress cannot exercise it.

Let the question be asked, then, whether the power over the press, exercised in the Sedition Act, be found among the powers expressly vested in Congress. This is not pretended.

Is there any express power, for executing which it is a necessary and proper power ?

The power which has been selected, as least remote, in answer to this question, is that " of suppressing insurrections ; " which is said to imply a power to prevent insurrections, by punishing whatever may lead or tend to them.   But it surely cannot, with the least plausibility, be said, that the regulation of the press, and punishment of libels, are exercises of a power to suppress insurrections.   The most that could be said would be, that the punishment of libels, if it had the tendency ascribed to it, might prevent the occasion of passing or executing laws necessary and proper for the suppression of insurrections.

Has the federal government no power, then, to prevent as well as to punish resistance to the laws ?

They have the power, which the Constitution deemed most proper, in their hands for the purpose.   The Congress has power, before it happens, to pass laws for punishing it ; and the executive and judiciary have power to enforce those laws when it does happen.

It must be recollected by many, and could be shown to the satisfaction of all, that the construction here put on the terms " necessary and proper " is precisely the construction which prevailed during the discussions and ratifications of the Constitution.   It may be added, and cannot too often be repeated, that it is a construction absolutely necessary to maintain their consistency with the peculiar character of the government, as possessed of particular and definite powers only, not of the general and indefinite powers vested in ordinary governments ; for, if the power to suppress insurrections includes the power to punish libels, or if the power to punish includes a power to prevent, by all the means that may have that tendency, such is the relation and influence among the most remote subjects of legislation, that a power over a very few would carry with it a power over all. And it must be wholly immaterial whether unlimited powers be exercised under the name of unlimited powers, or be exercised under the name of unlimited means of carrying into execution limited powers.

This branch of the subject will be closed with a reflection which must have weight with all, but more especially with those who place peculiar reliance on the judicial exposition of the Constitution, as the bulwark provided against an undue extension of the legislative power.   If it be understood that the powers implied in the specified powers have an immediate and appropriate relation to them, as means necessary and proper for carrying them into execution, questions on constitutionality of laws passed for this purpose will be of a nature sufficiently precise and determinate for judicial cognizance and control.   If, on the other hand, Congress are not limited, in the choice of means, by any such appropriate relation of them to the specified powers, but may employ all such means as they may deem fitted to prevent, as well as to punish, crimes subjected to their authority, (such as may have a tendency only to promote an object for which they are authorized to provide,) every one must perceive that questions relating to means of this sort must be questions for mere policy and expediency ; on which legislative discretion alone can decide, and from which the judicial interposition and control are completely excluded.

2. The next point which the resolution requires to be proved is, that the power over the press, exercised by the Sedition Act, is positively forbidden by one of the amendments to the Constitution.

The amendment stands in these words : "Congress shall make no law respecting an establishment of religion, or prohibiting the free exercise thereof, or abridging the freedom of speech, or of the press, or of the right of the people peaceably to assemble, and to petition the government for a redress of grievances."

In the attempts to vindicate the Sedition Act, it has been contended, 1. That the "freedom of the press" is to be determined by the meaning of these terms in the common law ; 2. That the article supposes the power over the press to be in Congress, and prohibits them only from abridging the freedom allowed to it by the common law.

Although it will be shown, on examining the second of these positions, that the amendment is a denial to Congress of all power over the press, it may not be useless to make the following observations on the first of them : —

It is deemed to be a sound opinion that the Sedition Act, in its definition of some of the crimes created, is an abridgment of the freedom of publication, recognized by principles of the common law in England.

The freedom of the press, under the common law, is, in the defences of the Sedition Act, made to consist in an exemption from all previous restraint on printed publications, by persons authorized to inspect or prohibit them. It appears to the committee that this idea of the freedom of the press can never be admitted to be the American idea of it; since a law inflicting penalties on printed publications would have a similar effect with a law authorizing a previous restraint on them. It would seem a mockery to say that no laws should be passed preventing publications from being made, but that laws might be passed for punishing them in case they should be made.

The essential difference between the British government and the American constitutions will place this subject in the clearest light.

In the British government, the danger of encroachments on the rights of the people is understood to be confined to the executive magistrate. The representatives of the people in the legislature are not only exempt themselves from distrust, but are considered as sufficient guardians of the rights of their constituents against the danger from the executive. Hence it is a principle, that the Parliament is unlimited in its power ; or, in their own language, is omnipotent. Hence, too, all the ramparts for protecting the rights of the people, — such as their Magna Charta, their bill of rights, &c., — are not reared against the Parliament, but against the royal prerogative. They are merely legislative precautions against executive usurpation. Under such a government as this, an exemption of the press from previous restraint by licensers appointed by the king, is all the freedom that can be secured to it.

In the United States, the case is altogether different. The people, not the government, possess the absolute sovereignty. The legislature, no less than the executive, is under limitations of power. Encroachments are regarded as possible from the one as well as from the other. Hence, in the United States, the great and essential rights of the people are secured against legislative as well as executive ambition. They are secured, not by laws paramount to prerogative, but by constitutions paramount to laws. This security of the freedom of the press requires that it should be exempt, not only from previous restraint of the executive, as in Great Britain, but from legislative restraint also; and this exemption, to be effectual, must be an exemption, not only from the previous inspection of licensers, but from the subsequent penalty of laws.

The state of the press, therefore, under the common law, cannot, in this point of view, be the standard of its freedom in the United States.

But there is another view under which it may be necessary to consider this subject. It may be alleged that, although the security for the freedom of the press be different in Great Britain and in this country, — being a legal security only in the former, and a constitutional security in the latter, — and although there may be a further difference, in an extension of the freedom of the press, here, beyond an exemption from previous restraint, to an exemption from subsequent penalties also, — yet the actual legal freedom of the press, under the common law, must determine the degree of freedom which is meant by the terms, and which is constitutionally secured against both previous and subsequent restraints.

The committee are not unaware of the difficulty of all general questions, which may turn on the proper boundary between the liberty and licentiousness of the press. They will leave it, therefore, for consideration only, how far the difference between the nature of the British government, and the nature of the American government, and the practice under the latter, may show the degree of rigor in the former to be inapplicable to, and not obligatory in, the latter.

The nature of governments elective, limited, and responsible, in all their branches, may well be supposed to require a greater freedom of animadversion, than might be tolerated by the genius of such a government as that of Great Britain. In the latter, it is a maxim, that the king — an hereditary, not a responsible magistrate — can do no wrong; and that the legislature, which, in two thirds of its composition, is also hereditary, not responsible, can do what it pleases. In the United States, the executive magistrates are not held to be infallible, nor the legislatures to be omnipotent; and both, being elective, are both responsible. Is it not natural and necessary, under such different circumstances, that a different degree of freedom in the use of the press should be contemplated?

Is not such an inference favored by what is observable in Great Britain itself? Notwithstanding the general doctrine of the common law, on the subject of the press, and the occasional punishment of those who use it with a freedom offensive to the government, it is well known that, with respect to the responsible measures of the government, where the reasons operating here become applicable there, the freedom exercised by the press, and protected by public opinion, far exceeds the limits prescribed by the ordinary rules of law. The ministry, who are responsible to impeachment, are at all times animadverted on, by the press, with peculiar freedom; and during the elections for the House of Commons, the other responsible part of the government, the press is employed with as little reserve towards the candidates.

The practice in America must be entitled to much more respect. In every state, probably, in the Union, the press has exerted a freedom in canvassing the merits and measures of public men, of every description, which has not been confined to the strict limits of the common law. On this footing the freedom of the press has stood; on this foundation it yet stands; and it will not be a breach, either of truth or of candor, to say that no persons or presses are in the habit of more unrestrained animadversions on the proceedings and functionaries of the state governments, than the persons and presses most zealous in vindicating the act of Congress for punishing similar animadversions on the government of the United States.

'The last remark will not be understood as claiming for the state governments an immunity greater than they have heretofore enjoyed.   Some degree of abuse is inseparable from the proper use of every thing; and in no instance is this more true than in that of the press.   It has accordingly been decided, by the practice of the states, that it is better to leave a few of its noxious branches to their luxuriant growth, than, by pruning them away, to injure the vigor of those yielding the proper fruits.   And can the wisdom of this policy be doubted by any one who reflects that to the press alone, checkered as it is with abuses, the world is indebted for all the triumphs which have been gained by reason and humanity over error and oppression; who reflects that to the same beneficent source the United States owe much of the lights which conducted them to the rank of a free and independent nation and which have improved their political system into a shape so auspicious to their happiness? Had Sedition Acts, forbidding every publication that might bring the constituted agents into contempt or disrepute, or that might excite the hatred of the people against the authors of unjust or pernicious measures, been uniformly enforced against the press, might not the United States have been languishing, at this day, under the infirmities of a sickly Confederation ?   Might they not, possibly, be miserable colonies, groaning under a foreign yoke?

To these observations one fact will be added, which demonstrates that the common law cannot be admitted as the universal expositor of American terms, which may be the same with those contained in that law.   The freedom of conscience, and of religion, is found in the same instrument which asserts the freedom of the press.   It will never be admitted that the meaning of the former, in the common law of England, is to limit their meaning in the United States.

Whatever weight may be allowed to these considerations, the committee do not, however, by any means intend to rest the question on them. They contend that the article of the amendment, instead of supposing in Congress a power that might be exercised over the press, provided its freedom was not abridged, meant a positive denial to Congress of any power whatever on the subject.

To demonstrate that this was the true object of the article, it will be sufficient to recall the circumstances which led to it, and to refer to the explanation accompanying the article.

When the Constitution was under the discussions which preceded its ratification, it is well known that great apprehensions were expressed by many, lest the omission of some positive exception, from the powers delegated, of certain rights, and of the freedom of the press particularly, might expose them to danger of being drawn, by construction, within some of the powers vested in Congress; more especially of the power to make all laws necessary and proper for carrying their other powers into execution.   In reply to this objection, it was invariably urged to be a fundamental and characteristic principle of the Constitution, that all powers not given by 't were reserved; that no powers were given beyond those enumerated in the Constitution, and such as were fairly incident to them ; that the power over the rights in question, and particularly over the press, was neither among the enumerated powers, nor incident to any of them : and consequently that an exercise of any such power would be manifest usurpation. It is painful to remark how much the arguments now employed in behalf of the Sedition Act, are at variance with the reasoning which then justified the Constitution, and invited its ratification.

From this posture of the subject resulted the interesting question, in so many of the conventions, whether the doubts and dangers ascribed to the Constitution should be removed by any amendments previous to the ratification, or be postponed, in confidence that, as far as they might be proper, they would be introduced in the form provided by the Constitution. The latter course was adopted; and in most of the states, ratifications were followed by the propositions and instructions for rendering the Constitution more explicit, and more safe to the rights not meant to be delegated by it. Among those rights, the freedom of the press, in most instances, is particularly and emphatically mentioned. The firm and very pointed manner in which it is asserted in the proceedings of the Convention of this state will hereafter be seen.

In pursuance of the wishes thus expressed, the first Congress that assembled under the Constitution proposed certain amendments, which have since, by the necessary ratifications, been made a part of it; among which amendments is the article containing, among other prohibitions on the Congress, an express declaration that they should make no law abridging the freedom of the press.

Without tracing farther the evidence on this subject, it would seem scarcely possible to doubt that no power whatever over the press was supposed to be delegated by the Constitution, as it originally stood, and that the amendment was intended as a positive and absolute reservation of it.

But the evidence is still stronger. The proposition of amendments made by Congress is introduced in the following terms: —

"The conventions of a number of the states having, at the time of their adopting the Constitution, expressed a desire, in order to prevent misconstruction or abuse of its powers, that further declaratory and restrictive clauses should be added; and as extending the ground of public confidence in the government will best insure the beneficent ends of its institutions."

Here is the most satisfactory and authentic proof that the several amendments proposed were to be considered as either declaratory or restrictive, and, whether the one or the other, as corresponding with the desire expressed by a number of the states, and as extending the ground of public confidence in the government.

Under any other construction of the amendment relating to the press, than that it declared the press to be wholly exempt from the power of Congress, the amendment could neither be said to correspond with the desire expressed by a number of the states, nor be calculated to extend the ground of public confidence in the government.

Nay, more; the construction employed to justify the Sedition Act would exhibit a phenomenon without a parallel in the political world. It would exhibit a number of respectable states, as denying, first, that any power over the press was delegated by the Constitution; as proposing, next, that an amendment to it should explicitly declare that no such power was delegated; and, finally, as concurring in an amendment actually recognizing or delegating such a power.

Is, then, the federal government, it will be asked, destitute of every authority for restraining the licentiousness of the press, and for shielding itself against the libellous attacks which may be made on those who administer it ?

The Constitution alone can answer this question. If no such power be expressly delegated, and if it be not both necessary and proper to carry into execution an express power; above all, if it be expressly forbidden, by a declaratory amendment to the Constitution, — the answer must be, that the federal government is destitute of all such authority.

And might it not be asked, in turn, whether it is not more probable, under all the circumstances which have been reviewed, that the authority should be withheld by the Constitution, than that it should be left to a vague and violent construction, whilst so much pains were bestowed in enumerating other powers, and so many less important powers are included in the enumeration ?

Might it not be likewise asked, whether the anxious circumspection which dictated so many peculiar limitations on the general authority would be unlikely to exempt the press altogether from that authority ? The peculiar magnitude of some of the powers necessarily committed to the federal government; the peculiar duration required for the functions of some of its departments; the peculiar distance of the seat of its proceedings from the great body of its constituents ; and the peculiar difficulty of circulating an adequate knowledge of them through any other channel ; — will not these considerations, some or other of which produced other exceptions from the powers of ordinary governments, altogether, account for the policy of binding the hands of the federal government from touching the channel which alone can give efficacy to its responsibility to its constituents, and of leaving those who administer it to a remedy, for their injured reputations, under the same laws, and in the same tribunals, which protect their lives, their liberties, and their properties ?

But the question does not turn either on the wisdom of the Constitution or on the policy which gave rise to its particular organization. It turns on the actual meaning of the instrument, by which it has appeared that a power over the press is clearly excluded from the number of powers delegated to the federal government.

3. And, in the opinion of the committee, well may it be said, as the resolution concludes with saying, that the unconstitutional power exercised over the press by the Sedition Act ought, "more than any other, to produce universal alarm; because it is levelled against that right of freely examining public characters and measures, and of free communication among the people thereon, which has ever been justly deemed the only effectual guardian of every other right."

Without scrutinizing minutely into all the provisions of the Sedition Act, it will be sufficient to cite so much of section 2d as follows : — " And be it further enacted, that if any shall write, print, utter, or publish, or shall cause or procure to be written, printed, uttered, or published, or shall knowingly and willingly assist or aid in writing, printing, uttering, or publishing, any false, scandalous, and malicious writing or writings against the government of the United States, or either house of the Congress of the United States, with an intent to defame the said government, or either house of the said Congress, or the President, or to bring them or either of them into contempt or disrepute, or to excite against them, or either or any of them, the hatred of the good people of the United States, &c., — then such persons, being thereof convicted before any court of the United States having jurisdiction thereof, shall be punished by a fine not exceeding two thousand dollars, and by imprisonment not exceeding two years."

On this part of the act, the following observations present themselves: —

1. The Constitution supposes that the President, the Congress, and each of its Houses, may not discharge their trusts, either from defect of judgment or other causes. Hence they are all made responsible to their constituents, at the returning periods of elections; and the President, who is singly intrusted with very great powers, is, as a further guard, subjected to an intermediate impeachment.

2. Should it happen, as the Constitution supposes it may happen, that either of these branches of the government may not have duly discharged its trust, it is natural and proper, that, according to the cause and degree of their faults, they should be brought into contempt or disrepute, and incur the hatred of the people.

3. Whether it has, in any case, happened that the proceedings of either or all of those branches evince such a violation of duty as to justify a contempt, a disrepute, or hatred among the people, can only be determined by a free examination thereof, and a free communication among the people thereon.

4. Whenever it may have actually happened that proceedings of this sort are chargeable on all or either of the branches of the government, it is the duty, as well as the right, of intelligent and faithful citizens to discuss and promulgate them freely — as well to control them by the censorship of the public opinion, as to promote a remedy according to the rules of the Constitution. And it cannot be avoided that those who are to apply the remedy must feel, in some degree, a contempt or hatred against the transgressing party.

5. As the act was passed on July 14, 1798, and is to be in force until March 3, 1801, it was of course that, during its continuance, two elections of the entire House of Representatives, an election of a part of the Senate, and an election of a President, were to take place.

6. That, consequently, during all these elections, — intended, by the Constitution, to preserve the purity or to purge the faults of the administration, — the great remedial rights of the people were to be exercised, and the responsibility of their public agents to be screened, under the penalties of this act.

May it not be asked of every intelligent friend to the liberties of his country, whether the power exercised in such an act as this ought not to produce great and universal alarm? Whether a rigid execution of such an act, in time past, would not have repressed that information and communication among the people which is indispensable to the just exercise of their electoral rights? And whether such an act, if made perpetual, and enforced with rigor, would not, in time to come, either destroy our free system of government, or prepare a convulsion that might prove equally fatal to it?

In answer to such questions, it has been pleaded that the writings and publications forbidden by the act are those only which are false and malicious, and intended to defame; and merit is claimed for the privilege allowed to authors to justify, by proving the truth of their publications, and for the limitations to which the sentence of fine and imprisonment is subjected.

To those who concurred in the act, under the extraordinary belief that the option lay between the passing of such an act, and leaving in force the common law of libels, which punishes truth equally with falsehood, and submits fine and imprisonment to the indefinite discretion of the court, the merit of good intentions ought surely not to be refused. A like merit may perhaps be due for the discontinuance of the corporal punishment, which the common law also leaves to the discretion of the court. This merit of intention, however, would have been greater, if the several mitigations had not been limited to so short a period; and the apparent inconsistency would have been avoided, between justifying the act, at one time, by contrasting it with the rigors of the common law otherwise in force; and at another time, by appealing to the nature of the crisis as requiring the temporary rigor exerted by the act.

But, whatever may have been the meritorious intentions of all or any who contributed to the Sedition Act, a very few reflections will prove that its baleful tendency is little diminished by the privilege of giving in evidence the truth of the matter contained in political writings.

In the first place, where simple and naked facts alone are in question, there is sufficient difficulty in some cases, and sufficient trouble and vexation in all, in meeting a prosecution from the government with the full and formal proof necessary in a court of law.

But in the next place, it must be obvious to the plainest minds, that opinions and inferences, and conjectural observations, are not only in many cases inseparable from the facts, but may often be more the objects of the prosecution than the facts themselves; or may even be altogether abstracted from particular facts; and that opinion, and inferences, and conjectural observations, cannot be subjects of that kind of proof which appertains to facts, before a court of law.

Again: it is no less obvious that the intent to defame, or bring into contempt, or disrepute, or hatred, — which is made a condition of the offence created by the act, — cannot prevent its pernicious influence on the freedom of the press. For, omitting the inquiry, how far the malice of the intent is an inference of the law from the mere publication, it is manifestly impossible to punish the intent to bring those who administer the government into disrepute or contempt, without striking at the right of freely discussing public characters and measures; because those who engage in such discussions must expect and intend to excite these unfavorable sentiments, so far as they may be thought to be deserved. To prohibit the intent to excite those unfavorable sentiments against those who administer the government, is equivalent to a prohibition of the actual excitement of them; and to prohibit the actual excitement of them is equivalent to a prohibition of discussions having that tendency and effect; which, again, is equivalent to a protection of those who administer the government, if they should at any time deserve the contempt or hatred of the people, against being exposed to it, by free animadversions on their characters and conduct. Nor can there be a doubt, if those in public trust be shielded by penal laws from such strictures of the press as may expose them to contempt, or disrepute, or hatred, where they may deserve it, that, in exact proportion as they may deserve to be exposed, will be the certainty and criminality of the intent to expose them, and the vigilance of prosecuting and punishing it; nor a doubt that a government thus intrenched in penal statutes against the just and natural effects of a culpable administration, will easily evade the responsibility which is essential to a faithful discharge of its duty.

Let it be recollected, lastly, that the right of electing the members of the government constitutes more particularly the essence of a free and responsible government. The value and efficacy of this right depends on the knowledge of the comparative merits and demerits of the candidates for public trust, and on the equal freedom, consequently, of examining and discussing these merits and demerits of the candidates respectively. It has been seen that a number of important elections will take place while the act is in force, although it should not be continued beyond the term to which it is limited. Should there happen, then, as is extremely probable in relation to some one or other of the branches of the government, to be competitions between those who are, and those who are not, members of the government, what will be the situations of the competitors ? Not equal ; because the characters of the former will be covered by the Sedition Act from animadversions exposing them to disrepute among the people, whilst the latter may be exposed to the contempt and hatred of the people without a violation of the act. What will be the situation of the people ? Not free ; because they will be compelled to make their election between competitors whose pretensions they are not permitted by the act equally to examine, to discuss, and to ascertain. And from both these situations will not those in power derive an undue advantage for continuing themselves in it ; which, by impairing the right of election, endangers the blessings of the government founded on it ?

It is with justice, therefore, that the General Assembly have affirmed, in the resolution, as well that the right of freely examining public characters and measures, and of communication thereon, is the only effectual guardian of every other right, as that this particular right is levelled at by the power exercised in the Sedition Act.

The resolution *next* in order is as follows : —

" That this state having, by its Convention, which ratified the Federal Constitution, expressly declared that, among other essential rights, ' the liberty of conscience and of the press cannot be cancelled, abridged, restrained, or modified, by any authority of the United States ;' and, from its extreme anxiety to guard these rights from every possible attack of sophistry and ambition, having, with other states, recommended an amendment for that purpose, which amendment was in due time annexed to the Constitution, it would mark a reproachful inconsistency, and criminal degeneracy, if an indifference were now shown to the most palpable violation of one of the rights thus declared and secured, and to the establishment of a precedent which may be fatal to the other."

To place this resolution in its just light, it will be necessary to recur to the act of ratification by Virginia, which stands in the ensuing form : —

" We, the delegates of the people of Virginia, duly elected in pursuance of a recommendation from the General Assembly, and now met in Convention, having fully and freely investigated and discussed the proceedings of the Federal Convention, and being prepared, as well as the most mature deliberation hath enabled us, to decide thereon, — DO, in the name and in behalf of the people of Virginia, declare and make known, that the powers granted under the Constitution, being derived from the people of the United States, may be resumed by them whensoever the same shall be perverted to their injury or oppression ; and that every power not granted thereby remains with them, and at their will. That, therefore, no right of any denomination can be cancelled, abridged, restrained, or modified, by the Congress, by the Senate or the House of Representatives, acting in any capacity, by the President, or any department or officer of the United States, except in those instances in which power is given by the Constitution for those purposes ; and that, among other essential rights, the liberty of conscience and of the press cannot be cancelled, abridged, restrained, or modified, by any authority of the United States."

Here is an express and solemn declaration by the Convention of the state, that they ratified the Constitution in the sense that no right of any denomination can be cancelled, abridged, restrained, or modified, by the government of the United States, or any part of it, except in those instances in which power is given by the Constitution ; and in the sense, particularly, " that among other essential rights, the liberty of conscience and freedom of the press cannot be cancelled, abridged, restrained, or modified, by any authority of the United States."

Words could not well express, in a fuller or more forcible manner, the understanding of the Convention, that the liberty of conscience and freedom of the press were *equally* and *completely* exempted from all authority whatever of the United States.

Under an anxiety to guard more effectually these rights against every possible danger, the Convention, after ratifying the Constitution, proceeded to prefix to certain amendments proposed by them, a declaration of rights, in which are two articles providing, the one for the liberty of conscience, the other for the freedom of speech and of the press.

Similar recommendations having proceeded from a number of other states; and Congress, as has been seen, having, in consequence thereof, and with a view to extend the ground of public confidence, proposed, among other declaratory and restrictive clauses, a clause expressly securing the liberty of conscience and of the press; and Virginia having concurred in the ratifications which made them a part of the Constitution, — it will remain with a candid public to decide whether it would not mark an inconsistency and degeneracy, if an indifference were now shown to a palpable violation of one of those rights — the freedom of the press; and to a precedent, therein, which may be fatal to the other — the free exercise of religion.

That the precedent established by the violation of the former of these rights may, as is affirmed by the resolution, be fatal to the latter, appears to be demonstrable by a comparison of the grounds on which they respectively rest, and from the scope of reasoning by which the power of the former has been vindicated.

First, Both of these rights, the liberty of conscience, and of the press, rest equally on the original ground of not being delegated by the Constitution, and consequently withheld from the government. Any construction, therefore, that would attack this original security for the one, must have the like effect on the other.

Secondly, They are both equally secured by the supplement to the Constitution; being both included in the same amendment, made at the same time and by the same authority. Any construction or argument, then, which would turn the amendment into a grant or acknowledgment of power, with respect to the press, might be equally applied to the freedom of religion.

Thirdly, If it be admitted that the extent of the freedom of the press, secured by the amendment, is to be measured by the common law on this subject, the same authority may be resorted to for the standard which is to fix the extent of the "free exercise of religion." It cannot be necessary to say what this standard would be — whether the common law be taken solely as the unwritten, or as varied by the written law of England.

Fourthly, If the words and phrases in the amendment are to be considered as chosen with a studied discrimination, which yields an argument for a power over the press, under the limitation that its freedom be not abridged, the same argument results from the same consideration, for a power over the exercise of religion, under the limitation that its freedom be not prohibited.

For, if Congress may regulate the freedom of the press, provided they do not abridge it, because it is said only, " they shall not abridge it," and is not said " they shall make no law respecting it," the analogy of reasoning is conclusive, that Congress may *regulate,* and even *abridge,* the free exercise of religion, provided they do not *prohibit it;* because it is said only, " they shall not prohibit it;" and is *not* said, " they shall make no law *respecting,* or no law *abridging* it."

The General Assembly were governed by the clearest reason, then, in considering the Sedition Act, which legislates on the freedom of the press, as establishing a precedent that may be fatal to the liberty of conscience; and it will be the duty of all, in proportion as they value the security of the latter, to take the alarm at every encroachment on the former.

The two concluding resolutions only remain to be examined. They are in the words following: —

" That the good people of this commonwealth, having ever felt, and continuing to feel, the most sincere affection for their brethren of the other states, the truest anxiety for establishing and perpetuating the union of all, and the most scrupulous fidelity to that Constitution which is the pledge of mutual friendship and the instrument of mutual happiness, — the General Assembly doth solemnly appeal to the like dispositions in the other states, in confidence that they will concur with this commonwealth in declaring, as it does hereby declare, that the acts aforesaid are unconstitutional; and that the necessary and proper measures will be taken, by each, for coöperating with this state, in maintaining, unimpaired, the authorities, rights, and liberties, reserved to the states respectively, or to the people.

" That the governor be desired to transmit a copy of the foregoing resolutions to the executive authority of each of the other states, with a request that the same may be communicated to the legislature thereof; and that a copy be furnished to each of the senators and representatives representing this state in the Congress of the United States."

The fairness and regularity of the course of proceeding here pursued, have not protected it against objections even from sources too respectable to be disregarded.

It has been said that it belongs to the judiciary of the United States, and not the state legislatures, to declare the meaning of the Federal Constitution.

But a declaration that proceedings of the federal government are not warranted by the Constitution, is a novelty neither among the citizens nor among the legislatures of the states; nor are the citizens or the legislature of Virginia singular in the example of it.

Nor can the declarations of either, whether affirming or denying the constitutionality of measures of the federal government, or whether made before or after judicial decisions thereon, be deemed, in any point of view, an assumption of the office of the judge. The declarations in such cases are expressions of opinion, unaccompanied with any other effect than what they may produce on opinion, by exciting reflection. The expositions of the judiciary, on the other hand, are carried into immediate effect by force. The former may lead to a change in the legislative expression of the general will — possibly to a change in the opinion of the judiciary; the latter enforces the general will, whilst that will and that opinion continue unchanged.

And if there be no impropriety in declaring the unconstitutionality of proceedings in the federal government, where can there be the impropriety of communicating the declaration to other states, and inviting their concurrence in a like declaration? What is allowable for one, must be allowable for all; and a free communication among the states, where the Constitution imposes no restraint, is as allowable among the state governments as among other public bodies or private citizens. This consideration derives a weight that cannot be denied to it, from the relation of the state legislatures to the federal legislature as the immediate constituents of one of its branches.

The legislatures of the states have a right also to originate amendments to the Constitution, by a concurrence of two thirds of the whole number, in applications to Congress for the purpose. When new states are to be formed by a junction of two or more states, or parts of states, the legislatures of the states concerned are, as well as Congress, to concur in the measure. The states have a right also to enter into agreements or compacts, with the consent of Congress. In all such cases a communication among them results from the object which is common to them.

It is lastly to be seen, whether the confidence expressed by the Constitution, that the *necessary and proper measures* would be taken by the other states for coöperating with Virginia in maintaining the rights reserved to he states, or to the people, be in any degree liable to the objections raised against it.

If it be liable to objections, it must be because either the object or the means are objectionable.

The object, being to maintain what the Constitution has ordained, is in itself a laudable object.

The means are expressed in the terms " the necessary and proper measures." A proper object was to be pursued by the means both necessary and proper.

To find an objection, then, it must be shown that some meaning was annexed to these general terms which was not proper ; and, for this purpose, either that the means used by the General Assembly were an example of improper means, or that there were no proper means to which the terms could refer.

In the example, given by the state, of declaring the Alien and Sedition Acts to be unconstitutional, and of communicating the declaration to other states, no trace of improper means has appeared. And if the other states had concurred in making a like declaration, supported, too, by the numerous applications flowing immediately from the people, it can scarcely be doubted that these simple means would have been as sufficient as they are unexceptionable.

It is no less certain that other means might have been employed which are strictly within the limits of the Constitution. The legislatures of the states might have made a direct representation to Congress, with a view to obtain a rescinding of the two offensive acts ; or they might have represented to their respective senators in Congress their wish that two thirds thereof would propose an explanatory amendment to the Constitution ; or two thirds of themselves, if such had been their opinion, might, by an application to Congress, have obtained a convention for the same object.

These several means, though not equally eligible in themselves, nor probably to the states, were all constitutionally open for consideration. And if the General Assembly, after declaring the two acts to be unconstitutional, (the first and most obvious proceeding on the subject,) did not undertake to point out to the other states a choice among the further measures that might become necessary and proper, the reserve will not be misconstrued by liberal minds into any culpable imputation.

These observations appear to form a satisfactory reply to every objection which is not founded on a misconception of the terms employed in the resolutions. There is one other, however, which may be of too much importance not to be added. It cannot be forgotten that, among the arguments addressed to those who apprehended danger to liberty from the establishment of the general government over so great a country, the appeal was emphatically made to the intermediate existence of the state governments between the people and that government, to the vigilance with which they would descry the first symptoms of usurpation, and to the promptitude with which they would sound the alarm to the public. This argument was probably not without its effect ; and if it was a proper one then to recommend the establishment of a constitution, it must be a proper one now to assist in its interpretation.

The only part of the two concluding resolutions that remains to be noticed, is the repetition, in the first, of that warm affection to the Union and its members, and of that scrupulous fidelity to the Constitution, which have been invariably felt by the people of this state. As the proceedings were introduced with these sentiments, they could not be more properly closed than in the same manner. Should there be any so far misled as to call in question the sincerity of these professions, whatever regret may be excited by the error, the General Assembly cannot descend into a discussion of it.   Those who have listened to the suggestion can only be left to their own recollection of the part which this state has borne in the establishment of our national independence, or the establishment of our national Constitution, and in maintaining under it the authority and laws of the Union, without a single exception of internal resistance or commotion. By recurring to the facts, they will be able to convince themselves that the representatives of the people of Virginia must be above the necessity of opposing any other shield to attacks on their national patriotism, than their own conscientiousness, and the justice of an enlightened public; who will perceive in the resolutions themselves the strongest evidence of attachment both to the Constitution and the Union, since it is only by maintaining the different governments, and the departments within their respective limits, that the blessings of either can be perpetuated.

The extensive view of the subject, thus taken by the committee, has led them to report to the house, as *the result of the whole*, the following resolution : —

Resolved, That the General Assembly, having carefully and respectfully attended to the proceedings of a number of the states, *in answer to the resolutions of December 21, 1798, and having accurately and fully reëxamined and reconsidered the latter, find it to be their indispensable duty* to adhere to the same, as founded in truth, as consonant with the Constitution, and as conducive to its preservation; and more especially to be their duty to renew, as they do hereby renew, their PROTEST against Alien and Sedition Acts, as palpable and alarming infractions of the Constitution.

THE TARIFF. SOUTH CAROLINA. PROTEST.

The Senate and House of Representatives of South Carolina, now met, and sitting in General Assembly, through the Hon. William Smith and the Hon. Robert Y. Hayne, their representatives in the Senate of the United States, do, in the name and on behalf of the good people of the said commonwealth, solemnly *PROTEST* against the system of protecting duties, lately adopted by the federal government, for the following reasons : —

1st. *Because* the good people of this commonwealth believe that the powers of Congress were delegated to it in trust for the accomplishment of certain specified objects which limit and control them, and that every exercise of them for any other purposes, is a violation of the Constitution as unwarrantable as the undisguised assumption of substantive, independent powers not granted or expressly withheld.

2d. *Because* the power to lay duties on imports is, and in its very nature can be, only a means of effecting objects specified by the Constitution; since no free government, and least of all a government of enumerated powers, can of right impose any tax, any more than a penalty, which is not at once justified by public necessity, and clearly within the scope and purview of the social compact; and since the right of confining appropriations of the public money to such legitimate and constitutional objects is as essential to the liberties of the people as their unquestionable privilege to be taxed only by their own consent.

3d. *Because* they believe that the tariff law passed by Congress at its last session, and all other acts of which the principal object is the protection of manufactures, or any other branch of domestic industry, if they be considered as the exercise of a power in Congress to tax the people at its own good will and pleasure, and to apply the money raised to objects not specified in the Constitution, is a violation of these fundamental principles, a breach of a well-defined trust, and a perversion of the high powers vested in the federal government for federal purposes only.

4th. *Because* such acts, considered in the light of a regulation of commerce, are equally liable to objection; since, although the power to regulate commerce may, like other powers, be exercised so as to protect domestic manufactures, yet it is clearly distinguishable from a power to do so *eo nomine*, both in the nature of the thing and in the common acceptation of the terms; and because the confounding of them would lead to the most extravagant results, since the encouragement of domestic industry implies an absolute control over all the interests, resources, and pursuits of a people, and is inconsistent with the idea of any other than a simple, consolidated government.

5th. *Because*, from the contemporaneous exposition of the Constitution in the numbers of the Federalist, (which is cited only because the Supreme Court has recognized its authority,) it is clear that the power to regulate commerce was considered by the Convention as only incidentally connected with the encouragement of agriculture and manufactures; and because the power of laying imposts and duties on imports was not understood to justify, in any case, a prohibition of foreign commodities, except as a means of extending commerce, by coercing foreign nations to a fair reciprocity in their intercourse with us, or for some other *bona fide* commercial purpose.

6th. *Because*, whilst the power to protect manufactures is nowhere expressly granted to Congress, nor can be considered as necessary and proper to carry into effect any specified power, it seems to be expressly reserved to the states, by the 10th section of the 1st article of the Constitution.

7th. *Because*, even admitting Congress to have a constitutional right to protect manufactures by the imposition of duties, or by regulations of commerce, designed principally for that purpose, yet a tariff of which the operation is grossly unequal and oppressive, is such an abuse of power as is incompatible with the principles of a free government and the great ends of civil society, justice, and equality of rights and protection.

8th. *Finally*, because South Carolina, from her climate, situation, and peculiar institutions, is, and must ever continue to be, wholly dependent upon agriculture and commerce, not only for her prosperity, but for her very existence as a state; because the valuable products of her soil — the blessings by which Divine Providence seems to have designed to compensate for the great disadvantages under which she suffers in other respects — are among the very few that can be cultivated with any profit by slave labor; and if, by the loss of her foreign commerce, these products should be confined to an inadequate market, the fate of this fertile state would b: poverty and utter desolation; her citizens, in despair, would emigrate to more fortunate regions, and the whole frame and constitution of her civil polity be impaired and deranged, if not dissolved entirely.

Deeply impressed with these considerations, the representatives of the good people of this commonwealth, anxiously desiring to live in peace with their fellow-citizens, and to do all that in them lies to preserve and perpetuate the union of the states, and liberties of which it is the surest pledge, but feeling it to be their bounden duty to expose and resist all encroachments upon the true spirit of the Constitution, lest an apparent acquiescence in the system of protecting duties should be drawn into precedent — do, in the name of the commonwealth of South Carolina, claim to enter upon the Journal of the Senate their *protest* against it as unconstitutional, oppressive, and unjust.

PRESIDENT JACKSON'S PROCLAMATION,

OF THE 10TH DECEMBER, 1833,

CONCERNING

THE ORDINANCE OF SOUTH CAROLINA. ON THE SUBJECT OF THE TARIFF,

ON THE 24TH NOVEMBER, 1832.

WHEREAS a convention assembled in the state of South Carolina have passed an ordinance, by which they declare "that the several acts, and parts of acts, of the Congress of the United States, purporting to be laws for the imposing duties and imposts on the importation of foreign commodities, and now having actual operation and effect within the United States," and more especially, two acts for the same purposes, passed on the 29th of May, 1828, and on the 14th of July, 1832, " are unauthorized by the Constitution of the United States, and violate the true meaning and intent thereof, and are null and void, and no law," not binding on the citizens of that state or its officers; and by the said ordinance it is further declared to be unlawful for any of the constituted authorities of the state, or of the United States, to enforce the payment of the duties imposed by the said acts within the same state, and that it is the duty of the legislature to pass such laws as may be necessary to give full effect to the said ordinance:

. And whereas, by the said ordinance, it is further ordained, that, in any case of law or equity decided in the courts of said state, wherein shall be drawn in question the validity of the said ordinance, or of the acts of the legislature that may be passed to give it effect, or of the said laws of the United States, no appeal shall be allowed to the Supreme Court of the United States, nor shall any copy of the record be permitted or allowed for that purpose, and that any person attempting to take such appeal shall be punished as for a contempt of court:

And, finally, the said ordinance declares that the people of South Carolina will maintain the said ordinance at every hazard; and that they will consider the passage of any act, by abolishing or closing the ports of the said state, or otherwise obstructing the free ingress or egress of vessels to and from the said ports, or any other act of the federal government to coerce the state, shut up her ports, destroy or harass her commerce, or to enforce the said acts otherwise than through the civil tribunals of the country, as inconsistent with the longer continuance of South Carolina in the Union; and that the people of the said state will thenceforth hold themselves absolved from all further obligation to maintain or preserve their political connection with the people of the other states, and will forthwith proceed to organize a separate government, and do other acts and things which sovereign and independent states may of right do:

And whereas the said ordinance prescribes to the people of South Carolina a course of conduct in direct violation of their duty as citizens of the United States, contrary to the laws of their country, subversive of its Constitution, and having for its object the destruction of the Union — that Union which, coeval with our political existence, led our fathers, without any other ties to unite them than those of patriotism and a common cause, through a sanguinary struggle, to a glorious independence — that sacred Union, hitherto inviolate, which, perfected by our happy Constitution, has brought us, by the favor of Heaven, to a state of prosperity at home, and high consideration abroad, rarely, if ever, equalled in the history of nations. To preserve this bond of our political existence from destruction, to maintain inviolate this state of national honor and prosperity, and to justify the confidence my fellow-citizens have reposed in me, I, Andrew Jackson, President of the United States, have thought proper to issue this my Proclamation, stating my views of the Constitution and laws applicable to the measures adopted by the Convention of South Carolina, and to the reasons they have put forth to sustain them, declaring the course which duty will require me to pursue, and, appealing to the understanding and patriotism of the people, warn them of the consequences that must inevitably result from an observance of the dictates of the Convention.

Strict duty would require of me nothing more than the exercise of those powers with which I am now, or may hereafter be, invested for preserving the peace of the Union, and for the execution of the laws. But the imposing aspect which opposition has assumed in this case, by clothing itself with state authority, and the deep interest which the people of the United States must all feel in preventing a resort to stronger measures, while there is a hope that any thing will be yielded to reasoning and remonstrance, perhaps demand, and will certainly justify, *a full exposition*, to South Carolina and the nation, of the views I entertain of this important question, as well as a distinct enunciation of the course which my sense of duty will require me to pursue.

The ordinance is founded, not on the indefeasible right of resisting acts which are plainly unconstitutional, and too oppressive to be endured, but on the strange position that any one state may not only declare an act of Congress void, but prohibit its execution; that they may do this consistently with the Constitution; that the true construction of that instrument permits a state to retain its place in the Union, and yet be bound by no other of its laws than those it may choose to consider as constitutional. It is true, they add that, to justify this abrogation of a law, it must be palpably contrary to the Constitution; but it is evident that, to give the right of resisting laws of that description, coupled with the uncontrolled right to decide what laws deserve that character, is to give the power of resisting all laws. for, as by the theory, there is no appeal: the reasons alleged by the state, good or bad, must prevail. If it should be said that public opinion is a sufficient check against the abuse of this power, it may be asked why it is not deemed a sufficient guard against the passage of an unconstitutional act by Congress. There is, however, a restraint, in this last case, which makes the assumed power of a state more indefensible, and which does not exist in the other. There are two appeals from an unconstitutional act passed by Congress — one to the judiciary, the other to the people and the states. There is no appeal from the state decision in theory, and the practical illustration shows that the courts are closed against an application to review it, both judges and jurors being sworn to decide in its favor. But reasoning on this subject is superfluous when our social compact, in express terms, declares that the laws of the United States, its Constitution, and treaties made under it, are the supreme law of the land; and, for greater caution, adds, " that the judges in every state shall be bound thereby, any thing in the Constitution or laws of any state to the contrary notwithstanding." And it may be asserted, without fear of refutation, that no federative government could exist without a similar provision. Look, for a moment, to the consequence. If South Carolina considers the revenue laws unconstitutional, and has a right to prevent their execution in the port of Charleston, there would be a clear constitutional objection to their collection in every other port, and no revenue could be collected any where ; for all imposts must be equal. It is no answer to repeat, that an unconstitutional law is no law, so long as the question of its legality is to be decided by the state itself; for every law operating injuriously upon any local interest will be perhaps thought, and certainly represented, as unconstitutional; and, as has been shown, there is no appeal.

If this doctrine had been established at an earlier day, the Union would have been dissolved in its infancy. The excise law in Pennsylvania, the embargo and non-intercourse law in the Eastern States, the carriage tax in Virginia, were all deemed unconstitutional, and were more unequal in their operation than any of the laws now complained of; but, fortunately, none of those states discovered that they had the right now claimed by South Carolina. The war into which we were forced, to support the dignity of the nation and the rights of our citizens, might have ended in defeat and disgrace, instead of victory and honor, if the states who supposed it a ruinous and unconstitutional measure had thought they possessed the right of nullifying the act by which it was declared, and denying supplies for its prosecution. Hardly and unequally as those measures bore upon several members of the Union, to the legislatures of none did this efficient and peaceable remedy, as it is called, suggest itself. The discovery of this important feature in our Constitution was reserved to the present day. To the statesmen of South Carolina belongs the invention, and upon the citizens of that state will unfortunately fall the evils of reducing it to practice.

If the doctrine of a state veto upon the laws of the Union carries with it internal evidence of its impracticable absurdity, our constitutional history will also afford abundant proof that it would have been repudiated with indignation, had it been proposed to form a feature in our government.

In our colonial state, although dependent on another power, we very early considered ourselves as connected by common interest with each other. Leagues were formed for common defence ; and, before the declaration of independence, we were known in our aggregate character as the United Colonies of America. That decisive and important step was taken jointly. We declared ourselves a nation by a joint, not by several acts; and when the terms of our confederation were reduced to form, it was in that of a solemn league of several states, by which they agreed that they would collectively form one nation, for the purpose of conducting some certain domestic concerns and all foreign relations. In the instrument forming that Union is found an article which declares that "every state shall abide by the determinations of Congress on all questions which by that confederation, should be submitted to them."

Under the Confederation, then, no state could legally annul a decision of the Congress, or refuse to submit to its execution; but no provision was made to enforce these decisions. Congress made requisitions, but they were not complied with. The government could not operate on individuals. They had no judiciary, no means of collecting revenue.

But the defects of the Confederation need not be detailed. Under its operation we could scarcely be called a nation. We had neither prosperity at home nor consideration abroad. This state of things could not be endured, and our present happy Constitution was formed — but formed in vain, if this fatal doctrine prevails. It was formed for important objects, that are announced in the preamble made in the name and by the authority of the people of the United States, whose delegates framed, and whose conventions approved it. The most important among these objects — that which is placed first in rank, on which all the others rest — is "*to form a more perfect union*." Now, is it possible that, even if there were no express provision giving supremacy to the Constitution and laws of the United States over those of the states, — can it be conceived, that an instrument made for the purpose of "*forming a more perfect union*" than that of the Confederation, could be so constructed by the assembled wisdom of our country, as to substitute for that Confederation a form of government dependent for its existence on the local interest, the party spirit, of a state, or the prevailing faction of a state? Every man of plain, unsophisticated understanding, who hears the question, will give such an answer as will preserve the Union. Metaphysical subtlety, in pursuit of an impracticable theory, could alone have devised one that is calculated to destroy it.

I consider, then, the power to annul a law of the United States, assumed by one state, *incompatible with the existence of the Union, contradicted expressly by the letter of the Constitution, unauthorized by its spirit, inconsistent with every principle on which it was founded, and destructive of the great object for which it was formed.*

After this general view of the leading principle, we must examine the particular application of it which is made in the ordinance.

The preamble rests its justification on these grounds: It assumes as a fact that the obnoxious laws, although they purport to be laws for raising revenue, were, in reality, intended for the protection of manufactures, which purpose it asserts to be unconstitutional; that the operation of these laws is unequal; that the amount raised by them is greater than is required by the wants of the government; and, finally, that the proceeds are to be applied to objects unauthorized by the Constitution. These are the only causes alleged to justify an open opposition to the laws of the country, and a threat of seceding from the Union, if any attempt should be made to enforce them. The first virtually acknowledges that the law in question was passed under a power expressly given by the Constitution to lay and collect imposts; but its constitutionality is drawn in question from the *motives* of those who passed it.   However apparent this purpose may be in the present case, nothing can be more dangerous than to admit the position that an unconstitutional purpose, entertained by the members who assent to a law enacted under a constitutional power, shall make that law void; for how is that purpose to be ascertained?   Who is to make the scrutiny?   How often may bad purposes be falsely imputed — in how many cases are they concealed by false professions — in how many is no declaration of motive made!   Admit this doctrine, and you give to the states an uncontrolled right to decide; and every law may be annulled under this pretext.   If, therefore, the absurd and dangerous doctrine should be admitted, that a state may annul an unconstitutional law, or one that it deems such, it will not apply to the present one.

The next objection is, that the laws in question operate unequally. This objection may be made with truth to every law that has been or can be passed.   The wisdom of man never yet contrived a system of taxation that would operate with perfect equality.   If the unequal operation of a law makes it unconstitutional, and if all laws of that description may be abrogated by any state for that cause, then, indeed, is the Federal Constitution unworthy of the slightest effort for its preservation.   We have hitherto relied on it as the perpetual bond of our union.   We have received it as the work of the assembled wisdom of the nation.   We have trusted to it as to the sheet anchor of our safety in the stormy times of conflict with a foreign or domestic foe.   We have looked to it with sacred awe as the palladium of our liberties; and with all the solemnities of religion have pledged to each other our lives and fortunes here, and our hopes of happiness hereafter, in its defence and support.   Were we mistaken, my countrymen, in attaching this importance to the Constitution of our country? Was our devotion paid to the wretched, inefficient, clumsy contrivance which this new doctrine would make it?   Did we pledge ourselves to the support of an airy nothing — a bubble that must be blown away by the first breath of disaffection?   Was this self-destroying, visionary theory the work of the profound statesmen, the exalted patriots, to whom the task of constitutional reform was intrusted?

Did the name of Washington sanction, did the states deliberately ratify, such an anomaly in the history of fundamental legislation?   No.   We were not mistaken.   The letter of this great instrument is free from this radical fault.   Its language directly contradicts the imputation; its spirit, its evident intent, contradicts it.   No, we did not err!   Our Constitution does not contain the absurdity of giving power to make laws, and another power to resist them.   The sages, whose memory will always be reverenced, have given us a practical, and, as they hoped, a permanent constitutional compact.   The Father of his Country did not affix his revered name to so palpable an absurdity.   Nor did the states, when they severally ratified it, do so, under the impression that a veto on the laws of the United States was reserved to them, or that they could exercise it by implication. Search the debates in all their conventions; examine the speeches of the most zealous opposers of federal authority; look at the amendments that were proposed: they are all silent — not a syllable uttered, not a vote given, not a motion made, to correct the explicit supremacy given to the laws of the Union over those of the states, or to show that implication, as is now contended, could defeat it.   No, we have not erred!   The Constitution is still the object of our reverence, the bond of our union, our de-

fence in danger, the source of our prosperity in peace : it shall descend as
we have received it, uncorrupted by sophistical construction, to our pos
terity ; and the sacrifices of local interest, of state prejudices, of personal
animosities, that were made to bring it into existence, will again be patri
otically offered for its support.

The two remaining objections made by the ordinance to these laws
are, that the sums intended to be raised by them are greater than are
required, and that the proceeds will be unconstitutionally employed.

The Constitution has given expressly to Congress the right of raising
revenue, and of determining the sum the public exigencies will require.
The states have no control over the exercise of this right, other than that
which results from the power of changing the representatives who abuse
it, and thus procuring redress.   Congress may, undoubtedly, abuse this
discretionary power ; but the same may be said of others with which they
are vested.   Yet the discretion must exist somewhere.   The Constitution
has given it to the representatives of all the people, checked by the representatives of the states, and by the executive power.   The South Carolina
construction gives it to the legislature, or the convention, of a single state,
where neither the people of the different states, nor the states in their separate capicity, nor the chief magistrate elected by the people, have any
representation.   Which is the most discreet disposition of the power?
I do not ask you, fellow-citizens, which is the constitutional disposition :
that instrument speaks a language not to be misunderstood.   But if you
were assembled in general convention, which would you think the safest
depository of this discretionary power, in the last resort?   Would you add
a clause giving it to each of the states, or would you sanction the wise
provisions already made by your Constitution?   If this should be the
result of your deliberations, when providing for the future, are you, can
you be, ready to risk all that we hold dear, to establish, for a temporary
and a local purpose, that which you must acknowledge to be destructive,
and even absurd, as a general provision?   Carry out the consequences of
this right vested in the different states, and you must perceive that the
crisis your conduct presents at this day would recur whenever any law of
the United States displeased any of the states, and that we should soon
cease to be a nation.

The ordinance, with the same knowledge of the future that character-
izes a former objection, tells you that the proceeds of the tax will be unconstitutionally applied.   If this could be ascertained with certainty, the
objection would, with more propriety, be reserved for the law so applying
the proceeds, but surely cannot be urged against the laws levying the duty.

These are the allegations contained in the ordinance.   Examine them
seriously, my fellow-citizens — judge for yourselves.   I appeal to you to
determine whether they are so clear, so convincing, as to leave no doubt
of their correctness ; and even if you should come to this conclusion, how
far they justify the reckless, destructive course, which you are directed to
pursue.   Review these objections, and the conclusions drawn from them,
once more.   What are they?   Every law, then, for raising revenue, according to the South Carolina ordinance, may be rightfully annulled, unless it
be so framed as no law ever will or can be framed.   Congress have a right
o pass laws for raising revenue, and each state has a right to oppose their
execution — two rights directly opposed to each other ; and yet is this
absurdity supposed to be contained in an instrument drawn, for the express
purpose of avoiding collisions between the states and the general govern-

ment, by an assembly of the most enlightened statesmen and purest patriots ever imbodied for a similar purpose!

In vain have these sages declared that Congress shall have power to lay and collect taxes, duties, imposts, and excises; in vain have they provided that they shall have power to pass laws which shall be necessary and proper to carry those powers into execution; that those laws and that Constitution shall be the "supreme law of the land, and that the judges in every state shall be bound thereby, any thing in the constitution or laws of any state to the contrary notwithstanding;" in vain have the people of the several states solemnly sanctioned these provisions, made them their paramount law, and individually sworn to support them whenever they were called on to execute any office; — vain provisions! ineffectual restrictions! vile profanation of oaths! miserable mockery of legislation! — if a bare majority of the voters in any one state may, on a real or supposed knowledge of the intent with which a law has been passed, declare themselves free from its operation — say, "Here it gives too little, there too much, and operates unequally — here it suffers articles to be free that ought to be taxed — there it taxes those that ought to be free — in this case the proceeds are intended to be applied to purposes which we do not approve — in that, the amount raised is more than is wanted.

"Congress, it is true, are vested by the Constitution with the right of deciding these questions according to their sound discretion.   Congress is composed of the representatives of all the states, and of all the people of all the states; but WE, part of the people of one state, to whom the Constitution has given no power on the subject, from whom it has expressly taken it away, — *we*, who have solemnly agreed that this Constitution shall be our law, — *we*, most of whom have sworn to support it, — *we* now abrogate this law, and swear, and force others to swear, that it shall not be obeyed. And we do this, not because Congress have no right to pass such laws,— this we do not allege, — but because they have passed them with improper views.   They are unconstitutional from the motives of those who passed them, which we can never with certainty know; from their unequal operation, although it is impossible, from the nature of things, that they should be equal; and from the disposition which we presume may be made of their proceeds, although that disposition has not been declared."   This is the plain meaning of the ordinance in relation to laws which it abrogates for alleged unconstitutionality.   But it does not stop there   It repeals, in express terms, an important part of the Constitution itself, and of laws passed to give it effect, which have never been alleged to be unconstitutional.   The Constitution declares that the judicial powers of the United States extend to cases arising under the laws of the United States, and that such laws, the Constitution, and treaties, shall be paramount to the state constitutions and laws.   The judiciary act prescribes the mode by which the case may be brought before a court of the United States, by appeal, when a state tribunal shall decide against this provision of the Constitution.   The ordinance declares there shall be no appeal: makes the state law paramount to the Constitution and laws of the United States; forces judges and jurors to swear that they will disregard their provisions; and even makes it penal in a suitor to attempt relief by appeal.   It further declares that it shall not be lawful for the authorities of the United States, or of that state, to enforce the payment of duties imposed by the revenue laws within its limits.

Here is a law of the United States, not even pretended to be unconstitutional, repealed by the authority of a small majority of the voters of a single state.   Here is a provision of the Constitution which is solemnly abrogated by the same authority.

On such expositions and reasonings, the ordinance grounds not only an assertion of the right to annul the laws of which it complains, but to enforce it by a threat of seceding from the Union if any attempt is made to execute them.

This right to secede is deduced from the nature of the Constitution, which, they say, is a compact between sovereign states, who have preserved their whole sovereignty, and, therefore, are subject to no super or; that, because they made the compact, they can break it when, in their opinion, it has been departed from by the other states.   Fallacious as this course of reasoning is, it enlists state pride, and finds advocates in the honest prejudices of those who have not studied the nature of our government sufficiently to see the radical error on which it rests.

The people of the United States formed the Constitution, acting through the state legislatures in making the compact to meet and discuss its provisions, and acting in separate conventions when they ratified those provisions; but the terms used in its construction show it to be a government in which the people of all the states collectively are represented.   We are ONE PEOPLE in the choice of the President and Vice-President.   Here the states have no other agency than to direct the mode in which the votes shall be given.   The candidates having the majority of all the votes are chosen.   The electors of a majority of states may have given their votes for one candidate, and yet another may be chosen.   The people, then, and not the states, are represented in the executive branch.

In the House of Representatives there is this difference, that the people of one state do not, as in the case of President and Vice-President, all vote for the same officers.   The people of all the states do not vote for all the members, each state electing only its own representatives.   But this creates no material distinction.   When chosen, they are all representatives of the United States, not representatives of the particular state from whence they come.   They are paid by the United States, not by the state, nor are they accountable to it for any act done in the performance of their legislative functions; and however they may, in practice, as it is their duty to do, consult and prefer the interests of their particular constituents when they come in conflict with any other partial or local interest, yet it is their first and highest duty, as representatives of the United States, to promote the general good.

The Constitution of the United States, then, forms a *government*, not a league; and whether it be formed by compact between the states, or in any other manner, its character is the same.   It is a government in which all the people are represented, which operates directly on the people individually, not upon the states.   They retained all the power they did not grant: but each state, having expressly parted with so many powers as to constitute, jointly with the other states, a single nation, cannot, from that period, possess any right to secede, because such secession does not break a league, but destroys the unity of a nation; and any injury to that unity is not only a breach which would result from the contravention of a compact, but it is an offence against the whole Union.   To say that any state may at pleasure secede from the Union, is to say that the United States are not a nation; because it would be a solecism to contend that any part of a nation might dissolve its connection with the other parts, to their injury or ruin, without committing any offence.   Secession, like any other revolutionary act, may be morally justified by the extremity of oppression; but to call it a constitutional right, is confounding the meaning of terms, and can only be done through gross error, or to deceive those who are willing to assert a right, but would pause before they made a revolution, or incur the penalties consequent on a failure.

Because the Union was formed by compact, it is said the parties to that compact may, when they feel themselves aggrieved, depart from it; but it is precisely because it is a compact that they cannot.   A compact is an agreement or binding obligation.   It may, by its terms, have a sanction or penalty for its breach, or it may not.   If it contains no sanction, it may be broken with no other consequence than moral guilt : if it have a sanction, then the breach insures the designated or implied penalty.   A league between independent nations, generally, has no sanction other than a moral one ; or if it should contain a penalty, as there is no common superior, it cannot be enforced.   A government, on the contrary, always has a sanction, express or implied ; and, in our case, it is both necessarily implied and expressly given.   An attempt, by force of arms, to destroy a government, is an offence, by whatever means the constitutional compact may have been formed ; and such government has the right, by the law of self-defence, to pass acts for punishing the offender, unless that right is modified, restrained, or resumed, by the constitutional act.   In our system, although it is modified in the case of treason, yet authority is expressly given to pass all laws necessary to carry its powers into effect, and, under this grant, provision has been made for punishing acts which obstruct the due administration of the laws.

It would seem superfluous to add any thing to show the nature of that union which connects us ; but, as erroneous opinions on this subject are the foundation of doctrines the most destructive to our peace, I must give some further development to my views on this subject.   No one, fellow-citizens, has a higher reverence for the reserved rights of the states than the magistrate who now addresses you.   No one would make greater personal sacrifices, or official exertions, to defend them from violation ; but equal care must be taken to prevent, on their part, an improper interference with, or resumption of, the rights they have vested in the nation. The line has not been so distinctly drawn as to avoid doubts, in some cases, of the exercise of power.   Men of the best intentions and soundest views may differ in their construction of some parts of the Constitution ; but there are others on which dispassionate reflection can leave no doubt. Of this nature appears to be the assumed right of secession.

It rests, as we have seen, on the alleged undivided sovereignty of the states, and on their having formed, in this sovereign capacity, a compact which is called the Constitution, from which, because they made it, they have the right to secede.   Both of these positions are erroneous, and some of the arguments to prove them so have been anticipated.

The states severally have not retained their entire sovereignty.

It has been shown that, in becoming parts of a nation, not members of a league, they surrendered many of their essential parts of sovereignty. The right to make treaties, declare war, levy taxes, exercise exclusive judicial and legislative powers, were all of them functions of sovereign power.   The states, then, for all these purposes, were no longer sovereign. The allegiance of their citizens was transferred, in the first instance, to the government of the United States : they became American citizens, and owed obedience to the Constitution of the United States, and to laws made in conformity with the powers it vested in Congress. This last position has not been, and cannot be, denied. How, then, can that state be said to be sovereign and independent whose citizens owe obedience to laws not made by it, and whose magistrates are sworn to disregard those laws when they come in conflict with those passed by another? What shows conclusively that the states cannot be said to have reserved an undivided sovereignty, is, that they expressly ceded the right to punish treason, — not treason against their separate power, but treason against the United States. Treason is an offence against sovereignty, and sovereignty must reside with the power to punish it. But the reserved rights of the states are not less sacred because they have, for their common interest, made the general government the depository of these powers.

The unity of our political character (as has been shown for another purpose) commenced with its very existence. Under the royal government we had no separate character: our opposition to its oppressions began as united colonies. We were the United States under the Confederation; and the name was perpetuated, and the union rendered more perfect, by the Federal Constitution. In none of these stages did we consider ourselves in any other light than as forming one nation. Treaties and alliances were made in the name of all. Troops were raised for the joint defence. How, then, with all these proofs that, under all changes of our position, we had, for designated purposes and defined powers, created national governments — how is it that the most perfect of those several modes of union should now be considered as a mere league that may be dissolved at pleasure? It is from an abuse of terms. Compact is used as synonymous with league, although the true term is not employed, because it would at once show the fallacy of the reasoning. It would not do to say that our Constitution was only a league, but it is labored to prove it a compact, (which in one sense it is,) and then to argue that, as a league is a compact, every compact between nations must of course be a league, and that from such an engagement every sovereign power has a right to recede. But it has been shown that, in this sense, the states are not sovereign, and that, even if they were, and the national Constitution had been formed by compact, there would be no right in any one state to exonerate itself from its obligations.

So obvious are the reasons which forbid this secession, that it is necessary only to allude to them. The union was formed for the benefit of all. It was produced by mutual sacrifices of interests and opinions. Can those sacrifices be recalled? Can the states, who magnanimously surrendered their title to the territories of the west, recall the grant? Will the inhabitants of the inland states agree to pay the duties that may be imposed without their assent by those on the Atlantic or the Gulf, for their own benefit? Shall there be a free port in one state, and onerous duties in another? No one believes that any right exists in a single state to involve the other in these and countless other evils, contrary to the engagements solemnly made. Every one must see that the other states, in self-defence, must oppose it at all hazards.

These are the alternatives that are presented by the convention — a repeal of all the acts for raising revenue, leaving the government without the means of support; or an acquiescence in the dissolution of our Union by the secession of one of its members. When the first was proposed, it was known that it could not be listened to for a moment. It was known, if force was applied to oppose the execution of the laws, that it must be repelled by force; that Congress could not, without involving itself in disgrace, and the country in ruin, accede to the proposition; and yet, if this is not done on a given day, or if any attempt is made to execute the laws, the state is, by the ordinance, declared to be out of the Union. The majority of a convention assembled for the purpose have dictated these terms, or rather this rejection of all terms, in the name of the people of South Carolina. It is true that the government of the state speaks of the submission of their grievances to a convention of all the states, which, he says, they "sincerely and anxiously seek and desire." Yet this obvious and constitutional mode of obtaining the sense of the other states on the construction of the federal compact, and amending it, if necessary, has never been attempted by those who have urged the state on to this destructive measure. The state might have proposed the call for a general convention to the other states, and Congress, if a sufficient number of them concurred, must have called it. But the first magistrate of South Carolina, when he expressed a hope that, "on a review, by Congress and the functionaries of the general government, of the merits of the controversy," such a convention will be accorded to them, must have known that neither Congress, nor any functionary of the general government, has authority to call such a convention, unless it may be demanded by two thirds of the states. This suggestion, then, is another instance of the reckless inattention to the provisions of the Constitution with which this crisis has been madly hurried on; or of the attempt to persuade the people that a constitutional remedy had been sought and refused. If the legislature of South Carolina "anxiously desire" a general convention to consider their complaints, why have they not made application for it in the way the Constitution points out? The assertion that they "earnestly seek it" is completely negatived by the omission.

ON THE TARIFF.

SUMMARY OF THE ARGUMENT ON THE SOUTH CAROLINA EXPOSITION.

(See p. 580.)

"The argument against the constitutional authority [to lay taxes, except for the purposes of revenue] is understood to be maintained on the following grounds, which, though applied to the protection of manufactures, are equally applicable to all other cases, where revenue is not the object. The general government is one of specific powers, and it can rightfully exercise only the powers expressly granted, and those which may be 'necessary and proper' to carry them into effect; all others being reserved expressly to the states, or to the people. It results, necessarily, that those who claim to exercise a power under the Constitution are bound to show that it is expressly granted, or that it is 'necessary and proper,' as a means to execute some of the granted powers. No such proof has been offered in regard to the protection of manufactures.

"It is true that the 8th section of the 1st article of the Constitution authorizes Congress to lay and collect an impost duty; but it is granted as tax power, for the sole purpose of revenue — a power in its nature essen tially different from that of imposing protective or prohibitory duties. The two are incompatible ; for the prohibitory system must end in destroying the revenue from imports. It has been said that the system is a violation of the spirit, and not of the letter, of the Constitution. The distinction is not material. The Constitution may be as grossly violated by acting against its meaning, as against its letter. The Constitution grants to Congress the power of imposing a duty on imports for revenue, which power is abused by being converted into an instrument for rearing up the industry of one section of the country on the ruins of another. The violation, then, consists in using a power, granted for one object, to ad vance another, and that by a sacrifice of the original object. It is, in a word, a *violation of perversion*, the most dangerous of all, because the most insidious, and difficult to resist. Such is the reasoning emanating from high legislative authority." — *Story.*

MR. CALHOUN'S REPORT

ON

THE CIRCULATING, THROUGH THE MAILS, OF INFLAMMATORY APPEALS.

SENATE, *February 4, 1836.*

The message recommends that Congress should pass a law to punish the transmission, through the mail, of incendiary publications intended to instigate the slaves to insurrection. It of course assumes for Congress a right to determine what papers are incendiary and intended to excite insur rection. The question, then, is, Has Congress such a right ? — a question of vital importance to the slaveholding states.

After examining this question with due deliberation, in all its bearings, the committee are of opinion, not only that Congress has not the right, but to admit it would be fatal to those states. Nothing is more clear than that the admission of the right, on the part of Congress, to determine what papers are incendiary, and, as such, to prohibit their circulation through the mail, necessarily involves the right to determine what are not incendi ary, and to enforce their circulation. Nor is it less certain that to admit such a right would be virtually to clothe Congress with the power to abolish slavery, by giving it the means of breaking down all the barriers which the slaveholding states have erected for the protection of their lives and prop erty. It would give Congress, without regard to the prohibition laws of the states, the authority to open the gates to the flood of incendiary publi cations which are ready to break into those states, and to punish all who dare resist as criminals. Fortunately, Congress has no such right. The internal peace and security of the states are under the protection of the states themselves, to the entire exclusion of all authority and control on the part of Congress. It belongs to them, and not to Congress, to de termine what is, or is not, calculated to disturb their peace and security ; and, of course, in the case under consideration, it belongs to the slave holding states to determine what is incendiary and intended to incite to insurrection, and to adopt such defensive measures as may be necessary for their security, with unlimited means of carrying them into effect, except such as may be expressly inhibited to the states by the Constitution. To establish the truth of this position, so essential to the safety of those states, it would seem sufficient to appeal to their constant exercise of this right, at all times, without restriction, or question, both before and since the adoption of the Constitution.

That the states which form our federal Union are sovereign and independent communities, bound together by a constitutional compact, and are possessed of all the powers belonging to distinct and separate states, excepting such as are delegated to be exercised by the general government, is assumed as unquestionable. The compact itself expressly provides that all powers not delegated are reserved to the states and the people. To ascertain, then, whether the power in question is delegated or reserved, it is only necessary to ascertain whether it is to be found among the enumerated powers or not. If it be not among them, it belongs, of course, to the reserved powers. On turning to the Constitution, it will be seen that, while the power of defending the country against external danger is found among the enumerated, the instrument is wholly silent as to the power of defending the internal peace and security of the states, and, of course, reserves to the states this important power, as it stood before the adoption of the Constitution, with no other limitations, as has been stated, except such as are expressly prescribed by the instrument itself. From what has been stated, it may be inferred that the right of a state to defend itself against internal dangers is a part of the great primary and inherent right of self-defence, which, by the laws of nature, belongs to all communities; and so jealous were the states of this essential right, without which their independence could not be preserved, that it is expressly provided by the Constitution, that the general government shall not assist a state, even in case of domestic violence, except on the application of the authorities of the state itself; thus excluding, by a necessary consequence, its interference in all other cases.

ABOLITION. — RECEPTION OF PETITIONS.

HOUSE, *January,* 1836.

Mr. CUSHING. Looking into the Constitution, I find, among the amendments proposed by the Congress of 1789, and in the very first of the number, the following article : —

" Congress shall make no law respecting an establishment of religion, or prohibiting the free exercise thereof, or abridging the freedom of speech or of the press, *or the right of the people peaceably to assemble and to petition the government for a redress of grievances.*"

Long before I had imagined that such a right would ever be called in question, I remember to have read the remark of a distinguished jurist and magistrate of the state of Virginia, (Tucker's Notes on Blackstone,) complaining that the concluding words of the clause I have cited from the Constitution did not so strongly guard the great right of petition as the liberties of the people demanded. On the other hand, a still more distinguished jurist and magistrate of my own state, Massachusetts, (Story,) in remarking upon the same article, expresses the opinion that it is ample in terms; because, he adds, " It [the right of petition] results from the very nature of the structure and institutions of a republican government; it is impossible that it should be practically denied until the spirit of liberty had wholly disappeared, and the people had become so servile and debased as to be unfit to exercise any of the privileges of freemen." These eminent constitutional lawyers agreed in opinion of the importance of the provision; they differed only in thinking, the one, that the right of petition could not be too clearly defined; the other, that, whether defectively defined or not in the letter, the people would take care that it should in spirit be faithfully observed. While the first entertained a wise jealousy of the encroachments of the people's representatives, the other looked for the protection of the public rights to the people themselves, the masters of the people's representatives; and, as the fears of the former have been verified too speedily, I trust the hopes of the latter will be not less truly realized.

When the Constitution was submitted to the people of the respective states, for their adoption or rejection, it awakened the warmest debates of the several state conventions. Some of them, in accepting the proposed plan of government, coupled their acceptance with a recommendation of various additions to the Constitution, which they deemed essential to the preservation of the rights of the states, or of the people. The commonwealth of Massachusetts insisted, among other things, on the adoption of that memorable amendment.

New York, North Carolina, and Rhode Island, proposed, either literally or in substance, the same provision; and the consequence was, the addition to the Constitution of the article, which I am now discussing, on the right of conscience, speech, and petition. And, such being the history of this clause, I look to the gentlemen from Virginia especially, constant and honorable as they are in their attachment to constitutional principles at whatever hazard, to go with me in maintaining inviolate this great original right of the people.

SENATE, 1836.

Mr. PRENTISS. If Congress, under the clause giving it "exclusive legislation, in all cases whatsoever," over the District, has authority to impose taxes, and provide how they shall be raised, for local and municipal purposes, I do not see why it has not the power, by means of taxation, to effect the abolition of slavery here. I say nothing of the right or justice of exerting the power for such a purpose. I speak only of the power, and of its capacity to be used to accomplish such an end. But, however this may be, I hold that Congress, if the public interest and welfare require it, may directly, and at once, emancipate the slaves, on making a just compensation to the owners. The clause in the Constitution which regulates the taking of private property for public use, is not, in my opinion, restricted to such property, merely, as may be converted and applied to the actual use and emolument of the public. I think the word *use*, in the Constitution, is to be understood, in a liberal sense, as equivalent to purpose or benefit; and that whatever is taken for public purposes, or for the public benefit, is taken for public use, within the meaning of the Constitution. Neither justice, nor the security of private rights would seem to demand any other or different construction. No principle of justice can be violated, nor can private property be exposed to wrongful and unjust invasions of power, when an equivalent is required to be rendered. A more strict, narrow, and limited interpretation would be obviously less beneficial, and does not appear to be called for either by the words or the intent of the Constitution. Such an interpretation would not only be an unnecessary and inconvenient restraint upon the power of the legislature, but might prevent, in many instances, the accomplishment of objects of the greatest importance — objects of the highest interest and utility to the community. The equivalent prescribed and guarantied by the Constitution is a sure and sufficient security against any abuse of the power; and it certainly is not unreasonable that private rights should yield, on terms of just compensation, to the paramount rights of the public, so far, and to such extent, as the interest and welfare of the public may require, or as may be necessary to effectuate great and useful public purposes.

Mr. HUGH L. WHITE. When the Constitution was framed, the great and leading interests of the whole country were considered, and, in the spirit of liberality and compromise, were adjusted and settled. They were settled upon principles that ought to remain undisturbed so long as the Constitution lasts, which I hope will be forever; for although liberty may be preferable to the Union, yet I think the Union is indispensable to the security of liberty. At the formation of the Constitution, slavery existed in many of the states; it was one of the prominent interests that was then settled. It, in all its domestic bearings, was left exclusively to the respective states to do with as they might think best, without any interference on the part of the federal government. This, it is admitted by every gentleman who has addressed you, is now the case, in every slaveholding state; therefore it is only urged that Congress has the power to abolish slavery in the District of Columbia. It should never be forgotten that when the Constitution was formed and adopted, what is now the District of Columbia was then comprehended within two of the slaveholding states, Maryland and Virginia.

In my opinion, we should refuse to receive these petitions. It is a mere question of expediency what disposition we shall make of them. All who have yet spoken admit that Congress has no power whatever over slavery in the respective states. It is settled. Whether slavery is right or wrong, we have now no power to consider or discuss. Suppose, then, a petition were presented to abolish slavery in the states; should we receive it? Assuredly we ought not, because it would be asking us to act upon a subject over which we have no power.

Slaves are property in this District. Congress cannot take private property, even for public use, without making just compensation to the owner. No fund is provided by the Constitution to pay for slaves which may be liberated; and the Constitution never gives Congress the power to act upon any subject, without, at the same time, furnishing the means for its accomplishment. To liberate slaves is not taking them for public use. It is declaring that neither individuals nor the public shall use them.

Congress sits here as the legislature of the whole Union, and also as the only legislature for the local concerns of the District of Columbia. These petitions do not ask us to make a general law, operating throughout the whole Union; but a law the operations of which are to be spent entirely upon property within the ten miles square. Now, if we were in form, as well as in substance, a local legislature when acting on this question which gentlemen say is to affect slavery in the District, and nowhere else, should we be bound to receive these petitions? No more than we are bound to receive petitions from France or Germany. Would gentlemen, if sitting as members of the legislature of Alabama, feel bound to receive petitions from citizens of Maine or Pennsylvania to emancipate slaves within their own state? Assuredly not. If that be so, is it not most rea sona'le, when we are called upon to pass an act confined exclusively to this District, that we should conduct towards the people here as if in this matter they were our constituents?

Mr. GRUNDY. He would not go into an examination of the constitutional power of Congress. For his own part, he should consider himself as culpable, were he to vote for such a measure, if the constitutional power existed, as were he to vote for it in the absence of such power. He considered the faith of the government pledged not to interfere with this subject in this District, and the faith of the government should be preserved as sacredly as the Constitution.

It would be recollected that, by the Constitution of the United States, Congress is expressly prohibited from interfering with the slave trade, which might be carried on by the citizens of the different states for the space of twenty-one years; yet in 1790, the society of Quakers, or Friends, forwarded their petition to Congress praying their interference upon that subject. This petition, although in direct opposition to the Constitution, was received, and a motion was made to send it to a committee. This was opposed, and a proposition was made to lay it upon the table. Those most opposed to the object of the petition sustained the latter proposition, Mr. Madison, of Virginia, a slaveholding state, advocated the reference to a committee.

Mr. KING, (of Alabama.) The cession (of the District of Columbia) was made with a clear understanding, implied or otherwise, that no such power (abolition) would ever be claimed. This was apparent from the fact that, at the time of the cession, the states of Virginia and Maryland had, as they still have, a large slave population; and they never would have been so blind to their own safety as to make this cession, could they have believed that Congress thereby acquired the power to produce a state of things in this District that would operate on their slaves in so dangerous a manner. If such, then, was the understanding with which this cession was made, would it not be a violation of the faith pledged to these two states, if government was now to attempt any interference with the prohibited subject?

Mr. BUCHANAN. Although the Constitution, as it came from the hands of its framers, gave to Congress no power to touch the right of petition, yet some of the states to whom it was submitted for ratification, apprehending that the time might arrive when Congress would be disposed to act like the British Parliament, (in Charles II.'s time,) expressly withdrew the subject from our control. Not satisfied with the fact, that no power over it had been granted by the Constitution, they determined to prohibit us, in express terms, from ever exercising such a power.

The proposition [the right of petition] is almost too plain for argument, that, if the people have a constitutional right to petition, a corresponding duty is imposed upon us to receive their petitions. From the very nature of things, rights and duties are reciprocal. The human mind cannot conceive of the one without the other. They are relative terms. If the people have a right to command, it is the duty of their servants to obey. If I have a right to a sum of money, it is the duty of my debtor to pay it to me. If the people have a right to petition their representatives, it is our duty to receive their petition.

This question was solemnly determined by the Senate more than thirty years ago. Neither before nor since that time, so far as I can learn, has the general right of petition ever been called in question; until the motion now under consideration was made by the senator from South Carolina

Mr. KING, (of Georgia.) Congress, under this article, [the first amendment] can pass no law to " abridge " the right of the people to petition the government.   A modern commentator on the Constitution, of some note and much ability, in noticing this part of the article, dismissed it with the remark, that it was totally unnecessary.   This is obvious to every one who will consider for a moment the relation between a free people and the government of their own choice.   The privilege belonged (Mr. K. said) to the form of government — was united with it, and inseparable from it. ' It as clearly belonged to the people, on the formation of the government, as did the right to use the English language without any constitutional provision for that purpose ; and, said Mr. K., if gentlemen will only look at the Constitution, and not evade it, they will see that the right was not ACQUIRED by the Constitution, but only SECURED by it. The right, as a preëxisting one, was expressly recognized by the language of the Constitution itself.   What was the language applicable to the question before the Senate ?   It prevented Congress from passing any law " abridging the right of the people to petition," &c.

The right belonged to the people as inseparably incident to their form of government ; was acknowledged to exist by the language of the Constitution ; and was guardedly secured by the provisions of that instrument.

Mr. CALHOUN.   The first amended article of the Constitution, which provides that Congress shall pass no law to prevent the people from peaceably assembling and petitioning for a redress of grievances, was clearly intended to prescribe the limits within which the right might be exercised. It is not pretended that to refuse to receive petitions, touches, in the slightest degree, on these limits.   To suppose that the framers of the Constitution — no, not the framers, but those jealous patriots who were not satisfied with that instrument as it came from the hands of the framers, and who proposed this very provision to guard what they considered a sacred right — performed their task so bunglingly as to omit any essential guard, would be to do great injustice to the memory of those stern and sagacious men.

If the Constitution makes it our duty to receive, we should have no discretion left to reject, as the motion presupposes.   Our rules of proceeding must accord with the Constitution.   Thus, in the case of revenue bills, which, by the Constitution, must originate in the other house, it would be out of order to introduce them here; and it has accordingly been so decided.   For like reasons, if we are bound to receive petitions, the present motion would be out of order ; and, if such should be your opinion, it is your duty, as the presiding officer, to call me to order, and to arrest all further discussion on the question of reception.

EXPUNGING RESOLUTION.

SENATE, 1836.

Mr. LEIGH.   The original manuscript journal is *the journal* — that journal which the Constitution commands us to *keep*.   But gentlemen insist that the constitutional provision, that " each house shall *keep* a journal," imports only that they shall *make* one, without requiring that they shall *preserve* it.

This Anglo-Saxon word *to keep* is generally used in a strict literal sense, and then always imports *to preserve*, and nothing else or more.   It is used in divers metaphorical senses, which, from frequency, have the appearance, at first view, of being literal; but it always imports the idea of preservation or indefinite continuation, requested or commanded. It is never used as synonymous with *making* any thing.

I think myself well warranted in saying that the expunging of the resolution of the Senate of the 23th of March, 1834, from the journal, literally or figuratively, is wholly irreconcilable with the Constitution, upon any fair construction of its words; and that no authority for such expunction can be found in any precedent whatever at all applicable to the purpose, or entitled to the least weight. I think myself warranted in saying, too, that, if the Senate shall adopt this proposition, and carry it into execution, it will set a precedent fraught with the most dangerous and pernicious consequences.

Mr. RIVES. In the jealous apprehensions which were entertained, at the time of the adoption of the Constitution, of the encroachments and abuses of the new government, this objection was strongly urged against the clause in question; but it was replied, and with success, that every legislative body must have the power of concealing important transactions, the publication of which might compromise the public interests; and as it was impossible to foresee and enumerate all the cases in which such concealment might be necessary, they should be left to the sound discretion of the body itself, subject to the constitutional responsibility of its members, and the other securities provided by the Constitution against the abuse of power. These securities have hitherto been found sufficient; and, in point of fact, the journals of both houses have been published from day to day, with such special and limited exceptions as have been universally approved by the public judgment.

This publication, when made, is the practical fulfilment and consummation of the design of the Constitution in requiring a journal to be kept, by either house, of its proceedings. It is agreed, on all hands, that the great object for which a journal is required to be kept is, to give authentic information to our constituents of our proceedings; and that information is to be given, as the Constitution provides, by means of a publication, from time to time, of the journal itself. The requisition to keep a journal, on which gentlemen have laid so much stress, is therefore merely introductory, or what the lawyers call matter of *inducement* only, to that which forms the life and substance of the provision, to wit, the *publication*, from time to time, of the journal. The whole structure and sequence of the sentence sustains this interpretation: " each house shall keep a journal of its proceedings, and, from time to time, *publish* the same." It is evident that the whole practical virtue and effect of the provision is in the latter member of the sentence, and that the former would have been implied and comprehended in it, though not expressed.

The requisition in the present Constitution, to keep a journal, is but an expression, for the sake of greater fulness, of what would otherwise have been implied, and serves only as a more formal introduction to the practical end and substance of the constitutional provision on the subject, and that with which it emphatically concludes, to wit, *the publication*, from time to time, of the journal. That publication once made, and the people put in possession of the authentic evidence of the proceedings of their agents, the purposes of the Constitution are fulfilled, and the preservation of the original manuscript journal becomes thenceforward an official formality.

APPENDIX.

MADISON ON THE TARIFF.

LETTER I.

Montpelier, *September* 18, 1828.

Dear Sir: Your late letter reminds me of our conversation on the constitutionality of the power in Congress to impose a tariff for the encouragement of manufactures, and of my promise to sketch the grounds of the confident opinion I had expressed that it was among the powers vested in that body.

The Constitution vests in Congress, expressly, "the power to lay and collect taxes, duties, imposts, and excises," and "the power to regulate trade."

That the former power, if not particularly expressed, would have been included in the latter as one of the objects of a general power to regulate trade, is not necessarily impugned by its being so expressed. Examples of this sort cannot sometimes be easily avoided, and are to be seen elsewhere in the Constitution. Thus the power "to define and punish offences against the law of nations" includes the power, afterwards particularly expressed, "to make rules concerning captures, &c., from offending neutrals." So also a power "to coin money" would doubtless include that of "regulating its value," had not the latter power been expressly inserted. The term *taxes*, if standing *alone*, would certainly have included duties, imposts, and excises. In another clause, it is said, "no tax or duties shall be laid on exports," &c. Here the two terms are used as synonymous. And in another clause, where it is said, "No state shall lay any impost, or duties," &c., the terms *imposts* and *duties* are synonymous. Pleonasms, tautologies, and the promiscuous use of terms and phrases, differing in their shades of meaning, (always to be expounded with reference to the context, and under the control of the general character and manifest scope of the instrument in which they are found,) are to be ascribed, sometimes to the purpose of greater caution, sometimes to the imperfections of language, and sometimes to the imperfection of man himself. In this view of the subject, it was quite natural, however certainly the general power to regulate trade might include a power to impose duties on it, not to omit it in a clause enumerating the several modes of revenue authorized by the Constitution. In few cases could the "*ex majori cautela*" occur with more claim to respect.

Nor can it be inferred that a power to regulate trade does not involve a power to tax it, from the distinction made in the original controversy with Great Britain, between a power to regulate trade with the colonies, and a power to tax them. A power to regulate trade between different parts of the empire was confessedly *necessary*, and was admitted to lie, as far as that was the case, in the British Parliament; the taxing part being at the same time denied to the Parliament, and asserted to be necessarily inherent in the colonial legislatures, as sufficient, and the only safe depositories of the taxing power. So difficult was it, nevertheless, to maintain the distinction in practice, that the ingredient of revenue was occasionally overlooked or disregarded in the British regulations, as in the duty on sugar and molasses imported into the colonies. And it was fortunate that the attempt at an internal and direct tax, in the case of the stamp act, produced a radical examination of the subject before a regulation of trade, with a view to revenue, had grown into an established authority. One thing at least is certain — that the main and admitted object of the parliamentary *regulations* of trade with the colonies was the encouragement of manufactures in Great Britain.

But the present question is unconnected with the former relations between

Great Britain and her colonies, which were of a peculiar, a complicated, an I, in several respects, of an undefined character. It is a simple question, under the Constitution of the United States, whether "the power to regulate trade with foreign nations," as a distinct and substantive item in the enumerated powers, embraces the object of encouraging by duties, restrictions, and prohibitions, the manufactures and products of the country. And the affirmative must be inferred from the following considerations: —

1. The meaning of the phrase "to regulate trade" must be sought in the general use of it; in other words, in the objects to which the power was generally understood to be applicable when the phrase was inserted in the Constitution.

2. The power has been understood and used, by all commercial and manufacturing nations, as embracing the object of encouraging manufactures. It is believed that not a single exception can be named.

3. This has been particularly the case with Great Britain, whose commercial vocabulary is the parent of ours. A primary object of her commercial regulations is well known to have been, the protection and encouragement of her manufactures.

4. Such was understood to be a proper use of the power by the states most prepared for manufacturing industry, whilst retaining the power over their foreign trade.

5. Such a use of the power by Congress accords with the intention and expectation of the states, in transferring the power over trade from themselves to the government of the United States. This was emphatically the case in the Eastern, the more manufacturing members of the confederacy. Hear the language held in the Convention of Massachusetts.

By Mr. Dawes, an advocate for the Constitution, it was observed — "Our manufactures are another great subject which has received no encouragement by national duties on foreign manufactures, and they never can by any authority in the old Confederation." Again — "If we wish to encourage our own manufactures, to preserve our own commerce, to raise the value of our own lands, we must give Congress the powers in question."

By Mr. Wilgery, an opponent — "All we hear is, that the merchant and farmer will flourish, and that the mechanic and tradesman are to make their fortunes directly, if the Constitution goes down."

The Convention of Massachusetts was the only one in New England whose debates have been preserved.* But it cannot be doubted that the sentiment there expressed was common to the other states in that quarter, more especially to Connecticut and Rhode Island, the most thickly-peopled of all the states, and having, of course, their thoughts most turned to the subject of manufactures. A like inference may be confidently applied to New Jersey, whose debates in Convention have not been preserved. In the populous and manufacturing state of Pennsylvania, a partial account only of the debates having been published, nothing certain is known of what passed in her Convention on this point. But ample evidence may be found elsewhere, that regulations of trade, for the encouragement of manufactures, were considered as within the powers to be granted to the new Congress, as well as within the scope of the national policy. Of the states south of Pennsylvania, the only two in whose Conventions the debates have been preserved are Virginia and North Carolina; and from these no adverse inferences can be drawn; nor is there the slightest indication that either of the two states farthest south, whose debates in Convention, if preserved, have not been made public, viewed the encouragement of manufactures as not within the general power over trade to be transferred to the government of the United States.

6. If Congress have not the power, it is annihilated for the nation — a policy without example in any other nation, and not within the reason of the solitary one in our own. The example alluded to is the prohibition of a tax on exports, which resulted from the apparent impossibility of raising, in that mode, a revenue from the states, proportioned to the ability to pay it — the ability of some

* Except a portion of the Convention of Connecticut.   See vol. ii

being derived, in a great measure, not from their exports, but from their fisheries, from their freights, and from commerce at large, in some of its branches altogether external to the United States; the profits from all which, being invisible and intangible, would escape a tax on exports. A tax on imports, on the other hand, being a tax on consumption, which is in proportion to the ability of the consumers, whencesoever derived, was free from that inequality.

7. If revenue be the sole object of a legitimate impost, and the encouragement of domestic articles be not within the power of regulating trade, it would follow that no monopolizing or unequal regulations of foreign nations could be counteracted; that neither the staple articles of subsistence, nor the essential implements for the public safety, could, under any circumstances, be insured or fostered at home, by regulations of commerce, the usual and most convenient mode of providing for both; and that the American navigation, though the source of naval defence, of a cheapening competition in carrying our valuable and bulky articles to market, and of an independent carriage of them during foreign wars, when a foreign navigation might be withdrawn, must be at once abandoned, or speedily destroyed; it being evident that a tonnage duty, in foreign ports, against our vessels, and an exemption from such a duty in our ports, in favor of foreign vessels, must have the inevitable effect of banishing ours from the ocean.

To assume a power to protect our navigation, and the cultivation and fabrication of all articles requisite for the public safety, as incident to the war power, would be a more latitudinary construction of the text of the Constitution, than to consider it as embraced by the specified power to regulate trade — a power which has been exercised by all nations for those purposes, and which effects those purposes with less of interference with the authority and conveniency of the states than might result from internal and direct modes of encouraging the articles, any of which modes would be authorized, as far as deemed " necessary and proper," by considering the power as an incidental power.

8. That the encouragement of manufactures was an object of the power to regulate trade, is proved by the use made of the power for that object, in the first session of the first Congress under the Constitution; when among the members present were so many who had been members of the Federal Convention which framed the Constitution, and of the state Conventions which ratified it; each of these classes consisting also of members who had opposed, and who had espoused, the Constitution in its actual form. It does not appear, from the printed proceedings of Congress on that occasion, that the power was denied by any of them; and it may be remarked that members from Virginia, in particular, as well of the anti-federal as the federal party, — the names then distinguishing those who had opposed and those who had approved the Constitution, — did not hesitate to propose duties, and to suggest even prohibitions in favor of several articles of her productions. By one a duty was proposed on mineral coal, in favor of the Virginia coal-pits; by another, a duty on hemp was proposed, to encourage the growth of that article; and by a third, a prohibition even of foreign beef was suggested, as a measure of sound policy.

A further evidence in support of the constitutional power to protect and foster manufactures by regulations of trade, — an evidence that ought of itself to settle the question, — is the uniform and practical sanction given to the power, by the general government, for nearly forty years, with a concurrence or acquiescence of every state government throughout the same period, and, it may be added, through all the vicissitudes of party which marked the period. No novel construction, however ingeniously devised, or however respectable and patriotic its patrons, can withstand the weight of such authorities, or the unbroken current of so prolonged and universal a practice. And well it is that this cannot be done without the intervention of the same authority which made the Constitution. If it could be so done, there would be an end to that stability in government, and in laws, which is essential to good government and good laws — a stability, the want of which is the imputation which has at all times been levelled against republicanism, with most effect, by its most dexterous adversaries.

The imputation ought never, therefore, to be countenanced, by innovating constructions, without any plea of precipitancy, or a paucity of the constructive precedents they oppose; without any appeal to material facts newly brought to light; without any claim to a better knowledge of the original evils and inconveniences for which remedies were needed — the very best keys to the true object and meaning of all laws and constitutions.

And may it not be fairly left to the unbiased judgment of all men of experience and of intelligence, to decide, which is most to be relied on for a sound and safe test of the meaning of a constitution, — a uniform interpretation by all the successive authorities under it, commencing with its birth, and continued for a long period, through the varied state of political contests; or the opinion of every new legislature, heated as it may be by the strife of parties — or warped, as often happens, by the eager pursuit of some favorite object — or carried away, possibly, by the powerful eloquence or captivating addresses of a few popular statesmen, themselves, perhaps, influenced by the same misleading causes? If the latter test is to prevail, every new legislative opinion might make a new constitution, as the foot of every new chancellor would make a new standard of measure.

It is seen, with no little surprise, that an attempt has been made, in a highly-respectable quarter, and at length reduced to a resolution, formally proposed in Congress, to substitute, for the power of Congress to regulate trade so as to encourage manufactures, a power in the several states to do so, with the consent of that body; and this expedient is derived from a clause in the 10th section of article 1st of the Constitution, which says, "No state shall, without the consent of Congress, lay any imposts or duties on imports or exports, except what may be absolutely necessary for executing its inspection laws; and the net produce of all du ies and imposts, laid by any state on imports and exports, shall be for the use of the treasury of the United States; and all such laws shall be subject to the revision and control of the Congress."

To say nothing of the clear indications in the Journal of the Convention of 1787, that the clause was intended merely to provide for expenses incurred by particular states, in their inspection laws, and in such improvements as they might choose to make in their harbors and rivers, with the sanction of Congress, — objects to which the reserved power has been applied, in several instances, at the request of Virginia and Georgia, — how could it ever be imagined that any state would wish to tax its own trade for the encouragement of manufactures, if possessed of the authority — or could, in fact, do so, if wishing it?

A tax on imports would be a tax on its own consumption; and the net proceeds going, according to the clause, not into its own treasury, but into the treasury of the United States, the state would tax itself separately for the equal gain of all the other states; and as far as the manufactures, so encouraged, might succeed in ultimately increasing the stock in market, and lowering the price by competition, this advantage, also, procured at the sole expense of the state, would be common to all the others.

But the very suggestion of such an expedient to any state would have an air of mockery, when its *experienced* impracticability is taken into view. No one, who recollects or recurs to the period when the power over commerce was in the individual states, and separate attempts were made to tax, or otherwise regulate it, need be told that the attempts were not only abortive, but, by demonstrating the necessity of general and uniform regulations, gave the original impulse to the constitutional reform which provided for such regulations.

To refer a state, therefore, to the exercise of a power, as reserved to her by the Constitution, the impossibility of exercising which was an inducement to adopt the Constitution, is, of all remedial devices, the last that ought to be brought forward. And what renders it the more extraordinary is, that, as the tax on commerce, as far as it could be separately collected, instead of belonging to the treasury of the state, as previous to the Constitution, would be a tribute to the United States, the state would be in a worse condition, after the adoption of the Constitution, than before, in reference to an important interest, the improvement of which was a particular object in adopting the Constitution.

Were Congress to make the proposed declaration of consent to state tariffs in favor of state manufactures, and the permitted attempts did not defeat them selves, who would be the situation of states deriving their foreign supplies through the ports of other states? It is evident that they might be compelled to pay, in their consumption of particular articles imported, a tax for the common treasury, not common to all the states, without having any manufacture or product of their own, to partake of the contemplated benefit.

Of the impracticability of separate regulations of trade, and the resulting necessity of general regulations, no state was more sensible than Virginia. She was accordingly among the most earnest for granting to Congress a power adequate to the object. On more occasions than one, in the proceedings of her legislative councils, it was recited, "that the relative situation of the states had been found, on *trial*, to require *uniformity* in their commercial regulations, as the *only* effectual policy for obtaining, in the ports of foreign nations a stipulation of privileges reciprocal to those enjoyed, by the subjects of such nations, in the ports of the United States; for preventing animosities which cannot fail to arise among the several states from the interference of partial and separate regulations; and for deriving from commerce such aids to the public revenue as it ought to contribute, &c.

During the delays and discouragements experienced in the attempts to invest Congress with the necessary powers, the state of Virginia made various trials of what could be done by her individual laws. She ventured on duties and imposts as a source of revenue; resolutions were passed, at one time, to encourage and protect her own navigation and ship-building; and in consequence of complaints and petitions from Norfolk, Alexandria, and other places, against the monopolizing navigation laws of Great Britain, particularly in the trade *between the United States and the British West Indies*, she deliberated, with a purpose controlled only by the inefficacy of separate measures, on the experiment of forcing a reciprocity by prohibitory regulations of her own.

The effect of her separate attempts to raise revenue by duties on imports soon appeared in representations from her merchants that the commerce of the state was banished by them into other channels, especially of Maryland, where imports were less burdened than in Virginia.

Such a tendency of separate regulations was, indeed, too manifest to escape anticipation. Among the projects prompted by the want of a federal authority over commerce, was that of a concert, first proposed on the part of Maryland, for a uniformity of regulations between the two states; and commissioners were appointed for that purpose. It was soon perceived, however, that the concurrence of Pennsylvania was as necessary to Maryland as of Maryland to Virginia, and the concurrence of Pennsylvania was accordingly invited. But Pennsylvania could no more concur without New York than Maryland without Pennsylvania, nor New York without the concurrence of Boston, &c.

These projects were superseded, for the moment, by that of the Convention at Annapolis in 1786, and forever by the Convention at Philadelphia in 1787, and the Constitution which was the fruit of it.

There is a passage in Mr. Necker's work on the finances of France which affords a signal illustration of the difficulty of collecting, in contiguous communities, indirect taxes, when not the same in all, by the violent means resorted to against smuggling from one to another of them. Previous to the late revolutionary war in that country, the taxes were of very different rates in the different provinces; particularly the tax on salt, which was high in the interior provinces and low in the maritime, and the tax on tobacco, which was very high in general, whilst in some of the provinces the use of the article was altogether free. The consequence was, that the standing army of patrols against smuggling had swollen to the number of twenty-three thousand; the annual arrest of men, women, and children, engaged in smuggling, to five thousand five hundred and fifty; and the number annually arrested on account of salt and tobacco alone, to seventeen or eighteen hundred, more than three hundred of whom were consigned to the terrible punishment of the galleys.

May it not be regarded as among the providential blessings to these states, that their geographical relations, multiplied as they will be by artificial channels of intercourse, give such additional force to the many obligations to cherish that union which alone secures their peace, their safety, and their prosperity! Apart from the more obvious and awful consequences of their entire separation into independent sovereignties, it is worthy of special consideration, that, divided from each other as they must be by narrow waters and territorial lines merely, the facility of surreptitious introductions of contraband articles would defeat every attempt at revenue, in the easy and indirect modes of impost and excise: so that, whilst their expenditures would be necessarily and vastly increased by their new situation, they would, in providing for them, be limited to direct taxes on land or other property, to arbitrary assessments on invisible funds, and to the odious tax on persons.

You will observe that I have confined myself, in what has been said, to the constitutionality and expediency of the power in Congress to encourage domestic products by regulations of commerce. In the exercise of the power, they are responsible to their constituents, whose right and duty it is, in that as in all other cases, to bring their measures to the test of justice and of the general good. With great esteem and cordial respect,

Jos. C. Cabell, Esq. JAMES MADISON.

LETTER II.

Montpelier, *October* 30, 1828.

In my letter of September 18th, I stated briefly the grounds on which I rested my opinion, that a power to impose duties and restrictions on imports, with a view to encourage domestic productions, was constitutionally lodged in Congress. In the observations then made was involved the opinion, also, that the power was properly there lodged. As this last opinion necessarily implies that there are cases in which this power may be usefully exercised by Congress, — the only body within our political system capable of exercising it with effect, — you may think it incumbent on me to point out cases of that description.

I will premise that I concur in the opinion, that, as a *general* rule, individuals ought to be deemed the best judges of the best application of their industry and resources.

I am ready to admit, also, that there is no country in which the application may, with more safety, be left to the intelligence and enterprise of individuals, than the United States.

Finally, I shall not deny, that, in all doubtful cases, it becomes every government to lean rather to a confidence in the judgment of individuals, than to interpositions controlling the free exercise of it.

With all these concessions, I think it can be satisfactorily shown that there are exceptions to the general rule, now expressed by the phrase " Let us alone," forming cases which call for the interposition of the competent authority, and which are not inconsistent with the generality of the rule.

1. The theory of " Let us alone " supposes that all nations concur in a perfect freedom of commercial intercourse. Were this the case, they would, in a commercial view, be but one nation, as much as the several districts composing a particular nation; and the theory would be as applicable to the former as to the latter. But this golden age of free trade has not yet arrived; nor is there a single nation that has set the example. No nation can, indeed, safely do so, until a reciprocity, at least, be insured to it. Take, for a proof, the familiar case of the navigation employed in a foreign commerce. If a nation, adhering to the rule of never interposing a countervailing protection of its vessels, admits foreign vessels into its ports free of duty, whilst its own vessels are subject to a duty in foreign ports, the ruinous effect is so obvious, that the warmest advocate for the theory in question must shrink from a *universal* application of it.

A nation leaving its foreign trade, in all cases, to regulate itself, might soon find it regulated, by other nations, into a subserviency to a foreign interest. In the interval between the peace of 1783 and the establishment of the present Constitution of the United States, the want of a general authority to regulate trade is known to have had this consequence. And have not the pretensions and policy latterly exhibited by Great Britain given warning of a like result from a renunciation of all countervailing regulations on the part of the United

States? Were she permitted, by conferring on certain portions of her domain the name of colonies, to open from there a trade for herself to foreign countries, and to exclude, at the same time, a reciprocal trade to such colonies, by foreign countries, the use to be made of the monopoly need not be traced. Its character will be placed in a just relief by supposing that one of the colonial islands, instead of its present distance, happened to be in the vicinity of Great Britain; or that one of the islands in that vicinity should receive the name and be regarded in the light of a colony, with the peculiar privileges claimed for colonies. Is it not manifest that, in this case, the favored island might be made the sole medium of the commercial intercourse with foreign nations, and the parent country thence enjoy every essential advantage, as to the terms of it, which would flow from an *unreciprocal* trade from her other ports with other nations?

Fortunately, the British claims, however speciously colored or adroitly managed, were repelled at the commencement of our commercial career as an independent people, and at successive epochs under the existing Constitution, both in legislative discussions and in diplomatic negotiations. The claims were repelled on the solid ground that the colonial trade, as a *rightful* monopoly, was limited to the intercourse between the parent country and its colonies, and between one colony and another; the whole being, strictly, in the nature of a coasting trade from one to another port of the same nation — a trade with which no other nation has a right to interfere. It follows, of necessity, that the parent country, whenever it opens a colonial port for a direct trade to a foreign country, departs, itself, from the principle of colonial monopoly, and entitles the foreign country to the same reciprocity, in every respect, as in its intercourse with any other ports of the nation.

This is common sense and common right. It is still more, if more could be required. It is in conformity with the established usage of all nations, other than Great Britain, which have colonies. Some of those nations are known to adhere to the monopoly of their colonial trade, with all the vigor and constancy which circumstances permit. But it is also known that, whenever, and from whatever cause, it has been found necessary or expedient to open their colonial ports to a foreign trade, the rule of reciprocity in favor of the foreign party was not refused, nor, as is believed, a right to refuse it pretended.

It cannot be said that the reciprocity was dictated by a deficiency in the commercial marine. France, at least, could not be, in every instance, governed by that consideration; and Holland still less, to say nothing of the navigating states of Sweden and Denmark, which have rarely, if ever, enforced a colonial monopoly. The remark is, indeed, obvious, that the shipping liberated from the usual conveyance of supplies from the parent country to the colonies might be employed, in the new channels opened for them, in supplies from abroad.

Reciprocity, or an equivalent for it, is the only rule of intercourse among independent communities; and no nation ought to admit a doctrine, or adopt an invariable policy, which would preclude the counteracting measures necessary to enforce the rule.

2. The theory supposes, moreover, a perpetual peace — a supposition, it is to be feared, not less chimerical than a universal freedom of commerce.

The effect of war, among the commercial and manufacturing nations of the world, in raising the wages of labor and the cost of its products, with a like effect on the charges of freight and insurance, need neither proof nor explanation. In order to determine, therefore, a question of economy, between depending on foreign supplies and encouraging domestic substitutes, it is necessary to compare the probable periods of war with the probable periods of peace, and the cost of the domestic encouragement in time of peace with the cost added to foreign articles in time of war.

During the last century, the periods of war and peace have been nearly equal. The effect of a state of war in raising the price of imported articles cannot be estimated with exactness. It is certain, however, that the increased price of particular articles may make it cheaper to manufacture them at home.

Taking, for the sake of illustration, an equality in the two periods, and the cost of an imported yard of cloth in time of war to be nine and a half dollars, and in time of peace to be seven dollars, whilst the same could at all times be manufactured at home for eight dollars, it is evident that a tariff of one dollar and a quarter on the imported yard would protect the home manufacture in time of peace, and avoid a tax of one dollar and a half imposed by a state of war.

It cannot be said that the manufactures which could not support themselves against foreign competition, in periods of peace, would spring up of themselves at the recurrence of war prices. It must be obvious to every one, that, apart from the difficulty of great and sudden changes of employment, no prudent capitalists would engage in expensive establishments of any sort, at the commencement of a war of uncertain duration, with a certainty of having them crushed by the return of peace.

The strictest economy, therefore, suggests, as exceptions to the general rule, an estimate, in every given case, of war and peace, periods and prices, with inferences therefrom of the amount of a tariff which might be afforded during peace, in order to avoid the tax resulting from war; and it will occur at once that the inferences will be strengthened by adding, to the supposition of wars wholly foreign, that of wars in which our own country might be a party.

3 It is an opinion in which all must agree, that no nation ought to be unnecessarily dependent on others for the munitions of public defence, or for the materials essential to a naval force, where the nation has a maritime frontier, or a foreign commerce, to protect. To this class of exceptions to the theory may be added the instruments of agriculture, and of the mechanic arts which supply the other primary wants of the community. The time has been, when many of these were derived from a foreign source, and some of them might relapse into that dependence, were the encouragement of the fabrication of them at home withdrawn. But, as all foreign sources must be liable to interruptions too inconvenient to be hazarded, a provident policy would favor an internal and independent source, as a reasonable exception to the general rule of consulting cheapness alone.

4. There are cases where a nation may be so far advanced in the prerequisites for a particular branch of manufactures, that this, if once brought into existence, would support itself; and yet, unless aided, in its nascent and infant state, by public encouragement and a confidence in public protection, might remain, if not altogether, for a long time, unattempted without success. Is not our cotton manufacture a fair example? However favored by an advantageous command of the raw material, and a machinery which dispenses in so extraordinary a proportion with manual labor, it is quite probable that, without the impulse given by a war cutting off foreign supplies, and the patronage of an early tariff, it might not even yet have established itself; and pretty certain that it would be far short of the prosperous condition which enables it to face, in foreign markets, the fabrics of a nation that defies all other competitors. The number must be small that would now pronounce this manufacturing boon not to have been cheaply purchased by the tariff which nursed it into its present maturity

5. Should it happen, as has been suspected, to be an object, though not of a foreign government itself, of its great manufacturing capitalists, to strangle in the cradle the infant manufactures of an extensive customer, or an anticipated rival, it would surely, in such a case, be incumbent on the suffering party so far to make an exception to the " let alone " policy, as to parry the evil by opposite regulations of its foreign commerce.

6. It is a common objection to the public encouragement of particular branches of industry, that it calls off laborers from other branches found to be more profitable; and the objection is in general a weighty one. But it loses that character in proportion to the effect of the encouragement in attracting skilful laborers from abroad. Something of this sort has already taken place among ourselves, and much more of it is in prospect; and, as far as it has taken or may take place, it forms an exception to the general policy in question.

The history of manufactures in Great Britain, the greatest manufacturing nation in the world, informs us that the woollen branch — till of late her greatest branch — owed both its original and subsequent growths to persecuted exiles from the Netherlands; and that her silk manufactures — now a flourishing and favorite branch — were not less indebted to emigrants flying from the persecuting edicts of France. — *Anderson's History of Commerce.*

It appears, indeed, from the general history of manufacturing industry, that the prompt and successful introduction of it into new situations has been the result of emigration from countries in which manufactures had gradually grown up to a prosperous state; as into Italy on the fall of the Greek empire; from Italy into Spain and Flanders, on the loss of liberty in Florence and other cities; and from Flanders and France into England, as above noticed. — *Franklin's Canada Pamphlet.*

In the selection of cases here made as exceptions to the "let alone" theory, none have been included which were deemed controvertible. And if I have viewed them, or a part of them only, in their true light, they show, what was to be shown, that the power granted to Congress to encourage domestic products, by regulations of foreign trade, was properly granted, inasmuch as the power is, in effect, confined to that body, and may, when exercised with a sound legislative discretion, provide the better for the safety and prosperity of the nation.

With great esteem and regard,

Jos. C. Cabell, Esq.   JAMES MADISON.

BANKS.

LETTER FROM J. MADISON TO CHAS. J. INGERSOLL,

OF THE PENNSYLVANIA LEGISLATURE,

ON THE SUBJECT OF "BILLS OF CREDIT;"

Dated Montpelier, *February* 22, 1831.

Dear Sir: I have received your letter of January 21, asking —

1. *Is there any state power to make banks?*

2. *Is the federal power, as has been exercised, or as proposed to be exercised, by President Jackson, preferable?*

The evil which produced the prohibitory clause in the Constitution of the United States, was the practice of the states in making bills of credit, and, in some instances, appraised property, a "legal tender." If the notes of state banks, therefore, whether chartered or unchartered, be made a legal tender, they are prohibited; if not made a legal tender, they do not fall within the prohibitory clause. The number of the Federalist referred to was written with that view of the subject; and this, with probably other contemporary expositions, and the uninterrupted practice of the states in creating and permitting banks, without making their notes a legal tender, would seem to be a bar to the question, if it were not inexpedient now to agitate it.

A virtual and incidental enforcement of the depreciated notes of the state banks, by their crowding out a sound medium, though a great evil, was not foreseen; and, if it had been apprehended, it is questionable whether the Constitution of the United States, (which had many obstacles to encounter,) would have ventured to guard against it, by an additional provision. A virtual, and, it is hoped, an adequate remedy, may hereafter be found in the refusal of state paper, when debased, in any of the federal transactions, and the control of the federal bank; this being itself controlled from suspending its specie payments by the public authority.

On the other question, I readily decide *against* the project recommended by the President. Reasons, more than sufficient, appear to have been presented to the public in the reviews, and other comments, which it has called forth. How far a hint for it may have been taken from Mr. Jefferson, I know not. The kindred ideas of the latter may be seen in his Memoirs, &c., vol. iv. pp. 196, 207, 526 ; * and his view of the state banks, vol. iv. pp. 199, 220.

There are sundry statutes in Virginia, prohibiting the circulation of notes, payable to bearer, whether issued by individuals, or unchartered banks.

JAMES MADISON.

IDEAS OF MR. JEFFERSON ON BANKS;

REFERRED TO BY MR. MADISON IN THE PRECEDING LETTER.

[EXTRACT.]

The bill for establishing a national bank, in 1791, undertakes, among other things, —

1. To form the subscribers into a corporation.

2. To enable them, in their corporate capacities, to receive grants of lands ; and, so far, is against the laws of *mortmain.* †

3. To make *alien* subscribers capable of holding lands; and, so far, is against the laws of *alienage.*

4. To transmit these lands, on the death of a proprietor, to a certain line of successors; and, so far, changes the course of *descents.*

5. To put the lands out of the reach of forfeiture, or escheat ; and, so far, is against the laws of *forfeiture* and *escheat.*

6. To transmit personal chattels to successors, in a certain line; and, so far, is against the laws of *distribution.*

7. To give them the sole and exclusive right of banking, under the national authority ; and, so far, is against the laws of *monopoly.*

8. To communicate to them a power to make laws, paramount to the laws of the states; for so they must be construed, to protect the institution from the control of the state legislatures; and so, probably, they will be construed.

I consider the foundation of the Constitution as laid on this ground — that *all powers not delegated to the United States, by the Constitution, nor prohibited by it to the states, are reserved to the states, or to the people,* (12th amend.) To take a single step beyond the boundaries thus specially drawn around the powers of Congress, is to take possession of a boundless field of power, no longer susceptible of any definition.

The incorporation of a bank, and the powers assumed by this bill, have not, in my opinion, been delegated to the United States by the Constitution.

* *Extract from President Jackson's Message of December 7, 1830.* — "It becomes us to inquire, whether it be not possible to secure the advantages afforded by the present bank, through the agency of a bank of the United States, so modified, in its principles and structure, as to obviate *constitutional* and other objections. It is thought practicable to organize such a bank, with the necessary officers, as a branch of the treasury department, based on the public and individual deposits, without power to make loans or purchase property, which shall remit the funds of the government, and the expenses of which may be paid, if thought advisable, by allowing its officers to sell bills of exchange to private individuals, at a moderate premium. Not being a corporate body, having no stockholders, debtors, or property, and but few officers, it would not be obnoxious to the *constitutional objections* which are urged against the present bank ; and having no means to operate on the hopes, fears, or interests, of large masses of the community, it would be shorn of the influence which makes that bank formidable. The states would be strengthened by having in their hands the means of furnishing the local paper currency through their own banks, while the Bank of the United States, though issuing no paper, would check the issues of the state banks, by taking their notes in deposit, and for exchange, only so long as they continue to be redeemed with specie."

† Though the Constitution controls the laws of mortmain so far as to permit Congress itself to hold lands for certain purposes, yet not so far as to permit them to communicate a similar right to other corporate bodies.

1. *They are not among the powers specially enumerated. For these are,* —

1. A power to *lay taxes* for the purpose of paying the debts of the United States.   But no debt is paid by this bill, nor any tax laid.   Were it a bill to raise money, its organization in the Senate would condemn it by the Constitution.

2. To "borrow money."   But this bill neither borrows money nor insures the borrowing of it.   The proprietors of the bank will be just as free as any other money-holders to lend, or not to lend, their money to the public.   The operation proposed in the bill, first to lend them two millions, and then borrow them back again, cannot change the nature of the latter act, which will still be a payment, and not a loan, call it by what name you please.

3. "To regulate commerce with foreign nations, and among the states, and with the Indian tribes."   To erect a bank, and to regulate commerce, are very different acts.   He who erects a bank creates a subject of commerce in its bills; so does he who makes a bushel of wheat, or digs a dollar out of the mines: yet neither of these persons regulates commerce thereby.   To make a thing which may be bought and sold, is not to prescribe regulations for buying and selling. Besides, if this were an exercise of the power of regulating commerce, it would be void, as extending as much to the internal commerce of every state, as to its external.   For the power given to Congress by the Constitution does not extend to the internal regulation of the commerce of a state, (that is to say, of the commerce between citizen and citizen,) which remains exclusively with its own legislature ; but to its external commerce only, that is to say, its commerce with another state, or with foreign nations, or with the Indian tribes.   Accordingly, the bill does not propose the measure as a "regulation of trade," but as "productive of considerable advantage to trade."

Still less are these powers covered by any other of the special enumerations. II. *Nor are they within either of the general phrases, which are the two following :* —

1. "To lay taxes to provide for the general welfare of the United States ;" that is to say, "to lay taxes *for the purpose* of providing for the general welfare ;" for the laying of taxes is the *power,* and the general welfare the *purpose* for which the power is to be exercised.   Congress are not to lay taxes *ad libitum, for any purpose they please ;* but only to *pay the debts, or provide for the welfare, of the Union.*   In like manner, they are not *to do any thing they please,* to provide for the general welfare, but only *to lay taxes* for that purpose.   To consider the latter phrase, not as describing the purpose of the first, but as giving a distinct and independent power to do any act they please which might be for the good of the Union, would render all the preceding and subsequent enumerations of power completely useless.   It would reduce the whole instrument to a single phrase — that of instituting a Congress with power to do whatever would be for the good of the United States ; and, as they would be the sole judges of the good or evil, it would be also a power to do whatever evil they pleased.   It is an established rule of construction, where a phrase will bear either of two meanings, to give it that which will allow some meaning to the other parts of the instrument, and not that which will render all the others useless.   Certainly no such universal power was meant to be given them.   It was intended to lace them up straitly within the enumerated powers, and those without which, as means, these powers could not be carried into effect.   It is known that the very power now proposed *as a means,* was rejected *as an end by the Convention which formed the Constitution.*   A proposition was made to them, to authorize Congress to open canals, and an amendatory one to empower them to incorporate. But the whole was rejected ; and one of the reasons of objection urged in debate was, that they then would have a power to erect a bank, which would render great cities, where there were prejudices and jealousies on that subject, adverse to the reception of the Constitution.

2. The second general phrase is, "to make all laws *necessary* and proper for carrying into execution the enumerated powers."   But they can all be carried into execution without a bank.   A bank, therefore, is not *necessary,* and consequently not authorized by this phrase.

It has been much urged that a bank will give great facility or convenience in tne collection of taxes. Suppose this were true; yet the Constitution allows only the means which are "necessary," not those which are merely "convenient," for effecting the enumerated powers. If such a latitude of construction be allowed to this phrase as to give any non-enumerated power, it will go to every one; for there is no one which ingenuity may not torture into a *convenience, in some way or other, to some one* of so long a list of enumerated powers. It would swallow up all the delegated powers, and reduce the whole to one phrase, as before observed. Therefore it was that the Constitution restrained them to the *necessary* means; that is to say, to those means without which the grant of the power would be nugatory.

Perhaps bank bills may be a more *convenient* vehicle than treasury orders. But a little *difference* in the degree of convenience cannot constitute the necessity which the Constitution makes the ground for assuming any non-enumerated power.

Can it be thought that the Constitution intended that, for a shade or two of *convenience*, more or less, Congress should be authorized to break down the most ancient and fundamental laws of the several states, such as those against mortmain, the laws of alienage, the rules of descent, the acts of distribution, the laws of escheat and forfeiture, and the laws of monopoly?

Nothing but a necessity invincible by any other means, can justify such a prostration of laws, which constitute the pillars of our whole system of jurisprudence. Will Congress be too strait-laced to carry the Constitution into honest effect, unless they may pass over the foundation laws of the state governments, for the slightest convenience to theirs?

The negative of the President is the shield provided by the Constitution to protect, against the invasions of the legislature, 1. *The rights of the executive;* 2. *Of the judiciary;* 3. *Of the states and state legislatures.* The present is the case of a right remaining exclusively with the states, and is, consequently, one of those intended by the Constitution to be placed under his protection.

It must be added, however, that, unless the President's mind, on a view of every thing which is urged for and against this bill, is tolerably clear that it is unauthorized by the Constitution, if the *pro* and the *con* hang so even as to balance his judgment, a just respect for the wisdom of the legislature would naturally decide the balance in favor of their opinion. It is chiefly for cases where they are clearly misled by error, ambition, or interest, that the Constitution has placed a check in the negative of the President. *February 15, 1791.*

THOMAS JEFFERSON.

NOTES — ON BANKS.

March 11, 1798. When the bank bill was under discussion, in the House of Representatives, Judge Wilson came in, and was standing by Baldwin. Baldwin reminded him of the following fact, which passed in "*the grand Convention.*" Among the enumerated powers given to Congress, was one to erect corporations. It was, on debate, struck out. Several particular powers were then proposed. Among others, *Robert Morris* proposed to give Congress a power to establish a national bank. *Gouverneur Morris* opposed it, observing that it was extremely doubtful whether the Constitution they were framing could ever be passed at all by the people of America; that, to give it its best chance, however, they should make it as palatable as possible, and put nothing into it, not very essential, which might raise up enemies; that his colleague (Robert Morris) well knew that "a bank" was in their state (Pennsylvania) the very watchword of party; that *a bank* had been the great bone of contention between the two parties of the state from the establishment of their Constitution; having been erected, put down, erected again, as either party preponderated; that, therefore, to insert this power would instantly enlist against the whole instrument the whole of the anti-bank party in Pennsylvania. Whereupon it was rejected, as was every other special power, except that of giving copyrights to authors, and patents to inventors; the general power of incorporating being whittled down to this shred. Wilson agreed to the fact. — *Jefferson's Memoirs.*

———————

LETTER OF MR. MADISON TO MR. STEVENSON,

DATED 27TH NOVEMBER, 1830,

EXAMINING THE ORIGIN AND PROGRESS OF THE CLAUSE OF THE CONSTITUTION "*TO PAY THE DEBTS,* AND PROVIDE FOR THE COMMON DEFENCE, &c."

[EXTRACT.]

A special provision, says Mr. Madison, could not have been necessary for the *debts* of the new Congress; for a power to provide money, and a power to perform certain acts, of which money is the ordinary and appropriate means, must, of course, carry with them a power to pay the expense of performing the acts Nor was any special provision for debts proposed till the case of the revolutionary debts was brought into view; and it is a fair presumption, from the course of the varied propositions which have been noticed, that but for the old debts, and their association with the terms " common defence and general wel fare," the clause would have remained, as reported in the first draft of a constitution, expressing, generally, " a power in Congress to lay and collect taxes, duties, imposts, and excises," without any addition of the phrase " to provide for the common defence and general welfare." With this addition, indeed, the language of the clause being in conformity with that of the clause in the Articles of Confederation, it would be qualified, as in those Articles, by the specification of powers subjoined to it. But there is sufficient reason to suppose that the terms in question would not have been introduced, but for the introduction of the old debts, with which they happened to stand in a familiar, though inoperative, relation. Thus introduced, however, they pass, undisturbed, through the subsequent stages of the Constitution.

If it be asked why the terms "common defence and general welfare," if not meant to convey the comprehensive power which, taken literally, they express, were not qualified and explained by some reference to the particular power subjoined, the answer is at hand — that, although it might easily have been done, and experience shows it might be well if it had been done, yet the omission is accounted for by an inattention to the phraseology, occasioned, doubtless, by the identity with the harmless character attached to it in the instrument from which it was borrowed.

But may it not be asked, with infinitely more propriety, and without the possibility of a satisfactory answer, why, if the terms were meant to embrace not only all the powers particularly expressed, but the indefinite power which has been claimed under them, the intention was not so declared; why, on that supposition, so much critical labor was employed in enumerating the particular powers, and in defining and limiting their extent?

The variations and vicissitudes in the modification of the clause in which the terms " common defence and general welfare " appear, are remarkable, and to be no otherwise explained than by differences of opinion concerning the necessity or the form of a constitutional provision for the debts of the revolution ; some of the members apprehending improper claims for losses, by depreciated bills of credit; others, an evasion of proper claims, if not positively brought within the authorized functions of the new government; and others, again, considering the past debts of the United States as sufficiently secured by the principle that no change in the government could change the obligations of the nation. Besides the indications in the Journal, the history of the period sanctions this explanation.

But it is to be emphatically remarked, that, in the multitude of motions, propositions, and amendments, there is not a single one having reference to the terms "common defence and general welfare," unless we were so to understand the proposition containing them, made on August 25th, which was disagreed to by all the states except one.

The obvious conclusion to which we are brought is, that these terms, copied from the Articles of Confederation, were regarded in the new, as in the old instrument, merely as general terms, explained and limited by the subjoined specifications, and therefore requiring no critical attention or studied precaution.

If the practice of the revolutionary Congress be pleaded in opposition to this view of the case, the plea is met by the notoriety, that, on several accounts, the practice of that body is not the expositor of the "Articles of Confederation." These Articles were not in force till they were finally ratified by Maryland in 1781. Prior to that event, the power of Congress was measured by the exigencies of the war, and derived its sanction from the acquiescence of the states. After that event, habit, and a continued expediency, amounting often to a real or apparent necessity, prolonged the exercise of an undefined authority, which was the more readily overlooked, as the members of the body held their seats during pleasure; as its acts, particularly after the failure of the bills of credit, depended, for their efficacy, on the will of the state; and as its general impotency became manifest. Examples of departure from the prescribed rule are too well known to require proof. The case of the old Bank of North America might be cited as a memorable one. The incorporating ordinance grew out of the inferred necessity of such an institution to carry on the war, by aiding the finances, which were starving under the neglect or inability of the states to furnish the assessed quotas. Congress was at the time so much aware of the deficient authority, that they recommended it to the state legislatures to pass laws giving due effect to the ordinance, which was done by Pennsylvania and several other states.

Mr. Wilson, justly distinguished for his intellectual powers, being deeply impressed with the importance of a bank at such a crisis, published a small pamphlet, entitled "Considerations on the Bank of North America," in which he endeavored to derive the power from the nature of the Union, in which the colonies were declared and became independent states, and also from the tenor of the "Articles of Confederation" themselves. But what is particularly worthy of notice is, that, with all his anxious search in those Articles for such a power, he never glanced at the terms "common defence and general welfare," as a source of it. He rather chose to rest the claim on a recital in the text, "that, for the more convenient management of the general interests of the United States, delegates shall be annually appointed to meet in Congress," which, he said, implied that the United States had general rights, general powers, and general obligations, not derived from any particular state, nor from all the particular states, taken separately, but "resulting from the Union of the whole;" these general powers not being controlled by the article declaring that each state retained all powers not granted by the Articles, because "the individual states never possessed, and could not retain, a general power over the others."

The authority and argument here resorted to, if proving the ingenuity and patriotic anxiety of the author, on one hand, show sufficiently, on the other, that the term "common defence and general welfare" could not, according to the known acceptation of them, avail his object.

That the terms in question were not suspected, in the Convention which formed the Constitution, of any such meaning as has been constructively applied to them, may be pronounced with entire confidence; for it exceeds the possibility of belief, that the known advocates, in the Convention, for a jealous grant and cautious definition of federal powers, should have silently permitted the introduction of words or phrases in a sense rendering fruitless the restrictions and definitions elaborated by them.

Consider, for a moment, the immeasurable difference between the Constitution, limited in its powers to the enumerated objects, and expanded as it would be by the import claimed for the phraseology in question. The difference is equivalent to two constitutions, of characters essentially contrasted with each other ; the one possessing powers confined to certain specified cases, the other extended to all cases whatsoever.   For what is the case that would not be embraced by a general power to raise money, a power to provide for the general welfare, and a power to pass all laws necessary and proper to carry these powers into execution — all such provisions and laws superseding, at the same time, all local laws and constitutions at variance with them?   Can less be said, with the evidence before us furnished by the Journal of the Convention itself, than that it is impossible that such a constitution as the latter would have been recommended to the states by all the members of that body whose names were subscribed to the instrument ?

Passing from this view of the sense in which the terms "common defence and general welfare" were used by the framers of the Constitution, let us look for that in which they must have been understood by the conventions, or rather by the people, who, through their conventions, accepted and ratified it.   And here the evidence is, if possible, still more irresistible, that the terms could not have been regarded as giving a scope to federal legislation infinitely more objectionable than any of the specified powers which produced such strenuous opposition, and calls for amendments which might be safeguards against the dangers apprehended from them.

Without recurring to the published debates of those conventions, which, as far as they can be relied on for accuracy, would, it is believed, not impair the evidence furnished by their recorded proceedings, it will suffice to consult the list of amendments proposed by such of the conventions as considered the powers granted to the government too extensive, or not safely defined.

Besides the restrictive and explanatory amendments to the text of the Constitution, it may be observed, that a long list was premised under the name and in the nature of "Declarations of Rights;" all of them indicating a jealousy of the federal powers, and an anxiety to multiply securities against a constructive enlargement of them.   But the appeal is more particularly made to the number and nature of the amendments proposed to be made specific and integral parts of the constitutional text.

No less than seven states, it appears, concurred in adding to their ratifications a series of amendments, which they deemed requisite.   Of these amendments, nine were proposed by the Convention of Massachusetts, five by that of South Carolina, twelve by that of New Hampshire, twenty by that of Virginia, thirty-three by that of New York, twenty-six by that of North Carolina, and twenty-one by that of Rhode Island.

Here are a majority of the states proposing amendments, in one instance thirty-three by a single state, all of them intended to circumscribe the power granted by them to the general government, by explanations, restrictions, or prohibitions, without including a single proposition from a single state referring to the terms "common defence and general welfare;" which, if understood to convey the asserted power, could not have failed to be the power most strenuously aimed at, because evidently more alarming in its range than all the powers objected to put together.   And that the terms should have passed altogether unnoticed by the many eyes which saw danger in terms and phrases employed in some of the most minute and limited of the enumerated powers, must be regarded as a demonstration that it was taken for granted that the terms were harmless, because explained and limited, as in the "Articles of Confederation," by the enumerated powers which followed them.

A like demonstration that these terms were not understood in any sense that could invest Congress with powers not otherwise bestowed by the constitutional charter, may be found in what passed in the first session of Congress, when the subjects of amendment were taken up, with the conciliatory view of freeing the Constitution from objections which had been made to the extent of its powers, or to the unguarded terms employed in describing them.   Not only were the terms "common defence and general welfare" unnoticed in the long list of amendments brought forward in the outset, but the Journals of Congress show that, in the progress of the discussions, not a single proposition was made, in either branch of the legislature, which referred to the phrase as admitting a constructive enlargement of the granted powers, and requiring an amendment guarding against it. Such a forbearance and silence on such an occasion, and among so many members who belonged to the part of the nation which called for explanatory and restrictive amendments, and who had been elected as known advocates for them, cannot be accounted for without supposing that the terms "common defence and general welfare" were not, at that time, deemed susceptible of any such construction as has since been applied to them.

It may be thought, perhaps, due to the subject, to advert to a letter of October 5, 1787, to Samuel Adams, and another, of October 16, of the same year, to the governor of Virginia, from R. H. Lee, in both of which it is seen that the terms had attracted his notice, and were apprehended by him "to submit to Congress every object of human legislation." But it is particularly worthy of remark that, although a member of the Senate of the United States, when amendments to the Constitution were before that house, and sundry additions and alterations were there made to the list sent from the other, no notice was taken of those terms as pregnant with danger. It must be inferred that the opinion formed by the distinguished member, at the first view of the Constitution, and before it had been fully discussed and elucidated, had been changed into a conviction that the terms did not fairly admit the construction he had originally put on them, and therefore needed no explanatory precaution against it.

Note: Against the opinion of Mr. Madison, there are the opinions of men of great eminence ; and among these may be enumerated Presidents Washington, Jefferson, and Monroe, and Mr. Hamilton.

MADISON'S LETTER

ON THE

CONSTITUTIONALITY OF THE BANK OF THE UNITED STATES;

Dated MONTPELIER, *June* 25, 1831.

DEAR SIR : I have received your friendly letter of the 18th inst. The few lines which answered your former one, of the 21st of January last, were written in haste and in bad health ; but they expressed, though without the attention in some respects due to the occasion, a dissent from the views of the President, as to a Bank of the United States, and a substitute for it ; to which I cannot but adhere. The objections to the latter have appeared to me to preponderate greatly over the advantages expected from it, and the constitutionality of the former I still regard as sustained by the considerations to which I yielded, in giving my assent to the existing bank.

The charge of inconsistency between my objection to the constitutionality of such a bank in 1791, and my assent in 1817, turns on the question, how far legislative precedents, expounding the Constitution, ought to guide succeeding legislatures.

Some obscurity has been thrown over the question, by confounding it with the respect due from one legislature to laws passed by preceding legislatures. But the two cases are essentially different. A Constitution, being derived from a superior authority, is to be expounded and obeyed, not controlled or varied by the *subordinate* authority of a legislature. A law, on the other hand, resting on no higher authority than that possessed by every successive legislature, its expediency, as well as its meaning, is within the scope of the latter.

The case in question has its true analogy in the obligation arising from judicial expositions of the law on succeeding judges, the Constitution being a *law* to the legislator, as the law is a *rule* of decision to the judge.

And why are judicial precedents, when formed on due discussion and consideration, and deliberately sanctioned by reviews and repetitions. regarded as of binding influence, or rather of authoritative force, in settling the meaning of a law? It must be answered, 1. Because it is a reasonable and established axiom, that the good of society requires that the rules of conduct of its members should be certain and known; which would not be the case if any judge, disregarding the decisions of his predecessors, should vary the rule of law according to his individual interpretation of it. *Misera est servitus ubi jus est aut vagum aut incognitum.* 2. Because an exposition of the law publicly made, and repeatedly confirmed by the constituted authority, carries with it, by fair inference, the sanction of those who, having made the law through their legislative organ, appear, under such circumstances, to have determined its meaning through their judiciary organ.

Can it be of less consequence that the meaning of a Constitution should be fixed and known, than that the meaning of a law should be so? Can, indeed, a law be fixed in its meaning and operation, unless the Constitution be so? On the contrary, if a particular legislature, differing, in the construction of the Constitution, from a series of preceding constructions, proceed to act on that difference, they not only introduce uncertainty and instability in the Constitution, but in the laws themselves; inasmuch as all laws preceding the new construction, and inconsistent with it, are not only annulled for the future, but virtually pronounced nullities from the beginning.

But it is said that the legislator, having sworn to support the Constitution, must support it in his own construction of it, however different from that put on it by his predecessors, or whatever be the consequences of the construction. And is not the judge under the same oath to support the law? Yet has it ever been supposed that he was required, or at liberty, to disregard all precedents, however solemnly repeated and regularly observed, and, by giving effect to his own abstract and individual opinions, to disturb the established course of practice in the business of the community? Has the wisest and most conscientious judge ever scrupled to acquiesce in decisions in which he has been overruled by the matured opinions of the majority of his colleagues, and subsequently to conform himself thereto, as to authoritative expositions of the law? And is it not reasonable that the same view of the official oath should be taken by a legislator, acting under the Constitution, which is his guide, as is taken by a judge, acting under the law, which is his?

There is, in fact, and in common understanding, a necessity of regarding a course of practice, as above characterized, in the light of a legal rule of interpreting a law; and there is a like necessity of considering it a constitutional rule of interpreting a constitution.

That there may be extraordinary and peculiar circumstances controlling the rule in both cases, may be admitted; but with such exceptions, the rule will force itself on the practical judgment of the most ardent theorist. He will find it impossible to adhere to, and act officially upon, his solitary opinions, as to the meaning of the law or Constitution, in opposition to a construction reduced to practice during a reasonable period of time; more especially where no prospect existed of a change of construction by the public or its agents. And if a reasonable period of time, marked with the usual sanctions, would not bar the individual prerogative, there could be no limitation to its exercise, although the danger of error must increase with the increasing oblivion of explanatory circumstances, and with the continued changes in the import of words and phrases.

Let it, then, be left to the decision of every intelligent and candid judge, which, on the whole, is most to be relied on for the true and safe construction of the Constitution: — that which has the uniform sanction of successive legislative bodies through a period of years, and under the varied ascendency of parties; not that which depends upon the opinions of every new legislature, heated as it may be by the spirit of party, eager in the pursuit of some favorite object, or led away by the eloquence and address of popular statesmen, themselves, perhaps, under the influence of the same misleading causes.

It was in conformity with the view here taken of the respect due to deliberate and reiterated precedent, that the Bank of the United States, though on the original question held to be unconstitutional, received the executive signature in the year 1817. The act originally establishing a bank had undergone ample discussions in its passage through the several branches of the government. It had been carried into execution through a period of twenty years, with annual legislative recognition, — in one instance, indeed, with a positive ramification of it into a new state, — and with the entire acquiescence of all the local authorities, as well as of the nation at large; to all of which may be added, a decreasing prospect of any change in the public opinion adverse to the constitutionality of such an institution. A veto from the executive, under these circumstances, with an admission of the expediency, and almost necessity, of the measure, would have been a defiance of all the obligations derived from a course of precedents amounting to the requisite evidence of the national judgment and intentions.

It has been contended that the authority of precedents was, in that case, invalidated by the consideration, that they proved only a respect for the stipulated duration of the bank, with a toleration of it until the law should expire, and by the casting vote given in the Senate by the Vice-President, in the year 1811, against a bill for establishing a national bank, the vote being expressly given on the ground of unconstitutionality. But if the law itself was unconstitutional, the stipulation was void, and could not be constitutionally fulfilled or tolerated. And as to the negative of the Senate by the casting vote of the presiding officer, it is a fact, well understood at the time, that it resulted, not from an equality of opinions in that assembly on the power of Congress to establish a bank, but from a junction of those who *admitted* the power, but *disapproved* the plan, with those who denied the power. On a simple question of constitutionality there was a decided majority in favor of it.

JAMES MADISON.

Mr. Ingersoll.

HAMILTON'S ARGUMENT

ON THE

CONSTITUTIONALITY OF A BANK OF THE UNITED STATES.

February, 1791.

[EXTRACTS.]

It remains to show, that the incorporation of a bank is within the operation of the provision which authorizes Congress to make all needful rules and regulations concerning the property of the United States. But it is previously necessary to advert to a distinction which has been taken up by the attorney-general. He admits that the word *property* may signify personal property, however acquired; and yet asserts that it cannot signify money arising from the sources of revenue pointed out in the Constitution, "because," says he, "the disposal and regulation of money is the final cause for raising it by taxes." But it would be more accurate to say that the *object* to which money is intended to be applied is the *final cause* for raising it, than that the disposal and regulation of it is such. The support of a government, the support of troops for the common defence, the payment of the public debt, are the true final causes for raising money. The disposition and regulation of it, when raised, are the steps by which it is applied to the *ends* for which it was raised, not the ends themselves. Hence, therefore, the moneys to be raised by taxes, as well as any other personal property, must be supposed to come within the meaning, as they certainly do within the letter, of authority to make all needful rules and regulations concerning the property of the United States. A case will make this plainer. Suppose the public debt discharged, and the funds now pledged for it liberated. In some instances, it would be found expedient to repeal the taxes; in others, the repeal might injure our own industry — our agriculture and manufactures. In these cases, they would, of course, be retained. Here, then, would be moneys, arising from the authorized sources of revenue, which would not fall within the rule by which the attorney-general endeavors to except them from other personal property, and from the operation of the clause in question. The moneys being in the coffers of government, what is to hinder such a disposition to be made of them as is contemplated in the bill; or what an incorporation of the parties concerned, under the clause which has been cited?

It is admitted that, with regard to the western territory, they give a power to erect a corporation; that is, to constitute a government. And by what rule of construction can it be maintained that the same words, in a constitution of government, will not have the same effect when applied to one species of property as to another, as far as the subject is capable of it? or that a legislative power to make all needful rules and regulations, or to pass all laws necessary and proper concerning the public property, which is admitted to authorize an incorporation, in one case, will not authorize it in another; will justify the institution of a government over the western territory, and will not justify the incorporation of a bank for the more useful management of the money of the nation? If it will do the last as well as the first, then, under this provision alone, the bill is constitutional, because it contemplates that the United States shall be joint proprietors of the stock of the bank. There is no observation of the secretary of state to this effect, which may require notice in this place. — Congress, says he, are not to lay taxes *ad libitum, for any purpose they please*, but only to pay the debts, or provide for the welfare, of the Union. Certainly no inference can be drawn from this against the power of applying their money for the institution of a bank. It is true that they cannot, without breach of trust, lay taxes for any other purpose than the general welfare; but so neither can any other government. The welfare of the community is the only legitimate end for which money can be raised on the community. Congress can be considered as only under one restriction, which does not apply to other governments. They cannot rightfully apply the money they raise to any purpose merely or purely local. But, with this exception, they have as large a discretion, in relation to the application of money, as any legislature whatever.

The constitutional *test* of a right application must always be, whether it be for a purpose of *general* or *local* nature. If the former, there can be no want of constitutional power. The quality of the object, as how far it will really promote, or not, the welfare of the Union, must be matter of conscientious discretion; and the arguments for or against a measure, in this light, must be arguments concerning expediency or inexpediency, not constitutional right; whatever relates to the general order of the finances, to the general interests of trade, &c., being general objects, are constitutional ones, for the *application of money*. A bank, then, whose bills are to circulate in all the revenues of the country, is evidently a general object; and, for that very reason, a constitutional one, as far as regards the appropriation of money to it. Whether it will really be a beneficial one, or not, is worthy of careful examination, but is no more a constitutional point, in the particular referred to, than the question, whether the western lands shall be sold for twenty or thirty cents per acre. A hope is entertained that, by this time, it has been made to appear to the satisfaction of the President, that the bank has a natural relation to the power of collecting taxes; to that of regulating trade; to that of providing for the common defence; and that, as the bill under consideration contemplates the government in the light of a joint proprietor of the stock of the bank, it brings the case within the provision of the clause of the Constitution which immediately respects the property of the United States. Under a conviction that such a relation subsists, the secretary of the treasury, with all deference, conceives that it will result as a necessary consequence from the position, that all the specified powers of government are sovereign, as to the proper objects; that the incorporation of a bank is a constitutional measure; and that the objections, taken to the bill in this respect, are ill founded.

But, from an earnest desire to give the utmost possible satisfaction to the mind of the President, on so delicate and important a subject, the secretary of the treasury will ask his indulgence, while he gives some additional illustrations of cases in which a power of erecting corporations may be exercised, under some of those heads of the specified powers of the government which are alleged to include the right of incorporating a bank. 1. It does not appear susceptible of a doubt, that, if Congress had thought proper to provide, in the collection law, that the bonds, to be given for the duties, should be given to the collector of the District A, or B, as the case might require, to enure to him and his successors in office, in trust for the United States, it would have been consistent with the Constitution to make such an arrangement. And yet this, it is conceived, would amount to an incorporation. 2. It is not an unusual expedient of taxation to form particular branches of revenue; that is, to sell or mortgage the product of them for certain definite sums, leaving the collection to the parties to whom they are mortgaged or sold. There are even examples of this in the United States. Suppose that there was any particular branch of revenue which it was manifestly expedient to place on this footing and there were a number of persons willing to engage with the government, upon condition that they should be incorporated, and the funds vested in them, as well for their greater safety as for the more convenient recovery and management of the taxes; is it supposable that there could be any constitutional obstacle to the measure? It is presumed that there could be none. It is certainly a mode of collection which it would be in the discretion of the government to adopt, though the circumstances must be very extraordinary that would induce the secretary to think it expedient. 3. Suppose a new and unexplored branch of trade should present itself with some foreign country; suppose it was manifest that to undertake it with advantage required a union of the capitals of a number of individuals, and that those individuals would not be disposed to embark without an incorporation, as well to obviate the consequences of a private partnership, which makes every individual liable in his whole estate for the debts of the company to their utmost extent, as for the more convenient management of the business; what reason can there be to doubt that the national government would have a constitutional right to institute and incorporate such a company? None. They possess a general authority to regulate trade with foreign countries. This is a mean which has been practised to that end by all the principal commercial nations, who have trading companies to this day, which have subsisted for centuries. Why may not the United States *constitutionally* employ the means usual in other countries for attaining the ends intrusted to them? A power to make all needful rules and regulations concerning territory has been construed to mean a power to erect a government. A power to regulate trade is a power to make all needful rules and regulations concerning trade. Why may it not, then, include that of erecting a trading company, as well as in other cases to erect a government?

It is remarkable that the state conventions, who have proposed amendments in relation to this point, have, most, if not all of them, expressed themselves nearly thus: Congress shall not grant monopolies, nor *erect any company* with exclusive advantages of commerce! Thus at the same time expressing their sense that the power to erect trading companies, or corporations, was inherent in Congress, and objecting to it no further than as to the grant of *exclusive* privileges. The secretary entertains all the doubts which prevail concerning the utility of such companies; but he cannot fashion to his own mind a reason to induce a doubt that there is a constitutional authority in the United States to establish them. If such a reason were demanded, none could be given, unless it were this — that Congress cannot erect a corporation; which would be no better than to say they cannot do it because they cannot do it; first presuming an inability without reason, and then assigning that inability as the cause of itself. The very general power of laying and collecting taxes, and appropriating their proceeds; that of borrowing money indefinitely; that of coining money and regulating foreign coins; that of making all needful rules and regulations respecting the property of the United States; — these powers combined, as well as the reason and nature of the thing, speak strongly this language — that it is the manifest design and scope of the Constitution to vest in Congress all the powers requisite to the effectual administration of the finances of the United States. As far as concerns this object, there appears to be no parsimony of power.

To suppose, then, that the government is precluded from the employment of so usual and so important an instrument for the administration of its finances as that of a bank, is to suppose, what does not coincide with the general tenor and complexion of the Constitution, and what is not agreeable to the impressions that any mere spectator would entertain concerning it.   Little less than a prohibitory clause can destroy the strong presumptions which result from the general aspect of the government.   Nothing but demonstration should exclude the idea that the power exists.   The fact that all the principal commercial nations have made use of trading corporations or companies, for the purpose of *external commerce*, is a satisfactory proof that the establishment of them is an incident to the regulation of commerce.   This other fact, that banks are a usual engine in the administration of national finances, and an ordinary and the most effectual instrument of loans, and one which, in this country, has been found essential, pleads strongly against the supposition that a government, clothed with most of the important prerogatives of sovereignty, in relation to its revenues, its debt, its credit, its defence, its trade, its intercourse with foreign nations, is forbidden to make use of that instrument, as an appendage to its own authority.   It has been usual, as an auxiliary test of constitutional authority, to try whether it abridges any preëxisting right of any state, or any individual.   Each state may still erect as many banks as it pleases: every individual may still carry on the banking business to any extent he pleases.   *   *   *

Surely a bank has more reference to the objects intrusted to the national government than to those left to the care of the state governments.   The common defence is decisive in this comparison.

A SHORT HISTORY OF THE VETO.*

Upon the proceedings of the American colonial assemblies, there existed a double negative or veto — one vested in the royal governor, the other in the king By the royal governors the right was often exercised, and the king frequently signified his disallowance of acts which had not only passed the colonial assemblies, but even been sanctioned by the governor.   This feature was one strongly set forth as a prime grievance, in recounting the injuries and usurpations of the British monarch, in the Declaration of Independence, and its exercise was highly repugnant to the interests of America.

Dr. Franklin, in the Debates of the Federal Convention, thus shows the influence of the veto power under the proprietary government of Penn: —

---

* HISTORICAL MEMORANDA OF THE VETO.

The veto power originated with the ancient Romans, and was the first essay of the common people of the republic towards the securing of their proper liberties.   The Plebeians, having long been oppressed by the Patricians, at the instigation of Sicinius, 200 years after the founding of the city, made secession to a mountain three miles distant from Rome, (ever after termed *Mons Sacer*,) and would not return to the city until they had received from the Patricians compliance with their demand, and the solemn assurance, that the common people should elect magistrates, whose persons should be sacred and inviolable, to whom they could commit the protection of their rights.   These magistrates were called *tribunes*; a name given by Romulus to the three military officers in chief, selected from the three tribes into which he had divided the city.   The civic tribunes were originally chosen from the Plebeians, and no Patrician could hold the office, unless he had been first adopted into a Plebeian family.   Their power was at first limited, but at the same time extraordinary.   It was *preventive*, rather than enforcing; it was to interpose and protect the people from the oppressions and tyranny of their superiors; to assist them in redressing their wrongs, and in maintaining their liberties; and consisted in the utterance of but one word, and that one, "VETO," (I forbid.)   These officers could prevent the discussion of any question, the passage of any law, the execution of any sentence, the levying of any taxes, the enlisting of any troops, and almost arrest the entire machinery of govern

"The negative of the governor was constantly made use of to extort money. No good law whatever could be passed without a private bargain with him. An increase of salary, or some donation, was always made a condition; till, at last, it became the regular practice to have orders in his favor on the treasury presented along with the bills to be signed, so that he might actually receive the former before he should sign the latter. When the Indians were scalping the western people, and notice of it arrived, the concurrence of the governor in the means of self-defence could not be got, until it was agreed that his estate should be exempted from taxation; so that the people were to fight for the security of his property, whilst he was to have no share of the burdens of taxation."

At first sight, then, it appears strange that the framers of our Constitution, when they were originating a new government, which should combine the experience of the past, without borrowing any of its defects, should bring in such a power, the operation of which had proved so baneful, and which had already been so strongly reprobated. But such was the fact. The war of the revolution over, the Articles of Confederation alone bound the states together; and the reaction which took place in several places urgently demanded some new form of compact more adequate for the purposes of government, and more consonant with the altered condition of affairs. Upon the 25th May, 1787, the Federal Convention met in the city of Philadelphia. Having organized themselves by the choice of proper officers, and the adoption of necessary rules, Mr.

---

ment, by standing up and speaking that one word, *Veto.* No reasons were required of them; no one dared oppose them; their *Veto* was supreme! As originally designed, it was emphatically the *people's* measure, for the *people's* protection; the necessary balance-wheel, to equalize the powers of the government, which had hitherto been engrossed by the rich, and give the people that interposing check, which the alarming tyranny of the Patricians made necessary. It was the first attempt at a democratic, *i. e.* a people-ruling institution, and in all its features, save that of unlimited power, showed the humility of its origin. The tribunes must be not only of the Plebeian order, but they had no insignia of office, save a kind of beadle, who went before them; were not allowed to use a carriage, had no tribunal, but sat on benches. Their doors were open night and day for the people to prefer their requests or complaints. They were not allowed to enter the senate, and were not even dignified with the name of magistrate. As designed by Sicinius, it was the mere unadorned majesty of the people's voice, assimilated to the lowly pretensions of the people — the visible exponent of their will. These popular traits did not, however, long remain. The grasping ambition of some, the restlessness for change in others, soon abused the power; the tribunes became themselves a greater evil than they remedied, and their authority was more tyrannous than the edicts of those they were created to oppose.

Veto became a word of despotic power. The decrees of the senate, the ordinances of the people, the entire arrangements of government, bowed to its supremacy; and such was the force of the word, that not only could it stop the proceedings of all the magistrates. which Cæsar well calls "*extremum jus tribunorum,*" but whoever. senator or consul, Patrician or Plebeian, dared oppose it, was immediately led to prison to answer for his crime. And so sacred were the persons of the tribunes, that whoever hurt them was held accursed, and his goods were confiscated. Sylla was the first who resisted the gross encroachments of the tribunes; but on his death they regained their influence, and henceforth it became but the tool of ambitious men, who used it almost to the ruin of the state. Such was its abuse, that, as Cicero says, the popular assemblies became the scenes of violence and massacre, in which the most daring and iniquitous always prevailed. The perversion of the original design of the veto was now completed by the arts of the emperor Augustus, who got the tribuneship conferred on himself, which concentrated in his person the entire and uncontrolled disposition of the state. This was the first instance of the combination of royal and veto power, and its assumption was all that was wanting to make the king a tyrant. From this time it was conferred upon the emperors, though the tribunes still continued to be elected, without, however, the exercise of tribunitian power, until the time of Constantine, when the office was abolished.

The early operation of the veto power in Rome was good, the subsequent disastrous. At first. it protected the people, gave them a voice in the legislative as emblies, and secured their liberties; ultimately, it oppressed the lower orders, excluded them from the councils of the nation, and made them the passive instruments of power-lusting demagogues. The first civil blood shed at Rome was the blood of Tiberius; the tribune battling, inprudently indeed, against the oppressions of the nobility. The

Randolph, of Virginia, opened the business of the Convention by proposing, on the 29th May, a series of resolutions, imbodying his views as to what the crisis required; and on the same day General Charles Pinckney, of South Carolina, laid before the delegates the draught of a federal government, to be agreed upon between the free and independent states of America. The veto power entered into the schemes of both these gentlemen, though centred by them in different points. The 8th resolution of Mr. Randolph says:—

"*Resolved*, That the executive and a convenient number of the national judiciary ought to compose a council of revision, with authority to examine every act of the national legislature before it shall operate, and every act of a particular legislature before a negative thereon shall be final; and that the dissent of the said council shall amount to a rejection, unless the act of the national legislature be again passed, or that of a particular legislature be again negatived by ——— of the members of each branch."

The article embracing this feature, in the draft of Mr. Pinckney, reads thus:—

"Every bill which shall have passed the legislature shall be presented to the President of the United States for his revision. If he approve it, he shall sign it; but if he does not approve it, he shall return it, with his objections, to the house it originated in; which house, if two thirds of the members present, notwithstanding the President's objections, agree to pass it, shall send it to the other house, with the President's objections; where, if two thirds of the members present also agree to pass it, the same shall

---

last but closed the sanguinary series of intestine wars, created, continued, and tragically ended, by the very perversion of that power which was at first designed to give peace and unity to the Roman nation. So true has it ever been, that the delegated power of the people, when abused, has always reverted to their own destruction. Having traced the veto power, from the simple word of the tribune to the imperial exercise of its rights in Rome, we are prepared to come down to modern times, and cite a few instances of its adoption and influence in European states.

The king of Great Britain possesses the veto right, upon the resolutions of parliament, though no instance of its exercise has occurred since 1692. In fact, constituted as the British government is, the veto is entirely unnecessary. Such is the powerful agency of money and influence, that they will prevent the passage of any law obnoxious to the crown, and the king can, through his ministers, so trim and shape the proceedings of those bodies, as to accommodate them to his views; while, on the other hand, the taking away responsibility from the monarch, and resting it with the cabinet, which varies with the changes of public sentiment, never creates an emergency for the exercise of the royal negative. The same power is also vested with the king of Norway; but if three successive storthings or diets repeat the resolution or decree, it becomes a law without the king's assent, though he may have negatived it twice before. As the storthing, however, sits only every third year, the veto of the king, though it may not eventually be ratified, has yet a prohibitory operation on any given law for six years. It was thus that nobility was abolished in Norway in 1821. The king had twice vetoed the law, passed by the storthing, against the further continuance of the nobility; but the third diet confirmed the resolutions of the two former, and the law became established, notwithstanding the royal negative.

The constituent assembly of France conferred the veto power on the king in 1789, but the very first exercise of it proved his ruin. It was preposterous for such a body, and at such a time, to make such a provision in the constitution they were then passing, and as affairs then stood, when judicious temporizing, and not royal prerogative, was required. It was equally preposterous in Louis to employ it. It but showed the waywardness of the popular will, which could at one time grant such a right, and at another punish the exercise of it. The negative is, however, held by the present king, though it has never yet been put into requisition.

By the constitution of the cortes, the king of Spain was vested with the same power, and it still forms a provision of the Spanish government. In Poland, the veto power assumed another shape. It was centred, not in the king, but in the former republic. Each member of the diet could, by his "*Nie Pozwalam*," (I do not permit it,) prevent the passage of any resolution, and defeat the operations of the rest. On the partition of Poland, Russia confirmed this *liberum veto* to the Polish assembly, with the sinister design of thereby frustrating any effective or independent legislation; well knowing that, in its then distracted state, the continuance of this individual veto, would be, as it proved, destructive to harmony of action and unity of design, and the "*Nie Pozwalam*" of the Polish representative has been but an apple of discord to that noble but suffering people.

become a law. And all bills sent to the President, and not returned by him within ——— days, shall be laws, unless the legislature, by their adjournment, prevent their return, in which case they shall not be laws."

Mr. Randolph's views were evidently based on the suggestions of Mr. Madison; for that gentleman, in a letter to Mr. Randolph, a few weeks previous, urged the same idea of a negative by the national government, "in all cases whatsoever, on the legislative acts of the states, as the king of Great Britain heretofore had."

The resolutions of Mr. Randolph became the basis on which the proceedings of the Convention commenced, and, as Mr. Madison says, "to the developments, narrations, and modifications of which the plan of government proposed by the Convention may be traced."

Let us, then, follow out the discussions of this body until the suggested joint revision by the executive and judiciary became altered to the single negative of the President. On the 4th of June, the first clause of Mr. Randolph's eighth resolution was taken up; but Mr. Gerry, from Massachusetts, doubting whether the judiciary ought to have any thing to do with it, moved to postpone the clause, and introduced the following amendment : —

" That the national executive shall have a right to negative any legislative act which shall not afterwards be passed by ——— parts of each branch of the national legislature."

Rufus King, from Massachusetts, seconded the motion, and the proposition of Mr. Gerry was taken up. Mr. Wilson, of Pennsylvania, and Alexander Hamilton, of New York, wished to strike out the latter clause, so as to give the executive *an absolute* negative on the laws; but, though supported by these gentlemen, it was opposed by Dr. Franklin, Roger Sherman, of Connecticut, Madison, Butler, of South Carolina, and Mason, of Virginia; and was therefore negatived.

Mr. Butler and Dr. Franklin then wished to give a *suspending* instead of a *negative* power; but this was overruled, and the blank of Mr. Gerry's resolution was filled up, *sub silentio*, with *two thirds*; and the question being taken on the motion, as thus stated, it received the votes of eight states, Connecticut and Maryland voting in the negative. On the 6th June, according to previous notice, Mr. Wilson and Mr. Madison moved to reconsider the vote excluding the judiciary from a share in the revision and negative of the executive, with the view of reënforcing the latter with the influence of the former. But though Mr. Madison urged the plan of associating the judges in the revisionary function of the executive, as thereby doubling the advantages and diminishing the dangers, and as enabling the judiciary better to defend itself against legislative encroachments, it was as eloquently opposed by Mr. Gerry, and others, who thought that the executive, while standing alone, would be more impartial than when he could be covered by the sanction and seduced by the sophistry of the judges; and it was finally rejected. Two days after, at the conclusion of an animated debate, the subject of giving the national legislature a negative on the several state laws, which was first suggested to the convention by Mr. Randolph's resolutions, and subsequently brought up for reconsideration by Mr. Pinckney and Mr. Madison, was also voted down, — three states in the affirmative, seven in the negative, Delaware divided.

On the 18th of June, Mr. Hamilton offered to the Convention a plan of government, in the fourth article of which the veto power was unqualifiedly conferred on the executive. The next day, Mr. Gorham, from Massachusetts, reported from the committee appointed to reconsider the various propositions before the Convention, and the tenth resolution of that report says: " That the national executive shall have a right to negative any legislative act, which shall not be afterwards passed, unless by two thirds of each branch of the national legislature." The Convention proceeded to take up the several articles and clauses of this report, and it was not till the 18th July, that the tenth resolution became the order of the day; it was then passed *nem. con.* On the 21st, however, Mr. Wilson, still entertaining his original views, as to the union of the judiciary with the executive on the veto power, moved an amendment to the resolution, which gave rise to a most interesting debate, in which Mr. Ellsworth, from Connecticut, Mr. Mason, from Virginia, and Mr. Madison and M. Gouverneur Morris, of Pennsylvania, sustained the views of Mr. Wilson; and Messrs. Gorham, Gerry, and Strong, of Massachusetts, Mr. Martin, of Maryland, and Mr. Rutledge, of South Carolina, opposed them, and the amendment was lost. The original resolution, therefore, was again passed.

Having gone critically through with the report of the committee, the various resolutions which had been agreed to were, on Thursday, 26th July, referred to a committee of detail, to report on Monday, August 6th, a draft of the Constitution. This committee, of which Mr. Rutledge was chairman, reported on the day assigned, and the veto power was conferred by the 13th section of the sixth article. This paragraph, as reported by the committee, came under discussion on Wednesday, 15th August, when Mr. Madison moved an amendment, which revived the previously agitated question of uniting the judges of the Supreme Court with the President in his revision and rejection of laws passed by Congress. Much debate followed. Mr. Wilson and Mr. Mercer supported Mr. Madison, and Mr. Pinckney opposed. The amendment was lost — three states voting for it, and eight against it. Having thus surveyed the subject in all its bearings, the Constitution, amended, altered, and perfected, was, on the 17th September, 1787, signed by the Convention, and constitutes to this day the basis of our government. The veto power in this Constitution is thus expressed, article 1, section 7: —

" Every bill which shall have passed the House of Representatives shall, before it becomes a law, be presented to the President of the United States. If he approve, he shall sign it; but if not, he shall return it, with his objections, to that house in which it shall have originated, who shall enter the objections at large on their Journal, and proceed to reconsider it."

The first use of this constitutional power was by Washington, who, on the 5th April, 1792, vetoed the " Representation Bill," which originated in the House of Representatives. As this, from its priority, is an event worthy of extended notice, we give the circumstances of the case, as briefly related by Jefferson, then secretary of state: —

" *April 6th.* The President called on me before breakfast, and first introduced some other matter, then fell on the Representation Bill, which he had now in his possession for the 10th day. I had before given him my opinion, in writing, that the method of apportionment was contrary to the Constitution. He agreed that it was contrary to the common understanding of that instrument, and to what was understood at the time by the makers of it; that yet it would bear the construction which the bill put; and he observed that the vote for and against the bill was perfectly geographical — a northern against a southern vote -- and he feared he should be thought to be taking side with a southern party. I admitted the motive of delicacy, but that it should not induce him to do wrong, and urged the dangers to which the scramble for the fractionary members would always lead. He here expressed his fear that there would, ere long, be a separation of the Union; that the public mind seemed dissatisfied, and tending to this. He went home, sent for Randolph, the attorney-general, desired him to get Mr. Madison immediately, and come to me; and if we three concurred in opinion, that he would negative the bill. He desired to hear nothing more about it, but that we would draw up the instrument for him to sign. They came; — our minds had been before made up; — we drew the instrument. Randolph carried it to him, and told him we all concurred in it. He walked with him to the door, and, as if he still wished to get off, he said, " And you say you approve of this yourself?" " Yes, sir," says Randolph; " I do, upon my honor." He sent it to the House of Representatives instantly. A few of the hottest friends of the bill expressed passion, but the majority were satisfied, and both in and out of doors it gave pleasure to have at length an instance of the negative being exercised. Written this, the 9th April."

LIST OF THE VETOES.

1. Returned to the House of Representatives, by GEORGE WASHINGTON, April 5, 1792 — " An Act for an apportionment of representatives among the several states, according to the first enumeration."

2. Returned to the House of Representatives, by GEORGE WASHINGTON,

March 1, 1797 — "An Act to alter and amend an act, entitled, An Act to ascertain and fix the military establishment of the United States."

3. Returned to the House of Representatives, by JAMES MADISON, February 21, 1811 — "An Act for incorporating the Protestant Episcopal Church in the town of Alexandria, in the District of Columbia."

4. Returned to the House of Representatives, by JAMES MADISON, February 28, 1811 — "An Act for the relief of Richard Tervin, William Coleman, Edwin Lewis, Samuel Mims, Joseph Wilson, and the Baptist Church at Salem meeting-house, in the Mississippi territory."

5. Returned to the House of Representatives, by JAMES MADISON, April 3, 1812 — "An Act providing for the trial of causes pending in the respective District Courts of the United States, in case of the absence or disability of the judges thereof."

6. Bill not approved, nor returned with objections, for want of time; retained, and notice thereof sent to Congress, by JAMES MADISON, November 5, 1812 — "An Act supplementary to the acts heretofore passed on the subject of a uniform rule of naturalization."

7. Returned to the Senate, by JAMES MADISON, January 30, 1815 — "An Act to incorporate the subscribers to the Bank of the United States of America."

8. Returned to the House of Representatives, by JAMES MADISON, March 3, 1817 — "An Act to set apart and pledge certain funds for internal improvement."

9. Returned to the House of Representatives, by JAMES MONROE, May 4, 1822 — "An Act for the preservation and repair of the Cumberland road."

10. Returned to the House of Representatives, by ANDREW JACKSON, May 27, 1830 — "An Act authorizing a subscription of stock in the Maysville, Washington, Paris, and Lexington Turnpike Road Company."

11. Returned to the Senate, by ANDREW JACKSON, May 31, 1830 — "An Act authorizing a subscription of stock in the Washington Turnpike Road Company."

12. Returned to the Senate, by ANDREW JACKSON, July 10, 1832 — "An Act to incorporate the subscribers to the Bank of the United States."

13. Returned to the Senate, by ANDREW JACKSON, December 6, 1832 — "An Act providing for the final settlement of the claims of states for interests on advances to the United States, made during the last war."

14. Returned to the House of Representatives, by ANDREW JACKSON, December 6, 1832 — "An Act for the improvement of certain harbors, and the navigation of certain rivers."

15. Bill not approved, nor returned with objections, for want of time; retained, and notice sent to the Senate, by ANDREW JACKSON, December 5, 1833 — "An Act to appropriate, for a limited time, the proceeds of the sales of the public lands of the United States, and for granting lands to certain states."

16. Returned to the Senate, by ANDREW JACKSON, March 3, 1835 — "An Act to authorize the secretary of the treasury to compromise the claims allowed by the commissioners under the treaty with the king of the Two Sicilies, concluded October 14, 1832."

17. Bill not approved, nor returned with objections, for want of time; retained, and notice thereof sent to Congress, by ANDREW JACKSON, December 2, 1834 — "An Act to improve the navigation of the Wabash River."

18. Returned to the Senate, by ANDREW JACKSON, June 10, 1836 — "An Act to appoint a day for the annual meeting of Congress."

19. Returned to the Senate, by JOHN TYLER, August 16, 1841 — "An Act to incorporate the subscribers to the Fiscal Bank of the United States."

20. Returned to the House of Representatives, by JOHN TYLER, September 9, 1841 — "An Act to provide for the better collection, safe keeping, and disbursement, of the public revenue, by means of a corporation, to be styled the 'Fiscal Corporation of the United States.'"

21. Returned to the House of Representatives, by JOHN TYLER, June 29, 1842 — "An Act to extend, for a limited period, the present laws for laying and collecting duties on imports;" (containing a proviso about distribution of proceeds of lands.)

22. Returned to the House of Representatives, by JOHN TYLER, August 9,

1842 — "An Act to provide revenue from imports, and to change and modify the existing laws imposing duties on imports, and for other purposes." (This bill was afterwards revived, with alterations and modifications; and, thus amended, finally passed, and received the President's signature.)

Recapitulation of Vetoes.

By George Washington,	2
" James Madison,	6
" James Monroe,	1
" Andrew Jackson,	9
" John Tyler,	4
Total,	22

Such is a plain history of the veto power. As it respects the several states, the executives in some have the power, in others not. Those which possess the negative power, such as is given to the President, are New York, New Hampshire, Massachusetts, Pennsylvania, Georgia, Louisiana, Mississippi, Missouri, and Maine. The other states do not have it at all, or the bill, when returned by the governor, may be repassed by a mere *majority.*

Of the ten Presidents, five have made use of the veto power and five have not.

f acts approved, upwards of 6,000.

DIGEST OF DECISIONS

IN THE COURTS OF THE UNION,

INVOLVING

CONSTITUTIONAL PRINCIPLES.

1. The individual states have a constitutional right to pass naturalization laws, provided they do not contravene the rule established by the authority of the Union. *Collett* v. *Collett*, 2 Dall. 294. But see *United States* v. *Villatto*, Ibid. 370.

2. The 2d section of the 3d article of the Constitution, giving original jurisdiction to the Supreme Court in cases affecting consuls, does not preclude the legislature from vesting a concurrent jurisdiction in inferior courts. *United States* v. *Ravara*, Dall. 297.

Every act of the legislature repugnant to the Constitution is, *ipso facto*, void; and it is the duty of the court so to declare it. *Vanhorne's Lessee* v. *Dorrance*, 2 Dall. 304.

3. It is contrary to the letter and spirit of the Constitution to divest one citizen of his right, and vest it in another, without full compensation; and if the legislature may do so, upon full indemnification, it cannot of itself constitutionally determine upon the amount of the compensation. *Ibid.*

4. The constitution of England is at the mercy of Parliament. Every act of Parliament is transcendent, and must be obeyed. *Ibid.* 308.

5. In America, the case is widely different. Every state of the Union has its constitution, reduced to written exactitude. A constitution is the form of government delineated by the mighty hand of the people, in which certain first principles of fundamental law are established. The Constitution is certain and fixed; it contains the permanent will of the people, and is the supreme law of the land; it is paramount to the power of the legislature, and can be revoked or altered only by the power that made it. The life-giving principle and the death-dealing stroke must proceed from the same hand. The legislatures are creatures of the Constitution; they owe their existence to the Constitution; they derive their powers from the Constitution. It is their commission, and

therefore all their acts must be conformable to it, or else they will be void. The Constitution is the work or will of the people themselves, in their original, sovereign, and unlimited capacity. Law is the work or will of the legislature, in their derivative and subordinate capacity. The one is the work of the creator, and the other of the creature. The Constitution fixes limits to the exercise of the legislative authority, and prescribes the orbit in which it must move. Whatever may be the case in other countries, yet in this there can be no doubt that every act of the legislature repugnant to the Constitution is absolutely void. *Ibid.*

6. The right of trial by jury is a fundamental law, made sacred by the Constitution, and cannot be legislated away. *Ibid.* 309.

7. Whether the individual states have concurrent authority with the United States to pass naturalization laws, *quære?* *United States* v. *Villatto,* 2 Dall. 370. See *ante,* No. 1.

8. Congress cannot by law assign the judicial department any duties but such as are of a judicial character ; *e. g.,* appointing the judges of the Circuit Court to receive and determine upon claims of persons to be placed on the pension list. *Hayburn's Case,* 2 Dall. 409.

9. A tax on carriages is not a direct tax, within the meaning of the Constitution ; and the act of Congress of 5th June, 1794, ch. 219, (2 Bior. 414,) laying a tax on carriages, was constitutional and valid. *Hylton* v. *United States,* 3 Dall. 171.

10. A treaty, under the 6th article, sect. 2, of the Constitution, being the supreme law of the land, the treaty of peace, in 1783, operates as a repeal of all state laws, previously created, inconsistent with its provisions. *Ware, Adm'r.* v. *Hylton,* 3 Dall. 199.

11. The prohibition, in the Federal Constitution, of *ex post facto* laws, extends to penal statutes only, and does not extend to cases affecting only the civil rights of individuals. *Calder et Ux.* v. *Bull et Ux.,* 3 Dall. 386.

12. A resolution or law of the legislature of Connecticut, setting aside a decree of a court, and granting a new trial, to be had before the same court, is not void, under the Constitution, as an *ex post facto* law. *Ibid.*

13. It is a self-evident proposition that the several state legislatures retain all the powers of legislation delegated to them by the state constitutions, which are not expressly taken away by the Constitution of the United States. Per CHASE, J. *Ibid.*

14. A law that punishes a citizen for an innocent action, or, in other words, for an act which, when done, was in violation of no existing law ; a law that destroys or impairs the lawful private contracts of citizens ; a law that makes a man judge in his own cause ; or a law that takes property from A, and gives it to B, is contrary to the great first principles of the social compact, and cannot be considered as a rightful exercise of legislative authority. The genius, the nature, the spirit of our state governments amount to a prohibition of such acts of legislation, and the general principles of law and reason forbid them. Per CHASE, J. *Ibid.*

15. The words and intent of the prohibition embrace, 1st, every law that makes an action done before the framing of the law, and which was innocent when done, criminal, and punishes such action ; 2d, every law that aggravates a crime, or makes it greater than it was when committed ; 3d, every law that changes the punishment, and inflicts a greater punishment than the law annexed to the crime when committed ; 4th, every law that alters the legal rules of evidence, and receives less or different testimony than the law required at the time of the commission of the offence, in order to convict the offender. Per CHASE, J. *Ibid.*

16. If any act of Congress, or of the legislature of a state, violates the constitutional provisions, it is unquestionably void. If, on the other hand, the legislature of the Union, or the legislature of any member of the Union, shall pass a law within the general scope of their constitutional power, the court cannot pronounce it to be void, merely because it is, in their judgment, contrary to the principles of natural justice. If the legislature pursue the authority delegated to them, their acts are valid ; if they transgress the boundaries of that authority, their acts are invalid. Per IREDELL, J. *Ibid.*

17. An act of a state legislature, banishing the person and confiscating the property of certain individuals therein named as traitors, passed before the establishment of the Federal Constitution, is not void. *Cooper* v. *Telfair*, 4 Dall. 14.

18. The words of the Constitution, declaring that "the judicial power shall extend to all cases of admiralty and maritime jurisdiction," must be taken to refer to the admiralty and maritime jurisdiction of England. *United States* v. *M'Gill*, 4 Dall. 426, 429.

19. The Constitution, art. 2, sect. 2, 3, with regard to the appointment and commissioning of officers by the President, seems to contemplate three distinct operations — 1. The nomination: this is the sole act of the President, and is completely voluntary. 2. The appointment: this is also the act of the President, though it can only be performed by and with the advice and consent of the Senate. 3. The commission: to grant a commission to a person appointed, might perhaps be deemed a duty enjoined by the Constitution. *Marbury* v. *Madison*, 1 Cranch, 137, 155.

20. The acts of appointing to office, and commissioning the person appointed, are distinct acts. *Ibid.* 156.

21. The Constitution contemplates cases where the law may direct the President to commission an officer appointed by the courts, or by the heads of departments. In such a case, to issue a commission would be apparently a duty distinct from the appointment, the performance of which, perhaps, could not be legally refused. *Ibid.*

22. Where the officer is not removable at the will of the executive, the appointment is not revocable, and cannot be annulled; it has conferred legal rights which cannot be resumed. *Ibid.* 162.

23. The question whether the legality of the act of the heads of departments be examinable in a court of justice, or not, must always depend on the nature of that act. *Ibid.* 165. Where the heads of departments are the political or confidential agents of the executive, merely to execute the will of the President, or rather to act on cases in which the executive possesses a confidential or legal discretion, nothing can be more perfectly clear than that their acts are only politically examinable. But where a specific duty is assigned by law, and individual rights depend on the performance of that duty, it seems equally clear that the individual who considers himself injured has a right to resort to the laws of his country for a remedy. *Ibid.*

24. Where the head of a department acts in a case in which executive discretion is to be exercised, in which he is the mere organ of executive will, any application to a court to control, in any respect, his conduct, would be rejected without hesitation. But where he is directed by law to do a certain act affecting the absolute rights of individuals, in the performance of which he is not placed under the particular direction of the President, and the performance of which the President cannot lawfully forbid, and therefore is never presumed to have forbidden, — as, for example, to record a commission, or a patent for land, which has received all the legal solemnities, or to give a copy of such record, — in such cases, the courts of the country are no further excused from the duty of giving judgment that right be done to an injured individual, than if the same services were performed by a person not at the head of a department. *Ibid.* 171.

25. The authority given to the Supreme Court, by the act establishing the judicial courts of the United States, to issue writs of *mandamus* to public officers, is not warranted by the Constitution. *Ibid.* 176.

26. An act of Congress repugnant to the Constitution cannot become the law of the land. *Ibid.* 176, 177, 180.

27. An act of Congress cannot invest the Supreme Court with an authority not warranted by the Constitution. *Ibid.* 175, 176.

28. A contemporary exposition of the Constitution, practised and acquiesced under for a period of years, fixes the construction, and the Court will not shake or control it. *Stuart* v. *Laird*, 1 Cranch, 299.

29. An act of Congress giving to the United States a preference over all other creditors, in all cases, is constitutional and valid. *United States* v. *Fisher et Al.* 2 Cranch, 358, 395.

30. Such preference exists in a case where no suit has been instituted ; as, upon an assignment by a bankrupt, the United States must be first paid. *Ibid.*

31. The legislature of a state cannot annul the judgment, or determine the jurisdiction, of the courts of the United States. *United States* v. *Peters*, 5 Cranch, 115.

32. In an action of ejectment between two citizens of the state where the lands lie, if the defendant set up an outstanding title in a British subject, which he contends is protected by treaty, and that therefore the title is out of the plaintiff, and the highest state court decides against the title thus set up, it is not a case in which a writ of error lies to the Supreme Court of the United States. *Owing* v. *Norwood's Lessee*, 5 Cranch, 344.

33. This is not a case arising under the treaty, and the words of the judiciary act must be restrained by those of the Constitution. *Ibid.*

34. Whenever a right grows out of, or is protected by, a treaty, it is sanctioned against all the laws and judicial decisions of the states ; and whoever may have this right, it is protected. But if the person's title is not affected by the treaty, if he claims nothing under the treaty, his title cannot be protected by the treaty. *Ibid.* 348.

35. If a title be derived from a legislative act, which the legislature might constitutionally pass, if the act be clothed with all the requisite forms of law, a court sitting as a court of law cannot sustain a suit by one individual against another, founded on the allegation that the act is a nullity in consequence of the impure motives which influenced certain members of the legislature which passed the act. *Fletcher* v. *Peck*, 6 Cranch, 87, 131.

36. One legislature, so far as respects general legislation, is competent to repeal any act which a former legislature was competent to pass ; and one legislature cannot abridge the powers of a succeeding legislature. But if an act be done under a law, a succeeding legislature cannot undo it. *Ibid.* 135.

37. When a law is, in its nature, a contract, and absolute rights have vested under that contract, a repeal of the law cannot divest those rights. *Ibid.*

38. It may well be doubted whether the nature of society and government does not prescribe some limits to the legislative power : and if any be prescribed, where are they to be found, if the property of an individual, fairly and honestly acquired, may be seized without compensation ? *Ibid.*

39. The question whether a law be void for its repugnancy to the Constitution, is a question which ought seldom, if ever, to be decided in the affirmative in a doubtful case. The opposition between the Constitution and the law should be such that the judge feels a clear and strong conviction of their incompatibility with each other. *Ibid.* 128.

40. Where an estate has passed, under a legislative grant, into the hands of a purchaser for a valuable consideration, without notice, the state is restrained, either by general principles which are common to our free institutions, or by the particular provisions of the Constitution of the United States, from passing a law whereby the estate so purchased can be impaired and invalidated. *Ibid.* 139.

41. The appellate powers of the Supreme Court are given by the Constitution ; but they are limited and regulated by the judiciary act and other acts of Congress. *Durousseau* v. *United States*, 6 Cranch, 307.

42. An act of the legislature, declaring that certain lands which should be purchased for the Indians should not thereafter be subject to any tax, constituted a contract, which could not be rescinded by a subsequent legislative act ; such repealing act being void under that clause of the Constitution of the United States which prohibits a state from passing any law impairing the obligation of contracts. *New Jersey* v. *Wilson*, 7 Cranch, 164.

43. In expounding the Constitution of the United States, a construction ought not lightly to be admitted which would give to a declaration of war an effect in this country it does not possess elsewhere, and which would fetter that exercise of entire discretion respecting enemy's property, which may enable the government to apply to the enemy the rule that he applies to us. *Brown* v. *United States*, 8 Cranch, 110.

44. The power of making " rules concerning captures on land and water

which is superadded, in the Constitution, to that of declaring war, is not confined to captures which are extra-territorial, but extends to rules respecting enemy's property found within the territory, and is an express grant to Congress of the power of confiscating enemy's property, found within the territory at the declaration of war, as an independent substantive power, not included in that of declaring war.   *Ibid.*

45. The legislature may enact laws more effectually to enable all sects to accomplish the great objects of religion, by giving them corporate rights for the management of their property, and the regulation of their temporal as well as spiritual concerns.   *Terret et Al.* v. *Taylor et Al.* 6 Cranch, 43.

46. Consistently with the Constitution of Virginia, the legislature could not create or continue a religious establishment which should have exclusive rights and prerogatives, or compel the citizens to worship under a stipulated form or discipline, or to pay taxes to those whose creed they do not conscientiously believe.   But the free exercise of religion is not restrained by aiding, with equal attention, the votaries of every sect to perform their own religious duties, or by establishing funds for the support of ministers, for public charities, for the endowment of churches, or for the sepulture of the dead.   Nor did either public or constitutional principles require the abolition of all religious corporations.   *Ibid.*

47. The public property acquired by the Episcopal churches under the sanctions of the law did not, at the revolution, become the property of the state. The title was indefeasibly vested in the churches, or their legal agents.   The dissolution of the form of government did not involve in it a dissolution of civil rights, or an abolition of the common law.   *Ibid.*

48. A legislative grant and confirmation vests an indefeasible, irrevocable title ; is not revocable in its own nature, or held only *durante bene placito.* *Ibid.*

49. In respect to public corporations, which exist only for public purposes, as counties, towns, cities, &c., the legislature may, under proper limitations, have a right to change, modify, enlarge, or restrain them ; securing, however, the property for the uses of those for whom, and at whose expense, it was originally purchased.   *Ibid.*

50. But the legislature cannot repeal statutes creating private corporations, or confirming to them property already acquired under the faith of previous laws, and by such repeal vest the property exclusively in the state, or dispose of the same to such purposes as they may please, without the consent or default of the corporators.   *Ibid.*

51. Congress cannot vest any portion of the judicial power of the United States, except in courts ordained and established by itself.   *Martin* v. *Hunters' Lessee,* 1 Wheat. 304, 380.

52. The 25th sect. of the judiciary act of September 24, 1789, ch. 20, (2 Bior. 56,) is supported by the letter and spirit of the Constitution.   *Ibid.*

The Constitution of the United States was ordained and established, not by the United States in their sovereign capacities, but, as the preamble declares, by the people of the United States.   *Ibid.* 324.

53. It was competent for the people to invest the national government with all the powers which they might deem proper and necessary, to extend or limit these powers at their pleasure, and to give to them a paramount and supreme authority.   *Ibid.*

54. The people had a right to prohibit to the states the exercise of any powers which were, in their judgment, incompatible with the objects of the general compact ; to make the powers of the state governments, in given cases, subordinate to those of the nation ; or to reserve to themselves those sovereign authorities which they might not choose to delegate to either.   *Ibid.*

55. The Constitution was not, therefore, necessarily carved out of existing state sovereignties, nor a surrender of powers already existing in the state governments.   *Ibid.*

56. On the other hand, the sovereign powers vested in the state governments by their respective constitutions, remain unaltered and unimpaired, except so far as they are granted to the government of the United States.   *Ibid.*

57 The government of the United States can claim no powers which are not granted to it by the Constitution, either expressly or by necessary implication. *Ibid.*

58. The Constitution, like every other grant, is to have a reasonable construction, according to the import of its terms; the words are to be taken in their natural and obvious sense, and not in a sense either unreasonably restricted or enlarged. *Ibid.*

59. The power of naturalization is exclusively in Congress. *Chirac v. Chirac,* 2 Wheat. 359.

See *ante*, No. 1.

60. The grant, in the Constitution, to the United States, of all cases of admiralty and maritime jurisdiction, does not extend to a cession of the waters in which those cases may rise, or of the general jurisdiction over them. *United States* v. *Bevans*, 3 Wheat. 336.

61. Congress may pass all laws which are necessary for giving the most complete effect to the exercise of the admiralty and maritime jurisdiction, granted in the Constitution to the United States; but the general jurisdiction, subject to this grant, adheres to the territory, as a portion of sovereignty not yet given away, and the residuary powers of legislation still remain in the state. *Ibid.*

62. Congress has power to provide for the punishment of offences committed by persons serving on board a ship of war of the United States, wherever that ship may be; but Congress has not exercised that power in the case of a ship lying in the waters of the United States. *Ibid.*

63. Since the adoption of the Constitution of the United States, a state has authority to pass a bankrupt law, (provided such law does not impair the obligation of contracts,) provided there be no acts of Congress in force to establish a uniform system of bankruptcy conflicting with such law. *Sturges v. Crowninshield*, 4 Wheat. 122. Contra, *Golden v. Prince*, 3 Wash. C. C. R. 313, 5 Hall's Am. L. Journ. 502. S. C. Accord, *Adams* v. *Storey*, 6 Hall's Am. L. Journ. 474.

64. The mere grant of a power to Congress does not imply a prohibition on the states to exercise the same power. *Ibid.*

65. Whenever the terms in which a power is granted to Congress require that it should be exercised exclusively by Congress, the subject is as completely taken from the state legislatures, as if they had been expressly forbidden to act upon it. *Ibid.*

66. To release the future acquisitions of a debtor from liability to a contract, impairs its obligation. *Ibid.* 198.

67. Statutes of limitation, and usury laws, unless retroactive in their effect, do not impair the obligation of contracts, within the meaning of the Constitution. *Ibid.*

68. The right of the states to pass bankrupt laws is not extinguished by the enactment of a uniform bankrupt law throughout the Union by Congress; it is only suspended. The repeal of that law cannot confer that power upon the states, but it removes a disability to exercise, which was created by the act of Congress. *Ibid.*

69. The act of the legislature of the state of New York, of April 3d, 1811, which not only liberated the person of the debtor, but discharged him from all liability for any debt contracted previous to his discharge, on his surrendering his property in the manner prescribed, so far as it attempted to discharge the contract, is a law impairing the obligation of contracts within the meaning of the Constitution of the United States, and is not a good plea in bar of an action brought upon such contract. *Ibid.*

70. A state bankrupt or an insolvent law, which not only liberates the person of the debtor, but discharges him from all liability for the debt, so far as it attempts to discharge the contract, is repugnant to the Constitution of the United States; and it makes no difference whether the law was passed before or after the debt was contracted. *M'Millan v. M'Neil*, 4 Wheat. 209.

71. The act of Assembly of Maryland, of 1793, incorporating the Bank of Columbia, and giving to the corporation a summary process by execution, in the nature of an attachment, against its debtors, who have, by an express con

sent in writing, made the bonds, bills, or notes, by them drawn or endorsed negotiable at the bank, is not repugnant to the Constitution of the United States, or of Maryland. *Bank of Columbia* v. *Okely*, 4 Wheat. 316.

72. Congress has power to incorporate a bank. *M'Culloch* v. *Maryland*, 4 Wheat. 316.

73. The government of the Union is a government of the people ; it emanates from them ; its powers are granted by them, and are to be exercised directly on them, and for their benefit. *Ibid.*

74. The government of the Union, though limited in its powers, is supreme within its sphere of action ; and its laws, when made in pursuance of the Constitution, form the supreme laws of the land. *Ibid.*

75. The government, which has a right to do an act, and has imposed on it the duty of performing that act, must, according to the dictates of reason, be allowed to select the means. *Ibid.*

76. There is nothing in the Constitution of the United States, similar to the Articles of Confederation, which excludes incidental or implied powers. *Ibid.*

77. If the end be legitimate, and within the scope of the Constitution, all the means which are appropriate, which are plainly adapted to that end, and which are not prohibited, may constitutionally be employed to carry it into effect. *Ibid.*

78. The power of establishing a corporation is not a distinct sovereign power or end of government, but only the means of carrying into effect other powers which are sovereign. Whenever it becomes an appropriate means of exercising any of the powers given by the Constitution to the government of the Union, it may be exercised by that government. *Ibid.*

79. If certain means to carry into effect any of the powers expressly given by the Constitution to the government of the Union, be an appropriate measure, not prohibited by the Constitution, the degree of its necessity is a question of legislative discretion, not of judicial cognizance. *Ibid.*

80. The act of April 10, 1816, ch. 44. (3 Stor. 1547,) to " incorporate the subscribers to the Bank of the United States," is a law made in pursuance of the Constitution. *Ibid.*

81. The Bank of the United States has, constitutionally, a right to establish its branches, or offices of discount and deposit, within any state. *Ibid.*

82. The state within which such branch may be established cannot constitutionally tax that branch. *Ibid.*

83. The state governments have no right to tax any of the constitutional means employed by the government of the Union to execute its constitutional powers. *Ibid.*

84. The states have no power, by taxation otherwise, to retard, impede, burden, or in any manner control, the operation of the constitutional laws enacted by Congress to carry into effect the powers vested in the national government. *Ibid.*

85. This principle does not extend to a tax paid by the real property of the Bank of the United States, in common with the other real property in a particular state ; nor to a tax imposed on the proprietary interest which the citizens of that state may hold in this institution, in common with other property of the same description throughout the state. *Ibid.*

86. The charter granted by the British crown to the trustees of Dartmouth College, in New Hampshire, in the year 1769, is a contract within the meaning of that clause of the Constitution of the United States, (art. 1, sect. 10,) which declares that no state shall make any law impairing contracts ; and this charter was not dissolved by the revolution. *Trustees of Dartmouth College* v. *Woodward*, 4 Whent. 518.

87. An act of the legislature of New Hampshire, altering the charter in a material respect, without the consent of the corporation, is an act impairing the obligation of a contract, and is unconstitutional and void. *Ibid.*

88. The act of Congress of March 3, 1819, ch. 76, § 35, referring to the law of nations for a definition of the crime of piracy, is a constitutional exercise of the power of Congress to define that crime. *United States* v. *Smith*, 5 Wheat. 153.

89. Congress has authority to impose a direct tax on the District of Columbia.

in proportion to the census directed to be taken by the Constitution. *Lufborough* v. *Blake*, 5 Wheat. 317.

90. The power of Congress to levy and collect taxes, duties, imposts, and excise, is coextensive with the territory of the United States. *Ibid.*

91. The power of Congress to exercise exclusive legislation, in all cases whatsoever, within the District of Columbia, includes the power of taxing it. *Ibid.*

92. Congress has no power to exempt any state from its due share of the burden of taxes, but is not bound to extend a direct tax to the District and territories. *Ibid.*

93. The present Constitution of the United States did not commence its operation until the first Wednesday in March, 1789; and the provision that "no state shall make any law impairing the obligation of contracts," does not extend to a law enacted before that day, and operating upon rights of property vested before that time. *Owings* v. *Speed et Al.* 5 Wheat. 420.

94. An act of a state legislature, which discharges a debtor from all liability for debts contracted previous to his discharge, on his surrendering his property for the benefit of his creditors, is a law impairing the obligation of a contract, within the meaning of the Constitution of the United States; and it is immaterial that the suit was brought in a state court of a state of which both parties were citizens, where the contract was made, and the discharge obtained, and where they continued to reside until the suit was brought. *Farmers' and Mechanics' Bank of Pennsylvania* v. *Smith*, 6 Wheat. 131.

95. The Supreme Court has, constitutionally, appellate jurisdiction, under the 25th sect. of the judiciary act of September 24, 1789, ch. 20, (2 Bior. 56,) from the final judgment or decree of the highest court of law or equity of a state having jurisdiction of the suit, where is drawn in question the validity of a treaty, or statute of, or an authority exercised under, the United States, and the decision is against their validity; or where is drawn in question the validity of a statute of, or an authority exercised under, any state, on the ground of their being repugnant to the Constitution, treaties and laws of the United States, and the decision is in favor of their validity; or of the Constitution, or of a treaty of, or of a statute of, or a commission held under, the United States, and the decision is against the title, right, privilege, or exemption, specially set up or claimed by either party, under the Constitution, treaty, statute, or commission. *Cohens* v. *Virginia*, 6 Wheat. 264.

96. It is no objection to the exercise of this appellate jurisdiction, that one of the parties is a state, and the other a citizen of that state. *Ibid.*

97. The 2d section of the 3d article of the Constitution defines the extent of the judicial power of the United States. Jurisdiction is given to the courts of the United States in two classes of cases. In the first, their jurisdiction depends on the *character of the cause*, whoever may be the parties. This class comprehends "all cases in law and equity arising under this Constitution, the laws of the United States, and treaties made, or which shall be made, under their authority." In the second class, the jurisdiction depends entirely on the *character of the parties*. In this class are comprehended "controversies between two or more states, between a state and citizens of another state," and "between a state and foreign states, citizens, or subjects." If these be the parties, it is entirely unimportant what may be the subject of the controversy; be it what it may, these parties have a constitutional right to come into the courts of the Union. *Ibid.* 378.

98. A case in law or equity consists of the rights of the one party as well as of the other, and is said to arise under the Constitution or a law of the United States, whenever its correct decision depends on the construction of either. *Ibid.*

99. The judicial power of every well-constituted government must be coextensive with the legislative, and must be capable of deciding every judicial question which grows out of the Constitution and laws. *Ibid.*

100. Where the words of the Constitution confer only appellate jurisdiction upon the Supreme Court, original jurisdiction is most clearly not given; but where the words admit of appellate jurisdiction, the power to take cognizance

of the suit originally does not necessarily negative the power to decide upon it on an appeal, if it may originate in a different court. *Ibid.* 397.

101. In every case to which the judicial power extends, and in which original jurisdiction is not expressly given, that power shall be exercised in the appellate, and only in the appellate, form. The original jurisdiction of the Supreme Court cannot be enlarged, but its appellate jurisdiction may be exercised in every case, cognizable under the 3d article of the Constitution, in the federal courts, in which original jurisdiction cannot be exercised. *Ibid.*

102. Where a state obtains a judgment against an individual, and the court rendering such judgment overrules a defence set up under the Constitution or laws of the United States, the transfer of the record into the Supreme Court, for the sole purpose of inquiring whether the judgment violates the Constitution or laws of the United States, cannot be denominated a suit commenced or prosecuted against the state whose judgment is so far reëxamined, within the 11th amendment of the Constitution of the United States. *Ibid.*

103. The act of Kentucky, of February 27, 1797, concerning occupying claimants of land, whilst it was in force, was repugnant to the Constitution of the United States. It was, however, repealed by a subsequent act of January 31, 1812. This last act is also repugnant to the Constitution of the United States, being in violation of the compact between the states of Virginia and Kentucky, contained in the act of the legislature of Virginia, December 18, 1789, and incorporated into the Constitution of Kentucky. *Green et Al.* v. *Biddle,* 8 Wheat. 1.

104. The objection to a law, on the ground of its impairing the obligation of a contract, can never depend on the extent of the change which the law may make in it; any deviation from its terms, by postponing or accelerating the period of performance which it prescribes, imposing conditions not expressed in the contract, or dispensing with the performance of those which are, however minute, or apparently immaterial in their effect upon the contract of the parties, impairs its obligation. *Ibid.*

105. The compact between the states of *Kentucky* and *Virginia* of 1789–1790, is valid and binding upon the parties, and has, within the meaning of the Constitution of the United States, received the assent of Congress, by act of February 4, 1791, ch. 78, (2 Bior. 191.) *Ibid.*

106. This compact is not invalid on the ground of its containing limitations, or a surrender of sovereign rights. *Ibid.*

107. A compact between two states is a contract within that clause of the Constitution which prohibits states from passing any laws impairing the obligation of contracts. *Ibid.*

108. The several acts of the legislature of the state of New York, granting and securing to Robert R. Livingston and Robert Fulton the exclusive right of navigating the waters within the jurisdiction of that state, with boats moved by fire or steam, for the periods therein specified, are in collision with a constitutional act of Congress, and so far repugnant to the Constitution of the United States, and void. *Gibbons* v. *Ogden,* 9 Wheat. 1, 209, 210.

109. The framers of the Constitution must be understood to have employed words in their natural sense, and to have intended what they have said : and in construing the extent of the powers which it creates, there is no other rule than to consider the language of the instrument which confers them, in connection with the purposes for which they were conferred. *Ibid.* 188, 189.

110. In the clause of the Constitution of the United States, which declares that " Congress shall have power to regulate *commerce* with foreign nations, and among the several states, and with the Indian tribes," the word " commerce " comprehends " navigation ;" and a power to regulate navigation is as expressly granted as if that term had been added to the word " commerce." *Ibid.* 189 193.

111 It is a rule of construction that exceptions from a power mark its extent. *Ibid.* 191.

112. The power to regula.e commerce extends to every species of commercial intercourse between the United States and foreign nations, and among the several states. *Ibid.* 193.

113. It does not comprehend that commerce which is completely internal — which is carried on between man and man in a state, or between different parts of the same state, and which does not extend to or affect other states. *Ibid.* 194.

114. But it does not stop at the jurisdictional lines of the several states; it must be exercised wherever the subject exists, and must be exercised within the territorial jurisdiction of the several states. *Ibid.* 195, 196.

115. This power to regulate commerce is the power to prescribe the rule by which commerce is to be governed. *Ibid.*

116. Like all other powers vested in Congress, it is complete in itself, may be exercised to its utmost extent, and has no other limitations than such as are prescribed in the Constitution. *Ibid.*

117. The authority of Congress to lay and collect taxes does not interfere with the power of the states to tax for the support of their own governments; nor is the exercise of that power by the states an exercise of any portion of the power that is granted to the United States. *Ibid.* 199.

118. But when a state proceeds to regulate commerce with foreign nations, or among the several states, it is exercising the very power that is granted to Congress.

119. The power of laying duties on imports or exports is considered, in the Constitution, as a branch of the taxing power, and not of the power to regulate commerce. *Ibid.* 201.

120. The inspection laws, quarantine laws, health laws of every description, laws for regulating the internal commerce of a state, and those which respect turnpike roads, ferries, &c., are not in the exercise of a power to regulate commerce, within the language of the Constitution. *Ibid.* 203.

121. Although Congress cannot enable a state to legislate, it may adopt the provisions of a state on any subject. *Ibid.* 207.

122. *It seems* that the power to regulate implies, in its nature, full power over the thing to be regulated, and excludes necessarily the action of all others that would perform the same operation on the same thing. *Ibid.* 209.

123. When the legislature attaches certain privileges and exemptions to the exercise of a right over which its control is absolute, the law must imply the power to exercise the right; and therefore the act on the subject of the coasting trade implies an authority to licensed vessels to carry on that trade. *Ibid.* 212.

124. The license, under that law, is a legislative authority to the licensed vessel to be employed in the coasting trade, and is not intended merely to confer the national character: that character is conferred by the enrolment, not by the license. *Ibid.* 214.

125. The power to regulate commerce extends as well to vessels employed in carrying passengers as to those employed in transporting property. *Ibid.* 215.

126. It extends equally to vessels propelled by steam, or fire, as to those navigated by the instrumentality of wind and sails. *Ibid.* 219.

127. The clause in the act of incorporation of the Bank of the United States which authorizes the bank to sue in the federal courts, is warranted by the 3d article of the Constitution of the United States, which declares " that the judicial power shall extend to all cases in law and equity arising under the Constitution, the laws of the United States, or treaties made, or which shall be made, under their authority." *Osborn et Al.* v. *Bank of the United States,* 9 Wheat. 733.

128. The executive department may constitutionally execute every law which the legislature may constitutionally make, and the judicial department may receive from the legislature the power of construing every such law. *Ibid.*

129. The 3d article of the Constitution of the United States enables the judicial department to receive jurisdiction to the full extent of the Constitution, laws, and treaties of the United States, when any question respecting them shall assume such a form that the judicial power is capable of acting on it. That power is capable of acting only when the subject is submitted to it by a

party who asserts his rights in the form prescribed by law.   It then becomes a case. *Ibid.*

130. In those cases in which original jurisdiction is given to the Supreme Court, the judicial power of the United States cannot be exercised in its appellate form.   In every other case, the power is to be exercised in its original or appellate form, or both, as the wisdom of Congress may direct.   *Ibid.*

131. With the exception of those cases in which original jurisdiction is given to the Supreme Court, there is none to which the judicial power extends from which the original jurisdiction of the inferior courts is excluded by the Constitution.   *Ibid.*

132. The Constitution establishes the Supreme Court, and defines its jurisdiction.   It enumerates cases in which jurisdiction is original and exclusive, and then defines that which is appellate, but does not insinuate that, in any such case, the power cannot be exercised in its original forms by courts of original jurisdiction.

133. The postmaster-general cannot sue in the federal courts under that part of the Constitution which gives jurisdiction to those courts in consequence of the character of the party, nor is he authorized to sue by the judiciary act: he comes into the courts of the United States under the authority of an act of Congress, the constitutionality of which rests upon the admission that his suit is a case arising under the law of the United States. *Ibid.*

134. The clause in the patent law authorizing suits in the Circuit Courts stands on the principle that they are cases arising under a law of the United States. *Ibid.*

135. Jurisdiction is neither given nor ousted by the relative situation of the parties concerned in interest, but by the relative situation of the parties named on the record; consequently the 11th amendment to the Constitution, which restrains the jurisdiction of the federal courts over suits against states, is limited to those suits in which a state is a party on the record. *Ibid. Bank of the United States* v. *Planters' Bank of Georgia.* *Ibid.* 904, S. P.

136 The Circuit Courts of the United States have jurisdiction of a bill in equity, filed by the Bank of the United States for the purpose of protecting the bank in the exercise of its franchises, which are threatened with invasion and destruction under an unconstitutional state law; and, as the state itself cannot be made a defendant, it may be maintained against the officers and agents of the state who are appointed to execute such law.   *Ibid.*

137. The act of February 28, 1795, ch. 277, (2 Bior. 479,) to provide for calling out the militia, to execute the laws of the Union, to suppress insurrections, and repel invasions, is within the constitutional authority of Congress. *Martin* v. *Mott*, 12 Wheat. 19.

138. The power granted to Congress, by the Constitution, "to establish uniform laws on the subject of bankruptcy throughout the United States," does not exclude the right of the states to legislate on the same subject, except when the power is actually exercised by Congress, and the state laws conflict with those of Congress. *Ogden* v. *Saunders*, 12 Wheat. 213.

139. A state bankrupt or insolvent law, which discharges both the person of the debtor and his future acquisitions of property, is not "a law impairing the obligation of contracts" so far as respects debts contracted subsequent to such law. *Ibid.*

140. But a certificate of discharge under such law cannot be pleaded in bar of an action brought by a citizen of another state in the courts of the United States, or of any other state than that where the discharge was obtained. *Ibid.*

141. The states have a right to regulate or abolish imprisonment for debt, as a part of the remedy for enforcing the performance of contracts. *Mason* v. *Haile*, 12 Wheat. 370.

142. An act of a state legislature, requiring all importers of foreign goods by the bale or package, &c., and other persons selling the same by wholesale, bale or package, &c., to take out a license, for which they shall pay fifty dollars, and in case of neglect or refusal to take out such license, subject them to certain forfeitures and penalties, is repugnant to that provision of the Constitution of the

United States which declares that "no state shall, without the consent of Congress, lay any impost, or duty on imports and exports, excepting what may be absolutely necessary for executing its own inspection laws;" and also to that which declares that Congress shall have power to regulate commerce with foreign nations, among the several states, and with the Indian tribes. *Brown et Al.* v. *State of Maryland,* 12 Wheat. 419.

143. It is extremely doubtful whether the legislature can constitutionally impose upon a judge of the Supreme Court of the United States the authority or duty to hold a District Court. There is a great difference between giving new jurisdiction to a court of which such judge is a member, and appointing him *pro hac vice* to a new office. Nor is there any sound distinction between an appointment to a new office, and an appointment to perform the duties of another office, while it remains a separate and distinct office. *Ex parte United States,* 1 Gallis. 338.

144. The act of New Hampshire of June 19, 1805, which allows to tenants the value of improvements, &c., on recoveries against them, if it applies to past improvements, is so far unconstitutional and void. *Society for the Propagation, &c.* v. *Wheeler et Al.* 2 Gallis. 105.

145. The expressions "admiralty and maritime jurisdiction," in the Constitution of the United States, give jurisdiction of all things done upon and relating to the sea, or, in other words, all transactions and proceedings relative to commerce and navigation, and to damages or injuries upon the sea. *De Corvio* v *Boit et Al.* 2 Gallis. 308, 468.

146. The delegation of cognizance "of all civil causes of admiralty and maritime jurisdiction" to the courts of the United States, comprehends all maritime contracts, torts, and injuries. The latter branch is necessarily bounded by locality; the former extends over all contracts, wheresoever they may be made or executed, or whatsoever may be the form of the stipulations, which relate to the navigation, business, or commerce of the sea. *Ibid.* 474, 475.

147. The 9th section of the 1st article of the Constitution of the United States, which restrained Congress from forbidding the migration or importation of slaves prior to the year 1808, did not apply to state legislatures, who might at any time prohibit the introduction of such persons. *Butler* v. *Hoppen,* 1 Wash. C. C. R. 499.

148. The 2d section of the 4th article of the Constitution of the United States does not extend to a slave voluntarily carried by his master into another state, and there left under the protection of a law declaring him free, but to slaves escaping from one state into another. *Ibid.*

149. The powers bestowed by the Constitution upon the government of the United States were limited in their extent, and were not intended, nor can they be construed with other powers before vested in the state governments, which of course were reserved to those governments, impliedly, as well as by an express provision of the Constitution. *Golden* v. *Prince,* 3 Wash. C. C. R. 313. 5 Hall's Am. L. Journ. 502 S. C.

150. The state governments therefore retained the right to make such laws as they might think proper within the ordinary functions of legislation, if not inconsistent with the powers vested exclusively in the government of the United States, and not forbidden by some article of the Constitution of the United States or of the state; and such laws were obligatory upon all the citizens of that state, as well as others who might claim rights or redress for injuries under those laws, or in the courts of that state. *Ibid.*

151. The establishment of federal courts, and the jurisdiction granted to them in certain specified cases, could not, consistently with the spirit and provisions of the Constitution, impair any of the obligations thus imposed by the laws of the state, by setting up in those courts a rule of decision at variance with that which was binding upon the citizens, and which they were bound to obey. *Ibid.*

152. Thus the laws of a state affecting contracts, regulating the disposition and transmission of property, real or personal, and a variety of others, which in themselves are free from all constitutional objections, are equally valid and obligatory within the state, since the adoption of the Constitution of the United

54

States, as they were before.   They provide rules of civil conduct for every individual who is subject to their power.   *Ibid.*

153. With respect to rules of practice for transacting the business of the courts, a different principle prevails.   These rules form the law of the court; and it is, in relation to the federal courts, a law arising under the Constitution of the United States, consequently not subject to state regulations.   It is in reference to this principle that the 17th section of the judicial act authorizes the courts of the United States to make all necessary rules for the orderly conducting of business in the said courts, provided the same are not repugnant to the laws of the United States; and under this power the different Circuit Courts, at their first session, adopted the state practice as it then existed, which continues to this day in all the states, except so far as the courts have thought proper, from time to time, to alter or amend it.   *Ibid.*

154. A law may be unconstitutional, and of course void, in relation to particular cases, and yet valid, to all intents and purposes, in its application to other cases within the scope of its provisions, but varying from the former in particular circumstances.   Thus a law prospective in its operation, under which a contract afterwards made may be avoided in a way different from that provided by the parties, would be clearly constitutional; because the stipulations of the parties, which are inconsistent with such a law, never had a legal existence, and of course could not be impaired by the law.   But if the law act retrospectively as to other contracts, so as to impair their obligation, the law is invalid, or, in milder terms, affords no rule of decision in these latter cases.   *Ibid.*

155. A law of a state, which declares that a debtor, by delivering up his estate for the benefit of his creditors, shall be forever discharged from the payment of his debts, due or contracted before the passage of the law, whether the creditor do any act or not in aid of the law, cannot be set up to bar the right of such creditor to recover his debt either in a federal or state court; such law impairs the obligation of the contract.   *Ibid.*

156. A law which authorizes the discharge of a contract by a smaller sum, or at a different time, or in a different manner, than the parties have stipulated, impairs its obligation, by substituting, for the contract of the parties, one which they never entered into, and to the performance of which, of course, they never had consented.   *Ibid.*

157. A state law, directing that the court before whom an insolvent debtor is discharged, shall make an order, that whenever a majority of the creditors shall consent, the debtor shall be released, and his future acquisitions exempted from all liability for seven years, is unconstitutional and void.   *United States v. Kederickson,* C. C. U. S. P. Oct. 1821. M. S.

158. There is nothing in the Constitution of the United States which forbids Congress to pass laws violating the obligation of contracts, though such power is denied to the states individually.   *Evans* v. *Eaton,* 1 Peters's C. C. R. 322.

159. If the local ordinances of a city are in collision with an act of Congress, the former must give way.   The laws of Congress, made in pursuance of the Constitution of the United States, are the supreme laws of the land, any thing in the constitution or laws of the particular state notwithstanding.   *United States* v. *Hart,* 1 Peters's C. C. R. 390.

160. An act of Congress, laying an embargo for an indefinite period of time, is constitutional and valid.   *United States* v. *The William,* 2 Hall's Am. L. Journ. 255.

161. There is nothing in the Constitution of the United States which forbids the legislature of a state to exercise judicial functions.   *Satterlee* v. *Mathewson,* Peters's Reports, vol. ii. 413.

162. There is no part of the Constitution of the United States, which applies to a state law, which divested rights vested by law in an individual, provided its effect be not to impair the obligation of the contract.   *Ibid.* 413.

163. A tax imposed by a law of any state of the United States or under the authority of such a law, on stock issued for loans made the United States, is unconstitutional.   *Weston et Al.* v. *The City Council of Charleston, Ibid.* 449.

164. It is not the want of original power in an independent sovereign state to prohibit loans to a foreign government, which restrains the state legislature

from direct opposition to those made by the United States. The restraint is imposed by our Constitution. The American people have conferred the power of borrowing money on the government; and, by making that government supreme, have shielded its action, in the exercise of that power, from the action of the local governments. The grant of the power, and the declaration of supremacy, are a declaration that no such restraining or controlling power shall be exercised. *Ibid.* 468.

165. The provision in the 5th amendment to the Constitution of the United States, declaring that private property shall not be taken for public use without just compensation, is intended solely as a limitation on the exercise of power by the government of the United States, and is not applicable to the legislation of the states. *Barron* v. *The Mayor and City Council of Baltimore,* 7 Peters Sup. Ct. U. S.

e

6/19

CPSIA information can be obtained
at www.ICGtesting.com
Printed in the USA
BVHW082211260819
556819BV00004B/577/P